Essentials of Conservation Biology

ESSENTIALS OF
CONSERVATION BIOLOGY FOURTH EDITION

RICHARD B. PRIMACK

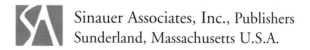

Sinauer Associates, Inc., Publishers
Sunderland, Massachusetts U.S.A.

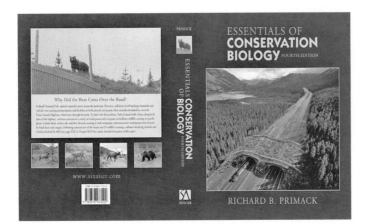

About the Cover

The cover depicts a wildlife overpass at Banff National Park located in the province of Alberta, Canada. This overpass was one of a series of overpasses and underpasses built to reduce the frequency of collisions involving large mammals and vehicles when animals attempted to cross the Trans-Canada Highway. The back cover shows animals using these new crossing points. (Front cover photograph © Joel Sartore; large back cover photograph by Laurel Hicks; small back cover photographs courtesy of Tony Clevenger.)

Essentials of Conservation Biology, *Fourth Edition*

Copyright © 2006 by Sinauer Associates, Inc.

For information, address:
Sinauer Associates, Inc., 23 Plumtree Road, Sunderland, MA 01375 USA
Fax: 413-549-1118
E-mail: orders@sinauer.com; publish@sinauer.com
Internet: www.sinauer.com

Credits for Part Opener Photographs

Part I: Photograph courtesy of Projeto TAMAR Image Bank. **Part II**: Photograph by Scott Kraus, New England Aquarium. **Part III**: Photograph by Milla Jung. **Part IV**: Photograph by Bill Campbell. **Part V**: Photographs courtesy of David Polster, Polster Environmental Services. **Part VI**: Photograph by Merlin Tuttle, Bat Conservation International.

Library of Congress Cataloging-in-Publication Data

Primack, Richard B., 1950-
  Essentials of conservation biology / Richard B. Primack.— 4th ed.
      p. cm.
  Includes bibliographical references.
  ISBN 0-87893-720-X (hardcover : alk. paper)
  1. Conservation biology. I. Title.

QH75.P752 2006
333.95'16—dc22

2006008306

54321

To Margaret, Dan, Will, and Jasper

Brief Contents

Contents

Preface

In 2005, hundreds of scientists came together to evaluate the Earth's health in the Millenium Ecosystem Assessment, which recognized the immense value of the living world. Conservation biology is the field that seeks to study and protect the living world and its biological diversity. The field emerged during the last 25 years as a major new discipline to address the alarming loss of biological diversity. The threats to biological diversity are all too real, as most recently demonstrated by the recognition of severe declines in fully one-third of amphibian species. At the same time, our need to remain hopeful was highlighted by the 2004 discovery of a population of the Ivory-billed woodpecker, a conspicuous species not previously seen for over 60 years.

Evidence of the explosive increase of interest in conservation biology is shown by the rapidly increasing membership in the Society for Conservation Biology, the great intellectual excitement displayed in many journals and newsletters, and the large numbers of new edited books and advanced texts that appear almost weekly. In the United States, a major grant by one of the founders of the Intel Corporation has been used to establish a Center for Applied Biodiversity Science, and a Global Biodiversity Information Facility is being developed as an online resource to coordinate international conservation efforts.

Such interest extends to university students, who continue to enroll enthusiastically and in large numbers in conservation biology courses. The publication of the first (1993), second (1998), and third (2002) editions of *Essentials of Conservation Biology* provided a comprehensive textbook for this subject. (The *Primer of Conservation Biology*'s first [1995], second [2000], and third [2004] editions fill the need for a "quick" guide for those who want a basic familiarity with conservation biology.) This fourth edition of *Essentials* provides a thorough introduction to the major concepts and problems of the field. Like its predecessors, it is designed for use in conservation biology courses, and also as a supplemental text for general biology, ecology, wildlife biology, and environmental policy courses. The book is also intended to serve as a detailed guide for professionals who require a comprehensive background in the subject.

The fourth edition reflects the excitement and new developments in the field. It provides coverage of the latest information available on a number of topics, including the global hot spots of biodiversity that have been identified as targets for conservation efforts and a new system of classification for endangered species. The fourth edition also highlights new approaches culled from the literature on topics such as species reintroductions, population viability analysis, protected areas management, and payments for ecosystem services. Also new to this edition is an Instructor's Resource CD, available to qualified adopters of the text. This IRCD includes electronic versions of all the line-art figures, photos, and tables from the textbook.

In keeping with the international approach of conservation biology, I feel it is important to make the field accessible to as wide an audience as possible. With the assistance of Marie Scavotto and the staff of Sinauer Associates, I have arranged an active translation program, beginning in 1995 with translations into German (as

Naturschutzbiologie) and Chinese in 1997. However, it became clear to me that the best way to make the material accessible was to create regional or country-specific translations, identifying local scientists to become coauthors and to add case studies, examples, and illustrations from their own countries and regions that would be more relevant to the intended audience. To that end, in the past seven years, editions of *Essentials* have appeared in Arabic (with Mohamed El-Demerdash), Hungarian (with Tibor Standovar), and Spanish with a Latin American focus (with Ricardo Rozzi, Peter Feinsinger, Rodolfo Dirzo, and Francisca Massardo); and the *Primer* has appeared in Brazilian Portuguese (with Efraim Rodrigues), Chinese (with Weizhu Ji), Czech (with Pavel Kindlmann and Jena Jersakova), French with a Madagascar focus (with Joelisoa Ratsirarson), Indonesian (with Jatna Supriatna, Mochammad Indrawan, and Padmi Kramadibrata), Italian (with Luciana Carotenuto), Japanese (with Hiromi Kobori), Korean (with Dowon Lee, Z. Kim, Y. Sohn, J. H. Shin, and J. C. Chae), Mongolian (with Batbold Otgoid, Samiya Khiad, and Batsaikhan Tsagaan-aduut), Romanian (with Maria Patroescu, Laurentiu Rozylowicz, and Cristian Ioja), Russian, Spanish (with Joandomenec Ros), and Vietnamese (with Pham Binh Quyen, Vo Quy, and Hoang Van Thang). Editions of the *Primer* for South Asia and Greece are currently in production. It is my hope that these translations will help conservation biology develop as a discipline with a global scope. At the same time, examples from these translations find their way back into the English language editions, thereby enriching the presentation.

I hope that readers of this book will want to find out more about the extinction crisis facing species and biological communities and how they can take action to halt it. I encourage readers to take the field's activist spirit to heart—use the Appendix to find organizations and sources of information on how to help. If readers gain a greater appreciation for the goals, methods, and importance of conservation biology, and if they are moved to make a difference in their everyday lives, this textbook will have served its purpose.

Acknowledgments

I sincerely appreciate the contributions of Elizabeth Platt, who read and commented on the entire manuscript, and Les Kaufman, who provided expertise on marine ecosystems. Individual chapters or groups of chapters in this edition were reviewed by Katrina Brandon, Aaron Bruner, Mark Burgman, Phil Cafaro, Linus Chen, Richard Corlett, Brian Czech, Binna Davidsdottir, Elizabeth Farnsworth, Richard Frankham, Ulf Gärdenfors, Kevin Gaston, Ed Guerrant, Bill Laurance, Svata Louda, Kathy MacKinnon, Jeffrey McNeely, Rick Ostfeld, David Pimentel, Robert Pressey, Dan Simberloff, Brandie Smith, John Stinchcombe, Don Waller, Tony Whitten, and Joy Zedler.

Numerous people offered specialized input that helped make the boxes and case studies current and accurate. I would particularly like to recognize the contributions of Mary Ashley, Jason Baker, Kamal Bawa, Chris Belden, Joel Berger, Andrew Blaustein, Ivan Bond, Marlin Bowles, David Bray, Erwin Bulte, Tom Cade, Tina Carlsen, Peter Daszak, Carlos Davidson, Julie Denslow, Jim Estes, Jerry Franklin, Paul Gobster, Eric Harley, Kay Havens, Rob Horwich, Mike Hutchings, Susan Jacobson, Daniel Janzen, Beth Kaplin, Karen Lips, Colby Loucks, Meg Lowman, Irv Mendelssohn, Nalini Nadkarni, Fred Nelson, Jim Petterson, Tom Power, Walt Reid, Rob Riordan, Doug Smith, Lisa Sorenson, Caroline Stem, David Wilcove, and Gary Williams.

Diana Bierschenk was the principal research assistant and organizer for the project, with additional help from Kiruba Dharaneeswaran, Emilie Heilig, Abe Miller-Rushing, Anica Miller Rushing, Sharda Mukunda, Daniel Primack, Vikki Rogers, and Carolyn Zyloney. Sydney Carroll and Kerry Falvey provided invaluable help in the production of the book, with numerous suggestions on how to make the book friendlier to student readers. Joanne Delphia did a fine job laying out the book and creating new figures, and Andy Sinauer and the rest of the Sinauer staff helped to transform the manuscript into a finished book. Special thanks are due to my wife Margaret and my children Daniel, William, and Jasper for encouraging me to fulfill an important personal goal by completing this book. I would like to recognize Boston University for providing me with the facilities and environment that made this project possible and the many Boston University students who have taken my conservation biology courses over the years. Their enthusiasm and suggestions have helped me to find new ways to present this material. And lastly, I would like to express my great appreciation to my coauthors in other countries who have worked with me to produce conservation biology textbooks in their own languages, which are critical for spreading the message of conservation biology to a wider audience.

RICHARD PRIMACK
BOSTON, MA
APRIL, 2006

Major Issues That Define the Discipline

What Is Conservation Biology?

Popular interest in protecting the world's biological diversity—including its amazing range of species, its complex biological communities, and the genetic variation within species—has intensified during the last few decades. It has become increasingly evident to both scientists and the general public that we are living in a period of unprecedented biodiversity loss. Around the globe, biological communities that took millions of years to develop, including tropical rain forests, coral reefs, temperate old-growth forests, and prairies, are being devastated by human actions. Thousands, if not tens of thousands, of species and millions of unique populations are predicted to go extinct in the coming decades (Wilson 1992, Levin 2001, Millennium Ecosystem Assessment 2005; Brown and Laband 2006). Unlike mass extinctions in the geological past, in which tens of thousands of species died out following massive catastrophes such as asteroid collisions with the Earth and dramatic temperature changes, today's extinctions have a human face. Never before in the history of life have so many species and biological communities been threatened with extinction in so short a period of time. Never before has such devastation been caused by beings who claim reason, a moral sense, and free will as their unique and defining characteristics. Worse still, the threats to biological diversity are accelerating due to the demands of a rapidly increasing human population and its rising material consumption.

Unless something is done to reverse the trend of human-caused extinctions, wonderful species that exemplify the natural world for us—such as giant pandas, butterflies, songbirds, and whales—soon will be lost forever from their wild habitats. Additionally, many thousands, possibly millions, of less conspicuous plant, fungi, and invertebrate species and uncountable numbers of microorganisms will join them in extinction unless their habitats and populations are protected. The loss of these inconspicuous species may prove to be devastating to the planet and its human inhabitants because of the roles these species play in maintaining biological communities.

In addition to species extinctions, the natural hydrologic and chemical cycles that people depend on for clean water and clean air have been disrupted by deforestation and land clearing (MEA 2005). Soil erosion and pollution from agriculture and sewage discharges cause massive damage to rivers, lakes, and oceans. The very climate of our planet Earth has been disrupted by a combination of atmospheric pollution and deforestation. Genetic diversity within species has decreased as populations are reduced in size, even among species with seemingly healthy populations.

The main threat humans pose to the diversity of life is our destruction of natural habitat, which stems from the growth of the human population and our ever-increasing use of resources (WRI 2005). Such habitat destruction includes the clear-cutting of old-growth forests in the temperate zone and in rain forests in the Tropics, overuse of grasslands for pasture, draining of wetlands, and pollution of freshwater and marine ecosystems. Even when parcels of natural habitat are preserved as national parks, nature reserves, and marine protected areas, extreme vigilance is required to prevent the extinction of their remaining species, whose numbers have been so dramatically reduced in the past that they are now particularly vulnerable to extinction. Also, the environment in the preserved habitat fragments is so altered from its original condition that a site may no longer be suitable for the continued existence of certain species.

There are many other threats facing modern ecosystems, including climate change and invasive species. Efforts to protect a species in one area may be severely crippled as a result of a rapid climate change to which the species cannot adapt (see Chapter 9). Also, biological communities have been particularly devastated by the introduction of exotic species, which are either deliberately brought in from another area and established by people, such as domesticated animals and ornamental plants, or are brought in accidentally, such as weed species, insect pests, and new diseases. In many cases, particularly on islands, these species have become invasive (see Chapter 10) and have displaced and eliminated native species.

Another major threat to biological diversity is the use of modern technology to overharvest animals and plants for local and international markets. Entire forest, grassland, and ocean communities have been emptied of their animal life, and in many cases, their plant life as well.

Powerful technologies allow alteration of the environment on a regional and even a global scale. Some of these transformations are intentional, such as the creation of dams and the development of new agricultural land, but other changes, such as air pollution, overgrazing of grasslands, and damage to seabed habitats during fishing, are by-products of our activities. Unregulated dumping of chemicals and sewage into streams, rivers, and lakes has polluted major freshwater and coastal marine systems throughout the world and has driven significant numbers of species toward extinction. Pollution has reached such high levels that even large marine environments, such as the Mediterranean Sea, the Gulf of Mexico, and the Persian Gulf, which were once assumed to be able to absorb pollution with no negative effects, are threatened with the loss of whole suites of formerly common species. Some inland water bodies, such as the Aral Sea, have been completely destroyed, along with the many unique fish species that lived in them. Air pollution from factories and cars has turned rainwater into an acid solution that weakens and kills plant life and, in turn, the animals that depend on those plants. Scientists have warned that levels of air pollution have become severe enough to alter global climate patterns and strain the capacity of the atmosphere to filter out harmful ultraviolet radiation. The impacts of these events on biological communities are enormous and ominous; they have also stimulated the growth of conservation biology.

Scientists now realize that many of the threats to biological diversity are synergistic—that is, the negative effects of several independent factors such as logging, fire, poverty, and overhunting—combine additively or even multiplicatively. They also know that the threats to biological diversity directly threaten human populations, because people are dependent on the natural environment for raw materials, food, medicines, and even the water they drink. And the poorest people are the ones who will experience the greatest hardship from damaged environments (WRI 2005).

additive /cumulative effects — synergies among activities.

The New Science of Conservation Biology

Some people feel discouraged by the avalanche of species extinctions and the wholesale habitat destruction occurring in the world today (Morell 1999; Orr 2004). But it is possible—and indeed necessary—to feel challenged in order to find ways to stop the destruction. Actions taken—or bypassed—during the next few decades will determine how many of the world's species and natural areas will survive. People may someday look back on the closing years of the twentieth century and the first decade of the twenty-first century as an extraordinarily exciting time, when a handful of determined people saved numerous species and some entire biological communities.

Conservation biology is a new, integrated science that has developed in response to this challenge. It has three goals: first, to document the full range of biological diversity on Earth; second, to investigate human impact on species, communities, and ecosystems; and third, to develop practical approaches to prevent the extinction of species, to maintain genetic variation within species, and to protect and restore biological communities and their associated ecosystem functions (Levin 2001; Groom et al. 2006).

Conservation biology goals —

Despite the threats to biological diversity, we can detect many positive signs that allow conservation biologists to remain cautiously hopeful. The number of people living in poverty has declined over the last few decades and the rate of human population growth has slowed (Sachs 2005). The number of protected areas around the globe continues to increase, with a dramatic expansion in the number of marine protected areas. Moreover, our ability to protect biological diversity has been strengthened due to a wide range of local, national, and international efforts. Certain endangered species are now recovering as a result of conservation measures. We can point to an expansion of our knowledge base and the science of conservation biology, the developing linkages with rural development and social sciences, and our increased ability to restore degraded environments. All of these suggest that progress is being made despite the enormous tasks still ahead.

Conservation Biology Complements the Traditional Disciplines

Conservation biology arose because the traditional applied disciplines of resource management alone were not comprehensive enough to address the critical threats to biological diversity. Agriculture, forestry, wildlife management, and fisheries biology have been concerned primarily with developing methods to manage a small range of species for the marketplace and for recreation. These disciplines generally were not concerned with the protection of the full range of species and biological communities, or at best, they regarded this as a secondary issue. Conservation biology complements the applied disciplines and provides a more general theoretical approach to the protection of biological diversity. It differs from these disci-

~~plines in its primary goal of long-term preservation of entire biological communities, with economic factors secondary.~~

The academic disciplines of population biology, taxonomy, ecology, and genetics constitute the core of conservation biology, and many conservation biologists have been drawn from these ranks. In addition, many leaders in conservation biology have come from zoos and botanical gardens, bringing with them experience in maintaining and propagating species in captivity. Because much of the biodiversity crisis arises from human pressures, conservation biology also incorporates ideas and expertise from a broad range of other fields (Figure 1.1) (Levin 2001; Groom et al. 2006). For example, environmental law and policy provide the basis for government protection of rare and endangered species and critical habitats. Environmental ethics provides a rationale for preserving species. Ecological economists provide analyses of the economic value of biological diversity to support arguments for preservation. Ecosystem ecologists and climatologists monitor the biological and physical characteristics of the environment and develop models to predict environmental responses to disturbance. Social sciences, such as anthropology, sociology, and geography, provide methods to involve local people in actions to protect their immediate environment. Conservation education links academic study and field work to solve environmental problems, teaching people about science and helping them realize the value of the natural environment. Because it draws on the ideas and skills of so many separate fields, conservation biology can be considered a truly multidisciplinary approach.

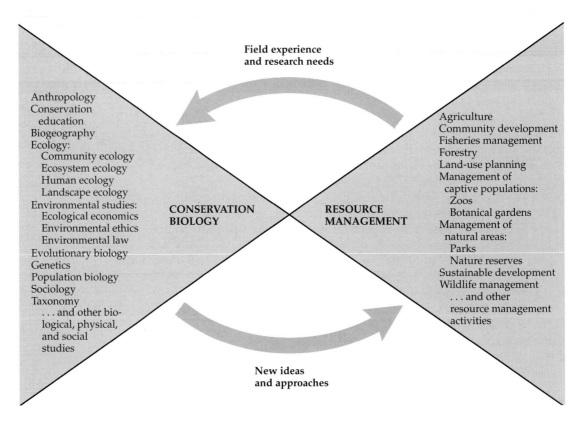

FIGURE 1.1 Conservation biology represents a synthesis of many basic sciences (left) that provide principles and new approaches for the applied fields of resource management (right). The experiences gained in the field, in turn, influence the direction of the basic sciences. (After Temple 1991.)

Another crucial difference between conservation biology and other purely academic disciplines is that conservation biology attempts to address specific issues with solutions that can be applied in actual field situations (Box 1.1). These issues involve determining the best strategies for protecting rare species, designing nature reserves, developing programs to maintain genetic variability in small populations, and reconciling conservation concerns with the needs of local people. The critical test for conservation biology is whether it can preserve and restore species and biological communities. While much of conservation research remains overly academic, the goal is still to provide practical solutions that managers can use in real situations (Fazey et al. 2005).

BOX 1.1

Conservation Biology's Interdisciplinary Approach: A Case Study with Sea Turtles

■ Sea turtles are in trouble: In many countries of the world, sea turtle populations have shrunk to less than 1% of their original sizes. Turtle populations have been devastated by a combination of factors, including destruction of their habitat due to coastal development, harvesting of adult turtles and turtle eggs for food, and high mortality due to entanglement in fishing gear. Like many tropical countries, Brazil has come to recognize the importance of protecting its sea turtles. Brazil's comprehensive approach to saving these fascinating, mysterious creatures provides a powerful illustration of the interdisciplinary nature of conservation biology. The hope is that Brazil can be one of the key places in the world where sea turtles can recover their numbers.

Sea turtles spend their whole lives at sea, with only the females returning to land to lay eggs on remote, sandy beaches. When the Brazilian government set out to design its conservation program, it soon discovered that no one knew which sea turtles were found in Brazil, how many there were, where they lived, and how local people were affecting them. To overcome this lack of basic information, in 1980 the Brazilian government established the National Marine Turtle Conservation Program, called Projeto TAMAR (TAMAR is an acronym for the Portuguese TArtarugas MARinas: "marine turtles" in English) (Marcovaldi and Marcovaldi 1999; Marcovaldi et al. 2005). The project began with a two-year survey of Brazil's 6000-km long coastline, using boats, horses, and foot patrols, combined with hundreds of interviews with villagers. TAMAR divers aided in these efforts by tagging and monitoring sea turtle populations in the water. This phase of data-gathering is an important initial step of many conservation projects.

In a protected feeding and nesting area around Rocas Atoll, about 220 km from the coast of Brazil, Brazilian scientists measure the length of an endangered green turtle (*Chelonia mydas*). They will permanently tag the turtle as part of a comprehensive conservation effort by Projeto TAMAR. (Photograph courtesy of Projeto TAMAR Image Bank.)

The survey found three main zones of turtle nesting beaches along 1100 km of the coastline between Rio de Janeiro and Recife, with loggerhead turtles (*Careta careta*) the most abundant and four other species also pres-

(continued)

BOX 1.1 *(continued)*

ent. The green turtle (*Chelonia mydas*) was the only species nesting on Brazil's offshore islands.

Interviews with villagers and observations of beaches revealed that adult turtles and turtle eggs were being intensively harvested, with 100% of the eggs often collected. In many areas, the construction of resorts, houses, commercial developments, and beach roads directly damaged and reduced the available nesting area on beaches. The shadows cast by the buildings also changed the temperature of the sand, which is a critical determinant of sex in hatching turtles. In certain developed beaches, most of the emerging turtles were males. Additionally, the light from the buildings at night disoriented emerging hatchlings; instead of heading straight to the ocean, they often would wander in different directions and become exhausted. For the young turtles that did make it to sea, many were caught in the nets of fishermen, both in Brazil's coastal waters and throughout the Atlantic Ocean, and suffocated to death.

Student interns and a child release turtle hatchlings. Interns gain valuable experience through their participation, in the process furthering project objectives. (Photograph courtesy of Projeto TAMAR Image Bank.)

Information from the TAMAR survey was critical to legislation passed in 1986 in Brazil that led to the complete protection of sea turtles and the establishment of two new Biological Reserves and a Marine National Park to protect nesting beaches on the islands.

While creating protected areas is important in conservation efforts, ongoing management activities are also needed. Projeto TAMAR also chose an innovative and comprehensive approach to protecting the turtles on the ground. First, they established 21 conservation stations at each of the main nesting beaches. Within these areas, the Brazilian government allowed TAMAR complete responsibility for and control of the beaches. Each station has a manager, several university interns, and local employees. Over 85% of TAMAR's 1000 employees are coastal residents, many of whom are former fishermen, who bring their knowledge of turtles to bear on conservation. The local employees have become strong advocates for the sea turtles, because their wages from Projeto TAMAR and the related tourist industry are linked to the continuing presence of these animals.

The stations' personnel regularly patrol the conservation areas on foot and by vehicle, measuring turtles for size and permanently flipper-tagging all adults observed on the beach. In places where predators are abundant, nests are covered with wire mesh fitted with small gaps to allow natural hatching, or the eggs are collected and brought to nearby hatchery areas for reburial. These measures allow baby turtles emerging from the hatcheries to enter the ocean just as if they were emerging from a natural nest. TAMAR protects over 4000 turtle nests each year, and has protected around 100,000 nests and approximately 7 million hatchlings in total over the years since its inception.

TAMAR is also working with the Brazilian government to protect and manage the nesting beaches on the offshore islands. The project has extended its mission to include protecting turtles caught in fishing nets while in the coastal feeding grounds. TAMAR provides fishermen with information about the importance of turtles and fishing gear designed to avoid capturing turtles. Fishermen are also taught techniques for reviving turtles caught in their nets so the turtles will not suffocate. Due to their increasing appreciation of turtles and their awareness of the new laws, fishermen are cooperating with these policies.

Projeto TAMAR plays a highly positive role in the villages where it operates. In many areas, TAMAR is the primary source of income for the local people, and it often provides for child care facilities and small medical and dental clinics. Villagers are employed in making crafts for sale to tourists, based on turtle themes. To increase awareness of the program at the local level, TAMAR per-

BOX 1.1 *(continued)*

sonnel give talks about marine conservation in village schools and organize hatchling-release ceremonies and local festivals.

The project reaches a wide audience in Brazil through coverage in popular articles and on television programs. In addition, TAMAR operates special sea turtle educational centers where hundreds of thousands of tourists visit each year. The tourists get to see conservation in action, they receive a large dose of conservation education and, in turn, they support the project through their purchase of souvenirs.

Projeto TAMAR has tried to involve the next generation of concerned conservationists in current projects, help-

ing student interns experience success with a real-life conservation project. Hopefully the awareness raised by Projeto TAMAR will gradually extend to other conservation programs.

Projeto TAMAR has slowed population decline dramatically by protecting thousands of adult turtles, tens of thousands of nests, and millions of hatchlings. The project has also changed people's attitudes, both in coastal villages and in the wider Brazilian society. By integrating conservation goals with local community development, Brazil's Projeto TAMAR has improved the future for sea turtles and for local people involved with their conservation.

Conservation Biology Is a Crisis Discipline

Decisions on conservation questions are being made every day under severe time pressures. Conservation biologists and scientists in related fields are well-suited to provide the advice that governments, businesses, and the general public need in order to make crucial decisions, but because of time constraints, scientists are often compelled to make decisions on matters such as park design and species management without the thorough investigations that would normally be required. If they are unable or unwilling to offer such advice, decisions to act or not to act will be made with even less knowledge and concern for the needs of biological communities and endangered species (Barry and Oelschlager 1996). Conservation biologists must also be able to articulate a long-term vision that extends beyond the immediate crisis (Redford and Sanjayan 2003; Granek et al. 2005). Consequently, they must be willing to express an opinion and take a stand based on available evidence, accepted theory, comparable examples, and informed judgment.

Conservation Biology's Ethical Principles

Conservation biology rests on an underlying set of principles that are generally agreed on by members of the discipline (Soulé 1985). These principles cannot be proved or disproved, and accepting all of them is not a requirement for conservation biologists. Religious fundamentalists who are active in the conservation movement but do not believe in the theory of evolution, for instance, probably will not accept some of these principles. Nonetheless, this set of ethical and ideological statements forms the philosophical foundation of the discipline and suggests research approaches and practical applications. As long as one or two of these principles are accepted, there is enough rationale for conservation efforts.

- *The diversity of species and biological communities should be preserved.* The rich diversity of life should be protected. In general, most people agree with this principle because they enjoy biological diversity. The hundreds of millions of visitors each year to zoos, national parks, botanical gardens, and aquariums testify to the general public's interest in observing different species and biological communities. Genetic variation within species also sparks popular interest, as shown by the wide appeal of pet shows, agricultural expositions, flower exhibitions, and large numbers of specialty clubs (African violet societies, rose societies, etc.). Home gardeners pride themselves on how many types of plants they have in their gardens, while birdwatchers compete to see how many species they can identify in one day or in their lifetimes. It has even been suggested that humans may have a genetic predisposition to like biological diversity, called **biophilia** (Kellert and Wilson 1993; Kellert 1997).

- *The untimely extinction of populations and species should be prevented*. The ordinary extinction of species and populations as a result of natural processes is an ethically neutral event. Through the millennia of geological time, the natural extinction of each species has tended to be balanced by the evolution of new species. The local loss of a population of a species likewise is usually offset by the establishment of a new population through dispersal. However, as a result of human activity the rate of extinction has increased by more than a hundredfold (see Chapter 7) (Lövei 2001; MEA 2005). Virtually all of the hundreds of vertebrate species—and the presumed tens of thousands of invertebrate species—that have gone extinct in the last few centuries have been wiped out by humans. Many people now recognize their role and responsibility in causing and, more important, in preventing extinctions.

- *Ecological complexity should be maintained*. Many of the most interesting properties of biological diversity are only expressed in natural environments. For example, complex coevolutionary and ecological relationships exist among some tropical flowers, the hummingbirds that visit the flowers to drink nectar, and the mites that live in the flowers and use the hummingbirds' beaks as "buses" to travel from flower to flower. These relationships would no longer exist if the hummingbirds, mites, and plants were housed separately and in isolation at zoos and botanical gardens. While the biological diversity of species may be partially preserved in zoos and gardens, the ecological complexity that exists in natural communities will be largely lost without the preservation of wild lands and aquatic environments.

- *Evolution should continue*. Evolutionary adaptation is the process that eventually leads to new species and increased biological diversity. Therefore, it is important to allow populations to continue to evolve in nature. Human processes that limit or even prevent populations from evolving, such as elimination of unique high-level populations or populations at the northern edge of a species range should be avoided. Preserving species in captivity when they are no longer able to survive in the wild is a possible stop-gap means of rescue, but such species are then cut off from the ecological processes that allowed them to evolve. In those cases, the species may no longer be able to survive in the wild if released.

- *Biological diversity has intrinsic value*. Species and the biological communities in which they live possess value of their own ("intrinsic value") regardless of their economic, scientific, or aesthetic value to human society. This value is conferred not only by their evolutionary history and unique ecological role, but also by their very existence. This position is in sharp contrast to an economic viewpoint, which would assign a monetary value to each species or biological community on the basis of the goods and services that it provides or potentially could provide to humans. A purely economic viewpoint often leads to a decision to move forward with a highly destructive development project and to ignore the intrinsic value of biological diversity.

The Origins of Conservation Biology

The origins of conservation biology can be traced to religious and philosophical beliefs concerning the relationship between human societies and the natural world (Berkes 1999, 2001; McNeely 2001; also see Chapter 6). In many of the world's religions, people are seen as both physically and spiritually connected to the plants and animals in the surrounding environment (Figure 1.2). In Chinese Taoism, Japanese Shinto, Indian Hinduism, and Buddhist philosophies, some sacred wilderness areas and natural settings are valued and protected for their capacity to provide intense spiritual experiences. These philosophies see a direct connection between the natural world and the spiritual world, a connection that breaks when the natural world is altered or destroyed by human activity. Strict adherents to the Jain and Hindu religions in India believe that *all* killing of animal life is wrong. In Islamic, Judaic, and Christian teachings alike, people are given the sacred responsibility to be guardians of nature.

Biological diversity often has immediate significance to traditional societies whose people live close to the land and water. In Native American tribes of the Pacific Northwest, hunters undergo purification rituals in order to be considered worthy of hunting animals. The Iroquois, a Native American group, considered how their actions would affect the lives of their descendants after seven generations. Hunting and gathering societies, such as the Penan of Borneo, give thousands of names to individual trees, animals, and places in their surroundings to create a cultural landscape that is vital to the well-being of the tribe. This type of relationship to the natural world was described eloquently at the Fourth World Wilderness Congress in 1987 by the delegate from the Kuna people of Panama (Gregg 1991):

> For the Kuna culture, the land is our mother and all living things that we live on are her brothers in such a manner that we must take care of her and live in a harmonious manner on her, because the extinction of one thing is also the end of another.

FIGURE 1.2 Tanah Lot is a Hindu temple on the island of Bali in Indonesia. Its coastal setting allows worshippers to experience the connection of the human spirit with the natural world. (Photograph by Gary J. James/Biological Photo Service.)

In an ecological and cultural history of the Indian subcontinent, Gadgil and Guha (1992) argue that the belief systems, religions, and myths of hunter-gatherer societies and stable agricultural societies tend to emphasize conservation themes and the wise use of natural resources because these groups have learned over time to live within the constraints of a fixed resource base. In contrast, the belief systems of communities that raise livestock and rapidly expanding agricultural and industrial societies emphasize the rapid consumption and destruction of natural resources as a way to maximize growth and assert control over other groups. These groups move to new localities when the resources of any one place are exhausted. Modern industrial states represent the extreme of such societies. Their excessive and wasteful consumption requires the transportation of resources to urban centers in ever-widening circles of resource depletion. However, what will we do when the resources are all gone?

European Origins

To the European mind, the prevalent view has been that God created nature for humans' use and benefit. In Genesis, the first book of the Bible, God instructs Adam and Eve to "be fruitful and multiply and fill the Earth and subdue it; have dominion over every living thing that moves upon the Earth." The Biblical instruction supports a dominant tenet of Western philosophy: Nature should be converted into wealth as rapidly as possible and used for the benefit of humans. This point of view justifies nearly all land uses and implies that to leave land unused is to misuse God's gift—a foolish, if not downright sinful, mistake. In medieval Europe, wilderness was perceived to be useless land and was often believed to be inhabited by evil spirits or monsters, in contrast to the orderly qualities and appearance of agricultural landscapes (Nash 1990).

This anthropocentric (human-centered) view of nature led to the exploitation and degradation of vast resources in the regions colonized by European countries from the sixteenth century onward (Diamond 1999). In practice, the wealth and benefits that came from this policy accrued primarily to the citizens of the colonial powers, while the needs of non-European native peoples were largely disregarded. The long-term ramifications for the forests, fisheries, and other natural resources themselves were not considered at all; the unexplored territories of the Americas, Asia, Africa, and Australia seemed so vast and rich that it was inconceivable to the colonial powers that their natural resources could ever be depleted.

An important element of the conservation movement did develop in Europe, however, based on the experiences of scientific officers—often imbued with Romantic idealism—who were sent to assist in the development of colonies in the eighteenth and nineteenth centuries (Grove and Rackham 2001). These scientists were trained to make detailed observations on the biology, natural history, geography, and anthropology of the colonial regions. Many of them expected to find the indigenous people living in wonderful harmony with nature. Instead, they found devastated forests, damaged watersheds, and newly created poverty.

In European colonies throughout the world, perceptive scientific officers came to see that protection of forests was necessary to prevent soil erosion, provide water for irrigation and drinking, maintain wood supplies, and prevent famine. Some colonial administrators also argued that certain intact forests should remain uncut because of their necessary role in ensuring a steady supply of rainfall in adjacent agricultural areas—foreshadowing modern concern with global climate change. Such arguments led directly to conservation ordinances. On the Indian Ocean island of Mauritius, for example, the French colonial administration in 1769 stipulated that 25% of landholdings remain forested to prevent erosion, degraded areas be planted with trees, and forests growing within 200 meters of water be protected. On the Caribbean island of Tobago, British officers set aside 20% of the land so as to maintain rainfall (Grove and Rackham 2001). In order to prevent water pollution and the destruction of fish populations, various colonial governments passed laws in the late eighteenth century regulating the pollutants being discharged by indigo and sugar mills. The experiences and experiments on small tropical island colonies had considerable influence on British scientists working in India, who issued a report in 1852 urging the establishment of forest reserves throughout the vast subcontinent in order to avert environmental calamities and economic losses. In particular, the report linked deforestation to decreased rainfall and water supplies, which resulted in famine among the local people. The report was embraced by the leadership of the British East India Company, who could see that conservation made good economic sense. During the mid-nineteenth century, Indian state governments established an extensive system of forest reserves protected and managed by professional foresters. This system was widely adopted in other parts of the colonial world, such as Southeast Asia, Australia, and Africa, and it influenced forestry in North America as well. The irony is that, prior to colonization, indigenous peoples in these regions often had well-developed systems of natural resource management that were swept aside by the colonial governments (Poffenberger 1990; Gadgil and Guha 1992).

FIGURE 1.3 Humans witnessed the extinction of the dodo, a flightless bird found only on the remote island of Mauritius in the Indian Ocean. The dodo was extinct within 80 years of humans colonizing the island.

Many of the themes of contemporary conservation biology were established in European scientific writings of a century or more ago (Grove 1992). The possibility of species extinction was demonstrated by the loss of wild cattle (*Bos primigenius*, also known as the aurochs) from Europe in 1627 and the extinction of the dodo bird (*Raphus cucullatus*) in Mauritius in the 1680s (Figure 1.3). To address the problem of the decline and possible extinction of wild cattle, Polish authorities in 1564 established a nature reserve that prohibited hunting. This nature reserve represented one of the earliest deliberate European efforts to conserve a species. While this action failed to preserve wild cattle (the progenitor of modern cattle), the nature reserve protected the sole remaining population of the wisent, also known as the European bison (*Bison bonasus*) and remains today one of Europe's most important nature reserves.

In Europe, expression of concern for the protection of wildlife began to spread widely in the late nineteenth century (Galbraith et al. 1998). The combination of both an increasing area of land under cultivation and more widespread use of firearms for hunting led to a marked reduction in wild animals. In Britain, many culturally and ecologically significant species became extinct in the wild around this time: great bustards (*Otis tarda*), ospreys (*Pandion haliaetus*), sea eagles (*Haliaeetus albicilla*), and the great auk (*Pinguinus impennis*). Other species showed similar rapid declines. These dramatic changes stimulated the formation of the British conservation movement, leading to the founding of the Commons, Open Spaces and Footpaths Preservation Society in 1865, the National Trust for Places of Historic Interest and Natural Beauty in 1895, and the Royal Society for the Protection of Birds in 1899. Altogether, these groups have preserved around 900,000 hectare*

---

*For an explanation of the term "hectare" and other measurements, see Table 1.1.

TABLE 1.1 *Some useful units of measurement*

LENGTH

1 meter (m)	1 m = 39.4 inches
1 kilometer (km)	1 km = 1000 m = 0.62 mile
1 centimeter (cm)	1 cm = 1/100 m = 0.39 inch
1 millimeter (mm)	1 mm = 1/1000 m = 0.039 inch

AREA

square meter (m^2)	Area encompassed by a square, each side of which is 1 meter
1 hectare (ha)	1 ha = 10,000 m^2 = 2.47 acres 100 ha = 1 square kilometer (km^2)

MASS

1 kilogram (kg)	1 kg = 2.2 pounds
1 gram (g)	1 g = 1/1000 kg = 0.035 ounce

TEMPERATURE

$0°C = \frac{5}{9} (°F - 32)$

degree Celsius (°C)	0°C = 32° Fahrenheit (the freezing point of water) 100°C = 212° Fahrenheit (the boiling point of water) 23°C = 72° Fahrenheit ("room temperature")

(ha) of open land. In the twentieth century, government action produced laws such as the National Parks and Access to the Countryside Act, passed in 1949 for the "protection and public enjoyment of the wider countryside" and the Wildlife and Countryside Act, passed in 1981, for the protection of endangered species, their habitat, and the marine environment. Because of the intensive human use of the British landscape, conservation efforts in Britain have traditionally emphasized the preservation and management of relatively small fragments of land. Rare and declining habitats, such as the chalk grasslands of eastern and southern England, continue to be a major concern in conservation efforts.

Many other European countries also have strong traditions of nature conservation and land protection, most notably Denmark, Austria, the Netherlands, Germany, and Switzerland. In these countries as well, conservation is enacted by both the government and private conservation organizations. Over the last two decades, regional initiatives to protect species, habitats, and ecosystem processes have been coordinated by the European Union.

American Origins

Among the first major intellectual figures in the United States arguing for the protection of natural areas were the nineteenth-century philosophers Ralph Waldo Emerson and Henry David Thoreau (Callicott 1990). Emerson, in his transcendentalist writings, saw nature as a temple in which people could commune with the spiritual world and achieve spiritual enlightenment (Emerson 1836). Thoreau was both an advocate for nature and an opponent of materialistic society, believing that people needed far fewer possessions than they sought. To prove his point, he lived simply in a cabin near Walden Pond, writing about his ideas and experiences in a book—*Walden*, published in 1854—that has had a significant impact on many generations of students and environmentalists. Thoreau believed that the experience of nature was a necessary counterweight to the over-refining tendencies of civilization. In his collection of essays (1863) he argued emphatically that

[in] wilderness is the preservation of the world. . . . The story of Romulus and Remus [the founders of the Roman Empire] being suckled by a wolf is not a meaningless fable. The founders of every state which has risen to eminence have drawn their nourishment and vigor from a similar wild source.

This concern for preserving wilderness, large areas that remain essentially unoccupied, unmanaged, and unmodified by human beings, is a continuing and dominant theme in the American conservation movement up to the present time (Meine 2001). It contrasts sharply with the traditional European view that because landscapes developed over thousands of years of human interaction, further management is appropriate to reach conservation objectives (Cooper 2000).

Eminent American wilderness advocate John Muir used the transcendental themes of Emerson and Thoreau in his campaigns to preserve natural areas. According to Muir's **preservationist ethic**, natural areas such as forest groves, mountaintops, and waterfalls have spiritual values that are generally superior to the tangible material gain obtained by their exploitation (Muir 1901). This philosophy emphasized the needs of philosophers, poets, artists, and spiritual seekers—who require the beauty and stimulus of nature for their development—over the needs of the mass society, who require jobs and material goods from the natural environment. Some see this view as undemocratic and elitist, arguing that it disregards the very real material needs of food, clothing, shelter, and employment, which may require economic exploitation of the wilderness. Yet one does not have to be a member of the elite in order to appreciate natural beauty: All human beings share these impulses, and Muir's arguments for the spiritual and artistic value of nature did not limit its accessibility or its benefits to a single stratum of society. That wilderness can benefit all of society can be seen today in special programs such as Outward Bound that use experiences with nature and wilderness to challenge and enrich the character development and self-confidence of teenagers and young adults, some of whom might otherwise succumb to drugs, crime, despair, or apathy.

In addition to advocating the preservation of nature on the grounds of human spiritual needs, Muir was among the first American conservationists to explicitly state that nature has **intrinsic value**—value in and of itself, apart from its value to humanity. Muir argued on biblical grounds that, since God had created nature and individual species, to destroy them was undoing God's work. In Muir's view, people have an equal place with all other species in God's scheme of nature (Muir 1916, p. 139):

> Why should man value himself as more than a small part of the one great unit of creation? And what creature of all that the Lord has taken the pains to make is not essential to the completeness of that unit—the cosmos? The universe would be incomplete without the smallest transmicroscopic creature that dwells beyond our conceitful eyes and knowledge.

JOHN MUIR
(1838–1914)

Muir also viewed biological communities as assemblages of species evolving together and dependent on one another, foreshadowing the views of modern ecologists.

An alternative view of nature, known as the **resource conservation ethic**, was developed by Gifford Pinchot, the dynamic first head of the U.S. Forest Service (Callicott 1990; Norton 1991). According to Pinchot, the world consists essentially of two components, human beings and natural resources. He defined natural resources as the commodities and qualities found in nature, including timber, fodder, clean water, wildlife, and even beautiful landscapes (Pinchot 1947). The proper use of natural resources, according to the resource conservation ethic, is whatever will further "the greatest good of the greatest number [of people] for the longest time." Its first principle is that resources should be fairly distributed among present individuals, and between present and future generations. In this definition, we see the origins of sustainable use doctrines and modern attempts by ecological economists

GIFFORD PINCHOT
(1865–1946)

ALDO LEOPOLD
(1887–1948)

to put a monetary value on natural resources. As defined by the World Commission on the Environment and Development (1987), "sustainable development is development that meets the needs of the present without compromising the ability of future generations to meet their own needs." From the perspective of conservation biology, **sustainable development** is development that best meets present and future human needs without damaging the environment and biological diversity (Lubchenco et al. 1991).

The second principle of the resource conservation ethic is that resources should be used with efficiency—that is, they should be put to the best possible use and not wasted. Efficiency implies that there can be an ordering of uses, with some favored over others, or possibly a "multiple use" of resources. In this view, appreciation of natural beauty and other aesthetic and intellectual experiences can be considered competing uses of nature, which in some situations will take precedence over material uses, although in practice, "multiple use" land managers have usually given precedence to material uses

Although the resource conservation ethic can be linked to resource economics to determine the "best" or most profitable use of the land, such methods use market forces to determine value and thus have a tendency to minimize or even disregard the costs of environmental degradation and to discount the future value of resources. Consequently, Pinchot argued that government bodies are needed to regulate and control natural resources such as forests and rivers with a long-term perspective to prevent their destruction. The resource conservation ethic came to dominate American thinking in the twentieth century because of its democratic social philosophy and because it supported American efforts to increase control over nature. Government bodies that manage natural resources for multiple use, such as the Bureau of Land Management and the U.S. Forest Service, are the legacy of this conservationist approach, in contrast to the generally preservationist philosophy of the National Park Service.

The resource conservation ethic was the philosophy initially embraced by the influential biologist Aldo Leopold in his early years as a government forester. Eventually, however, he came to believe that the resource conservation ethic was inadequate and untrue, because it viewed the land merely as a collection of individual goods that can be used in different ways. Leopold began to consider nature as a landscape organized as a system of interrelated processes (Leopold 1939a) and remarked that

> The emergence of ecology has placed the economic biologist in a peculiar dilemma: with one hand he points out the accumulated findings of his search for utility, or lack of utility, in this or that species; with the other he lifts the veil from a biota so complex, so conditioned by interwoven cooperations and competitions, that no man can say where utility begins or ends.

Leopold eventually came to the conclusion that the most important goal of conservation is to maintain the health of natural ecosystems and ecological processes (Leopold 2004). As a result, he and many others lobbied successfully for certain parts of national forests to be set aside as wilderness areas (Rolston 2000; Shafer 2001). He also considered humans part of the ecological community rather than standing apart from and exploiting nature, as the proponents of the resource conservation ethic argued. Despite Leopold's philosophical shift, he remained committed to the idea that humans should be involved in land management, seeking a middle ground between overexploitation and total control over nature on the one hand, and complete preservation of land with no human presence or activity on the other.

Leopold's synthesis has been termed the **evolutionary–ecological land ethic**. In his writings and in practice at his family farm, Leopold advocated a land use policy in which human use of natural resources was compatible with, or even enhanced, biological diversity (Leopold 1939b, 1949). Integrating human activity into preservationist philosophy also makes practical sense because complete exclusion of human impact from natural reserves has always been very difficult and is now becoming impossible due to human population growth, air pollution, and global climate change. An approach that combines ideas of both Leopold and Pinchot has been developed, known as **ecosystem management**, which places the highest management priority on maintaining the health of wild species and ecosystems.

Development of these philosophies has taken place alongside the growth of many U.S. conservation organizations, such as the Wilderness Society, the Audubon Society, Ducks Unlimited, and the Sierra Club; the development of the national and state park systems; and the passing of numerous environmental laws. Elements of each of these differing philosophies are present in contemporary writings, the stated goals of conservation organizations, and government policy in both the United States and in other countries. Disagreements over policy and practice among and within conservation organizations, individual conservationists, and government departments continue to reflect these long-term philosophical differences. This continuing debate over elements of conservation philosophy and ethics is necessary in deciding how to balance the long-term needs of protecting biological diversity with the more immediate needs of modern society for natural resources.

Environmental activists, writers, and educators have applied these diverse philosophies in ways that have benefited and transformed society. Ellen Swallow Richards (1842–1911) was one of the most influential individuals, though she had great difficulty obtaining a professional position as a chemist, a field not open to women at that time. After being appointed a chemistry instructor at the Massachusetts Institute of Technology, she developed the first course in the new subject of ecology. In her many public activities she emphasized the need to protect the natural environment as a key element in maintaining public health. Richards was particularly concerned with how water quality was affected by sewage and industrial wastes, and she began to test the quality of water in rivers and lakes. Her procedures led to the first water-quality standards in the country and eventually to the development of modern sewage treatment plants that help protect public drinking supplies as well as the natural environment.

Another key figure was Rachel Carson (1907–1964). In her widely read book *Silent Spring* (1962), she documented the role of pesticides and the chemical industry in the loss of bird populations. At first she was heavily criticized by representatives of the chemical industry. However, her tireless campaigning led to bans on DDT in many countries and to better regulation of other toxic chemicals, and it was crucial to the development of the modern environmental movement. The recovery of numerous bird species, such as falcons, eagles, and ospreys in the years following the ban on DDT, proved that her observations were correct (see Box 9.1).

Within the American conservation movement, other writers have prophetically warned about the increasing destruction of biological diversity and the natural environment (Nash 1990; Meine 2001). Key authors include G. P. Marsh, with his *Man and Nature: Or, Physical Geography as Modified by Human Action* (1864); Fairfield Osborn, author of *Our Plundered Planet* (1948); Paul Ehrlich and Anne Ehrlich, authors of *The Population Bomb* (1968); former U.S. Vice-President Albert Gore, author of *Earth in the Balance: Ecology and the Human Spirit* (1992); E. O. Wilson, and his book, *The Diversity of Life* (1992); and Jared Diamond's decisive historical analysis, *Collapse* (2005). These authors have found a receptive general audience and have galvanized citizens by the millions to join efforts to protect birds and other wildlife; to conserve mountains, seashores, wetlands, and other habitats; and to limit environmental pollution.

ELLEN SWALLOW RICHARDS
(1842–1911)

RACHEL CARSON
(1907–1964)

A New Science Is Born

By the early 1970s, scientists throughout the world were aware of an accelerating biological diversity crisis, but there was no central forum or organization to address the issue. The growing number of people thinking about conservation issues and conducting research needed to be able to communicate with each other to develop new ideas and approaches (Takacs 1996). Ecologist Michael Soulé organized the First International Conference on Conservation Biology in 1978, which met at the San Diego Wild Animal Park, so that wildlife conservationists, zoo managers, and academics could discuss their common interests. At that meeting, Soulé proposed a new interdisciplinary approach that could help save plants and animals from the threat of human-caused extinctions. Subsequently, Soulé, along with colleagues including Paul Ehrlich of Stanford University and Jared Diamond of the University of California at Los Angeles, began to develop conservation biology as a discipline that would combine the practical experience of wildlife, forestry, and fisheries management with the theories of population biology and biogeography. In 1985, this core of scientists founded the Society for Conservation Biology.

Conservation Biology: A Dynamic and Growing Field

The field of conservation biology has set itself some imposing—and absolutely critical—tasks: to describe the Earth's biological diversity, to restore what is degraded, and to protect what is remaining. Fortunately, the field is up to such tasks. The indicators listed below show just how dynamic the field is today.

- *Conservation biology has resulted in government action, both nationally and internationally.* The protection of biological diversity has emerged as a major goal of many national governments, as shown by the widespread government action being taken on behalf of conservation biology: laws such as the U.S. Endangered Species Act; Red Lists of endangered species in the European Union; new national parks and protected areas; international treaties, such as the Convention on Biological Diversity; and increased regulations on trade and harvesting of endangered species, most notably the Convention on Trade in Endangered Species (CITES).

- *Conservation biology programs and activities are being funded as never before.* Major funding agencies have made conservation biology a primary recipient for funding. For example, projects involving conservation and environmental protection worth $4.7 billion are currently supported by the Global Environment Facility, a special program established by the United Nations and the World Bank. Major foundations, such as the MacArthur Foundation, the Ford Foundation, and the Pew Charitable Trusts, also make conservation activities a major priority.

- *Conservation biology's goals have been adopted by traditional conservation organizations.* Large, established conservation organizations such as The Nature Conservancy, the World Wildlife Fund, and the Audubon Society, which formerly had a restricted set of priorities, have embraced the broader goals of conservation biology, making science central to decision-making.

- *Conservation biology's goals are being incorporated into international scientific activity and policy.* For example, in 2005, over 1300 scientists from 95 countries completed the Millennium Ecosystem Assessment, promoting the value of biodiversity to the public, government officials, and funding agencies as well as describing actions needed to protect it. In addition, two projects, Species 2000 and the Global Biodiversity Information Facility, are producing a comprehensive list of all known species in the world and related databases of species distribution, conservation status, habitat, and documented museum specimens (Edwards et al. 2000).

- *Conservation biology's aims and goals are reaching a broader audience through increased media coverage.* The latest findings of the field reach an even wider audience through popular magazines such as *National Geographic, National Wildlife, Scientific American,* and *Environment;* newspapers such as the *New York Times;* and nature television programs such as those found on Nova and on the National Geographic Channel.

- *Conservation biology courses and curricula are expanding in academia.* More than 195 American, Canadian, European, and Australian universities, and numerous universities in other countries, have established graduate programs in conservation biology and biological diversity; large numbers of courses are being taught at all levels (van Heezik and Seddon 2005). This development in academe is driven by the interests of students, the changing research activities of professors, and the willingness of foundations to support new programs.

FIGURE 1.4 The Society for Conservation Biology has a simple, yet powerful, logo showing the circle of life, within which we live. The ocean waves in the center symbolize the changes that lie ahead. The logo can also be viewed as a singing bird, providing us with beauty and tranquility; on closer look, we see that its wings are really rustling leaves. (Courtesy of The Society for Conservation Biology.)

- *Conservation biology has a rapidly expanding professional society.* The Society for Conservation Biology (SCB) has become one of the fastest-growing and most exciting societies in biology (Figure 1.4). The SCB now has approximately 10,000 professional members, in 120 countries, equaling the size of the Ecological Society of America, which was founded more than 90 years ago. The growing membership in the SCB reflects the perceived relevance of this new discipline.

Ultimately, however, conservation biology must be judged by its ability to preserve biological diversity. When conservation biologists can confidently point to successful examples of species and biological communities that have been protected and restored, only then will we be able to consider conservation biology a success.

Summary

1. Thousands of species are going extinct, genetic variation is being lost, millions of populations are disappearing, and entire biological communities are being destroyed as a result of human activities. Conservation biology is a relatively new, synthetic discipline combining basic and applied research to describe biological diversity, document the threats it faces from human activities, and develop methods to protect and restore biological diversity.

2. Conservation biology rests on a number of underlying assumptions that are accepted by most conservation biologists: biological diversity, including the range of species, genetic variation, biological communities, and ecosystem interactions, should be preserved; the extinction of species by human activities should be prevented; the complex interaction of species in natural communities should be maintained; evolutionary change should continue; and biological diversity has value in and of itself.

3. Conservation biology draws on both scientific and religious/philosophical traditions. European scientists in the eighteenth and nineteenth centuries reacted to the destruction of forests and water pollution in their colonies by proposing some of the first environmental legislation. The decline and extinction of species in Europe

led to the establishment of the first nature reserves and an active popular interest in conservation. In the United States, Henry David Thoreau and John Muir argued for the preservation of wilderness and the intrinsic value of species. Gifford Pinchot proposed developing a balance among competing natural resource needs for present and future societies. Aldo Leopold advocated striking a balance between managing land for ecological processes and satisfying human needs. These philosophies still guide land management, and elements of them can be found in the current doctrines of conservation organizations and government departments.

For Discussion

1. What do you think are the major conservation and environmental problems facing the world today? What are the major problems facing your local community? How do you think these problems can be solved?

2. Consider the public land management and private conservation organizations with which you are familiar. Would you consider their guiding philosophies to be closest to the resource conservation ethic, the preservation ethic, or the evolutionary–ecological land ethic? What factors allow them to be successful or limit their effectiveness? Learn more about these organizations through their publications and websites.

3. How would you characterize your own conservation philosophy? How did you come to hold those beliefs? How do you, or could you, put these beliefs into practice?

4. Which do you think teaches us the most about nature: science, watching nature programs on television, or direct personal experience?

Suggested Readings

Brown, R. M. and D. N. Laband. 2006. Species imperilment and spatial patterns of development in the United States. *Conservation Biology* 20: 239–244. Increasing human activity threatens species with extinction.

Callicott, J. B. 1990. Whither conservation ethics? *Conservation Biology* 4: 15–20. A summary of some major themes in conservation biology.

Cooper, N. 2000. How natural is a native reserve? An ideological study of British conservation landscapes. *Biological Conservation* 9: 1131–1152. Public attitudes strongly influence what societies decide to protect.

Groom, M. J., G. K. Meffe, and C. R. Carroll (eds.). 2006. *Principles of Conservation Biology*, 3rd ed. Sinauer Associates, Inc., Sunderland, MA. Excellent, advanced treatment, with dozens of case studies.

Grove, A. T. and O. Rackham. 2001. *The Nature of Mediterranean Europe: An Ecological History*. Yale University Press, New Haven. Humans have been shaping the European lands for thousands of years.

Kellert, S. R. and E. O. Wilson (eds.). 1993. *The Biophilia Hypothesis*. Island Press, Washington, D.C. A discussion of the hypothesis that people have an inherent predisposition to value biological diversity.

Levin, S. A. (ed.). 2001. *Encyclopedia of Biodiversity*. Academic Press, San Diego, CA. An amazing, comprehensive guide to the whole field; see individual essay on conservation, ethics, and religion.

Millenium Ecosystem Assessment. 2005. *Ecosystems and Human Well-Being*. 4 Volumes. Island Press, Covelo, CA. Detailed report and summary by the world's leading scientists documenting the importance of ecosystem services.

Morell, V. 1999. The variety of life. *National Geographic* 195 (February): 6–32. Special issue on biodiversity includes this and other beautifully illustrated articles about biological diversity, threats to its existence, and key conservation projects.

Redford, K. H. and M. A. Sanjayan. 2003. Retiring Cassandra. *Conservation Biology* 17: 1473–1474. In a short essay, the authors argue that conservation biology needs to develop a positive, long-term vision.

Rolston, H. III. 2000. The land ethic at the turn of the millennium. *Biodiversity and Conservation* 9: 1045–1058. Aldo Leopold's land ethic is now evolving into a more all-encompassing Earth ethic.

Takacs, D. 1996. *The Idea of Biodiversity.* The Johns Hopkins University Press, Baltimore. Critical evaluation of the philosophical and political basis of conservation biology, including interviews with leading figures.

Van Heezik, Y. and P. J. Seddon. 2005. Conservation education structure and content of graduate wildlife management and conservation biology programs: An international perspective. *Conservation Biology* 19: 7–14. Conservation education programs are increasing and are highly diverse.

Wilson, E. O. 1992. *The Diversity of Life.* Belknap Press of Harvard University Press, Cambridge, MA. An outstanding description of biological diversity, written for the general public.

World Resource Institute. 2005. *World Resources 2005: The Wealth of the Poor-Managing Ecosystems to Fight Poverty.* World Resource Institute, Washington, D.C. Massive body of data on biodiversity and the human condition.

What Is Biological Diversity?

The protection of biological diversity is central to conservation biology, but the phrase "biological diversity" (or simply "biodiversity") can have different meanings. In the field of conservation biology, biological diversity is often used to encompass the complete range of species, the genetic variation within species, and all biological communities, including their ecosystem interactions. By this definition, which we will use in this book, biological diversity must be considered on three levels:

1. *Species diversity.* All the species on Earth, including single-celled bacteria and protists as well as the species of the multicellular kingdoms (plants, fungi, and animals).

2. *Genetic diversity.* The genetic variation within species, both among geographically separate populations and among individuals within single populations.

3. *Ecosystem diversity.* The different biological communities and their associations with the chemical and physical environment ("the ecosystem") (Figure 2.1).

All three levels of biological diversity are necessary for the continued survival of life as we know it, and all are important to people (MEA 2005). Species diversity reflects the entire range of evolutionary and ecological adaptations of species to particular environments. It provides people with resources and resource alternatives—for example, a tropical rain forest or a temperate swamp

Genetic diversity in a rabbit population

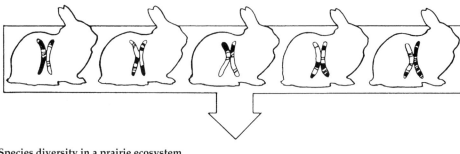

Species diversity in a prairie ecosystem

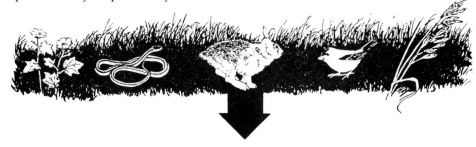

Community and ecosystem diversity across an entire region

FIGURE 2.1 Biological diversity includes genetic diversity (the genetic variation found within each species), species diversity (the range of species in a given ecosystem), and community/ecosystem diversity (the variety of habitat types and ecosystem processes extending over a given region). (From Temple 1991; drawing by T. Sayre.)

with many species produces a wide variety of plant and animal products that can be used as food, shelter, and medicine. Genetic diversity is necessary for any species to maintain reproductive vitality, resistance to disease, and the ability to adapt to changing conditions. In domestic plants and animals, genetic diversity is of particular value in the breeding programs necessary to sustain and improve modern agricultural species and resist diseases. Community-level diversity results from the collective response of species to different environmental conditions. Biological communities found in deserts, grasslands, wetlands, and forests support the continuity of proper ecosystem functioning, which provides crucial services to people, such as water for drinking and agriculture, flood control, protection from soil erosion, and filtering of air and water. We will now examine each level of biodiversity in turn.

Species Diversity

Species diversity includes the entire range of species found on Earth. Recognizing and classifying species is one of the major goals of conservation biology. Yet how do biologists separate out individual species from the mass of creatures living on Earth, many of them small in size with few distinguishing features?

What Is a Species?

A species is generally defined in one of two ways. First, a species can be defined as a group of individuals that is morphologically,* physiologically, or biochemically distinct from other groups in some important characteristic (the **morphological definition of species**). Increasingly, differences in DNA sequences and other molecular markers distinguish species that look almost identical, such as bacteria (Tautz et al. 2003). And second, a species can be defined as a group of individuals that can potentially breed among themselves in the wild and that do not breed with individuals of other groups (the **biological definition of species**). Because the methods and assumptions used are different, these two approaches to distinguishing species sometimes do not give the same results.

The morphological definition of species is the one most commonly used by **taxonomists**, biologists who specialize in the identification of unknown specimens and the classification of species (Box 2.1). Taxonomists collect specimens in the field and store them in one of the world's 6500 natural history museums (Figure 2.2). These permanent collections of approximately eight billion specimens form the basis of species descriptions and systems of classification. The biological definition of a species is the one most commonly used by **evolutionary biologists** because it emphasizes breeding and genetic relationships rather than physical features, which can be affected by the environment. In practice, however, the biological definition

---

*An individual's morphology is its form and structure—or, to put it more simply (if not totally accurately), its appearance.

FIGURE 2.2 (A) A botanist preparing a plant specimen while collecting in the Atlantic Coastal Forest of Brazil. The specimen will be flattened, dried, and mounted on paper. (B) Natural history collections are stored in museums for use by scientists, such as these preserved birds in the Smithsonian Institution. (A, photograph by Donat Agosti; B, photograph © Chip Clark/ National Museum of Natural History.)

BOX 2.1

Naming and Classifying Species

▧ **Taxonomy** is the science of classifying living things. The goal of modern taxonomy is to create a system of classification that reflects the evolution of groups of species from their ancestors . By identifying the relationships between species, taxonomists help conservation biologists identify species or groups that may be evolutionarily unique and/or particularly worthy of conservation efforts. Information about the taxonomy, ecology, morphology, distribution, and status of species is being organized into central databases, accessible via the Internet (Bisby 2000). In modern classification:

Similar species are grouped into a **genus** (plural, **genera**): the Blackburnian warbler (*Dendroica fusca*) and many similar warbler species belong to the genus *Dendroica*.

Similar genera are grouped into a **family**: all wood warbler genera belong to the family Parulidae.

Similar families are grouped into an **order**: all songbird families belong to the order Passeriformes.

Similar orders are grouped into a **class**: all bird orders belong to the class Aves.

Similar classes are grouped into a **phylum** (plural, **phyla**): all vertebrate classes belong to the phylum Chordata.

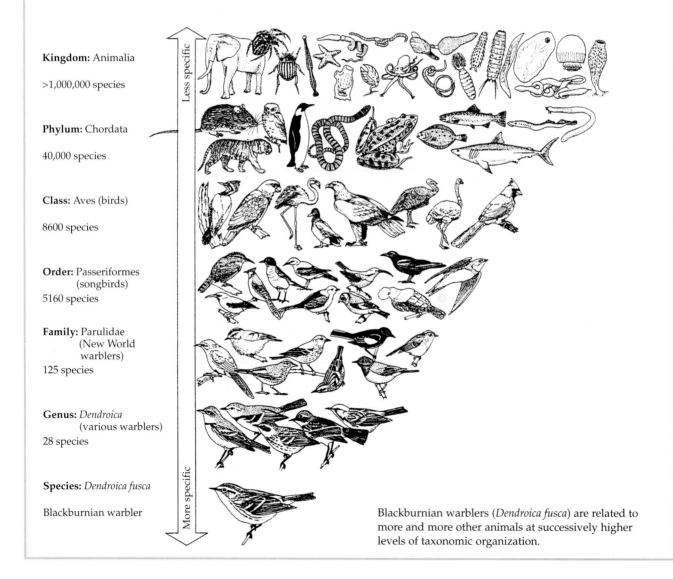

Kingdom: Animalia

>1,000,000 species

Phylum: Chordata

40,000 species

Class: Aves (birds)

8600 species

Order: Passeriformes
(songbirds)
5160 species

Family: Parulidae
(New World
warblers)
125 species

Genus: *Dendroica*
(various warblers)
28 species

Species: *Dendroica fusca*

Blackburnian warbler

Blackburnian warblers (*Dendroica fusca*) are related to more and more other animals at successively higher levels of taxonomic organization.

BOX 2.1 *(continued)*

Similar phyla are grouped into a **kingdom***: all animal classes belong to the kingdom Animalia.

Biologists throughout the world have agreed to use a standard set of scientific, or Latin, names when discussing species. The use of scientific names avoids the confusion that can occur when using common names; the Latin names are standard across countries and languages. Scientific species names consist of two words. This naming system, known as **binomial nomenclature**, was developed in the eighteenth century by the Swedish biologist Carolus Linnaeus. In the scientific name for the Black-burnian warbler, *Dendroica fusca, Dendroica* is the genus name and *fusca* is the species name. The genus name is somewhat similar to a person's family name in that many people can have the same family name (Sullivan), while the species name is similar to a person's given name (Margaret).

Scientific names are written in a standard way to avoid confusion. The first letter of the genus name is always capitalized, whereas the species name is almost always lowercased. Scientific names are either italicized or underlined. Sometimes scientific names are followed by a person's name, as in *Homo sapiens* Linnaeus, indicating that Linnaeus was the person who first proposed the scientific name given to the human species. When many species in a single genus are being discussed, or if the identity of a species within a genus is uncertain, the abbreviations spp. or sp., respectively, are sometimes used (e.g., *Dendroica* spp.). If a species has no close relatives, it may be the only species in its genus. Similarly, a genus that is unrelated to any other genera may form its own family.

---

*Until recently, most modern biologists recognized five kingdoms in the living world: plants, animals, fungi, monerans (single-celled species without a nucleus and mitochondria, such as bacteria), and protists (more complex single-celled species with a nucleus and mitochondria). With the increasing sophistication of molecular techniques, many biologists now use a system of classification with three domains containing six kingdoms: Bacteria (common bacteria), Archaea (ancient bacteria that live in extreme environments, such as hypersaline pools, hot springs, and deep sea vents), and the Eucarya (all organisms with a membrane-bound nucleus, including animals, plants, fungi, and protists) (Coleman 2001).

---

of species is difficult to use because it requires a knowledge of which individuals actually have the potential to breed with one another and their relationships to each other—information that is rarely available. As a result, practicing field biologists learn to recognize one or more individuals that look different from other individuals and might represent a different species, sometimes referring to them as "**morpho-species**" or another such term until taxonomists can give them official scientific names (Derraik et al. 2002).

Problems in distinguishing and identifying species are more common than many people realize. For example, a single species may have several varieties that have observable morphological differences, yet the varieties are similar enough to be considered a single biological species. Different varieties of dogs, such as German shepherds, collies, and beagles, all belong to one species and readily interbreed despite the conspicuous morphological differences among them (Figure 2.3). Alternatively, closely related "sibling" species appear very similar in morphology and physiology, yet are biologically separate and do not interbreed. In practice, biologists often find it difficult to distinguish variation *within* a single species from variation *between* closely related species. For example, genetic analysis of New Zealand's unique reptile, the tuatara (*Sphenodon punctatus*), revealed that there are actually two distinct species of tuatara, both deserving scientific recognition and conservation protection (Hay et al. 2003). And scientists are still debating whether the African elephant is one widespread, variable species or is actually three separate species: a savannah species, a forest species, and a desert species.

To further complicate matters, individuals of related but distinct species may occasionally mate and produce **hybrids**, intermediate forms that blur the distinction between species. Sometimes hybrids are better suited to their environment than either parent species, and they can go on to form new species. Hybridization is particularly common among plant species in disturbed habitats. Hybridization in both

(A)

(B)

(C)

(D)

(E)

FIGURE 2.3 Dogs are all one species and readily interbred despite their differences in appearance. Artificial selection by people has led to dogs bred for special purposes. (A) Dogs originated from wolves which were domesticated by people. (B) Great danes have long legs and a large body size for hunting wild boars. (C) Shih-tzus are bred as cute house pets. (D) Welsh corgis have short legs and herd cattle. (E) Border collies herd sheep. (A, photograph © Gerry Ellis/DigitalVision/PictureQuest; B,C, and D, photographs courtesy of David McIntyre; E, photograph courtesy of Denise Leonard.)

plants and animals frequently occurs when a few individuals of a rare species are surrounded by large numbers of a closely related species. For example, the endangered Ethiopian wolf (*Canis simensis*) frequently mates with domestic dogs, and declining British populations of the European wildcat (*Felis silvestris*) are being swamped with genetic material due to matings with domestic cats. In the United States, protection of the endangered red wolf (*Canis rufus*) was almost withdrawn because morphological and genetic evidence demonstrated that many of the remaining individuals are hybrids formed from extensive mating with common coyotes (*Canis latrans*) (Brownlow 1996; www.redwolves.com).

Much more work is needed to catalog and classify the world's species. At best, taxonomists have described only one-third of the world's species, and perhaps as little as 1%. The inability to clearly distinguish one species from another, whether due to similarities of characteristics or to confusion over the correct scientific name, often slows down efforts at species protection. It is difficult to write precise, effective laws to protect a species if scientists and lawmakers are not certain what name should be used. At the same time, species are going extinct before they are even described. Tens of thousands of new species are being described each year, but even this rate is not fast enough. The key to solving this problem is to train more taxonomists, especially for work in the species-rich Tropics (Wilson 2003). We'll return to this topic later in the chapter.

The Origin of New Species

The biochemical similarity of all living species and the uniform use of DNA as the genetic code indicate that life on Earth originated only once, about 3.5 billion years ago. From one original species came the millions of species found on Earth today. The process of new species formation, known as **speciation**, continues today and will most likely continue into the future.

This process, whereby one original species evolves into one or more new and distinct species, was first described by Charles Darwin and Alfred Russel Wallace more than 100 years ago (Darwin 1859; Futuyma 1998). Their theory of the origin of new species is widely accepted today in the scientific community* and continues to be further refined and developed, along with the science of genetics. The wealth of new information that is continuously provided by the fossil record, along with the extensive modern research in molecular biology, has provided additional support for the ideas of Darwin and Wallace.

The theory of evolution is both simple and elegant. Imagine a population of a species—mountain rabbits living in Canada, for example. Individuals in the population tend to produce more offspring than can survive in that place. Most offspring will die before reaching maturity. In the population, each pair of rabbits will produce numerous litters of six or more offspring, yet on average, in a stable population, only two of those offspring will survive. Individuals in the population show variations in certain characteristics (such as fur thickness), and some of these characteristics are inherited; that is, they are passed from parents to offspring via genes. These genetic variations are caused both by mutations—spontaneous changes in the chromosomes—and by the rearrangement of chromosomes that occurs during sexual reproduction. Within the rabbit population, some individuals have thicker fur than others because of such genetic differences. These differences will enable some individuals to grow, survive, and reproduce better than others, a phenomenon sometimes referred to as "survival of the fittest." Our hypothetical thick-furred rabbits will be more likely to survive cold winters than rabbits with thinner fur. As a result of the improved survival ability associated with a certain genetic characteristic, the individuals possessing that characteristic will be more likely to produce offspring than the others; over time, the genetic composition of the population will change. After a series of cold winters, more thick-furred rabbits will have survived and produced thick-furred offspring, while more thin-furred rabbits will have died. Consequently, more rabbits in the population will have thicker fur than in previous generations. At the same time, another population of the same species living in a lowland area or further south could be undergoing selection for individuals with thinner fur in response to warming conditions.

In the process of evolution, populations often genetically adapt to changes in their environment. These changes may be biological (new food sources, new competitors, new predators) as well as environmental (climate, water availability, soil characteristics). When a population has undergone so much genetic change that it is no longer able to interbreed with the original species from which it derives, the population can be considered a new species. This gradual transformation into another species is termed **phyletic evolution**.

In order for two or more new species to evolve from one original ancestor, there is usually a geographical barrier that prevents the movement of individuals between the various populations of a species (Bush 2001). For terrestrial species, these barriers may be rivers, mountain ranges, or oceans that the species cannot readily

*That evolution occurs is regarded by virtually all biologists as fact. Several popular and scholarly books (e.g., Futuyma 1998; Shanks 2004) discuss religion-based arguments (and intelligent-design arguments) against evolution and why most scientists do not accept such arguments.

cross. Aquatic species adapt to particular lakes, rivers, or estuaries, which are separated from one another by land. Speciation is particularly rapid on islands. Island groups, such as the Galápagos and the Hawaiian Islands, are homes to many examples of insects and plants that were originally local populations of a single colonizing species. These local populations adapted genetically to the distinctive environments of particular unoccupied islands, mountains, and isolated valleys. Often in the absence of the competitors, predators, and parasites that affected them on the mainland, they diverged sufficiently from the original species to be considered separate species. This process of local adaptation and subsequent speciation is known as **adaptive radiation**. One of the best-known examples of adaptive radiation is that of the Hawaiian honeycreepers, a group of specialized bird species that apparently derives from a single pair of birds that arrived by chance in the Hawaiian Islands tens of thousands of years ago (Figure 2.4).

The origination of new species is normally a slow process, taking place over hundreds, if not thousands, of generations. The evolution of new genera and families is an even slower process, lasting hundreds of thousands, or even millions, of years. However, there are mechanisms whereby new species can arise in just one generation without geographical separation. Unusual, unequal divisions of chromosome sets during reproduction may result in offspring with extra sets of chromosomes; these offspring are known as **polyploids**. Polyploid individuals may be morphologically and physiologically different from their parents and, if they are well suited to the environment, may form a new species within the range of the parent

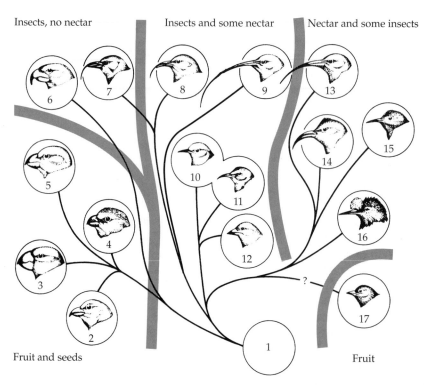

FIGURE 2.4 The Hawaiian honeycreeper family, a spectacular example of adaptive radiation, is thought to have arisen from one pair of birds that arrived on the Hawaiian islands (indicated by #1). The shape and size of bills are related to foods eaten: sharp for eating insects, thick for cracking seeds and eating fruit, long for feeding on nectar. Black lines indicate evolutionary relationships; gray bars indicate shifts in feeding habits. Numbered birds indicate different species. (After Cox 1993.)

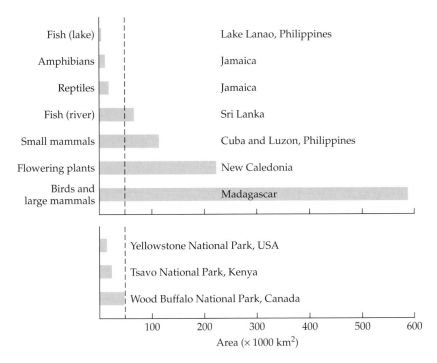

FIGURE 2.5 Certain groups of organisms apparently need a minimum area in order to undergo the process of speciation (upper graph). For example, for small mammals, the smallest islands (Cuba and Luzon) on which a single species is known to have given rise to two species are 100,000 km². The bottom graph shows the areas of some national parks. Even the largest national park shown (dotted line) is probably too small to allow for the evolution of new species of river fish, flowering plants, birds, or mammals, although it might be large enough for the continued evolution of lake fishes, amphibians, and reptiles. (After Soulé 1980.)

species. Hybrids that result from mating between individuals of two different species can also form new species, especially when they have different characteristics from their parents and mate among themselves. Polyploid species are particularly common in plants.

Even though new species are arising all the time, the present rate of species extinction is probably more than 100 times faster than the rate of speciation and may even be 1000 times faster. The situation is actually worse than this grim statistic suggests. First, the rate of speciation may actually be slowing down because so much of the Earth's surface has been taken over for human use and no longer supports evolving biological communities. As habitats decline, fewer populations of each species exist, and thus there are fewer opportunities for evolution (Myers and Knoll 2001). Many of the existing protected areas and national parks may be too small to allow the process of speciation to occur (Figure 2.5). Second, many of the species threatened with extinction in the wild are the sole remaining representatives of their genus or family; examples include the gorilla (*Gorilla gorilla*), rapidly declining throughout its range in Africa, and the giant panda (*Ailuropoda melanoleuca*) in China. The extinction of taxonomically unique species representing ancient lineages is not balanced by the appearance of new species.

Species Diversity and Its Measurement

Conservation biologists often want to identify locations of high species diversity. In the broadest sense, species diversity is simply the number of different species in a place. However, there are many other specialized, quantitative definitions of species diversity that ecologists have developed as a means of comparing the overall diversity of different communities at varying geographical scales (Summerville et al. 2003; Legendre et al. 2005). Ecologists have used these quantitative measures to test the assumption that increasing levels of diversity lead to increasing community stability and biomass production. In controlled experiments in the greenhouse or gardens, or in simple grassland plant communities, increasing the number of species growing together generally leads to greater biomass production and resistance to drought. However, the significance of this result to the broader range of natural communities, such as forests and coral reefs, still needs to be convincingly demonstrated. Measures of biological diversity used by field ecologists are often most useful for comparing particular groups of species within or among communities and determining patterns of distribution. These researchers typically consider the diversity of plants, birds, or frogs separately.

At its simplest level, diversity has been defined as the number of species found in a community, a measure often called **species richness**. Quantitative indexes of biodiversity have been developed primarily to denote species diversity at three different geographical scales. The number of species in a certain community or designated area is described as **alpha diversity**. Alpha diversity comes closest to the popular concept of species richness and can be used to compare the number of species in particular places or ecosystem types, such as lakes or forests. For example, a 100-ha forest in Wisconsin has fewer tree species than a 100-ha patch of the Amazon rain forest; that is, the alpha diversity of the rain forest is greater. More highly quantitative indexes such as the Shannon diversity index take the relative abundance of different species into account and assign the highest diversity to communities with large numbers of species that are equally abundant and the lowest scores to communities in which there are either few species, or a large number of species, one or a few of which are much more abundant than the others. Because there is no universal agreement about which quantitative indexes are best to use or how to interpret them, they may be of less value to conservation biology than simply using the number of species.

Gamma diversity applies to larger geographical scales. It refers to the number of species in a large region or on a continent. Gamma diversity allows us to compare large areas that encompass diverse landscapes or a wide geographical area. For example, Kenya, with 1000 species of forest birds, has a higher gamma diversity than Britain, which has only 200 species.

Beta diversity links alpha and gamma diversity. It represents the rate of change of species composition along an environmental or geographical gradient. For example, if each lake in a region contained different fish species, or if the bird species on one mountain were entirely different from the birds on neighboring mounts, then beta diversity would be high. However, if the species composition along the gradient does not change much ("the birds on this mountain are the same as the birds on the mountain we visited yesterday"), then beta diversity will be low. Beta diversity is sometimes calculated as the gamma diversity of a region divided by the average alpha diversity, though other measures also exist.

We can illustrate the three types of diversity with a theoretical example of three mountain ranges (Figure 2.6). Region 1 has the highest alpha diversity, with more species per mountain on average (6 species) than the other two regions. Region 2 has the highest gamma diversity, with a total of 10 species. Dividing gamma by alpha, region 3 has a higher beta diversity (3.0) than region 2 (2.5) or region 1 (1.2), because all of its species are found on only one mountain each. In practice, indexes of diversity are often highly correlated. The plant communities of the eastern foothills of the Andes Mountains, for instance, show high levels of diversity at the alpha, beta, and gamma scales (Gentry 1986). These quantitative definitions of di-

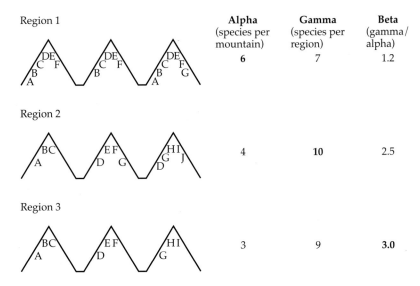

	Alpha (species per mountain)	Gamma (species per region)	Beta (gamma/ alpha)
Region 1	6	7	1.2
Region 2	4	10	2.5
Region 3	3	9	3.0

FIGURE 2.6 Biodiversity indexes for three regions, each with three mountains. Each letter represents a population of a species. Some species are found on only one mountain, while others are found on two or three mountains. Alpha, beta, and gamma diversity are shown for each region. If funds were available to protect only one mountain range, region 2 should be selected because it has the greatest gamma (total) diversity. However, if only one mountain can be protected, a mountain in region 1 should be selected because these have the highest alpha (local) diversity, with region 2 in second place because of the restricted distribution of its species, as shown by a high beta diversity. Each mountain in region 3 has a more distinct assemblage of species than those in the other two regions, as shown by the higher beta diversity. Overall, region 3 would be a lower conservation priority, unless the entire region can be protected.

versity are used primarily in the technical ecological literature and capture only part of the broad definition of biological diversity used by conservation biologists. However, they are useful for talking about patterns of species distribution and for comparing regions of the world. They are also valuable for highlighting areas that have large numbers of species that require conservation protection.

Genetic Diversity

At each level of biological diversity—genetic, species, and community—conservation biologists study the mechanisms that alter or maintain diversity. Genetic diversity within a species is often affected by the reproductive behavior of individuals within populations (Wayne and Morin 2004). A **population** is a group of individuals that mate with one another and produce offspring; a species may include one or more separate populations. A population may consist of only a few individuals or millions of individuals, provided that the individuals actually produce offspring. A single individual of a sexual species would not constitute a population. Neither does a group of individuals that cannot reproduce; for example, the last 10 dusky seaside sparrows (*Ammodramus maritimus nigrescens*), native to the southeastern United States, did not constitute a true population because all of them were male.

What Is Genetic Diversity?

Individuals within a population usually are genetically different from one another. Genetic variation arises because individuals have slightly different forms of their **genes** (or **loci**), the units of the chromosomes that code for specific proteins. These different forms of a gene are known as **alleles**, and the differences originally arise through **mutations**—changes that occur in the deoxyribonucleic acid (DNA) that constitutes an individual's chromosomes. The various alleles of a gene may affect the development and physiology of an individual organism. Crop and animal breeders take advantage of this genetic variation to breed higher yielding, pest-resistant strains of domesticated species such as wheat, corn, cattle, and poultry.

Genetic variation increases when offspring receive unique combinations of genes and chromosomes from their parents via the **recombination** of genes that occurs during sexual reproduction. Genes are exchanged between chromosomes, and new combinations are created when chromosomes from two parents combine to form a genetically unique offspring. Although mutations provide the basic material for genetic variation, the random rearrangement of alleles in different combinations that characterizes sexually reproducing species dramatically increases the potential for genetic variation.

The total array of genes and alleles in a population is the **gene pool** of the population, while the particular combination of alleles that any individual possesses is its **genotype**. The **phenotype** of an individual represents the morphological, physiological, anatomical, and biochemical characteristics of the individual that result from the expression of its genotype in a particular environment (Figure 2.7). Some characteristics of humans, such as the amount of body fat and tooth decay, are strikingly influenced by the environment, while other characteristics, such as eye color, blood type, and forms of certain enzymes, are determined predominantly by an individual's genotype.

Sometimes individuals that differ genetically also differ in ways related to their survival or ability to reproduce—such as their ability to tolerate cold, as in our hypothetical thick-furred rabbits; resistance to disease; or the speed at which they can run away from danger. If individuals with certain alleles are better able to survive and produce offspring than individuals without these alleles, then **gene frequencies** in the population will change in subsequent generations. This phenomenon is called **natural selection**. Our hypothetical rabbits in the cold climate are experiencing natural selection against thin, short fur.

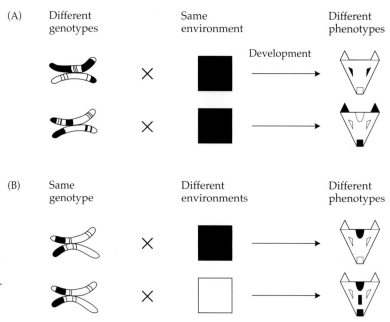

FIGURE 2.7 (The physical, physiological, and biochemical characteristics of an individual—its phenotype—are determined by its genotype and by the environment (e.g., hot vs. cold climate; abundant vs. scarce food) in which the individual lives. (After Alcock 1993.)

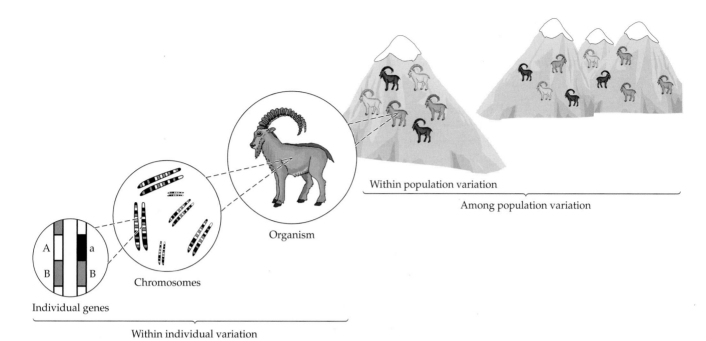

FIGURE 2.8 Genetic variation occurs within individuals due to variation in the alleles found at particular loci or genes and variation between chromosomes. Genetic variation also occurs between individuals within populations and among separate populations. (From Groom et al. 2006.)

The amount of genetic variability in a population is determined by both the number of genes that have more than one allele (**polymorphic genes**) and the number of alleles for each of these genes (Figure 2.8). The existence of a polymorphic gene also means that some individuals in the population will be **heterozygous** for the gene; that is, they will receive a different allele of the gene from each parent. All these levels of genetic variation contribute to a population's ability to adapt to a changing environment. Rare species often have less genetic variation than widespread species and, consequently, are more vulnerable to extinction when environmental conditions change.

In a wide variety of plant and animal populations, it has been demonstrated that individuals that are heterozygous have greater **fitness** than comparable homozygous individuals. This means that heterozygous individuals have greater growth, survival, and reproduction rates than homozygotes. The reasons for this appear to be that (1) having two different alleles gives the individual greater flexibility in dealing with life's challenges, and (2) nonfunctional or harmful alleles received from one parent are masked by the functioning alleles received from the other parent. This phenomenon of increased fitness in highly heterozygous individuals, also referred to as **hybrid vigor**, or **heterosis**, is widely known in domestic animals. As populations of wild species get smaller due to habitat destruction and other human activities, genetic variation will be lost and individuals will have a lower average fitness.

Populations of a species may differ genetically from one another in relative frequencies of alleles and even in types of allele forms for particular genes. These genetic differences may result from adaptation of each population to its local environment or simply from random chance. Unique populations of a species, particularly those found at the edges of a species range, are considered an important component of biological diversity and conservation biologists often recommend their protection. Such populations are sometimes designated as distinct varieties or sub-species, especially when they are morphologically distinct (Zink 2004). Furthermore, distinctive alleles from these populations can sometimes be used as markers to determine the geographical origin of individuals collected in the wild (Wayne and Morin 2004; Kelly et al. 2005).

Although most mating occurs within populations, individuals occasionally move from one population to another, resulting in the transfer of new alleles and genetic combinations between populations. This genetic transfer is referred to as **gene flow**. Natural gene flow between populations is sometimes interrupted by human activities, causing a reduction in the genetic variation in each population (Wofford et al. 2005). The importance of genetic variability to conservation biology is discussed at length in Chapters 11 and 12.

Genetic variation also occurs within domesticated plants and animals. In traditional societies, people preserved new plant forms that were well suited to their needs. Through generations of this process of **artificial selection**, varieties of species were developed that were productive and adapted to local conditions of soil, climate, and crop pests. This process has greatly accelerated in modern agriculture, which makes use of scientific breeding programs that manipulate genetic variation to meet present human needs. Without genetic variation, improvements in agriculture would be more difficult. Advanced techniques of biotechnology enable even more precise use of genetic variation by allowing the transfer of genetic material between unrelated species. Thousands of varieties of crops, such as rice, potatoes, and wheat, have been incorporated into the breeding programs of modern agriculture. Among animals, the huge numbers of breeds of domestic dogs, cats, chickens, cattle, sheep, and pigs are evidence of the ability of artificial selection to alter gene pools for the benefit of people (see Figure 2.3).

Genetic variation is also maintained in specialized collections of species used in scientific research, such as the *Drosophila* fruit fly stocks used in genetic studies; the tiny, fast-growing *Arabidopsis* mustard plants that are used in plant research; and the mice used in physiological and medical research.

Recent evidence suggests the intensive harvesting of fish in the ocean is beginning to impose artificial selection on fish populations; by harvesting the largest fish in the population, selection tends to favor individuals that grow slowly and reproduce at an earlier age and smaller size (Raloff 2005).

Ecosystem Diversity

Communities are diverse, and this diversity is apparent even across a particular landscape. As we climb a mountain, for example, the structure of the vegetation and kinds of plants and animals present gradually change from those found in a tall forest to those found in a low, moss-filled forest to alpine meadow to cold, barren rock. As we move across the landscape, physical conditions (soil, temperature, precipitation, and so forth) change, and one by one the species present at the original location drop out and we encounter new species that were not found at the starting point. The landscape as a whole is dynamic and changes in response to the overall environment and the types of human activities that are associated with it.

What Are Communities and Ecosystems?

A **biological community** is defined as the species that occupy a particular locality and the interactions among those species. A biological community, together with its associated physical and chemical environment, is termed an **ecosystem**. Many characteristics of an ecosystem result from ongoing processes, including water cycles, nutrient cycles, and energy capture. Water evaporates from leaves, the ground, and other surfaces, to fall again elsewhere as rain or snow and replenish terrestrial and aquatic environments. Soil is built up from parent rock material and decaying organic matter. Photosynthetic plants absorb light energy, which fuels the plants' growth. This energy may be captured by animals that eat the plants, and it may be released as heat when the plants (or the animals that eat them) die and decompose. Plants absorb carbon dioxide and release oxygen during photosynthesis, while animals and fungi absorb oxygen and release carbon dioxide during respiration. Mineral nutrients, such as nitrogen and phosphorus, cycle between the living and the nonliving compartments of the ecosystem. These processes occur at geographical scales that range from square meters to hectares to square kilometers all the way to regional scales involving tens of thousands of square kilometers (Poiani et al. 2000; Kratochwil 2005; MEA 2005).

The physical environment, especially annual cycles of temperature and precipitation and the characteristics of the land surface, affects the structure and characteristics of a biological community and profoundly influences whether a site will support a forest, grassland, desert, or wetland. In aquatic ecosystems, physical characteristics such as water turbulence and clarity, and water chemistry, temperature, and depth affect the characteristics of the associated **biota** (a region's flora and fauna). The biological community can also alter the physical characteristics of an environment. For example, in a terrestrial ecosystem, wind speed, humidity, and temperature in a given location can be affected by the vegetation present there. Marine communities such as kelp forests and coral reefs can affect the physical environment as well (Box 2.2).

BOX 2.2

Kelp Forests and Sea Otters: Shaping an Ocean Ecosystem

Although the effects of human activities on the world's tropical and temperate forests have been given a lot of media attention in recent years, a third kind of forest has received very little notice—marine kelp forests. Although unsung in magazines and newspapers, these forests provide essential habitat for a diversity of species. Kelp forests are communities that develop mostly in the high-latitude coastal waters of the world's oceans around any of a number of species of marine brown algae, such as southern bull kelp (*Durvillaea antarctica*) and giant kelp (*Macrocystis pyrifera*). Enormous numbers of ocean fish, shellfish, and invertebrates depend on these forests for food and shelter (Estes et al. 2001; Steneck et al. 2003). Like terrestrial forests, kelp and seaweed communities inhibit erosion: The presence of kelp reduces the impact of waves and currents upon the shoreline, preventing destruction of coastal land. Despite their recognized value, kelp forests have disappeared over the last century at many localities in Alaska, British Columbia, and the Pacific Northwest of the United States.

The source of reduction is not as apparent as clear-cutting of terrestrial forests. Kelp is harvested in many countries by local people for subsistence, but this type of exploitation is fairly small-scale and does little harm to the kelp beds. Even large-scale harvesting of kelp for the food processing industry appears to have little long-term effect. The principal cause for kelp forest declines began over a century ago, with the harvesting of sea otters.

Sea otters (*Enhydra lutris*), once widespread throughout the Pacific, were all but exterminated by fur traders. Sea otters eat large quantities of shellfish—as much as 25% of their body weight each day. In the absence of otters, populations of mussels, abalone, other shellfish, and sea urchins exploded, providing a greater harvest for the shellfish industry. However, sea urchins feed voraciously on kelp; unchecked by predators, they created large "urchin barrens" where kelp forests formerly swayed.

Confined mostly to the far northern Pacific islands for decades, the sea otter is now protected in the United States and has begun to recolonize parts of its former range. The return of the sea otters has initiated a cascade of effects throughout the ecosystem with implications for the economy of the region's fisheries. Reductions in shellfish populations from sea otter predation have angered fishermen (Fanshawe et al. 2003), but at the same

(continued)

BOX 2.2 *(continued)*

time, the reduced herbivory by sea urchins has allowed kelp and other algae to grow back. Wherever otters have returned or have been reintroduced, significant changes have taken place in kelp communities: Within one, two, or more years of the otters' return, formerly deforested areas are again dominated by kelp. Enhanced production of kelp has increased fish production and growth rates of suspension feeders, benefiting commercial and recreational fishing, though in many areas fish populations have been significantly reduced due to overharvesting (Paddack and Estes 2000). The disappearance of kelp beds in the last century and their subsequent recovery following the restoration of the sea otter demonstrates an important feature of ocean ecosystems: The loss of a single keystone species, no matter what its position on the food chain, can have a profound effect on every aspect of the system's ecological interactions. The sea otter recovery is still fragile, however. Over the last decade, off the coast of western Alaska, killer whales have switched to feeding on sea otters, because their preferred prey of seals and sea lions has declined, perhaps in part due to overfishing (Estes et al. 2001). As a consequence the entire marine community is again changing in structure and composition.

Forests of giant kelp provide the starting point and structure for a diverse biological community off the Pacific coast of North America. Sea otters are vital to the kelp community because they feed on invertebrates, such as sea urchins, that graze on the kelp. When the sea otters decline in number, sea urchin populations soar, resulting in grave damage to the kelp forests. (Illustration © Abigail Rorer. Reproduced with permission from *The Work of Nature* by Yvonne Baskin, Island Press, Washington, D.C.)

Within a biological community, species play different roles and differ in what they require to survive. For example, a given plant species might grow best in one type of soil under certain conditions of sunlight and moisture, be pollinated only by certain types of insects, and have its seeds dispersed by certain bird species. Similarly, animal species differ in their requirements, such as the types of food they eat and the types of resting places they prefer (Figure 2.9). Even though a forest may be full of vigorously growing green plants, an insect species that feeds only on one rare plant species may be unable to develop and reproduce because it cannot get the specific food that it requires. Any of these requirements may become a **limiting resource** when it restricts population size of the species. For example, a bat species with specialized roosting requirements—forming colonies only in small grottoes on the ceilings of limestone caves—will be restricted by the number of caves with the proper conditions for roosting sites. If people damage the caves to collect limestone, then the bat

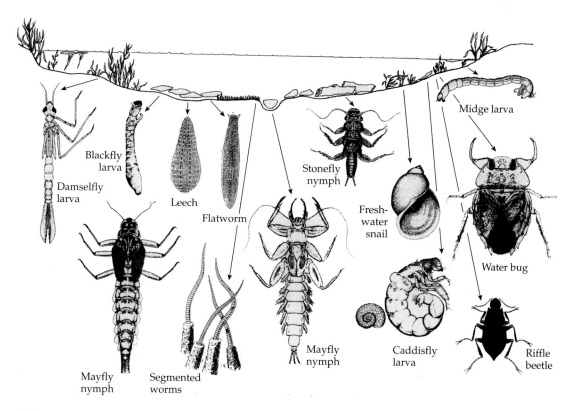

FIGURE 2.9 In this illustration of a stream community in the Andean mountains, each animal species lives at different depths and in association with certain structural features. (From Roldán 1988.)

population will likely decline; however, if the bats are able to adapt to human presence and roost under bridges, their population might increase.

In many communities, there may be occasional episodes when one or several resources become limited and vulnerable species are eliminated from the site. For example, although water is not normally a limiting resource to organisms living in a rain forest, episodes of drought lasting for weeks and even months occasionally do occur, even in the wettest forests. At these times, animal and plant species that need a constant supply of water may vanish. Or, bird species that are specialized to feed on flying insects may be unable to eat or to feed their young during days or weeks when unusually cold, wet, or windy weather prevents insects from flying; in this situation, the flying insects suddenly become the limiting resource for the bird population.

Ecological Succession

As a result of its particular requirements, behaviors, or preferences, a given species often ends up appearing in a given site at a particular time during the process of ecological succession. **Succession** is the gradual process of change in species composition, community structure, soil chemistry, and microclimatic characteristics that occur following natural and human-caused disturbance in a biological community. For example, sun-loving butterflies and annual plants most commonly are found early in succession, in the months or few years immediately following a hurricane or after a logging operation has destroyed an old-growth forest. At this time, with the tree canopy disrupted, the ground is receiving high levels of sunlight, with high temperatures and low humidity during the day. Over the course of decades, the forest canopy is gradually reestablished. Different species, including shade-tolerant, moisture-requiring wildflowers, butterflies whose caterpillars feed on these plants, and birds that nest in holes in dead trees, thrive in these mid- and late-successional stages. Similar cases of species firmly associated with early, mid-, or late succession are found in other ecosystems, such as grasslands, lakeshores, and the intertidal zones of oceans. Human management patterns often upset the natural pattern of succession; for instance, grasslands that have been overgrazed by cattle and forests from which all the large trees have been cut for timber no longer contain certain late-successional species.

Successional processes in modern landscapes might represent a combination of natural and human-caused disturbances. A grassland and forest community in the Rocky Mountains of Colorado, for instance, might be affected by natural fires, cycles of drought, and grazing by elk. Now succession in such a community is increasingly dominated by human-caused fires, cattle grazing, and road construction.

Species Interactions within Communities

The composition of communities is often affected by **competition** and **predation** (Gotelli 2001; Huxel and Polis 2001; Ricklefs 2001). Predators may dramatically reduce the densities of certain prey species and even eliminate some species from particular habitats. Indeed, predators may indirectly increase the number of prey species in a community by keeping the density of each species so low that severe competition for resources does not occur. A good example of this is the marine intertidal ecosystem in which a large sea star (starfish), *Pisaster*, feeds on 15 species of mollusks that cling to the rocks (Paine 1966). As long as the predatory sea star is present, competition among the mollusks for space on the rocks is reduced, since the mollusks are eaten too fast to achieve high population densities. Under these circumstances, all 15 species are able to occupy the intertidal rocks. If *Pisaster* is removed, however, the mollusks increase in abundance and start competing for space on the rocks. In the absence of predation, competition between species reduces the number of species; eventually only a few of the original 15 species remain, with some rocks taken over by just one species. In plant communities as well, species diversity is often higher when grazing by animals lessens competition than when grazers are absent. Of course, overgrazing may completely destroy a community if all plants are eaten and the soil washes away. It is also possible that disease-causing organisms, including species we barely notice unless they attack us directly, profoundly influence community structure, reducing many species to low densities.

In many communities, predators keep the number of individuals of a particular prey species below the number that the resources of an ecosystem can support, a number termed the habitat's **carrying capacity**. If the predators (e.g., wolves) are removed by hunting, fishing, or some other human activity, the prey population (e.g., deer) may increase to carrying capacity, or it may increase beyond carrying capacity to a point at which crucial resources are overtaxed and the population crashes.

In addition, the population size of a species may often be controlled by other species that compete with it for the same resources; for example, the population size of terns that nest on a small island may decline or grow if a seagull species that uses the same nesting sites becomes abundant or is eliminated from the community. When the population of a species is sufficiently large to have an impact on the other species in a community, it is termed **ecologically functional**.

Community composition is also affected when two species benefit each other in a **mutualistic relationship**. Mutualistic species reach higher densities when they occur together than when only one of the species is present. Common examples of mutualism are: fruit-eating birds and plants with fleshy fruit, flower-pollinating insects and flowering plants, the fungi and algae that together form lichens, and plants that provide both food and homes for the ants that protect them from pests (Figure

(A) (B)

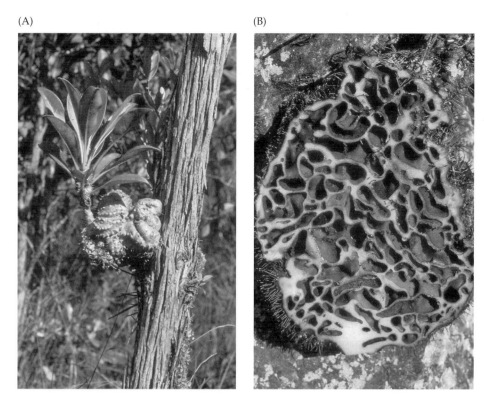

FIGURE 2.10 Mutualistic relationships. (A) This *Myrmecodia* in Borneo is an epiphyte—a plant growing on the surface of another plant. The plant produces a tuber at its base that is filled with hollow chambers, as seen in (B). The chambers are occupied by ant colonies, which use some chambers as nesting sites and some as "dumps" for wastes and dead ants. The plant absorbs the mineral nutrients it needs for growth from these "dumps," while the ants obtain a safe nest. In the epiphyte–tree relationship shown in (A), the epiphyte benefits while the tree it grows on neither benefits nor is harmed. (Photographs by K. M. Wong and R. Primack.)

2.10). At the extreme of mutualism, two species that are always found together and apparently cannot survive without each other form a **symbiotic relationship**. For example, the death of certain types of coral-inhabiting algae in unusually high water temperatures in tropical areas, due to natural causes or human activities, may be followed by the weakening and subsequent death of their associated coral species.

Principles of Community Organization

Examining the feeding relationships among species provides an important way to understand how a community is organized. Further investigations demonstrate how these relationships can be disrupted by human activities.

TROPHIC LEVELS   Biological communities can be organized into trophic levels that represent ways in which energy is obtained from the environment (Figure 2.11).

- **Photosynthetic species** (also known as **primary producers**) obtain their energy directly from the sun. In terrestrial environments, higher plants, such as flowering plants, gymnosperms, and ferns, are responsible for most photosynthesis, while in aquatic environments, seaweeds, single-celled algae, and cyanobacteria (blue-green algae) are the most important. All of these species use solar energy to build the organic molecules they need to live and grow. Without the primary producers, species at the higher levels could not exist.

FIGURE 2.11 A model of a field ecosystem showing its trophic levels and simplified energy pathways.

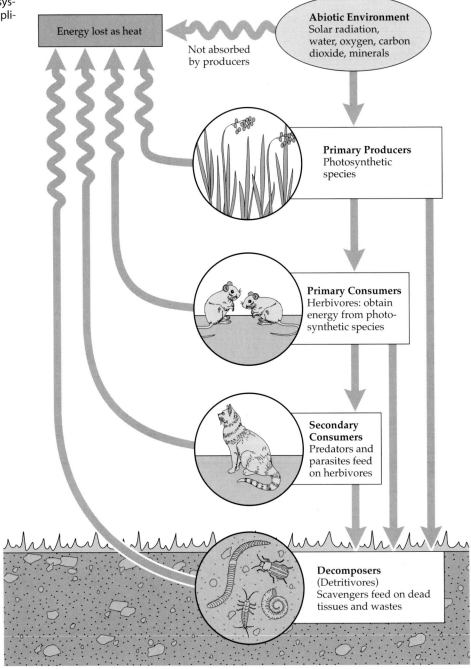

- **Herbivores** (also known as **primary consumers**) eat photosynthetic species. For example, in terrestrial environments, gazelles and grasshoppers eat grass, while in aquatic environments, crustaceans and fish eat algae. Because much plant material, such as cellulose and lignin, is indigestible to many animal species or is simply not eaten, only a small percentage of the energy captured by photosynthetic species is actually transferred to the herbivore level. The intensity of grazing by herbivores often determines the relative abundance of plant species and even the mass of plant material present (Wardle and Bardgett 2004).

- **Carnivores** (also known as **secondary consumers** or **predators**) kill and eat other animals. Primary carnivores (e.g., foxes) eat herbivores (e.g., rabbits), while secondary carnivores (e.g., bass) eat other carnivores (e.g., frogs). Because carnivores do not catch all of their potential prey, and because many body parts of the prey are indigestible, again only a small percentage of the energy of the herbivore trophic level is transferred to the carnivore level. Carnivores usually are predators, though some combine direct predation with scavenging behavior, and others, known as **omnivores**, include a substantial proportion of plant foods in their diets. In general, predators are larger and stronger than the species they prey on, but they usually occur in lower densities than their prey. In many biological communities, carnivores play a crucial role in keeping herbivore numbers in check and preventing overgrazing of plants.

- **Parasites** form an important subclass of predators. Parasites of animals, including mosquitoes, ticks, intestinal worms, protozoans, bacteria, and viruses, are small in size and do not kill their hosts immediately, if ever. Plants can also be attacked by parasites that include fungi, other plants (such as mistletoe), nematode worms, insects, bacteria, and viruses. The effects of parasites range from imperceptibly weakening their hosts to totally debilitating or even killing their hosts over time. The term "parasite" includes many of the organisms that cause disease, and that we call "pests." Parasites can strongly affect the density of host species. When host densities are low, parasites are less able to move from one host to another, and their effects on the host population are correspondingly weak. When host populations are at a high density, parasites spread readily from one host individual to the next, causing an intense local infestation of the parasite and a subsequent decline in host density. High densities of host populations are sometimes maintained in zoos and small nature reserves, making these places hazardous for many endangered species due to the easy spread of parasites.

- **Decomposers** and **detritivores** are species that feed on dead plant and animal tissues and wastes ("detritus"), breaking down complex tissues and organic molecules. In the process, decomposers release minerals such as nitrates and phosphates back into the soil and water, where they can be taken up again by plants and algae. The most important decomposers are fungi and bacteria, but a wide range of other species plays a role in breaking down organic materials. For example, vultures and other scavengers tear apart and feed on dead animals, dung beetles feed on and bury animal dung, and worms break down fallen leaves and other organic matter. Crabs, worms, mollusks, fish, and numerous other organisms eat detritus in aquatic environments. If decomposers were not present, organic material would accumulate and plant growth would decline greatly.

FOOD CHAINS AND FOOD WEBS   Because less and less energy is transferred to each successive trophic level in biological communities, the greatest **biomass** (living weight) in a terrestrial ecosystem is usually that of the primary producers. In any community there tends to be more individual herbivores than primary carnivores, and more primary carnivores than secondary carnivores. For example, a forest community generally contains more insects and insect biomass than insectivorous birds, and more insectivorous birds than raptorial birds (birds such as hawks that feed on other birds). Most energy accumulated by each level is eventually broken down by decomposers.

Although species can be organized into these general trophic levels, their actual requirements or feeding habits within the trophic levels may be quite restricted.

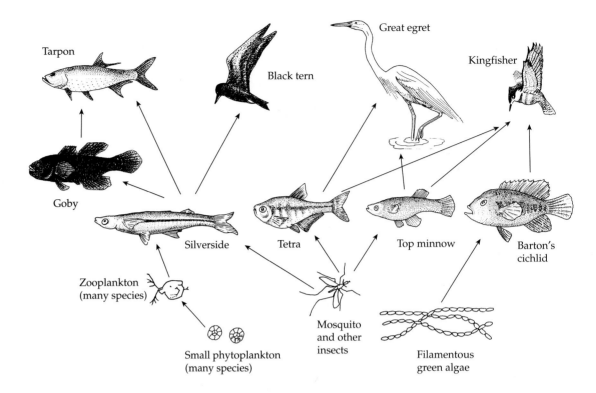

FIGURE 2.12 A diagram of an actual food web studied in Gatun Lake, Panama. Phytoplankton ("floating plants") such as green algae are the primary producers at the base of the web. Zooplankton are tiny, often microscopic, floating animals; they are primary consumers, not photosynthesizers, but they, along with insects and algae, are crucial food sources for fish in aquatic ecosystems. (Courtesy of G. H. Orians.)

For example, a certain aphid species may feed on only one type of plant, and a certain lady beetle species may feed on only one type of aphid. These specific feeding relationships are termed **food chains**. The more common situation in many biological communities, however, is for one species to feed on several other species at the lower trophic level, to compete for food with several species at its own trophic level, and, in turn, to be preyed upon by several species at the next higher trophic level. Consequently, a more accurate description of the organization of biological communities is a **food web**, in which species are linked together through complex feeding relationships (Yodzis 2001) (Figure 2.12). Species at the same trophic level that use approximately the same environmental resources are considered to be a **guild** of competing species. For example, the many bird species that eat fruit in the temperate woodland make up a guild.

Humans can substantially alter the relationships in food webs (Valladares et al. 2006; Becker and Beissinger 2006). In urban settings, bird populations may increase due to reduced predation, in the process reducing insect abundance (Faeth et al. 2005).

Keystone Species and Guilds

Within biological communities, certain species or groups of species with similar ecological features (guilds) may determine the ability of large numbers of other species to persist in the community. These **keystone species** affect the organization of the community to a far greater degree than one would predict, if considering only the number of individuals or the biomass of the keystone species (Figure 2.13) (Gittleman et al. 2000; Soulé et al. 2003, 2005; Mumby et al. 2006). Protecting key-

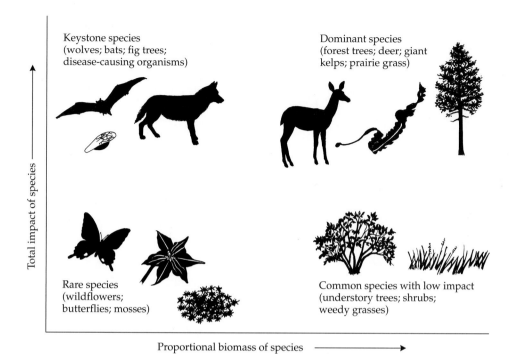

Total impact of species →

Keystone species
(wolves; bats; fig trees;
disease-causing organisms)

Dominant species
(forest trees; deer; giant
kelps; prairie grass)

Rare species
(wildflowers;
butterflies; mosses)

Common species with low impact
(understory trees; shrubs;
weedy grasses)

Proportional biomass of species →

FIGURE 2.13 Keystone species, such as wolves, fig trees, bats, and disease-causing organisms, make up only a small proportion of the total biomass of a biological community, yet have a huge impact on the community's organization and survival. Many other species are not considered to be keystone species: rare species, such as some wildflowers, butterflies, and mosses, may have minimal impact on the biomass and on other species in the community; dominant species constitute a large proportion of the biomass and affect many other species in proportion to their biomass; some common species are plentiful in biomass, but have a relatively low impact on the community organization. (After Power et al. 1996.)

stone species and guilds is a priority for conservation efforts, because loss of a keystone species or guild will lead to loss of numerous other species as well (see Box 2.2). While we can sometimes identify such keystone species, it is also true that less obvious species may be significant for ecosystem functioning in ways that are not immediately obvious (Lyons et al. 2005). Top predators are often considered to be keystone species, because predators can markedly influence herbivore populations. The elimination of even a small number of individual predators, even though they constitute only a minute amount of the community biomass, may result in dramatic changes in the vegetation and a great loss in biological diversity (Berger et al. 2001; Pedersen and Wallis 2004). For example, in some localities where gray wolves and other predators have been hunted to extinction by humans, deer populations have exploded. The deer severely overgraze the habitat, eliminating many herb and shrub species. The loss of these plants, in turn, is detrimental to the deer and to other herbivores, including insects. The reduced plant cover may lead to soil erosion, also contributing to the loss of species that inhabit the soil.

Bats called "flying foxes," of the family Pteropodidae, are another example of a keystone species (Figure 2.14). These bats are the primary pollinators and seed dispersers of many economically important tree species in the Old World tropics and Pacific Islands (Fujita and Tuttle 1991; Nyhagen et al. 2005). When bat colonies are overharvested by hunters, and the trees in which the bats roost are cut down, the bat populations decline. As a result, many of the tree species in the remaining forest fail to reproduce.

FIGURE 2.14 Flying foxes—bats out of the family Pteropodidae, such as this *Pteropus samoensis*, a fruit bat—are vital pollinators and seed dispersers in Old World tropical forest communities. (Photograph © Barry Bland/Alamy.)

Species that extensively modify the physical environment through their activities, often termed "ecosystem engineers," are considered keystone species also (McLaren and Peterson 1994; Wright et al. 2003). For example, beavers build dams that flood temperate forests, creating new wetland habitat for many species. Earthworms may turn over many tons of soil per hectare each year, dramatically affecting soil fertility and thereby the plant and animal community. Leaf cutter ants in tropical and subtropical American forests dig extensive tunnels through the soil to build fungal gardens and, in the process, create new habitats for many subterranean species; their leaf-cutting activities also have a profound effect on the vegetation.

The importance of grazing animals in physically shaping communities is illustrated by the case of Caribbean coral reefs (Hughes 1994; Burke and Maidens 2004). On these reefs, many species of fish and sea urchins of the genus *Diadema* included algae in their diets, particularly those species of large, fleshy algae that were fairly uncommon prior to 1980. However, in the 1980s, overharvesting greatly depleted fish populations, and there was a massive die-off of *Diadema,* apparently caused by a viral epidemic. Without the fish and *Diadema* to control their numbers, the fleshy algae increased dramatically in abundance, covering and damaging the coral reefs. Pollution of coastal waters by human activities may have helped tip the ecological balance in favor of the algae by providing abundant nutrients for growth.

The importance of a keystone species or guild may hinge upon highly specialized relationships between the keystone species and other organisms. In many tropical forests, fig trees and fig vines (*Ficus* spp.) appear to be keystone species in the functioning of vertebrate communities. Fig flowers are pollinated by small, highly specialized fig wasps, which mature inside the developing fig fruit. Mature fig trees produce continuous fig crops, and generations of wasps are continually coming to maturity. As a consequence of this continuous fruit production, figs provide a reliable source of fruit to primates, birds, and other fruit-eating vertebrates throughout the year, even during dry seasons. While fig fruits do not have the high energy content of many preferred lipid-rich fruits or the high protein content of an insect diet, during periods of drought the fig fruits serve as "famine food," which allows vertebrates to survive until their preferred foods are once more available. Even though fig trees and vines may be uncommon in the forest, and the fruit may constitute only a small percentage of the total vertebrate diet, their persistence is necessary to the continued functioning of many species in the vertebrate community. In this case, the fig trees are a keystone guild because so many other species rely on them for food, and the health of the fig tree population rests on the health of their wasp pollinators. The mutualistic relationship between the trees and the wasps forms the foundation of the entire community's health.

Many keystone species play less obvious roles that are nevertheless essential to maintaining biological diversity. In addition to worms, other inconspicuous detritivores also play a significant role in the functioning of communities. For example, dung beetles exist at low density levels in tropical forests and constitute only a fraction of the biomass (Klein 1989), yet these beetles are crucial to the community because they create balls of dung and carrion and bury them as a food source for their larvae (Figure 2.15). These buried materials break down rapidly, making

FIGURE 2.15 Dung beetles, also known as scarabs, are important keystone species in many communities. The beetles disperse and bury balls of dung and carrion, allowing the waste material to decompose quickly and making nutrients available for plant growth. Seeds are dispersed along with the dung, allowing new plants to flourish. (Illustration © Abigail Rorer. Reproduced with permission from *The Work of Nature* by Yvonne Baskin, Island Press, Washington, D.C.)

nutrients available for plant growth. Seeds contained in the dung of fruit-eating animals are also buried, which facilitates seed germination and the establishment of new plants. In addition, by burying and feeding on dung, the beetles kill the vertebrate parasites contained in the dung, thus helping to keep the vertebrate populations healthy. Disease-causing organisms and parasites can also be examples of inconspicuous but nevertheless crucial species, because their presence reduces the density of their host species and keeps the biological community in balance.

As should be evident from our discussion thus far, the identification of keystone species has several important implications for conservation biology. First, the elimination of a keystone species or group from a community may precipitate the loss of other species (Letourneau et al. 2004). Losing keystones can create a series of linked extinction events, known as an **extinction cascade**, that results in a degraded ecosystem with much lower biological diversity at all trophic levels. This may already be happening in tropical forests where overharvesting has drastically reduced the populations of birds and mammals that act as predators, seed dispersers, and herbivores. While such a forest appears to be green and healthy at first glance, it is really an "empty forest" in which ecological processes have been irreversibly altered such that the species composition of the forest will change over succeeding decades or centuries (Redford 1992).

Nonetheless, in some cases, if the few keystone species in a community being affected by human activity can be identified, they can be carefully protected or even encouraged. For example, during selective logging operations, figs and other important fruit trees should be protected, while common trees that are not keystone species could be reduced in abundance with little permanent loss of biological diversity. Likewise, hunting of keystone animal species in the logging area should be limited or stopped altogether.

Keystone Resources

Often nature reserves are compared and valued in terms of their size because, on average, larger reserves contain more species and habitats than smaller reserves. However, area alone does not ensure that a nature reserve contains the full range of crucial habitats and resources. Particular habitats may contain critical **keystone resources**, often physical or structural, that occupy only a small area yet are crucial to many species in the community (Pykala 2004; Hunter 2005). For example:

- *Salt licks and mineral pools* provide essential minerals for wildlife, particularly in inland areas with heavy rainfall. The distribution of salt licks can determine the abundance and distribution of vertebrates in an area.

- *Deep pools* in streams and springs may be the only refuge for fish, certain plant species, and other aquatic species during the dry season, when water levels drop. For terrestrial animals, these water sources may provide the only available drinking water for a considerable distance.

- *Hollow tree trunks* are needed as breeding sites for many bird and mammal species. Suitable tree cavities are the limiting resource on the population size of many vertebrate species. The significance of nesting sites is demonstrated by the increase in breeding pairs that occurs when nesting boxes are provided and by the decline in population size of many species when dead and hollow trees are removed in managed forests.

- *Rotting wood* provides habitat for a wide range of animals, plants, and fungi in both terrestrial and aquatic environments (Gurnell et al. 2005). Fallen trees in streams are important refuges for fish; they provide both shelter from predators and create well-oxygenated ripples that nourish both fish and their invertebrate prey. When such wood is cleared away, the species richness of the system declines.

Keystone resources may occupy only a small proportion of a conservation area, yet they are of crucial importance in maintaining many animal populations. The loss of a keystone resource could mean the rapid loss of animal species, particularly certain birds and mammals. When vertebrate species are lost, there could be an extinction cascade of plant species that depend on those animals for pollination and seed dispersal.

Ecosystem Dynamics

In the interaction of the biological community with the physical and chemical environment, key ecosystem processes include transfer of energy; production of biomass; cycling of carbon, nitrogen, and other nutrients; and the movement of water (Chu and Karr 2001; Diaz 2001; MEA 2005). The concept of **ecosystem integrity** is important to conservation (but is challenging to evaluate objectively and quantitatively). Ecosystem integrity is the condition in which an ecosystem is complete and functional. An ecosystem that has been damaged by human activity and has lost some of its species and certain processes, such as the ability to retain water after storms and then release it slowly, has lost some of its integrity.

An ecosystem in which the processes are functioning normally, whether or not there are human influences, is referred to as a **healthy ecosystem**. In many cases, ecosystems that have lost some of their species will remain healthy because there is often some redundancy in the roles performed by ecologically similar species. Ecosystems that are able to remain in the same state are referred to as **stable ecosystems**. These systems remain stable either because of lack of disturbance or because they have special features that allow them to remain stable in the face of disturbance. Such stability despite disturbance could result from one or both of two features: resistance and resilience. **Resistance** is the ability to maintain the same state even with ongoing disturbance; that would be the case if after an oil spill, a river ecosystem retains its major ecosystem processes. **Resilience** is the property of being able to return to the original state quickly after disturbance has occurred; that would be true if following contamination by an oil spill and the deaths of many animals and plants, a river ecosystem eventually returns to its original condition. For example, when fish are introduced in previously fish-free ponds, the number of native animal species declines, indicating low resistance; but when the fish die out, the number of native species soon recovers, indicating high resilience (Knapp et al. 2005).

Conclusion

The concepts of biological diversity described in this chapter can help identify species and places in need of protection. In addition, ecological principles are being used to formulate management strategies for biological communities. These topics will be further developed in later chapters. The next chapter will explore the global distribution of biological diversity.

Summary

1. The Earth's biological diversity includes the entire range of living species, the genetic variation that occurs among individuals within a species, and, at a higher level, the biological communities in which species live, and their ecosystem-level interactions with the physical and chemical environment.

2. Species richness, one component of species diversity, refers to the number of species found in a particular location. Species diversity is also measured across landscapes and at regional scales with the goal of examining and comparing large-scale patterns of species distribution. These measures are used chiefly for examining particular groups of species.

3. Genetic variation within species arises through the mutation of genes and the recombination of genes during sexual reproduction. Species with high levels of genetic variation may adapt most readily to a changing environment through the process of natural selection. In some cases, this process leads to the evolution of new species. In artificial selection, people alter gene pools to make domestic plants and animals more suitable for human use.

4. Within biological communities, species interact through processes such as competition, predation, and mutualism, and occupy distinct trophic, or feeding, levels that represent the ways in which they obtain energy. Individual species often have specific feeding relationships with other species that can be represented as food chains and food webs.

5. Certain keystone species or groups may determine the ability of other species to persist in a community. These keystone species are sometimes top carnivores but also may be inconspicuous species. The loss of a keystone species from a community might result in a cascade of extinctions of other species.

6. Certain keystone resources, such as water holes, nesting sites, and salt licks, may occupy only a small fraction of a habitat, but they can be crucial to the persistence of many species in an area.

For Discussion

1. How many species of birds, plants, insects, mammals, and mushrooms can you identify in your neighborhood? How could you learn to identify more? Do you believe that the present generation of people is more or less able to identify species than past generations?

2. Conservation efforts usually target genetic variation, species diversity, biological communities, and ecosystems for protection. Can you think of other components of natural systems that need to be protected? What do you think is the most important component of biological diversity?

3. Some examples of keystone species are top predators. Can examples of keystone species be found at all trophic levels and in each kingdom of the living world?

4. How could you manage a property, such as a degraded rangeland, a forest plantation, or a polluted lake, to restore all levels of biological diversity?

Suggested Readings

Becker, B. H. and S. R. Beissinger. 2006. Centennial decline in the trophic level of an endangered seabird after fisheries decline. *Conservation Biology* 20: 470–479. Commercial fishing practices have altered the trophic relationships of marine species.

Bisby, F. A. 2000. The quiet revolution: Biodiversity informatics and the Internet. *Science* 289: 2309–2314. Databases are accumulating and organizing information on every known species and then making the information available on the Internet.

Buchmann, S. L. and G. P. Nabhan. 1996. *The Forgotten Pollinators.* Island Press, Washington, D.C. Wild species are vital pollinators of many crop species and endangered plants, as shown in this beautiful book.

Gittleman, J. L., S. M. Funk, D. MacDonald, and R. K. Wayne. (eds.). 2000. *Carnivore Conservation.* Cambridge University Press, Cambridge. Carnivores are the subject of intense research as symbols of wildness and for their role as keystone species.

Gotelli, N. J. 2001. *A Primer of Ecology,* 3rd Edition. Sinauer Associates, Sunderland, MA. Concise introduction, emphasizing theory and lucidly explained mathematics.

Kratochwil, A. (ed.). 2000. *Biodiversity in Ecosystems.* Kluwer Academic Publishers, Dordrecht, Netherlands. Focus on landscape conservation in southern and central Europe.

Legendre P., D. Borcard, and P. R. Peres-Neto. 2005. Analyzing beta diversity: Partitioning the spatial variation of community composition data. *Ecological Monographs* 75: 435–450. Biological diversity can be measured at different levels using different methods.

Letourneau, D. K., L. A. Dyer, and G. C. Vega. 2004. Indirect effects of a top predator on a rainforest understory plant community. *Ecology* 85: 2144–2152. Extinction cascades can be caused by the loss of a single species.

Mumby, P. J., C. P. Dahlgren, A. R. Harborne, C. V. Kappel, F. Micheli, D. R. Brumbaugh, et al. 2006. Fishing, trophic cascades, and the process of grazing on coral reefs. *Science* 311: 98–101. Interactions among trophic levels have important conservation implications.

Myers, N. and A. Knoll. 2001. The biotic crisis and the future of evolution. *Proceedings of the National Academy of Sciences of the U.S.A.* 98: 5389–5392. Human alteration of the world is changing the process of evolution and may lead to unpredictable results.

Nyhagen, D. F., S. D. Turnbull, J. M. Olesen, and C. G. Jones. 2005. An investigation into the role of the Mauritian flying fox, *Pteropus niger*, in forest regeneration. *Biological Conservation* 122: 491–497. Flying foxes have been identified as keystone species.

Pedersen, B. S. and A. M. Wallis. 2004. Effects of white-tailed deer herbivory on forest gap dynamics in a wildlife preserve, Pennsylvania, USA. *Natural Areas Journal* 24: 82–94. Without wolves to control their numbers, deer are having a harmful effect on many forest ecosystems.

Poiani, K. A., B. D. Richter, M. G. Anderson, and H. E. Richter. 2000. Biodiversity conservation at multiple scales: Functional sites, landscapes and networks. *BioScience* 50: 133–146. Biodiversity needs to be considered at the local scale but also at larger landscape and regional scales.

Power, M., D. Tilman, J. A. Estes, B. A. Menge, et al. 1996. Challenges in the quest for keystones. *BioScience* 46: 609–620. An excellent review article, with strong coverage of theory and examples.

Purvis, A. and A. Hector. 2000. Getting the measure of biodiversity. *Nature* 405: 212–219. Biological diversity can be measured at different levels using different methods.

Soulé, M. E., J. A. Estes, B. Miller, and D. L. Honnold. 2005. Strongly interacting species: Conservation policy, management, and ethics. *BioScience* 55: 168–176. Keystone species need to be the focus of management efforts and decisions on new protected areas.

Tautz, D., P. Arctander, A. Minelli, R. H. Thomas, and A. P. Vogler. 2003. A plea for DNA taxonomy. *Trends in Ecology and Evolution* 18: 70–74. In the past morphological characters were the major tools of taxonomists; increasingly DNA markers are being used.

Valladares, G., A. Salvo, and L. Cagnolo. 2006. Habitat fragmentation effects on trophic processes of insect-plant food webs. *Conservation Biology* 20: 212–217. Food webs can be dramatically altered by human activities.

Wayne, R. K. and P. A. Morin. 2004. Conservation genetics in the new molecular age. *Frontiers in Ecology and the Environment* 2: 89–97. Modern molecular techniques can be used to assess population characteristics and suggest conservation strategies.

Wilson, E. O. 2003. The encyclopedia of life. *Trends in Ecology and Evolution* 18: 77–80. One of the founders of conservation biology argues that there is an urgent need for more taxonomists to describe new species.

Where Is the World's Biological Diversity Found?

Although the planet Earth has an abundance of biological diversity, certain ecosystems have far more species than others. Certain groups of organisms are also especially rich in species, and scientists are discovering entire new biological communities in previously unexplored places. In this chapter we will examine the factors that determine the abundance and distribution of species throughout the world.

The most species-rich environments appear to be tropical rain forests and deciduous forests, coral reefs, large tropical lakes, and perhaps the deep sea (Heywood 1995; Levin 2001; Groombridge and Jenkins 2002). Much of the diversity of tropical forests is due to their great abundance of insects, but they also have many species of birds, mammals, and plants. In coral reefs and the deep sea, diversity is spread over a much broader range of phyla and classes. These marine systems contain representatives of 28 of the 33 animal phyla that exist today; 13 of these phyla exist only in the marine environment (Grassle 2001). In contrast, only one phylum is found exclusively in the terrestrial environment. Diversity in the ocean may be due to great age, enormous area, the degree of isolation of certain seas by intervening land masses, the stability of the environment, and specialization on particular sediment types (Waller 1996; Lambshead and Schalk 2001). However, the traditional view of the "unchanging" sea is being reevaluated as a result of evidence that shows decreased deep sea biodiversity during postglacial episodes and recent shifts in species distribution associated with global climate change. Diversity in large tropical lakes is accounted for by the rapid evolutionary radiation of fishes and other species in a series of isolated, productive habitats. High freshwater diversity is also found in complex river systems, with individual species having restricted distribution.

In temperate communities, great diversity is found among plant species in southwestern Australia, the Cape Region of South Africa, California, central Chile, and the Mediterranean Basin, all of which are characterized by a Mediterranean climate of moist winters and hot, dry summers (Groombridge and Jenkins 2002). The Mediterranean Basin is the largest in area (2.3 million km^2) and has the most plant species (25,000); the Cape Region of South Africa has an extraordinary concentration of unique plant species (8550) in a relatively small area (70,000 km^2). The shrub and herb communities in these areas are apparently rich in species due to their combination of considerable geological age, complexity of site conditions, and severe environmental conditions. The frequency of fire in these areas also may favor rapid speciation (Cowling et al. 1996; Richardson et al. 2001; Rundel 2001).

Two of the Most Diverse Ecosystems on Earth

Species richness is greatest in tropical ecosystems. Tropical rain forests on land and coral reefs in marine systems are among the most biologically diverse ecosystems on Earth and have become the focus of popular attention.

Tropical Rain Forests

Even though the world's tropical forests occupy only 7% of the land area, they contain over half the world's species (Caulfield 1985; Whitmore 1990; Primack and Corlett 2005). This estimate is based on limited sampling of insects and other arthropods, groups that are thought to contain the majority of the world's species (Figure 3.1). Reasonable estimates (we could call them educated guesses) of the number of insect species in tropical forests range from 5 million to 10 million, though some estimates have been as high as 30 million species (May 1992). Such numbers suggest that insects found in tropical forests may constitute the majority

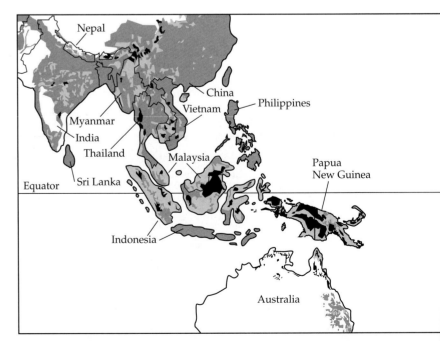

FIGURE 3.1 Tropical rain forests are found predominantly in wet, equatorial regions of America, Africa, and Asia. Eight thousand years ago, tropical forests covered the entire shaded area, but human activities have resulted in the loss of a great deal of forest cover, shown in the darkest shade. In the lighter shaded area forests remain, but they are no longer true tropical forests; instead they are (1) secondary forests that have grown back following cutting, (2) plantation forests such as rubber and teak, or (3) forests degraded by logging and fuelwood collection. Only in the regions shown in black are there still blocks of intact natural tropical forest large enough to support all of their biodiversity. (After Bryant et al. 1997.)

of the world's species. Information on other groups, such as plants and birds, is much more accurate. For flowering plants, gymnosperms, and ferns, about 40% of the world's 275,000 species occur in the world's tropical forest areas in the Americas, Africa, Madagascar, Southeast Asia, New Guinea, Australia, and various tropical islands.

About 30% of the world's bird species—1300 species in the American tropics, 400 species in tropical Africa, and 900 in tropical Asia—depend on tropical forests. This figure is probably an underestimate, since it does not include species that are only partially dependent on tropical forests (such as migratory birds), nor does it reflect the high concentrations of tropical forest birds living in restricted habitats, such as islands, that may be more vulnerable to habitat loss. In forested islands such as New Guinea, 78% of the nonmarine birds depend on the tropical forest for their survival.

Coral Reefs

Colonies of tiny coral animals build the large coral reef ecosystems—the marine equivalent of tropical rain forests in both species richness and complexity (Spalding et al. 2001; Porter and Tougas 2001) (Figure 3.2). One explanation for this richness is the high primary productivity of coral reefs, which produce 2500 grams of biomass per square meter per year in comparison with 125 $g/m^2/yr$ in the open ocean. The clarity of the water in the reef ecosystem allows sunlight to penetrate deeply so that high levels of photosynthesis occur in the algae that live mutualistically inside the coral. Extensive niche specialization among coral species and adaptations to varying levels of disturbance may also account for the high species richness found in coral reefs.

The world's largest coral reef is Australia's Great Barrier Reef, with an area of 349,000 km^2. The Great Barrier Reef contains over 400 species of coral, 1500 species of fish, 4000 species of mollusks, and 6 species of turtles, and it provides breeding sites for some 252 species of birds. Although the Great Barrier Reef occupies only 0.1% of the ocean surface area, it contains about 8% of the world's fish species. The Great Barrier Reef is part of the rich Indo–West Pacific region. The great diversity

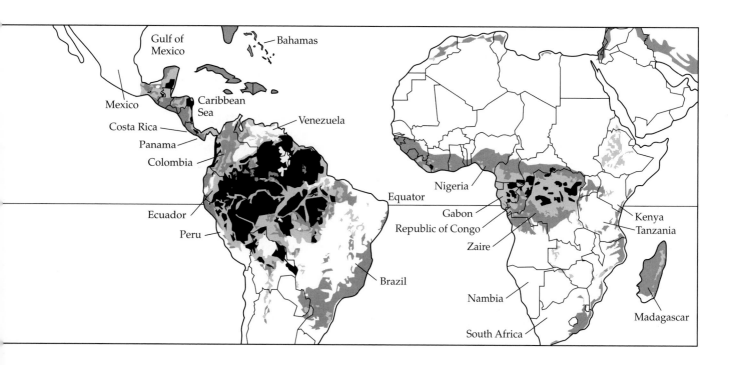

FIGURE 3.2 Coral reefs in tropical waters are built up from the skeletons of billions of tiny individual animals. The intricate coral landscapes create a habitat for many other marine species, such as these French grunts shoaling near the Elkhorn coral off Little Cayman, British West Indies. (Photograph © David Wrobel/ Biological Photo Service.)

of species in this region is illustrated by the fact that more than 2000 fish species are found in the Philippine Islands, compared with 448 species found in the mid-Pacific Hawaiian Islands, and 500 species around the Bahama Islands. In comparison to tropical coral reefs, the number of marine fishes in temperate areas is low: the mid-Atlantic seaboard of North America has only 250 fish species, and the Mediterranean has fewer than 400 species.

Most of the animals inhabiting coral reefs are small in size and not yet studied; tens of thousands of species still await discovery and description. Scientists are also now beginning to learn about deep sea corals that live in the deep, cold environments without light (Roberts and Hirshfield 2004). These deep sea coral communities are still poorly known, but they appear to be rapidly declining due to destructive trawling practices.

One notable difference between tropical forest species and coral reef species is that, unlike many tropical forest species that occupy tropical forests in a specific part of the world, coral reef species are often widely dispersed, yet occupy a tiny percentage of the ocean's surface area. Only isolated islands, such as Hawaii, have numerous restricted-range endemic species—species that are found in a particular location and nowhere else; fully 25% of Hawaiian coral species are endemic to the area (Pacific Whale Foundation 2003). Because most coral reef species are more widely distributed than rain forest species, they may be less prone to extinction by the destruction of a single locality. However, this assertion may be a taxonomic bias, because coral reef species are not as well known as terrestrial species. Recent research suggests that some widely distributed tropical marine species have genetically unique populations in certain geographical areas (Palumbi 2004); eventually these populations might be considered to be a single species and warrant protection for that reason.

Patterns of Diversity

Patterns of diversity are known primarily through the efforts of taxonomists, who have methodically collected organisms from all areas of the world. These patterns, however, are known only in broad outline for many groups of organisms because the great majority of species-rich groups, such as beetles, bacteria, and fungi, remain undescribed. It is clear that local variation in climate, environment, topography, and geological age are factors that affect patterns of species richness (Huston 1994; Gaston 2000).

Variation in Climate and Environment

In terrestrial communities, species richness tends to increase with decreasing elevation, increasing solar radiation, and increasing precipitation. These factors act in combination; for example, deserts are species poor due to their low precipitation, even though they have high solar radiation. In some localities, species abundance is greatest at mid-elevations. The lower richness of plants and animals in Africa, in comparison with South America and Asia, may be due to a combination of lower past and present rainfall, the smaller total area of rain forest, and a longer period of human impact in Africa (Primack and Corlett 2005). Even within tropical Africa itself, areas of low rainfall in the Sahel have fewer species than forested areas with higher rainfall to the south. However, the extensive savannah areas of East and Central Africa have a richness and abundance of antelopes and other ungulate grazers not found on other continents. The greatest abundance of mammal species may occur at intermediate levels of precipitation rather than in the wettest or driest habitats (Mares 1992). In the open ocean, species diversity reaches a peak at 2000 to 3000 m, with lower diversity closer to the surface and at greater depths.

Variation in Topography, Geological Age, and Habitat Size

Species richness can be greater where complex topography and great geological age provide more environmental variation, which allows genetic isolation, local adaptation, and speciation to occur. For example, a species able to colonize a series of isolated mountain peaks in the Andes during a period of favorable climate may eventually evolve into several different species, each adapted to its local mountain environment. A similar process could occur for fish and invertebrates occupying large drainage systems and lakes that become divided into several smaller systems. Examples include the Tennessee River system in the United States, the Mekong River in southeast Asia, and Lake Baikal in Siberia (Strayer 2001). Geologically complex areas can produce a variety of soil conditions with very sharp boundaries between them, leading to multiple communities and species adapted to one specific soil type or another.

At various spatial scales, there are concentrations of species in particular places, and there is a rough correspondence in the distribution of species richness between different groups of organisms (Lamoreux et al. 2006). For example, in Africa, concentrations of birds, amphibians, and mammal species are each found in the same general areas: southern African shrubland, West African tropical forests and rivers, the Great Lakes region, and the Ethiopian highlands (Figure 3.3) (Bibby et al. 1992). In North America, large-scale patterns of species richness are highly correlated for amphibians, birds, butterflies, mammals, reptiles, land snails, trees, all vascular plants, and tiger beetles; that is, a region with numerous species of one group will tend to have numerous species of the other groups (Ricketts et al. 1999). On a local scale, this relationship may break down; for example, amphibians may be most diverse in wet, shady habitats, whereas reptiles may be most diverse in drier, open habitats. These patterns are also greatly weakened when the effects of latitude are removed. This is because greater concentrations of species tend to be found further

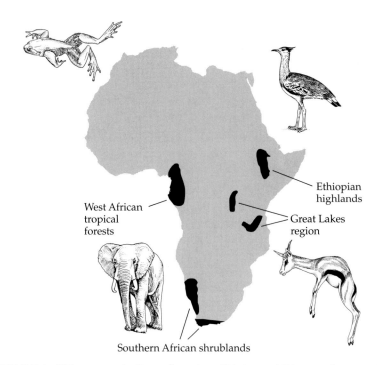

FIGURE 3.3 In Africa, concentrations of species of birds, amphibians, and mammals are found in the same general areas: the Ethiopian highlands, the African Great Lakes, West African tropical rain forests, and in the Mediterranean climate of southern Africa's shrublands. (Map after Bibby et al. 1992.)

south in North America. At a global scale, each group of living organisms may reach its greatest species richness in a different part of the world due to historical circumstances or the suitability of the site to its needs.

Larger areas also can provide a greater range of habitats in which species can evolve and live. For example, coral species richness is several times greater in the Indian and West Pacific Oceans than in the western Atlantic Ocean, which is much smaller in area (Figure 3.4). More than 50 genera of coral exist in many of the Indo–Pacific areas, but only about 20 genera occur in the reefs of the Caribbean Sea and the adjacent Atlantic Ocean.

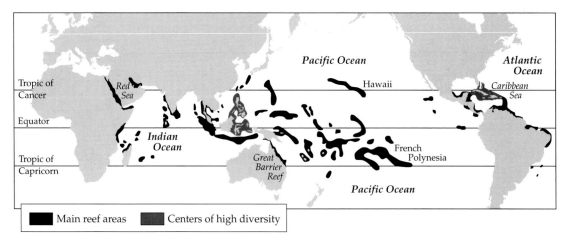

FIGURE 3.4 Global distribution of the coral reef biome. (After Wells and Hanna 1992.)

Why Are There So Many Species in the Tropics?

Almost all groups of organisms show an increase in species diversity toward the Tropics. For example, Thailand has 265 species of mammals, while France has only 93, despite the fact that both countries have roughly the same land area (Table 3.1). The contrast is particularly striking for trees and other flowering plants: 10 ha of forest in Amazonian Peru or Brazil might have 300 or more tree species, whereas an equivalent forest area in temperate Europe or the United States would probably contain 30 species or less. Within a given continent, the number of species increases toward the Equator (Figure 3.5).

Patterns of diversity in terrestrial species are paralleled by patterns in marine species, again with an increase in species diversity toward the Tropics. For example, the Great Barrier Reef off the eastern coast of Australia has 50 genera of reef-building coral at its northern end where it approaches the Tropics, but only 10 genera at its southern end, farthest away from the Tropics. These increases in richness of coastal species toward the Tropics and in warmer waters are paralleled by increases in open ocean species, such as plankton and predatory fish (Worm et al. 2005), though there are some groups of species that are most diverse in temperate waters.

Many theories have been advanced to explain the greater diversity of species in the Tropics (Gaston 2000; Noble and Roxburgh 2001; Willig 2001; Hubbell 2001; Pimm and Brown 2004). Following are some of the most reasonable theories:

1. Tropical regions receive more solar energy over the course of a year than temperate regions. As a result, many tropical communities have a higher rate of productivity than temperate communities, in terms of the number of kilograms of living material (biomass) produced each year per hectare of habitat. This high productivity results in a greater resource base that can support a wider range of species.

2. The large geographical area of the Tropics, in comparison with the temperate zone, may account for the greater rates of speciation and lower rates of extinction in the Tropics than in the temperate zones (Chown and Gaston 2000). This follows from the fact that the tropical areas north and south of the Equator are next to each other, while the temperate areas outside the Tropics are divided in two by the Tropics themselves.

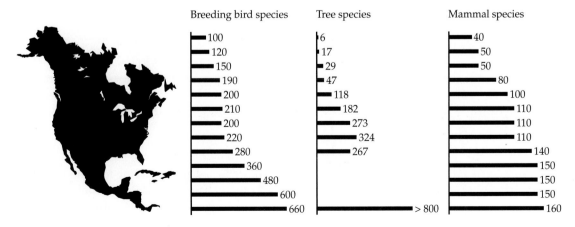

FIGURE 3.5 In North America, as in all the continents, the numbers of bird, tree, and mammal species increase toward the Tropics. The numbers of species indicated in the bar graphs correspond to latitude in the map at left. Tree species diversity is not available for some lower latitudes. (From Briggs 1995.)

TABLE 3.1 *Number of mammal species in selected tropical and temperate countries paired for comparable size*

Tropical country	Area (1000 km²)	Number of mammal species	Temperate country	Area (1000 km²)	Number of mammal species
Brazil	8456	417	Canada	9220	193
DRC[a]	2268	450	Argentina	2737	320
Mexico	1909	491	Algeria	2382	92
Indonesia	1812	457	Iran	1636	140
Colombia	1039	359	South Africa	1221	255
Venezuela	882	323	Chile	748	91
Thailand	511	265	France	550	93
Philippines	298	158	United Kingdom	242	50
Rwanda	25	151	Belgium	30	58

Source: Data from WRI 2000.
[a]DRC = Democratic Republic of the Congo.

3. Tropical communities have had longer periods of stability than temperate communities, which have had to disperse in response to periods of glaciation. This greater stability has allowed the processes of evolution and speciation to occur uninterrupted in tropical communities in response to local conditions. In temperate areas, the scouring actions of glaciers and the frigid climate destroyed many local species that might have evolved and favored those species able to disperse long distances. Thus, a relatively more stable climate has allowed a greater degree of evolutionary specialization and local adaptation to occur in tropical areas.

4. The warm temperatures and high humidity in many tropical areas provide favorable conditions for the growth and survival of many species. Entire communities of species can also develop in the tree canopies. In contrast, species living in temperate zones must have physiological mechanisms that allow them to tolerate cold and freezing conditions. These species may also have specialized behaviors, such as dormancy, hibernation, burrowing into the ground, or migration, to help them survive the winter. The inability of many groups of plants and animals to live outside the Tropics suggests that adaptations to cold do not evolve easily or quickly.

5. Due to a predictable environment, species interactions in the Tropics are more intense, leading initially to greater competition among species and later to niche specialization. Also, tropical species may face greater pressure from parasites and disease because there is no freezing weather in winter to reduce pest populations. Ever-present populations of these parasites prevent any single species or group of species from dominating communities, creating an opportunity for numerous species to coexist at low individual densities. For example, tree seedlings are often killed by fungi and insects when they grow near other trees of the same species, often leading to wide spaces between adult trees of the same species (Harms et al. 2000). In many ways, the biology of the Tropics is the biology of rare species. In contrast, temperate-zone species may face reduced parasite pressure because the winter cold suppresses parasite populations, allowing one or a few competitively superior species of plants and animals to dominate the community and exclude many other, less competitive species.

How Many Species Exist Worldwide?

Any strategy for conserving biological diversity must be based on a firm grasp of the numbers of species that exist in the world today and how those species are distributed (Figure 3.6A). At the present time, about 1.5 million species have been described in total. It is certain that *at least twice* this number of species remain undescribed, primarily in the Tropics, leading to an estimate of nearly 5 million species worldwide. We will return to this number later in the chapter when we examine the problems involved in estimating species.

(A)

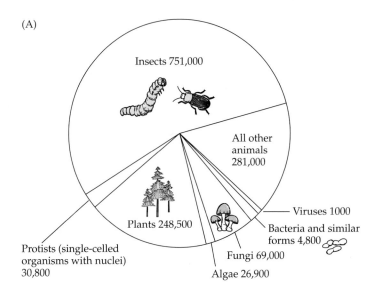

Insects 751,000

All other animals 281,000

Viruses 1000

Plants 248,500

Bacteria and similar forms 4,800

Protists (single-celled organisms with nuclei) 30,800

Fungi 69,000

Algae 26,900

FIGURE 3.6 (A) Approximately 1.5 million species have been identified and described by scientists; the majority of these are insects and plants. (B) For major groups of organisms estimated to contain over 100,000 species, the numbers of described species are indicated by the shaded portions of the bars; the unshaded portions are estimates of the numbers of undescribed species. (Vertebrates are included for comparison.) The column on the right shows the accuracy of the estimates. The number of undescribed species is particularly speculative for the various groups of microorganisms. The number of identified species could eventually reach 5 to 10 million, or even 20 to 40 million. (A, data from Wilson 1992; B, after Hammond 1992.)

(B)

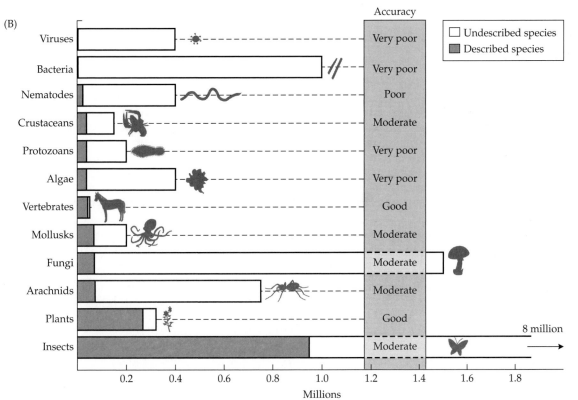

	Accuracy
Viruses	Very poor
Bacteria	Very poor
Nematodes	Poor
Crustaceans	Moderate
Protozoans	Very poor
Algae	Very poor
Vertebrates	Good
Mollusks	Moderate
Fungi	Moderate
Arachnids	Moderate
Plants	Good
Insects	Moderate

☐ Undescribed species
■ Described species

8 million

0.2 0.4 0.6 0.8 1.0 1.2 1.4 1.6 1.8

Millions

New Species Are Being Discovered All the Time

Amazingly, around 20,000 new species are described each year. While certain groups of organisms such as birds, mammals, and temperate flowering plants are relatively well known, a small but steady number of new species in these groups are being discovered each year (Donoghue and Alverson 2000; Peres 2005). Since 1990, 10 new species of primates have been found in Brazil, and three new species of lemurs in Madagascar have been discovered. Five hundred to six hundred new species of amphibians are described each decade. More species of all groups will be found if scientists keep looking for them (Morell 1996).

In groups such as insects, spiders, mites, nematodes, and fungi, the number of described species is still increasing at the rate of 1–2% per year (Donoghue and Alverson 2000). Huge numbers of species in these groups, mostly in tropical areas but also in the temperate zone, have yet to be discovered and described (Figure 3.6B). Compounding the problem is the fact that, though most of the world's remaining undescribed species are probably insects and other invertebrates, only one-third of the world's 5000 taxonomists are now studying these groups.

Species are typically discovered when taxonomists collect specimens while on field trips, but are unable to identify them despite looking at all available published descriptions. Taxonomists will then make a description of each new species and give them a new scientific name. New species are also discovered when further research, often involving the techniques of molecular systematics, reveals that what was originally thought to be a single species with a number of geographically distinct populations is really two or more species.

Sometimes new species are discovered via "living fossils"—species known only from the fossil record and believed to be extinct until living examples are found in modern times. In 1938, ichthyologists throughout the world were stunned by the report of a strange fish caught in the Indian Ocean. This fish, subsequently named *Latimeria chalumnae,* belonged to a group of marine fish known as coelacanths that were common in ancient seas but were thought to have gone extinct 65 million years ago (Thomas 1991). Coelacanths are of particular interest to evolutionary biologists because they show certain features of muscles and bones in their fins that are comparable to the limbs of the first land animals. Biologists searched the Indian Ocean for 14 years before another coelacanth was found, off Grand Comoro Island between Madagascar and the African coast. Subsequent investigation has shown that there is a single population of about 200 individuals living in underwater caves approximately 200 m offshore of Grand Comoro Island (Fricke and Hissmann 1990). In recent years, the Republic of Comores implemented a conservation plan to protect the coelacanths, including a ban on catching and selling the fish. In a remarkable footnote to this story, in 1998 a marine biologist working in Indonesia was astonished to see a dead coelacanth for sale in a local fish market. Subsequent investigations demonstrated that this was a new species of coelacanth (Inoue et al. 2005) unknown to science but well known to the local fishermen, illustrating how much is still waiting to be discovered in the world's oceans.

In 2002, scientists exploring in the remote Brandberg Mountains of Namibia in southwestern Africa discovered insects in an entirely new order, distantly related to grasshoppers, stick insects, and praying mantids, subsequently named the Mantophasmatodea (Figure 3.7) (Klass et al. 2002). The last time a new order of insects had been described was in 1915. Further searches in other African countries have found additional species in this order.

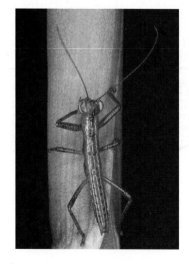

FIGURE 3.7 In 2002 a new order of insects, Mantophasmatodea, was discovered in Namibia. These predators are now also known as gladiator insects. (Photograph by M. Picker.)

Recently Discovered Communities

In addition to new species, entire biological communities continue to be discovered, often in extremely remote and inaccessible localities. These communities often consist of inconspicuous species, such as bacteria, protists, and small invertebrates, that have escaped the attention of earlier taxonomists. Specialized exploration techniques have aided in these discoveries, particularly in the deep sea and in the forest canopy. Some recently discovered communities include:

- Diverse communities of animals, particularly insects, that are adapted to living in the canopies of tropical trees and rarely, if ever, descend to the ground (Wilson 1991; Moffat 1994; Lowman 1999). The use of technical climbing equipment, canopy towers and walkways, and tall cranes, is opening up this habitat to exploration (Figure 3.8).

- Investigations of bacterial communities in remote locations using new sampling techniques have revealed a diversity of species previously unsuspected. The floor of the deep sea has unique communities of bacteria and animals that grow around geothermal vents (Box 3.1). Undescribed, active bacteria unrelated to any known species have even been found in marine sediments at depths of up to 6.5 km (4 mi.), where they undoubtedly play a major chemical and energetic role in this vast ecosystem (Li et al. 1999). Drilling projects have shown that diverse bacterial communities exist 2.8 km deep in the Earth's crust, at densities ranging from 100 to 100 million bacteria per gram of solid rock. Molecular genetic techniques have revealed these communities to be

(A)

(B)

FIGURE 3.8 (A) Biologists are gaining access to the diverse world of the rain forest canopy by using techniques borrowed from technical rock climbing. (B) Research is carried out in the tree canopy from a mobile platform attached to the arm of a tall crane. (A, photograph courtesy of Meg Lowman; B, photograph by Marcos Guerra, courtesy of Joe Wright.)

composed of numerous species, each with their own characteristic DNA (Fredrickson and Onstott 1996; Fisk et al. 1998). These bacterial communities are being actively investigated as a source of novel chemicals, for their potential usefulness in degrading toxic chemicals, and for insight into whether life could exist on other planets.

- Recent investigations of healthy tropical tree leaves have revealed an extraordinarily rich group of fungi that live inside the leaves. In a sample of 83 leaves, there appears to be over 340 distinct species of fungi (Arnold et al. 2003; Arnold and Lewis 2005). These fungi appear to aid the plant in excluding harmful bacteria and fungi in exchange for receiving a place to live and perhaps some carbohydrates.

BOX 3.1

Conserving a World Unknown: Hydrothermal Vents and Oil Plumes

Biologists are aware that many species exist that have not been adequately studied and described, a fact that frequently hampers conservation. In recent years, it has become apparent that there are entire communities that remain undiscovered in the more remote parts of the Earth. It is clear from the example of deep sea hydrothermal vents that species, genera, and even families of organisms exist about which scientists know nothing. The biota of these vents were investigated in detail only in the last 15 years with the invention of technology that enables scientists to photograph and collect specimens from depths of over 2000 meters (Van Dover et al. 2002). Such organisms pose a significant problem for conservationists: How does one go about conserving undiscovered or barely known species and communities?

Hydrothermal vents are temporary underwater openings in the Earth's crust. Extremely hot water (in excess of 150°C), sulfides, and other dissolved minerals escape from these vents and support a profusion of species in the deepest parts of the ocean. Specialized chemosynthetic bacteria are the primary producers of the vent community, using the minerals as an energy source. Communities of large animals such as clams, crabs, fishes, and 2-m long tube worms (also known as pogonophorans) in turn feed on the bacteria directly or the bacteria live symbiotically inside their bodies. The vents themselves are short-lived, spanning a few decades at most; however, the communities supported by these vents are thought to have evolved over the past 200 million years or more. Until deep sea submersibles were developed in the 1970s, scientists were completely unaware of the communities that live around the vents. Since 1979, however, when the submersible *Alvin* was first used to examine the

vents around the Galápagos Rift in the Pacific Ocean, 150 new species, 50 new genera, and 20 new families and subfamilies of animals—not including microorganisms—have been described (Lambshead and Schalk 2001). As investigation of deep sea vents continues, more families will certainly be discovered, encompassing many new genera and species.

Like many terrestrial communities, hydrothermal communities vary according to differences in their local environment. Distribution of hydrothermal communities is dependent upon the character of the vents, including the temperature, chemical composition, and flow pattern of hydrothermal fluid issuing from the vents. Scientists studying hydrothermal species may work for decades, yet only acquire minimal knowledge of the dynamics of these communities because of the unique nature of the study sites: The vents are ephemeral, sometimes existing for only a few years, and inaccessible—they can be reached only with the use of expensive, specialized equipment. Work is just starting on the genetics of these species to determine their ability to disperse and colonize new vents.

Petroleum-seep communities, another little-known ecosystem like the assemblages at hydrothermal vents, exist at ocean depths far below the reach of sunlight. In this case, the initial source of energy comes from petrochemicals—oil—seeping from cracks in the ocean floor. Some of the same species that congregate around hydrothermal and petroleum-seep vents may also colonize the carcasses of large fish and marine mammals, such as whales, which sink to the bottom of the ocean floor; these unpredictable bonanzas of organic matter may provide crucial stepping stones for organisms to

Diversity Surveys: Collecting and Counting Species

Describing the diversity of major groups of organisms represents an enormous undertaking. Large institutions and teams of scientists often undertake biological surveys of entire countries or regions, which may involve decades—such work includes specimen collection in the field, identification of known species, descriptions of new species, and, finally, publication of the results so that others can use the information. Two such examples are the massive Flora of North America Project, based at the Missouri Botanical Garden, and the Flora Malesiana in the Indo–Pacific region, organized by the Rijksherbarium in the Netherlands.

In conducting such surveys, scientists determine the identity and numbers of species present in an area by means of a thorough collection of specimens that has

---

BOX 3.1 *(continued)*

Part of a hydrothermal vent community. Large tube worms (*Riftia pachyptila*) dominate the ecosystem. Crabs and mussels also make their home here. The energy and nutrients that support this community are derived from the hydrogen sulfide and minerals emitted by volcanic vents. (Photograph courtesy of Cindy Lee Van Dover.)

disperse among widely scattered hydrothermal vents and petroleum seeps.

Hampered by the inaccessibility of the sites and the cost of investigation, biologists nevertheless need to think ahead to conservation problems that might face these species in the future. Industrial pollutants, for example, have damaged ocean species in shallower waters and in theory could harm these communities as well. Deep sea oil rigs might pump dry oil seeps and cause local extinctions. As whale and fish stocks decline, the corresponding decrease in carcasses on the sea bottom may remove a

critical resource necessary for the dispersal and maintenance of certain populations. How would conservationists respond to such a situation?

Though as yet these problems are strictly hypothetical, they illustrate a frustrating aspect of conservation biology: Too little is known about too many species and ecosystems to develop and implement specific measures that might prevent future extinctions. As time passes, new species, genera, and families continue to be added to the list of known organisms living on the Earth, but many others are probably lost before they are even discovered. How does conservation biology account for species and perhaps whole communities that are still unknown but are nonetheless in need of conservation? Experience has shown that a specific conservation program created in ignorance of a species' behavior and biological needs can sometimes be worse than no program at all. Do we develop conservation programs despite our lack of information and hope for the best? Or do we continue our studies in the hope that the time lost will not prove fatal to the species? At this stage, there is only one definitive statement that can address these dilemmas: we know that restricting pollution has broadly positive effects on natural communities, so pollution abatement programs may offer the best conservation strategy in these situations, even when the biological communities are not thoroughly understood.

been compiled over an extended period of time (Forkner et al. 2006). The collection is then carefully sorted and classified by specialists, often at museums. For example, a team from the Natural History Museum of London collected over one million beetles from a 500-ha lowland rain forest in the Dumoga–Bone National Park on Sulawesi, Indonesia, in 1985. This effort led to an initial list of 3488 species, large numbers of which were previously unknown to science. Subsequent museum work allowed the identification of 1000 more species, with as many as 2000 species remaining to be identified over the coming years and decades.

Estimating the Number of Species

Worldwide, the most diverse group of organisms appears to be the insects, with about 750,000 species described already—about half the world's total species (see Figure 3.6A). If we assume the number of insect species can be accurately estimated in tropical forests where they are most abundant, then it may be possible to estimate the total number of species in the world. Various entomologists have attempted this by sampling entire insect communities in tropical forests using insecticidal fogging of whole trees and intensive hand collection (Figure 3.9) (Ødegaard 2000; Novotny et al. 2002). These studies have revealed an extremely rich and largely undescribed insect fauna in the tree canopies. Using the results of such intensive collecting, these entomologists have attempted to calculate the number of insect species. In one approach, they begin with the fact that there are

(A)

(B)

FIGURE 3.9 (A) A researcher uses insecticidal fog to sample the vast number of insect species in the canopy of a tropical forest. (B) Back in the lab, a Costa Rican researcher begins the process of sorting, describing, and identifying specimens. (A, photograph © Mark Moffett/Minden Pictures; B, photograph by Robert Colwell.)

55,000 species of tropical trees and woody vines (lianas). Based on detailed field sampling by entomologists, an average of 9 species of specialized beetle each feed only on plant species, leading to an estimated 400,000–500,000 species of canopy beetles. Canopy beetles represent about 44% of all beetle species, yielding an estimate of around 1 million beetle species. Because beetles are about 20% of all insects, it can be estimated that there are about 5 million insects in tropical forests. Such calculations give values comparable to earlier estimates of 5 to 10 million species for the entire Earth (Gaston and Spicer 2004).

Such "rules" can be used to determine how many species are involved in other biological relationships (May 1992; Schmit et al. 2005). For example, in Britain and Europe, where species have been extensively studied, there are about six times more fungus species than plant species. If this general ratio is applicable throughout the world, there may be as many as 1.6 million fungus species, in addition to the estimated 250,000 plant species worldwide. Since only 69,000 fungus species have been described so far, it is possible that there are over 1.5 million fungus species waiting to be discovered, most of them in the Tropics. If it turns out that fungal diversity increases more rapidly toward the Equator, as some scientists have suggested (Frohlich and Hyde 1999), there may be as many as 9 million undescribed fungus species.

Yet another approach is to assume that each species of plant and insect, which together form the majority of currently known species, has at least one species of specialized bacteria, protist, and nematode (round worm); hence the estimate of the number of total species worldwide should be multiplied by four—bringing it to 20 million using the figure of 5 million species as the starting point, or 40 million if 10 million species is the starting point. Developing such preliminary approaches allows estimates to be made of the number of species in communities while more rigorous sampling and identification is being performed.

UNDERREPRESENTED SPECIES The difficulty of making estimates of species numbers is exacerbated by the fact that inconspicuous species have not received their proper share of taxonomic attention. Since inconspicuous species constitute the majority of species on Earth, the difficulty of finding and cataloging them delays a thorough understanding of the full extent of the planet's biological diversity.

Inconspicuous organisms, including small rodents, most insects, and microorganisms, are much less likely to be observed by chance outside their natural habitats, as the coelacanth was, or even *within* their native environments. For example, mites in the soil, soft-bodied insects such as bark lice, and nematodes in both soil and water are small and hard to study. If properly studied, these groups could number in the hundreds of thousands of species or even millions. Since demonstrating the role of nematode species as root parasites of agricultural plants, scientists have dramatically increased their efforts to collect and describe these minute roundworms. Consequently, the catalog of this one group of organisms has grown from the 80 species known in 1860 to around 20,000 species known today. Most of the described nematode species are from northwestern European coastal regions; some experts estimate that there may be millions more species waiting to be described (Boucher and Lambshead 1995), though this number should be considered highly speculative. As is the case with so many other taxonomic groups, the number of trained specialists is the limiting factor in unlocking the diversity of this enormous group of species.

Bacteria are also very poorly known (Dunlap 2001; Azam and Worden 2004) and thus underrepresented in estimates of the total species on Earth. Only about 5000 species of bacteria are currently recognized by microbiologists, because they are difficult to grow and identify. However, work analyzing bacterial DNA indi-

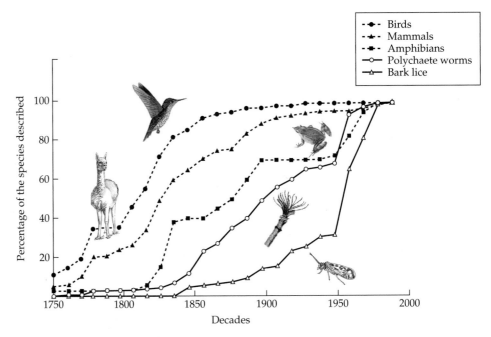

FIGURE 3.10 For five groups of Chilean animals, the cumulative percentage of the known species described from 1750 to 2000. Note that the majority of birds and mammals were largely described by 1900, and probably few new species remain to be discovered. In contrast, polychaete worms and bark lice were largely neglected by early taxonomists and are only now being investigated and described. Amphibians are intermediate in their intensity of study. (After Primack et al. 2001.)

cates that there may be from 6400 to 38,000 species in a single gram of soil and 160 species in a liter of seawater (Nee 2003). Such high diversity in small samples suggests that there could be thousands or even millions of undescribed bacteria species. Many of these unknown bacteria are probably very common and of major environmental importance. In the ancient kingdom of Archaea, which has been less studied in the past, even new bacteria *phyla* continue to be discovered.

Many inconspicuous species that live in remote habitats will not be found and cataloged unless biologists search for them. A lack of collecting, especially, has hampered our knowledge of the species richness of the marine environment (Grassle 2001)—a great frontier of biological diversity, with huge numbers of species and even entire communities still unknown—at least in part because it poses challenges for study. Marine invertebrate animals such as polychaete worms, for instance, are not well studied because they make the ocean bottom their home (Figure 3.10). Additionally, an entirely new animal phylum, the Loricifera, was described in 1983 based on specimens from the deep sea (Kristensen 1983), and another new phylum, the Cycliophora, was first described in 1995 based on tiny, ciliate creatures found on the mouthparts of the Norway lobster (Figure 3.11) (Funch and Kristensen 1995). In 1999, the world's largest bacteria was discovered off the Namibian coast, with individual cells as large as the eyes of fruit flies (Schulz et al. 1999). Undoubtedly, more species, genera, families, orders, classes, and phyla (and perhaps even kingdoms!) are waiting to be discovered.

Considering that around 20,000 new animal species are described each year and perhaps 5 million more are waiting to be identified, the task of describing the world's species will not be completed for over 250 years if continued at the present rate! This underlines the absolutely critical need for more taxonomists.

FIGURE 3.11 A new phylum, the Cycliophora, was first described in 1995. The phylum contains one vase-shaped species, *Symbion pandora* (around 40 of which are shown below), which attaches itself on the mouthparts of the Norway lobster, *Nephrops norvegicus* (inset). (Photographs courtesy of Reinhardt Kristensen, University of Copenhagen.)

The Need for More Taxonomists

A major problem the scientific community faces in describing and cataloging the biological diversity of the world is the lack of trained taxonomists able to take on the job. At the present time, there are only about 1500 taxonomists in the world who are competent to work with tropical species, and many of them are based in temperate countries. Unfortunately, this number is declining rather than increasing. When academic taxonomists retire, universities have a tendency to either close the position due to financial difficulties or replace the retiring biologist with a nontaxonomist. Many members of the younger generation of taxonomists are so preoccupied with the technology of molecular systematics and associated data analysis that they are neither interested in nor capable of continuing the great tradition of discovering and cataloging the world's biological treasures. A substantial increase in the number of field taxonomists focused primarily on describing and identifying tropical and marine species is needed to complete the task of describing the world's biological diversity. Much of this effort should be directed to lesser-known groups, such as fungi, bacteria, and invertebrates. And where possible, these taxonomists need to be based in tropical countries where this diversity is located. Natural history societies and clubs that combine professional and amateur naturalists also can play a valuable role in assisting these efforts and in exposing the general public and student groups to the issues and excitement of biological diversity and encouraging people to become taxonomists.

Summary

1. In general, species richness is greatest in tropical rain forests, coral reefs, tropical lakes, the deep sea, and shrublands with a Mediterranean climate. In terrestrial habitats, species richness tends to be greatest at lower elevations and in areas with abundant rainfall. Areas that are geologically old and topographically complex also tend to have more species.

2. Tropical rain forests occupy only 7% of the Earth's land area, yet they are estimated to contain most of the Earth's species. The great majority of these species are insects not yet described by scientists. Coral reef communities are also rich in species, with many of the species widely distributed. The deep sea also appears to be rich in species, but is still not adequately explored.

3. About 1.5 million species have been described and at least twice that number remains to be described. Intensive collecting of insects in tropical forest has yielded estimates of species numbers ranging from 5 to 10 million, but it could be higher.

4. While conspicuous groups, such as flowering plants, mammals, and birds, are reasonably well known to science, other inconspicuous groups, particularly insects, bacteria, and fungi, have not been thoroughly studied. New biological communities are still being discovered, especially in the deep sea and the forest canopy. For example, spectacular communities that occupy deep sea hydrothermal vents are major, recent discoveries.

5. There is a vital need for more taxonomists and field biologists to study, collect, classify, and help protect the world's biological diversity before it is lost.

For Discussion

1. What are the factors promoting species richness? Why is biological diversity diminished in particular environments? Why aren't species able to overcome these limitations and undergo the process of speciation?

2. Develop arguments for both low and high estimates of the total number of species in particular groups, such as bacteria, fungi, or nematodes. Read more about groups that you don't know well. Why is it important to identify and name all the species in a particular group?

3. If taxonomists are so important to documenting and protecting biological diversity, why are their numbers declining instead of increasing? How could societal and scientific priorities be readjusted to reverse this trend? Is the ability to identify and classify species a skill that every conservation biologist should possess?

4. Some scientists have argued that life may have existed on Mars, and recent drilling demonstrates that bacteria actually flourish in rocks deep under the Earth's surface. Speculate, as wildly as you can, about where to search for previously unsuspected species, communities, or novel life forms.

Suggested Readings

Arnold, A. E. and L. C. Lewis. 2005. Evolution of fungal endophytes, and their roles against insects. *In* F. Vega and M. Blackwell (eds.), *Ecological and Evolutionary Advances in Insect Fungus*, pp. 74–96. Oxford University Press, Oxford. An amazing diversity of fungi live inside leaves and they may benefit their host plants.

Cowling, R. M., P. W. Rundel, B. B. Lamont, M. K. Arroyo, and M. Arianoutsou. 1996. Plant diversity in Mediterranean climate regions. *Trends in Ecology and Evolution* 11: 362–366. A succinct review of patterns of species richness in these communities and threats to their continued existence.

Donoghue, M. J. and W. S. Alverson. 2000. A new age of discovery. *Annals of the Missouri Botanical Garden* 87: 110–126. In this article and others in the same special issue, scientists describe the numerous species still being discovered and described, even in the developed countries of the world.

Forkner, R. E., R. J. Marquis, J. T. Lill, and J. Le Corff. 2006. Impacts of alternative timber harvest practices on leaf-chewing herbivores of oak. *Conservation Biology* 20: 429–440. Species richness of insects can be affected by management practices.

Gaston, J. K. and J. I. Spicer. 2004. *Biodiversity: An Introduction, 2nd Edition.* Blackwell, Oxford. Concise treatment of terms and patterns of abundance.

Groombridge, B. and M. D. Jenkins. 2002. *World Atlas of Biodiversity: Earth's Living Resources in the 21st Century.* University of California Press, Berkeley, CA. Description of the world's biodiversity, with lots of maps and tables.

Heywood, V. H. (ed.). 1995. *Global Biodiversity Assessment.* Cambridge University Press, Cambridge. This massive book treats the subject comprehensively, with chapters by leading scientists and a huge bibliography.

Hubbell, S. P. 2001. *Unified Theory of Biodiversity and Biogeography.* Princeton University Press, Princeton, NJ. Innovative new theory that seeks to combine biogeography and biodiversity theory to explain patterns of species richness.

Lamoreux, J. F., J. C. Morrison, T. H. Ricketts, D. M. Olson, et al. 2006. Global tests of biodiversity concordance and the importance of endemism. *Nature* 440: 212–214. Concentrations of species are found in similar places for many major groups of organisms.

Lowman, M. D. 1999. *Life in the Treetops: Adventures of a Woman in Field Biology.* Yale University Press, New London, CT. Account of scientific research in the tropical forest canopy conducted while balancing work and family.

Nee, S. 2003. Unveiling prokaryotic diversity. *Trends in Ecology and Evolution* 18: 62–63. Scientists keep uncovering amazing diversity in the bacteria.

Ødegaard, F. 2000. How many species of arthropods? Erwin's estimate revised. *Biological Journal of the Linnean Society* 71: 583–597. A careful analysis of tropical insect diversity leads to calculations of the total number of insect species.

Pimm, S. L. and J. H. Brown. 2004. Domains of diversity. *Science* 304: 831–833. Various theories of global diversity are critically examined.

Primack, R. and R. Corlett. 2005. *Tropical Rainforests: An Ecological and Biogeographical Comparison.* Blackwell Publishing, Malden, MA. Rainforests on each continent have distinctive assemblages of animal and plant species.

Spalding, M. D., C. Ravilious, and E. P. Green. 2001. *World Atlas of Coral Reefs.* The University of California Press, Berkeley, CA. Outstanding account of coral reefs in each area of the world.

Wilson, E. O. 1991. Rain forest canopy: The high frontier. *National Geographic* 180 (December): 78–107. An authoritative and vivid account of diversity in the forest canopy.

Worm, B., M. Sandow, A. Oschlies, H. K. Lotze, and R. A. Myers. 2005. Global patterns of predator diversity in the open oceans. *Science* 309: 1365–1369. Species diversity in the ocean declines with distance from the Equator.

Valuing Biodiversity

Ecological Economics and Direct Economic Values

Decisions on protecting species, communities and ecosystems, and genetic variation often come down to arguments over money: How much will it cost? And how much is it worth? The economic value of something is generally accepted as the amount of money people are willing to pay for it. But this is only one possible way of assigning value to things, including biological diversity. Ethical, aesthetic, scientific, and educational methods of valuation are available as well. However, government and corporate officials currently base major policy decisions on economic valuation. As a result, conservation biologists now use the methodology and vocabulary of economics in their arguments for the protection of diversity: It is easier to convince governments and corporations to protect biological diversity when there is an economic incentive to do so. When the loss of biological diversity is perceived to cost money, governments and corporations may act more aggressively to prevent it.

Why Economic Valuation Is Needed

A major problem for conservation biology is that natural resources have often been undervalued. Thus, the costs of environmental damage have been ignored, the depletion of natural resource stocks disregarded, and the future value of resources discounted (MEA 2005). Because the underlying causes of environmental damage are so often economic in nature, the solution must incorporate economic principles. **Ecological economics** is an emerging discipline that studies the interaction between economic and ecological systems. It facilitates understanding between economists and ecologists and seeks to integrate their thinking into a trans-discipline aimed at developing a sustainable world. One of the core agenda items of this new discipline is to develop methods to value biological diversity by integrating economic valuation with ecology, environmental science, sociology, and ethics, and based on those new valuations, design welfare-enhancing public policy (Costanza et al. 1996; Edwards-Jones 2000; Dasgupta 2001; Nunes et al. 2003; Common and Stagl 2005). Governments need to allocate their resources in the most efficient manner possible, and a well-considered argument for the conservation of biological diversity that is grounded in economics will often effectively support arguments based on biological, ethical, and emotional grounds.

Before the trend of biodiversity loss can be reversed, its fundamental causes must be understood. What factors induce humans to act in a nonsustainable—and therefore—destructive manner? Usually, environmental degradation and species loss occur as a by-product of human economic activities. Forests are logged for revenue from timber sales. Species are hunted for personal consumption, sale, and sport. Marginal land is converted into cropland because people have nowhere else to farm. Species, either transported accidentally by commercial vessels or brought purposefully by people, invade islands and continents, often killing the local flora and fauna. Factories and towns release their pollutants into nearby water bodies.

An understanding of a few fundamental economic principles will clarify the reasons why people treat the environment in what appears to be a shortsighted, wasteful manner. One of the most universally accepted tenets of modern economic thought centers on the "voluntary transaction"—the idea that a monetary transaction takes place only when it is beneficial to both of the parties involved. For example, a baker who sells his loaves of bread for 50 dollars will find few customers. Likewise, a customer who is willing to pay only 5 cents for a loaf will soon go hungry. A transaction between seller and buyer will only occur when a mutually agreeable price is set that benefits both parties. Adam Smith, the eighteenth-century philosopher whose ideas are the foundation of much modern economic thought, wrote, "It is not upon the benevolence of the butcher, the baker, or the brewer that we eat our daily bread, but upon his own self-interest" (Smith 1909). All parties involved in an exchange expect to improve their own situation. The sum of each individual acting in his or her self-interest results in a more prosperous society. Smith likened this effect to an "invisible hand" guiding the market—turning selfish, uncoordinated actions into increased prosperity and relative social harmony.

However, there is a notable exception to Smith's principle that directly applies to environmental issues. Smith assumed that the costs and benefits of free exchange are accepted and borne by the participants in the transaction. In some cases, however, associated costs or benefits sometimes befall individuals not directly involved in the exchange. These hidden costs or benefits are known as negative and positive **externalities** (Loucks and Gorman 2004). Perhaps the most important and frequently overlooked negative externality is the environmental damage that occurs as a consequence of human economic activity, such as the dumping of industrial sewage into a river as a by-product of manufacturing. The externalities of this activity are degraded drinking water, fewer fish that are safe to eat, and the loss of many species unable to survive in the polluted river. Where externalities exist, the market fails to benefit society as a whole. **Market failure** occurs when resources are misallocated, which allows a few individuals or businesses to benefit at the expense of the larger society. As a result, the society as a whole becomes *less* prosperous from certain economic activities, not more prosperous.

The fundamental challenge facing conservation biologists is to ensure that all the costs of economic behavior, as well as the benefits, are understood and taken into account when decisions are made that will affect biological diversity. Companies, individuals, or other stakeholders involved in production that results in ecological damage generally do not bear the full cost of their activities, but gain substantial private economic benefits. For example, the company that owns an electric power plant that burns coal and emits toxic fumes benefits from the sale of low-cost electricity, as does the consumer. Yet the hidden costs of this transaction—decreased air quality and visibility, increased respiratory disease for people and animals, damage to plant life, and a polluted environment—are distributed throughout society and do not affect decisions made by the company.

Another example is the almost unstoppable movement to convert undeveloped land into agricultural land, residential neighborhoods, and industrial sites. Such activities create great individual and corporate wealth, often increasing the value of the land by 200 to 2500 times (Hulse and Ribe 2000). Yet the loss in species, ecosystem services, and quality of life for the surrounding human community is rarely considered in the rush to make a profit, and is borne by the society as a whole. Understanding this imbalance is central to understanding market failure: The wide distribution of economic cost, combined with the concentrated benefit to a small group, creates conflict between private benefit and public cost, and results in the overuse of natural resources, loss of biodiversity and ecosystem services, and even harm to the welfare of the society.

When people and organizations must pay for the consequences of their actions—that is, be forced to take into account the negative externalities that result from their activities—they will be much more likely to stop damaging, or at least minimize their damage to, the environment (Arrow et al. 1995; Loucks and Gorman 2004). Some suggestions designed to discourage behavior that damages the environment include: charging taxes on air pollution caused by using fossil fuels; charging higher rates for water use and sewage discharge; preserving open land as compensation when another nearby site is developed; and paying for the damage caused when insecticides, herbicides, and fertilizers are released into the environment. Many countries of northern Europe have already put such ideas into action. In addition, policy makers could create penalties for damaging biological diversity and subsidies for preserving it, to make industries more mindful of how their actions impact the environment.

Assigning Economic Value to Biological Diversity

Most natural resources, such as clean air, clean water, soil quality, rare species, and even scenic beauty, are considered to be **common property**, or **open access**, **resources**. Common property resources are not controlled by individuals, but are collectively owned by society at large or owned by no one, with open access to everyone who is part of that society. Open access resources are available for everyone to use. These resources are rarely assigned a monetary value. In the absence of regulations, people, industries, and governments use and damage these resources without paying more than a minimal cost, or sometimes paying nothing at all. This is a situation in which market failure occurs, described as **the tragedy of the commons**—in which the value of the common property resources is lost to all of society (Hardin 1985; WRI 2005).

In the more complete systems of "green" accounting (such as national resource accounting) that are being developed, the costs of depleting and damaging common property resources are included as part of the *internal cost* of doing business instead of being regarded as externalities. When such accounting methods are used, the value of maintaining natural resources is often greater than the short-term benefit realized through resource extraction (Box 4.1).

In developing new accounting systems, conservation biologists and ecological economists also need to address **discount rates**, which are commonly used by economists to calculate the value natural resources will have at some point in the future (Goulder and Stavins 2002; Naidoo and Adamowicz 2006). Economists use discount

BOX 4.1

Industry, Ecology, and Ecotourism in Yellowstone Park

▨ Yellowstone National Park is the oldest and most famous of the protected areas of the U.S. National Parks System. While federal policies affecting the natural landscape of the park often attract intense public scrutiny, policies that support the extraction of timber, oil, natural gas, and other natural resources within the park and in nearby parts of Wyoming, Montana, and Idaho generally go unchallenged.

The industries that benefit from these policies argue that such activities are necessary for the economic health of the local communities surrounding the park and even the entire country, but studies indicate that this argument is increasingly less valid. The economic health of the communities surrounding Yellowstone has gradually become primarily dependent on the tourism industry and on the new residents and businesses that have moved to the area because of a perceived higher quality of life (Power 1991; Power and Barrett 2001; Gude et al. 2005). Though extractive industry was a significant force in the regional economy four decades ago, it may now be detrimental to the economic well-being of local residents because it harms what has become their major economic resource: the wildlife and natural landscape of Yellowstone Park.

One of the industries in Yellowstone that presently provides the largest boost to the economy of the region—ecotourism—is also the one that does the least damage to the ecosystem of the park. Ecotourism is not without drawbacks. The noise and pollution brought by the passage of millions of tourists annually, the disruption and alteration of animal behavior from constant exposure to the human presence, and the threat of human-caused soil erosion and fire are all side effects of the tourist trade. Accidental fires are perhaps the most visible and fearsome form of disturbance related to ecotourism; nevertheless, even the damage caused by these anthropogenic fires pales in comparison to the damage done by logging and mining activities. The reason that extractive industry is so much more damaging than ecotourism is simple: ecotourism, while it can pollute and alter habitats, does not actively destroy them.

In contrast, logging and mining have many detrimental effects. Clear-cutting, a common logging practice in which forested slopes are simply cleared of trees, can induce massive sheet erosion, particularly if steps are not immediately taken to replace the vegetation

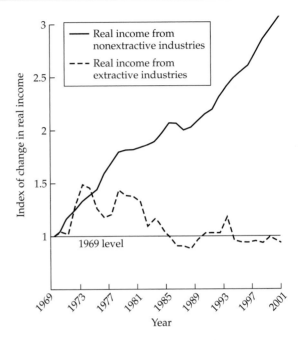

In the greater Yellowstone region, real income from extractive industries has fluctuated widely over the last 30 years but has not grown significantly, while real income from the rest of the economy—including recreation industries, tourism, service industries, and new residents, including retirees—has grown steadily, expanding by almost 200%. The region's economy has become increasingly independent of the extractive industries. The two income lines shown in the graph are standardized to equal a value of 1 in 1969, when extractive industries provided about 23% of the region's total income. By 2001 extractive industries provided only 9% of the region's total income. (From Power 1991, with updates from author.)

removed during logging. The eroded silt builds up in streams, killing fish and other aquatic species, and the loss of nutrients retards regrowth of vegetation. Mining practices often introduce into the environment harmful chemical by-products, including cyanide. These practices are ultimately not cost-effective for several reasons: (1) they lower the potential for future extraction by damaging the soil and water resources needed to regenerate timber; (2) they lower the region's potential for tourism, retirement communities, and new businesses by damaging the natural beauty of the area; and (3) they create hidden costs by lowering water quality for residents of the area, who must then pay more to have clean drinking water. However, the previously sparse resident human population of the greater Yellowstone area has increased by 58% from 1970 to 1999, with an even greater increase in rural housing construction. With

BOX 4.1 *(continued)*

exurban housing development encroaching on park boundaries, management of residential growth is now needed to maintain the quality of life and natural landscapes that brought people to the region in the first place (Gude et al. 2005).

Many people and businesses have been moving to the Yellowstone National Park area because of its natural beauty. People value a lifestyle filled with outdoor experiences, such as these visitors on the Yellowstone River boardwalk. (Photograph courtesy of U.S. National Park Service.)

rates to assign a *lower current value* to resources or materials that will be used in the future (on the grounds that it is better for the society to have money now and invest it for greater wealth rather than leave natural resources unused). Economists often assign high discount rates (higher discount rates = lower current values) to natural resources (trees, wood, water, fish, wild game, etc.) in developing countries; that is, resources harvested at some point in the future will have a much lower value than equivalent resources harvested now. Such an approach leads to short-sighted decisions to use resources right away, and it minimizes the value of resources used in the future. This use of discounting propels development projects forward, when a more cautious approach would be to lower discount rates for natural resources in general, especially in developing countries, where local people rely on natural resources to survive.

Assigning monetary values to species, communities, and ecosystems has strengthened the conservation movement (Daily 1997; Jenkins et al. 2004; WRI 2005; MEA 2005). Researchers are now able to assign economic values to variables such as the amelioration of global climate change and the future use of presently unused or even unknown species. The hidden costs of environmental degradation that occur during income-producing activities, such as logging, agriculture, commercial fishing, and development of wetlands for commercial use, are now being incorporated into discussions of the costs of large-scale projects.

Evaluating Development Projects

In order to ensure that the costs of development are taken into account and carefully weighed, it is essential to review such projects and evaluate their potential effects *before* they proceed. Such reviews are the standard practice in most developed countries and are increasingly carried out in developing countries as well. International donor agencies often require such evaluations before projects are funded.

Cost–Benefit Analysis

Economists evaluate large development projects using **environmental** and **economic impact assessments**, which consider the present and future effects of the projects on the environment and the economy. The environment is often broadly defined to include not only harvestable natural resources, but also air and water quality, the quality of life for local people, and the preservation of endangered species. In its most comprehensive form, **cost–benefit analysis** compares the values gained against the costs of the project or resource use (Hanley and Splash 1994; Perrings

1995). For example, during feasibility studies for a large logging operation that would remove a forest, an economist might compare the income obtained during the logging with the income and resources lost due to damage to game animals, medicinal plants, clean water and fish, a scenic walk through a grove of large trees, rare bird species, and wildflower populations. Alternatively, an economist might estimate what it would cost to restore the biological community or resource to its original condition. These different strategies are likely to have very different costs and produce very different results.

In one cost–benefit analysis, the competing uses of the terrestrial and marine environments in Bacuit Bay, Palawan, Philippines were modeled against three alternatives (Table 4.1). In the first option, logging, tourism, and fishing occur together. While logging provides more revenue than tourism and fishing when all three activities occur simultaneously, logging has strong negative impacts on the fishing industry and on tourism because it results in increased sedimentation that kills coral communities and the fish that depend on them. The second option protects forests through a ban on logging, and the fishing and tourist industries provide more revenue than when all three industries operate together. The third possible option involves the techniques of sustainable forestry. Logging is undertaken in a responsible and limited way to minimize environmental damage (such as by logging in small patches and avoiding steep slopes, streams, rivers, and the coast). If this third option were chosen, fishing, tourism, and logging might coexist without one industry compromising the economic benefits of the others. Although based on this analysis sustainable forestry appears to be the best long-term option, ultimately this was not considered realistic. In the end, Bacuit Bay was established as a marine sanctuary and has become a major tourist resort.

In theory, the outcome of such analysis is simple: If cost–benefit analysis shows that a project will be profitable, it should go forward, while unprofitable projects should be stopped. In practice, though, cost–benefit analyses are notoriously difficult to calculate because benefits and costs change over time and are hard to measure. For example, when a new paper mill is being constructed in a forested area, it is difficult to predict the future price of paper, the profitability of the industry, the future need for clean water, and the value of other plant and animal species in the forests being harvested. In the past, the natural resources used or damaged by large development projects were either ignored or were grossly undervalued. Now, there is an in-

TABLE 4.1 *Cost-benefit analysis of three development options in Bacuit Bay, Palawan, Phillipines*

Development option	Amount of revenue[a] generated by:			Total revenue
	Tourism	Fisheries	Logging	
Option 1: Intensive logging until timber depleted[b]	$6	$9	$10	$25
Option 2: Logging banned; protected area established[c]	$25	$17	$0	$42
Option 3: Sustainable logging[d]	$24	$16	$4	$44

Source: After Hodgson and Dixon 1988.

[a] Revenues are in millions of dollars over a 10-year period.

[b] In this option, logging substantially decreases the revenues from tourism and fisheries. Timber is completely depleted after 5 years.

[c] In this option, tourism and fisheries are major sustainable industries, no logging.

[d] In this option, logging is allowed to proceed in an environmentally responsible manner. A buffer of trees is maintained near wetlands and streams, logging does not occur on steep slopes, construction of logging roads is minimized, and hunting is banned. There is minimal impact on fisheries and tourism, and the overall economic benefits are enhanced. (Real-life logging practices are rarely as benign as portrayed here.)

creasing tendency by governments, conservation groups, and economists to apply the **precautionary principle**; when there is uncertainty about the risks associated with a project, it is better to err on the side of doing no harm to the environment. In some cases this may mean not approving a project (Matsuda 2003; Prato 2005).

It would be highly beneficial to apply cost–benefit analysis to many of the basic industries and practices of modern society. Many economic activities appear to be profitable even when they are actually losing money, because governments subsidize industries involved in environment-damaging activities with tax breaks, direct payments or price supports, cheap fossil fuels, free water, and road networks—sometimes referred to as "perverse subsidies" (Myers and Kent 2001). These government subsidies promote specific industries, such as agriculture, fishing, automobile manufacturing, and energy production, and they may amount to $1.4 trillion dollars per year, or roughly 5% of the world economy (Myers and Kent 2001). Subsidies in agriculture and fisheries can be as high as 20–30% of the production value (MEA 2005). Without these subsidies, many environmentally damaging or expensive activities, such as farming in areas with high labor, energy, and water costs, overfishing in the ocean, and inefficient and highly polluting energy use, would be reduced.

Natural Resource Loss and the Wealth of Societies

Attempts have been made to include the loss of natural resources in calculations of gross domestic product (GDP) and other indexes of national production (Balmford et al. 2005; Dobson 2005). The problem with GDP is that it measures economic activity in a country without accounting for all the costs of nonsustainable activities (such as overfishing of coastal waters and poorly managed strip-mining), which cause the GDP to increase, even though these activities may be destructive to a country's long-term economic well-being. In actuality, the economic costs associated with environmental damage can be considerable and often offset the gains attained through agricultural and industrial development.

In Costa Rica, for example, the value of the forests destroyed during the 1980s greatly exceeded the income produced from forest products, so that the forestry sector actually represented a drain on the wealth of the country. Similarly, the costs associated with soil erosion in that country decreased the value of agriculture by 17%. In the United Kingdom, hidden environmental costs in agriculture are estimated to be worth about $2.6 billion per year, or 9% of the value of the country's agriculture (MEA 2005). In the United States, one controversial estimate shows that soil erosion costs the economy $44 billion every year in direct damage to agricultural lands and indirect damage to waterways and to human and animal health (Pimentel et al. 1995). For the entire world, the cost of soil erosion is estimated to approach $400 billion per year. Even if these controversial estimates are eventually revised downward, the hidden costs of soil erosion and other environmental damage are enormous by any standard—and all such costs are underappreciated and excluded from GDP calculations. Alternatively, if farmers were paid based solely on how well their land provided soil protection, flood control, and contributed to water quality, they might improve their farming practices (Robertson and Swinton 2005) (Figure 4.1).

By excluding environmental costs and the loss of natural resources from economic analyses, many countries that appear to be achieving impressive economic gains actually may be on the verge of economic collapse. Unregulated national fisheries are a classic example of the need to monitor assets. Increased investment in fishing fleets may result in higher catches and impressive profits, but it gradually leads to the overharvesting and destruction of one commercial species after another and, eventually, to the collapse of the entire industry. It would be easier to justify this activity if the profits were used to improve society through increased infrastructure, industrial development, job training, and education. However, often a small num-

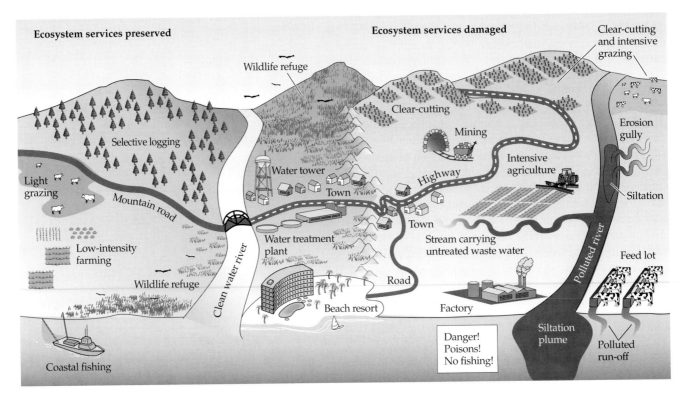

Ecosystem services preserved

Ecosystem services damaged

Clear-cutting and intensive grazing

Wildlife refuge

Selective logging

Clear-cutting

Mining

Erosion gully

Light grazing

Water tower

Intensive agriculture

Highway

Mountain road

Town

Siltation

Low-intensity farming

Town

Feed lot

Water treatment plant

Stream carrying untreated waste water

Polluted river

Wildlife refuge

Road

Clean water river

Beach resort

Factory

Danger! Poisons! No fishing!

Siltation plume

Polluted run-off

Coastal fishing

FIGURE 4.1 Agricultural ecosystems, forestry activities, and industries are usually valued by the products that they produce. In many cases these activities have negative externalities in that they erode soil, degrade water quality, and contribute to flooding (right side of figure). But farms, forests, and other human activities could also be valued on the basis of their public benefits, such as flood control, soil retention, and water quality, and receive subsidies for these benefits (left side of figure).

ber of people or companies take most of the profits, while society as a whole realizes only minor and temporary improvements.

The hidden costs associated with superficial economic gains are effectively demonstrated by the case of the *Exxon Valdez* oil spill in Alaska in 1989. The spill cost billions of dollars to clean up; damaged the environment; killed a large number of birds, fish, and marine mammals; and wasted 11 million gallons of oil. Yet the event was recorded as a *net economic gain* because expenditures associated with the cleanup increased the U.S. GDP and provided employment for cleanup crews hired throughout the United States. Without consideration of the hidden environmental costs and long-term damage to natural resources, a disaster like the *Valdez* spill can easily be misrepresented as economically beneficial!

One attempt to account for natural resource depletion, pollution, and unequal income distribution in measures of national production is the development of the Index of Sustainable Economic Welfare (ISEW), the updated version of which is called the Genuine Progress Indicator (Cobb et al. 1995). This index includes factors such as the loss of farmlands, the loss of wetlands, the impact of acid rain, the number of people living in poverty, and the effects of pollution on human health. Using the GPI, the U.S. economy apparently did not improve during the period from 1956 to 1986, and it actually declined from 1986 to 1997, even though the standard GDP index showed a dramatic gain. The GPI suggests what conservation biologists have long feared: Many modern economies are achieving their growth only through the nonsustainable consumption of natural resources. As these resources run out, the economies on which they are based may be seriously disrupted.

Another measure is the Environmental Sustainability Index (ESI), which has 21 environmental indicators that rank countries according to the health of, and threats to, their ecosystems, the vulnerability of their human population to an adverse environment, the ability of their society to protect the environment, and participation in global environmental protection efforts (Esty et al. 2005).There is a concern among many economists and business people that a country that rigorously protects its environment as shown by a high ESI may not be competitive in the world economy as measured by a competitiveness index that includes worker productivity and a country's ability to grow and prosper. However, Figure 4.2 shows that environmental sustainability is not linked to a country's economic competitiveness. Countries such as Finland can have an economy that is both sustainable and competitive, whereas Belgium is competitive but ranks poorly in sustainability. The rapidly growing economies of China and India are intermediate in competitiveness but rank low in environmental sustainability.

In Britain, an index that combines many factors related to the quality of life now incorporates the number of wild birds as one of the factors (Bazilchuk 2004). This index shows that while the number of wild birds has remained constant, the number of farmland birds has declined precipitously due to farming intensification, a shift toward monocultures, and increased pesticide use.

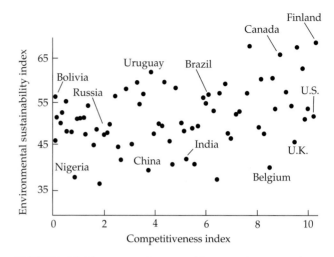

FIGURE 4.2 The economic competitiveness of a country is not closely related to its environmental sustainability, as measured by five sets of indicators: healthy ecosystems, low stress on ecosystems, low human vulnerability to environmental change, ability of the society and institutions to cope with environmental changes, and cooperation in international environmental initiatives. (From Esty et al. 2005.)

An awareness of, and involvement in, assigning economic value to biological diversity is important for conservation biologists, although many would argue that any attempt to place a strictly monetary value on biological diversity is inappropriate and potentially corrupting, since many aspects of the natural world are unique and thus truly priceless (Ehrenfeld 1989; Bulte and van Kooten 2000). Supporters of this position point out that there is no way to assign monetary value to the wonder people experience when they see an animal in the wild or a beautiful natural landscape; nor can economic value realistically be assigned to the human lives that have been and will be saved through the medicinal compounds derived from wild species. In fact, economic models contribute much to the debate over the protection of biological diversity. It is to the advantage of conservationists to develop economic models—both to improve such models' accuracy and to appreciate their limitations—since these models often provide surprisingly strong support for the crucial role of biological diversity in local economies and for the need to protect ecosystems. Economic models need to be presented to policy makers and incorporated into the regulations that will affect how development proceeds.

One Approach to Assigning Economic Value

A number of methods have been developed to assign economic values to genetic variability, species, communities, and ecosystems. In these methods, assignment of economic value can be done on three levels—the marketplace (or harvest) value of resources, the value provided by unharvested resources in their natural state, and the future value of resources (Kareiva and Levin 2003). For example, we can assign economic value to the Southeast Asian wild guar (*Bos frontalis*), a wild relative of domestic cattle, based on: the meat currently harvested from its wild populations, the animal's value in the wild for nature tourism, and its future potential in domestic cattle breeding programs. As yet there is no universally accepted framework for assigning values to biological diversity, but a variety of approaches have been proposed. Among the most useful is the framework used by McNeely et al. (1990) and Barbier et al. (1994), in which the use values of biodiversity are divided between **direct use values** (also known in other frameworks as **commodity values** and **private goods**) and **indirect use values** (in economics, **public goods**). Direct use values are assigned to products harvested by people, such as timber, seafood, and medicinal plants from the wild, while indirect use values are benefits provided by biological diversity that do not involve harvesting or destroying the resource, such as water quality, pollution control, ecosystem productivity, soil protection, recreation, education, scientific research, and regulation of climate. (Indirect use values are discussed in Chapter 5.) This framework also includes **option value**—the prospect for possible future benefits for human society, such as new medicines, possible future food sources, and future genetic resources. (Option value is discussed further in Chapter 5.) **Existence value** is another kind of value that can be assigned to biodiversity—for example, economists can attempt to measure how much people are willing to pay to protect a species from going extinct (Box 4.2). A related concept is **bequest value**, how much people are willing to pay to protect something for their children or future generations. The combination of all these individual values can be used to calculate the total economic value of biodiversity. Figure 4.3 describes how these different values can be applied to a tropical wetland ecosystem.

Total Economic Value of a Tropical Wetland Ecosystem

Use Values

Direct Use Values	Indirect Use Values
Fish and meat	Flood control
Fuelwood	Soil fertility
Timber and other building materials	Pollution control
Medicinal plants	Drinking water
Edible wild fruits and plants	Transportation
Animal fodder	Recreation and tourism (e.g., birdwatching)
	Education
	Biological services (pest control, pollination)

Option Value

Future products:
  Medicines
  Genetic resources
  Biological insights
  Food sources
  Building supplies
  Water supplies

Existence Value

Protection of biological diversity

Maintaining culture of local people

Continuing ecological and evolutionary process

FIGURE 4.3 Evaluating the success of a development project must incorporate the full range of its environmental effects. This figure shows the total economic value of a tropical wetland ecosystem, including direct and indirect use value, option value, and existence value. A development project such as an irrigation project lowers the value of the wetland ecosystem when water is removed for crop irrigation. When that lowered value is taken into account, the irrigation project may represent an economic loss. (From Groom et al. 2006; based on data in Barbier 1993.)

BOX 4.2

How Much Is a Species Worth?

Imagine that a new species of lily has been discovered growing in a 25-ha meadow slated to be dug up for commercial development. Extensive searches of the area fail to find any other populations of the lily. Conservation organizations would like to save this species from extinction in the wild, but are not sure of its value. How much money is this species worth? How much money should be spent to save it? Some possible answers follow.

1. The species has no known value to people, and therefore no money should be spent to save it. Value: $0.

2. The species' value might be considered as equal to the cost of purchasing the land on the open market, because saving the land is the key to saving the species. The willingness of conservation organizations to buy the land on which the species grows is an indication of the existence value of the species. Existence value: 25 ha at $4000 per ha = $100,000.

3. A local horticulturist is willing to pay for the exclusive right to collect 10% of the seeds of this species each year in order to propagate the species and sell the resulting plants for five years. He is willing to pay $5000 each year for this privilege. Productive use value: $5000 per year for 5 years = $25,000.

4. An average of two hundred botanists and nature lovers visit the site each year to see the plant, spending roughly $80 per person on local food, lodging, and supplies. Using the travel cost method, we estimate the nature tourism value as 200 people at $80 = $16,000 per year.

5. The species' value might also be determined by calculating its future usefulness. Protecting this species preserves its option value. If we divide the estimated value of newly discovered plant products and genetic variation over the last 10 years by the estimated total number of plant species, we get an indication of the average value of each species. Option value: $100 billion of new plant products divided by 250,000 plant species = $400,000.

6. Suppose this particular species is found to produce a chemical that could have an enormous impact on human health and well-being. Perhaps the chemical prevents disease transmission in humans. Such a compound would be effective against a multitude of illnesses ranging from the minor (such as the common cold and chicken pox) to the devastating (such as malaria and AIDS). Or it might contain compounds that break down air- and water-borne toxins, rendering dangerous pollutants harmless. Such compounds would give this species incalculable value, as they could eliminate disease or reverse ecological damage caused by pollution. The lily might be the key to saving humanity from devastation. In such cases, the species would have a value equal to the total monetary value of all human economic activity. Estimated value: $100 trillion, or infinitely large.

How do we determine what a newly discovered species might be worth?

Direct Use Values

Direct use values can often be readily calculated by observing the activities of representative groups of people, by monitoring collection points for natural products, and by examining import and export statistics. Direct use values are further divided into **consumptive use value** for goods that are consumed locally, and **productive use value** for products that are sold in markets.

Consumptive Use Value

Goods such as fuelwood and game that are consumed locally and do not appear in the national and international marketplace are assigned consumptive use value (Godoy 2001). People living close to the land often derive a considerable proportion of the goods they require for their livelihood from the surrounding environment. These goods do not appear in the GDP of countries because they are neither bought nor sold. However, if rural people are unable to obtain these products, as might occur following environmental degradation, overexploitation of natural resources, or even creation of a protected reserve, their standard of living will decline, possibly to the point where they are forced to relocate.

Studies of traditional societies in the developing world show how extensively these people use their natural environment to supply themselves with fuelwood, vegetables, fruit, meat, medicine, rope and string, and building materials (Figure 4.4A) (Myers 1983; Balick and Cox 1996; Cox 2001). One study of Amazonian Indians found that 79% of the species of rain forest trees in the area were used for some specific product other than fuel (Prance et al. 1987; Dobson 1995). About 80% of the world's population still relies principally on traditional medicines derived from plants and animals as their primary source of treatment (Tuxill 1999; Shanley and Luz 2003). More than 5000 species are used for medicinal purposes in China, 6000 species are used in India, and 2000 species are used in the Amazon basin.

One of the most crucial requirements of rural people is protein, which they obtain by hunting wild animals for meat. In many areas of Africa, wild meat constitutes a significant portion of the protein in the average person's diet—about 40% in Botswana and about 75% in the Democratic Republic of the Congo (formerly Zaire) (Rao and McGowan 2002). In Nigeria, over 100,000 tons of giant rats (*Cricetomys* sp.)

(A)

(B)

FIGURE 4.4 (A) A wide variety of plants and other natural products are used in Chinese medicine. (B) Wild animals, such as this wild bearded pig in Borneo, provide people with a crucial source of protein in many areas of the world. (A, photograph © Catherine Pringle/Biological Photo Service; B, photograph by R. Primack.)

are consumed each year, while in Botswana over three million kg of springhare (*Pedetes capensis*) are eaten per year. Estimates of annual harvesting rates are 74,000 to 181,000 tons (around 200 million pounds) for the Brazilian Amazon (Peres 2000a) and an astonishing 1 to 4 million tons (2 to 8 billion pounds) for Central Africa (Fa et al. 2001). Extraction rates for Africa are definitely unsustainable, perhaps by a factor of six. This wild meat includes not only birds, mammals, and fish, but adult insects, snails, caterpillars, and grubs. In certain areas of Africa, insects may constitute the majority of the dietary protein and supply critical vitamins.

In areas along coasts, rivers, and lakes, wild fish represent an important source of protein. Throughout the world, 130 million tons of fish, crustaceans, and mollusks, mainly wild species, are harvested each year, with 100 million tons constituting marine catch and 30 million tons constituting freshwater catch (WRI 2000). Much of this catch is consumed locally. In coastal areas fishing is often the most important source of employment, and seafood is the most widely consumed protein (WRI 2005). Even though fish farming is increasing rapidly, much of the feed used is fish meal derived from wild-caught fish (Goldburg and Naylor 2005).

Consumptive use value can be assigned to a product by considering how much people would have to pay if they had to buy an equivalent product when their local source was no longer available. This is sometimes referred to as a **substitute cost approach**. One example of this approach was an attempt to estimate the number of wild pigs harvested by native hunters in Sarawak, East Malaysia. The study involved counting the number of shotgun shells used in rural areas and interviewing hunters to obtain two independent measures of animal harvest rates (Figure 4.4B). This pioneering study estimated that the consumptive value of the wild pig meat was a surprisingly large $40 million per year (Caldecott 1988). In many cases local people do not have the money to buy products in the market. In remote regions, markets may not exist at all. When the local resource is depleted, local people may be forced to change their livelihoods, migrate to other rural areas or cities, or may simply be faced with rural poverty.

Consumptive use value can also be assigned to fuelwood used for heating and cooking, which is gathered from forests and shrublands (Figure 4.5). Around 2.6 billion people rely on fuelwood as the primary energy source for heating and cooking (MEA 2005). This accounts for over half of all global wood use. The value of these fuels, in places such as Nepal, Tanzania, and Peru, can be determined by considering how much people would have to pay for kerosene or other fuels if they were unable to obtain fuel from their environment. In many areas of the world, rural people have consumed all local fuel sources but do not have the money to buy fuel from the market. This situation, the "poor man's energy crisis," forces the poor—in particular poor women—to walk ever greater distances to obtain fuel and leads to ever-widening circles of deforestation. People also end up burning crop remains and dung for fuel, leading to a loss of mineral nutrients needed to maintain agricultural productivity.

In the past, people developed ways of extracting resources from the natural environment that prevented overuse of renewable resources (Berkes 1999, 2001).

FIGURE 4.5 One of the most important natural products required by local people is fuelwood, particularly in Africa and southern Asia. Here a woman in Nepal carries a load of kindling. (Photograph © Bill Kamin/Visuals Unlimited.)

Certain species of wild fruit trees were never allowed to be cut down; the breeding season of the year was taboo for hunting certain animals; families owned hunting territories that other families were not allowed to enter. These systems were organized at the village and tribal levels and were enforced through strong social pressures. For example, traditional Sherpa villages in Nepal had the custom of "shin-go nava," in which men were elected to be forest guards. These men determined how much fuelwood people could collect and what trees could be cut and hence protected the common resources. People violating the village rules were made to pay fines, which were used to fund village activities.

Most of these traditional conservation systems have broken down as cash economies and national governments have developed. Local conservation strategies have also been eliminated by centralized or "top down" government decisions. People now frequently sell natural resources in town markets for money. As social controls break down at the village level, the villagers, as well as outsiders, may begin to extract local resources in a destructive and nonsustainable manner. If the resources become depleted, many villagers may be forced to pay high prices in town markets for many of the products that they formerly obtained free from their natural environment. It is also true that access to town markets sometimes provides advantages to villagers that balance the loss of some local resources. For example, it sometimes allows local people to obtain higher prices for their products. With the cash, people may be able to establish their own businesses, educate their children, and have access to modern medical care.

Although dependency on local natural products is primarily associated with the developing world, there are rural areas of the United States, Canada, and other developed countries where hundreds of thousands of people are dependent on fuelwood for heating and on wild game and seafood for their protein needs. Many of these people would be unable to survive in these locations if they had to buy these necessities.

Productive Use Value

Products that are harvested from the wild and sold in both national and international commercial markets are assigned productive use value. Standard economic methods value these products at the price paid at the first point of sale minus the costs incurred up to that point, but they could also be valued at the final retail price of the products. The two methods give a wide range of values for the same product. For example, bark from the wild cascara (*Rhamnus purshiana*) gathered in the western United States is the major ingredient in certain brands of laxatives. The purchase price of the bark is about $1 million, but the final retail price of the medicine is $75 million (Prescott-Allen and Prescott-Allen 1986). Deciding the appropriate value for this product represents a basic problem for ecological economics.

The productive use value of natural resources is significant, even in industrial nations. Approximately 4.5% of the U.S. GDP—about $350 billion for the year 2001—depends in some way on wild species. The percentage would be far higher for developing countries that have less industry and a higher percentage of the population living in rural areas.

The range of products obtained from the natural environment and sold in the marketplace is enormous: fuelwood, construction timber, fish and shellfish, medicinal plants, wild fruits and vegetables, wild meat and skins, fibers, rattan (a vine used to make furniture and other household articles), honey, beeswax, natural dyes, seaweed, animal fodder, natural perfumes, and plant gums and resins (Radmer 1996; Baskin 1997). Additionally, there are large international industries associated with collecting tropical fish for the aquarium trade; tropical cacti, orchids, and other plants for the horticultural industry; and birds, mammals, amphibians, and reptiles for zoos and private collections.

In many cases, species have to be collected just once or a few times, because then they can be propagated in captivity. Only a few individuals are needed to establish entirely new populations, to be used for display purposes, to be used in the development of new medicines and industrial products, and to be used as biological control agents. Wild relatives of domesticated crops can be collected and incorporated into modern breeding programs for genetic improvement. This occasional collection can be considered productive use value, or perhaps as option value, for its ability to maintain and improve economic activity. Species collected only in small numbers from the wild will be treated in the next chapter, in the section on option value. Products gathered in large quantities from the wild are described below.

FOREST PRODUCTS Wood is one of the most significant products obtained from natural environments, with an export value of around $135 billion per year (WRI 2003). The total value of wood products is far greater, perhaps around $400 billion per year, because most wood is used locally and is not exported. Wood products from the forests of tropical countries, including timber, plywood, and wood pulp, are being exported at a rapid rate to earn foreign currency, to provide capital for industrialization, to pay foreign debt, and to provide employment. In tropical countries such as Indonesia, Brazil, and Malaysia, timber products earn billions of dollars per year (Primack and Corlett 2005) (Figure 4.6A).

Nonwood products from forests, including game, fruits, gums and resins, rattan, and medicinal plants, also have a large productive use value (Figure 4.6B). These nontimber products are sometimes erroneously called "minor forest products"; in reality they are often very important economically and may even rival the value of timber. In India, nontimber forest products account for 40% of forestry revenues and 55% of the forestry employment. One study from rural Zimbabwe demonstrated that 35% of village income was derived from natural products. What was espe-

(A)

(B)

FIGURE 4.6 The timber industry is a major source of revenue in many tropical countries. Here trees are harvested from rain forest in the Brazilian Amazon. (B) Nontimber products are often important in local and national economies. Many rural people supplement their incomes by gathering natural forest products to sell in local markets. Here a Land Dayak family in Sarawak (Malaysia) sells wild honey and edible wild fruits. (A, photograph courtesy of William Laurance; B, photograph by R. Primack.)

cially noteworthy was that dependence on natural products was even greater in the poorest households, showing the value of ecosystems in providing resources to people with nothing else (WRI 2005).

Many other studies similarly show that natural ecosystems provide resources to rural people in goods and services that do not appear in official government figures. When the ecosystem value of the forest as a source of drinking water, flood control, and soil protection is combined with the value of nontimber products, maintaining and utilizing natural communities may still prove to be more productive than intensive logging, converting the forest into commercial plantations, or establishing cattle ranches (Daily 1997; WRI 2005). Careful tree harvesting that minimizes damage to the surrounding biological community and the ecosystem services it provides, combined with gathering nontimber products, may be a profitable approach that justifies maintaining the land in forest.

THE NATURAL PHARMACY Effective drugs are needed to keep people healthy, and they represent an enormous industry, with worldwide sales of around $300 billion per year (Grifo and Rosenthal 1997; Mateo et al. 2001). The natural world is an important source of medicines currently in use and possible future medicines. One species with great medicinal use is the rose periwinkle (*Catharanthus roseus*) from Madagascar (Table 4.2). Two potent drugs derived from this plant are effective in treating Hodgkin's disease, leukemia, and other blood cancers. Treatment using these drugs has increased the survival rate of childhood leukemia from 10% to 90%. How many more such valuable plants will be discovered in the years ahead—and how many will go extinct before they are discovered?

Even in the case of medicines that are now produced synthetically by chemists, many were first discovered in a wild species used in traditional medicine (Cox 2001; Gerwick et al. 2001) (Figure 4.7). Extracts of willow tree bark (*Salix* sp.) were used by the ancient Greeks and by tribes of Native Americans to treat pain, leading to the discovery of acetylsalicylic acid—the painkilling ingredient in modern aspirin, one of our most important and widely used medicines. Similarly, the use of coca (*Erythoxylum coca*) by natives of the Andean highlands eventually led to the development of synthetic derivatives such as Novocaine and Xylocaine, commonly used as local anesthetics in dentistry and surgery. Many other important medicines were first identified in animals. Poisonous animals such as rattlesnakes, bees, and cone snails have been especially rich sources of chemicals with valuable medical and biological applications (Carte 1996).

All of the 20 most frequently used pharmaceuticals in the United States are based on chemicals first identified in natural products. These drugs have a combined sales value of $6 billion per year. Twenty-five percent of the prescriptions filled in the United States contain active ingredients derived from plants, and many of the most important antibiotics, including penicillin and tetracycline, are derived from fungi and other microorganisms (Dobson 1998; Taylor

FIGURE 4.7 Carrying on the traditions of his Mayan ancestors, Antonio Cue of Belize prepares useful medicines from plants that are growing in the local area. As is the case with many local people in the developing world who have knowledge of their flora and fauna, he is now working with scientists to determine if chemicals in these plants can be developed for use in modern medicine. (Photograph courtesy of M. J. Balick.)

TABLE 4.2 *Twenty drugs first discovered in traditional medical practice*

Drug	Medical use	Plant source	Common name
Ajmaline	Treats heart arrhythmia	*Rauwolfia* spp.	Rauwolfia
Aspirin	Analgesic, anti-inflammatory	*Spiraea ulmaria*	Meadow Sweet
Atropine	Dilates eyes during examination	*Atropa belladonna*	Belladonna
Caffeine	Stimulant	*Camellia sinensis*	Tea plant
Cocaine	Ophthalmic analgesic	*Erythroxylum coca*	Coca plant
Codeine	Analgesic, antitussive	*Papaver somniferum*	Opium poppy
Digitoxin	Cardiac stimulant	*Digitalis purpurea*	Foxglove
Ephedrine	Bronchodilator	*Ephedra sinica*	Ephedra plant
Ipecac	Emetic	*Cephaelis ipecachuanha*	Ipecac plant
Morphine	Analgesic	*Papaver somniferum*	Opium poppy
Pseudoephedrine	Decongestant	*Ephedra sinica*	Ephedra plant
Quinine	Antimalarial prophylactic	*Cinchona pubescens*	Chinchona
Reserpine	Treats hypertension	*Rauwolfia serpentina*	Rauwolfia
Sennoside A,B	Laxative	*Cassia angustifolia*	Senna
Scopolamine	Treats motion sickness	*Datura stramonium*	Thorn Apple
Strophanthin	Treats congestive heart failure	*Strophanthus gratus*	Rose Allamanda
THC	Antiemetic	*Cannabis sativa*	Marijuana
Toxiferine	Relaxes muscles during surgery	*Strychnos guianensis*	Strychnos plant
Tubocurarine	Muscle relaxant	*Chondrodendron tomentosum*	Curare
Vincristine	Treats pediatric leukemia	*Catharanthus roseus*	Rose periwinkle

Source: After Balick and Cox 1996.

2000). More recently, the fungus-derived drug cyclosporine has proved to be a crucial element in the success of heart and kidney transplants. As will be discussed in the next chapter, the natural world is being actively searched for the next generation of medicines and industrial products.

Even seemingly unimportant species often possess tremendous value. Horseshoe crabs, for instance, are usually noticed only as clumsy creatures that seemed to move with difficulty in shallow seawater. In the United States, people also use them as cheap fish bait. In recent years, however, we have realized that horseshoe crab eggs and juveniles are greatly important as a food source to shorebirds and coastal fish, which have a major role in local tourism related to bird watching and sport fishing (Figure 4.8). Without horseshoe crabs, bird populations and sport fish would decline in abundance. Additionally, horseshoe crab blood is now collected to make limulus amoebocyte lysate (LAL), which is used to detect bacterial contamination in medicines administered by injection (Odell et al. 2005). This chemical cannot be synthesized, and there is no other source for it besides horseshoe crabs. Without horseshoe crabs as a source of LAL, our ability to determine the purity of injected medicines would be com-

FIGURE 4.8 Horseshoe crabs gather in great numbers to reproduce in shallow coastal waters. These aggregations have significant value for contending groups of people. (Photograph by © Nick Greaves/Alamy.)

promised. Currently, commercial fishing and sport fishing interests, environmental groups, birdwatching groups, and the biomedical industry are contending over access to horseshoe crabs along the coastlines of the United States and struggling to find a working compromise.

Summary

1. Conservation biologists and ecological economists are developing new methods to assign monetary value to biological diversity and, in the process, are providing arguments for its protection. While some conservation biologists would argue that biological diversity is priceless and cannot and should not be assigned economic value, economic justification for biological diversity will play an increasingly important role in debates on the use of natural resources.

2. Many countries that appear to have annual increases in gross domestic product may have stagnant or even declining economies when the costs of development—depletion of natural resources and damage to the environment—are included in the calculations. Increasingly, large development projects are being analyzed through environmental and economic impact assessments and cost–benefit analyses before being approved. In addition, assigning economic value gives both the public and policy makers a frame of reference for understanding the magnitude of environmental degradation.

3. A number of methods have been developed to assign economic value to biological diversity. In one method, resources are divided between direct values, which are assigned to products harvested by people; indirect values, which are assigned to benefits provided by biological diversity that do not involve harvesting or destroying the resource; option value, which is assigned to the potential future value of biological diversity; and existence value, based on the willingness of society to pay for the protection of biological diversity.

4. Direct values can be further divided into consumptive use value and productive use value. Consumptive use value is assigned to products that are consumed locally, such as fuelwood, wild meat, fruits and vegetables, medicinal plants, and building materials. These goods can be valued by determining how much money people would have to pay for them if they were unavailable in the wild. When these wild products become unavailable, the living standard of the people who depend on them declines. Productive use value is assigned to products harvested in the wild and sold in markets, such as commercial timber, fish and shellfish, and wild meat.

For Discussion

1. Choose a recent large development project from your area, such as a dam, sewage treatment plant, shopping mall, highway, or housing development, and learn all you can about it. Estimate the costs and benefits of this project in terms of biological diversity, economic prosperity, and human health. Who pays the costs and who receives the benefits? Consider other projects carried out in the past and determine their impact on the surrounding biological and human communities. (These are challenging questions that may be appropriate to tackle as a group activity.)

2. How do traditional (or rural) societies use and value biological diversity? What is the relative importance of biological diversity in both traditional and modern societies? How do these societies value biodiversity knowledge?

3. Suppose a medicinal plant used by traditional people in a remote area in Indonesia is investigated by a European pharmaceutical company and found to have huge potential as a new cancer medicine. Who will profit from the sale of this medicine under current practices? Can you suggest alternative methods to distribute the profits in a way that would be more equitable and that would increase the possibility of preserving Indonesia's biological diversity?

Suggested Readings

Aguirre, A. A., R. S. Ostfeld, G. M. Tabor, C. House, and M. C. Pearl (eds.). 2002. *Conservation Medicine: Ecological Health in Practice*. Oxford University Press, New York. Relationships among ecosystem health, human health, and wildlife biology.

Balick, M. J. and P. A. Cox. 1996. *Plants, People and Culture: The Science of Ethnobotany*. *Scientific American* Library, New York. Fascinating story of traditional use of plants, filled with anecdotes and beautifully illustrated.

Balmford, A., A. Bruner, P. Cooper, R. Costanza, S. Farber, R. E. Green, et al. 2002. Economic reasons for conserving wild nature. *Science* 297: 950–953. Ecosystem services provide strong economic arguments for conserving biodiversity.

Bulte, E. H. and G. C. van Kooten. 2000. Economic science, endangered species, and biodiversity loss. *Conservation Biology* 14: 113–119. Considers the limitations of economic arguments in preserving biological diversity; a good starting point for discussions.

Common, M. and S. Stagl. 2005. *Ecological Economics An Introduction*. Cambridge University Press, New York. Assumes no prior knowledge of economics.

Cox, P. A. 2001. Pharmacology, biodiversity and. *In* S. A. Levin (ed.), *Encyclopedia of Biodiversity*, Vol. 4, pp. 523–536. Academic Press, San Diego, CA. Good historical account of the contributions of the natural world to modern medicine.

Daily, G. C. (ed.). 1997. *Nature's Services: Societal Dependence on Ecosystem Services*. Island Press, Washington, D.C. Clear explanations of why maintaining species and ecosystems is critical to human societies.

Esty, D. C., M. Levy, T. Srebotnjak, and A. de Sherbinin. 2005. *Environmental Sustainability Index: Benchmarking National Environmental Stewardship*. Yale Center for Environmental Law & Policy, New Haven, CT. The loss of ecosystem services and natural resources reduces the apparent gains in productivity and prosperity of many countries.

Godoy, R. A. 2001. *Indians, Markets, and Rainforests: Theoretical, Comparative, and Quantitative Exploration in the NeoTropics*. Columbia University Press, New York. An examination of the value of forest products and factors contributing to deforestation in tropical Latin America; valuable for its descriptive method.

Myers, N. and J. Kent. 2001. *Perverse Subsidies: How Tax Dollars Can Undercut the Environment and the Economy*. Island Press, Washington, D.C. Governments are paying for destructive industries to continue.

Naidoo, R. and W. L. Adamowicz. 2006. Modeling opportunity costs of conservation in transitional landscapes. *Conservation Biology* 20: 490–500. Information about land prices and discount rates is needed to protect biological diversity.

Nunes, P., J. Van Den Bergh, and P. Nijkamp. 2003. *The Ecological Economics of Biodiversity*. Edward Elgar, UK. Textbook for those who want to learn more.

Odell, J., M. E. Mather, and R. M. Muth. 2005. A biosocial approach for analyzing environmental conflicts: a case study of horseshoe crab allocation. *BioScience* 55: 735–748. Until previously, horseshoe crabs were considered to be almost worthless; now everyone thinks they are valuable but for different reasons.

Shanley, P. and L. Luz. 2003. The impacts of forest degradation on medicinal plant use and implications for health care in Eastern Amazonia. *BioScience* 53: 573–584. The loss of traditional medicinal plants threatens the health of people.

Tuxill, J. 1999. *Nature's Cornucopia: Our Stake in Plant Diversity*. World Watch Institute, Washington, D.C. Plants are crucial to both traditional and modern societies.

Indirect Economic Values

As we discussed in Chapter 4, some components of biological diversity provide economic benefits without being harvested and destroyed during use. These components are said to have indirect use value, and they are crucial to the continued availability of the natural products on which economies depend and societies function. Mountain forests, for example, prevent soil erosion and flooding that could damage human settlements and farmlands in nearby lowland areas; coastal estuaries provide rich harvests of fish and shellfish worth billions of dollars annually, and during severe storms, they provide protection for human coastal developments worth billions more.

Nonconsumptive Use Value

The great variety of environmental services that biological communities provide can be classified as having a particular type of indirect use value called **nonconsumptive use value** (because these services are not consumed). The nonconsumptive use value of ecosystem services is huge.

Economists are just beginning to calculate the nonconsumptive use value of ecosystem services at regional and global levels (Table 5.1; Figure 5.1) (Daily and Ellison 2002; Balmford et al. 2003; Wang et al. 2005). These calculations are still at a preliminary stage, but they suggest that the nonconsumptive use value of ecosystem services is enormous and often exceeds the value of the natural products harvested from the same place (MEA 2005). One estimate of

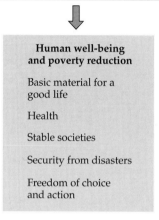

FIGURE 5.1 Ecosystem services are necessary for human well-being. (After MEA 2005.)

the value of the world's ecosystem services is around $33 trillion per year, which greatly exceeds the direct use value of biological diversity (Costanza et al. 1997). Because this amount is greater than the global gross national product of around $18 trillion, it can be argued that human societies are totally dependent on natural ecosystems and would not persist if these ecosystem services were permanently degraded or destroyed (Diamond 2005). The most important ecosystem services not accounted for in the current market system are waste treatment and nutrient retention, which are provided by wetlands and coastal areas and total $18 trillion per year. Many ecological economists are in sharp disagreement about

TABLE 5.1 *Estimated value of the world's ecosystems using ecological economics*

Ecosystem[a]	Total area (millions of ha)	Annual local value (dollars/ha/year)	Annual global value (trillions of dollars/year)
Coastal	3102	4052	12.6
Open ocean	33,200	252	8.4
Wetlands	330	14,785	4.9
Tropical forests	1900	2007	3.8
Lakes, rivers	200	8498	1.7
Other forests	2955	302	0.9
Grasslands	3898	232	0.9
Cropland	1400	92	0.1

Source: After Costanza et al. 1997

[a]Desert, tundra, urban, and ice/rock ecosystems not included.

how such calculations should be done, or if they even should be done at all. Using a different approach, Pimentel et al. (1997) and Balmford et al. (2002) came up with a lower estimate for the value of ecosystem services, though still trillions of dollars per year, indicating that much more work needs to be done on this topic.

The following is a discussion of some of the general benefits, derived from conserving biological diversity, that do not usually appear on the balance sheets of environmental impact assessments or in national GDPs.

Ecosystem Productivity and Carbon Sequestration

The photosynthetic capacity of plants and algae allows the energy of the sun to be captured in living tissue. The energy stored in plants is sometimes harvested by humans for use as food, fuelwood, and hay and other fodder for animals. This plant material is also the starting point for innumerable food chains, from which many animal products are harvested by people. Human needs for natural resources dominate approximately 40% of the productivity of the terrestrial environment (Vitousek et al. 1997; Chapin et al. 1998; DeFries et al. 2004). The destruction of the vegetation in an area through overgrazing by domestic animals, overharvesting of timber, or frequent fires will destroy the system's ability to make use of solar energy. Eventually it leads to the loss of production of plant biomass and the deterioration of the animal community (including humans) that lives at that site.

Likewise, coastal estuaries are areas of rapid plant and algal growth that provide the starting point for food chains leading to commercial stocks of fish and shellfish (see Table 5.1). The U.S. National Marine Fisheries Service has estimated that damage to coastal estuaries has cost the United States more than $200 million per year in lost productive value of commercial fish and shellfish and in lost nonconsumptive value of fish caught for sport (McNeely et al. 1990). Even when degraded or damaged ecosystems are rebuilt or restored at great expense, they often do not function as well as before and almost certainly do not contain their original species composition or species richness.

Scientists are actively investigating how the loss of species from biological communities affects ecosystem processes such as the total growth of plants, the ability of plants to absorb atmospheric carbon dioxide (CO_2), and the ability to adapt to global climate change (Loreau et al. 2002; Díaz et al. 2003; Zavaleta and Hulvey 2004). This question was addressed experimentally at a grassland in Minnesota in which either 1, 2, 6, 8, 12, or 24 species were grown on 3m × 3m plots (Tilman 1999). The growth of plant material and the uptake of soil nutrients such as nitrogen were greater in plots with more species, clearly demonstrating the importance of species diversity to productivity (Figure 5.2). These results were further supported by similar observations of nearby native grasslands. Plots with greater diversity of species showed an increased ability to withstand drought and resist invasion by outside species. This research has been extensively replicated in European grasslands, pasture communities, and wetlands with similar results.

We know that species diversity is being reduced in major ecosystems as a result of human activities (Foley et al. 2005). At what point will the productivity of these ecosystems decline as well? We need to know the

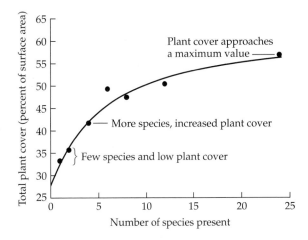

FIGURE 5.2 Varying numbers of prairie plant species were grown in experimental plots. The plots containing the most species had the greatest overall amount of growth, as measured by the total plant cover (the percentage of the total surface area occupied by plants) and total plant productivity (the total dry weight of plants on the plot). (After Tilman 1999.)

answer to this question before the world's forestry, ranching, agriculture, and fishing industries become critically damaged by the consequences of species decline. It is safe to assume that ecosystems with a lower diversity of species will be less able to adapt to the altered weather conditions associated with rising CO_2 levels and global climate change. For example, temperate forest ecosystems with few tree species to start with will likely show the effects of species loss quickly as their resident species are eliminated by exotic diseases and insects.

The value of intact and restored forests in retaining carbon and absorbing atmospheric carbon dioxide is now being recognized by environmental economists. As countries and corporations reduce their carbon dioxide emissions as part of the worldwide effort to address global climate change, they are paying to protect and restore forests and other ecosystems (Jenkins et al. 2004; Beedlow et al. 2004; MEA 2005). The payments for carbon reduction offset their own carbon production. In some cases, the value of ecosystems for carbon sequestration and watershed management often appears to be greater than their ability to produce harvestable products. Regenerating forests in the temperate zone, especially in North America, appear to play a particularly important role in slowing the increase of atmospheric carbon dioxide. The current market in carbon sequestration payments is around $350 million per year, but is projected to increase by 30 to 100 times over the next 5 years.

FIGURE 5.3 Logging and road construction on steep slopes leads to massive soil erosion and landslides, destroying a great deal of the economic value of the forest ecosystem. (Photograph by R. Primack.)

Protection of Water and Soil Resources

Biological communities are of vital importance in protecting watersheds, buffering ecosystems against extremes of flood and drought, and maintaining water quality (Pimental et al. 2000a). Plant foliage and dead leaves intercept the rain and reduce its impact on the soil; plant roots and soil organisms aerate the soil, increasing its capacity to absorb water. This increased water-holding capacity reduces the flooding that would otherwise occur after heavy rains and allows a slow release of water for days and weeks after the rains have ceased. The value of just the U.S. national forests in contributing to the water supply has been estimated at $4 billion per year.

When vegetation is disturbed by logging, farming, and other human activities, the rates of soil erosion and even occurrences of landslides increase rapidly, decreasing the value of the land for human activities (Figure 5.3) (Quist et al. 2003). Damage to the soil limits the ability of plant life to recover from disturbance and can render the land useless for agriculture. In addition, silt (soil particles suspended in water from runoff) can kill freshwater fish and other animals, coral reef organisms, and the marine life in coastal estuaries. Erosion and flooding also contaminate drinking water supplies for humans in the communities along the rivers, leading to an increase in human health problems. Soil erosion increases sediment loads into the reservoirs behind dams, causing a loss of electrical output, and creates sandbars and islands, which reduces the navigability of rivers and ports.

Floods are currently the most common natural disaster in the world, killing almost 100,000 people in recent years. The incidence of major floods has increased many-fold during the last few decades, which can be attributed to the concentration of people living in coastal areas and to the destruction of wetlands and upland ecosystems (MEA 2005). Unprecedented catastrophic floods and landslides in Bangladesh, India, the Philippines, Thailand, and Central America have been associated with recent extensive logging in watershed areas. Flood damage to India's agricultural areas has led to massive government and private tree-planting programs in the Himalayas. In the industrial nations of the world, wetlands protection has become a priority in order to prevent flooding of developed areas. Wetlands are estimated to have a value of $6,000 per ha per year in reducing flood damage and other ecosystem services, which is three times the value of farmland created on the same site (MEA 2005). The conversion of floodplain habitat to farmland along the Mississippi, Missouri, and Red Rivers, and along the Rhine River in Europe, is considered a major factor in the massive, damaging floods in past years, including the devastating flooding of the city of New Orleans in 2005 after Hurricane Katrina struck the Mississippi Delta, which has undergone heavy conversion for urban and agricultural development. The risk of flooding would be substantially reduced if even a small proportion of the wetlands along these rivers were restored to their original condition (Box 5.1).

BOX 5.1

Prophecy Fulfilled: How Ecosystem Services Became Front Page News

As the whirling maelstrom approached the coast, more than a million people evacuated to higher ground. Some 200,000 remained, however—the carless, the homeless, the aged and infirm....The storm hit Breton Sound with the fury of a nuclear warhead, pushing a deadly storm surge into Lake Pontchartrain. ...As it reached 25 feet (eight meters) over parts of the city, people climbed onto roofs to escape it. Thousands drowned in the murky brew that was soon contaminated by sewage and industrial waste.... It took two months to pump the city dry, and by then the Big Easy was buried under a blanket of putrid sediment, a million people were homeless... It was the worst natural disaster in the history of the United States.

▓ This *National Geographic* excerpt might be any of the now-familiar narratives of the devastation wreaked on New Orleans by Hurricane Katrina but for one fact: it was published in October 2004, almost a year before its description became reality on August 29, 2005 (Bourne 2004). Other major scientific publications and newspapers, including *Scientific American, Popular Mechanics,* and *The Houston Chronicle,* had written similar articles warning of the pending catastrophe, echoing an earlier 1998 Louisiana task force report by government officials, engineers, and scientists.

How did New Orleans reach the point at which impending disaster could be so clearly predicted? The answer lies partly in the geological and ecological processes by which the Mississippi Delta and its marshes were formed, and partly in the man-made systems that carved dry land from the marsh.

The delta surrounding New Orleans would have long ago sunk below sea level but for the contributions of the river. For millennia, the sediment load carried by the muddy Mississippi River was deposited in the delta marshes and swamps, nourishing the plants that grow there; these plants acted as anchors to protect the landscape against erosion, and the added new sediment and new plant matter compensated for the tendency of the old sediment to subside. These wetlands absorbed the fury of storms before they reached New Orleans. The construction of levees in the twentieth century, however, changed the equation. As the levees prevented sediment from reaching the coastal wetlands, the balance between land lost and land gained was tipped, and the slow subsidence of the landscape became a self-sustaining situation. Because New Orleans was continually pumping out water to stay dry, the city itself was subsiding even faster than the marshes.

To make matters worse, the remaining wetlands along the coast were being filled in for coastal development and carved up by engineers creating canals for ship traffic and oil drilling. Over 12,800 km (8000 miles) of canals were cut into the marshes, increasing soil ero-

(continued)

BOX 5.1 *(continued)*

sion and introducing salt water into the freshwater wetlands—salt water that further degraded the health of the wetland ecosystems.

By the 1990s, New Orleans had become a shallow depression almost 5 m (14 feet) below sea level, ringed by levees to protect it from the Mississippi River to its south and Lake Pontchartrain to the north. The city had sunk so much that the levees could no longer protect it from a major storm; the 1998 task force noted that a storm above category 3 would be sufficient to overcome the levees. However, data from earlier hurricanes suggested that an intact system of coastal wetlands and barrier islands could reduce storm surge by anywhere from 15 to 100 cm (half a foot to 3 feet) in some locations. In its conclusion, the task force stressed that the imminent danger to the wetlands ecosystems—and by extension New Orleans—required an immediate commitment to restore the overall health of the existing wetlands and, if possible, expand their extent.

Subsequent proposals in 2003 called for radical—and expensive—action, to the tune of about $14 billion worth of marsh restoration over 30 years; instead, a $2 billion/10 year project was started, a choice that, in hindsight, proved tragically shortsighted. These early efforts were small in scale and experimental in nature—nothing to match the 64 square kilometers of wetlands that were lost each year. When the hurricane struck in 2005, New Orleans was virtually an island, its marshes gone, exposed to the full fury of the ocean's wrath.

Katrina has left behind great damage, and its horrific destruction has shown indelibly the great value of the ecosystem services provided by coastal wetlands. If coastal wetlands had been in place to absorb the storm surge, much of the damage to property and the loss of life and livelihoods could have been avoided. As the rebuilding of New Orleans gets slowly underway, government authorities are asking questions about how to protect the city from another disaster—and are recognizing, in the process, just how valuable the lost wetlands could be if restored.

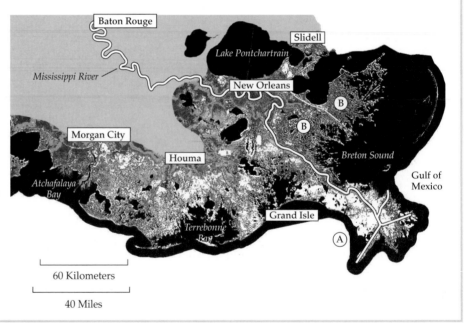

The loss of coastal wetlands from 1932 to 2000 (shown in white) has been severe in the southern Louisiana area, leaving New Orleans unprotected from hurricanes. Note the almost total loss of wetlands where the Mississippi River enters the Gulf of Mexico (A), and the severe degradation of wetlands south, east, and southeast of New Orleans and Lake Pontchartrain (B). (After 100 Years of Land Change for Coastal Louisiana [map ID: USGS-NWRC02003-03-085]; http://www.nwrc.usgs.gov/special/landloss.htm)

In many areas of the developing world, people settle near natural water sources to obtain water for drinking, washing, and irrigation. As hydrologic cycles are disrupted by deforestation, soil erosion, and dam projects, and as water quality deteriorates due to pollution, people are increasingly unable to obtain their water needs from natural systems. Water scarcity affects over 1 billion people throughout the world (MEA 2005). The cost of boiling water, buying bottled water, or building new wells, rain catchment systems, water treatment plants, pipes, and water pumps gives some measure of the consumptive use value of water from surface sources. The government of New York City, for instance, paid $1.5 billion in the late 1980s to county and town governments in rural New York state to maintain forests on the watersheds surrounding its reservoirs and to improve agricultural practices. Water filtration plants doing the same job would have cost $8 to $9 billion (McKibben 1996).

Increases in waterborne disease and intestinal ailments, such as cholera and dysentery, which currently affect half of the world's population, and the subsequent deaths and lost days of work that result from such illnesses, add to estimates of the economic value of water and the natural systems that provide it.

There is growing recognition of the fact that development of dams, reservoirs, and new croplands needs to include protection measures for natural communities located on the highlands above these projects in order to ensure a steady supply of high-quality water. For example, in Sulawesi, the Indonesian government established the Dumoga–Bone National Park to protect the watershed above a major agricultural project in the adjacent lowland.

Waste Treatment and Nutrient Retention

Aquatic communities such as swamps, lakes, rivers, floodplains, tidal marshes, mangroves, estuaries, the coastal shelf, and the open ocean are capable of breaking down and immobilizing toxic pollutants, such as heavy metals and pesticides that have been released into the environment by human activities. Fungi and bacteria are particularly important in this role. The waste treatment services performed by these biological communities is estimated to be valued at around $2.4 trillion per year (Costanza et al. 1997; Balmford et al. 2002). When these ecosystems are damaged and degraded, expensive pollution treatment facilities must be installed and operated to assume these functions.

Aquatic biological communities also play an important role in processing, storing, and recycling the large amount of nutrients that enter the ecosystem as sewage or agricultural runoff, allowing these nutrients to be absorbed by photosynthetic organisms. These communities also provide a matrix for the bacteria that fix atmospheric nitrogen. These roles in nutrient processing and retention have an estimated value of $15.9 trillion per year, with coastal marine areas accounting for most of the total (Costanza et al. 1997).

An excellent example of the value of such an ecosystem is provided by the New York Bight, a 5200 km^2 (2000 square mile) bay at the mouth of the Hudson River. For hundreds of years, the New York Bight provided a free sewage disposal system into which was dumped the waste produced by the millions of people in the New York metropolitan area (Friedman et al. 2000; Pearce 2000). However, as the volume of sewage increased in the 1960s and 1970s, the water quality and species diversity of the Bight began deteriorating, and the region was becoming less suitable for swimming and sport fishing. To deal with this situation, the ocean disposal of sewage sludge was stopped by the government in 1987, and the water quality began to improve, beaches became more acceptable for swimming, and marine species increased in abundance. However, the government had to spend billions of dollars on alternative waste treatment facilities.

Climate Regulation

Plant communities are important in moderating local, regional, and probably even global climate conditions (Couzin 1999; Fearnside 2005). At the local level, trees provide shade and transpire water, which reduces the local temperature in hot weather. This cooling effect reduces the need for fans and air conditioners and increases people's comfort and work efficiency. Trees are also locally important because they act as windbreaks for agricultural fields and homes and reduce heat loss from buildings in cold weather.

At the regional level, transpiration from plants recycles rainwater back into the atmosphere, creating new rain-producing clouds. A loss of vegetation from large forested regions of the world such as the Amazon Basin and West Africa may result in less transpiration into the atmosphere and a resulting reduction of average annual rainfall (Fearnside 2005).

Species Relationships

Many of the species harvested by people for their productive use value depend on other wild species for their continued existence. For example, the wild game and fish harvested by people are dependent on wild insects and plants for their food. A decline in insect and plant populations will result in a decline in animal harvests. Thus, a decline in a wild species of little immediate value to humans may result in a corresponding decline in a harvested species that is economically important.

Crop plants also benefit from birds and predatory insects, such as praying mantises, which feed on pest insect species that attack the crops (Jones et al. 2005). Insects act as pollinators for numerous crop species (De Marco and Coelho 2004). About 150 species of crop plants in the United States require insect pollination of their flowers, often involving a mixture of wild insects and honeybees (Buchmann and Nabhan 1996; Kremen et al. 2004; Kremen and Ostfeld 2005). The value of these pollinators has been estimated to be around $20 billion to $40 billion per year. The value of wild insect pollinators will increase in the near future if they take over the pollination role of domestic honeybees, whose populations are declining due to disease and pests. Many useful wild plant species depend on fruit-eating animals, such as bats, birds, and primates, to act as seed dispersers. Where these animals have been overharvested, fruits remain uneaten, seeds are not dispersed, and species head toward local extinction. However, it should be noted that there is redundancy in guilds of similar species, and the service of one pollinator or seed disperser may be carried out equally well by another species.

One of the most economically significant relationships in biological communities is that between many forest trees and crop plants and the soil organisms that provide them with essential nutrients (Hart and Trevors 2005). Fungi and bacteria break down dead plant and animal matter, which they use as their energy source. In the process, the fungi and bacteria release mineral nutrients such as nitrogen into the soil. These nutrients are used by plants for further growth. Mycorrhizal fungi that extend from the soil into tree roots greatly increase the ability of plant roots to absorb water and minerals, and certain mutualistic bacteria convert nitrogen into a form that can be taken up by plants (Figure 5.4). In return, the plants provide the mutualists with photosynthetic products that help them grow (Moore et al. 2001). The poor growth and dieback of many trees in certain areas of North America and Europe is attributable in part to the deleterious effects of acid rain and air pollution on soil fungi. Without fungi in their root systems, these plants are more susceptible to drought, disease, and insect attack.

FIGURE 5.4 The presence of different mycorrhizal fungi greatly enhances the growth and health of tree seedlings. Seedlings of a savannah tree, *Clusia grandiflora*, from Venezuela were grown with various species of mycorrhizal fungi. The spindly, small seedlings on the left were grown as a control without fungi. Fungi in the species *Acaulospora spinosa* and *Scutellospora heterogama* greatly enhanced seedling growth, whereas two species of fungi in the genus *Gigaspora* (*G. rosea* and *G. margarita*) had minimal effects. The inset shows the spores of a mycorrhizal fungus. (Photographs courtesy of Gisela Cuena.)

Environmental Monitors

Species that are particularly sensitive to chemical toxins serve as "early warning indicators" for monitoring the health of the environment. Some species can even substitute for expensive detection equipment. Among the best-known indicator species are rock lichens, which absorb large amounts of chemicals in rainwater and airborne pollution (Jovan and McCune 2005). High levels of toxic materials kill certain lichens, so the distribution and abundance of lichens can identify areas of contamination around sources of air pollution, such as smelters and urban areas. Conversely, certain conspicuous lichens grow only in old-growth forests and can be used to identify areas likely to contain rare and endangered species that are less conspicuous. Aquatic filter feeders, such as mollusks, are also effective in monitoring pollution because they process large volumes of water and concentrate toxic chemicals such as poisonous metals, PCBs, and pesticides in their tissues. The California Mussel Watch Program, started in 1977, has expanded to include 280 coastal and freshwater sites in which mussel (*Mytilus* sp.) and clam (*Corbicula fluminea*) tissues are sampled and analyzed for toxic compounds, highlighting areas of serious water pollution (Persson et al. 2000). Monitoring algal blooms in shallow marine waters can provide a warning of the contamination of shellfish by toxic species and potential health impacts on swimmers from encounters with poisonous species (Epstein 1998).

Recreation and Ecotourism

Ecosystems provide many recreational services for humans, such as the nonconsumptive enjoyment of nature through hiking, photography, and birdwatching (Harmon and Putney 2003). The monetary value of these activities, sometimes called their **amenity value**, can be considerable (Figure 5.5). In the United States, there are 350 million visitors each year to U.S. national parks, wildlife refuges, and other protected public lands. These visitors engage in nonconsumptive activities such as sport fishing and camping, and in the process spend $4 billion on fees, travel, lodging, food, and equipment. Recreation represents over 75 % of the value of the U.S. national forests, far greater than the value of the wood being extracted (Groom et al. 2006).

In national and international sites known for their conservation value or exceptional scenic beauty nonconsumptive recreational value often dwarfs the value generated or captured by all other economic enterprises, including extractive industries. This value is even larger when the money spent off-site on food, lodging, equipment, and other goods and services purchased in the local area is included. Even sport hunting and fishing, which in theory are consumptive uses, are in practice nonconsumptive, because the food value of the animals caught by fishermen and hunters is insignificant compared with the time and money spent on these activities. The increasingly common practice of sport fishermen releasing fish rather than keeping them emphasizes the recreational and nonconsumptive aspect of the activity. In many rural economies, such as those of East Africa, Alaska, and the southern United States, sport fishing and hunting are sources of tens of thousands of jobs. In the United States, the recreational hunting and fishing industries have been estimated to be worth around $100 billion per year (MEA 2005).

Consumptive Uses
Commercial hunting • Sport hunting • Subsistence hunting • Commercial fishing • Sport fishing • Subsistence fishing • Fur trapping • Hunting for animal parts and pet trade • Indirect kills through other activities (pollution, by-catch, road kills) • Eradication programs for animals posing real or perceived threats

Low-Consumptive Uses
Zoos and animal parks • Aquariums • Scientific research

Nonconsumptive Uses
Birdwatching • Whale-watching • Photography trips • Nature walks • Commercial photography and cinematography • Wildlife viewing in parks, reserves, and recreational areas

FIGURE 5.5 Wildlife is used in a variety of consumptive and nonconsumptive ways by both traditional and modern societies. The range of this use and the value of wildlife to people are increasing all the time. (After Duffus and Dearden 1990.)

The potential value of these recreational activities may be even greater than this number suggests, because many park visitors, fishermen, and hunters indicate that they would be willing to pay even higher usage fees to continue their activities.

Ecotourism is a special category of recreation that involves people visiting places and spending money wholly or in part to experience unusual biological communities (such as rain forests, African savannahs, coral reefs, deserts, the Galápagos Islands, and the Everglades) and to view particular "flagship" species (such as elephants on safari trips) (Marvell 2005; Kruger 2005). Tourism is among the world's largest industries (on the scale of the petroleum and motor vehicle industries). Ecotourism currently represents around 20% of the $600 billion dollar per year tourist industry (Braithwaite 2001).

Ecotourism is growing rapidly in many developing countries because people want to experience tropical biodiversity for themselves. One example of ecotourism's potential is Rwanda, which developed a gorilla tourism industry that at one point was the country's third largest foreign-currency earner. Ecotourism has traditionally been a key industry in East African countries such as Kenya and Tanzania, and is now a large part of tourism in many American and Asian countries.

The revenue provided by ecotourism has the potential to provide one of the most immediate justifications for protecting biological diversity, particularly when ecotourism activities are integrated into overall management plans (Lindsey et al. 2005). In Integrated Conservation Development Projects (ICDPs), local communities develop accommodations, expertise in nature guiding, local handicraft outlets, and other sources of income; the revenue income from ecotourism allows the local people to give up unsustainable or destructive hunting, fishing, or grazing practices (Figure 5.6). The local community benefits from learning new skills, employment opportunities, greater protection for their environment, and the development of additional community infrastructure such as schools, roads, medical clinics, and stores.

To help protect biological diversity, ecotourism must provide a significant and secure income for its destination location. However, in a typical ecotourist package, only 20–40% of the retail price of the trip remains in the destination country, and only 0.01–1% is paid in entrance fees to native parks (Gössling 1999). For example,

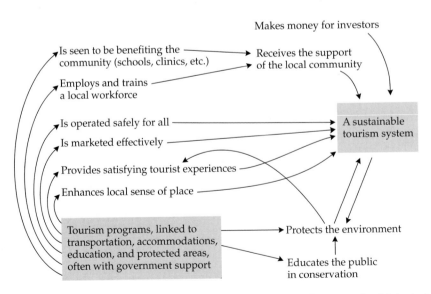

FIGURE 5.6 Ecotourism can provide an economic justification for protecting biological diversity and also can provide benefits to people living nearby. This diagram illustrates some of the main elements in a successful ecotourism program. (After Braithwaite 2001.)

for a two-week trip costing $4000, somewhere between 40 cents and $40 would typically be paid in entrance fees. Even in well-known destinations, such as Komodo National Park in Indonesia, tourist revenues account for less than 10% of the park management budget (Walpole et al. 2001). Obviously, raising entrance fees and increasing tourist spending in parks and adjacent countryside is a priority for this industry.

A danger of ecotourism is that tourists themselves will unwittingly damage these sites—by trampling wildflowers, breaking coral, or disrupting nesting bird colonies, for instance—thereby contributing to the degradation and disturbance of sensitive areas (Bouton and Frederick 2003; Walker et al. 2005). To take one example, hatching success was reduced by 47% when Adelie penguins (*Pygoscelis adeliae*) in the Antarctic were exposed to the typical activities of tourists (Giese 1996). Tourists might also indirectly damage sites by creating a demand for fuelwood for heating

Courtesy: EG Magazin

FIGURE 5.7 In developing countries, facilities for ecotourists sometimes create a fantasyland that disguises and ignores the real problems those countries face. (From E. G. Magazin, Germany.)

and cooking, thus contributing to deforestation (Laiolo 2004). In addition, the presence, affluence, and demands of tourists can transform traditional human societies in tourist areas by changing employment opportunities and often serving as a magnet for outside people looking for work (Carrier and Macleod 2005; Dahles 2005). As local people increasingly enter a cash-based economy, their values, customs, and relationship to nature might be lost along the way. A final potential danger of this industry is that ecotourist facilities may provide a sanitized fantasy experience rather than help visitors understand the serious social and environmental problems that endanger biological diversity (Figure 5.7). To respond to these problems, travel companies are promoting measures to minimize their impacts and provide increased benefits to local people. Ecotourism activities can even become certified as sustainable through programs such as Green Globe 21.

Educational and Scientific Value

Many books, television programs, and movies produced for educational and entertainment purposes are based on nature themes (Osterlind 2005). These natural history materials are being incorporated continually into school curricula. Such educational materials are probably worth billions of dollars per year. These represent a nonconsumptive use value of biodiversity because nature is used as intellectual content in these materials. A considerable number of professional scientists, as well as highly motivated amateurs, are engaged in making ecological observations and preparing educational materials. In rural areas, these activities often take place in scientific field stations, which are sources of training and employment for local people. While these scientific activities provide economic benefits to the areas surrounding field stations, their real value lies in their ability to increase human knowledge, enhance education, and enrich the human experience.

Other Ways of Valuing Biodiversity

In addition to nonconsumptive use value, option value and existence value are two other ways of valuing biological diversity. In this section we discuss these values in more detail.

Option Value

Recall from Chapter 4 that a species' potential to provide an economic benefit to human society at some point in the future is its option value. As the needs of society change, so must the methods of satisfying those needs, and such methods often lie in previously untapped animal or plant species. For example, the continued genetic improvement of cultivated plants is necessary not only for increased yield, but also to guard against pesticide-resistant insects and more virulent strains of fungi, viruses, and bacteria (Rommens and Humara 2004; Sairim et al. 2005). Catastrophic crop failures often can be directly linked to low genetic variability: the 1846 potato blight in Ireland, the 1922 wheat failure in the Soviet Union, and the 1984 outbreak of citrus canker in Florida were all related to low genetic variability among crop plants. To overcome this problem, scientists are constantly substituting new, resistant varieties of agricultural species for susceptible varieties. The source of resistance often comes from genes obtained from wild relatives of crop plants, and from local varieties of the domestic species grown by traditional farmers.

The genetic improvement of crops is an ongoing process, and past improvements can give an indication of the potential for future improvements. Development of new crop varieties has a huge economic impact, and the option value of future improvements is similarly great. Genetic improvements in U.S. crops are responsible for increasing harvest values by an average of $8 to $15 billion per year (Frisvold et al. 2001). In developing countries, genetic improvements of rice, wheat, and other crops increased harvests by an estimated $6 to $11 billion per year. As one example, the discovery of a wild perennial relative of corn in the Mexican state of Jalisco has a huge option value: It is potentially worth billions of dollars to modern agriculture because it could lead to the development of a high-yielding perennial corn crop, thus eliminating the need for annual plowing and planting. This example demonstrates the considerable option value of biodiversity for agricultural improvement alone.

Wild species also have option value as biological control agents. Biologists often can control exotic, invasive species by searching the pest species' original habitat for a control species that limits its population. This control species is then brought to the new locality, where it can be released to act as a biological control agent. A classic example is the case of the prickly pear cactus (*Opuntia inermis*), a South American species introduced into Australia for use as a hedgerow plant. The cactus spread out of control and took over millions of hectares of rangeland. In the prickly pear's native habitat, the larvae of a particular moth species (*Cactoblastis cactorum*) feed on the cactus. The moth was successfully introduced into Australia, where it has reduced the cactus to comparative rarity and allowed native species to recover. Thus pristine habitats can be of great value as reservoirs of natural pest control agents.

As was discussed in Chapter 4, we are continually searching the biological communities of the world for new plants, animals, fungi, and microorganisms that can be used to fight human diseases or to provide some other economic value*, an activity referred to as "bioprospecting" (Box 5.2) (Plotkin 1993; Balick and Cox 1996; Cox 2001; Coley et al. 2003). These searches are generally carried out by government research institutes and pharmaceutical companies. In 1987, the U.S. National Cancer Institute initiated a program costing $8 million to test extracts of thousands of wild species for their effectiveness in controlling cancer cells and the AIDS virus. To facilitate the search for new medicines and to profit financially from new products, the Costa Rican government established the National Biodiversity Institute (INBio) to collect biological products and supply samples to drug companies

---

*We discussed the productive use value of natural materials in Chapter 4; however, their future value as new products also gives them value in the present time, so in this chapter we will discuss their option value.

BOX 5.2

Mighty Multitudes of Microbes: Not To Be Ignored!

■ They're out there, and there are billions of them. They occupy cities, suburbs, countrysides, and forests; they're equally at home in spiffy high-rise hotels, filthy shanty towns, and barren deserts. They live in hospitals, restaurants, parks, theaters, and your digestive tract, as well as on mountaintops, in rain forests, and on seashores. They can be found swimming in the ocean's depths and warming themselves near volcanoes—they may even exist on Mars. The living world's quintessential jet-setters, we find them everywhere we look—or we would, if we could see at the microscopic level. Fortunately for the peace of mind of most people, we can't, so the billions of microbes that inhabit our world go unnoticed, out of sight and out of mind, except when we're bothered by a cold or have gone too long without cleaning out the vegetable drawer in the refrigerator.

The word "microbe" is a catchall for thousands of species of bacteria, yeasts, protozoans, fungi, and the bacterialike species in the primitive kingdom Archaea.* A handful of soil can contain thousands, millions, even billions of each of these different types of microbes (Coleman 2001; Dunlap 2001), except for the Archaea, which at present are known only from extreme environments such as deep-sea thermal vents, coal deposits, highly salty environments, and hot springs (see Box 3.1). Few people realize how utterly essential these invisible critters are to our day-to-day existence. We tend to look on microbes as nuisances that pose a potential threat to our health—hence the proliferation of antibacterial soaps and antibiotic sprays on supermarket shelves.

In truth, most microbes either actively help us or at the very least do us little harm. Those microbes that do harm us—pathogens that range from the annoying fungus that causes athlete's foot to the deadly viruses and protozoans that cause killer diseases such as AIDS and malaria—are fairly few in number when compared to the total collection of microbes present in the world. On the other hand, we literally could not live without some of them. Microbes play a vital role in the production of foods such as bread, cheese, vinegar, yogurt, soy sauce, and tofu, and alcoholic beverages such as beer and wine. Bacteria in our gastrointestinal tract help

break down the food we eat. A few species of bacteria perform the vital biochemical function of transforming nitrogen gas from the atmosphere into a form that plants can take up from the soil as a nutrient (Morrissey et al. 2004). Such "fixed" nitrogen is essential for plant growth. Bacteria and fungi in the soil also aid in the decomposition of organic wastes, freeing up more nutrients such as phosphates, nitrates, carbon dioxide, and sulphates for plants to use as they grow. In short, without bacteria, there would be no plants—and thus no food or oxygen available for the animal kingdom, including humans.

In recent years, scientists have begun to appreciate that these organisms are important not only to sustain life as we know it, but also to assist in the conservation of threatened species. Some microbes have uses that may ultimately help reduce environmental pollution and habitat degradation. For instance, a major cause of the decline of many insect and bird species is the presence of harmful compounds in sprays used to control agricultural pests and pathogens. These chemicals harm important nonpest species either by killing them outright or by interfering with their ability to forage and reproduce; at the same time, many pests and pathogens have grown resistant to the compounds. As pesticides have become less effective, agronomists have begun turning to microbial solutions to solve pest problems. For example, the bacterial species *Bacillus thuringiensis* produces a toxin that kills some insect pests and *Agrobacterium radiobacter* inhibits the growth of a bacterial pathogen that attacks several important fruit and flower species. These bacteria can be sprayed on crops, or by using the techniques of molecular biology, specific genes from bacteria can be incorporated into the cells of crop plants such as corn, potato, and tomato. The use of transgenic crops has improved crop yield, but some people believe that such dramatic alteration of species is morally wrong and potentially dangerous because of its unknown effects on other species.

Using microbes as biological controls is advantageous for two important reasons: First, they tend to be highly specific in what they will attack, so unlike chemicals, they are likely to harm only a narrow range of species. Though a microbe that causes disease in cabbage moth caterpillars could not be used, for instance, in an area also inhabited by an endangered butterfly, it

---

*The term "microbe" also encompasses viruses, fragments of genetic material surrounded by a protective protein coat, which can invade the cells of other species and make copies of themselves. Viruses are not generally considered to be living, independent organisms.

(continued)

BOX 5.2 *(continued)*

Bacteria can be genetically engineered to "eat" crude oil. In this laboratory simulation of an oil spill (left), adapted bacteria added to the spill (top, right) quickly reduce the area of the damaging pollutant (bottom right). (Photographs by Charles O'Rear.)

could be used elsewhere without concern that it would harm beneficial insects such as bees or dragonflies. A second advantage is that, like the pathogens they attack, microbes are capable of mutating into many different varieties. Unlike chemical pesticides, a microbe can be genetically altered to counteract the mutations of the pathogen; thus, although the pest species might become resistant to one strain of the bacterium used for biological control, additional strains of the microbe can be developed to counteract the resistance.

In addition, scientists are currently developing technologies involving bacteria to extract metals from ore in mines, and even to generate electricity from wastewater (Burton 2005). Bioengineering has also allowed us to "train" microbes to perform tasks that are not feasible using technological means. For example, bacteria engineered to attack pollutants such as cyanide, crude oil, and creosote are used more and more often in cleaning up toxic waste sites. This use of

microbes may become an important factor in reclaiming damaged habitat, possibly an essential component of future conservation efforts. It is ironic that the simplest, "lowest" life forms on Earth should be in a position to address problems created by the most complex and "highest" life form, humankind.

(Figure 5.8). The Merck Company has signed an agreement to pay INBio $1 million for the right to screen samples and will pay royalties to INBio on any commercial products that result from the research (Mateo et al. 2001; Castree 2003). Expected royalties are difficult to calculate, but one estimate suggests a figure of $4.8 million per new drug developed (Reid et al. 1993). The GlaxoSmithKline corporation, a Brazilian biotechnology company, and the Brazilian government signed a contract in 1999 worth $3 million to sample, screen, and investigate approximately 40,000 plants, fungi, and bacteria from Brazil, with part of the royalties going to support scientific research and local community-based conservation and development projects. Another approach has been to target traditional medicinal plants and other natural products for screening, often in collaboration with local healers. Programs such as these provide financial incentives for countries to protect their natural resources and the biodiversity knowledge that is possessed by indigenous inhabitants.

One discovery in this search is a potent anticancer chemical in the Pacific yew (*Taxus brevifolia*), a tree native to North American old-growth forests. This chemical, called taxol, has greatly reduced the mortality rate from ovarian cancer. Another discovery is the ginkgo tree (*Ginkgo biloba*), a species that occurs in the wild in a few isolated localities in China. This species has long been used in tradition-

FIGURE 5.8 Taxonomists and technicians at INBio sort and classify Costa Rica's rich array of species. In the offices shown here many species of plants and insects are cataloged. (Photograph by Steve Winter.)

al Chinese medicine. During the last 30 years, an industry valued at $500 million a year has developed around the cultivation of the ginkgo tree (Figure 5.9) and the manufacture of medicines made from its leaves, which are widely used in Europe, Asia, and increasingly in North America, to treat circulatory problems, including strokes, and to restore and maintain memory function.

The search for valuable natural products is wide-ranging: Entomologists search for insects that can be used as biological control agents, microbiologists search for bacteria that can assist in biochemical manufacturing processes, and wildlife biologists search for species that can potentially produce animal protein more efficiently and with less environmental damage than existing domestic species. The growing biotechnology industry is finding new ways to reduce pollution, to develop alternative industrial processes, and to fight diseases threatening human health. Innovative techniques in molecular biology are allowing unique, valuable genes found in one species to be transferred to another species. Both newly discovered and well-known species are often found to have exactly those properties needed to address some significant human problem. If biological diversity is reduced, the ability of scientists to locate and utilize a broad range of species will also be reduced.

A question currently being debated among conservation biologists, governments, environmental economists, and corporations is, "Who owns the commercial development rights to the world's biological diversity?" In the past, species were freely collected from wherever they occurred (often in the developing world) by corporations (almost always headquartered in the developed world). Whatever these corporations found useful in the species was then processed and sold at a profit, which was entirely kept by the corporation. An excellent example is provided by the immunosuppressant drug cyclosporine. Using the fungus *Tolypocladium inflatum*, the drug cyclosporine was developed into a family of drugs with sales of $1.2 billion

(A)

(B)

FIGURE 5.9 (A) Ginkgo trees are preserved in the wild in the Tian Mu Shan forest reserve in China; no other wild populations exist. This species is the basis of a pharmaceutical business worth hundreds of millions of dollars each year. (B) Because of the valuable medicines made from their leaves, ginkgo trees are now cultivated as a crop. Each year the woody stems sprout new shoots and branches, which are harvested. (Photographs by Peter Del Tredici, Arnold Arboretum of Harvard University.)

per year by the Swiss company Sandoz, which later merged to become Novartis (Svarstad et al. 2000). The fungus was in a sample of soil that was collected in Norway without permission by a Sandoz biologist on vacation. As of yet, Norway has not received any payment for the use of this fungus in drug production.

Countries in both the developing and developed world now frequently demand a share in the commercial activities derived from the biological diversity contained within their borders, and rightly so. Local people in developing countries who possess knowledge of the species, protect them, and show them to scientists, should also share in the profits from any use of them. Writing treaties and developing procedures to guarantee participation in this process will be a major diplomatic challenge in the coming years.

How can the option value of species be determined? One way involves examining the impact on the world economy of wild species only recently utilized by humans. Consider a hypothetical example: Imagine that during the last 20 years, newly discovered uses of 100 previously unused plant species accounted for $100 billion of new economic activity in the form of increased agriculture, new industrial products, and improved medicines. Since there are presently 250,000 unused plant species, a rough calculation might demonstrate that each presently unused plant species has the potential to provide an average of $400,000 worth of benefits to the world economy in the next 20 years. These types of calculations are now at a very preliminary stage, and they assume, for the sake of convenience, that the average value of a species can be determined.

While most species may have little or no direct economic value and little option value, a small proportion may have enormous potential value to supply medical treatments, to support a new industry, or to prevent the collapse of a major agricultural crop. If just one of these species goes extinct before it is discovered, it could be a tremendous loss to the global economy, even if the majority of the world's species were preserved. As Aldo Leopold commented:

If the biota, in the course of aeons, has built something we like but do not understand, then who but a fool would discard seemingly useless parts? To keep every cog and wheel is the first precaution of intelligent tinkering.

The diversity of the world's species can be compared to a manual on how to keep the Earth running effectively. The loss of a species is like tearing a page out of the manual. If we ever need the information from that page in the manual to save ourselves and the Earth's other species, the information will have been irretrievably lost.

Existence Value

Many people throughout the world care about wildlife and plants and are concerned for their protection. This concern may be associated with a desire to someday visit the habitat of a unique species and see it in the wild; alternatively, concerned individuals may not expect, need, or even desire to see these species personally or experience the wilderness in which they live. In either case, these individuals recognize an **existence value** in wild nature—the amount that people are willing to pay to prevent species from going extinct, habitats from being destroyed, and genetic variation from being lost (Tisdell et al. 2005). A component of existence value is **beneficiary value**, how much people are willing to pay to protect something of value for their own children and descendants, or for future generations.

Particular species, the so-called "charismatic megafauna"—such as pandas, whales, lions, elephants, bison, manatees, and many birds—elicit strong responses in people (Figure 5.10). Special groups have been formed to appreciate and pro-

FIGURE 5.10 For many people, the existence value of charismatic species, such as whales, is clear. Here people greet a minke whale that is being rescued after it became entangled in a trawler's gill net; the float behind the whale was attached to the net to keep the whale at the surface so it could breathe. Later, rescuers were able to release the whale from the netting. Most people find interacting with other species to be an educational and uplifting experience. Such meetings (which usually take place at greater distances, as in a more traditional "whale watch" setting, or on "photo safaris" in Africa) can enrich human lives. (Photograph by Scott Kraus, New England Aquarium.)

FIGURE 5.11 The bald eagle is a symbol of the United States. Many people have indicated a willingness to pay to protect its continued existence. (Photograph © Stockbyte/PictureQuest.)

tect butterflies and other insects, wildflowers, and fungi. People place value on wildlife and wild lands in a direct way by joining and contributing billions of dollars each year to conservation organizations that protect species. In the United States, billions of dollars are contributed each year to conservation and environmental organizations, with The Nature Conservancy ($700 million), the World Wildlife Fund ($110 million), Ducks Unlimited ($180 million), and the Sierra Club ($51 million) high on the list. Citizens also show their concern by directing their governments to spend money on conservation programs and to purchase land for habitat and landscape protection. For example, the government of the United States has spent more than $20 million to protect a single rare species, the California condor (*Gymnogyps californianus*). The citizens of the United States have indicated in surveys that they are willing to spend around $31 per person per year (more than $9 billion per year in total) to protect a national symbol, the bald eagle (*Haliaeetus leucocephalus*), a bird whose populations have suffered significant declines in the past but are now rebounding (Figure 5.11) (Groom et al. 2006).

Existence value can be attached to biological communities, such as temperate old-growth forests, tropical rain forests, coral reefs, and prairie remnants, and to areas of scenic beauty. Growing numbers of people and organizations contribute large sums of money annually to ensure the continuing existence of these habitats. Over the last 20 years and continuing into the present, surveys taken in the United States and the United Kingdom show that the public regards environmental protection as a high priority. Further, people want environmental education included in public scholl education (www.neetf.org; www.defra.gov.uk/environment/statistics/pubatt/index.htm).

At present, many people do not extend existence value to include the full range of the world's species (Kellert 1996). Although a few insect species, such as the monarch butterfly (*Danaus plexippus*), receive protection and attention, the need to protect other invertebrates, much less single-celled bacteria and protists, is not even part of the public discussion. Conservation biologists need to continue to educate the public on the subject of biological diversity to raise awareness of the need to protect *all* species, not just mammals and birds. Similarly, people need to learn the value of protecting all biological communities, including ones that are not as well-known or popular, and populations that are genetically unique or have special value due to their proximity to urban centers.

Is Economic Valuation Enough?

Although the more complete systems of accounting being developed by ecological economics value common property resources and include them in the cost of doing business (instead of leaving them out, as in traditional accounting methods), many environmentalists feel that ecological economics does not go far enough. For some, the use of green accounting methods still means acceptance of the present world economic system. These environmental thinkers advocate much stronger changes in our economic system, which is responsible for pollution, environmental degradation, and species extinctions at unprecedented rates.

They argue that the most damning aspect of this system is the unnecessary over-consumption of resources by a minority of the world's citizens at the same time that the majority of the world's people face poverty. Given a world economic system in which millions of children die each year from disease, malnutrition, warfare, crime, and other factors strongly correlated with poverty, and in which thousands of unique species go extinct each year due to habitat destruction, these thinkers suggest that major structural changes—not just minor adjustments—are needed.

As we will discuss in the next chapter, proponents of this view favor an alternative approach, one that will dramatically lower the consumption of resources in the developed world, reduce the need to exploit natural resources, and greatly increase the value placed on the natural environment and biological diversity. Some suggestions for bringing this about include stabilization or reduction of the number of people in the world, much higher taxes on fossil fuels, penalties for inefficient energy use and pollution, support for public transportation and fuel-efficient vehicles, and mandatory recycling programs. Lands on which endangered species are present would have to be managed for biodiversity; private landowners would receive a government subsidy for maintaining the habitat. One of the greatest inefficiencies in the agricultural economies of Western countries is the production of meat and dairy products, so a switch to (or at least toward) vegetarianism would be more healthy for people and would reduce the impact on the environment. Restrictions could be placed on trade, so that only those products derived from sustainable activities could be bought or sold on national and international markets. Debts of developing countries could be reduced or dismissed and investment redirected to activities that provide the most benefits to the greatest number of impoverished people. Finally, financial penalties for damaging biological diversity and incentives for protecting biological diversity could be established and made so compelling that industries would be forced to protect the natural world. While the political will to carry out these policies may not be present today, perhaps at some point in the future such policies can be implemented and biological diversity can be truly protected.

Summary

1. Indirect use values can be assigned to aspects of biological diversity that provide economic benefit to people but are not harvested or damaged during use. One major group of indirect use values is nonconsumptive use values of ecosystems. These include ecosystem productivity (important as the starting point for all food chains and carbon sequestration); protection of water resources and soils; regulation of local, regional, and global climates; waste treatment and nutrient retention; the enhancement of commercial crops by wild species; and recreation.

2. Biological diversity features prominently in the growing recreation and ecotourism industry. The number of people involved in nature recreation and the amount of money spent on such activities are surprisingly large. In many countries, particularly in the developing world, ecotourism represents one of the major sources of foreign income. Even in industrialized countries, the economy in areas around national parks is increasingly dominated by the recreation industry. Educational materials and the mass media draw heavily on themes of biological diversity and create materials of considerable value.

3. Biological diversity also has an option value in terms of its potential to provide future benefits to human society, such as new and improved medicines, biological control agents, and crops. The biotechnology industry is developing innovative techniques to take advantage of new chemicals and physiological properties found in the living world.

4. People are often willing to pay money in the form of taxes and voluntary contributions to ensure the continued existence of unique species, biological communities, and landscapes; this amount represents the existence value of biological diversity.

For Discussion

1. Consider the natural resources people use where you live. Can you place an economic value on those resources? If you can't think of any products harvested directly, consider basic ecosystem services such as flood control, fresh water, and soil retention.

2. Ask people how much money they spend on nature-related activities. Also ask them how much they would be willing to spend each year to protect well-known species, such as bald eagles, grizzly bears, and songbirds; to save a rare, endangered freshwater mussel; and to protect water quality and forest health. Multiply the average values by the number of people in your city, your country, or the world to obtain estimates as to how much these components of biological diversity are worth. Is this an accurate method for gauging the economic value of biodiversity? How might you improve this simple methodology?

3. Imagine that the only known population of a dragonfly species will be destroyed unless money can be raised to purchase the pond where it lives and the surrounding land. How much is this species worth? Consider different methods for assigning a monetary value to this species and compare the different outcomes. Which method is best?

Suggested Readings

Balmford, A., A. Bruner, P. Cooper, R. Costanza, S. Farber, R. E. Green, et al. 2003. Economic reasons for conserving wild nature. *Science* 297: 950–953. Ecosystem services often provide enormous economic benefits to society.

Buchmann, S. L. and G. P. Nabhan 1996. *The Forgotten Pollinators*. Island Press, Washington, D. C. Wild pollinators are crucial to agricultural production, as described in this wonderful book.

Carte, B. K. 1996. Biomedical potential of marine natural products. *BioScience* 46: 271–286. Describes search for valuable new chemicals in marine organisms, from bacteria to mollusks.

Chapin III, F. S., O. E. Sala, I. C. Burke, J. P. Grime, et al. 1998. Ecosystem consequences of changing biodiversity. *BioScience* 48: 45–52. Investigations throughout the world provide evidence that reduced species diversity lowers ecosystem productivity.

Costanza, R., R. d'Arge, R. de Gros, S. Farber, et al. 1997. The value of the world's ecosystem services and natural capital. *Nature* 387: 253–260. High-profile article by top ecological economists estimates the total ecosystem services worldwide as worth around $33 trillion a year.

Daily, G. C. and K. E. Ellison. 2002. *New Economy of Nature: The Quest to Make Conservation Profitable*. Island Press, Washington, D.C. Ways of providing increased funding for the protection of biodiversity.

Fearnside P. M. 2005. Deforestation in Brazilian Amazonia: history, rates, and consequences. *Conservation Biology* 19: 680–688. The transformation of the Amazon by human activities will have enormous economic and environmental consequences.

Harmon, D. and A. Putney (eds.). 2003. *The Full Value of Parks: From Economics to the Intangible*. Rownman & Littlefield Publishers, Inc., Oxford. Protected areas provide substantial economic benefits to society.

Jenkins, M., S. J. Scherr, and M. Inbar. 2004. Markets for biodiversity services: Potential roles and challenges. *Environment*: 33–42. Direct payments to landowners for absorbing and retaining carbon dioxide may provide incentives to protect ecosystems.

Kremen, C. and R. S. Ostefeld. 2005. A call to ecologists: measuring, analyzing and managing ecosystem services. *Frontiers in Ecology and the Environment* 10: 539–548. A good overview of the value of the natural world to human activities, especially agriculture.

Kruger, O. 2005. The role of ecotourism in conservation: Panacea or Pandora's Box? *Biodiversity and Conservation* 14: 579–600. Ecotourism may help to protect biodiversity, but it will not work everywhere and it has some serious drawbacks.

Mateo, N., W. Nader, and G. Tamayo. 2001. Bioprospecting. *In* S. A. Levin (ed.), *Encyclopedia of Biodiversity* Vol. 1, pp. 471–488. Academic Press, San Diego, CA. The best examples of bioprospecting are described, along with a summary of how the approach works.

Pimentel, D. C., L. Westra, and R. F. Noss (eds.). 2000a. *Ecological Integrity: Integrating Environment, Conservation, and Health.* Island Press, Washington, D.C. Investigates the linkages between conservation and social justice.

Plotkin, M. J. 1993. *Tales of a Shaman's Apprentice.* Viking/Penguin, New York. Vivid account of ethnobotanical exploration and efforts to preserve medical knowledge.

Svarstad, H., H. C. Bugge, and S. S. Dhillion. 2000. From Norway to Novartis: cyclosporine from *Tolypocladium inflatum* in an open access bioprospecting regime. *Biodiversity and Conservation* 9: 1521–1541. Without any collecting permit or permission, a biologist collected the soil sample that led to a new group of drugs worth over $1 billion in annual sales.

Tilman, D. 1999. The ecological consequences of change in biodiversity: A search for general principles. *Ecology* 80: 1455–1474. Mixture of field data, experiments, and models used to demonstrate relationships among biodiversity, stability, productivity, and susceptibility to invasion, with implications for management.

Wang, Z., B. Zhang, S. Zhang, X. Li, D. Liu, K. Song, et al. 2006. Changes of land use and of ecosystem service values in Sanjiang Plain, northeast China. *Environmental Monitoring and Assessment* 112: 69–91.

Zavaleta, E. S., and K. B. Hulvey. 2004. Realistic species losses disproportionately reduce grassland resistance to biological invaders. *Science* 306: 1175–1177. The loss of species will increase ecosystem vulnerability to invasive species.

Ethical Values

A s was discussed in Chapters 4 and 5, the new discipline of ecological economics provides positive arguments in support of conservation that can be put to use in the policy arena. Although such economic arguments can be advanced to justify the protection of biological diversity, there are also strong ethical arguments for doing so (Schmidtz and Willott 2001; Vandeveer and Pierce 2002). While economic arguments often are assumed to be more objective or more convincing, ethical arguments have unique power: They have foundations in the value systems of most religions and philosophies and are readily understood by the general public (McPhee 1971; Bassett 2000). They may appeal to a general respect for life; a reverence for nature or specific aspects of it; a sense of the beauty, fragility, uniqueness, or antiquity of the living world; or a belief in divine creation. Indeed, to many people, ethical arguments provide the most convincing reasons for conservation.

Ethical Values of Biological Diversity

Many hunter/gatherer and pastoral cultures have successfully coexisted with rich local flora and fauna for hundreds of years because their societal ethics encourage personal responsibility and thoughtful use of resources. People in these societies feel duty-bound to respect wild animals and plants even as they harvest them or "borrow" their habitat for human purposes. Traditional beliefs often treat rivers, mountains, and other ecosystems as sacred places to be approached with reverence and an appreciation for what they are, rather than for what human beings can make of them (Callicott 1994; Barnhill and Gottlieb 2001).

Even in Western industrial societies, ethical arguments can and do convince people to conserve biodiversity. For example, in the United States the right of all species to continue to exist is strongly protected under the Endangered Species Act, and a judge ruling in a major court decision stated "that Congress intended endangered species to be afforded the highest of priorities" (Rolston 1988). The E.S.A. states that the justification for this protection is the "aesthetic, ecological, educational, historical, recreational and scientific value" of species. As will be described in this chapter, the full range of ethical arguments includes many of these aspects of value. Significantly, economic value is not included in this legal rationale, and economic interests are explicitly stated to be of secondary importance when protecting species from extinction. According to the law, profits and economic values must be set aside when their pursuit threatens to extinguish a species. (The law does allow economic values to prevail in rare cases, but only if a so-called "God squad" of senior government officials rules that economic concerns are of overriding national interest.)

Ethical arguments are also important because although economic arguments by themselves provide a basis for valuing species (and biological communities), economic valuation can also provide grounds for extinguishing species or for saving one species and not another (Bulte and van Kooten 2001; Sagoff 2004). According to conventional economic thinking, a species with low population numbers, a limited geographical range, small physical size or unattractive appearance, no immediate use to people, and no relationship to any species of economic importance will be given a low value. Such qualities may characterize a substantial proportion of the world's species, particularly insects and other invertebrates, fungi, nonflowering plants, bacteria, and protists. Halting profitable developments or making costly attempts to preserve these species may not have any obvious economic justification. In fact, in some circumstances, economic justification could exist for destroying an endangered species, particularly an organism that causes disease or attacks crop plants.

Despite the economic justification, though, many people would make a case against species extinction on ethical grounds, arguing that the conscious destruction of a natural species is morally wrong, even if it is economically profitable. Similar arguments would be advanced for protecting unique biological communities and genetic variation. Ethical arguments for preserving biological diversity resonate with people because they appeal to our nobler instincts, which do play a role in societal decision-making. Human societies have often made decisions based more on ethical values than on economic ones. Outlawing slavery, limiting child labor, and preventing cruelty to animals are three examples. The linkages among environmental ethics, conservation, and social and economic justice have been incorporated into a unique and uncompromising document, The Earth Charter, put forward by Mikhail Gorbachev, the former President of the Soviet Union, and other world leaders (WRI 2003).

If modern society adopted values that strongly support preserving the natural environment and maintaining biological diversity, we could expect to see lower consumption of scarce resources, greater care in the use of those resources, and efforts to limit human population growth. Unfortunately, however, modern Western societies generally take a different view. While demanding that human beings treat one another ethically, their primary attitude toward nature is "anything goes"— people can use or destroy it as they see fit, as long as they do not harm human beings or take their property. In recent years, this attitude has been questioned. **Environmental ethics**, a vigorous new discipline within philosophy, has grown out of this questioning. It articulates a sense of the ethical value of the natural world (Armstrong and Botzler 2004; Primack and Cafaro 2001; Wenz 2001).

Ethical Arguments for Preserving Biological Diversity

Ethical arguments can form the basis for political action and changes in laws and corporate management (Minteer and Collins 2005). The following arguments, based on the intrinsic value of species and on our duties to other people, are important to conservation biology because they provide the rationale for protecting all species, including rare species and species of no obvious economic value.

EACH SPECIES HAS A RIGHT TO EXIST   All species represent unique biological solutions to the problem of survival. All are the living representatives of grand historical lineages, and all have their own beauty and fitness. For these reasons, the survival of each species must be guaranteed, regardless of its importance to humans. This statement is true whether the species is large or small, simple or complex, ancient or recently evolved; whether it is economically important or of little immediate economic value to humans; or whether it is loved or hated by humans (Box 6.1). Each species has value for its own sake—an **intrinsic value** unrelated to human needs or desires (Lee 1996; Agar 2001). This argument suggests not only that we have no right to destroy any species, but also that we have a moral responsibility to actively protect species from going extinct as the result of our activities. It recognizes

BOX 6.1

Sharks: A Feared Animal in Decline

■ Of the many plants and animals threatened by human exploitation, one of the least loved is the shark. Public perception of these animals is based almost entirely upon news reports of attacks on humans (which are actually quite rare; in the year 2000, only 79 shark attacks were confirmed worldwide, which resulted in 10 deaths) and gruesome media images that portray sharks as merciless, indiscriminate killers (e.g., the movies *Jaws, Finding Nemo,* and *Open Water*). For most people, a shark is little more than a terrifying triangular fin and a mouthful of very sharp teeth. For conservationists concerned with rapidly dwindling shark populations worldwide, the shark's bad reputation is a public relations nightmare. However, a recent international agreement to regulate trade in great white sharks is a major step in the right direction.

When we contrast the 10 people killed worldwide per year by sharks with the estimated 100 million sharks killed per year by people, it is clear that people, by far, are the more dangerous species (Lemonick 1997). Sharks actually help people far more than they harm them. For example, shark's liver oil was an important source of vitamin A until it was synthesized in 1947; it is also used in cosmetics and is highly effective at shrinking human hemorrhoids, and is widely used in medicines for that purpose. The chemical squalamine found in the internal organs of dogfish has the ability to inhibit the growth of

Shark fishing in Florida. These sharks were caught by vacationers on a pleasure cruise, displayed for photographs, and then discarded. (Photograph © Paige Chichester.)

certain brain tumors in humans, and shark cartilage is being used as an alternative treatment for kidney cancer. The immune system of sharks is being intensively studied to learn the secret of why sharks have an unusually low incidence of cancer even when experimentally exposed to known carcinogens, information that may

(continued)

BOX 6.1 *(continued)*

prove invaluable to humans in our battle against cancer (Raloff 2005). Their grace and power in the water, along with the medical benefits they provide or may provide in the future to people, would seem to warrant that sharks should be more appreciated by the public.

One quality that redeems these animals in the public eye is not one that encourages conservation: Sharks are a popular item on menus in Chinese restaurants. Shark fishing has become a booming business in the past decade. In Asia, shark-fin soup is a delicacy that has created high demand for several species of shark; dried shark fins may bring up to $300/kg (Fowler 2000; Clarke et al. 2006). At these prices, a single fin of the giant basking shark (also known as the whale shark) could bring up to $10,000. The cruel and wasteful practice called "finning," in which a captured shark is flung back into the water to die after its fins are amputated, has spurred some public sympathy for sharks and has led to a call for banning the practice. A more serious problem, however, is the tendency for sharks to become "by-catches" of commercial fishing using drift gill nets. More than half of the annual shark kills are related to accidental gill net catches; sharks caught in this manner are usually simply discarded.

High shark mortality has conservationists concerned for several reasons (Otway et al. 2004; Campana et al. 2005). Sharks mature very slowly, have long reproductive cycles, and produce only a few young at a time. Fish such as salmon (which have also been overharvested) can recover rapidly because of the large numbers of offspring they produce annually; sharks do not have this ability. A second problem is that harvesting of sharks by commercial and private fishing concerns is largely unregulated in many countries. Sharks are increasingly harvested for their meat, often used in fish-and-chips. Sharks are also targeted by sport fishermen because of their size and fierce reputation. A few countries, notably the United States, Australia, New Zealand, and Canada, have enacted legislation to stem shark losses, including

a ban on finning, but other countries involved in commercial shark fishing either see no need for action or are delaying proposed regulations. The recent bans on catching large coastal sharks in United States waters is a step in the right direction, but allowing continued harvesting of smaller individuals and open-ocean sharks may prevent vulnerable species from recovering to their original numbers.

Finally, the decimation of shark populations is occurring at a time when very little is known about more than a handful of individual species. Though more than 350 species of sharks exist, management proposals often treat all sharks as a single entity because, lacking specific information, management by species is impossible. Species in the heavily fished Atlantic Ocean that have been studied have demonstrated a precipitous decrease of 40 to 99% in the last 20 years (Baum et al. 2003; Baum and Myers 2004).

The decline of shark populations is a matter for concern in and of itself, but it is also an important factor in a larger problem. Sharks are among the most important predators in marine ecosystems; they feed upon a variety of organisms and are distributed throughout oceans, seas, and lakes worldwide. Terrestrial ecologists have already observed the benefits of predation for prey populations and the problems that occur when predators are removed from an ecosystem. The decline of sharks could have a significant, and possibly catastrophic, cascade effect upon marine ecosystems, allowing unwanted species to rapidly increase in numbers. Ironically, sharks have fulfilled their role for some 400 million years, making them one of the longest-lived groups of organisms on the planet; yet their future depends upon a change in human attitudes and perceptions. Conservationists have their work cut out for them. They must persuade world governments to look beyond the shark's terrifying aspect and act to preserve this diverse group of species that is vital to the health of the world's oceans.

humans are part of the larger biotic community and reminds us that we are not the center of the universe.

Robert Elliot (1992) suggests that wild nature has the following properties that show its intrinsic value: "diversity, stability, complexity, beauty, harmony, creativity, organization, intricacy, elegance, and richness." These qualities of natural organisms are ones that we can appreciate—and that call forth responses of personal restraint and active protection. In addition, "naturalness" itself might be seen as a valuable property, particularly in societies where wild nature is becoming more rare.

Opponents to this view counter that even though some people do value these qualities in nature, they are not morally required to do so (Ferry 1995). They argue that humans have a value beyond all other species' value, because only we are fully conscious, rational, and moral beings, and unless our actions affect other people, directly or indirectly, any treatment of the natural world is morally acceptable. It might seem strange to assign rights of existence and legal protection to nonhuman species, especially simple organisms, when they lack the self-awareness that we usually associate with the morality of rights and duties. How can a lowly moss or fungus have rights when it doesn't even have a nervous system? However, whether or not we allow them rights, species carry great value as the repositories of the accumulated experience and history of millions of previous life forms through their continuous, evolutionary adaptation to a changing environment (Rolston 2000). The premature extinction of a species due to human activities destroys this history and could be regarded as a "superkilling" (Rolston 1989) because it kills future generations of the species and eliminates the processes of evolution and speciation.

Other writers, especially many animal rights activists, have difficulty assigning rights to species, even if they value the rights of individual animals (Regan 2004). Singer (1979), for one, argues that "species as such are not conscious entities and so do not have interests above and beyond the interest of individual animals that are members of a species." However, Rolston (1994) counters that on both biological and ethical grounds, species, rather than individual organisms, are the appropriate targets of conservation efforts. All individuals eventually die; it is the species that continues, evolves, and sometimes forms new species. In a sense, individuals are temporary representatives of species, thus species are more important than individuals.

This focus on species challenges the modern Western ethical tradition of individualism. But the preservation of biodiversity seems to demand that the needs of endangered species take precedence over the needs of individuals. For example, the U.S. National Park Service killed hundreds of rabbits on Santa Barbara Island to protect a few plants of the endangered species Santa Barbara live-forever (*Dudleya traskiae*); in this case, one endangered plant species was judged to be more valuable than hundreds of individual animals of a common species (Figure 6.1).

ALL SPECIES ARE INTERDEPENDENT   Species interact in complex ways in natural communities. The loss of one species may have far-reaching consequences for other members of the community (Chapin et al. 2000; Tilman 2000): other species may become extinct in response, or the entire community may become destabilized as the result of cascades of species extinctions. For these reasons, if we value some parts of nature, we should protect all of nature. We are obligated to conserve the system as a whole because that is the appropriate survival unit (Rolston 2000; Aron and Patz 2001). Even if we only value human beings, our instincts toward self-preservation should impel us to preserve biodiversity. When the natural world prospers, we prosper. When the natural world is harmed, people suffer from widespread health problems—such as asthma, food poisoning, waterborne diseases, and cancer—that are caused or aggravated by environmental pollution.

FIGURE 6.1 Government agencies judged the continued existence of the endangered plant Santa Barbara live-forever (*Dudleya traskiae;* the tall plant at left) to be more valuable than the common rabbits on its island home. The rabbits, which fed on the plant's fleshy leaves (shown at the bottom right), were killed to stop their destruction of this fragile plant species. (Photograph by the U.S. National Park Service.)

In a colorful metaphor, Ehrlich and Ehrlich (1981) imagine that species are rivets holding together the "Earthship," which carries all species, including humans, in its travel through time. Species extinctions are like rivets popping out of the ship. While lost species may be more or less important, when enough species go extinct, the Earthship will crash, and all species on board will be harmed. This presents a new twist on the original Bible story, in which Noah built an ark at God's instruction to preserve each species. In this metaphor, the species (as rivets) prevent the Earthship/ark from crashing. Instead of people saving biodiversity, biodiversity saves people.

PEOPLE HAVE A RESPONSIBILITY TO ACT AS STEWARDS OF THE EARTH   Many religious adherents find it wrong to destroy species, because they are God's creations. If God created the world, then presumably the species God created have value. Within the Jewish and Christian traditions, human responsibility for protecting animal species is explicitly described in the Bible as part of the covenant with God. The Book of Genesis describes the creation of the Earth's biological diversity as a divine act, after which "God saw that it was good" and "blessed them." In the story of Noah's Ark, God commanded Noah to save two of all species, not just the ones human beings found useful. God provided detailed instructions for building the ark, an early species rescue project, saying "Keep them alive with

---

BOX 6.2

Religion and Conservation

In September 1986, an interfaith ceremony was held in the Basilica of St. Francis, in Assisi, Italy. It included "Declarations on Nature" by representatives of the five participating religions—Buddhism, Christianity, Hinduism, Islam, and Judaism. For the first time in history, leaders of these faiths declared that their religions mandate the conservation of nature. Excerpts from the five declarations follow.*

THE BUDDHIST DECLARATION ON NATURE
Venerable Lungrig Namgyal Rinpoche, Abbot, Gyuto Tantric University

The simple underlying reason why beings other than humans need to be taken into account is that, like human beings, they too are sensitive to happiness and suffering ... Many have held up usefulness to human beings as the sole criterion for the evaluation of an animal's life. Upon closer examination, one discovers that this mode of evaluation of another's life and right to existence has also been largely responsible for human indifference as well as cruelty to animals.

We regard our survival as an undeniable right. As co-inhabitants of this planet, other species too have this right for survival. And since human beings as well as

other non-human sentient beings depend upon the environment as the ultimate source of life and wellbeing, let us share the conviction that the conservation of the environment, the restoration of the imbalance caused by our negligence in the past, be implemented with courage and determination.

THE CHRISTIAN DECLARATION ON NATURE
Father Lanfranco Serrini, Minister General, Order of Friars Minor (Franciscans)

To praise the Lord for his creation is to confess that God the Father made all things visible and invisible; it is to thank him for the many gifts he bestows on all his children. . . . By reason of its created origin, each creature according to its species and all together in the harmonious unity of the universe manifest God's infinite truth and beauty, love and goodness, wisdom and majesty, glory and power.

Man's dominion cannot be understood as license to abuse, spoil, squander or destroy what God has made to manifest his glory. That dominion cannot be anything other than a stewardship in symbiosis with all creatures... Every human act of irresponsibility towards creatures is an abomination. According to its gravity, it is an offence against that divine wisdom which sustains and gives purpose to the interdependent harmony of the universe.

---

*Text excerpts from World Wildlife Fund, 1999; used with permission. Art from Bassett, 2000; used with permission.

you." The prophet Muhammad, founder of Islam, continued this theme of human responsibility: "The world is green and beautiful and God has appointed you as His stewards over it. He sees how you acquit yourselves." Belief in the value of God's creation supports a stewardship argument for preserving biodiversity: Human beings have been given responsibility for God's creation and must preserve, not destroy, what they have been given.

Other religious traditions also support the preservation of nature (Callicott 1994; Bassett 2000; Science and Spirit 2001). For example, Hinduism locates divinity in certain animals, and recognizes a basic kinship between humans and other beings (including the transmigration of souls from one species to another). A primary ethical concept in Hinduism and other Indian religions, such as Jainism and Buddhism, is *ahimsa*—nonviolence or kindness to all life. To live by this ideal, many religious people become vegetarians and live as simply as possible. Of course, some religions articulate views that put human beings at the center of creation, supporting a domineering attitude toward nature. Since many people base their ethical values on a religious faith, the development of religious arguments in support of conservation might be effective in motivating people to conserve biodiversity (Oelschlaeger 1994; Chapple and Tucker 2000; Foltz et al. 2003; Yaffe 2001; Wirzba 2003). Speakers for many major religions, in fact, have stated that their faiths mandate the conservation of nature (Box 6.2).

BOX 6.2 *(continued)*

THE HINDU DECLARATION ON NATURE
Dr. Karan Singh, President, Hindu Virat Samaj

The Hindu viewpoint on nature is permeated by a reverence for life, and an awareness that the great forces of nature—the earth, the sky, the air, the water and fire—as well as various orders of life including plants and trees, forests and animals, are all bound to each other within the great rhythms of nature. The divine is not exterior to creation, but expresses itself through natural phenomena. The *Mahabharata* says that 'even if there is only one tree full of flowers and fruits in a village, that place becomes worthy of worship and respect.'

Let us declare our determination to halt the present slide towards destruction, to rediscover the ancient tradition of reverence for all life and, even at this late hour, to reverse the suicidal course upon which we have embarked. Let us recall the ancient Hindu dictum: 'The Earth is our mother, and we are all her children.'

THE MUSLIM DECLARATION ON NATURE
Dr. Abdullah Omar Nasseef, Secretary General, Muslim World League

The essence of Islamic teaching is that the entire universe is God's creation. Allah makes the waters flow upon the earth, upholds the heavens, makes the rain fall and keeps the boundaries between day and night … It is God who created the plants and the animals in their pairs and gave them the means to multiply.

For the Muslim mankind's role on earth is that of a *khalifa*, viceregent or trustee of God. We are God's stewards and agents on Earth. We are not masters of this Earth; it does not belong to us to do what we wish. It belongs to God and He has entrusted us with its safekeeping …The *khalifa* is answerable for his/her actions, for the way in which he/she uses or abuses the trust of God.

THE JEWISH DECLARATION ON NATURE
Rabbi Arthur Hertzberg, Vice President, World Jewish Congress

The encounter of God and man in nature is conceived in Judaism as a seamless web with man as the leader and custodian of the natural world … Now, when the whole world is in peril, when the environment is in danger of being poisoned and various species, both plant and animal, are becoming extinct, it is our Jewish responsibility to put the defense of the whole of nature at the very centre of our concern.

We have a responsibility to life, to defend it everywhere, not only against our own sins but also against those of others. We are all passengers together in this same fragile and glorious world. Let us safeguard our rowboat—and let us row together.

PEOPLE HAVE A DUTY TO THEIR NEIGHBORS   Humans must be careful to minimize damage to their natural environment because such damage not only harms other species, it harms people as well. Much of the pollution and environmental degradation occurring today is unnecessary and could be minimized with better planning. Our duty to other humans requires us to live within sustainable limits (Norton 2003). This goal can be achieved by people in the industrialized countries taking strong actions to reduce their excessive and disproportionate consumption of natural resources. Why does an average person living in the United States or Canada use 9 times more energy per year than a person living in China, or 17 times more than a person living in India? If such energy use is not curbed, global warming could devastate low-lying areas from Bangladesh to the Mississippi Delta, with poor people bearing most of the harm. The government of the United States, where less than five percent of the world population uses twenty-five percent of the world's energy, has emerged as the primary opponent to international efforts to forestall global warming. But it is immoral for the government of the United States to avoid serious action on global warming when their inaction risks the lives and livelihoods of their poor neighbors at home and abroad (Brown 2002).

PEOPLE HAVE A RESPONSIBILITY TO FUTURE GENERATIONS   If in our daily living we degrade the natural resources of the Earth and cause species to become extinct, future generations will pay the price in terms of a lower standard of living and quality of life (Ellison 2003a). As species are lost and wild lands developed, children are deprived of one of the most exciting experiences in growing up—the wonder of seeing "new" animals and plants in the wild. Rolston (1995) predicts, "[I]t is safe to say that in the decades ahead, the quality of life will decline in proportion to the loss of biotic diversity, though it is often thought that one must sacrifice biotic diversity to improve human life." To remind us to act more responsibly, we might imagine that we are borrowing the Earth from future generations who expect to get it back in good condition.

RESPECT FOR HUMAN LIFE AND HUMAN DIVERSITY IS COMPATIBLE WITH A RESPECT FOR BIOLOGICAL DIVERSITY   Some people worry that recognizing an intrinsic value in nature requires taking resources and opportunities away from human beings. But a respect for biological diversity can be linked to greater opportunities for people (Kellert and Wilson 1993; Kelly 1994). Some of the most exciting developments in conservation biology involve supporting the economic development of disadvantaged rural people in ways that are linked to the protection of biological diversity. Helping poor people establish sustainable plots of cash crops and achieve a degree of economic independence sometimes reduces the need to overharvest wild species. Working with indigenous people to establish legal title to their land gives them the means to protect the biological communities in which they live, even though they may not choose to do so in practice. In developed countries, the environmental justice movement seeks to empower poor and politically weak people, who are often members of minority groups, to protect their own environment; in the process their well-being and the protection of biological diversity are enhanced. Working for the social and political benefit of poor and powerless people is compatible with efforts to preserve the natural environment (Westra and Lawson 2001).

Human maturity often leads to self-restraint and a respect for others. Environmentalists have argued that the further maturation of the human species will involve an "identification with all life forms" and "the acknowledgment of [their] intrinsic value" (Naess 1986). They envision an expanding circle of moral obligations, moving outward from oneself to include duties to relatives, local communities, one's nation, all humanity, animals, all species, ecosystems, and ultimately the whole Earth (Figure 6.2).

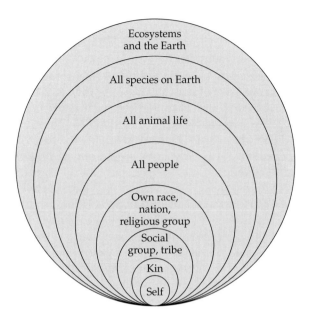

FIGURE 6.2 Environmental ethics holds that an individual has an expanding set of moral obligations, extending outward beyond the self to progressively more inclusive levels. (From Noss 1992.)

Actions taken to protect species and biological communities should, whenever possible, benefit people as well. Conservation biologists need to be sensitive to the public perception that they care *more* about birds, turtles, or nature in general than they do about people. In some situations, protecting biological diversity may be incompatible with promoting human needs or human cultures. For example, if a tribe needed to hunt the last remaining individuals of an endangered animal to maintain its way of life, environmental protection would demand real sacrifices from that tribe (Davradou and Namkoong 2001). In such a situation, the need to preserve a species from extinction should trump all other considerations.

Some people argue that recognizing an intrinsic value in nature leads to absurdity. Because we must use nature, they say, we cannot recognize its intrinsic value, since by definition that would limit the ways in which we use it. Even people who are sympathetic to environmentalism and appreciate wild nature often resist granting it intrinsic value since this demands so much. If nature is wonderful and complex, as science and our own experiences tell us it is, how can we go on using it? But we must do so to survive. In addition, the world is already filled with rules limiting our actions; adding another layer is tiresome. Finally, since so many modern lifestyles (especially in the developed world) depend to such a large extent on an ecologically destructive economic system, many despair of protecting the world and give up trying to live in an environmentally responsible manner.

These are legitimate concerns. Still, effective action to protect biological diversity is both possible and desirable (Schmidtz 2005). First, it is possible to use natural resources in a respectful and limited way: *It is necessary to use nature, but not all use of nature is necessary.* Second, while no one likes more rules, growing up and living moral lives involves recognizing our duty to others. Finally, it is possible to live in an environmentally responsible manner even in industrialized countries: it requires making a personal commitment to use less resources, have less of an impact on the environment, and help to change society in a positive manner. If nature does in fact have intrinsic value, we should respect that value—whether doing so is convenient or not.

Enlightened Self-Interest: Biodiversity and Human Development

Economic arguments stress that preserving biological diversity *is in our material self-interest*. Ethical arguments based on the intrinsic value of wild nature and our duties to others stress that we should act altruistically toward nature *regardless of our material self-interest*. A second ethical framework appeals to our *enlightened self-interest,* arguing that preserving biodiversity and developing our knowledge of it will make us better and happier people (Kellert 1996; Van Wensveen 2000; Sandler and Cafaro 2005). The following points describe how protecting biological diversity is in our enlightened self-interest.

PROTECTING OUR LIFE-SUPPORT SYSTEMS AND OUR ECONOMY   It cannot be repeated too often that biological diversity preserves our basic life-support systems of food production, water supply, oxygen replenishment, waste disposal, soil conservation, and more. People will be healthier and happier in a clean, intact environment. We depend on this and should value it. In addition to providing life-support, biodiversity allows us to create tremendous economic wealth, directly and indirectly, as detailed in Chapters 4 and 5.

FIGURE 6.3 Rare wildflowers and butterflies are the inspiration for botanical sculptor Patrick O'Hara. In his studio in western Ireland, O'Hara molds, sculpts, and paints delicate porcelain scenes from nature that inspire an appreciation of conservation in a worldwide audience. (Photograph courtesy of Patrick O'Hara.)

AESTHETIC AND RECREATIONAL ENJOYMENT   Nearly everyone enjoys wildlife and landscapes aesthetically, and joy increases the quality of our lives. Nature-related activities are important in childhood development (Kahn and Kellert 2002; Thomashow 2002). The beauty of a field of wildflowers in Glacier National Park or a migrating warbler on a spring morning in a city park enriches people's lives. And for many people, experiencing nature means experiencing it in an undisturbed setting— simply reading about species or seeing them in museums, gardens, and zoos does not suffice. Recreational activities such as hiking, canoeing, and mountain climbing are physically, intellectually, and emotionally satisfying. People spend tens of billions of dollars annually in these pursuits, proof enough of their value.

ARTISTIC AND LITERARY EXPRESSION   Throughout history, poets, writers, painters, and musicians of all cultures have drawn inspiration from wild nature (Leopold 1949; Burks 1994; Howarth 2001). Nature provides countless forms and symbols for painters and sculptors to render and interpret (Figure 6.3). Poets have often found their greatest inspiration in either wild nature or pastoral countryside. Preserving biological diversity preserves possibilities for all artists. It also allows those of us who appreciate such creativity access to the sources and experiences that inspire great artists. A loss in biological diversity could very well limit the creative energies of people in the future and thus restrict the development of human culture. For instance, if many species of whales, butterflies, and orchids go extinct in the next few decades, whole sets of imagery will be lost to the direct experience of future generations of artists.

SCIENTIFIC KNOWLEDGE   Science and our growing knowledge of nature are among humanity's greatest achievements. This knowledge is facilitated by the preservation of wild nature. Wild areas allow the study of natural ecological interactions. Wild species preserve the record of evolution. Young people are inspired to become scientists by personal contacts with wild nature (Carson 1998), and those who do not become professional scientists can apply their basic knowledge of science to understanding their own local fields, forests, and streams (Orr 1994).

Three of the central mysteries in the world of science are how life originated, how the diversity of life found on Earth today came about, and how humans evolved. Thousands of biologists are working on these problems and are coming ever closer to the answers. New techniques of molecular biology allow greater insight into the relationships of living species as well as some extinct species, which are known to us only from fossils. However, when species become extinct, important clues are lost, and the mysteries become harder to solve. For example, if *Homo sapiens'* closest living relatives—chimpanzees, bonobos, gorillas, and orangutans—disappear from the wild, we will lose important clues regarding human physical and social evolution (Whiten and Boesch 2001).

HISTORICAL UNDERSTANDING   Knowing nature, both scientifically and through personal experience, is key to an understanding of human history (Thomashow 1996): In walking the landscapes our ancestors walked, we gain insight into how they experienced the world at a slower pace and without mechanized aids. We often forget just how recently humankind has moved to ultrafast transportation, fully illuminated cities that shut out the night, and other aspects of modern life. We need to preserve natural areas in order to develop our historical imaginations.

RELIGIOUS INSPIRATION   Many religions have traditions of "wandering in the wilderness" in order to commune with God or with spirits and to "purify" themselves of the temptations and evils associated with life within human communities. From the Judeo-Christian tradition, Moses, Isaiah, St. John the Baptist, St. Francis of Assisi, and even Jesus, all sought out the solitude of wilderness to obtain spiritual strength and receive the guidance of God. Generations of Sioux, Ute, and Cheyenne vision seekers have done the same, albeit in accordance with different traditions. Being in nature allows us to clear and focus our minds and, sometimes, experience the transcendent. When we are surrounded by the artifacts of civilization, our minds stay fully focused on human purposes and our everyday lives. Religion probably would not disappear from an environment totally tamed by humans, but it might become diluted for many (Kellert and Farnham 2002).

Deep Ecology

Recognition of both the economic value and the intrinsic value of biological diversity leads to new limits on human action. This can make it seem like conservation is simply a never-ending list of "thou shalt nots," but many environmentalists believe that an understanding of our true self-interest would lead to a different conclusion:

> The crisis of life conditions on Earth could help us choose a new path with new criteria for progress, efficiency, and rational action. . . . The ideological change is mainly that of appreciating life quality rather than adhering to a high standard of living (Naess 1989).

In the past 200 years, the Industrial Revolution, with its accompanying technological advances and social changes, has generated tremendous material wealth and improved the lives of millions of people. But the law of diminishing returns seems to apply: For many in the developed world, heaping up further wealth at the expense of life quality makes little sense (Thoreau 1971; Segal 1999; Lane 2000). Similarly, the continued loss of biodiversity and taming of the natural landscape will not improve people's lives. What is being lost is unique and increasingly more precious as monetary wealth increases and opportunities to experience nature diminish. Human happiness and human development require preserving our remaining biodiversity, not sacrificing it for increased individual or corporate wealth.

During the twentieth century, ecologists, nature writers, religious leaders, and philosophers have increasingly articulated an appreciation of nature and have spoken of the need for changes in human lifestyles in order to protect it. Paul Sears, recognizing that a true belief in the value of nature would lead to questioning the destructive practices that are common in modern society and often taken for granted, called ecology a "subversive science." In the 1960s and 1970s, Paul Ehrlich and Barry Commoner demonstrated that professional biologists and academics could use their knowledge of environmental issues to create and lead political movements to protect species and ecosystems. Today religious leaders are revitalizing their followers with calls to combine social activism with environmental protection. Political movements such as these, Green political parties in Europe, and activist conservation organizations such as Greenpeace and EarthFirst! now exist throughout the world.

One well-developed environmental philosophy that supports this activism is known as **deep ecology** (Naess 1989; Sessions 1995; Witoszek and Brennan 1999). Deep ecology builds on the basic premise of biocentric equality, which expresses "the intuition . . . that all things in the biosphere have an equal right to live and blossom and to reach their own individual forms of unfolding" (Devall and Sessions 1985). Humans have a right to live and thrive, as do the other organisms with whom we share the planet. Deep ecologists oppose what they see as the dominant worldview, which places human concerns above all and views human happiness in materialistic terms (Table 6.1) (Shi 1985; McLaughlin 1993).

Deep ecologists see acceptance of the intrinsic value of nature less as a limitation than as an opportunity to live better lives. Because present human activities are destroying the Earth's biological diversity, existing political, economic, technological, and ideological structures must change. These changes entail enhancing the life quality of all people—emphasizing improvements in environmental quality, aesthetics, culture, and spirituality rather than higher levels of material consumption. Improving adult literacy, organizing active nature hiking, birdwatching, and natural history clubs, encouraging people to have healthier lifestyles, and lobbying

TABLE 6.1 *A comparison of beliefs of the dominant world view and those of deep ecology*

Dominant worldview	Deep ecology
Humans dominate nature	Humans live in harmony with nature
Natural environment and species are resources for humans	All nature has intrinsic worth, regardless of human needs
A growing human population with a rising standard of living	A stable human population living simply
Earth's resources are unlimited	Earth's resources are limited and must be used carefully
Ever-higher technology brings progress and solutions	Appropriate technology must be used with respect for the Earth
Emphasizes material progress	Emphasizes spiritual and ethical progress
Strong central government	Local control, organized according to ecosystems or bioregions

to reduce air pollution and sprawling development are some practical examples. The philosophy of deep ecology includes an obligation to work to implement needed programs through political activism and a commitment to personal lifestyle changes, in the process transforming the institutions in which we work, study, pray, and shop. Professional biologists, ecologists, and all concerned people (such as you?) are urged to escape from their narrow, everyday concerns and act and live "as if nature mattered" (Naess 1989).

Summary

1. Protecting biological diversity can be justified on ethical grounds as well as on economic grounds. The value systems of most religions, philosophies, and cultures provide justifications for preserving species. These justifications even support the protection of species that have no obvious economic or aesthetic value to people.

2. The most central ethical arguments assert that humans have a duty to protect species, biological communities, and other aspects of biodiversity based on their intrinsic value, unrelated to human needs. People do not have the right to destroy species and should take action to prevent their extinction.

3. Species, rather than individual organisms, are the appropriate target for conservation efforts; it is the species that evolves and undergoes speciation, whereas individuals are temporary representatives of the species.

4. Species interact in complex ways in biological communities. The loss of one species may have far-reaching negative consequences to that biological community and to human society.

5. People must learn to live within the ecological constraints of the planet, minimize environmental damage, and take responsibility for their actions, since they may harm humans as well as other species. People also have a responsibility to future generations to keep the Earth in good condition.

6. Protecting nature is in our enlightened self-interest. Biological diversity has provided generations of writers, artists, musicians, and religious thinkers with inspiration. A loss of species and natural areas cuts people off from this wellspring of creative experience and impoverishes human culture. It also curtails recreational enjoyment, scientific knowledge, and self-understanding.

7. Deep ecology is a philosophy that advocates major changes in the way society functions in order to protect biological diversity and promote genuine human growth. Advocates of this philosophy are committed to personal lifestyle changes and political activism in the environmental movement.

For Discussion

1. Do living creatures, species, biological communities, and physical entities, such as rivers, lakes, and mountains, have rights? Can we treat them any way we please? Where should we draw the line of moral responsibility?

2. Do human beings have a duty toward individual animals, most of which lack self-awareness, and toward plants, which lack a nervous system? Toward species of plants and animals? Biological communities? Mountains and streams? If so, what is the source of this duty? What is the sort of protection or respectful use appropriate for each of these groups?

3. What role does the consumption of resources, physical pleasure, the search for knowledge, artistic expression, recreation, and amusement play in your life? What role should it play in human life in general? Does the preservation of biodiversity set limits on these human activities, or is it a prerequisite for our continued enjoyment of them?

4. What is your own environmental ethic? What is the source of your ethic? Reason? Emotion? Faith? Does it affect your life in any important way? Is it easy or hard to live up to?

5. If your house were on fire, you would try to rescue every family member inside. If even one person died, you would be devastated. Should we try to save every species threatened with extinction? Is the comparison valid?

6. Suppose the proposed management plan for one endangered species threatens the existence of a second endangered species. How can we decide on which course of action to take?

Suggested Readings

Burks, D. C. (ed.). 1994. *Place of the Wild: A Wildlands Anthology.* Island Press/ Shearwater Books, Washington, D.C. Leading advocates for wilderness protection reflect on the meaning and value of wilderness.

Callicott, J. B. 1994. *Earth's Insights: A Multicultural Survey of Ecological Ethics from the Mediterranean Basin to the Australian Outback.* University of California Press, Berkeley, CA. Comparison of the environmental ethics of religions throughout the world, including conceptions of nature and the value given to nonhuman beings.

Carson, R. L. 1998. *A Sense of Wonder.* Harper Collins, New York. Rachel Carson's final book is an eloquent plea for adults to teach children about the natural world.

Clarke, S. C., J. E. Magnussen, D. L. Abercrombie, M. K. Mcallister, and M. S. Shivji. 2006. Identification of shark species composition and proportion in the Hong Kong shark fin market based on molecular genetics and trade records. *Conservation Biology* 20: 201–211. DNA technology is helping to identify the species from which shark fins are being taken.

Kahn, P. H., Jr. and S. R. Kellert (eds.). 2002. *Children and Nature: Psychological, Sociocultural, and Evolutionary Investigations.* The MIT Press, Cambridge, MA. Exposure to nature benefits children in many ways.

Kellert, S. R. 1996. *The Value of Life: Biological Diversity and Human Society.* Island Press/Shearwater Books, Washington, D.C. Insightful examination of people's attitudes toward biological diversity, as affected by class, ethnicity, sex, and nationality; also, eloquent statement of the importance of biodiversity to human happiness.

Leopold, A. 1949. *A Sand County Almanac.* Strong statement for the beauty and value of nature, and the many benefits that accrue for protecting it.

Leopold, A. C. 2004. Living with the land ethic. *BioScience.* 54: 149–154. An update of Leopold's ideas.

McPhee, J. 1971. *Encounters with the Archdruid.* Farrar, Straus, and Giroux, New York. Unique book describing an exchange of ideas between the leader of the Sierra Club and real-estate developers and mining engineers during wilderness backpacking trips.

Minteer, B. A. and J. P. Collins. 2005. Ecological ethics: Building a new tool kit for ecologists and biodiversity managers. *Conservation Biology* 1803–1812. Ethical issues arise when managers need to control non-native animal populations.

Naess, A. 1989. *Ecology, Community, and Lifestyle: Outline of an Ecosophy.* Cambridge University Press, Cambridge. Good explanation of, and argument for, deep ecology, by a leading proponent.

Rolston III, H. 1994. *Conserving Natural Value.* Columbia University Press, New York. A leading environmental philosopher lays out the ethical arguments for preserving biological diversity.

Schmidtz, D. and E. Willott (eds.). 2001. *Environmental Ethics: What Really Matters, What Really Works.* Oxford University Press, New York. Sixty-two selections, from classic articles to cutting-edge original research, that explore the principal issues in environmental ethics.

Scully, M. 2002. *Dominion: The Power of Man, the Suffering of Animals, and the Call to Mercy.* St. Martin's Press, New York. A powerful Christian statement on the obligations humans owe animals written by a former speechwriter for President George W. Bush.

Shi, D. E. 1985. *The Simple Life: Plain Living and High Thinking.* Oxford University Press, New York. Traces the many ways Americans have pursued the ideal of simple yet rich living, from the Puritans and Quakers to Thoreau and modern back-to-the land philosophies.

Thomashow, M. 1996. *Ecological Identity: Becoming a Reflective Environmentalist.* The MIT Press, Cambridge, MA. Through discussion and participatory learning, the author provides concerned teachers and students the tools needed to become reflective environmentalists.

Thoreau, H. D. 1971 [1854]. *Walden.* More than one hundred and fifty years after its publication, still the most eloquent and comprehensive brief for protecting nature.

Van Wensveen, L. 2000. *Dirty Virtues: The Emergence of Ecological Virtue Ethics.* Prometheus, New York. Provocative book that draws a strong connection between a healthy environment and human flourishing.

Wirtzba, N. 2003. *The Paradise of God: Renewing Religion in an Ecological Age.* Oxford University Press, New York. A delightful, imaginative book that seeks to reshape Christian thought and practice.

PART

III

Threats to Biological Diversity

Extinction

We live at a historic moment, a time in which the world's biological diversity is being rapidly destroyed. The present geological period has more species than any other, yet the current rate of extinction of species is greater now than at any time in the past. Ecosystems and communities are being degraded and destroyed, and species are being driven to extinction. The species that persist are losing genetic variation as the number of individuals in populations shrinks, unique populations and subspecies are destroyed, and remaining populations become increasingly isolated from one another.

The cause of this loss of biological diversity at all levels is the range of human activity that alters and destroys natural habitats to suit human needs. At present, approximately 40%, and perhaps as much as 55%, of the net primary productivity of the terrestrial environment—roughly 25% of the total primary productivity of the world—is used or wasted in some way by people (Vitousek et al. 1997; Haberl et al. 2002). Genetic variation is being lost even in domesticated species, such as wheat, corn, rice, chickens, cattle, and pigs, as farmers abandon traditional agriculture. In the United States, about 97% of the vegetable varieties that were once cultivated are now extinct (Cherfas 1993). In tropical countries, farmers are abandoning their local varieties in favor of high-yielding varieties for commercial sale. This loss of variability among food plants and animals, and its implications for world agriculture, are discussed further in Chapters 14 and 20.

FIGURE 7.1 Bachman's warbler (*Vermivora bachmanii*), last seen in the 1960s, is an example of a Neotropical songbird that became extinct as a result of tropical deforestation in its wintering grounds. The Cuban forests in which this species overwintered were almost entirely cleared for sugarcane fields. The warbler is shown in this Audubon print with the flowering Franklin tree (*Franklinia altamaha*). The tree is now extinct in the wild, although it can still be found in arboretums and other cultivated gardens. (By John James Audubon; photograph from the Ewel Stewart Library, The Academy of Natural Sciences of Philadelphia.)

E. O. Wilson, one of the leading advocates of conservation biology, has argued that the most serious aspect of environmental damage is the extinction of species. Biological communities can be degraded, reduced in area, and their value to people lessened, but as long as all of the original species survive, communities retain the potential to recover. Similarly, genetic variation within a species is reduced when population size drops, but species can regain genetic variation through mutation, natural selection, and recombination. Unfortunately, once a species is eliminated, the unique genetic information contained in its DNA and the special combination of characters that it possesses are forever lost—its populations cannot be restored, the communities that it inhabited become impoverished, and its potential value to humans will never be realized.

The word "extinct" has many nuances and can vary somewhat depending on the context. A species is **extinct** when no member of the species remains alive anywhere in the world: "Bachman's warbler is extinct" (Figure 7.1). If individuals of a species remain alive only in captivity or in other human-controlled situations, the species is said to be **extinct in the wild**: "The Franklin tree is extinct in the wild but grows well under cultivation." In both of these situations the species are also considered to be **globally extinct**. A species is **locally extinct** or **extirpated** when it is no longer found in an area it once inhabited but is still found elsewhere in the wild: "The gray wolf once occurred throughout North America; it is now locally extinct in Massachusetts." A species may also be considered **regionally extinct** if it is extinct in a country or region, but still persists in another part of its range. Some conservation biologists speak of a species being **ecologically extinct** if it persists at such reduced numbers that its effects on the other species in its community are negligible (Sekercioglu et al. 2004): "Tigers are ecologically extinct because so few remain in the wild that their impact on prey populations is insignificant." In order to successfully maintain species, conservation biologists must identify the human activities that affect the stability of populations and drive species to extinction.

Past Mass Extinctions

The diversity of species found on the Earth has been increasing since life first originated. This increase has not been steady; rather, it has been characterized by periods of high rates of speciation followed by periods of minimal change and episodes of mass extinction (Raup 1992; Lövei 2001). This pattern is visible in the fossil record, which has been examined by scientists interested in determining the number of species and families in particular geological periods.

The evolutionary history of marine animals is better studied than terrestrial organisms because they often have hard body parts that are preserved in rocks formed from marine sediments. Marine animals first arose about 600 million years ago during the Paleozoic era. According to the fossil record, new families of marine animals appeared in rapid and steady succession during the next 150 million years. For the 200 million years that followed, the number of families was more or less constant at around 400. For the last 250 million years of the Mesozoic and Cenozoic eras, the diversity of families has steadily increased to its present number of over 700 families (Figure 7.2). The fossil record of marine animals demonstrates the slow pace of evolution, with new families appearing at a rate of roughly one per million years.

In addition to this overall increase in the number of animal families there have been five episodes of mass extinction in the fossil record, occurring at intervals ranging from 60 to 155 million years in length (Figure 7.3). These episodes, which occurred during the Ordovician, Devonian, Permian, Triassic, and Cretaceous periods, could be called "natural mass extinctions." The most famous is the extinction of the

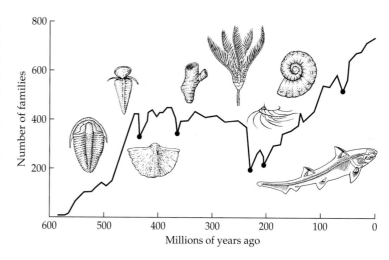

FIGURE 7.2 The number of families of marine organisms has been gradually increasing over geological time; this graph of their history clearly shows evidence of five episodes of mass extinction. (After Wilson 1989.)

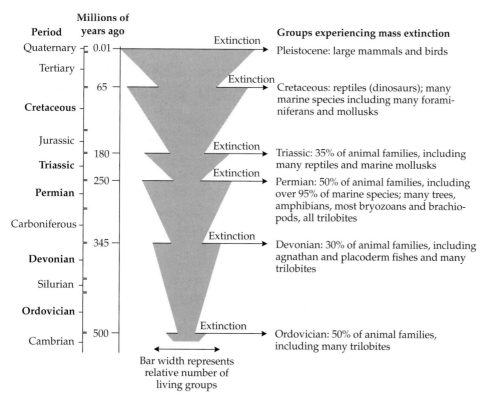

FIGURE 7.3 Although the total number of families and species of organisms has increased over the eons, during each of five episodes of natural mass extinction a large percentage of these groups disappeared. The most dramatic period of loss occurred about 250 million years ago, at the end of the Permian period. A sixth episode, beginning around 30,000 years ago up to the present time, incorporates the effects of hunting and habitat loss as human populations have spread across the continents.

dinosaurs during the late Cretaceous, 65 million years ago, after which mammals achieved dominance in terrestrial communities. The most massive extinction took place at the end of the Permian, 250 million years ago, when 77 to 96% of all marine animal species are estimated to have gone extinct, as well as half of all extant families of animals (Benton and Twitchett 2003). David Raup (1979) observed: "If these estimates are even reasonably accurate, global biology (for higher organisms at least) had an extremely close call." It is quite likely that some massive perturbation, such as widespread volcanic eruptions, a collision with an asteroid, or both, caused the dramatic change in the Earth's climate that resulted in the end of so many species. It took about 50 million years of evolution for Earth's biota to regain the number of families lost during the Permian extinction.

The Current, Human-Caused Mass Extinction

The global diversity of species reached an all-time high in the present geological period. The most advanced groups of organisms—insects, vertebrates, and flowering plants—reached their greatest diversity about 30,000 years ago. Since that time, however, species richness has slowly decreased as one species has asserted its dominance. Humans have increasingly altered terrestrial and aquatic environments at the expense of other species in their need to consume natural resources. We are presently in the midst of a *sixth extinction episode*, this one caused by human activities rather than a natural disaster (Leakey and Lewin 1996; Lövei 2001; Baillie et al. 2004; Mace et al. 2005).

The first noticeable effects of human activity on extinction rates can be seen in the elimination of large mammals from Australia and North and South America at the time humans first colonized these continents tens of thousands of years ago. Shortly after humans arrived, 74 to 86% of the megafauna—mammals weighing more than 44 kg (100 lbs)—became extinct. These extinctions probably were caused directly by hunting (Martin 2001; Barnosky et al. 2004) and indirectly by burning and clearing forests and grasslands and the introduction of invasive species and new diseases. On all continents, paleontologists and archaeologists have found an extensive record of prehistoric human alteration and destruction of habitat coinciding with high rates of species extinctions. For example, deliberate burning of savannahs, presumably to encourage plant growth for browsing wildlife and thereby improve hunting, has been occurring for 50,000 years in Africa (Baillie et al. 2004).

In the roughly 10,000 to 12,000 years since the domestication of herd animals such as goats, sheep, and cattle, and of wheat, corn, rice, and other crop plants, the total area of natural grassland and forest in North America, Central America, Europe, and Asia has been steadily reduced to create pastures and farmlands to supply human needs. It is not known what species went extinct because of these landscape alterations, but these changes almost certainly had a significant impact upon wild species, just as they do today.

Extinction rates during the last 2000 years are best known for land vertebrates, especially birds and mammals, because these species are conspicuous, that is, relatively large and well studied. Scientists have noted when these species are no longer found in the wild (Table 7.1). Extinction rates for the other 99% of the world's species are just rough guesses at present (Dunn 2005). However, extinction rates are uncertain even for birds and mammals because some species that were considered extinct have been rediscovered. For example, the Australian night parrot (*Pezoporus occidentalis*) was last seen in 1912, and was presumed extinct before being rediscovered in 1979. The North American Ivory-billed woodpecker was only rediscovered in 2005 after decades of searching by ornithologists (Fitzpatrick

TABLE 7.1 *Some species that have gone extinct from 1984 to 2004*

Species	Common name	Date of extinction	Place of extinction
Amphibians			
Atelopus ignescens	Jambato toad	1988 (last record)	Ecuador
Bufo baxteri	Wyoming toad	Mid 1990s[a]	United States
Bufo periglenes	Golden toad	1989 (last record)	Costa Rica
Rheobatrachus vitellinus	Northern gastric brooding frog	1985 (last record)	Australia
Cynops wolterstorffi	Yunnan Lake newt	1986 (last record)	China
Birds			
Corvus hawaiiensis	Hawaiian crow	2002[a]	Hawaiian Islands
Crax mitu	Alagoas curassow	Late 1980s	Brazil
Gallirallus owstoni	Guam rail	1987[a]	Guam
Moho braccatus	Kauai 'O'o	1987 (last report of vocalizations)	Hawaiian Islands
Myadestes myadestinus	Kama'o	1989 (last sighting)	Hawaiian Islands
Podilymbus gigas	Atitlán grebe	1986	Guatemala
Mammals			
Oryx dammah	Scimitar-horned oryx	1996[a]	Chad
Plants			
Argyroxiphium virescens	Silversword	1996	Hawaiian Islands
Commidendrum rotundifolium	Bastard gumwood	1986[a]	St. Helena Island
Nesiota elliptica	St. Helena olive	2003	St. Helena Island

Source: Baillie et al. 2004.
[a]Species still exists in captivity.

et al. 2005). It is also true that species presumed to be **extant** (still living) may actually be extinct. Some researchers have argued that the number of extinct species is probably higher than is generally known, because there are many remote areas scientists have not revisited to determine the status of rare species there (Whitten et al. 1987). In addition, in the last four centuries many species may have existed and gone extinct before we even discovered them.

How has human activity affected extinction rates in more recent times? One set of estimates based on the best available evidence indicates, for example, that about 77 species of mammals and 129 species of birds have become extinct since the year 1600, representing 1.6% of known mammal species and 1.3% of known birds* (Smith et al. 1993; Baillie et al. 2004). While these numbers may not seem alarming initially, the trend of these extinction rates is on the rise, with the majority of extinctions occurring in the last 150 years (Figure 7.4). The extinction rate for birds was about zero to five species every 25 years during the period from 1500 to 1725, but it rose to 8 to 12 species every 25 years from 1750 to 1850. After 1850, the extinction rate rose again to more than 16 species every 25 years. This increase in the rate of extinction indicates the seriousness of the threat to biological diversity. One trend to note is that all of the early extinctions were on islands. However,

---

*Only around 60 species of insects are known to have gone extinct, roughly 0.001% of the number of species in this taxon. However, this extremely low reported extinction rate is principally due to the poor state of our knowledge of this large group; many species may have gone extinct without scientists ever having been aware that they existed.

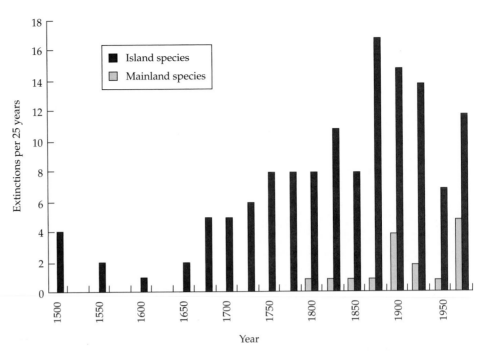

FIGURE 7.4 Rate of extinctions of birds during 25 year intervals since 1500. Extinction rates have been increasing from 1650 to the present. Initial extinctions were on islands, but extinctions of mainland species have been increasing since 1800. (After Baillie et al. 2004.)

extinctions of birds in mainland areas were first observed in the 1800 period, and have been increasing since then. Some of these species are extinct in the wild, but still remain alive in captivity. In the future, mainland species will be an increasing proportion of future extinctions.

The apparent decline in extinction rates since 1950 (see Figure 7.4) is due to the current practice of not declaring a species extinct until decades after they can no longer be found. In the coming years, numerous species will be declared extinct during the 1950 to 2000 period. In the last two years, a number of species not found despite intensive searches were finally declared extinct, including the golden toad of Costa Rica, the St. Helena's Olive and the Hawaiian crow. In the case of the golden toad, people have been looking for it for 17 years. Also the first extinction of a primate in the last 100 years, the Miss Waldron's colobus monkey (*Procolobus badius waldroni*) was reported from Ghana and Côte d'Ivoire (Oates et al. 2000). Many species not yet listed as extinct—and some that have not yet been documented at all—have been decimated by human activities and persist only in very low numbers. Our inability to locate any extant populations of many rare species provides further evidence that extinction rates are accelerating (Baillie et al. 2004).

Although for many species it is true that a few individuals in scattered small populations might persist for years, decades, or centuries (for woody plants in particular, isolated individuals can persist for hundreds of years), their ultimate fate is extinction (Adams and Carwardine 1990; Loehle and Li 1996). Remaining individuals of species that are doomed to extinction following habitat destruction have been called "the living dead" or "committed to extinction" (Figure 7.5). There are certainly many species in this category in the remaining fragments of forest in species-rich locations such as Madagascar and the Atlantic Forest of Brazil (Ferraz et al. 2003). Though technically the species is not extinct while these individuals live, the population is no longer reproductively viable, hence the species' future is limited to the lifespans of the remaining individuals (Gentry 1986; Janzen 1986, 2001). The loss of species over time in habitat fragments is sometimes called **relaxation**. Evidence from forest fragments and parks indicates that, following the destruction of the surrounding habitat, species diversity of vertebrates may actually show a temporary increase as animals flee into the few remaining patches of forest (Bierregaard et al. 1992). However, the number of species falls over the next few weeks, months, and years as species begin to go extinct on a local scale and are not replaced by other species. The predicted eventual loss of species following habitat destruction and fragmentation is called the **extinction debt** (Carroll et al. 2004; Berglund and Jonsson 2005).

Extinction rates will remain high in the coming century because of the large number of threatened species. About 12% of the world's remaining bird species are threatened with extinction. Mammal species are in even greater danger with 23% of species under threat; 31% of amphibians are threatened (Pounds et al. 2006). Table 7.2 shows certain animal groups for which the danger is even more severe, such as three orders that include turtles, manatees, and rhinos. Plant species are also at risk, with gymnosperms (conifers, ginkgos, and cycads) and palms among the especially vulnerable groups.

The threat of extinction is greater for some groups of species than for others (see Chapter 8). Some groups are especially vulnerable for a combination of reasons, including high levels of human exploitation. For example, 10 of the world's 23 crocodile and alligator species face extinction not only because their habitat is disappearing, but also because they are overhunted for their meat and skins. Almost half of the world's primate species and one-third of the parrot species are threatened with extinction for similar reasons (Chapman and Peres 2001). Throughout the world, large cat species (family Felidae) are hunted for sport, for their fur, and because they are perceived to be a threat to domestic animals and people. Slipper orchids, which have restrictive habitat requirements, are overharvested by plant collectors. In Europe, more mollusks have gone extinct than birds, mammals, reptiles, and amphibians together (Bouchet et al. 1999).

In most past geological periods, the extinction of existing species was balanced or exceeded by the evolution of new species. However, the present rate of human-caused extinction far surpasses the known rate of evolution. The known examples of recent rapid evolution—fruit flies adapting to localized environments or plants rapidly acquiring new characteristics when their chromosomes double during a peculiarity in meiosis—usually do not produce new families or orders. These unique evolutionary events require thousands of generations on a timescale over hundreds of thousands, if not millions, of years. The famous naturalist William Beebe said, "[W]hen the last individual of any race of living things breathes no more, another heaven and another earth must pass before such a one can be again."

FIGURE 7.5 The critically endagered cactus *Melocactus actinacanthus* is endemic to one rocky outcrop in Cuba. Despite its location in a protected area, the population continues to decline due to habitat destruction and illegal collecting by cactus enthusiasts. The current population of 3 adults and 33 juveniles is in imminent danger of extinction. (Photograph courtesy of the Team of the Project Conservation of *Melocactus actinacanthus*.)

TABLE 7.2 *Numbers of species threatened with extinction in major groups of animals and plants, and some key families and orders*

Group	Approximate number of species	Number of species threatened with extinction	Percentage of species threatened with extinction
Vertebrate animals			
Fishes	28,500	800	3[a]
Amphibians	5743	1770	31
Reptiles	8163	304	4[a]
Crocodiles	23	10	43
Turtles	205	128	62
Birds	9917	1213	12
Anseriformes (waterfowl)	168	26	16
Petrels and Albatrosses	131	60	45
Mammals	5416	1101	23
Primates	296	114	39
Manatees	5	4	80
Horses, tapirs, rhinos	17	12	71
Plants			
Gymnosperms	980	305	34
Angiosperms (flowering plants)	258,650	7796	3[a]
Palmae (palms)	357[b]	238	67

Source: Data from IUCN 2004.

[a]Low percentages are due in part to the small numbers of species that have been evaluated.

[b]Number of species for which information is available.

Background Extinction Rates

To better understand how calamitous present extinction rates are, it is useful to compare them to the natural extinction rates that would prevail regardless of human activity. What is the natural rate of extinction in the absence of human influence? Natural "background" extinction rates can be estimated by looking at the fossil record. In the fossil record, an individual species lasts about 1 to 10 million years before it goes extinct or evolves into a new species (Raup 1992; Pimm and Jenkins 2005). Since there are perhaps 10 million species on the Earth today, we can predict that 1 to 10 of the world's species would be lost per year as a result of a natural extinction rate of 0.0001 to 0.00001% per year. These estimates are derived from studies of wide-ranging marine animals, so they may be lower than natural extinction rates for species of narrow distribution, which are more vulnerable to habitat disturbance; however, they do appear to be applicable for terrestrial mammals. The current observed rate of extinction of birds and mammals of 1% per century (or 0.01% per year) is 100 to 1000 times greater than would be predicted based on background rates of extinction. Putting it another way, about 100 species of birds and mammals were observed to go extinct between 1850 and 1950, but the natural rate of extinction would have predicted that, at most, only 1 species would have gone extinct. Therefore, the other 99 extinctions can be attributed to the effects of human activity.

Some scientists have sharply questioned the accuracy of these estimates, saying that they are based on unfounded assumptions, such as the validity of comparing animals known from fossils with living animals and the validity of comparing marine mammals and terrestrial animals (Regan et al. 2001). However, even using a much more conservative approach with the available data, Regan and colleagues came up with a modern extinction rate that is still 36 to 78 times the background rate. Despite questions about the exact rates, no one disagrees that current extinction rates are far above background levels and that they are caused by human activity.

Extinction Rates on Islands

It should not come as a surprise that the highest species extinction rates during historic times have occurred on islands. These species often have a limited area, small population sizes, and a small number of populations (Young et al. 2004). The high extinction rates on islands include the extinctions of birds, mammals, and reptiles during the last 350 years (Pimm et al. 1995). Furthermore, numerous endemic plants of oceanic islands are extinct or in danger of extinction. (Endemic species, species found in one place and nowhere else, are particularly vulnerable to extinction; they are discussed in more detail in Chapter 8.)

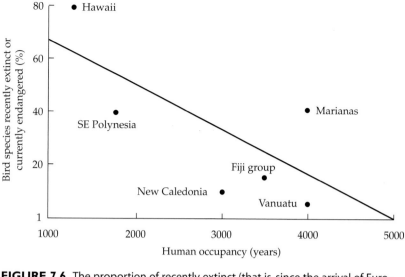

FIGURE 7.6 The proportion of recently extinct (that is, since the arrival of Europeans) or currently endangered bird species decreases as the length of time non-European peoples have occupied an island group increases. This probably means that most sensitive species have already disappeared from those islands with long histories of human occupation. The seeming anomaly of the high rate of recent extinctions in the Marianas group is due to the devastation caused by the recent introduction of the brown tree snake (see Chapter 10). (From Pimm et al. 1995.)

Island species usually have evolved and undergone speciation with a limited number of competitors, predators, and diseases. When predatory species from the mainland are introduced onto islands, they frequently decimate the endemic island species, which have not evolved any defenses against them (Box 7.1; see also Chapter 8). Species extinction rates peak soon after humans occupy an island and then decline after the most vulnerable species are eliminated (Figure 7.6). Island plant species are also threatened, mainly through habitat destruction (Table 7.3). In Madagascar, 68% of the 9500 plant species are endemic, and 255 species are threatened with extinction (WRI 2000). In general, the longer an island has been occupied by people, the greater the percentage of extinct biota.

TABLE 7.3 *Number of plant species and their status for various islands and island groups*

Island(s)	Native species	Endemic species	Percentage endemic	Number threatened	Percentage threatened
Fiji	1307	760	58	72	6
United Kingdom	1500	16	1	28	2
New Zealand	2160	1942	90	236	11
Jamaica	2746	923	33	371	14
Solomon Islands	2780	30	1	43	2
Sri Lanka	3000	890	30	436	15
Cuba	6004	3229	54	811	14
Philippines	8000	3500	44	371	5
Madagascar	9000	6500	72	189	2
Australia	15,000	14,074	94	1597	11

Source: Data from WRI 1998.

BOX 7.1

Invasive Species and Extinction in Island Ecosystems

The problem of invasive, exotic species (as described in Chapter 10) is most pronounced in islands and archipelagos. The evolution of species in isolation from the mainland makes island species particularly vulnerable when competitors, predators, and diseases are introduced by human colonists or visitors. The fragility of species endemic to islands and archipelagos has been dramatically illustrated by the history of multiple extinctions and species decline in the Hawaiian and Galápagos archipelagos.

The two archipelagos have several features in common. Both are volcanic in origin, and both are a substantial distance from the nearest mainland coast. However, the entire Hawaiian chain, including the western seamounts, is some 63 million years older than the Galápagos (Loope et al. 1988) and has greater humidity and topographical diversity. Though the Hawaiian islands are four times as far from the mainland as the Galápagos, their age, climate, and topography combine to permit a higher level of biological diversity. Nevertheless, both archipelagos share two features commonly found in island ecosystems: a high percentage of endemic species, and numerous species threatened with extinction due to invasive species. Evolutionary radiation from relatively few colonizing species can produce an array of new species (see Chapter 2). An extreme instance of this type of rapid evolution occurred in Hawaii, where one or two colonizing species of fruit fly evolved into more than 800 different species (Howarth 1990). In addition to their unusual diversity, island ecosystems have particular value for evolutionary biologists as natural laboratories for the study of evolution. Charles Darwin's observations of finches in the Galápagos—observations from which he developed and supported his theory of the origin of new species—is a classic study of the rapid speciation common to islands.

But the same factors that make these island ecosystems so unique also leave them particularly vulnerable to invasions by exotic species in addition to habitat destruction and overexploitation. Introductions of exotic species to the Hawaiian and Galápagos islands have had dramatic and devastating effects on the endemic biota. In Hawaii, an initial wave of introductions, including Polynesian pigs, dogs, Polynesian rats, and a variety of plants, accompanied the colonization of the islands by the Polynesians approximately 1300 years ago. The initial human colonization of the Hawaiian archipelago is thought to have resulted in a wave of extinctions. At present, paleontologists have documented at least 62 species of birds that became extinct after the arrival of the Polynesians; plant and invertebrate taxa have yet to be examined. Since the arrival of Europeans in 1778, many other alien species have had a powerful impact on native species. Black rats, domestic non-Polynesian pigs, cats, sheep, horses, cattle, goats, mongooses, and an estimated 2000 species of arthropods are some of the introduced species that have caused declines and extinctions among birds, insects, and plants in Hawaii in the past 200 years. In addition, numerous plant species brought to the islands have become naturalized, often outcompeting endemic taxa. The impact of exotic species and habitat destruction has been so severe and the area occupied by many native species is so small that Hawaii has the dubious distinction of having more recorded species extinctions than the entire rest of the United States.

The Galápagos archipelago has also experienced the effects of invasive, exotic species. Until recently, the overall inhospitality of these arid, rocky islands has limited the amount of human colonization, so the extent of destruction of endemic species is less than in Hawaii. Nonetheless, many species on these islands, particularly plants, are threatened by introduced species. Goats, cattle, and pigs are the primary culprits in the decline of many plant species; populations of goats on some islands are as high as 80,000, a number far in excess of what native plant species can withstand. Pigs consume the eggs of iguanas and turtles, including those of the endangered Pacific green turtle, which nests on the islands. Introduced cultivated plants that have escaped into the wild, including guava (*Psidium guajava*), quinine (*Cinchona succirubra*), and raspberries (*Rubus niveus*), crowd out many native species. The number of introduced plant species continues to increase and is strongly correlated with the rise in the human population (Mauchamp 1997). Even Darwin's famous finches are in decline, with several species having already gone extinct (Grant et al. 2005). The government of Ecuador, which has jurisdiction over the Galápagos islands, has declared the conservation of the Galápagos to be a national priority. However, this policy is constantly being challenged and ignored by commercial fisher folk who do not accept the government's authority.

As a first step toward protection, conservation biologists working in both archipelagos have been trying to eradicate some of the more prominent and destructive

BOX 7.1 *(continued)*

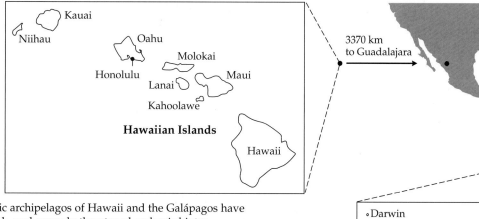

The oceanic archipelagos of Hawaii and the Galápagos have unique, rich, and severely threatened endemic biotas.

invasive species, particularly introduced mammals (Cruz et al. 2004). The hunting and removal of feral goats, pigs, and other ungulates is actively underway, while domestic stock is kept closely penned. Introduced herbs and trees are eliminated by herbicide sprays, felling, and burning. Over 75% of the management costs for Hawaii's protected areas are spent on the control of exotic species. These measures are sometimes effective against larger species. For example, when rat populations were controlled on Santa Cruz and Floreana in the Galápagos, nesting success of dark-rumped petrels increased from 1 success in 25 attempts to 2 successes in every 3 attempts (Powell and Gibbs 1995). Where pigs and other large animals have been eliminated from montane forests, the native species have recovered (Stone and Loope 1996). Control of invasive insects and other invertebrates and many herbaceous weeds is often far more difficult. Now that the problem of invasive species has been identified, the respective governments and conservation organizations are actively managing areas of the islands to protect, restore, and enlarge the original biological communities that remain.

European colonization of islands has sometimes been more destructive than colonization by other peoples because European colonization includes greater amounts of clearing and the wholesale introduction of non-native species. For instance, between 1840 and 1880, more than 60 species of vertebrates, particularly grazing animals such as sheep, were deliberately introduced into Australia, where they displaced native species and altered many communities. In the 1500s, the first European visitors to the Mascarene Islands (Mauritius, Reunion, and Rodrigues) released monkeys and pigs. These animals, and subsequent hunting and colonization by Dutch settlers, led to the extinction of the dodo bird, 19 other species of birds, and 8 species of reptiles. The impact of introduced predators on island species is highlighted by the example of the flightless Stephen Island wren, a bird that was endemic to a tiny island off New Zealand. Every Stephen Island wren on the island was killed by a single cat that belonged to the lighthouse keeper. Even one introduced predator can eliminate an entire species.

The vulnerability of island species is further illustrated when comparing the number of species that have gone extinct in mainland areas, on islands, and in the oceans from 1600 to the present. Of the 726 species of animals and plants known to have gone extinct, 351 (about half of the total) were island species, even though islands represent only a small fraction of the Earth's surface (Smith et al. 1993). Despite the documented danger to island species, however, in the coming decades a higher proportion of extinctions will occur in continental lowlands where many species occur and where human alteration of the landscape is rapid and extensive (Manne et al. 1999).

Extinction Rates in Water

In contrast with the large amount of information we have on extinct terrestrial species, there are no documented cases of marine fish or coral species that have gone extinct during the last few thousand years. Only around 12 species—three marine mammals, five marine birds, and four mollusks—are known to have gone extinct in the world's vast oceans during historic times (Carlton et al. 1999). This number of extinctions is almost certainly an underestimate, since marine species are not nearly as well known as terrestrial species (Edgar et al. 2005), but it may reflect a greater resiliency of marine species in response to disturbance. However, the significance of these losses may be greater than the numbers suggest. Many marine mammals are top predators, and their loss could have a major impact on marine communities. Some marine species are the sole species of their genus, family, or even order, so the extinction of even a few of them can possibly represent a serious loss to global biological diversity. The oceans were once considered so enormous that it seemed unlikely that marine species could go extinct; many people still share this viewpoint. However, as marine coastal waters become more polluted and species are harvested more intensely, even the vast oceans will not provide safety from extinction (Woodard 2000).

Also in contrast to terrestrial extinctions, the majority of freshwater fish extinctions have occurred in mainland areas rather than on islands because of the vastly greater number of species in mainland waters. In North America, over one-third of freshwater fish species are in danger of extinction. The fish of California are particularly vulnerable because of the state's scarcity of water and its intense development—7% of California's 115 types of native fish are already extinct and 56% are in danger of extinction (Moyle 1995). Large numbers of fish and aquatic invertebrates, such as mollusks, are in danger of extinction in the southeastern United States because of dams, pollution, irrigation projects, invasion of alien species, and general habitat damage (Figure 7.7).

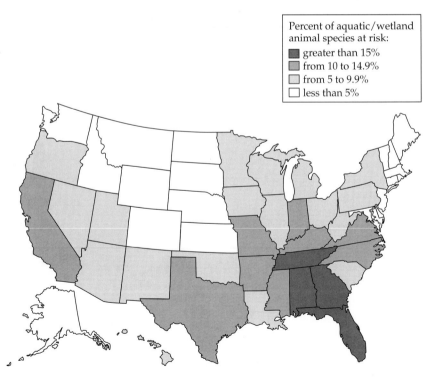

Percent of aquatic/wetland animal species at risk:
- greater than 15%
- from 10 to 14.9%
- from 5 to 9.9%
- less than 5%

FIGURE 7.7 Dams, irrigation systems, polluted runoff from industry and agriculture, introduced species, and habitat destruction threaten as many as 23% of the aquatic species in the United States, including dozens of species of freshwater mussels, fish, and crayfish. The many endemic species of restricted range in the southeastern section of the country are most at risk. (After Stolzenburg 1996.)

Estimating Extinction Rates with the Island Biogeography Model

Studies of island communities have led to general rules on the distribution of biological diversity, synthesized as the **island biogeography model** by MacArthur and Wilson (1967). This model can be used to estimate future extinction rates, as we will see later in this section. The central observation that this model was built to explain is the **species–area relationship**: Islands with large areas have more species than islands with smaller areas (Figure 7.8). This rule makes intuitive sense because large islands will tend to have a greater variety of local environments and community types than small islands. Also, large islands allow greater geographical isolation, a larger number of populations per species, and larger sizes of individual populations, increasing the likelihood of speciation and decreasing the probability of local extinction of newly evolved as well as recently arrived species. The species–area relationship can be accurately summarized by the empirical formula:

$$S = CA^Z$$

where S is the number of species on an island, A is the area of the island, and C and Z are constants. The exponent Z determines the slope of the curve. The values for C and Z will depend on the types of islands being compared (tropical versus temperate, dry versus wet, etc.) and the types of species involved (birds versus reptiles, etc.). Z values are typically around 0.25, with a range from 0.15 to 0.35 (Connor and McCoy 2001). Island species of restricted ranges, such as reptiles and amphibians, tend to have Z values near 0.35, while widespread mainland species tend to have Z values closer to 0.15. Values of C will be high in groups such as insects that are high in species numbers and low in groups such as birds that are low in species numbers.

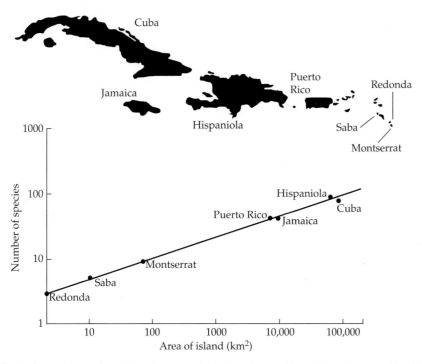

FIGURE 7.8 The number of species on an island can be predicted from the area of an island. In this figure, the number of species of reptiles and amphibians is shown for seven islands in the West Indies. The number of species on large islands such as Cuba and Hispaniola far exceeds that on the tiny islands of Saba and Redonda. (After Wilson 1989.)

The model has been empirically validated to the point of acceptance by most biologists (Quammen 1996): for numerous groups of plants and animals, it has been found to describe reasonably well the observed richness of species, explaining about half of the variation in numbers of species. Imagine the simplest situation, in which $C = 1$ and $Z = 0.25$, for raptorial birds on a hypothetical archipelago:

$$S = (1)A^{0.25}$$

The formula predicts that islands of 10, 100, 1000, and 10,000 km^2 in area would have 2, 3, 6, and 10 species, respectively. It is important to note that a tenfold increase in island area does not result in a tenfold increase in the number of species; with this equation, each tenfold increase in island area increases the number of species by a factor of approximately 2. Actual data from three Caribbean islands can be used to illustrate the relationship: with increasing area, St. Nevis (93 km^2), Puerto Rico (8959 km^2), and Cuba (114,524 km^2) have 2, 10, and 57 species of anolis lizard, respectively; with a C of 0.5 and a Z of 0.35, the islands would be predicted to have 2, 12, and 30 species, respectively.

In their classic text, MacArthur and Wilson (1967) hypothesized that the number of species occurring on an island represents a dynamic equilibrium between the arrival of new species (and also the evolution of new species) and the extinction rate of existing species. Starting with an unoccupied island, the number of species will increase over time, since more species will be arriving (or evolving) than are going extinct, until the rates of extinction and immigration are balanced (Figure 7.9). The arrival rate will be higher for large islands than small islands because large islands represent a larger target for dispersing animals to find and are more likely to have suitable open habitat available for colonization. The extinction rate will be lower on large islands than small islands because large islands have greater habitat diversity and a greater number of populations. The rate of immigration of new species will be higher for islands near the mainland than for islands farther away, since mainland species are able to disperse to near islands more easily than to distant islands. The model predicts that for any group of organisms, such as birds or trees, the number of species found on large islands near a continent will be greater than that on small islands far from a continent.

FIGURE 7.9 The island biogeography model describes the relationship between the rates of colonization and extinction on islands. The immigration rate (black curves) on unoccupied islands is initially high, as species with good dispersal abilities rapidly take advantage of the available open habitats. The immigration rate slows as the number of species increases and sites become occupied. The extinction rate (gray curves) increases with the number of species on the island; the more species on an island, the greater the likelihood that a species will go extinct at any time interval. Colonization rates will be highest for islands near a mainland population source, since species can disperse over shorter distances more easily than longer ones. Extinction rates are highest on small islands, where both population sizes and habitat diversity are low. The number of species present on an island reaches equilibrium when the colonization rate equals the extinction rate (circles). The equilibrium number of species is greatest on large islands near the mainland, and lowest on small islands far from the mainland. (After MacArthur and Wilson 1967.)

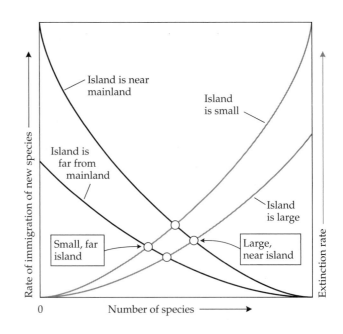

Extinction Rates and Habitat Loss

Species–area relationships have been used to predict the number and percentage of species that would become extinct if habitats were destroyed (Quammen 1996; Michalski and Peres 2005; Gurd 2006). The calculation assumes that, if an island has a certain number of species, reducing the area of natural habitat on the island would result in the island being able to support only a number of species corresponding to that on a smaller island (Figure 7.10). This model has great utility because it can be extended to national parks and nature reserves that are surrounded by damaged habitat. The reserves can be viewed as "habitat islands" in an inhospitable "sea" of unsuitable habitat. The model predicts that when 50% of an island (or habitat island) is destroyed, approximately 10% of the species occurring on the island will be eliminated. If these species are endemic to an area, they will become extinct. When 90% of the habitat is destroyed, 50% of the species will be lost; and when 99% of the habitat is gone, about 75% of the original species will be lost. The island of Singapore can be used as an example. Over the last 180 years, 95% of its original forest cover has been removed; the model estimates that around 30% of its forest species would be lost. In fact, between 1923 and 1998, 32% of Singapore's native birds were lost, with higher rates of loss for large ground birds and for insectivorous birds of the forest canopy (Castelleta et al. 2000).

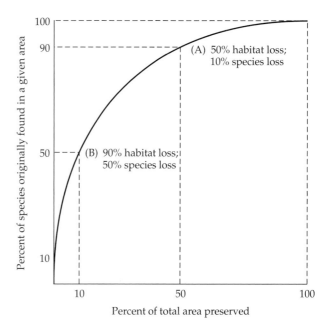

FIGURE 7.10 According to the island biogeography model, the number of species present in an area increases asymptotically to a maximum value. This means that if the area of habitat is reduced by 50%, the number of species lost may be 10% (A); if the habitat is reduced by 90%, the number of species lost may be 50% (B). The shape of the curve is different for each region of the world and for each group of species, but this model gives a general indication of the effect of habitat destruction on species extinctions and the persistence of species in the remaining habitat.

Predictions of extinction rates based on habitat loss vary considerably, because each species–area relationship is unique. Because insects and plants in tropical forests account for the great majority of the world's species, estimates of present and future rates of species extinction in rain forests gives an approximation of global rates of extinction. Using the conservative estimate that 1% of the world's rain forests is being destroyed each year, Wilson (1989) estimated that 0.2 to 0.3% of all species—10,000 to 15,000 species using a total of 5 million species worldwide—will be lost per year, or 34 species per day. This estimate predicts that over the 10-year period from 1996 to 2006, approximately 125,000 species will become extinct. Other methods applied to the rates of extinction in tropical rain forests estimate a loss of between 2 to 11% of the world's species per decade (Reid 1992; Koopowitz et al. 1994). The variation in rates is due to the use of different estimates of the rate of deforestation, different values for the species–area curves, and different mathematical approaches. The most recent estimates are that species extinctions by 2050 will be up to 35% in tropical Africa, 20% in tropical Asia, 15% in tropical America, and 8 to 10% elsewhere (MEA 2005). Extinction rates might in fact be higher because the highest rates of deforestation are occurring in countries with large concentrations of rare species, and large forest areas are increasingly being fragmented by roads and development projects (Laurance et al. 2001). We might lower extinction rates if these "hot spot" areas, particularly rich in endemic species, are targeted for conservation (Pimm and Raven 2000). Regardless of which estimate is the most accurate, all indicate that tens of thousands—if not hundreds of thousands—of species are headed for extinction within the next 50 years. Such a rate of extinction is without precedent since the great mass extinction of the Cretaceous period 65 million years ago.

Assumptions and Generalizations in the Island Biogeography Model

Estimates of extinction rates based on the island biogeography model include a number of assumptions and generalizations that may limit the validity of this approach (Simberloff 1992; Steadman and Martin 2003):

1. These estimates are based on typical values for the species–area curves. Groups of species with broad geographical ranges, such as marine animals and temperate tree species, will tend to have lower rates of extinction than species of narrow geographical distribution, such as island birds and freshwater fish.

2. The model assumes that all endemic species are eliminated from areas that have been largely cleared of forest. It is possible that many species can survive in isolated patches of forest and recolonize secondary forest that develops on abandoned land. A few primary forest species may also be capable of surviving in plantations and managed forests. Adaptation to managed forests is likely to be particularly significant in tropical forests that are being selectively logged on a large scale.

3. The species–area model assumes that areas of habitat are eliminated at random. In fact, areas of species richness are sometimes targeted for species conservation efforts and national park status. As a result, a greater percentage of species may be protected than is assumed in the species–area model.

4. The degree of habitat fragmentation may affect extinction rates. If remaining areas of land are divided into very small parcels or crossed by roads, then wide-ranging species or species requiring large population sizes may be unable to maintain themselves. Also, hunting, clearing land for agriculture, and the introduction of exotic species may increase in fragmented forests, leading to further loss of species.

Other Methods for Calculating Extinction Rates

Another approach to estimating extinction rates uses information on projected declines in habitat, numbers of populations, and the geographical range of well known individual species (Mace 1995). This approach uses empirical information to give a more accurate estimate of extinction rates for a smaller number of species. Applied to 725 threatened vertebrate species, this method predicts that some 15 to 20 species will go extinct in the world over the next 100 years. Extinction rates are expected to be much higher in certain groups; within 100 years it is likely that half of the 29 threatened species in the deer family (Cervidae) will be extinct, as will 3 of the world's 10 threatened hornbill species (Bucerotidae). Applied to specific geographical areas, the numbers of species predicted to go extinct using the estimated loss of habitat and the island biogeography models closely correspond with the current number of species extinct or threatened with extinction (Brooks et al. 2002).

The time required for a given species to go extinct following a reduction in area or fragmentation of its range is a vital question in conservation biology, and the island biogeography model makes no prediction as to how long it will take (Gibbs 2001). Small populations of some species may persist for decades or even centuries in habitat fragments, even though their eventual fate is extinction. One method to estimate when extinctions will occur compares predictions of species loss with historical examples. Comparing predictions with historical examples from forests in Kenya has estimated the rates at which remaining forest fragments will lose their bird species. Of the species that will eventually be lost, the best estimates predict that half will be lost in 50 years from a 1000-ha fragment, while half will be lost in 100 years from a 10,000-ha fragment (Brooks et al. 1999). Amazon forest fragments of 100 ha lost half their bird species in 15 years, but even isolated forest fragments as large as 10,000 ha will lose numerous species over a 100-year period (Ferraz et al. 2003). In situations in which there is widespread habitat destruction followed by recovery, such as in New England and Puerto Rico over the last several centuries, species may be able to survive in small numbers in isolated fragments and then reoccupy adjacent recovering habitat. Even though 98% of the forests of eastern North America were cut down, the clearing took place in a patchwork fashion over hundreds of years, so that forest always covered half of the area, providing refuges for mobile animal species such as birds.

Local Extinctions

In addition to the global extinctions that are a primary focus of conservation biology, many species are experiencing a series of local extinctions or extirpations across their range (Balmford et al. 2003; Rooney et al. 2004). When habitats are degraded and destroyed, populations of plants and animals go extinct (Scholes and Biggs 2004). Formerly widespread species are sometimes restricted to a few small pockets of their former habitat (Terborgh 1999). For example, the American burying beetle (*Nicrophorus americanus*), once found all across central and eastern North America, is now found in only four isolated populations (Figure 7.11) (Muths and Scott 2000). Biological communities are impoverished by such local extinctions. The Middlesex Fells, a local conservation area in metropolitan Boston,

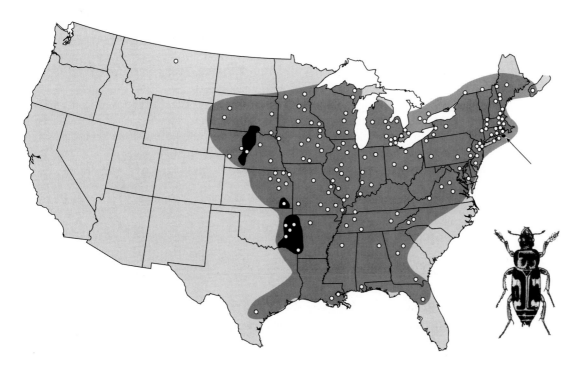

FIGURE 7.11 The American burying beetle (*Nicrophorus americanus*) was once widespread in the eastern and central United States (dark gray area) but is now found only in four isolated populations (black areas; Block Island, in Long Island Sound, is highlighted with an arrow). Open dots represent past sites of collection, based on museum specimens. Note the isolated collections from central Montana, southern Texas, and southern Nova Scotia. Intensive efforts have been initiated to determine the cause of this decline and develop a recovery plan. (After Muths and Scott 2000.)

contained 338 native wildflower species in 1894; only 227 native species remained when the area was surveyed 98 years later (Drayton and Primack 1996). Fourteen of the plant species that were lost had been listed as "common" in 1894. A combination of forest succession, ground fires, trampling by hikers and mountain bikers, invasions by exotic species, and habitat fragmentation contributed to species losses in the Fells. In the large Adelaide metropolitan area of Australia, 20 of 40 native mammal species and 89 of 1136 native plant species were lost between 1836 and 2002 (Tait et al. 2005).

According to surveys by the U.S. Natural Heritage program, 4 to 8% of the plant species formerly found in Hawaii, New York, and Pennsylvania can no longer be found. In Britain, where species distributions are often known with great accuracy due to decades of collecting and research, an analysis of butterflies in one county showed that local extinctions over the last 25 years had eliminated 67% of the previously known localities of species, an astonishingly high rate of local loss (Thomas and Abery 1995). And in a survey of one part of the Indonesian island of Sumatra, of 12 populations of Asian elephants known from the 1980s, only 3 populations were still present 20 years later (Hedges et al. 2005).

IMPOVERISHED COMMUNITIES   The world's 5 million species are estimated to consist of 1 billion distinct populations, or around 200 populations per species (Hughes and Roughgarden 2000). While some species have just a few populations, other species might have thousands of populations. The loss of populations is roughly equal to the proportion of a habitat that is lost, so that the world's populations are being lost at a far higher rate than the loss of species (see Figure 7.10). When 90% of an extensive grassland ecosystem is destroyed, 90% of the populations of plant, animal, and fungus species there will also be lost. Tropical rain forests contain at least half of the world's species, and they are being lost at the rate of around 1% per year. This represents a loss of 5 million populations per year (1% of 500 million tropical forest populations), or around 30,000 populations per day.

These large numbers of local extinctions serve as important biological warning signs that something is wrong with the environment. Action is needed to prevent further local extinctions, as well as global extinctions. The loss of local populations not only represents a loss of biological diversity, but it diminishes the value of an area for nature enjoyment, scientific research, and the provision of crucial materials to local people in subsistence economies.

Summary

1. There are more species on Earth in the present geological period than have ever existed in the past. However, the current rate of species extinction is rapid and is comparable to the five past episodes of natural mass extinction found at intervals in the geological record.

2. The effect of human activity has been to drive many species to extinction. Since 1600, around 1.6% of the world's mammalian species and 1.3% of its birds have gone extinct. The rate of extinction is accelerating, and many of the species still alive are teetering on the brink of extinction. The current observed rate of extinction for birds and mammals is estimated to be 100 to 1000 times greater than the rate that would be occurring naturally.

3. Island species have a higher rate of extinction than mainland species. Among aquatic species, freshwater species apparently have a higher extinction rate than marine species.

4. An island biogeography model has been developed to predict the equilibrium number of species that might be found on islands of different areas and distances from the mainland. This model has been used to estimate how many species would go extinct if human activity continues to destroy habitats at the present rate. The best evidence indicates that about 2 to 3% of the Earth's species will be lost over the next 10 years, with a loss of about 10,000 to 15,000 species per year. Other empirical evidence on population declines and reductions in range support the prediction that the rate of extinction will remain high over the coming decades.

5. Individuals of long-lived species that remain alive in disturbed and fragmented habitats can be considered "the living dead." The species may persist for many years but will eventually die out due to a lack of reproduction.

6. Many species are experiencing a loss of populations across their range leading to impoverished biological communities. These local extinctions, or extirpations, also represent a loss of biodiversity.

For Discussion

1. Calculate the number of species expected on islands of various sizes, using several values of C (0.5, 1, 2, 4, etc.) and several values of Z (0.15, 0.25, 0.35, etc.). How many species will be lost on the largest island if native habitat is completely destroyed on 30%, 70%, 97%, and 98% of the island? What are the assumptions on which these calculations are based?

2. Why should conservation biologists, or anyone else, care if species go locally extinct if they are still found somewhere else?

3. If 50% of the species present today go extinct within the next 200 years, what is your estimate of how long it would take for the process of speciation to replace the lost number of species?

Suggested Readings

Adams, D. and M. Carwardine. 1990. *Last Chance to See.* Harmony Books, New York. A light but poignant account of the threat of imminent extinction facing many well-known species.

Baillie, J. E. M., C. Hilton-Taylor, and S. N. Stuart. 2004. *2004 IUCN Red List of Threatened Species. A Global Assessment.* IUCN, Gland, Switzerland. Current information on the status of species and extinction; also available online.

Balmford, A., R. E. Green, and M. Jenkins. 2003. Measuring the changing state of nature. *Trends in Ecology and Evolution* 18: 326–330. Biodiversity is being lost on a wide variety of scales, from populations to species to entire biological communities.

Carroll, C., R. F. Noss, P. C. Paquet, and N. H. Schumaker. 2004. Extinction debt of protected areas in developing landscapes. *Conservation Biology* 18: 1110–1120. Many species will eventually go extinct because of current habitat loss.

Drayton, B. and R. B. Primack. 1996. Plant species lost in an isolated conservation area in metropolitan Boston from 1894 to 1993. *Conservation Biology* 10: 30–40. Species loss can be extensive over the course of a century, even in a protected area.

Ferraz, G., G. J. Russell, P. C. Stouffer, R. O. Bierregaard, S. L. Pimm, and T. E. Lovejoy. 2003. Rates of species loss from Amazonian forest fragments. *Proceedings of the National Academy of Sciences U.S.A.* 100: 14069–14073. Innovative attempt to calculate the rate of species extinction following habitat fragmentation.

Gurd, D. B. 2006. Variation in species losses from islands: artifacts, extirpation rates, or prefragmentation diversity? *Ecological Applications* 16: 176–185. The island biogeography model remains an effective method for calculating extinction risks.

Leakey, R. and R. Lewin. 1996. *The Sixth Extinction: Patterns of Life and the Future of Humankind.* Doubleday, New York. Popular account of the mass extinctions written by an anthropologist and a science writer.

MacArthur, R. H. and E. O. Wilson. 1967. *The Theory of Island Biogeography.* Princeton University Press, Princeton, NJ. This classic text outlining the island biogeography model has been highly influential in shaping modern conservation biology.

Mace, G., H. Masundire, J. Baillie, T. Ricketts, T. Brooks, M. Hoffmann, et al. 2005. Biodiversity. *In* R. Hassan, R. Scholes, and N. Ash (eds.), *Ecosystems and Human Well-being: Current State and Trends,* Vol. 1, pp. 77–122. Island Press, Washington, D.C. Comprehensive treatment of biodiversity and extinction by leading experts.

Michalski, F. and C. A. Peres. 2005. Anthropogenic determinants of primate and carnivore local extinctions in a fragmented forest landscape of southern Amazonia. *Biological Conservation* 124: 383–396. Certain large mammals are eliminated by habitat fragmentation, whereas other species can persist.

Pimm, S. L. and C. Jenkins. 2005. Sustaining the variety of life. *Scientific American* 293(3): 66–73. Colorful article about the modern high extinction rates.

Pounds, J. A., M. R. Bustamante, L. A. Coloma, J. A. Consuegra, et al. 2006. Widespread amphibian extinctions from epidemic disease driven by global warming. *Nature* 439: 161–167. Amphibians in montane areas are being driven to extinction by fungal disease.

Quammen, D. 1996. *The Song of the Dodo: Island Biogeography in an Age of Extinctions.* Scribner, New York. Popular account of early and modern explorations and of island biogeography theory.

Terborgh, J. 1999. *Requiem for Nature.* Island Press, Washington D.C. The multiple threats faced by biological diversity must be considered realistically and without illusions.

Wiles, G. J., J. Bart, R. E. Beck, Jr., and C. F. Aguon. 2003. Impacts of the brown tree snake: Patterns of decline and species persistence in Guam's avifauna. *Conservation Biology* 17: 1350–1360. One introduced species devastated the populations of many bird species.

Woodard, C. 2000. *Ocean's End: Travels through Endangered Seas.* Basic Books (Perseus Books Group), New York. A science journalist documents that even vast expanses of ocean are not protected from human impact.

Vulnerability to Extinction

Not all species have an equal chance of going extinct. Rare species are considered to be especially vulnerable to extinction, while common species are considered less so. But the term "rare" has a variety of meanings, each of which has a different implication for conservation biology (Goerck 1997; Stohlgren 2001).

Generally speaking, a species is considered rare if it (1) lives in a narrow geographical range, (2) occupies only one or a few specialized habitats, or (3) is found only in small populations (Rabinowitz et al. 1986). The first criterion, based on geographical area, is the most obvious: The Venus's-flytrap (*Dionaea muscipula*) is rare because it occurs only on the coastal plain of the Carolinas in eastern North America. Many geographically rare species occupy islands, and some may also occupy isolated habitats, such as high mountain peaks in the middle of lowlands or lakes surrounded by a terrestrial landscape. Within their limited geographical range, however, a rare species may be locally abundant.

Related to the concept of rarity is the concept of endemism—the idea that some species are found naturally in a single geographical area and no other place. This concept may seem similar to the properties of those rare species that live in a narrow geographical range. But a species may be endemic to a large area and abundant throughout it. In contrast, a rare species such as the Venus's-flytrap is typically found only in a limited area (and could be considered a narrowly distributed endemic) (Figure 8.1). Or a rare species may be

FIGURE 8.1 The Plymouth gentian (*Sabatia kennedyana*), a rare wildflower, is found only on the margins of coastal ponds in scattered locations in the eastern United States. At a few ponds, however, this species has large populations. (Photograph by Mark Primack.)

considered geographically rare in only part of its range. For example, the sweet bay magnolia (*Magnolia virginiana*) is reasonably common throughout the southeastern United States, but in the New England region this species is considered rare because it occurs in only one population of 100 individuals in one particular swamp in Magnolia, Massachusetts (Primack et al. 1986). Individual species may have always had a narrow geographical range, or they may have been more widespread at one time but became restricted due to human activities and habitat destruction, in which case they could be termed *artificially rare*.

A species may also be considered rare if it occupies only one or a few specialized habitats. Salt marsh cord grass (*Spartina patens*) is found only in salt marshes and not in other habitats; yet within this habitat, cord grass is quite common. This example contrasts with common species that are found in many different habitats, such as the dandelion (*Taraxacum officinale*), which occupies open meadows, roadsides, river edges, and mown lawns.

Finally, a species may be considered rare if it is found only in small populations. Mediterranean monk seals (*Monachus monachus*) are found over a wide area, but their populations are always small and isolated. A common species would have large populations at least occasionally.

These three criteria of rarity—narrow geographical range, specific habitat requirements, and small population size—can be applied to the entire range of species or to the distribution and abundance of species in a particular place. Such an approach can highlight priorities for conservation. Species with a narrow geographical range and specific habitat requirements that are always found in small populations require immediate habitat protection and, possibly, habitat management to maintain their few, fragile populations. This also applies, to a somewhat lesser degree, to species with larger populations. However, where species have a narrow geographical distribution but a broad habitat specificity, experiments in which individuals are transported to unoccupied but apparently suitable localities to create new populations may be a strategy worth considering (see Chapter 13), since these species may have been unable to disperse outside of their narrow geographical area. This suggestion is supported by a further study showing that plant species with poor dispersal abilities (no adaptation for long-distance dispersal) tend to have more aggregated populations in contrast to species with good dispersal ability (light, wind-dispersed seeds, or seeds dispersed by mammals and birds), which tend to have more widely dispersed populations (Quinn et al. 1994). Species with broad geographical ranges are less susceptible to extinction and less likely to need rescue efforts, since they tend to have more extant populations and more opportunities to colonize potentially suitable sites.

Endemic Species and Extinction

A species found naturally in a single geographical area and no other place is **endemic** to that location. Endemism is an extremely important factor in a species' risk of extinction. If the populations of an endemic species on Madagascar, or any isolated island, go extinct, the species will be globally extinct. In contrast, mainland species often have many populations distributed over a wide area, so the loss of one population is not catastrophic for the species. Even though 98% of the forests of eastern North America were logged or cleared for farming, for instance, no bird species went extinct because of habitat loss: presumably the remaining forest fragments were sufficient to allow the species to survive until the forest grew back following the widespread abandonment of farming.

Expansion of an endemic species' geographical distribution that is caused deliberately or accidentally by humans is not considered part of the species' natural distribution. For example, the giant panda (*Ailuropoda melanoleuca*) is endemic to China, even though it now lives in zoos throughout the world. The black locust tree (*Robinia pseudoaccacia*) is native to eastern and southern United States, but has been widely planted elsewhere in North America, Europe, and in other temperate regions as a timber tree and ornamental, and it has spread aggressively into native vegetation in these regions. A species may be endemic to a wide geographical area (the black cherry tree [*Prunus serotina*] is endemic to the Western Hemisphere and is found across North, Central, and South America), or a species may be endemic to a small geographical area (the giant Komodo dragon [*Varanus komodoensis*] is endemic to several small islands in the Indonesian archipelago). Species that occupy a small area because they have only recently evolved from closely related species are designated **neoendemics**; examples include the hundreds of species of cichlid fish that occupy Lake Victoria in East Africa. In contrast, **paleoendemics** are ancient species whose close relatives have all gone extinct; examples include the giant panda and the Indian Ocean coelacanth. All such narrowly distributed endemic species are of concern for their potential to become extinct.

Isolated geographical units, such as remote islands, old lakes, and solitary mountain peaks, often have high percentages of endemic species. A high level of endemism is also evident in geologically old, continental areas with Mediterranean climates, such as southern Africa and California (Table 8.1). The biota of the entire continent of Australia has evolved in almost complete isolation, with 94% of its native plant species endemic. Among the United States, it is not surprising that the geographically isolated Hawaiian islands have a large number of endemic species (Figure 8.2). Areas that are not geographically isolated typically have much lower percentages of endemic species. For example, Germany and Belgium have few endemic species because virtually all of their species are found in neighboring countries. Similarly, the Carolinas in the southeastern United States share most of their

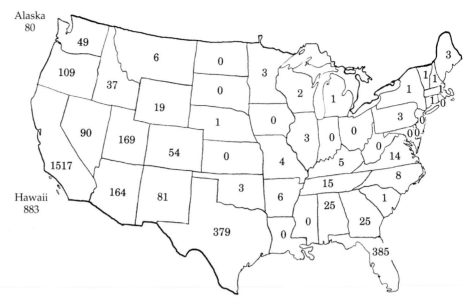

FIGURE 8.2 The number of plant species endemic to the different states varies greatly. For example, 379 plant species are found in Texas and nowhere else; New York, in contrast, has only one endemic plant species. California, with its large area and vast array of habitats, including deserts, mountains, seacoasts, old-growth forests, and myriad others, is home to more endemic species than any other state. There is a trend toward more endemic species in states further south. The island archipelago of Hawaii, far from the mainland, hosts many endemic species despite its small area. (From Gentry 1986.)

species with adjoining areas. One of the most notable concentrations of endemic species is on the island of Madagascar, where the moist tropical forests are spectacularly rich in endemic species: 93% of mammal species, 99% of frogs, and over 90% of the 15,000 plant species on the island are found nowhere else but on Madagascar (Mittermeier et al. 2004). About 80% of Madagascar's land has been altered or destroyed by human activity, possibly putting almost half of the endemic species of birds and mammals in danger of extinction.

TABLE 8.1 *Total plant species and endemic plant species in selected regions*

Region	Area (km²)	Total number of species	Number of endemic species	% endemic species
Europe	10,000,000	10,500	±3500	33
Australia	7,628,300	15,000	14,074	94
Southern Africa	2,573,000	18,550	±14,800	80
Texas	751,000	4196	379	9
California	411,000	5046	1517	30
Germany	349,270	2600	6	<1
North and South Carolina	217,000	2995	23	1
Cape Region of South Africa	90,000	8578	5850	68
Panama	75,000	9000	1222	14
Belgium	30,230	1400	1	<1

Source: After Gentry 1986; WRI 2000.

Species Most Vulnerable to Extinction

When environments are damaged by human activity, the ranges and population sizes of many species will be reduced, and some species will go extinct. Rare species must be carefully monitored and managed in conservation efforts. Ecologists have observed that particular categories of species are most vulnerable to extinction, many of which are the defining characteristics of rare species (Terborgh 1974; Gittleman 1994; Isaac and Colinshaw 2004). The five categories most frequently used in conservation planning are as follows:

FIGURE 8.3 Species of desert pupfish of the southwestern United States are highly endangered by the degradation and disappearance of their unique habitat—saline desert ponds. (Photograph by Ken Kelley, San Diego Zoo.)

- **Species with a very narrow geographical range.** Some species occur at only one or a few sites in a restricted geographical range, and if that whole range is affected by human activity, the species may become extinct (Brashares 2003; Dunn 2005; Ricketts et al. 2005). Bird species on oceanic islands are good examples of species with restricted ranges that have become extinct or are in danger of extinction (Grant and Grant 1997); many fish species confined to a single lake or a single watershed have also disappeared (Figure 8.3). Species with limited ranges are especially vulnerable to global climate change (see Chapter 9). Recent estimates suggest that more than 1 million species, mainly those with narrow ranges, could become extinct by 2050 as a result of climate change (Thomas et al. 2004).

- **Species with only one or a few populations.** Any one population of a species may become extinct as a result of chance factors, such as earthquakes, fire, an outbreak of disease, or human activity. Species with many populations are less vulnerable to extinction than are species with only one or a few populations (Pinto et al. 2005). This category is linked to the previous category, because species with few populations will also tend to have a narrow geographical range.

- **Species in which population size is small.** Sometimes called "the small population paradigm" (Caughley and Gunn 1996): Small populations are more likely to go locally extinct than large populations due to their greater vulnerability to demographic and environmental variation and loss of genetic variability (see Chapter 11); species that characteristically have small population sizes, such as large predators or extreme specialists, are more likely to become extinct than species that typically have large populations. At the extreme are species whose numbers have declined to just a few individuals.

    Population size by itself seems to be one of the best predictors of the extinction rate of isolated populations (see Chapter 7) (Pimm et al. 1988). An excellent example is provided by the survival of bird species at the Bogor Botanical Garden in Java, a woodland and arboretum that has been isolated for 50 years (Diamond et al. 1987). At this site, only 25% of the birds that had small population sizes during the period from 1932 to 1952 survived into the 1980s, while all of the species that were initially common survived. These results were confirmed in studies of isolated forest fragments in Brazil: The persistence of individual forest species, after several decades of isolation, was related to the size of the forest fragment, the number of habitats found in the fragment, and the initial abundance of the species (Bierregaard et al. 1992). Larger fragments with more habitat diversity had more forest species than smaller, less diverse fragments, and species with high initial populations were far more likely to persist than species with low initial populations.

- **Species in which population size is declining.** Population trends tend to continue, so a population showing signs of decline is likely to go extinct unless the cause of decline is identified and corrected (Peery et al. 2004); this is sometimes called "the declining population paradigm." As Charles Darwin pointed out almost 150 years ago in *On the Origin of Species* (1859):

  > To admit that species generally become rare before they become extinct, to feel no surprise at the rarity of the species, and yet to marvel greatly when the species ceases to exist, is much the same as to admit that sickness in the individual is the forerunner of death—to feel no surprise at sickness, but when the sick man dies, to wonder and to suspect that he died of some deed of violence.

- **Species that are hunted or harvested by people.** Overharvesting can rapidly reduce the population size of a species (see Chapter 10). If hunting and harvesting are not regulated, either by law or by local customs, the species can be driven to extinction. Utility has often been the prelude to extinction.

The following categories of species have also been linked to extinction, though they are not considered as all encompassing as the previous 5 categories.

- *Species that need a large home range.* Species in which individual animals or social groups need to forage over a wide area are prone to die off when part of their range is damaged or fragmented by human activity.

- *Animal species with a large body size.* Large animals tend to have large individual ranges, low reproductive rates, require more food, and are more often hunted by humans (Johnson 2002; Cardillo et al. 2005). Top carnivores, especially, are often killed by humans because they compete with humans for wild game, sometimes damage livestock, and are hunted for sport. Within groups of species, often the largest species will be the most prone to extinction—that is, the largest carnivore, the largest lemur, the largest whale. In Sri Lanka, for example, the largest species of carnivores—leopards and eagles—and the largest species of herbivores—elephants and deer—are at the greatest risk of extinction (Erdelen 1988). Countering this effect, to some degree, is the tendency for these large species to live longer than smaller species. For plants, species with large, short-lived seeds are more vulnerable than are species with smaller, long-lived seeds (Kolb and Diekmann 2005).

- *Species that are not effective dispersers.* Environmental changes prompt species to adapt, either behaviorally or physiologically, to the new conditions of their habitat. Species unable to adapt to changing environments must either migrate to more suitable habitat or face extinction. The rapid pace of human-induced changes often prevents adaptation, leaving migration as the only alternative. Species that are unable to cross roads, farmlands, and disturbed habitats are more likely to go extinct as their original habitat becomes affected by pollution, exotic species, and global climate change. In particular, many animal species in isolated forest fragments are unwilling or unable to cross pastures and colonize unoccupied areas of forest. Dispersal is important in the aquatic environment as well, where dams, point sources of pollution, channelization, and sedimentation can limit movement. Limited ability to disperse, as well as more specialized habitat requirements, may explain why in the United States 68% of the freshwater fauna of mussels and snails are extinct or threatened with extinction, in contrast to some 20% of dragonfly species (which can fly between the aquatic sites needed by their larval stages) (Stein and Flack 1997).

The importance of dispersal in preventing extinction is illustrated by two studies from Australia. The first, a detailed analysis of the vertebrates of Western Australia, revealed that modern extinctions were almost exclusively confined to nonflying mammals, with few extinctions recorded in birds and bats (Burbidge and McKenzie 1989). Among the birds, species that are unable to fly or are poor fliers showed the greatest tendency for extinction. In the second study, which examined 16 nonflying mammal species in Queensland rain forests, the most important characteristic that determined the ability of species to survive in isolated forest fragments was their ability to use, feed on, and move through the intervening matrix of secondary vegetation (Laurance 1991). This study highlights the importance of maintaining secondary vegetation to the survival of certain primary forest species.

- *Seasonal migrants.* Species that migrate seasonally depend on two or more distinct habitat types. If either one of those habitat types is damaged, the species may be unable to persist. The billion songbirds of 120 species that migrate each year between the northern United States and the American tropics depend on suitable habitat in both locations to survive and breed (see Figure 7.1). Also, if barriers to dispersal are created by roads, fences, or dams between the needed habitats, a species may be unable to complete its life cycle. Salmon species that are blocked by dams from swimming up rivers and spawning are a striking example of this problem. Many animal species migrate among habitats in search of food, often along elevational and moisture gradients. Herds of wild pigs, grazing ungulates, frugivorous vertebrates, and insectivorous birds are all examples of these. If these species are unable to migrate and thus are confined to one habitat type, they may not survive, or, if they do survive, they may be unable to accumulate the nutritional reserves needed to reproduce. Species that cross international barriers represent a special problem, in that conservation efforts must be coordinated by more than one country. Imagine the difficulties of conserving the tiny flock of Siberian cranes (*Grus leucogeranus*) that must migrate 4800 km each year from Russia to India and back, crossing six highly militarized, tense international borders.

- *Species with little genetic variability.* Genetic variability within a population can sometimes allow a species to adapt to a changing environment (see Chapters 2 and 11). Species with little or no genetic variability may have a greater tendency to become extinct when a new disease, a new predator, or some other change occurs in the environment.

- *Species with specialized niche requirements.* Once a habitat is altered, the environment may no longer be suitable for specialized species (Sigel et al. 2006). For example, wetland plants that require very specific and regular changes in water level may be rapidly eliminated when human activity affects the hydrology of an area. Species with highly specific dietary requirements are also at risk—for instance, there are species of mites that feed only on the feathers of a single bird species. If the bird species goes extinct, so do its associated feather mite species. Specialized insects that feed on only one type of plant species will go extinct if that plant species goes extinct. These types of linked extinctions are termed co-extinctions.

Some species are confined to a single unusual habitat type that is scattered and rare across the landscape (Koh et al. 2004). Unique species are found, for example, in vernal pools in California, granite outcrops in the southeastern United States, and isolated high mountains in the northeastern United States, illustrating the importance of habitat preservation to conserve species with narrow ranges.

- *Species that are characteristically found in stable, pristine environments.* Many species are found in environments where disturbance is minimal, such as in old stands of tropical rain forests and the interiors of rich temperate deciduous forests. When these forests are logged, grazed, burned, and otherwise altered, many native species are unable to tolerate the changed microclimatic conditions (more light, less moisture, greater temperature variation) and influx of exotic species. Also, species of stable environments tend to delay reproduction to an advanced age and produce only a few young. Following one or more episodes of habitat disturbance, such species are often unable to rebuild their populations fast enough to avoid extinction. When the environment is altered by air and water pollution, species unable to adapt to the destabilized physical and chemical environment will be eliminated from the community (Box 8.1). Coral reef species and freshwater invertebrates, such as crayfish, mussels, and snails, often cannot survive when their environments receive large inputs of sediment and sewage from human activities.

- *Species that form permanent or temporary aggregations.* Species that group together in specific places are highly vulnerable to local extinction (Reed 1999). For example, bats forage widely but typically roost together in particular caves. Hunters that enter these caves during the day can rapidly harvest every individual in the population. Herds of bison, flocks of passenger pigeons, and schools of spawning fish all represent aggregations that have been exploited and completely harvested by people. Temporary aggregations include schools of salmon and alewife moving up rivers to spawn; nets across rivers can catch virtually every fish and eliminate a species in a few days. Overly efficient harvesting of wild fruits from a cluster of neighboring trees for commercial markets can eliminate the seedlings that will grow into the next generation. Even though sea turtles may swim across vast stretches of ocean, egg collectors and hunters on a few narrow nesting beaches can threaten a species with extinction, as shown in Box 1.1. Many species of social animals may be unable to persist when their population size or density falls below a certain number; they may be unable to forage, find mates, or defend themselves; this is termed the **Allee effect**. Such species may be more vulnerable to habitat destruction than asocial species in which individuals are widely dispersed. On the other hand, monogamous animal species appear to be especially vulnerable to hunting pressures, perhaps due to their fixed mating system (Brashares 2003).

- *Species that have not had prior contact with people.* As we discussed in relation to islands in Chapter 7, species that have experienced prior human disturbance and persisted have a greater chance of surviving than species encountering people—along with their associated animals and plants—for the first time (see Figure 7.6) (Balmford 1996). The rate of recent bird extinction is far lower on Pacific islands colonized in the past by Polynesians than on islands not colonized by Polynesians (Pimm et al. 1995). Similarly, Western Australia, which has only recently experienced intense human impact, has a modern extinction rate for plant species that is 10 times higher than the Mediterranean region, which has a long history of heavy human impact (Greuter 1995).

BOX 8.1

Why Are Frogs and Toads Croaking?

At the First World Congress on Herpetology in 1989 in Canterbury, England, what had previously seemed like casual findings began to take on a disturbing significance: Scientists from around the world were seeing a decline in amphibian populations (Phillips 1990). Frogs, toads, salamanders, and other amphibians that had been common less than two decades ago were becoming rare, with some species even going extinct. This led to a call for action, to determine what was happening and what could be done to stop it. In the years since the meeting, hundreds of studies have been published, in addition to dozens of review articles and books. To pull together this vast body of new information, a Global Amphibian assessment was carried out from 2000 to 2004 (Stuart et al. 2004). This report shows that an astonishing 43% of amphibian species are declining in numbers.

These studies demonstrate that amphibians are particularly vulnerable to human disturbance, perhaps because many species require two separate habitats, aquatic and terrestrial, to complete their life cycles. If either habitat is damaged, the species will not be able to reproduce. Amphibians, like many other taxa, are also sensitive to a number of global environmental problems, including climate changes, increased ultraviolet radiation, habitat fragmentation, pesticides, chemical pollution, and acid rain (see Chapter 9). The latter two factors may be particularly dangerous to these animals: Chemical pollution and pesticides can easily penetrate the thin epidermis characteristic of amphibians, while slight decreases in pH can destroy eggs and tadpoles.

A major explanation continues to be loss of habitat, particularly wetlands. For instance, the number of farm ponds, a favorite habitat for amphibians in Britain, has declined by 70% over the last 100 years. Research on the natterjack toad (*Bufo calamita*) in England, one of the most intensively studied amphibians, also supported the acidification hypothesis: Ponds that had formerly supported significant populations of the species had become gradually more acidic due to industrial activities, a change that greatly increases the mortality of eggs and young toads (Beebee 1996). However, species in relatively undisturbed, protected areas elsewhere in the world have also exhibited declines. Introduced predatory fish, drought, unusual climatic events, and increased ultraviolet radiation due to a decrease in the protective ozone layer have subsequently been blamed for the decline of individual species; in many cases, these stress factors have apparent-

Studies of the natterjack toad (*Bufo calamita*) and its habitat in England pointed to pollution and acidification of pondwater as a cause for the decline in numbers of this species. (Photograph by Richard Griffiths.)

ly made species susceptible to fatal infections from waterborne fungi (Blaustein et al. 2003; Davidson et al. 2003; Stuart et al. 2004; McCallum 2005). Despite an abundance of recent studies, scientists are still not sure whether amphibian species are declining on a global scale due to global causes or if they are declining on a local scale due to numerous separate causes (Alford et al. 2001).

Much of the initial hubbub over amphibian declines occurred because amphibians are commonly perceived as being highly sensitive to environmental disturbance and could thus serve as an "indicator species" and give early warning of environmental damage. Recent reports suggest that amphibians have indeed been disproportionately affected (Stuart et al. 2004). Surveys suggest that around 32% of the world's amphibians are threatened with extinction, a figure that indicates a higher threat than the threat faced by both birds (12%) and mammals (23%) (Baillie et al. 2004). Since the time of the initial congress in 1989, a huge effort on the part of the conservation and herpetology communities have provided evidence for the crises facing amphibians, and many of the causes. Now that this information is available, people need to develop and implement an effective course of action. While we know what action to take to help certain species that are facing specific threats, for other species, we cannot develop a conservation strategy as long as the reason for the declines remains unknown or beyond our control.

- *Species that have closely related species that are recently extinct or are threatened with extinction.* Often groups of species are particularly vulnerable to extinction, such as primates, cranes, sea turtles, and cycads. The characteristics that make certain species vulnerable are often shared by related species.

Characteristics of extinction-prone species are not independent; rather, they group together into categories of characteristics. For example, species with a specialized diet also tend to have low population densities—both characteristics of extinction-prone species. The characteristics often vary among groups because of peculiarities of natural history: Butterflies differ from jellyfish and cacti in characters associated with vulnerability to extinction. By identifying characteristics of extinction-prone species, conservation biologists can anticipate the need for managing populations of vulnerable species. Those species most vulnerable to extinction may have the full range of characteristics, as David Ehrenfeld (1970) imagined:

> [A] large predator with a narrow habitat tolerance, long gestation period, and few young per litter [is] hunted for a natural product and/or for sport, but is not subject to efficient game management. It has a restricted distribution but travels across international boundaries. It is intolerant of man, reproduces in aggregates, and has nonadaptive behavioral idiosyncrasies.

There is another great need for identifying characteristics of threatened species: The greatest proportion of threatened species that have been identified so far are also in the most well-studied families, highlighting the point that only when we are knowledgeable about a species can we recognize the dangers it faces (Duncan and Lockwood 2001). A lack of knowledge about a group of species should not be taken to mean that the species are not threatened with extinction; rather, a lack of knowledge should be an argument for urgent study of those species.

Conservation Categories

Identifying those species most vulnerable to extinction is essential to the work of conservation. To mark the status of rare and endangered species for conservation purposes, the International Union for the Conservation of Nature (IUCN) has established 9 conservation categories (IUCN 2001); species in categories critically endangered (CR), endangered (EN), and vulnerable (VU) are considered to be threatened with extinction. For the three categories of threatened species, the IUCN has developed more quantitative measures of threat based on the probability of extinction (Gärdenfors 2001). These categories have proved to be useful at the national and international levels through published Red Data Books and Red Lists of threatened species (Figure 8.4), and by directing attention toward species of special concern and identifying species threatened with extinction for protection through international agreements, such as the Convention on International Trade in Endangered Species (CITES).

- *Extinct (EX).* The species (or other taxa, such as subspecies or varieties) is no longer known to exist.

- *Extinct in the Wild (EW).* The species exists only in cultivation, in captivity, or as a naturalized population well outside its original range.

- *Critically Endangered (CR).* Species that have an extremely high risk of going extinct in the wild, according to any of the criteria A to E (specified below).

- *Endangered (EN).* Species that have a very high risk of extinction in the wild, according to any of the criteria A to E.

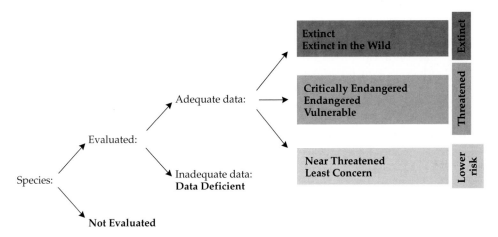

FIGURE 8.4 The IUCN categories of conservation status. This chart shows the distribution of the categories. Reading from left to right, they depend on (1) whether a species has been evaluated or not and (2) how much data is available for the species. If data are available, the species is then put into a category in the lower risk, threatened, or extinct areas. (After IUCN 2001.)

- *Vulnerable (VU)*. Species that have a high risk of extinction in the wild, according to any of the criteria A to E.

- *Near Threatened (NT)*. The species is close to qualifying for a threatened category, but is not currently considered threatened.

- *Least Concern (LC)*. The species is not considered near threatened or threatened. (Widespread and abundant species are included in this category.)

- *Data Deficient (DD)*. Inadequate information exists to determine the risk of extinction for the species.

- *Not Evaluated (NE)*. The species has not yet been evaluated against the Red List Criteria.

When used on a national or other regional level there are two additional Red List Categories (IUCN 2003):

- *Regionally Extinct (RE)*. The species no longer exists within the country (region), but is extant in other parts of the world.

- *Not Applicable (NA)*. The species is not eligible for the regional Red List, because, for example, it is not within its natural range in the region (it has been introduced) or because it is only a rare migrant to the region.

Assignment of categories depends on having at least one of the following types of information and comparing that data to threshold values given by the IUCN Red List Criteria (IUCN 2001):

A. Observable reduction in numbers of individuals.

B. The total geographical area occupied by the species.

C. The predicted decline in number of individuals.

D. The number of mature individuals currently alive.

E. The probability of the species going extinct in a certain number of years or generations.

The new criteria for assigning categories are based on the developing methods of population viability analysis (see Chapter 12) and focus particularly on population trends and habitat condition. For example, a critically endangered species has at least one of the following characteristics: its population has declined by 80% or more over the last 10 years or 3 generations, or is expected to decline that much (Red List criterion A); the species has a restricted range (for example, less than 100 km^2 at a single location), observed or predicted habitat loss, ecological imbalance, or commercial exploitation (B) (Figure 8.5); total population size is less than 250 mature, breeding individuals and is expected to decline by 25% or more within 3 years or 1 generation (C); population size is less than 50 mature individuals (D); or the overall extinction probability is greater than 50% in 10 years or 3 generations (E).

Using habitat loss as a criterion in assigning categories is particularly useful for many species that are poorly known biologically, since species can be listed as threatened if their habitat is being destroyed even if scientists know little else about them. In practice, species are most commonly assigned to an IUCN category based on the area it occupies, the number of mature individuals it has, or the rate of decline of the habitat or population; the probability of extinction is least commonly used (Gärdenfors 2001; Kindvall and Gärdenfors 2003). In any case, the probability of a species going extinct using population viability analysis is strongly correlated with its IUCN category and various other methods of risk assessment (O'Grady et al. 2004).

The advantage of the present system is that it provides a standard, quantitative method of classification by which decisions can be reviewed and evaluated by other scientists according to accepted quantitative criteria and using whatever information is available. However, this method can devolve into arbitrary assignment if decisions have to be made with insufficient data. Gathering the data needed for proper assignment is expensive and time-consuming, particularly for developing countries and in rapidly changing situations. Regardless of this limitation, this system of species classification is a distinct improvement over past methods that were more subjective and will assist attempts to protect species.

Using the new categories, the IUCN has evaluated and described the threats to plant and animal species in its series of Red Data Books and Red Lists (see Table 7.2; Baillie et al. 2004). For mammals, 1101 out of 5416 described species are listed as threatened; for birds, 1213 out of 9917 species are listed as threatened; and for amphibians 1770 out of 5743 species are listed as threatened. Although the IUCN evaluations have included numerous species of fish (800), reptiles (304), mollusks (974), insects (559), crustaceans (429), and plants (11,824) they are still not extensive enough. All bird and amphibian species and most mammal species have been evaluated using the IUCN system because they are well known, but the levels of evaluation are lower for reptiles, fish, and plants. The evaluations of insects and other invertebrates, mosses, algae, fungi, and microorganisms are even less adequate. For example, less than 0.1% of insects have been evaluated.

FIGURE 8.5 Yellow gentian (*Gentiana lutea*), a beautiful perennial herb of European mountain meadows, has roots that are collected for traditional medicine. Approximately 1500 tons of dried roots are used each year in a wide variety of preparations to stimulate digestion and to treat stomachache. Due to overharvesting and the resulting decline and destruction of many populations, the species is listed as endangered in Portugal, Albania, and certain regions of Germany and Switzerland, and as vulnerable in other countries, according to the IUCN's classification categories. Despite official regulation that restricts collection to designated areas, illegal harvesting continues. (Photograph by Bob Gibbons, Natural Image.)

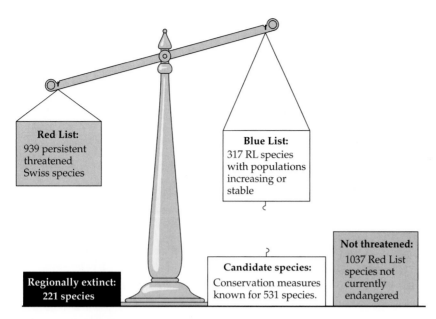

Red List:
939 persistent threatened Swiss species

Blue List:
317 RL species with populations increasing or stable

Regionally extinct:
221 species

Candidate species:
Conservation measures known for 531 species.

Not threatened:
1037 Red List species not currently endangered

FIGURE 8.6 An innovative approach is being developed in three Swiss cantons to evaluate the current status of the species of plants and animals that are currently on the Red List of threatened and extinct species. Of these, 317 species have been identified as stable or increasing in abundance, thanks to conservation and protection measures; these species form a "Blue List" of recovering species that have been removed from the Red List. Protection and conservation techniques are locally successful or known for 531 species: These species are future Candidate species for the Blue List. There are 939 Persistent Red List species that are still declining in size, and for which recovery efforts are not yet known. There are 1037 species on the Red List not currently listed as endangered, but in some cases abundances are declining, data are inadequate, or species are not responding to current conservation measures. The goal is to shift the balance as the Blue List lengthens. (After Gigon et al. 2000.)

The IUCN system has been applied to specific geographical areas and groups of species as a way of highlighting conservation priorities (Keller and Bollman 2004). As a group, mammals face a greater degree of threat than birds; comparing regions, in general, the species of Japan are more threatened than the species of South Africa, which are more threatened, in turn, than the species of the United Kingdom (Table 8.2). Using the IUCN system on a regional basis, species may be classified as threatened in a particular country, region (such as Europe), state, or province (Gärdenfors 2001; Eaton et al. 2005; Milner-Gulland et al. 2005).

By tracking the conservation status of species over time, it is possible to determine whether species are responding to conservation efforts or are continuing to be threatened. One such measure is the Red List Index, which demonstrates that the conservation status of birds has continued to decline during the period from 1988 to 2004, with particularly sharp declines for albatrosses and petrels and for amphibians (Butchart et al. 2004; Rodrigues et al. 2006). Another measure, the Living Planet Index, follows population sizes for 1100 vertebrate species; this index has shown a decline of 25 % from 1970 to 2000 (Loh et al. 2005).

In Switzerland, efforts are being made to identify those threatened (or Red List) species that are responding to conservation efforts (Gigon et al. 2000). The 317 species that have stable populations or are increasing in abundance are listed in a "Blue List." The Blue List highlights successful conservation efforts and suggests further projects that might succeed (Figure 8.6). A further development, suggested for other countries, is grouping together Red List species that occur in similar habitats so that they can be managed together (Pärtel et al. 2005).

TABLE 8.2 *Percentage of species in some temperate countries that are threatened[a] with global extinction*

Country	Mammals		Birds	
	Number of species	% threatened	Number of species	% threatened
Argentina	320	10.0	897	6.1
Canada	193	8.3	426	4.5
China	394	20.3	1100	7.5
Japan	132	28.0	>250	21.2
Russia	269	16.0	628	7.5
South Africa	247	11.7	596	6.0
United Kingdom	50	20.0	230	4.3
United States	428	9.3	650	10.9

Source: Data from WRI 1998 and Baillie et al. 2004.

[a]Threatened species include those in the IUCN categories "critically endangered," "endangered," and "vulnerable."

[b]Percentages are low for amphibians in certain countries and for plants in all countries because most species have not yet been evaluated using the updated system of assigning categories. Once all species have been evaluated, these percentages will increase substantially.

Natural Heritage Data Centers

A program similar to the efforts of the IUCN is the NatureServe network of Natural Heritage programs that covers all 50 of the United States, 3 provinces in Canada, and 14 Latin American countries (www.natureserve.org/explorer). This network, strongly supported by The Nature Conservancy, gathers, organizes, and manages information on the occurrence of "elements of conservation interest"—more than 50,000 species, subspecies, and biological communities (in addition to half a million precisely located populations) (De Grammont and Cuarón 2006). Elements are given status ranks based on a series of standard criteria: number of remaining populations or occurrences, number of individuals remaining (for species) or aerial extent (for communities), number of protected sites, degree of threat, and innate vulnerability of the species or community. On the basis of these criteria, elements are assigned an imperilment rank from 1 to 5, ranging from critically imperiled (1) to demonstrably secure (5), on a global, national, and regional basis. Species are also classified as "X" (extinct), "H" (known historically with searches ongoing), and "unknown" (uninvestigated elements). Data on these conservation elements is available on the NatureServe website.

The results of NatureServe's conservation status assessment for the United States are detailed in *Precious Heritage: The Status of Biodiversity in the United States* (Stein et al. 2000). The results demonstrate that aquatic species groups, including freshwater mussels, crayfish, amphibians, and fish, are in greater danger of extinction than well known groups of insects and vertebrates (Figure 8.7). Freshwater mussels are by far the most endangered species group, with 12% of these species presumed to be extinct already and almost 25% critically imperiled. Land plants are intermediate in degree of endangerment.

This system has also been applied to the 4500 distinct ecological communities recognized in the United States. Only 25% of these can be considered as secure, with 26% listed as vulnerable, 31% as imperiled or severely imperiled, less than 1% as presumably eliminated, and 18% as not possible to evaluate (Stein et al. 2000). Concentrations of endangered communities occur in Hawaii, the Willamette Valley of Oregon, and large areas of the Midwest and Southeast.

Reptiles		Amphibians[b]		Plants[b]	
Number of species	% threatened	Number of species	% threatened	Number of species	% threatened
220	2.3	145	20.7	9000	0.5
41	4.9	41	2.4	2920	0.0
340	9.1	263	32.7	30,000	1.5
66	16.7	52	38.5	4700	0.3
58	10.3	23	0.0	—	—
299	6.7	95	22.1	23,000	0.3
8	0.0	7	0.0	1550	0.8
280	9.6	233	21.5	16,302	1.5

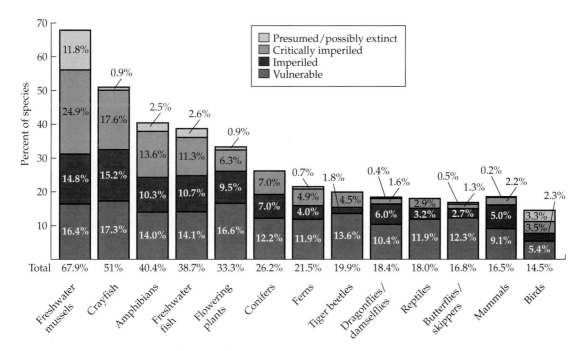

FIGURE 8.7 Some species groups from the United States ranked as critically imperiled, imperiled, or vulnerable (rankings 1–3, respectively, on a scale of 5) according to criteria endorsed by The Nature Conservancy and coordinated by NatureServe. The graph also shows the percentage of species in each class that are presumed to be extinct. The groups are arranged with those at greatest risk on the left. (From Stein and Flack 1997.)

This system has proved extremely successful and useful in organizing hundreds of thousands of records of species and ecosystems occurrence (Pearman et al. 2006). Regional data centers are maintained by hundreds of workers and are consulted approximately 200,000 times a year for information to assist with protection efforts on behalf of endangered species, environmental impact reports, scientific research, and land-use decisions. Organizing vast amounts of conservation information is an expensive, labor-intensive activity, but it is a crucial component of conservation efforts. It is imperative to know what species and biological communities are in danger and where they occur in order to protect them.

Summary

1. Rare species are more prone to extinction than common ones. A species can be considered rare if it has one of these three characteristics: it occupies a narrow geographical range, it occupies only one or a few specialized habitats, or it is always found in small populations. Isolated habitats such as islands, lakes, and mountaintops may have locally endemic species with narrow distributions.

2. Species most vulnerable to extinction have particular characteristics, including a very narrow range, one or only a few populations, small population size, declining population size, and an economic value to humans, which leads to overexploitation. Additional characteristics include: low population density, a large home range, large body size, low rate of population increase, poor dispersal ability, migration among different habitats, little genetic variability, specialized niche requirements, a need for a stable environment, or typically found in large aggregations. An extinction-prone species may display several of these characteristics.

3. To highlight the status of species for conservation purposes, the IUCN has established 9 conservation categories (plus 2 on the national level), including 3 categories of threatened species: critically endangered, endangered, and vulnerable. This system of classification is now widely used to evaluate the status of species and establish conservation priorities. Categorization depends on having quantitative information for species, such as number of individuals alive in the wild, number of extant populations, trends in population size, area occupied, and predicted future threats to the species.

4. Countries and regions of the world, as well as conservation organizations, are establishing additional lists of endangered species and biological communities.

For Discussion

1. Learn about a well known endangered species, such as the koala bear, the right whale, or the cheetah. Why are these particular species vulnerable to extinction? Use the IUCN criteria (IUCN 2001) to determine the appropriate conservation category for one or more species.

2. Develop an imaginary animal, recently discovered, that is extraordinarily vulnerable to extinction. Give your species a whole range of characteristics that make it vulnerable; then, consider what could be done to protect it. Give your species a hypothetical set of population characteristics, natural history, and geographical range. Then apply the recently developed IUCN system to the species to determine its conservation category.

Suggested Readings

Baillie, J. E. M., C. Hilton-Taylor, and S. N. Stuart. 2004. *2004 IUCN Red List of Threatened Species. A Global Assessment.* IUCN, Gland, Switzerland. Current information on the status of species and extinction; also available online.

Balmford, A. 1996. Extinction filters and current resilience: The significance of past selection pressures for conservation biology. *Trends in Ecology and Evolution* 11: 193–196. Current extinction rates are highest for groups of species encountering people for the first time.

Berger, J. 2004. The last mile: How to sustain long-distance migration in animals. *Conservation Biology* 18: 320–331. Migrating species need extra help to prevent their decline and extinction.

Butchart, S. H. M., A. J. Sattersfield, L. A. Bennun, S. M. Shutes, H. R. Akçakaya, J. E. M. Baillie, et al. 2004. Measuring global trends in the status of biodiversity: Red List Indices for birds. *PloS Biology* 2: 2294–2304. The conservation status for birds has gotten worse over time.

De Grammont, P. C. and A. D. Cuarón. 2006. An evaluation of threatened species categorization systems used on the American continent. *Conservation Biology* 20: 14–27. Legal and management efforts to project endangered species would be more effective if countries and organizations agreed on standard definitions of categories.

Gärdenfors, U. 2001. Classifying threatened species at national versus global levels. *Trends in Ecology and Evolution* 16: 511–516. IUCN Red Lists are being used at national levels to protect species.

Li, Y. and D. S. Wilcove. 2005. Threats to vertebrate species in China and the United States. *BioScience* 55: 147–153. Different economic systems and rural population densities result in different threats to biodiversity.

Loh, J., R. E. Green, T. Ricketts, J. Lamoreaux, M. Jenkins, V. Kapos, and J. Randers. 2005. The Living Plant Index: Using species population time series to track trends in biodiversity. *Philosophical Transactions of the Royal Society of London Series B* 360: 289–295. Populations of vertebrate species continue to decline over time.

NatureServe. 2005. http://www/natureserve.org. Organizes and presents data on biodiversity surveys in North America.

Pearman, P. B., M. R. Penskar, E. H. Schools, and H. D. Enander. 2006. Identifying potential indicators of conservation value using Natural Heritage occurrence data. *Ecological Applications* 16: 186–201. Databases of rare species occurrences can be used to identify areas for conservation.

Rabinowitz, D., S. Cairnes, and T. Dillon. 1986. Seven forms of rarity and their frequency in the flora of the British Isles. *In* M. E. Soulé (ed.), *Conservation Biology: The Science of Scarcity and Diversity*, pp. 182–204. Sinauer Associates, Sunderland, MA. An influential paper describing patterns of rarity and their significance to conservation.

Reed, J. M. 1999. The role of behavior in recent avian extinctions and endangerments. *Conservation Biology* 13: 232–241. Certain bird behaviors make species vulnerable to extinction.

Ricketts, T. H., E. Dinerstein, T. Boucher, T. M. Brooks, S. H. M. Butchart, M. Hoffmann, et al. 2005. Pinpointing and preventing imminent extinctions. *Proceedings of the National Academy of Sciences* 102: 18497–18501. Extinction rates will increase in coming decades because many threatened species are not in protected areas.

Rodrigues, A., J. D. Pilgrim, J. F. Lemoreux, M. Hoffman, and T. M. Brooks. 2006. The value of the IUCN Red List for conservation. *Trends in Ecology and Evolution* 21: 71–76. Red lists provide a standardized way to evaluate threats to biodiversity, both among countries and across time.

Sigel, B. J., T. W. Sherry, and B. E. Young. 2006. Avian community response to lowland tropical rainforest isolation: 40 years of change at La Selva Biological Station, Costa Rica. *Conservation Biology* 20: 111–121. Factors are identified that make certain tropical bird species vulnerable to extinction.

Stein, B. A., L. S. Kutner, and J. S. Adams (eds.). 2000. *Precious Heritage: The Status of Biodiversity in the United States*. Oxford University Press, New York. Analysis of the distribution of biodiversity in the United States and current threats.

Terborgh, J. 1974. Preservation of natural diversity: The problem of extinction-prone species. *BioScience* 24: 715–722. Why certain species are more vulnerable than others to extinction.

Thomas, J. A., M. G. Telfer, D. B. Roy, C. D. Preston, J. J. D. Greenwood, J. Asher, et al. 2004. Comparative losses of British butterflies, birds, and plants and the global extinction crisis. *Science* 303: 1879–1881. Millions of species face extinction due to global climate change.

Young, B. E., S. N. Stuart, J. S. Chanson, N. A. Cox, and T. M. Boucher. 2004. *Disappearing Jewels: The Status of New World Amphibians*. NatureServe, Arlington, VA. Island species are more vulnerable to extinction than mainland species.

Habitat Destruction, Fragmentation, Degradation, and Global Climate Change

As we've seen in Chapters 7 and 8, *Homo sapiens* poses a serious and growing threat of extinction to species and entire biological communities. Massive disturbances caused by people have altered, degraded, and destroyed the natural landscape on a vast scale, driving species and even entire communities to the point of extinction. The seven major threats to biological diversity that result from human activity are habitat destruction, habitat fragmentation, habitat degradation (including pollution), global climate change, the overexploitation of species for human use, the introduction of invasive species, and the increased spread of disease (Figure 9.1). In this chapter we will examine the first four threats we pose to the environment; in Chapter 10 we will discuss overexploitation, invasive species, and disease. Most threatened species face at least two or more of these threats, thus speeding their way to extinction and hindering efforts to protect them (Wilcove et al. 1998; Terborgh 1999; Stearns and Stearns 1999; IUCN 2004; MEA 2005). Typically, these threats develop so rapidly and on such a large scale that species are not able to adapt genetically to the changes or disperse to a more hospitable location. Moreover, multiple threats may interact additively or even synergistically, such that their combined impact on a species or an ecosystem is greater than their individual effects (Laurance and Cochrane 2001).

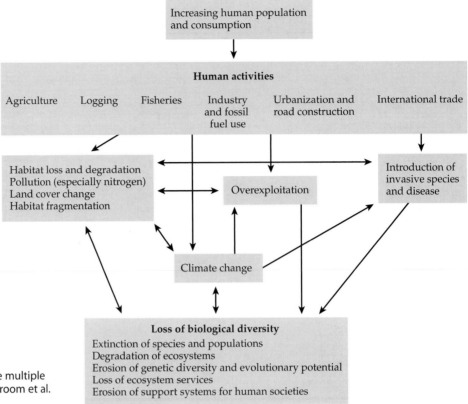

FIGURE 9.1 Human activities create multiple threats to biological diversity. (After Groom et al. 2006.)

The Problem of Human Population Growth

The seven major threats to biological diversity are all caused by an ever-increasing use of the world's natural resources by an expanding human population (Table 9.1). Up until the last few hundred years, the rate of human population growth had been relatively slow, with the birth rate only slightly exceeding the mortality rate. The greatest destruction of biological communities has occurred over the last 150 years, during which time the human population exploded from 1 billion in 1850 to 6.5 billion by March 2005 (Figure 9.2). World population will reach an estimated 10 billion by the year 2050. Humans have increased in such numbers because birth rates have re-

TABLE 9.1 *Three ways in which humans dominate the global ecosystem*

1. LAND SURFACE
Human land use and need for resources have transformed as much as half of the Earth's ice-free land surface.

2. NITROGEN CYCLE
Each year human activities, such as cultivating nitrogen-fixing crops, using nitrogen fertilizers, and burning fossil fuels, release more nitrogen into terrestrial systems than is added by natural biological and physical processes.

3. ATMOSPHERIC CARBON CYCLE
By the middle of this century, human use of fossil fuels will have resulted in a doubling of the level of carbon dioxide in the Earth's atmosphere.

Source: Data from Vitousek 1994; Vitousek 1997; MEA 2005.

mained high while mortality rates have declined—a result of both modern medical achievements (specifically the control of disease) and the presence of more reliable food supplies. Population growth has slowed in the industrialized countries of the world, as well as in some developing countries in Asia and Latin America, but it is still high in other areas, particularly in tropical Africa (Luck et al. 2004). If these countries implement immediate and effective programs of population control, human population numbers could possibly peak at "only" eight billion in 2050 and then gradually decline. Because human population density is a good predictor of the intensity of threats to biodiversity, this increase in human population is predicted to cause an additional 15% of bird and mammal species to be threatened with extinction by the year 2050 (McKee et al. 2003).

People use natural resources, such as fuelwood, wild meat, and wild plants, and convert vast amounts of natural habitat for agricultural and residential purposes. Agricultural systems now occupy one-quarter of the Earth's land surface. Because some degree of resource use is inevitable, population growth is partially responsible for the loss of biological diversity (McKee et al. 2003; Scharlemann et al. 2005). All else being equal, more people equals greater human impact and less biodiversity. Nitrogen pollution is greatest in rivers flowing through landscapes with high human population densities, and rates of deforestation are greatest in countries with the highest rates of human population growth. Therefore, some scientists have argued strongly that controlling the size of the human population is the key to protecting biological diversity (Hardin 1993; Johns 2003; Cohen 2004). However, population growth is not the only cause of species extinction and habitat destruction: overconsumption of resources is also responsible. Species extinctions and the destruction of ecosystems are not necessarily caused by individual citizens obtaining their basic needs. The rise of industrial capitalism and materialistic modern societies has greatly accelerated demands for natural resources, particularly in the developed countries. Moreover, industrialized countries have served as role models for developing nations, which now increasingly aspire to attain the same levels of overconsumption as the industrial countries. Inefficient and wasteful use and overconsumption of natural resources are major causes of the decline in biological diversity.

In many developing countries, local farm owners are often forced off their land by large landowners, business interests, and even the government, which is often backed up by the police and army. These local farmers often have no choice but to move to remote, undeveloped areas and attempt to eke out a living through shifting cultivation, destroying natural habitats, and hunting animals to local extinction. Political instability, lawlessness, and war also force farmers off their land and into remote, undeveloped areas where they feel safer. The one billion impoverished people of the world who live on less than $2 per day are too hungry and desperate to worry about protecting biodiversity (United Nations Millennium Project 2005). Until these people are given the opportunity to improve their lives in a sustainable manner, the environments in which they live will continue to deteriorate.

Whether motivated by greed, desperation, or indifference, once a community or nation begins exploiting resources for short-term gain, it is difficult to stop the process. Biological communities can often persist close to areas with high densities of people as long as human activities are regulated by local custom or government. The sacred groves that are preserved next to villages in Africa, India, and China are excel-

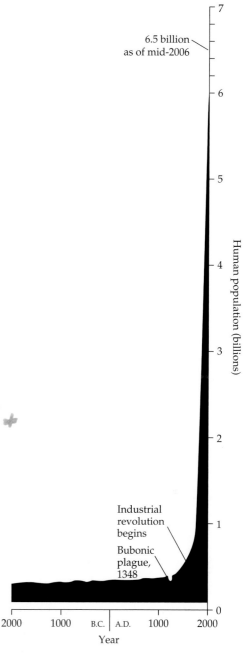

FIGURE 9.2 Human population has increased spectacularly since the seventeenth century. At current growth rates, the population will increase to 10 billion by the year 2050.

FIGURE 9.3 Citizens of the wealthy, developed countries of the world often criticize the poorer, developing nations for a lack of sound environmental policies but seem unwilling to acknowledge that their own excessive consumption of resources is a major part of the problem. (Cartoon by Scott Willis, © San Jose Mercury News.)

lent examples of locally managed biological communities (Chandrashekara and Sankar 1998). Sometimes this regulation breaks down during war, political unrest, and social instability. When this happens, there may be a scramble to use up and sell resources that had been sustainably used for generations. The higher the density of people, the more closely their activities must be regulated, and the greater the destruction that can result from a breakdown in authority. The devastation that occurred in China's forests during the Cultural Revolution is a revealing example: Strict regulations against cutting trees were no longer enforced, so farmers cut down trees at a tremendous rate, stockpiling wood for fuel, construction, and furniture-making (Primack 1988).

People in industrialized countries (and the wealthy minority in the developing countries) consume a disproportionate share of the world's energy, minerals, wood products, and food (Myers and Kent 2004), and therefore have a disproportionate impact on the environment (Figure 9.3). Each year, the United States, which has 5% of the world's human population, uses roughly 25% of the world's natural resources. Each year the average U.S. citizen uses 17 times more energy and 79 times more paper products than does the average citizen of India (WRI 2000).

The impact (I) of any human population on the environment is captured by the formula: $I = PAT$, where P is the number of people, A is the average income, and T is the level of technology (Rees 2001). It is important to recognize that this impact is often felt over a great distance; for example, a citizen of Germany, Canada, or Japan affects the environment in other countries through his/her use of foods and other materials produced elsewhere: The fish eaten quietly at home perhaps came from Alaskan waters, where its capture contributed to the population decline of sea lions, seals, and sea otters; the chocolate cake and coffee consumed at the end of a meal in Italy or France were made with cacao and coffee beans grown in plantations carved out of rain forests in West Africa, Indonesia, or Brazil. This linkage has been captured in the idea of the **ecological footprint**, defined as the influence a group of people has on both the surrounding environment and locations across the

TABLE 9.2 *A comparison of ecological footprints for selected countries*

Country	Population (millions)	Footprint (ha/person)[a]	Biocapacity (ha/person)[b]	Ecological deficit (if negative)[c]
India	950	1.1	0.7	–0.4
Indonesia	200	1.5	3.2	1.7
Brazil	161	2.5	11.5	9.0
China	1232	3.4	2.0	–1.4
Russia	148	5.3	4.0	–1.3
Japan	126	5.9	0.9	–5.0
Germany	82	6.2	2.4	–3.8
United Kingdom	58	6.2	1.8	–4.4
Canada	30	7.7	11.2	3.5
Australia	18	8.5	9.3	0.8
United States	269	12.2	5.5	–6.7
World[d]	5745	2.9	2.2	–0.7

Source: Redefining Progress, 2001.

[a]The ecological footprint is the number of hectares of land required to support the lifestyle of one person.

[b]Biocapacity is the number of hectares per person in a country.

[c]Countries with an ecological deficit (negative values) are using more natural resources than they have, resulting in environmental degradation within their own country and/or a need to obtain natural resources from other countries.

[d]The total ecological footprint of the world's human population.

globe (Table 9.2) (Rees 2001; Sanderson et al. 2002; Holden and Hoyer 2005). A modern city in a developed country typically has an ecological footprint of between 290 to 1130 times its area. For example, the city of Toronto, Canada, occupies an area of only 630 km^2, but each of its citizens requires the environmental services of 7.7 ha (0.077 km^2) to provide food, water, and waste disposal sites; with a population of 2.4 million people, Toronto has an ecological footprint of 185,000 km^2, an area equal to the state of New Jersey or the country of Syria. This excessive consumption of resources is not sustainable in the long term. Unfortunately, this pattern is now being adopted by the expanding middle class in the developing world, including the large, rapidly developing countries of China and India, which increases the probability of massive environmental disruption (Myers and Kent 2004). The affluent citizens of developed countries must confront their excessive consumption of resources and reevaluate their lifestyles while at the same time offering aid to curb population growth and protect biological diversity and increase energy efficiency in the developing world (Speth 2003).

Habitat Destruction

The primary cause of the loss of biological diversity, including species, biological communities, and genetic variation, is not direct human exploitation or malevolence, but the habitat destruction that inevitably results from the expansion of human populations and human activities (Figure 9.4). For the next few decades, land-use change will continue to be the main factor affecting biodiversity in terrestrial ecosystems (Tilman et al. 2001), probably followed by overexploitation, climate change, and the introduction of invasive species (IUCN 2004). Consequently, the most important means of protecting biological diversity is habitat preservation. Habitat loss does not necessarily mean wholesale habitat destruction—habitat damage associated with pollution and habitat fragmentation can also mean that the habitat is ef-

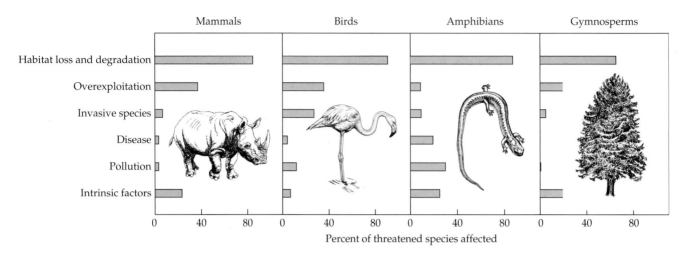

FIGURE 9.4 Habitat loss and degradation is the greatest threat to the world's species, followed by overexploitation. Groups of species face different threats; birds are more threatened by invasive species, whereas amphibians are more effected by disease and pollution. Percentages add up to more than 100 percent because species often face multiple threats. (After IUCN 2004.)

fectively "lost" to species that cannot tolerate these changes, even though to the casual onlooker the habitat appears intact. A pond contaminated by acid rain may still look like a healthy wetland habitat, but for frogs sensitive to these chemicals, it can be considered a lost habitat. When a habitat is degraded and destroyed, the plants, animals, and other organisms living there will have nowhere to go and will just die off (Scholes and Biggs 2004).

In many areas of the world, particularly on islands and in locations where human population density is high, most of the original habitat has been destroyed (WRI 2003; MEA 2005) (Figure 9.5). Fully 98% of the land suitable for agriculture has already been transformed by human activity (Sanderson et al. 2002). Because the world's population will continue to increase, we will increase agricultural output by 30 to 50% over the next 30 years; thus, the need to protect biological diversity will be forced to compete directly against the need for new agricultural lands (Tilman et al. 2001).

Habitat disturbance has been particularly severe throughout Europe; south and east Asia, including the Philippines, China, and Japan; southeastern and southwestern Australia; New Zealand; Madagascar; West Africa; the southeastern and northern coasts of South America; Central America; the Caribbean; and central and eastern North America. In many of these regions, more than 50% of the natural habitats have been disturbed or removed. Only 15% of the land area in Europe remains unmodified by human activities, and in some regions of Europe, the figure is even lower. In Germany or the U.K., for example, one can hardly find any habitat that has not been modified by humans at one time or another.

In the United States, only 42% of the natural vegetation remains, and in many regions of the East and Midwest, less than 25% remains (Stein et al. 2000). Surveys in the United States have documented certain biological communities that have declined in area by 98% or more since European settlement (Noss et al. 1995): old-growth stands in eastern deciduous forests, old-growth long-leaf pine (*Pinus palustris*) forests and savannahs in the southeastern coastal plain, ungrazed dry prairie in Florida, native grasslands in California, ungrazed sagebrush steppe in the Intermountain West, and streams in the Mississippi River floodplain. The principal threats to habitat that affect endangered species, in order of decreasing importance, are agriculture (affecting 38% of endangered species), commercial developments (35%), water projects (30%), outdoor recreation (27%), livestock grazing (22%), pollution

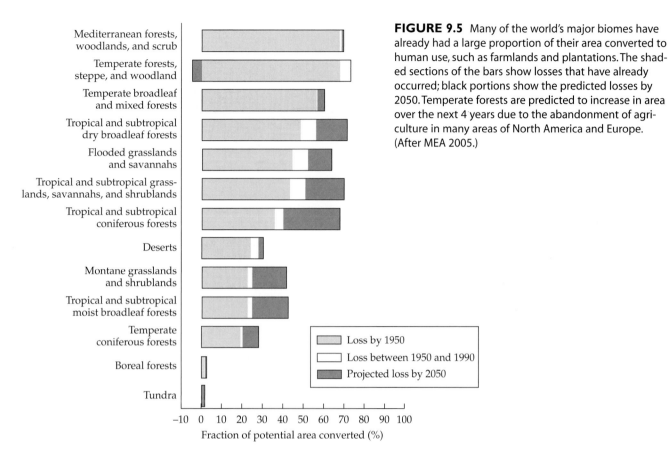

Mediterranean forests, woodlands, and scrub

Temperate forests, steppe, and woodland

Temperate broadleaf and mixed forests

Tropical and subtropical dry broadleaf forests

Flooded grasslands and savannahs

Tropical and subtropical grasslands, savannahs, and shrublands

Tropical and subtropical coniferous forests

Deserts

Montane grasslands and shrublands

Tropical and subtropical moist broadleaf forests

Temperate coniferous forests

Boreal forests

Tundra

Loss by 1950

Loss between 1950 and 1990

Projected loss by 2050

−10 0 10 20 30 40 50 60 70 80 90 100

Fraction of potential area converted (%)

FIGURE 9.5 Many of the world's major biomes have already had a large proportion of their area converted to human use, such as farmlands and plantations. The shaded sections of the bars show losses that have already occurred; black portions show the predicted losses by 2050. Temperate forests are predicted to increase in area over the next 4 years due to the abandonment of agriculture in many areas of North America and Europe. (After MEA 2005.)

(20%), infrastructure and roads (17%), disruption of fire ecology (13%), and logging (12%) (Stein et al. 2000).

More than 50% of the wildlife habitat has been destroyed in many Old World tropical countries (WRI 2000). In tropical Asia, fully 65% of the primary forest habitat has been lost (Table 9.3). The two biologically rich countries of Malaysia and Indonesia still have about half of their primary forest habitats and have established extensive protected areas, but the forces of habitat destruction and degradation continue apace. Sub-Saharan Africa has similarly lost a total of about 65% of its forests, with losses being most severe in Rwanda (80%), Gambia (89%), and Ghana (82%). Two biologically rich nations, Zimbabwe and the Democratic Republic of the Congo (formerly Zaire), are relatively better off, retaining about half of their forests, although the recent civil war in the latter country has halted efforts to protect and manage wildlife.

Present rates of deforestation vary considerably among countries, with particularly high annual rates of over 2% reported in such tropical countries as Malaysia (2.4%), the Philippines (3.5%), Thailand (2.6%), Costa Rica (3.1%), El Salvador (3.3%), Haiti (3.5%), Honduras (2.3%), Nicaragua (2.5%), Panama (2.2%), and Paraguay (2.6%) (WRI 1998). As a result of habitat fragmentation, farming, logging, and other human activities, very little **frontier forest**—intact blocks of undisturbed forest large enough to support all aspects of biodiversity—remains in most Old World tropical countries. In the New World, the situation is somewhat better; 42% of Brazilian forest and 59% of Venezuelan forest are frontier forest. In the Mediterranean region, which has been densely populated by people for thousands of years, only 10% of the original forest cover remains. An important point to remember here is that wildlife populations are lost in proportion to the amount of habitat that has been lost; even though the Mediterranean forest still exists in places, approximately 90% of its pop-

how much is enough?

TABLE 9.3 *Loss of forest habitat in some countries of the Old World tropics*

Country	Current forest remaining (× 1000 ha)	Percentage of habitat lost	Percentage of current forest as frontier forest
AFRICA			
Democratic Republic of the Congo	135,071	40	16
Gambia	188	38	0
Ghana	1694	91	0
Kenya	3423	82	0
Madagascar	6940	87	0
Rwanda	291	84	0
Zimbabwe	15,397	33	0
ASIA			
Bangladesh	862	92	4
India	44,450	80	1
Indonesia	88,744	35	28
Malaysia	13,007	36	14
Myanmar (Burma)	20,661	59	0
Philippines	2402	94	0
Sri Lanka	1581	82	12
Thailand	16,237	78	5
Vietnam	4218	83	2

Source: Data from WRI 2000.

ulations of birds, butterflies, wildflowers, frogs, and mosses that once existed are no longer there.

For many important wildlife species, the majority of habitat in their original range has been destroyed and very little of the remaining habitat is protected. For certain Asian primates, such as the Javan gibbon, more than 95% of the original habitat (and 95% of the populations!) has been destroyed, and some of these species are protected on less than 2% of their original ranges (WRI 2000). The orangutan, a great ape that lives in Sumatra and Borneo, has lost 63% of its range and is protected in only 2% of its range.

Threatened Rain Forests

The destruction of tropical rain forests has come to be synonymous with the rapid loss of species. Tropical moist forests occupy 7% of the Earth's land surface, but they are estimated to contain over 50% of its species (Primack and Corlett 2005). Many of these species are important to local economies and have the potential for greater use by the entire world population. Rain forests also have regional importance in protecting watersheds and moderating climate; they have local significance as the home to numerous indigenous cultures; and they have global importance as sinks to absorb some of the excess carbon dioxide that is produced by the burning of fossil fuels (Laurance 1999).

These evergreen (or partly evergreen) forests occur in frost-free areas below about 1800 m in altitude and have at least 100 mm (4 inches) of rain per month in most years. They are characterized by a great richness of species and a complexity of species interaction and specialization unparalleled in any other community. Tropical rain forests are easily degraded because the soils are often thin and nutrient-poor, and they erode readily in heavy rainfall. At present, there is considerable discussion in the scientific literature about the original extent and current area of tropical forests as well as rates of deforestation (WRI 2000; Jenkins et al. 2003; Primack and Corlett

2005). The original extent of tropical rain forests and related moist forests has been estimated at 16 million km^2, based on current patterns of rainfall and temperature (Sayer and Whitmore 1991). A combination of ground surveys, airplane photos, and remote-sensing data from satellites showed that in 1990 only 11.5 million km^2 remained. A further 58,000 km^2 per year was lost between 1990 and 1997 with particularly high absolute deforestation rates in the Brazilian Amazon, Madagascar, Borneo, and Sumatra. The current rate of deforestation represents approximately 1% of the original forest area lost per year (Laurance 1999). Despite the difficulty in obtaining accurate numbers for rain forest deforestation rates, due to varying definitions of forest cover and forest degradation and differing methods, the consensus is that tropical deforestation rates are alarmingly high. The loss of tropical forest habitat continues at a rate that guarantees that almost all tropical rain forests will be lost over the next few decades. The only forests that remain will be in protected areas and on rugged or remote terrain. The move to establish large new parks in many tropical countries is cause for some hope; however, these will need to be well-funded and managed to be effective, as described in Chapters 15 and 17. In many cases, these are only "paper parks" with few employees or facilities.

On a global scale, about 60% of rain forest destruction results from small-scale cultivation of crops by poor, landless farmers, most of whom moved to the agricultural frontier to practice temporary farming out of desperation or by way of government-sponsored resettlement programs (Fearnside 2001; Zarin et al. 2005). Some of this land is converted to permanent farm plantations and pastures, but much of the area is farmed using a method known as shifting cultivation (Figure 9.6). **Shifting cultivation** is a kind of subsistence farming, sometimes referred to as "slash-and-burn," or "swidden" agriculture, in which trees are cut down and then burned away and the cleared patches farmed for two or three seasons, after which soil fertility usually diminishes to the point where adequate crop production is no longer possible. The patches are then abandoned and new natural vegetation must be cleared. Shifting cultivation is often practiced because the farmers are unwilling or unable to spend the time and money necessary to develop more permanent forms of agriculture on land that they do not own and may not occupy for very long. Included in this discussion is land degraded each year for fuelwood production, mostly to supply local villagers with wood for cooking fires. More than two billion people cook their food with firewood, so their impact is significant. About another 20% of rain forest is damaged during commercial logging, primarily selective logging operations. Around 10% more is cleared for cattle ranches. Clearing for cash-crop plantations (oil palm, cocoa, rubber, etc.), plus road building, mining, and other activities account for the remaining 5 to 10%.

The relative importance of these enterprises varies by geographical region: logging is a significant activity in tropical Asia and America, cattle ranching is most prominent in tropical America, and farming is more important for the rapidly expanding population in tropical Africa (Nepstad et al. 1999; Fearnside 2005; Primack and Corlett 2005). In relative terms, the deforestation rate is greatest in Asia, at around 1.2% per year, while in absolute terms tropical America has the greatest amount of deforestation due to its larger total area. Extending the projection forward in time reveals that, at the current rate of loss, there will be little tropical forest left after the year 2040, except in the relatively small national parks and remote areas of the Amazon basin, Congo River basin, and New Guinea. The situation is actually more grim than these projections indicate, because the world's population is still increasing and poverty is on the rise in many developing tropical countries, putting ever-greater demands on the dwindling supply of rain forest.

The destruction of tropical rain forests is caused frequently by demand in industrialized countries for cheap agricultural products, such as rubber, palm oil, cocoa, soybeans, and beef, and for low-cost wood products (Figure 9.7) (Primack and Cor-

(A)

(B)

(C)

FIGURE 9.6 The displacement of rain forest for agricultural purposes can take many forms. (A) In this case, indigenous people in the Amazon have cut down trees and burned them in preparation for planting their crops. Here a local chief stands in front of land that has been cleared. (B) Shifting cultivation in West Africa: Gardens are hewn from the forest with slash-and-burn techniques. Indigenous peoples living at low densities have used such farming practices for centuries. However, when large numbers of people migrate into an area and practice shifting cultivation, rain forest destruction is vast. (C) Rice paddies take over rain forest in southwestern India. (A, photograph by Milla Jung; B, photograph © Charles Cecil/Visuals Unlimited; C, photograph by R. Primack.)

lett 2005). During the 1980s, Costa Rica and other Latin American countries had some of the world's highest rates of deforestation as a result of the conversion of rain forests into cattle ranches. Much of the beef produced on these ranches was sold to the United States and other developed countries to produce inexpensive hamburgers. Adverse publicity resulting from this "hamburger connection," followed by consumer boycotts, led major restaurant chains in the United States to stop buying tropical beef from these ranches. Even though deforestation continued in Latin America, the boycott was important in making people aware of the international connections that promote deforestation. A priority for conservation biology is to help provide the information, programs, and public awareness that will allow the greatest amount of rain forest to persist once the present cycle of destruction ends.

The story of Rondônia illustrates how rapid and serious rain forest destruction can be. This state in Amazonian Brazil was almost entirely covered by primary forest as late as 1975, with only 1200 km^2 cleared out of a total area of 243,000 km^2 (Fearnside 1990, 2005). In the 1970s, the Brazilian government built a major highway system through Rondônia, including a network of lateral roads leading away from the highway into the forest. The government also provided lucrative tax subsidies to allow corporations to establish cattle ranches in the region and encouraged poor, landless people from coastal states to migrate to Rondônia with offers of free land. These incentives were necessary because the soils of the Amazon region are low in mineral nutrients, so new pastures and farmlands are usually unproductive and unprofitable. During this land rush, 10,000 km^2 of the forest was cleared

1973

0   20
Kilometers

2004

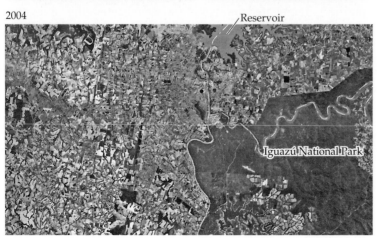

FIGURE 9.7 Due to intensive commercial agriculture, rain forest has been declining rapidly in South America, in this case at the border of Brazil, Paraguay, and Argentina on the edge of the tropics, as shown by the two satellite images taken in 1973 and 2004. In the 1973 image, large amounts of forest still exist, but a road network (as shown by the herringbone pattern) is extending westward from the town. By 2004, most of the forest has been converted to soybean fields except for the area surrounding Iguazú National Park. Also note the large reservoir in the 2004 image created after construction of a dam. (Satellite images courtesy of NASA. From Division of Early Warning and Assessment, United Nations Environment Programme 2004.)

by 1982, an additional 6000 km^2 was cleared by 1985, and a total of around 39,000 km^2 by 1993, representing 16% of the total land area. By the late 1980s, the population of the state was growing at 16% per year, with deforestation increasing at 37% per year. These rates of growth and deforestation are phenomenally high compared to most other parts of the world, whether industrial or developing. International protests against this environmental damage led the government to reduce its subsidies of the cattle industry. Reduced subsidies and a general economic recession somewhat decreased the rate of deforestation during the early 1990s, but the rate of deforestation due to cattle ranching, logging, and clearing for soybean cultivation increased thereafter (Nepstad et al. 2001). Deforestation in the Amazon will also increase if the Brazilian government proceeds with its plan to build 7500 km of new paved roads and associated transportation infrastructure, at a total cost of $45 billion (Laurance et al. 2001; Fearnside 2005).

Other Threatened Habitats

The plight of the tropical rain forests is perhaps the most widely publicized case of habitat destruction, but many other habitats are also in grave danger. Around 94% of temperate broadleaf forests have been disturbed by human activities, primarily farming and logging, with a comparable percentage for evergreen sclerophyllous forest consisting mainly of conifers. Certain biological communities have lost more than 98% of their previous area due to human activities; among these are old-growth forest stands in eastern North America, native grasslands in California, and streams in the Mississippi River floodplains. We discuss a few of these threatened habitats below:

TROPICAL DECIDUOUS FORESTS   The land occupied by tropical deciduous forests is more suitable for agriculture and cattle ranching than is the land occupied by tropical rain forests. The forests are also easier than rain forests to clear and burn. Moderate rainfall in the range of 250 to 2000 mm per year allows mineral nutrients to be retained in the soil where they can be taken up by plants. Consequently, human population density is five times greater in dry forest areas of Central America than in adjacent rain forests. Today, the Pacific Coast of Central America has less than 0.1% of its original extent remaining, and less than 8% remains in Madagascar (Laurance 1999; Gillespie et al. 2000).

GRASSLANDS   Temperate grasslands are another habitat type that has been almost completely destroyed by human activity. It is relatively easy to convert large areas of grassland to farmland and cattle ranches (Figure 9.8). Almost 97% of the tall grass prairie of North America has been converted to farmland (White et al. 2000). The remaining area of prairie is fragmented and widely scattered across the landscape.

WETLANDS AND AQUATIC HABITATS   Wetlands are critical habitats for fish, aquatic invertebrates, and birds. They are also a resource for flood control, drinking water, and power production (MEA 2005). Although many wetland species are widespread, some aquatic systems are known for their high levels of endemism.

Wetlands are often filled in or drained for development, or they are altered by channelization of watercourses, dams, and chemical pollution. All of these factors are affecting the Florida Everglades, one of the premier wildlife refuges in the United States, which is now on the verge of ecological collapse (and see Box 5.1 for the disastrous consequences of wetlands destruction in Louisiana). Over the last 200 years, over half of the wetlands in the United States have been destroyed, resulting in 40 to 50% of the freshwater snail species in the southeastern United States becoming either extinct or endangered (Stein et al. 2000). More than 97% of the ver-

(A)

(B)

(C)

FIGURE 9.8 Temperate grasslands are extremely valuable for protecting biological diversity and for agriculture. (A) A natural grassland with numerous native species on the National Bison Range, federally protected land in the state of Montana. (B) Cattle graze on natural grassland. (C) Overgrazed grassland takes on the appearance of a desert, and native species are eliminated. (Photographs courtesy of the U.S. Fish and Wildlife Service and the U.S. Forest Service.)

nal pools in California's San Diego County have been destroyed; these unusual wetlands fill up with water in the winter and dry out in the summer, and support a unique endemic biota. The majority of U.S. Pacific salmon stocks face moderate to high extinction risks as the rivers that they use to spawn are damaged and dammed (Naiman et al. 1995). In the United States, 98% of the country's 5.2 million km of streams have been degraded in some way to the point that they are no longer considered wild or scenic (Harrison and Stiassny 1999). Destruction of wetlands has been equally severe in other parts of the industrialized world, such as Europe and Japan. Around 60 to 70% of wetlands in Europe have been lost (Ravenga et al. 2000). Only 2 of Japan's 30,000 rivers can be considered wild, without dams or some other major modification. In the last few decades, one of the major threats to wetlands in developing countries has been massive development projects organized by governments and often financed by international aid agencies involving drainage, irrigation, and dams.

MARINE COASTAL AREAS   Human populations are increasingly concentrated in coastal areas. Already 20% of marine coastal areas have been degraded or highly modified by human activity (Burke et al. 2000). Throughout the world, intensive harvesting of fish, shellfish, seaweeds, and other marine products is transforming marine environments. Marine environments are also threatened by pollution, dredging, sedimentation, destructive fishing practices, and invasive species. Human impacts are less well-studied than in the terrestrial environment, but are probably equally as severe, especially in shallow coastal areas. Two coastal habitats of special note are mangroves and coral reefs.

MANGROVES   Mangrove forests are among the most important wetland communities in tropical areas. Composed of species that are among the few woody plants able to tolerate salt water, mangrove forests occupy coastal areas with saline or brackish water, typically where there are muddy bottoms. Such habitats are similar to salt marshes in the temperate zone. Mangroves are extremely important breeding grounds and feeding areas for shrimp and fish. In Australia, for example, two-thirds of the species caught by commercial fishermen depend to some degree on the mangrove ecosystem.

   Despite their great economic value and their utility for protecting coastal areas from storms and tsunamis, mangroves are often cleared for rice cultivation and commercial shrimp and prawn hatcheries, particularly in Southeast Asia, where as much as 15% of the mangrove area has been removed for aquaculture. Mangroves have also been severely degraded by overcollecting wood for fuel, construction poles, and timber throughout the region. Over 35% of the world's mangrove ecosystems have already been destroyed, and more are being destroyed every year (MEA 2005).

CORAL REEFS   Tropical coral reefs are particularly significant, as they contain an estimated one-third of the ocean's fish species in only 0.2% of its surface area (see Chapter 3). Already 20% of all coral reefs have been destroyed. A further 20% has been degraded by overfishing, overharvesting, pollution, and the introduction of invasive species (MEA 2005). The most severe destruction is taking place in the Philippines, where a staggering 90% of the reefs are dead or dying. The main culprits are pollution, which either kills the coral directly or allows excessive growth of algae; sedimentation following deforestation; overharvesting of fish, clams, and other animals; and, finally, blasting with dynamite and releasing cyanide to collect the few remaining living creatures.

   Extensive loss of coral reefs is expected within the next 40 years in tropical East Asia, the areas around Madagascar and East Africa, and throughout the Caribbean

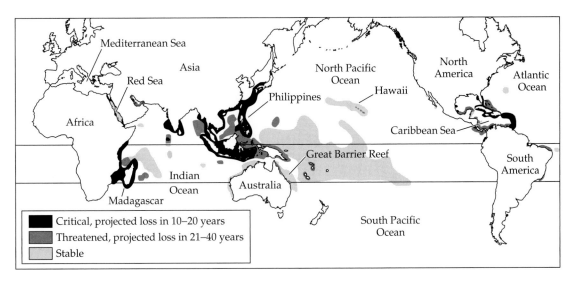

FIGURE 9.9 Extensive areas of coral will be damaged or destroyed by human activity over the next 40 years unless conservation measures can be implemented. (After Weber 1993.)

(Figure 9.9). In the Caribbean, a combination of overfishing, hurricane damage, pollution, and disease is responsible for a dramatic decline of a large proportion of the coral reefs and their replacement by fleshy macroalgae (Burke and Maidens 2004). Elkhorn and staghorn corals, which were formerly common in the Caribbean and gave structure to the community, have already become rare in many locations.

Over the last 10 years, scientists have discovered extensive coral reefs living in cold water at depths of 300 m or more, many of which are in the temperate zone of the North Atlantic. These coral reefs are rich in species, with numerous species new to science. Yet at the same time these communities are first being explored, they are being destroyed by trawlers, which drag nets across the seafloor to catch fish; the trawlers destroy the very coral reefs that protect and provide food for young fish. The damage to these cold water reefs by careless harvesting is costing the industry its resource base in the long run.

Desertification

Many biological communities in seasonally dry climates are degraded by human activities into man-made deserts, a process known as **desertification** (Reynolds 2001). These dryland communities include grasslands, scrub, and deciduous forest, as well as temperate shrublands, such as those found in the Mediterranean region, southwestern Australia, South Africa, central Chile, and California. Dry areas cover around 41% of the world's land area and are home to around 1 billion people. Approximately 10 to 20% of these drylands are at least moderately degraded, with more than 25% of the productive capacity of their plant growth having been lost (Kaufman and Pyke 2001). Although these areas may initially support agriculture, their repeated cultivation, especially during dry and windy years, often leads to soil erosion and loss of water-holding capacity in the soil (Figure 9.10). Land may also be chronically overgrazed by domestic livestock, and woody plants may be cut down for fuel (Nyssen et al. 2004; MEA 2005; Neff et al. 2005). Frequent fires during long dry periods often damage the remaining vegetation. The result is the progressive and largely irreversible degradation of the biological community and the loss of soil cover. Ultimately, formerly productive farmland and pastures take on the appearance of a desert. Desertification has been ongoing for thousands of years in the Mediterranean region and was known even to ancient Greek observers.

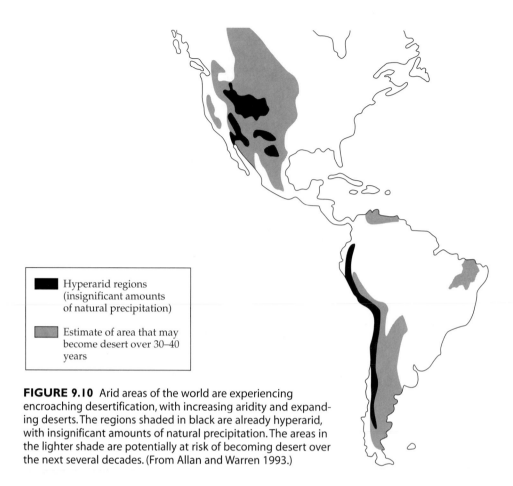

FIGURE 9.10 Arid areas of the world are experiencing encroaching desertification, with increasing aridity and expanding deserts. The regions shaded in black are already hyperarid, with insignificant amounts of natural precipitation. The areas in the lighter shade are potentially at risk of becoming desert over the next several decades. (From Allan and Warren 1993.)

Worldwide, 9 million km^2 of arid lands have been converted to man-made deserts. These areas are not functional desert ecosystems but are wastelands, lacking the flora and fauna characteristic of natural deserts. The process of desertification is most severe in the Sahel region of Africa, just south of the Saharan Desert, where most of the native large mammal species are threatened with extinction. The human dimension of the problem is illustrated by the fact that the Sahel region is estimated to have 2.5 times more people (100 million currently) than the land can sustainably support. The problem is magnified by the high population growth and poverty of people living in such areas, as well as by wars and civil unrest, which force thousands of people to eke out an existence using whatever resources and methods they can find whether sustainable or not (MEA 2005). Further desertification appears to be almost inevitable, unless programs can be implemented involving improved and sustainable agricultural practices, the elimination of poverty, the stabilization of civil society, and population control (Hassan and Dregné 1997).

Habitat Fragmentation

In addition to outright destruction, habitats that formerly occupied wide, unbroken areas are now often divided into pieces by roads, fields, towns, and a broad range of other human constructs. **Habitat fragmentation** is the process whereby a large, continuous area of habitat is both reduced in area and divided into two or more fragments (Figure 9.11) (Spellerberg 2002; Forman 2004; Harper et al. 2005; Radeloff et al. 2005; Siitonen et al. 2005). When habitat is destroyed, a patchwork of habitat fragments may be left behind. These fragments are often isolated from one another by a highly modified or degraded landscape, and their edges experience an altered set

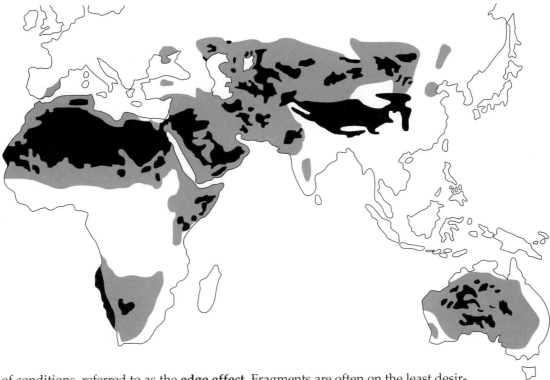

of conditions, referred to as the **edge effect**. Fragments are often on the least desirable land, such as steep slopes, poor soils, and inaccessible areas. Fragmentation almost always occurs during a severe reduction in habitat area, but it can also occur when area is reduced to only a minor degree if the original habitat is divided by roads, railroads, canals, power lines, fences, oil pipelines, fire lanes, or other barriers to the free movement of species (Figure 9.12). In many ways, the habitat fragments resemble islands of original habitats in an inhospitable, human-dominated landscape. Habitat fragmentation is now being recognized as a serious threat to biodiversity, as species are often unable to survive under the altered set of conditions.

Habitat fragments differ from the original habitat in three important ways: (1) fragments have a greater amount of edge for the area of habitat (and thus a greater

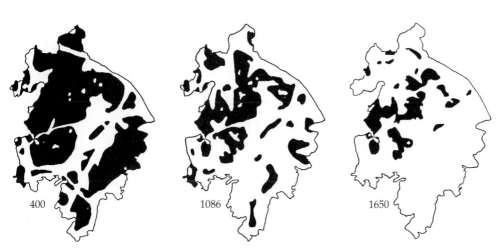

FIGURE 9.11 The forested areas of Warwickshire, England (shown in black), were fragmented and reduced in area—by paths, roads, agriculture, and human settlements—over the centuries from A.D. 400 (when Romans established villages and towns in the forested landscape and built roads between them) to A.D. 1960 (when only a few tiny forest fragments remained).

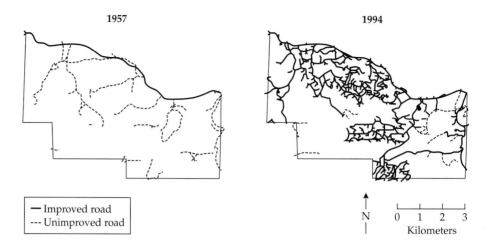

1957   1994

— Improved road
--- Unimproved road

N   0   1   2   3
Kilometers

FIGURE 9.12 Rural development in Colorado has led to the expansion of the road network and the fragmentation of the habitat. Formally widespread species are now restricted to small fragments. (From Knight et al. 2006.)

exposure to the edge effect), (2) the center of each habitat fragment is closer to an edge, and (3) a formerly continuous habitat with large populations is divided into pieces with smaller populations. A simple example will illustrate these characteristics and the problems they can cause.

Consider a square conservation reserve 1000 m (1 km) on each side (Figure 9.13). The total area of the park is 1 km² (100 ha). The perimeter (or edge) of the park totals 4000 m. A point in the middle of the reserve is 500 m from the nearest perimeter. If the principle edge effect for birds in the reserve is predation from domestic cats and introduced rats, which forage 100 m into the forest from the perimeter of the reserve and prevent forest birds from successfully raising their young, then only the reserve's interior—64 ha—is available to the birds for breeding. Birds can move freely across this entire area. Edge habitat, unsuitable for breeding, occupies 36 ha.

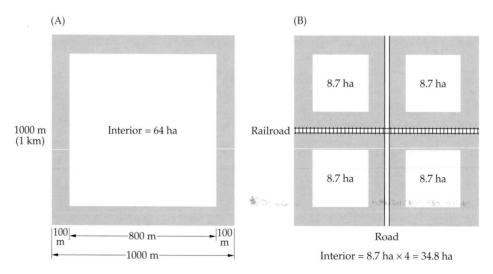

(A)

1000 m
(1 km)

Interior = 64 ha

100 m |←— 800 m —→| 100 m
|←——— 1000 m ———→|

(B)

8.7 ha   8.7 ha

Railroad

8.7 ha   8.7 ha

Road

Interior = 8.7 ha × 4 = 34.8 ha

FIGURE 9.13 A hypothetical example shows how habitat area is severely reduced by fragmentation and edge effects. (A) A 1-km² protected area. Assuming edge effects (gray) penetrate 100 m into the reserve, approximately 64 ha are available as usable habitat for nesting birds. (B) The bisection of the reserve by a road and a railway, although taking up little in actual area, extends the edge effects so that almost half the breeding habitat is destroyed. Effects are proportionately greater when forest fragments are irregular in shape, as is usually the case.

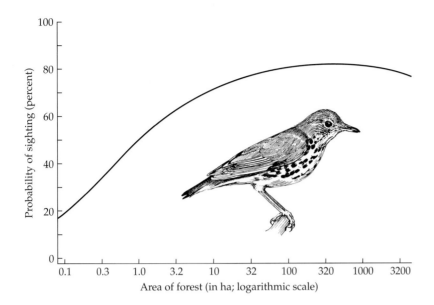

FIGURE 9.14 The probability of sighting a wood thrush in a mature forest in Maryland is only about 20% in a forest fragment of 0.1 ha; it increases to about 80% in a forest fragment over 100 ha in area. (From Decker et al.1991.)

Now imagine the park being divided into four equal quarters by a north–south road 10 m wide and by an east–west railroad track, also 10 m wide. The rights-of-way remove a total of 2 m × 1000 m × 10 m of area (2 ha) from the park. Since only 2% of the park is being removed by the road and railroad, government planners argue that the effects on the park are negligible. However, the reserve has now been divided into four fragments, each of which is 495 m × 495 m in area. If birds are unable or unwilling to leave forest areas, what was formerly one population is now divided into four small populations. The distance from the center of each fragment to the nearest point on the perimeter has been reduced to 247 m, which is less than half of the former distance. Since cats and rats can now forage into the forest from along the road and railroad as well as the perimeter, birds can successfully raise young only in the most interior areas of each of the four fragments. Each of these interior areas is now 8.7 ha, for a total of 34.8 ha. Even though the road and railroad removed only 2% of the reserve area, they reduced the habitat available to the birds by about half due to edge effects. The implications of this can be seen in the decreased ability of birds to live and breed in small forest fragments compared with larger blocks of forest (Figure 9.14). Comparable edge effects are known to impact many other groups of animals and plants in fragmented habitats.

LIMITS TO DISPERSAL AND COLONIZATION Fragmentation may limit a species' potential for dispersal and colonization (Bhattacharya et al. 2003; Driscoll 2004; Ito et al. 2005; Baur et al. 2005) by creating barriers to normal movements. In an undisturbed environment, seeds, spores, and animals move passively and actively across the landscape. When they arrive in a suitable but unoccupied area, new populations begin to develop at that site. Over time, populations of a species may build up and go extinct on a local scale as the species disperses from one suitable site to another and the biological community undergoes succession. At a landscape level, a series of populations exhibiting this pattern of extinction and recolonization is sometimes referred to as a metapopulation (see Chapter 12).

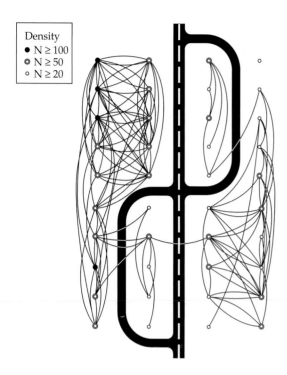

Density
- N ≥ 100
- N ≥ 50
- N ≥ 20

FIGURE 9.15 A road and its parking loops (shown as heavy black lines) block the movement of a forest-dwelling beetle species, effectively creating two subpopulations. The circles represent points where beetles were trapped, with darker circles indicating beetle populations with greater density. The lines indicate the movement of "tagged" beetles. (After Mader 1984.)

When a habitat is fragmented, the potential for dispersal and colonization is often reduced. Many bird, mammal, and insect species of the forest interior will not cross even very short distances of open area (Figure 9.15) (Laurance et al. 2002). If they do venture into the open, they may find predators such as hawks, owls, flycatchers, and cats waiting on the forest edge to catch and eat them. Agricultural fields 100 m wide may represent an impassable barrier to the dispersal of many invertebrate species. Roads in particular may be significant barriers to animal movement. Many species will avoid crossing roads, which represent a totally different environment for animals (S. G. Laurance et al. 2004). For animals that attempt to cross roads, motor vehicles are a major source of mortality.

As species go extinct within individual fragments through natural successional and metapopulation processes, new species will be unable to arrive due to barriers to colonization, and the number of species present in the habitat fragment will decline over time (Beier et al. 2002). In river systems, dams may fragment the habitat and prevent the migration of species (Pringle 2006). Extinction will be most rapid and severe in small habitat fragments (Hokit and Branch 2003). In Belgium, the area of heathland has declined by over 99% during the last 100 years, with the remaining habitat broken up into small fragments; the greatest loss of species is in the most isolated habitats, indicating the role of dispersal in maintaining species richness (Piessens et al. 2005).

Species that are able to live in and move across disturbed habitat will increase in abundance in small, isolated fragments of undisturbed habitat. This is particularly true when the spaces between forest fragments are occupied by secondary forests and tree plantations, rather than pastures and cultivated fields (Antongiovanni and Metzger 2005). Most of the world's national parks and nature reserves represent fragments of the original ecosystems which are now too small and isolated to maintain populations of many of the original species.

RESTRICTED ACCESS TO FOOD AND MATES   Many animal species, either as individuals or social groups, need to move freely across the landscape to feed on widely scattered resources. A given resource may be needed only for a few weeks each year, or even only once in a few years, and when a habitat is fragmented, species confined to a single habitat fragment may be unable to migrate in search of that scarce resource over their normal home range. For example, orangutans, gibbons, and other primates typically remain in forests and forage widely for fruits. Finding scattered trees with abundant fruit crops may be crucial during episodes of fruit scarcity. Clearings and roads that break up the forest canopy may prevent these primates from reaching nearby fruiting trees because the primates are unable or unwilling to descend to the ground and cross the intervening open landscape. Fences may prevent the natural migration of large grazing animals such as wildebeest and bison, forcing them to overgraze unsuitable habitat, which eventually leads to starvation and further degradation of the habitat (Berger 2004).

Barriers to dispersal can also restrict the ability of widely scattered species to find mates, leading to a loss of reproductive potential for many animal species. Plants also may have reduced seed production if butterflies and bees are less able to migrate among habitat fragments to pollinate flowers.

DIVISION OF POPULATIONS Habitat fragmentation may precipitate population decline and extinction by dividing an existing widespread population into two or more subpopulations in a restricted area (Diaz et al. 2005; Banks et al. 2005). These smaller populations are then more vulnerable to inbreeding depression, genetic drift, and other problems associated with small population size (see Chapter 11). Animals killed while crossing roads will further depress population size. While a large area may support a single large population, it is possible that none of the smaller subpopulations will be sufficiently large to persist for a long period. Connecting the fragments with properly designed movement corridors may be the key to maintaining populations.

Edge Effects

Habitat fragmentation also changes the microenvironment at the fragment edge. Some of the more important edge effects include microclimatic changes in light, temperature, wind, humidity, and incidence of fire (Laurance 2000; Laurance et al. 2002). Each of these edge effects can have a significant impact on the vitality and composition of the species in the fragment.

MICROCLIMATE CHANGES Sunlight is absorbed and reflected by the layers of leaves in forest communities and other communities with dense plant cover. In rainforests, often less than 1% of the light energy may reach the forest floor. The forest canopy buffers the microclimate of the forest floor, keeping it relatively cool, moist, and shaded during the day, reducing air movement, and trapping heat during the night. When the forest is cleared, these effects are removed. As the forest floor is exposed to direct sunlight, the ground becomes much hotter during the day; without the canopy to reduce heat and moisture loss, the forest floor is also much colder at night and generally less humid. Increased wind movement at the forest edge further dries out the vegetation and soil, leading to the death of trees and ground plants. These effects will be strongest at the edge of the habitat fragment and decrease toward the interior of the fragment. In studies of Amazonian forest fragments, microclimate changes had strong effects up to 60 m into the forest interior, and increased tree mortality could be detected within 100 to 300 m of forest edges (Laurance et al. 1998). Since species of plants and animals are often precisely adapted to temperature, humidity, and light levels, changes in these factors will eliminate many species from forest fragments. Shade-tolerant wildflower species of the temperate forest, late-successional tree species of the tropical forest, and humidity-sensitive animals such as certain insects and amphibians, often are rapidly eliminated by habitat fragmentation because of altered environmental conditions, leading to a shift in the species composition of the community.

In their place, a dense tangle of vines and fast-growing pioneer species may grow up at the forest edge in response to these altered conditions and often create a barrier that reduces the effects of environmental disturbance on the interior of the fragment. Over time, the forest edge may be occupied by species of plants and animals different from those found in the forest interior (Figure 9.16).

INCREASED INCIDENCE OF FIRE Increased wind, lower humidity, and higher temperatures make fires more likely. Fires may spread into habitat fragments from nearby agricultural fields that are being burned regularly, as in sugarcane harvesting, or from the irregular activities of farmers practicing slash-and-burn agriculture. Forest fragments may be particularly susceptible to fire damage when wood has accumulated on the edge of the forest where trees have died or have been blown down by the wind. In Borneo and the Brazilian Amazon, millions of hectares of tropical moist forest burned during unusually dry periods in 1997 and 1998 (Nepstad et al.

FIGURE 9.16 (A) Forest clearing for pasture in Brazil results in sharp edges that change the rain forest microclimate. (B) Various effects of habitat fragmentation, as measured from the edge into the interior of an Amazon rain forest fragment. For example, disturbance-adapted butterflies migrate 250 m into the forest from an edge, and the relative humidity of the air is lowered within 100 m of the forest edge. (A, photograph by R. Bierregaard; B, after Laurance and Bierregaard 1997.)

(A)

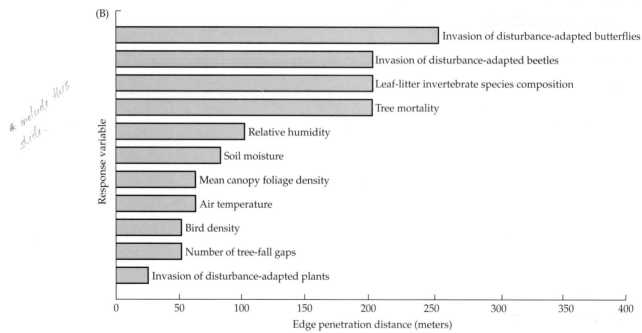

2001; Fuller et al. 2004). A combination of factors contributed to these environmental disasters: forest fragmentation due to farming and selective logging, the accumulation of brush following selective logging, and human-caused fires (Cochrane et al. 1999; Goldammer 1999). Once a forest burns, dead fuel accumulates and sunlight can more readily dry out the ground, leading to a greater likelihood of further fires. Eventually, a forest can be degraded into scrub.

INTERSPECIES INTERACTION Habitat fragmentation increases the vulnerability of the fragment to invasion by exotic and native pest species. The road edges themselves may represent dispersal routes for invasive species (Gelbard and Belnap 2003). The forest edge represents a high-energy, high-nutrient, disturbed environment in which many pest species of plants and animals can increase in number and then disperse into the interior of the fragment (Donoso 2004). For example, the seeds of wind-dispersed plants may be blown great distances into the interior of the fragment and then colonize open, sunny areas where trees and shrubs have recently died, either from natural causes or because of the newly altered growing conditions. Butterflies that are adapted to disturbed habitats migrate up to 250 m into the forest interior.

In the temperate regions of North America, omnivorous native animals such as raccoons, skunks, and blue jays may increase in population size along forest edges, where they can eat foods from both undisturbed and disturbed habitats. (Similar increases in nest predation occur on the edges of fragmented tropical forests.) These aggressive feeders seek out the nests of interior forest birds, often preventing successful reproduction for many bird species hundreds of meters from the nearest forest edge (Stephens et al. 2003; Lampila et al. 2005). Nest-parasitizing cowbirds, which live in fields and edge habitats, use habitat edges as an invasion point, flying up to 15 km into forest interiors, where they lay their eggs in the nests of forest songbirds (Lloyd et al. 2005). The combination of habitat fragmentation, increased nest predation, and destruction of tropical wintering habitats is probably responsible for the dramatic decline of certain migratory songbird species of North America, such as the cerulean warbler (*Dendroica cerulea*), particularly in the eastern half of the United States (Parker et al. 2005). In addition to these local effects, individual bird species in North America and Europe are both increasing and decreasing on regional scales in response to changing land use patterns, such as those caused by agricultural practices and forest management activities (James et al. 1996). For example, forest species increase in places where forests are increasing following agricultural abandonment. Similarly, predatory animals may decimate insect and amphibian populations that were inaccessible to them before fragmentation. Populations of deer and other herbivores can build up in edge areas, where plant growth is lush, eventually overgrazing the vegetation and selectively eliminating certain rare and endangered plant species for distances of several kilometers into the forest interior.

In settled areas with a fragmented landscape, domestic cats may be extremely important predators. In one area of Michigan, 26% of landowners had cats that went outside. Each cat killed an average of one bird per week, including species of conservation concern (Lepczyk et al. 2003). In many areas of the world, human hunters are the most important predators. When habitat is fragmented by roads, hunters can use the road network to hunt more intensively in the habitat fragments and reach remote areas. Without controls on hunting, there is no refuge for the animals and their populations decline (Michalski and Peres 2005).

POTENTIAL FOR DISEASE Habitat fragmentation puts wild populations of animals in closer proximity to domestic animals. Diseases of domestic animals can then spread more readily to wild species, which often have no immunity to them. There is also the potential for diseases to spread from wild species to domestic plants, animals, and even people, once the level of contact increases. The effects of disease, and of exotic species in general, are more thoroughly examined in Chapter 10. One recent study of fragmented forest habitats shows high densities and rates of infection of white-footed mice and black-legged ticks with Lyme disease and a corresponding increase in Lyme disease in people living in this fragmented habitat (Allan et al. 2003).

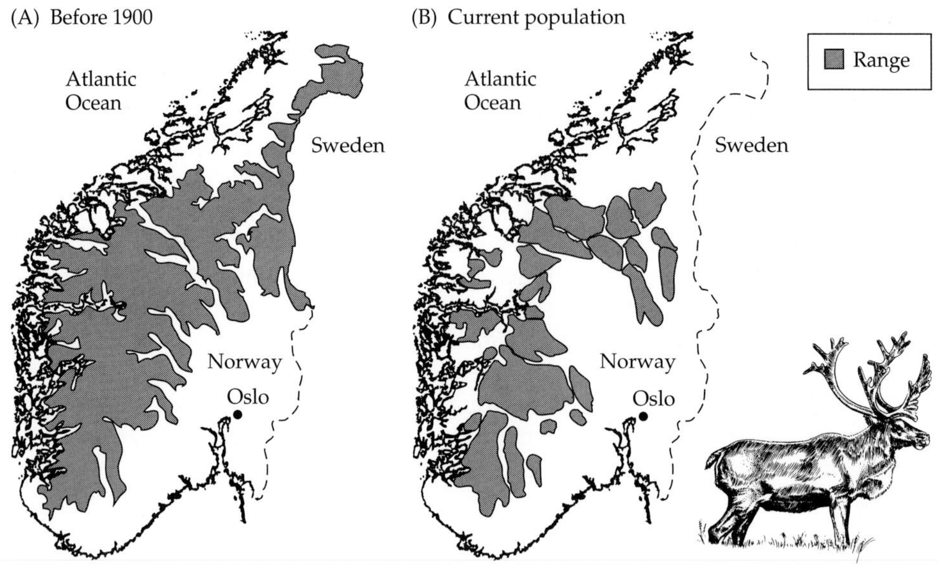

FIGURE 9.17 (A) Wild reindeer herds formerly roamed throughout the mountainous regions of southern Norway, with only one break in their range. (B) The range of reindeer has now been divided by roads, power lines, and other infrastructure, leading to 26 isolated subpopulations. (After Nelleman et al. 2001.)

Two Studies of Habitat Fragmentation

An extensive literature on habitat fragmentation has developed over the last 10 years. These studies show that habitat fragmentation changes the local environment, often resulting in the decline and loss of original species. The following are two such studies:

- The impact of habitat fragmentation was examined for eight bird species occupying chaparral and coastal sage scrub in southern California, an area undergoing rapid urban development (Crooks et al. 2001). In comparison with large fragments, small fragments (less than 10 ha in area) had higher rates of species extinction and lower rates of new species colonization. Bird species with high initial densities were less likely to go extinct in habitat fragments and were better able to persist in small fragments.

- Reindeer are one of the essential symbols of Scandinavian culture. The last remaining population of wild reindeer (*Rangifer tarandus tarandus*) lives in southern Norway (Nelleman et al. 2001). Prior to 1900, the reindeer lived as a continuous herd, freely migrating throughout the mountain ranges of this region. Infrastructure developments and the reindeer's tendency to keep 5 km away from human settlements and other structures, such as resort areas, roads, and power lines, have fragmented the population into 26 distinct herds (Figure 9.17). Only around 10% of the original range of reindeer is now found more than 5 km from such human structures. Because isolated herds are unable to migrate and consequently tend to overgraze the vegetation in their habitat fragment, herds must be actively managed by hunting to prevent local population increases. If additional roads, power lines, and resorts are built, the reindeer population will undergo further fragmentation and its long-term future will then be even more in doubt.

Habitat Degradation and Pollution

Even when a habitat is unaffected by overt destruction or fragmentation, the communities and species in that habitat can be profoundly affected by human activities (Smith 2001; Niemi and McDonald 2004). Biological communities can be damaged and species driven to extinction by external factors that do not change the structure of dominant plants in the community, so that the damage is not immediately apparent. For example, in temperate deciduous forests, physical degradation of a habitat might be caused by frequent, uncontrolled ground fires; these fires might not kill the mature trees, but the rich perennial wildflower community and insect fauna on the forest floor would gradually become impoverished. Keeping too many cattle in grassland communities gradually changes the biological community, often eliminating many native species and favoring exotic species that can tolerate grazing and trampling. Frequent boating and diving among coral reefs degrade the community, as fragile species are crushed by divers' flippers, boat hulls, and anchors. Out of sight from the public, fishing trawlers drag across an estimated 15 million km^2 of ocean floor each year, an area 150 times greater than the area of forest cleared in the same time period. The trawling destroys delicate creatures such as anemones and sponges and reduces species diversity, biomass, and community structure (see Figure 9.19) (Watling and Norse 1998).

The most subtle and universal form of environmental degradation is pollution, commonly caused by pesticides, herbicides, sewage, fertilizers from agricultural fields, industrial chemicals and wastes, emissions from factories and automobiles, and sediment deposits from eroded hillsides (Brown 2003; Relyea 2005). These types of pollution often are not visually apparent even when they occur all around us, every day, in nearly every part of the world. The general effects of pollution on water quality, air quality, and even the global climate are cause for great concern, not only because of the threats to biological diversity, but also because of their effects on human health (Sharpe and Irvine 2004; Eyles and Consitt 2004). Although environmental pollution is sometimes highly visible and dramatic, as in the case of the massive oil spill shown in Figure 9.18, it is the subtle, unseen forms of pollution that are probably the most threatening—primarily because they are so insidious.

FIGURE 9.18 In the year 2000, an oil pipeline broke in Southern Brazil, spilling 4 million liters (1 million gallons) of oil into the Rio Iguaçu. Shown here are the polluted waters of the Iguaçu (left) merging with another river. (Photograph from *Jornal Gazeta do Povo*.)

Pesticide Pollution

The dangers of pesticides were brought to the world's attention in 1962 by Rachel Carson's influential book *Silent Spring*. Carson described a process known as **biomagnification**, through which dichlorodiphenyltrichloroethane (DDT) and other organochlorine pesticides become concentrated as they ascend the food chain (Elliott et al. 2005). These pesticides, used on crop plants to kill insects and sprayed on water bodies to kill mosquito larvae, were harming wildlife populations, especially birds that ate large amounts of insects, fish, or other animals exposed to DDT and its by-products. Birds with high levels of concentrated pesticides in their tissues, particularly raptors such as hawks and eagles, became weak and tended to lay eggs with abnormally thin shells that cracked during incubation. As a result of the fail-

BOX 9.1

Pesticides and Raptors: Sentinel Species Warn of Danger

■ Birds of prey such as the American bald eagle, the osprey, and the peregrine falcon are symbols evocative of power, grace, and nobility to people worldwide. When populations of these and other raptors began an abrupt decline shortly after World War II, concern for the birds prompted urgent research into the cause. In retrospect, these birds of prey were acting as sentinels, warning human society of a serious danger in the environment that was broadly affecting biological communities. The culprit was eventually identified as the chemical pesticide DDT (dichlorodiphenyltrichloroethane) and related organochlorine compounds such as DDE and dieldrin. DDT was first used as an insecticide during World War II to combat insect-borne diseases among the troops. After the war ended, domestic use of the chemical exploded in an effort to control agricultural pests and mosquitoes; consequently, raptor populations plummeted.

A captive male peregrine falcon feeding young at the Cornell University "hawk barn" propagation facility. (Photograph courtesy of T. J. Clade, The Peregrine Fund.)

Raptors are particularly vulnerable to these compounds because of their position at the top of the food chain. Toxic chemicals become concentrated at the top of the food chain through biomagnification: Pesticides are ingested and absorbed by insects and other invertebrates and remain in their tissues at fairly low concentrations. When fish, birds, or mammals eat a diet of these insects, the pesticides are further concentrated, eventually to highly toxic levels. For example, DDT concentrations might be only 0.000003 parts per million (ppm) in lake water and 0.04 ppm in zooplankton, but the concentrations rise to 0.5 ppm in minnows that eat zooplankton, 2.0 ppm in fish that eat the minnows, and 25 ppm in the fish-eating osprey. Birds such as the osprey (*Pandion haliaetus*) and the bald eagle (*Haliaetus leucocephalus*) are particularly susceptible because they rely heavily on fish, which concentrate the toxins draining into rivers and lakes from agricultural watersheds. Peregrine falcons (*Falco peregrinus*), which frequently feed on insectivorous birds and bats, are also vulnerable to the effects of biomagnification. DDT and its breakdown products cause eggshell thinning, inhibit proper development of the embryo, change adult bird behavior, and may even cause direct adult mortality.

ure to raise young and the outright death of many adults, populations of these birds showed dramatic declines throughout the world (Box 9.1).

In lakes and estuaries, DDT and other pesticides became concentrated in predatory fish and in sea mammals such as dolphins. In agricultural areas, beneficial and endangered insect species were killed along with pest species. At the same time, mosquitoes and other targeted insects evolved resistance to the chemicals, so that ever-larger doses of DDT were required to suppress the insect populations. Recognition of this situation in the 1970s led many industrialized countries to ban the use of DDT and other chemically related pesticides. The ban eventually allowed the partial recovery of many bird populations, most notably peregrine falcons, ospreys, and bald eagles (Hoffman and Smith 2003). Nevertheless, the continuing massive

---

BOX 9.1 *(continued)*

Dramatic evidence of the damage done to raptors by DDT is the rapidity with which many U.S. populations recovered after DDT and other organochlorine pesticides were banned in 1972. The peregrine falcon has made an astonishingly strong recovery in many parts of the world (Enderson et al. 1995; Cade and Burnham 2003; Hoffman and Smith 2003). Captive-bred peregrine falcons released within their former range have successfully established new breeding populations, often nesting on skyscrapers in urban areas. Ospreys and bald eagles have made a similar comeback. There are now over 7000 breeding pairs of eagles in the lower 48 states of the U.S., following a low of 417 pairs in 1963.

The unanticipated decline of raptor populations illustrates the dangers of indiscriminately introducing chemicals into the environment. The unique sensitivity of raptors to pesticides warned of potential danger to humans as well. It should have been expected that a chemical toxic to

insects might have a negative impact on other organisms. Chemicals known to be toxic to human and animal life are still being produced and finding their way into the environment. It has long been known that PCBs cause cancer, yet they continue to be used, for example, in the manufacture of electric transformers. As the use of new chemicals multiplies, so do the chances of unanticipated, harmful side effects. In addition, lead poisoning from spent ammunition and fishing weights, an old but little recognized problem for humans and animals, is causing increased public concern because of the numbers of eagles, California condors, trumpeter swans, and other species dying from ingestion of lead shot and bullet fragments. Observation of sentinel species—in this case, top predators that accumulate contaminants—may alert us to rising levels of harmful chemicals in the environment. But it may take the threat of another "silent spring" to motivate humankind to stop contaminating the environment with chemicals.

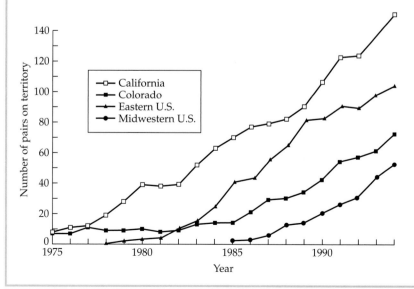

Following the banning of DDT in 1972, remnant peregrine populations in California and Colorado have gradually recovered with the help of population augmentation and nest protection. Populations in the East and Midwest were reestablished in their former range using captive-raised animals. (After Enderson et al. 1995.)

use of pesticides and even DDT itself in other countries is still cause for concern, not only for endangered animal species, but also for the potential long-term effects on people, particularly the workers who handle these chemicals in the field and the consumers of the agricultural products treated with these chemicals (Eyles and Consitt 2004). These chemicals are widely dispersed in the air and water and can harm plants, animals, and people living far from where the chemicals are actually applied (Davidson et al. 2002; Bustnes et al. 2003; Relyea 2005). In addition, even in countries that outlawed these pesticides decades ago, chemicals persist in the environment, where they have a detrimental effect on the reproductive and endocrine systems of aquatic vertebrates (Sapozhnikova et al. 2005).

PCBs and organochlorine chemicals used as pesticides are often carried by the wind for great distances and concentrated far from the source. High concentrations of these toxins are found even in the tissues of polar bears in northern Norway and Russia, where they have a harmful impact on bear health.

Water Pollution

Water pollution has negative consequences for people, animals, and all species that live in water: it destroys important food sources and contaminates drinking water with chemicals that can cause immediate and long-term harm to the health of people and other species that come into contact with the polluted water (Townsend et al. 2003; Niemi and McDonald 2004). In the broader picture, water pollution often severely damages aquatic communities (Figure 9.19). Rivers, lakes, and oceans are used as open sewers for industrial wastes and residential sewage. And higher densities of people almost always mean greater levels of water pollution. Pesticides, herbicides, oil products, heavy metals (such as mercury, lead, and zinc), detergents, and industrial wastes directly kill organisms, such as insect larvae, fish, and amphibians, living in aquatic environments (Relyea 2005). Pollution is a threat to 90% of the endangered fishes and freshwater mussels in the United States (Wilcove et al. 1998). An increasing source of pollution in coastal areas is the discharge of nutrients and chemicals from shrimp and salmon farms (Naylor et al. 1998).

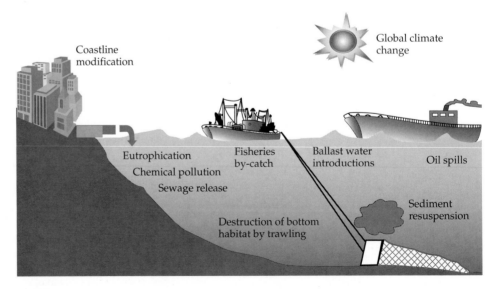

FIGURE 9.19 The aquatic environment faces multiple threats, as shown by this schematic view of damage to the ocean. Trawling is a fishing method in which a net is dragged along the ocean bottom by a boat, scooping up sea life but also damaging the structure of the community. (After Snelgrove 2001.)

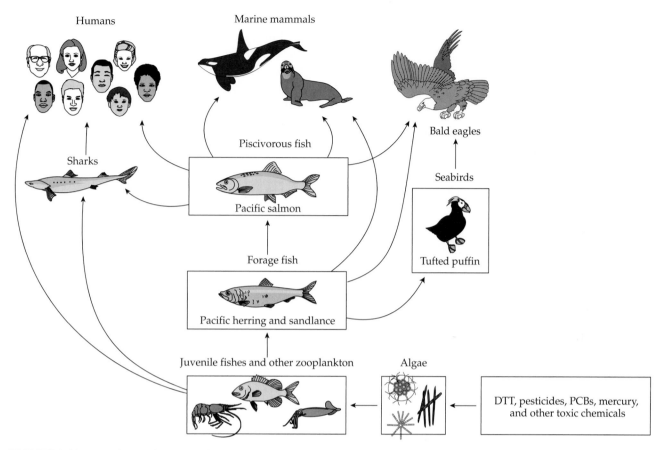

FIGURE 9.20 Toxic chemicals in water become successively concentrated at higher levels in the food chain, leading to health problems for humans, marine mammals, sea birds, and raptors. (After Groom et al. 2006.)

Even if aquatic organisms are not killed outright, these chemicals can make the environment so inhospitable that species can no longer thrive. In contrast to a dump in the terrestrial environment, which has primarily local effects, toxic wastes in aquatic environments diffuse over a wide area. Toxic chemicals, even at very low levels in the water, can be lethal to aquatic organisms through the process of biomagnification. Many aquatic environments are naturally low in essential minerals, such as nitrates and phosphates, and aquatic species have adapted to the natural absence of minerals by developing the ability to process large volumes of water and concentrate these minerals. When these species process polluted water, they concentrate toxic chemicals along with the essential minerals; the toxins eventually poison the plant or animal. Species that feed on these aquatic species ingest these concentrations of toxic chemicals. One of the most serious connections is the accumulation of mercury by long-lived predatory fish, such as swordfish and shark, and its impact on the nervous system of people who eat this type of fish frequently (Figure 9.20) (Ellison 2004).

Essential minerals that are beneficial to plant and animal life can become harmful pollutants at high levels (Smith et al. 1999; Haddad et al. 2000). Human sewage, agricultural fertilizers, detergents, and industrial processes often release large amounts of nitrates and phosphates into aquatic systems, initiating the process of **eutrophication**, the result of human activity. Humans release as much nitrate into the environment as are produced by all natural processes; and the human re-

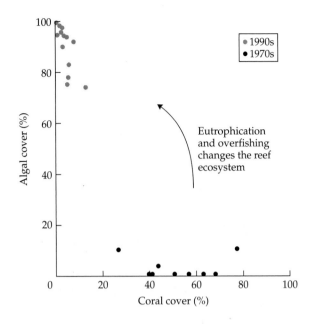

FIGURE 9.21 In the 1970s, coral dominated Jamaica's reef ecosystems; 20 years later, algae have taken over these same areas. The shift is due to water pollution and the overharvesting of algae-eating fish. (After Hughes 1994.)

lease of nitrogen is expected to keep increasing as the human population continues to increase (MEA 2005). From 1960 to 2003, the use of nitrogen fertilizers increased by 8 times, and the use of phosphate fertilizers increased by 3 times. Even small amounts of these nutrients can stimulate plant and animal growth, and high concentrations of nutrients released through human activities often result in thick "blooms" of algae at the surface of ponds and lakes. These algal blooms may be so dense that they outcompete other plankton species and shade bottom-dwelling plant species. As the algal mat becomes thicker, its lower layers sink to the bottom and die. The bacteria and fungi that decompose the dying algae grow in response to this added sustenance and consequently absorb all of the oxygen in the water. Without oxygen, much of the remaining animal life dies off, sometimes visibly in the form of masses of dead fish floating on the water's surface. The result is a greatly impoverished and simplified community, a "dead zone" consisting of only those species tolerant of polluted water and low oxygen levels.

This process of eutrophication can affect marine systems with large anthropogenic inputs of nutrients as well, particularly coastal areas and bodies of water in confined areas, such as the Gulf of Mexico, the Mediterranean, the North Sea and the Baltic Sea in Europe, and the enclosed seas of Japan (Beman et al. 2005). In warm tropical waters, eutrophication favors algae, which grow over coral reefs and completely change the biological community (Figure 9.21).

Eroding sediments from logged or farmed hillsides can also harm aquatic ecosystems (Thrush et al. 2004). The sediment covers submerged plant leaves and other green surfaces with a muddy film that reduces light availability and diminishes the rate of photosynthesis. Increasing water turbidity reduces the depth at which photosynthesis can occur and may prevent animal species from seeing, feeding, and living in the water. Sediment loads are particularly harmful to many coral species that require crystal-clear waters to survive. Corals have delicate filters that strain tiny food particles out of the clear water. When the water is filled with a high density of soil particles, the filters clog up and the animals cannot feed. Coral animals often have symbiotic algae that provide carbohydrates for the coral. When the water is filled with soil particles, there may be too little light for the algae to photosynthesize, and the corals will lose this source of energy.

Air Pollution

The effects of air pollution on forest communities have been intensively studied because of the great economic value of forests from wood production, protection of water supplies, and recreation (Hendrey 2001). In certain areas of the world, particularly northern Europe and eastern North America, air pollution damages and weakens many tree species—apparently both directly and indirectly—and makes them more susceptible to attacks by insects, fungi, and disease (Figure 9.22). When the trees die, many of the other species in a forest also become locally extinct. Even when communities are not destroyed by air pollution, species composition may be altered as more susceptible species are eliminated. Lichens—symbiotic organisms composed of fungi and algae that can survive in some of the harshest natural environments—are particularly susceptible to air pollution. Because each lichen species has distinct levels of tolerance to air pollution, the composition of the lichen community can be used as a biological indicator of the level of air pollution.

In the past, people assumed that the atmosphere was so vast that materials they released into the air would be widely dispersed and their effects would be minimal. But today several types of air pollution are so widespread that they damage whole ecosystems. These same pollutants also have severe impacts on human health, demonstrating again the common interests shared by people and nature. We discuss each of these air pollutants below.

ACID RAIN Industries such as smelting operations and coal- and oil-fired power plants release huge quantities of nitrogen and sulfur oxides into the air, where they combine with moisture in the atmosphere to produce nitric and sulfuric acids. These acids become part of cloud systems and dramatically lower the pH (the standard measure of acidity) of rainwater, leading to the weakening and deaths of trees over wide areas. Acid rain, in turn, lowers the pH of soil moisture and water bodies, such as ponds and lakes, and also increases the concentration of toxic metals such as aluminum.

Acid rain is currently a severe problem in eastern North America, throughout Europe, but particularly in central Europe, and east Asia, particularly in China and Korea; within the next 50 years acid rain will also affect Southeast Asia, western coastal India, and south central Africa (Kuylenstierna et al. 2001; Menz and Seip 2004). In the United States alone, around 40 million metric tons of these compounds are released

FIGURE 9.22 Forests in montane areas near concentrations of power plants and heavy industry are experiencing diebacks, thought to be caused in part by the effects of acid rain combined with nitrogen deposition, ozone damage, insect attack, and disease. These dead trees were photographed in Blue Ridge Parkway, North Carolina, in 1992. (Photograph © Cub Kahn/TERRAPHOTOGRAPHICS/Biological Photo Service.)

into the atmosphere each year (WRI 1998; Lynch et al. 2000). The heavy reliance of China on high-sulfur coal and the rapid increase in automobile ownership and industrialization in China, India, and elsewhere in Southeast Asia, represent serious threats to biological diversity in the region, with dramatic increases in acid rain and nitrogen deposition predicted over the next 50 years (MEA 2005).

Increased acidity alone damages many plant and animal species; as the acidity of water bodies increases, many fish either fail to spawn or die outright (Figure 9.23). Both increased acidity and water pollution are two contributing factors to the dramatic decline of many amphibian populations throughout the world. Most amphibian species depend on bodies of water for at least part of their life cycle, and a decline in water pH causes a corresponding increase in the mortality of eggs and young animals (Stuart et al. 2004). Acidity also inhibits the microbial process of decomposition, lowering the rate of mineral recycling and ecosystem productivity. Many ponds and lakes in industrialized countries have lost large portions of their animal communities as a result of acid rain. These damaged water bodies are often in supposedly pristine areas hundreds of kilometers from major sources of urban and industrial pollution, such as the North American Rocky Mountains. While acidity of rain is decreasing in many areas due to better pollution control, it still remains a serious problem. In developing countries, such as China, the acidity of rain is increasing as the country powers its rapid industrial development through the use of fuels high in sulfur.

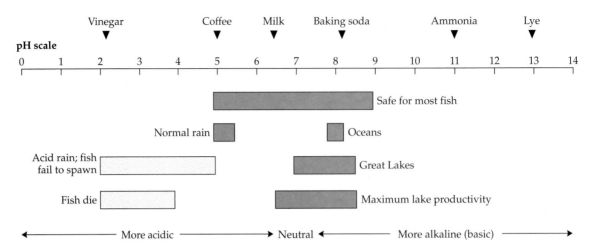

FIGURE 9.23 The pH scale, indicating ranges at which acidity becomes lethal to fish. Studies indicate that fish are indeed disappearing from heavily acidified lakes. (After Cox 1993, based on data from the U.S. Fish and Wildlife Service.)

OZONE PRODUCTION AND NITROGEN DEPOSITION Automobiles, power plants, and industrial activities release hydrocarbons and nitrogen oxides as waste products. In the presence of sunlight, these chemicals react with the atmosphere to produce ozone and other secondary chemicals, collectively called photochemical smog. Although ozone in the upper atmosphere is important in filtering out ultraviolet radiation, high concentrations of ozone at ground level damage plant tissues and make them brittle, harming biological communities and reducing agricultural productivity. Ozone and smog are detrimental to people and animals when inhaled, so both people and biological communities benefit from air-pollution controls. When airborne nitrogen compounds are deposited by rain and dust, biological communities throughout the world are damaged and altered by potentially toxic levels of this nutrient (Brys et al. 2005; Smart et al. 2005). In particular, the combination of nitrogen deposition and acid rain is responsible for a decline in the density of soil fungi that form beneficial relationships with trees.

TOXIC METALS Leaded gasoline (still used in many developing countries, despite its clear danger to human health), mining and smelting operations, coal burned for heat and power, and other industrial activities release large quantities of lead, zinc, mercury, and other toxic metals into the atmosphere. These compounds are directly poisonous to plant and animal life, and can cause permanent injury to children. The effects of these toxic metals are particularly evident in areas surrounding large smelting operations, where life has been destroyed for miles around.

Levels of pollution may sometimes be reduced by enforcing local and national policies and regulations; eliminating lead from gasoline is one such example. Levels of air pollution are declining in certain areas of North America and Europe, but continue to rise in many other areas of the world. Increases in air pollution will be particularly severe in many Asian countries with dense (and growing) human populations and expanding industrialization. Hope for controlling air pollution in the future depends on building motor vehicles with dramatically lower emissions, increasing the development and use of mass transit systems, developing more efficient scrubbing processes for industrial smokestacks, and reducing overall energy use through conservation and efficiency measures. Many of these measures are already being actively implemented in European countries and in Japan.

Global Climate Change

Carbon dioxide, methane, and other trace gases in the atmosphere are transparent to sunshine, allowing light energy to pass through the atmosphere and warm the surface of the Earth. These gases and water vapor (in the form of clouds) trap the energy radiating from the Earth as heat, slowing the rate at which heat leaves the Earth's surface and radiates back into space. These gases are called **greenhouse gases** because they function much like the glass in a greenhouse, which is transparent to sunlight but traps energy inside the greenhouse once it is transformed to heat (Figure 9.24). The similar warming effect of Earth by its atmospheric gases is called the **greenhouse effect**. We can imagine that these gases act as "blankets" on the Earth's surface: the denser the concentration of gases, the more heat trapped near the Earth, thus, the higher the planet's surface temperature.

(A)

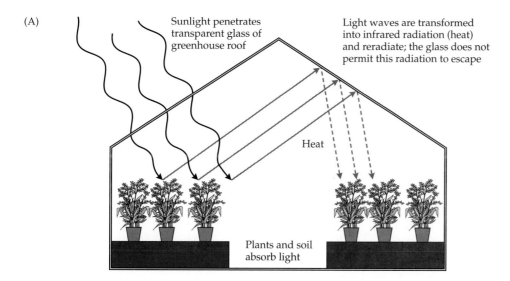

Sunlight penetrates transparent glass of greenhouse roof

Light waves are transformed into infrared radiation (heat) and reradiate; the glass does not permit this radiation to escape

Heat

Plants and soil absorb light

(B)

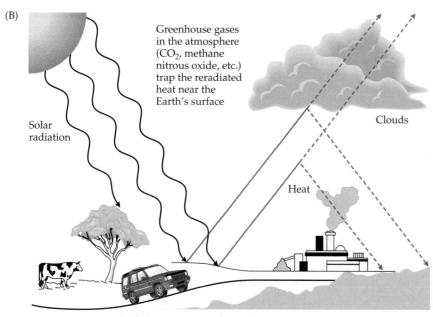

Greenhouse gases in the atmosphere (CO_2, methane nitrous oxide, etc.) trap the reradiated heat near the Earth's surface

Clouds

Solar radiation

Heat

Light waves are transformed into infrared radiation (heat) and reradiated

FIGURE 9.24 In the greenhouse effect, gases and water vapor form a blanket around the Earth that acts like the glass roof of a greenhouse, trapping heat near the Earth's surface. (From Gates 1993.)

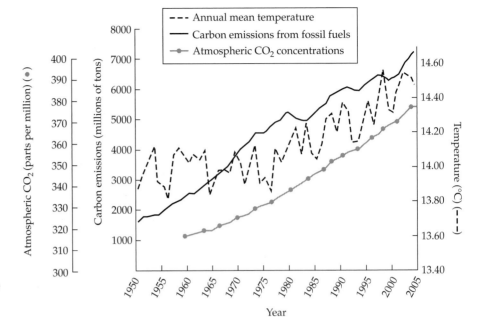

FIGURE 9.25 Over the last 55 years, the carbon emissions from fossil fuel use and forest destruction has increased dramatically resulting in greater atmospheric CO_2 concentrations. Most scientists believe the observed increase in global temperature is caused by this increased atmospheric concentration of carbon dioxide and other greenhouse gases. (Data from Worldwatch Institute.)

The greenhouse effect allows life to flourish on Earth—without it the temperature on the Earth's surface would fall dramatically. Today, however, as a result of human activity, concentrations of greenhouse gases are increasing so much that scientists believe they are already affecting the Earth's climate (IPCC 2001; Karl and Trenberth 2003). The term **global warming** is used to describe this increased temperature resulting from the greenhouse effect, and **global climate change** refers to the complete set of climate characteristics that are changing now and will continue to change in the future, including patterns of precipitation and wind.

During the past 100 years, global levels of carbon dioxide (CO_2), methane, and other trace gases have been steadily increasing, primarily as a result of burning fossil fuels—coal, oil, and natural gas (IPPC 2001). Clearing forests to create farmland and burning firewood for heating and cooking also contribute to rising concentrations of CO_2. Carbon dioxide concentration in the atmosphere has increased from 290 parts per million (ppm) to 380 ppm over the last 100 years (Figure 9.25), and it is projected to double at some point in the latter half of this century. Even if the plans to reduce CO_2 production that were agreed upon by many countries at the 1997 Kyoto conference were implemented tomorrow, there would be little immediate reduction in present atmospheric CO_2 levels, because each CO_2 molecule resides in the atmosphere for an average of 100 years before being removed by plants and natural geochemical processes. Because of this time lag, levels of CO_2 in the atmosphere will continue to rise in the medium term.

Another significant greenhouse gas is methane, which has increased from 0.8 to 1.7 ppm in the last 100 years as a result of rice cultivation, cattle production, microbial activity in dumps, the burning of tropical forests and grasslands, and release during fossil fuel production. Methane is far more efficient at absorbing heat than carbon dioxide, so that, even at low concentrations, methane is an important contributor to the greenhouse effect. Methane molecules persist in the atmosphere for even longer than does carbon dioxide. Reductions in methane levels will require changes in agricultural practices and improved pollution controls.

Most scientists believe that the increased levels of greenhouse gases have affected the world's climate and ecosystems already and that these effects will increase in the future (Table 9.4). An extensive review of the evidence supports the

TABLE 9.4 *Some evidence for global warming*

1. INCREASED INCIDENCE OF HEAT WAVES
Example: August 2003 heat wave in France kills 11,435 people, with temperatures reaching 40°C (104°F).

2. MELTING OF GLACIERS AND POLAR ICE
Example: In the Caucasus Mountains between the Black Sea and the Caspian Sea, half of all glacial ice has melted during the last 100 years.
Example: A 2992-km2 section of previously stable Antarctic ice shelf collapses in 1999.

3. RISING SEA LEVELS
Example: Since 1938, one-third of the coastal marshes in a wildlife refuge in Chesapeake Bay have been submerged by rising seawater.

4. EARLIER FLOWERING OF PLANTS.
Example: Two-thirds of plant species are now flowering earlier than they did several decades ago.

5. EARLIER SPRING ARRIVAL
Example: One-third of English birds are now laying eggs earlier in the year then they did 30 years ago, and oak trees are now leafing out earlier than they did 40 years ago.

6. SHIFTS IN SPECIES RANGES
Example: Two-thirds of European butterfly species studied are now found farther northward by 35 to 250 km than recorded several decades ago.

7. POPULATION DECLINES
Example: Adelie penguin populations have declined by one-third over the past 25 years as their sea ice habitat melts away.

Source: After Union of Concerned Scientists 1999; Parmesan and Yohe 2003.

conclusion that global surface temperatures have increased by 0.7°C during the last century (Schneider 1998; IPCC 2001; Karoly et al. 2003). Temperatures at high latitudes, such as in Siberia, Alaska, and Canada, have increased by 2 to 4°C. Some plant and animal species are changing their ranges and the timing of their reproductive behavior in response to these temperature changes (Grebmeier et al. 2006). Evidence indicates that ocean water temperatures have also changed over the last 50 years: the Atlantic, Pacific, and Indian Oceans have increased in temperature by an average of 0.06°C (Gillett et al. 2003). As a consequence, certain marine species are expanding their range to higher latitudes (Precht and Aronson 2004).

There is now a general consensus among climatologists that the world climate will increase in temperature by an additional 1.4° to 5.8°C by 2100 as a result of increased levels of carbon dioxide and other gases. The increase could be even greater if carbon dioxide levels rise faster than predicted; it could be slightly less if all countries reduced their emissions of greenhouse gases in the very near future. The increase in temperature will be greatest at high latitudes and over large continents (Wohlforth 2004) (Figure 9.26). Rainfall has already started to increase on a global scale and will continue to increase, but will vary by region, with some regions showing decreases in rainfall. There will also probably be an increase in extreme weather events, such as hurricanes, flooding, and regional drought, associated with this warming (IPCC 2001; Schärr et al. 2004). In dry forests and savannahs, warmer conditions will result in an increased incidence of fire. In coastal areas, storms will cause increased destruction of cities and other human settlements and will severely damage coastal vegetation, including beaches and coral reefs. The series of hurricanes that devastated the southern United States in 2005 could be an indication of what the future may bring.

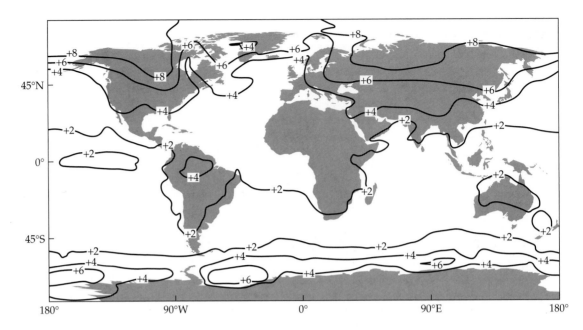

FIGURE 9.26 Complex computer models of global climate predict that temperatures will increase significantly (temperatures in 2071 to 2100 relative to the period from 1961 to 1990) when CO_2 levels double, which is projected to occur in the mid to late part of this century. Predicted temperature increases, shown in °C, are greatest over continents and at high latitudes (i.e., closer to the poles). (After IPCC 2001.)

The computer simulation models of future weather patterns are rapidly improving to include: the role of the ocean in absorbing atmospheric carbon dioxide, how plant communities will respond to higher carbon dioxide levels and temperatures, the effects of increased levels of anthropogenic aerosols (airborne particles resulting from burning fossil fuels, wood, and other sources), and the role of cloud cover in reflecting sunlight. Even though details of global climate change are being debated by scientists, there is a broad consensus that the world's climate has started to change already and will continue to change substantially in coming decades.

Changes in Temperate and Tropical Climates

Global climate change is not a new phenomenon. During the past 2 million years, there have been at least 10 cycles of global warming and cooling. When the polar ice caps melted during warm periods, sea levels rose to well above their earlier levels, and species extended their ranges closer to the poles and migrated to higher elevations on mountains. During cold periods, the ice caps enlarged, sea levels dropped, and species shifted their ranges closer to the equator and to lower elevations. While many species undoubtedly went extinct during these repeated episodes of range changes, the species we have today are survivors of global climate change. If species could adjust to changes in global climate in the past, will species be able to adjust to the predicted changes in global climate caused by human alteration of the atmosphere?

It seems likely that many species will be unable to adjust quickly enough to survive this human-caused warming, which will occur far more rapidly than previous, natural climate shifts. It is likely that the consequences of a rise in temperature will be profound, probably profoundly negative. Many species will be unable to disperse rapidly enough to track the changing climate and remain within their "climatic envelope" of temperature and precipitation (Hansen et al. 2001; Malcom

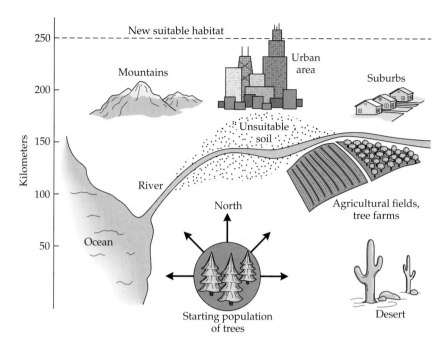

FIGURE 9.27 If global temperatures increase as models suggest, north-temperate tree species will have to disperse hundreds of kilometers northward in order to find sites with a hospitable climate. Not only will these species encounter natural barriers such as mountains, oceans, rivers, and unsuitable terrain, but they face barriers created by people, such as agricultural fields, cities, suburbs, roads, and fences. (After Peters and Lovejoy 1992.)

et al. 2006). Habitat fragmentation caused by human activities will further slow or prevent many species from migrating to new sites where suitable habitat exists (Figure 9.27). Many species of limited distribution and/or poor dispersal ability will undoubtedly go extinct, with widely distributed, easily dispersed species being favored in the new communities (Miller-Rushing and Primack 2004). Extinction rates for species of restricted range could be 9 to 13%, with over 1 million species predicted to go extinct by 2050 (Thomas et al. 2004). Entire biological communities may become altered and degraded if the dominant species are not able to adapt to the changing conditions (Sala et al. 2000). Experimental warming experiments in mountain meadows to simulate the effects of global climate change show that there will be a loss of species from these communities. Certain biological communities of the United States, such as the spruce–fir and the aspen–birch communities, may decline in area by more than 90% (Hansen et al. 2001).

As a result of global climate change, climatic regions in the northern and southern temperate zones will be shifted toward the poles. More than 10% of the plant species in many U.S. states will not be able to survive the new climatic conditions—if they are not able to migrate northward, they will die. This change has clearly begun already, with alpine plants found growing higher on mountains and migrating birds observed spending longer times at their summer breeding grounds (Walther et al. 2002). In the coming century, global climate change is predicted to have a great impact on arctic boreal and alpine ecosystems as a result of warmer conditions and a longer growing season.

The effects of global climate change on temperature and rainfall are expected to be less drastic in the Tropics than in the temperate zone (IPCC 2001). However, even small changes in the amount and timing of rainfall could have major effects on species composition, cycles of plant reproduction, and susceptibility to fire. Such changes have already been linked to the decline and extinction of amphibians in the mountains of Costa Rica (Pounds and Puschendorf 2004). Moreover, cool-adapted species that live atop tropical mountains could be highly vulnerable to increasing temperatures. Some models suggest that hurricanes could become more severe and frequent in tropical areas, which would have major consequences for forest structure.

Plants and Climate Change

Some plant species will adapt to utilize the increased carbon dioxide levels and higher temperatures to increase their growth rates, whereas other, less adaptable species will not and will decrease in abundance (Bezemer and Jones 1998). A substantial increase in plant growth has already been detected over large areas of northern high latitudes using satellite data (Myneni et al. 1997). Shifts in the populations of herbivorous insect species and pollinators may be pronounced as their plant resources change.

Finally, the large areas where temperate agricultural crops, such as wheat and maize (corn), are now grown may have to be moved farther from the equator and perhaps expanded as the climate changes. Many of the areas that will be potentially suitable for new agricultural land are currently protected conservation land such as national parks. This potentially creates a situation in which the protection of biological diversity directly competes with supplying the food needs of people.

Rising Sea Levels and Warmer Waters

Warming temperatures are already causing mountain glaciers to melt and the polar ice caps to shrink, and this process will continue and accelerate. As a result of this release of water and the thermal expansion of water, over the next 100 years sea levels are predicted to rise by 9 to 88 cm and flood low-lying, coastal communities (Gillett et al. 2003; Fish et al. 2005). Much of the current land area of low-lying countries such as Bangladesh could be under water within 100 years. There is evidence that this process has already begun; sea levels have already risen by 10 to 20 cm over the last 100 years (IPCC 2001). Many low islands that were previously just above water are now just below the water level.

Rising sea levels could destroy or radically alter 25 to 80% of the coastal wetlands of the United States. The rise will occur so rapidly that many species will be unable to migrate quickly enough to adjust to changing water levels. The migration of wetland species, in particular, species of coastal salt marshes, will be blocked where human settlements, roads, and flood control barriers have been built adjacent to wetlands. Squeezed between the rising sea and dense coastal developments, many species will no longer have a place to live (Fish et al. 2005; Feagin et al. 2005). This will have major economic impacts as well because salt marsh habitat is among the world's most productive habitat for plant and animal life, and is a major breeding and nursery ground for commercial fish and shellfish.

Rising sea levels are potentially detrimental to many coral reef species, which grow at a precise depth in the water with the right combination of light and water movement. Water levels rising at a rate of 88 cm per century translates into a rise in sea level of almost 1 cm per year—and 1 cm per year is about as fast as massive coral can grow (Grigg and Epp 1989). Slow-growing coral reefs will be unable to keep pace with the rise in sea level and will gradually be submerged and die; only fast-growing species will be able to survive. Compounding this, the pace of coral growth might be slower than normal; increasing absorption of CO_2 by the ocean will make the water more acidic and inhibit the ability of coral animals to deposit the calcium used to build the reef structure.

Warming waters are already affecting the marine environment (Field et al. 2006). In the coastal waters off California, warm-water, southern species are increasing in abundance, while cold-water, northern species are declining (Holbrook et al. 1997; Vilchis et al. 2005). Zooplankton are also declining due to warmer seas temperatures, with dire consequences for the marine animals that use them for food. In addition, coral reefs are threatened by rising seawater temperatures (Buddemier et al. 2004). Abnormally high water temperatures in the Pacific Ocean and Indian Ocean in 1998 caused the coral animals to sicken and expel the symbiotic algae that live inside the coral and provide them with essential carbohydrates; subsequently, these "bleached" coral then suffered a massive dieback, with an estimated 70% coral mortality in Indian Ocean reefs (West and Salm 2003), though scattered patches did survive. Even-warmer conditions in the coming decades could be a disaster for many coral reefs.

The Overall Effect of Global Warming

Global climate change has the potential to radically restructure biological communities and change the ranges of many species. The pace of this change could overwhelm the natural dispersal abilities of species. There is mounting evidence that this process has already begun (see Table 9.4), with poleward movements in the distribution of bird and plant species, and reproduction occurring earlier in the spring (Walther et al. 2002; Parmesan and Yohe 2003; Primack et al. 2004). Because the implications of global climate change are so far-reaching, biological communities, ecosystem functions, and climate need to be carefully monitored over the coming decades. Global climate change will also have an enormous impact on human populations in coastal areas affected by rising sea levels and increased hurricane impacts, and in areas that usually experience large changes in temperature and rainfall. In much of sub-Saharan Africa, growing seasons will get shorter, and crop yields will decline (WRI 2005). The poor people of the world will be least able to adjust to these changes and will suffer the consequences disproportionately. However, all countries of the world will be affected, and it is time for people to recognize the urgent need to address global climate change (Moser and Dilling 2004).

It is likely that, as the climate changes, many existing protected areas will no longer preserve the rare and endangered species that currently live there (Miller-Rushing and Primack 2004; Hannah et al. 2005; Pyke and Fischer 2005). We need to establish new conservation areas now to protect sites that will be suitable for these species in the future, such as sites with large elevational gradients (Figure 9.28). Potential future migration routes, such as north–south river valleys, need to be identified and established now. If species are in danger of going extinct in the wild because of global climate change, the last remaining individuals may have to be maintained in captivity. Another necessary strategy will be to transplant isolated populations of rare and endangered species to new localities at higher elevations and farther from the poles, where they can survive and thrive. Even if global climate change is not as severe as predicted, establishing new protected areas can only help to protect biological diversity.

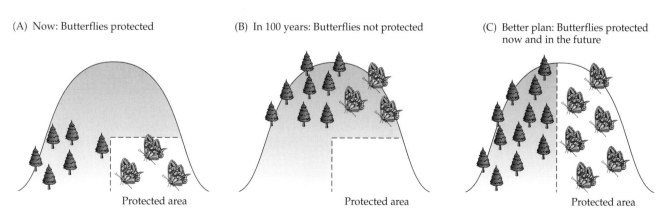

(A) Now: Butterflies protected

(B) In 100 years: Butterflies not protected

(C) Better plan: Butterflies protected now and in the future

Protected area   Protected area   Protected area

FIGURE 9.28 A rare butterfly now lives inside a protected area (A). However, due to a warming climate over the next 100 years, it migrates to a higher elevation where it is no longer protected (B). The solution is to establish more protected areas along elevational gradients and natural migration routes now in anticipation of future climate change (C).

Although the prospect of global climate change is cause for great concern, it should not divert our attention from the massive habitat destruction that is the principal current cause of species extinction (Kappelle et al. 1999; Pyke 2004): Preserving intact communities and restoring degraded ones are the most important and immediate priorities for conservation.

Summary

1. Massive disturbances to the environment caused by human activities are driving species, even communities, to the point of extinction. These impacts will increase in the future, mostly in the species-rich tropical countries, as the human population increases to 8 to 10 billion by the year 2050. Slowing human population growth and reducing the overconsumption of resources are important elements of the solution to the biological diversity crisis.

2. The major threat to biological diversity is the loss of habitat, so to protect biological diversity we must preserve habitat. Many unique and threatened species have lost most of their habitat and are protected on only a tiny percentage of their original range. Species-rich tropical rain forests are currently being destroyed at a rapid rate. Extensive habitat destruction has occurred in tropical dry forests, wetlands in all regions of the world, coral reefs, and temperate grasslands.

3. Habitat fragmentation is the process whereby a large continuous area of habitat is both reduced and divided into two or more fragments. These fragments are isolated from one another by modified or degraded habitat. Habitat fragmentation leads to the rapid loss of remaining species because it creates barriers to the normal processes of dispersal, colonization, and foraging. Particular fragments may lack the range of food types and other resources necessary to support permanent populations of certain species, or they may contain altered environmental conditions and increased levels of pests, which make them less suitable for the original species.

4. Environmental pollution eliminates many species from biological communities, even where the structure of the community is not obviously disturbed. Pesticides, sprayed to control insects, become concentrated in the bodies of birds, particularly raptors, leading to a decline in populations. Water pollution by petroleum products, sewage, and industrial wastes can kill species outright or gradually eliminate them. Excessive nutrient inputs can cause harmful algal blooms that damage aquatic communities. Acid rain, high ozone levels near the surface of the Earth, and airborne toxic metals are all damaging components of air pollution.

5. Global climate patterns will probably change within the coming century because of the large amounts of carbon dioxide and other greenhouse gases that are being produced by human activities such as the burning of fossil fuels. Predicted temperature increases could be so rapid during this coming century that many species will be unable to adjust their ranges and will go extinct. Low-lying coastal communities will be submerged by seawater as the polar ice caps continue to melt. Conservation biologists need to monitor these changes and take action when species cannot adapt to climate change.

For Discussion

1. Human population growth is often blamed for the loss of biological diversity. Is this valid? What other factors are responsible, and how do we weigh their relative importance?

2. Excessive consumption of resources by people in developed countries is a major cause of the loss of biological diversity. An alternative is to "live simply, so that others may simply live," or to "live as if life mattered." Consider the absolute minimum of food, shelter, clothing, and energy that you and your family need to survive and compare it with what you now use. Would you be willing to change your lifestyle to preserve the environment and help others? How could an entire society change enough to benefit the environment?

3. What can an individual citizen do to improve the environment and conserve biodiversity? Consider the options, which range from doing no harm to becoming actively involved in large conservation organizations.

4. Consider the most damaged and the most pristine habitats near where you live. Why have some been preserved and others allowed to degrade?

5. Examine maps of parks and nature reserves. Have these areas been fragmented by roads, power lines, and other human constructs? How has fragmentation affected the average fragment size, the area of interior habitat, and the total length of edge? Analyze the effects of adding new roads or eliminating existing roads and developments from the parks and consider their biological, legal, political, and economic implications.

Suggested Readings

Allan, B. F., F. Keesing, and R. S. Ostfeld. 2003. Effects of forest fragmentation on Lyme disease risk. *Conservation Biology* 17: 267–272. Habitat fragmentation increases the risk of Lyme disease; a frightening prospect.

Beman, J. M., K. R. Arrigo, and P. A. Matson. 2005. Agricultural runoff fuels large phytoplankton blooms in vulnerable areas of the ocean. *Nature* 434: 211–214. Dead zones are appearing in more of the world's marine areas due to pollution.

Carson, R. 1982. *Silent Spring*. Reprint, Penguin, Harmondsworth, England. This book describing the harmful effects of pesticides on birds heightened public awareness when it was first published.

Driscoll, D. A. 2004. Extinction and outbreaks accompany fragmentation of a reptile community. *Ecological Applications* 14: 220–240. Case study of impacts of fragmentation.

Fearnside P. M. 2005. Deforestation in Brazilian Amazonia: History, rates, and consequences. *Conservation Biology* 19: 680–688. The destruction of the Amazonian rainforests is a momentous environmental event.

Field, D. B., T. R. Baumgartner, C. D. Charles, V. Ferreira-Bartrina, and M. D. Ohman. Planktonic foraminifera of the California current reflect 20th-century warming. *Science* 311: 63–66. Global warming is already having an effect on the distribution of species in the ocean.

Forman, R. T., D. Sperling, J. H. Bissonette, A. P. Clevenger, C. D. Cutshall, V. H. Dale, et al. 2003. *Road Ecology: Science and Solutions*. Island Press, Washington, D.C. Roads have an enormous impact on the ecology of landscapes.

Grebmeier, J. M., J. E. Overland, S. E. Moore, E. V. Farley, E. C. Carmack, L. W. Cooper, et al. 2006. A major ecosystem shift in the northern Bering Sea. *Science* 311: 1461–1464. Major changes in the distribution and abundance of marine animals are associated with global climate change.

Hansen, A. J., R. P. Neilson, V. H. Dale, C. H. Flather, L. R. Iverson, D. J. Currie, et al. 2001. Global change in forests: Responses of species, communities, and biomes. *BioScience* 51: 765–779. Global climate change will have enormous effects in the distribution of species and communities.

Intergovernmental Panel on Climate Change (IPCC). 2001. *Climate Change 2001: Synthesis Report*. Cambridge University Press, Cambridge. A comprehensive presentation of the current state of our knowledge.

Laurance, W. F. and G. B. Williamson. 2001. Positive feedback among forest fragmentation, drought, and climate change in the Amazon. *Conservation Biology* 15: 1529–1535. Article from a symposium on habitat fragmentation.

Malcolm, J. R., C. Liu, R. P. Neilson, L. Hansen, and L. Hannah. 2006. Global warming and extinctions of endemic species from biodiversity hotspots. *Conservation Biology* 20: 538–548. Global warming is predicted to drive numerous species to extinction within the next 100 years.

McKee, J. K., P. W. Sciulli, C. D. Fooce, and T. A. Waite. 2003. Forecasting global biodiversity threats associated with human population growth. *Biological Conservation* 115: 161–164. Biodiversity will be most threatened in areas with rapid population growth.

Michalski, F. and C. A. Peres. 2005. Anthropogenic determinants of primate and carnivore local extinctions in a fragmented forest landscape of southern Amazonia. *Biological Conservation* 124: 383–396. Species vary in response to fragmentation.

Miller-Rushing, A. and R. Primack. 2004. Climate and plant conservation. *Plant Talk* 35: 34–38. Strategies for monitoring and dealing with the impact of climate change.

Parker, T. H., B. M. Stansberry, C. D. Becker, and P. S. Gipson. 2005. Edge and area effects on the occurrence of migrant forest songbirds. *Conservation Biology* 19: 1157–1167. Fragmentation causes the decline of many bird populations.

Parmesan, C. and G. Yohe. 2003. A globally coherent fingerprint of climate change impacts across natural systems. *Nature* 42: 37–42. Numerous bird, insect, and plant species are already showing the effects of climate change.

Pearson, R. G. 2006. Climate change and the migration capacity of species. *Trends in Ecology and Evolution* 21: 111–113. Discussion of the ability of species to migrate and persist in the face of climate change.

Precht, W. F. and R. B. Aronson. 2004. Climate flickers and range shifts of reef corals. *Frontiers in Ecology and the Environment* 2: 307–314. Climate change efffects are now evident in marine systems.

Pyke, C. R. and D. T. Fischer. 2005. Selection of bioclimatically representative biological reserve systems under climate change. *Biological Conservation* 121: 429–441. Protected areas must anticipate climate change.

Relyea, R. A. 2005. The impact of insecticides and herbicides on the biodiversity and productivity of aquatic communities. *Ecological Applications* 15: 618–627. A review of the effects of chemical pollution on aquatic communities.

Stephens, E. S., D. N. Koons, J. J. Rotella, and D. W. Willey. 2003. Effects of habitat fragmentation on avian nesting success: a review of evidence at multiple spatial scales. *Biological Conservation* 115: 101–110. A review of 86 studies shows that the effects of habitat fragmentation are most readily detectable at large landscape scales over a period of several years.

UN Millennium Project. 2005. *Investing in Development: A Practical Plan to Achieve the Millennium Development Goals.* New York. Businesses can help improve the human condition and the environment through responsible activities and investments.

Watling, L. and E. Norse. 1998. Disturbance of the seabed by mobile fishing gear: A comparison to forest clear-cutting. *Conservation Biology* 12: 1180–1197. Special section devoted to fishing impacts.

Overexploitation, Invasive Species, and Disease

Even when biological communities appear intact, they may be experiencing significant losses as a result of human activities. In this chapter, we will discuss three threats to biological communities that are less obvious, but not less damaging than more apparent threats such as habitat destruction and loss. These three threats are overexploitation of particular species, introduction of invasive species, and increased levels of disease transmission. These threats often follow habitat fragmentation and degradation, or are made worse by such factors. Global climate change will also make biological communities more vulnerable to these threats in the future.

Overexploitation

Overexploitation by humans has been estimated to currently threaten about a quarter of the endangered vertebrates in the United States, and fully three-quarters of the vertebrate species in China (Li and Wilcove 2005). A greater level of overexploitation in China results from its large, poor, rural population and the extensive use of wildlife for both food and traditional medicine. People have always hunted and harvested the food and other resources they need to survive, and as long as human populations were small and the methods of collection unsophisticated, people could sustainably harvest and hunt the plants and animals in their environment. However, as human populations have increased, our use of the

(A)

(B)

FIGURE 10.1 (A) These fishermen are pulling a net to harvest fish on Mahe Island, Seychelles. Such traditional methods are often sustainable. (B) Modern methods of harvesting wildlife, however, have become so efficient that catches seriously deplete populations. In this case, large quantities of herring are being pumped into the hold of a fishing vessel in Sitka, Alaska. Note the additional vessels in the background. (A, photograph © G. J. James/Biological Photo Service; B, photograph © Gary C. Will/Visuals Unlimited.)

environment has escalated, and our methods of harvesting have become dramatically more efficient (Figure 10.1) (Redford 1992; Bennett et al. 2002; Lewis 2004). In many areas, this has led to an almost complete depletion of large animals from many biological communities and the creation of strangely "empty" habitats.

Technological advances mean that, even in the developing world, guns are used instead of blowpipes, spears, or arrows for hunting in the tropical rain forests and savannahs. Powerful motorized fishing boats and enormous "factory ships" harvest fish from the world's oceans and sell them on the global market. Small-scale local fishermen now have outboard motors on their canoes and boats, allowing them to harvest wider areas more rapidly. However, even in preindustrial societies, intense exploitation has led to the decline and extinction of local species. For example, ceremonial cloaks worn by the Hawaiian kings were made from feathers of the mamo bird (*Drepanis* sp.); a single cloak used the feathers of 70,000 birds of this now-extinct species.

Traditional societies often have imposed restrictions on themselves to prevent overexploitation of natural resources. For example, the rights to specific harvesting territories were rigidly controlled; hunting and harvesting in certain areas was banned. There were often prohibitions against harvesting female, juvenile, and undersized animals. Certain seasons of the year and times of the day were closed for harvesting. Certain efficient methods of harvesting were not allowed. (Interestingly enough, these restrictions, which allowed traditional societies to exploit communal resources on a long-term, sustainable basis, are almost identical to the fishing restrictions regulators have imposed on or proposed for many fisheries in industrialized nations [Colding and Folke 2001].) Among the most highly developed restrictions were those of the traditional or artisan societies of the Pacific islands (Cinner et al. 2005). In these societies, the resources of the reef, lagoon, and forest were clearly defined, and the possible consequences of overharvesting readily apparent. This is still true today in Tonga, where only the King is permitted to hunt flying foxes because their numbers have shrunk precipitously due to overharvesting.

Exploitation in the Modern World

Few self-imposed restrictions on using resources remain effective today. In much of the world, resources are exploited opportunistically (Chapman and Peres 2001; Jennings et al. 2001). The lack of restraint applies to both ends of the economic scale—the poor and hungry as well as the rich and greedy. In previous chapters, we have seen how corporations and the developed world take advantage of natural resources for a profit. If a market exists for a product, local people will search their environment to find and sell it. Sometimes traditional groups will sell the rights to a resource, such as a forest or mining area, for a bit of cash to buy desired goods. In rural areas, the traditional controls that regulate the extraction of natural products have generally weakened. Whole villages are mobilized to remove systematically every usable animal and plant from an area of forest. Where there has been substantial human migration, civil unrest, or war, controls may no longer exist. In countries beset with civil conflict, such as Somalia, the former Yugoslavia, the Democratic Republic of the Congo, and Rwanda, firearms have come into the hands of rural people. The breakdown of food distribution networks in countries such as these leaves the resources of the natural environment vulnerable to whoever can exploit them (Hart and Hart 2003). The most efficient hunter can kill the most animals, sell the most meat, and make the most money for himself and his family. Animals are sometimes even killed for target practice or simply to spite the government.

On local and regional scales, hunters in most developing countries move into recently logged areas, national parks, and other areas near roads, where they legally and illegally shoot, trap, and collect wild mammals to sell as meat. Populations of large primates, such as gorillas and chimpanzees, ungulates, and other mammals, may be reduced by 80% or more by hunting, and certain species may be eliminated altogether, especially those that occur within a few kilometers of a road (Peres and Lake 2003). Hunters are extracting animals at a rate 6 times greater or more than the resource base can sustain. The result is an empty forest: land with a mostly intact plant community that is lacking its animal community (Milius 2005). The decline in animal populations caused by the intensive hunting of animals has been termed the **bushmeat crisis** and is a major concern for wildlife officials in Africa (Figure 10.2). Eating primate bushmeat also increases the possibility of new diseases being transmitted to human populations. Recent evidence indicates that in coastal Africa, the export of fish to supply European markets is creating greater demand for bushmeat to supply protein needs (Brashares et al. 2004).

Solutions involve restricting the sale and transport of bushmeat, restricting the sale of firearms and ammunition, closing roads following logging, extending legal protection to key endangered species, establishing protected reserves where hunting is not allowed, and most important, providing alternative protein sources to re-

FIGURE 10.2 Bushmeat hunters begin with the largest animals, and successively remove medium-sized and small animals, until there is an "empty forest." The monkey in this photograph is a red-tailed guenon (*Cercopithecus ascanius*). (Photograph © Martin Harvey/ Alamy.)

duce the demand for bushmeat (Milner-Gulland and Bennett 2003; Bushmeat Crisis Taskforce 2004; Pearce 2005; Wilkie et al. 2005). Projects with these goals are being initiated, with the premise that "Food secure, farm-based communities with alternative sources of income to illegal use of wildlife can contribute positively to wildlife protection" (Lewis 2004). However, it remains to be seen if the legal markets in wildlife and increasing domestic livestock production will reduce hunting pressure on (or halt declines in) wildlife populations.

Overexploitation of resources often occurs rapidly when a commercial market develops for a previously unexploited or locally used species. The legal and illegal trade in wildlife is responsible for the decline of many species. Worldwide trade in wildlife is valued at over $10 billion per year, not including edible fish. One of the most pervasive examples of this is the international trade in furs, in which hunted species, such as the chinchilla (*Chinchilla* spp.), vicuña (*Vicugna vicugna*), giant otter (*Pteronura brasiliensis*), and numerous cat species, have been reduced to low numbers. Overharvesting of butterflies by insect collectors; of orchids, cacti, and other plants by horticulturists; of marine mollusks by shell collectors; and of tropical fish by aquarium hobbyists are further examples of whole biological communities being targeted to supply an enormous international demand (Table 10.1). It has been estimated that 500 to 600 million tropical fish are sold worldwide for the aquarium market, and many times that number are killed during collection or shipping (Simpson 2001). Many rare animals such as bears and tigers are killed to obtain specific organs or body parts that are considered useful for medicines and aphrodisiacs, particularly in East Asia. Major exporters are primarily in the developing world, often in the Tropics; most major importers are in the developed countries and East Asia, including Canada, China, the European Union, Hong Kong, Japan, Singapore, Taiwan,

TABLE 10.1 *Major targeted groups of the worldwide trade in wildlife*

Group	Number traded each year[a]	Comments
Primates	35,000	Mostly used for biomedical research; also for pets, zoos, circuses, and private collections.
Birds	2–5 million	Zoos and pets. Mostly perching birds, but also legal and illegal trade of around 80,000 parrots.
Reptiles	2–3 million	Zoos and pets. Also 10–15 million raw skins. Reptiles are used in some 50 million manufactured products (mainly from the wild but increasingly from farms).
Ornamental fish	500–600 million	Most saltwater tropical fish come from the wild and may be caught using illegal methods that damage other wildlife and the surrounding coral reef.
Reef corals	1000–2000 tons	Reefs are being destructively mined to provide aquarium decor and coral jewelry.
Orchids	9–10 million	Approximately 10% of the international trade comes from the wild, sometimes deliberately mislabeled to avoid regulations.
Cacti	7–8 million	Approximately 15% of traded cacti come from the wild, with smuggling a major problem.

Source: Data from Hemley 1994, WRI 2000, WRI 2005.
[a]With the exception of reef corals, refers to number of individuals.

and the United States. The international trade in other animals is similarly large: 250,000 live snakes, 80,000 live parrots, and 35,000 primates are sold each year.

In an attempt to regulate and restrict this trade, many declining species are listed as protected under the Convention on International Trade in Endangered Species (CITES; see Chapter 21). Listing species with CITES has often protected species or groups of species from further exploitation.

Besides a surprisingly large legal trade, billions of dollars are involved in the illegal trade of wildlife. A black market links poor local people, corrupt customs officials, rogue dealers, and wealthy buyers who don't question the sources from whom they buy. This trade has many of the same characteristics, the same practices, and sometimes the same players, as the illegal trade in drugs and weapons. Confronting those who perpetuate illegal activities has become a major and dangerous job for international law enforcement agencies.

The pattern of overexploitation of plants and animals in many cases is distressingly similar. A wildlife resource is identified, a commercial market is developed for that resource, and the local human populace is mobilized to extract and sell the resource. Initial sales are used to buy guns, boats, trucks, tools, and whatever else will help extract the resource more quickly. A transportation network involving roads, cargo ships, and airplanes is built to connect harvesters, buyers, and stores. As the supply diminishes, the price rises, creating a strong incentive to overexploit the resource. The resource is extracted so thoroughly that it becomes rare or even extinct, and the market then turns to another species or another region to exploit. Commercial fishing and whaling demonstrates this pattern well, with the industry working one species after another to the point of diminishing returns, a process sometimes termed "fishing down the food chain" (Box 10.1).

BOX 10.1

Endangered Whales: Making a comeback?

Whales are among the largest and possibly most intelligent animals on Earth, with complicated social organization and communication systems. The discovery of the whale's complex, unique songs captured the public imagination, resulting in strong public support for research on whales and for legal measures to protect them. But as public support has increased, has the situation for whales really improved?

Scientists have only recently begun to comprehend the complexity of whale behavior and ecology because studies of many whale species are difficult for several reasons. First, radio tracking devices commonly used for land animals are difficult to use in water, making it difficult to observe individuals and populations. Second, whales are often very far-ranging, traveling throughout the year from tropical to polar seas. Finally, many whale species have become so rare that finding the animals in the open ocean is truly a needle-in-a-haystack search. Populations of numerous species, including blue (*Balaenoptera muscu-*

lus), bowhead (*Balaena mysticetus*), humpback (*Megaptera novaenglie*), gray (*Eschrichtius robustus*), and right whales (*Eubalaena glacialis, E. japonica,* and *E. australis*), are estimated to have fewer than 35,000 individuals remaining (Myers 1993; Sea World 2000).

Few ocean predators are capable of taking on the larger whales, so the greatest threat to all whale species for the last four centuries has been humans. Until as recently as 20 years ago, commercial whaling has been the single most significant factor leading to the decline of the larger whale species—a threat from which many have not yet recovered (Clapham et al. 2003).

Commercial whaling began in the sixteenth century and reached its apex in the nineteenth and early twentieth centuries, when "baleen" (whalebone), spermaceti oil (oil from sperm whales), and oil made from whale blubber became important commercial products in the international marketplace. Several species hunted preferen-

(continued)

BOX 10.1 *(continued)*

tially were pushed to the brink of extinction. Right whales—so named because they were slow, easy to capture, and provided up to 150 barrels of blubber oil as well as abundant baleen, thus making them the "right" whale for whalers—were the first to bear the brunt of the industry. As the right whale declined in the eighteenth century, whalers turned to other species: the gray, humpback, and bowhead, and later the blue, were decimated in their turn (Darling 1988).

Hunting of right whales was made illegal by international agreement in 1935, by which point they had been reduced to less than 5% of their original abundance. By 1946, faced with the imminent extinction of these and other important species, whaling nations created the International Whaling Commission (IWC) to regulate whale hunting. In 1974, the IWC instituted partial bans on whaling for parts of the world (and for certain species). These rules were violated so often that the IWC instituted a moratorium on all commercial killing of whales worldwide in 1986, against the protests of nations such as Japan, Norway, Russia, and Iceland. Some of these nations continued hunting by employing a loophole in the IWC agreement allowing hunting of some abundant whale species, such as the southern minke whale, for scientific studies, but hunters regularly kill more whales than the agreement permits (Clapham et al. 2003). The Japanese

fleet currently catches around 400 minke whales per year. Worse still, whalers frequently make illegal kills of protected species, often with the tacit approval of their governments (Taylor and Dunstone 1996; Twiss and Reeves 1999). Nevertheless, annual killings of whales have dropped dramatically since the 1986 ban.

Since the ban was instituted, different species have had variable recovery rates. Right whales, protected since 1936, have not recovered in either the North Atlantic or North Pacific. Humpback numbers, on the other hand, have more than doubled in some areas since the early 1960s, an increase of nearly 10% annually. Pacific gray whales appear to have recovered to their previous levels of about 23,000 animals after being hunted to less than 1000 whales. Despite continued hunting, minke whales appear to have recovered, with an estimated 850,000 individuals.

Though the whaling ban has greatly reduced the most direct threat, other factors now contribute to whale mortality. At greatest risk is the North Atlantic right whale population, currently estimated at 350 animals—far less than its original size (Kraus et al. 2005). Right whales tend to ignore boats when feeding on the surface and are injured during collisions with large ships or when they become tangled in fishing gear. Recent efforts to limit injury and deaths related to human activ-

Worldwide populations of whale species harvested by humans

Species	Numbers prior to whaling[a]	Present numbers	Main diet items
BALEEN WHALES			
Blue	200,000	9000	Plankton
Bowhead	56,000	8200	Plankton
Fin	475,000	123,000	Plankton, fish
Gray (Pacific stock)	23,000	21,000	Crustaceans
Humpback	150,000	25,000	Plankton, fish
Minke	140,000	850,000	Plankton, fish
Northern right	Unknown	1300	Plankton
Sei	100,000	55,000	Plankton, fish, squid
Southern right	100,000	1500	Plankton
TOOTHED WHALES			
Beluga	Unknown	50,000	Fish, crustaceans
Narwhal	Unknown	35,000	Fish, squid, crustaceans
Sperm	2,400,000	1,950,000	Fish, squid

Source: After Myers 1993; Sea World 2000.

[a]Preexploitation population numbers are highly speculative; recent evidence suggests that they might have been even greater (Roman and Palumbi 2003).

BOX 10.1 *(continued)*

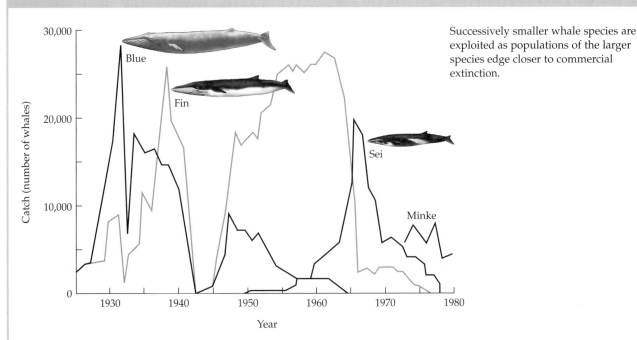

Successively smaller whale species are exploited as populations of the larger species edge closer to commercial extinction.

ities have included bans on gill nets in Florida calving grounds. In addition, information about whale distribution using bioacoustic monitoring is being used to keep fishing boats away from critical feeding areas off the coast of New England.

Many whales too small for large-scale commercial use, such as dolphins and porpoises, have shown substantial population declines as a result of deliberate as well as accidental capture. As fish become scarce due to overharvesting, people are hunting dolphins for food in increasing numbers (Parfit 1995). Other rare marine animals, such as manatees, are also being targeted by fishermen. Nevertheless, accidental catches by commercial fishing boats still account for a high proportion of dolphin deaths. Dolphins in tropical waters of the eastern Pacific Ocean are particularly vulnerable to fishing-related fatalities because they often travel with schools of tuna; thousands of dolphins die in tuna nets each year. One approach to limit the by-catch killing of dolphins has been to establish international certification that tuna have been caught using "dolphin-friendly" methods and to label the tuna caught with such methods.

Small whales and dolphins living in estuarine and riverine habitats face additional threats because these areas are heavily used for shipping and boating, increasing the possibility of direct harm from collisions or entanglements, as well as indirect harm caused by chemical and noise pollution. Small whales appear to be highly sensitive to pollutants and carcinogens (particu-

larly heavy metals and pesticides), which are present in greater concentrations in rivers and harbors than in the open sea. Tissue samples of St. Lawrence River belugas (*Huso huso*), for example, contain concentrations of carcinogenic PCBs 10 to 100 times higher than have been found in ocean-dwelling Arctic belugas (Beland 1996). Long-term exposure to high levels of pollutants exacts a heavy toll on the health of river-dwelling whales: Autopsies of over 70 beluga whales from the St. Lawrence indicate that the cancer rate among these whales was twice as high as in humans, with gastrointestinal cancers the most common form observed. Ailments found in these animals—illnesses not prevalent in Arctic Ocean belugas—include perforated stomach ulcers, thyroid and adrenal gland lesions, and a high incidence of infections.

In the coming years, whales and people will come into increasing conflict over marine resources. Fin, humpback, minke, and sperm whales eat the same fish and squid that commercial fishing fleets are harvesting intensively in the North Atlantic Ocean—in some cases, such as with cod and haddock stocks, to the point of collapse. Increasingly powerful sonar devices being tested by the U.S. navy may be responsible for recent episodes of whale stranding on beaches. As harvesting of marine resources becomes ever more efficient and as marine habitats are impacted by human activities and destroyed, it will grow increasingly difficult to find effective conservation strategies to protect whales and other marine species and to sustain ocean ecosystems.

FIGURE 10.3
Seahorses are widely used as an ingredient in Chinese medicine, and they have been overharvested for this purpose.

Any number of other examples could be given to illustrate this scenario of overexploitation: fisherfolk in the Philippines who supply ornamental fish to international buyers and exploitation leading to the depletion of wild game at increasing distances around mining towns in Africa. A striking example is the enormous increase in demand for seahorses (*Hippocampus* spp.; Figure 10.3) in China. The Chinese use dried seahorses in their traditional medicine, because it resembles a dragon and is believed to have a variety of healing powers. Around 45 tons of seahorses are consumed in China per year—roughly 16 million animals. Seahorse populations throughout the world are being decimated to supply this ever-increasing demand, with the result that international trade in seahorses is now carefully monitored and regulated by international treaty (Foster and Vincent 2005). Another example is the worldwide trade in frog legs; each year Indonesia exports the legs of around 94 to 235 million frogs to western European countries for luxury meals. There is no information on how this intensive harvesting affects frog populations, forest ecology, and agriculture; and perhaps not surprisingly, the names of the frog species on the shipping labels are often wrong, which adds to the difficulty in quantifying the extent of the problem (Veith et al. 2000). The United States similarly exports and imports millions of amphibians and reptiles every year for food, pets, and clothing products, and many shipments do not even identify the species involved (Schlaepfer et al. 2005). Such intense exploitation leads to decline; however species can recover when exploitation ceases (Figure 10.4).

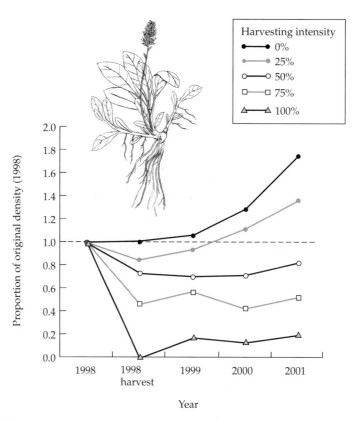

FIGURE 10.4 *Neopicrorhiza* is a Himalayan medicinal plant that is declining rapidly due to overharvesting. In experimental plots, the density was reduced in 1998 by various intensities of harvesting. Following no harvesting or light harvesting (25%), density increases over three subsequent years. Density remains low after intensive harvesting (75% and 100%) as virtually all plants have been removed, and other species grow in their place. (After Ghimire et al. 2005.)

Maximum Sustainable Yield

Governments and industries often claim that they can avoid the overharvesting of wild species by applying modern scientific management. As part of this approach, an extensive body of literature has developed in wildlife and fisheries management and in forestry to describe the **maximum sustainable yield**: the greatest amount of a resource, such as Atlantic bluefin tuna (*Thunnus thynnus*), that can be harvested each year and replaced through population growth without detriment to the population (Jennings et al. 2001). Calculations using the maximum population growth rate (r) and the carrying capacity (B; the largest population or biomass that a given area can support) are used to estimate the maximum sustainable yield (Y_{max}) (Essington 2001; Saltz 2001), which typically occurs when the population size is at around half the carrying capacity, or when the biomass is half of its maximum value. The maximum sustainable yield can be estimated as:

$$Y_{max} = rB/4$$

For a growing population with r having a value of 2 (meaning the population is capable of doubling each year until it reaches carrying capacity), half of the biomass could theoretically be harvested each year. In highly controlled situations where the resource can be quantified, such as with plantations of timber trees, it may be possible to approach maximum sustainable yield. However, in many real-world situations, harvesting a species at the theoretical maximum sustainable yield is not possible because of factors such as weather conditions, disease outbreaks, illegal harvesting, and damage to stock during harvesting (Ravenal et al. 2004). Attempts to harvest at high levels often lead to an abrupt species decline (Ghimire et al. 2006). Yield management of marine resources demonstrates some of the serious problems that can arise from unrealistic applications of maximum sustainable yield figures.

PROBLEMS WITH YIELD MANAGEMENT: THE FISHING INDUSTRY   Worldwide, one-third of the world's major fish stocks have been classified as overfished (Pauly and Maclean 2003; U.S. Commission of Ocean Policy 2004; Hilborn et al. 2006). As a consequence, consumption of fish, an important source of protein, has been declining in most developing countries. But fishing industry representatives use maximum sustainable yield calculations to support their position that harvesting levels of Atlantic bluefin tuna, for example, can be maintained at the present rate, even though the population of the species has declined by 97% in recent years (Safina 1993; www.bigmarinefish.com). In order to satisfy local business interests and protect jobs, governments often set harvesting levels too high, resulting in damage to the resource base. It is particularly difficult to coordinate international agreements and to monitor compliance with maximum sustainable yield limits when species migrate across national boundaries and through international waters. Illegal harvesting may result in additional resource removal not accounted for in official records (Berkes et al. 2006), as has been occurring in the whaling industry and in fishing operations in Antarctic waters.

Furthermore, a considerable proportion of the remaining juvenile stock may be damaged during harvesting operations. Another difficulty presents itself if harvest levels are kept fairly constant—often based on overly optimistic estimates of resource biomass—even though the resource base fluctuates; a normal harvest of a fish species during a year when fish stocks are low due to variable or poor weather conditions may severely reduce or destroy the species. In order to protect species from total destruction, governments are more frequently closing fishing grounds in the hopes that populations will recover (Safina 2001). For example, the Canadian fishing fleet continued to harvest large amounts of cod off Newfoundland during the 1980s, even as the population declined. As a result, cod stocks dropped to 1% of their original numbers, and the government was forced to close the fishery in 1992, eliminating 35,000 jobs (MEA 2005).

Many examples like these clearly demonstrate that management based on simplistic mathematical models of maximum sustainable yield are often inappropriate and invalid for the real world. Yield models should primarily be used to gain insight into fish stocks rather than to determine a single yield level that must be accepted. What *is* required is constant monitoring of stocks and the ability to adjust harvesting levels as appropriate. Once harvesting pressure is removed by government restrictions, fishing stocks may take years to recover, because fish density may be too low for successful reproduction, competing species may have established themselves, or most years may be unsuitable for reproduction. In some cases, fishing stocks have not recovered even many years after harvesting has been stopped completely.

For many marine species, direct exploitation is less important than the indirect effects of commercial fishing (Chuenpagdee et al. 2003; Kappel 2005; Read et al. 2006). Many marine vertebrates and invertebrates are caught incidentally as **by-catch** during fishing operations and are killed or injured in the process. Approximately 25% of the harvest in fishing operations is dumped back in the sea to die. The decline of skates, rays, and millions of seabirds have all been linked to their wholesale death as by-catch. The huge number of sea turtles and dolphins killed by commercial fishing boats as by-catch resulted in a massive public outcry and led to the development of improved nets to reduce these accidental catches. Even so, many marine animals die when they accidentally become entangled in discarded and lost fishing gear.

What Can Be Done To Stop Overexploitation?

Perhaps as many overexploited species become rare it will no longer be commercially viable to harvest them, and their numbers will have a chance to recover. Unfortunately, populations of many species, such as the rhinoceros and certain large wild cats, may already have been reduced so severely by the combination of hunting and habitat destruction that they will require vigilant conservation efforts to recover. In some cases, rarity even increases demand: As the rhinoceros becomes more rare, the price of its horn rises, making it an even more valuable commodity on the black market. In rural areas of the developing world, desperate people may search even more intensively for the last remaining marketable plants and animals to collect and sell in order to buy food for their families.

Finding the methods to protect and manage the remaining individuals in such situations is a priority for conservation biologists. As described in Chapter 20, conservation projects linking the conservation of biodiversity and local economic development represent one possible approach. In some cases, this linkage may be possible by acknowledging the sustainable harvesting of a natural resource with a special certification that allows producers to receive a higher price for their product. Certified timber products and coffee are already entering the market, but it remains to be seen if they will have a significant positive impact on biodiversity (Gulbrandsen 2005). National parks, nature reserves, marine sanctuaries, and other protected areas can also be established to conserve overharvested species. When harvesting can be reduced or stopped by the enforcement of international regulations, such as the CITES, and comparable national regulations, species may be able to recover. Sea otters, sea turtles, elephants, and certain whale species provide hopeful examples of species that have recovered once overexploitation was stopped.

Invasive Species

Human activities have distributed species throughout the world, obscuring past regional differences. This new, more homogeneous distribution of species is so significant that some scientists consider that we are entering a new era that could be called the "Homogeocene."

Exotic species are species that occur outside their natural ranges because of human activity. The great majority of exotics do not become established in the places in which they are introduced because the new environment is not suitable to their needs. However, a certain percentage of species do establish themselves in their new homes, and many of these can be considered **invasive species**—that is, they increase in abundance at the expense of native species (McNeely 2004; Knapp et al. 2005; Simberloff et al. 2005; Parker et al. 2006). These invasive species may displace native species through competition for limiting resources. Introduced animal species may prey upon native species to the point of extinction, or they may alter the habitat so that many natives are no longer able to persist. Invasive exotic species represent threats to 49% of the endangered species in the United States, with particularly severe impacts on bird and plant species (Wilcove et al. 1998). The thousands of non-native species in the United States are estimated to cause damages and losses amounting to $137 billion per year (Pimentel et al. 2000b). Many species introductions have occurred by the following means:

- Settlers arriving at new colonies released hundreds of different species of European birds and mammals into places like New Zealand, Australia, North America, and South Africa to make the countryside seem familiar and to provide game for hunting. Numerous species of fish (trout, bass, carp, etc.) have been widely released to provide food and recreation.

- Large numbers of plant species have been introduced and grown as ornamentals, as agricultural species, as pasture grasses, or as soil stabilizers. Many of these species have escaped from cultivation or their original habitat and have become established in local communities. As aquaculture develops there is a constant danger of more plant species escaping and becoming invasive in marine and freshwater environments (Chapman et al. 2003).

- Species are often transported unintentionally. For example, weed seeds are accidentally harvested with commercial seeds and sown in new localities; rats, snakes, and insects stow away aboard ships and airplanes; and disease, parasitic organisms, and insects travel along with their host species, particularly in the leaves and roots of plants and the soil of potted plants. Ships frequently carry exotic species in their water ballast, releasing vast numbers of bacteria, viruses, algae, invertebrates, and small fish into new locations. Large ships may hold up to 150,000 tons of ballast water (Ruiz et al. 2000). In one study, ballast water being released by ships into Coos Bay, Oregon, was found to contain 367 marine species originating in Japanese waters (Carlton and Geller 1993). Governments are now developing regulations to reduce the transport of species in ballast water, such as requiring ships to exchange their ballast water 320 km offshore in deep water before approaching a port.

- When an exotic species becomes invasive, a common solution is to release an animal species from its original range that will consume the pest and hopefully control its numbers. While biological control can be dramatically successful, there are many cases in which a biological control agent does not control its targeted pest, or the introduced species itself has become invasive, attacking native species along with, or instead of, its intended target species. For example, a parasitic fly species (*Compsilura cocinnata*) introduced into North America to control invasive gypsy moths has been found to parasitize more than 200 native moth species, in many cases dramatically reducing population numbers. In another example, an herbivorous

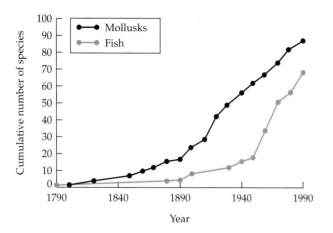
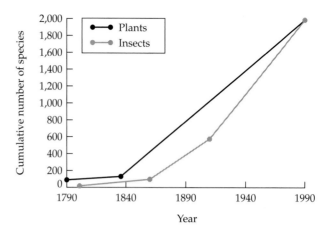

FIGURE 10.5 The number of exotic mollusk, fish, plant, and insect species in the United States has increased steadily over time. (After OTA 1993.)

weevil (*Rhinocyllus conicus*) introduced into North America to control invasive Eurasian thistles (*Carduus* spp.) has been found to attack native North American thistles (*Cirsium* spp.), and it is threatening populations of several uncommon and rare species (Louda et al. 2003). In order to minimize the chance of such effects, the species being considered as biological control agents are tested before release to determine if they will restrict their feeding to their intended target species. In most cases such tests have been successful in predicting at least the short-term direct effects of the biocontrol agent; however, this is not true in all cases, so further development of the protocols is being pursued. Furthermore, at present, no pre-release testing is done to evaluate potential community effects caused by the addition of a new species into the environment.

Many areas of the world are strongly affected by exotic species. The United States currently has more than 20 species of exotic mammals, 97 species of exotic birds, 70 species of exotic fish, 88 species of exotic mollusks, 2000 species of exotic plants, and 2000 species of exotic insects (Figure 10.5). Exotic perennial plants completely dominate many North American wetlands: purple loosestrife (*Lythrum salicaria*) from Europe dominates marshes in eastern North America, while Japanese honeysuckle (*Lonicera japonica*) forms dense tangles in bottomlands of the southeastern United States. In southern Florida, introduced melaleuca trees (*Melaleuca quinquenervia*) already cover vast areas and are increasing their coverage by 16 ha per day, while Brazilian pepper (*Shinus terebinthifolius*) occupies over 100,000 ha (Simberloff et al. 1997; Li and Norland 2001). Introduced annual grasses now cover extensive areas of western North America rangelands and increase the probability of ground fires in the summer. When invasive species dominate a community, the diversity of native plant species and the insects that feed on them shows a corresponding decline. Recent evidence also indicates that invasive plants can even reduce the diversity of soil microbe species (Callaway et al. 2004). Further, invasive species are many of the most serious agricultural weeds, costing farmers tens of billions of dollars a year in lost crop yield and extra weed control and herbicide expenses (Box 10.2).

Insects introduced deliberately, such as European honeybees (*Apis mellifera*) and the biocontrol weevil (*Rhinocyllus conicus*), and accidentally, such as fire ants (*Solenopsis invicta*) and gypsy moths (*Lymantria dispar*), can build up huge populations. The effects of such invasive insects on the native insect fauna can be devastating (Porter

BOX 10.2

GMOs and Conservation Biology

■ A special topic of concern for conservation biologists is the increasing use of genetically modified organisms (GMOs) in agriculture, forestry, aquaculture, and toxic waste cleanups (Snow et al. 2005). In such organisms, genes from a source species have been added into the GMO using the techniques of recombinant DNA technology. In some cases, the transfer even occurs across kingdoms, as when a bacterial gene toxic to insects is transferred into a crop, such as corn. Already, enormous areas—especially in the United States, Argentina, China, and Canada—have been planted with GMOs, the main crops being soybeans, corn (maize), cotton, and oilseed rape (canola). GMO animals are still under development, with salmon and pigs showing commercial potential. There is a concern among some people, espe-

Fear is that GM crops will harm birds, insects, soil organisms, other species, and even humans.

GMO crops have the potential to produce more abundant, cheaper food, while using less pesticides. However, there is a concern that these crops will hybridize with wild species to create new weeds and disease, that the crops will harm wild animals that eat them, and that eating food from GMO crops might harm people.

Hope is that GM crops will produce more food and use less pesticides, resulting in an improved water quality and healthier animals.

Runoff

River

cially in Europe, that GMOs will hybridize with related species, leading to new, aggressive weeds and virulent diseases. Also, the use of GMOs could potentially harm noncrop species, such as insects, birds, and soil organisms that live in or near agricultural fields. Further, some people want assurances that eating food from GMO crops will not harm their health, and especially not cause unusual allergic reactions. The fact that many species being investigated for genetic engineering, including viruses, bacteria, insects, fungi, and shellfish, have not previously been used in breeding programs has many people worried, and it has resulted in governments implementing special controls on this type of research and its commercial applications. It is also clear that GMO crop species have the potential to increase crop production, produce new and

cheaper medicines, and reduce the use of pesticides; such benefits are clearly potentially important in providing abundant food for the human population, increasing efficiency of drug production, and possibly reducing the use of chemicals on agricultural fields and the runoff associated with such use (but "Roundup Ready" herbicide-resistant GM soybeans are actually treated with more, rather than less, glyphosate herbicide, which is sold as the weed-killer "Roundup®") (www.sourcewatch.org). In sum, the actual benefits of GMOs need to be examined and weighed against the potential risks. The best approach involves proceeding cautiously, investigating GMOs thoroughly before commercial releases are authorized, and monitoring environmental and health impacts after release.

and Savignano 1990). At some localities in the southern United States, the diversity of insect species declined by 40% following the invasion of exotic fire ants, with a similarly large decline for native birds (Figure 10.6). Introduced European earthworm species are currently outcompeting native species in soil communities across North America, with potentially enormous consequences to the rich underground

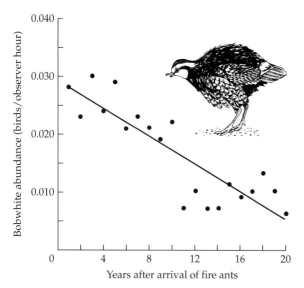

FIGURE 10.6 The abundance of northern bobwhites (*Colinas virginianus*) in Texas has been declining over a 20-year period following the arrival of the exotic red fire ant (*Solenopsis invicta*). The fire ants may directly attack and disturb bobwhites, particularly at the nestling stage, and may compete for food items, such as insects. (After Allen et al. 1995.)

biological communities and to the recycling of nutrients from the leaf litter to plants (Bohlen et al. 2004; Gundale et al. 2005). In areas of human settlement, domestic cats may be one of the most serious predators of birds and small mammals: A placid house cat may be a fearsome hunter when outdoors. Feral cats that must hunt for their own meals are especially damaging because of their ability to move far from human settlements.

Invasive Species on Islands

The isolation of island habitats encourages the development of a unique assemblage of endemic species (see Chapter 7), but it also leaves these species particularly vulnerable to depredations by invading species. Only a limited number of organisms are capable of crossing large expanses of water without human assistance. Thus, undisturbed island communities generally include few, if any, large mammalian grazers and predators, and organisms representing the highest trophic levels, such as mammalian carnivores, may be absent altogether. Because they evolved in the absence of selective pressures from mammalian grazers and predators, many endemic island plants and animals have evolutionarily lost or never developed defenses against these enemies and often lack a fear of them. Many island plants do not produce the bad-tasting, tough vegetative tissue that discourages herbivores, nor do they have the ability to resprout rapidly following damage. Some birds have lost the power of flight and build their nests on the ground.

Thriving endemic species on islands often succumb rapidly when the selective pressures that exotic invasive species represent are introduced. Animals introduced to islands have often efficiently preyed upon endemic animal species and have grazed some native plant species to extinction. Introduced plant species with tough, unpalatable foliage are better able to coexist with the introduced grazers than are the more palatable native plants, so the exotics often begin to dominate the landscape as the native vegetation dwindles. Moreover, island species often have no natural immunities to mainland diseases. When exotic species (e.g., chickens, domestic ducks, etc.) arrive, they frequently carry pathogens or parasites that, though relatively harmless to the carrier, devastate the native populations (e.g., wild birds).

The introduction of just one exotic species to an island may cause the local extinction of numerous native species. (Biogeographical models in which the arrival of one exotic species on an island results in the loss of one native species represent a great oversimplification.) Three examples illustrate the effects of introduced species on the biota of islands:

- *Plants of Santa Catalina Island.* Forty-eight native plant species have been eliminated from Santa Catalina Island off the coast of California, primarily due to grazing by introduced goats, pigs, and deer. One-third of the plant species currently found on the island are exotics. Almost complete removal of goats and pigs from part of the island has led to the reappearance of many rare wildflowers and the regrowth of woodlands.

- *Birds of the Pacific islands.* The brown tree snake (*Boiga irregularis*; Figure 10.7) has been introduced onto a number of Pacific islands where it is devastating endemic bird populations. The snake eats eggs, nestlings, and adult birds. On Guam alone, the brown tree snake has driven eight of eleven forest bird species extinct (Wiles et al. 2003). Visitors have remarked on the absence of birdsong: "between the silence and the cobwebs, the rain forests of Guam

FIGURE 10.7 The brown tree snake (*Boiga irregularis*) has been introduced onto many Pacific islands, where it devastates populations of endemic birds. This adult snake has just swallowed a bird. (Photograph by Julie Savidge.)

have taken on the aura of a tomb" (Jaffe 1994). Perhaps in an attempt to locate new prey, brown tree snakes have even attacked sleeping people. The government spends $4.6 million per year on attempts to control the brown tree snake population, so far without success.

- *Society Island snails.* The deliberate introduction of a predatory snail into the Society Islands as a biological control agent has resulted in the extinction of over 50 native snail species (www.zsl.org).

Invasive Species in Aquatic Habitats

Freshwater communities are somewhat similar to oceanic islands in that they are isolated habitats surrounded by vast stretches of inhospitable and uninhabitable terrain. Exotic species can have severe effects on vulnerable lake communities and isolated stream systems (Mills et al. 1994). There has been a long history of introducing exotic commercial and sport fish species into lakes, such as the introduction of the Nile Perch into Lake Victoria in East Africa, which was followed by the subsequent extinction of numerous endemic cichlid fish species. Although some of the introductions have been deliberate attempts to increase fisheries, most of the introductions were the unintentional result of canal building and the transport of ballast water in ships (MacIsaac et al. 2004). Often the introduced exotic fish are larger and more aggressive than the native fish fauna, and they may eventually drive the local fish to extinction (Maezono et al. 2005). The invasion of sea lampreys into the Great Lakes of North America severely damaged the commercial and sport fisheries, particularly lake trout; the United States and Canada spend $13 million each year to control the lampreys. In Madagascar, surveys of freshwater habitats were able to locate only 5 of the 28 known native freshwater fish of the island, with introduced fish dominating all of the freshwater habitats. But once these invasive species are removed from aquatic habitats, the native species are sometimes able to recover (Vredenburg 2004).

Large numbers of marine and estuarine fish species have been introduced throughout the world, both accidentally and deliberately, altering these ecosystems in the process. In the United States, every marine estuary that has been carefully surveyed has been found to contain between 70 and 235 exotic species; the actual numbers may be much higher because many of the species were probably not recognized as exotic or were absent from the specific locations surveyed (Carlton 2001).

One-third of the worst invasive species in aquatic environments are aquarium and ornamental species that are traded worldwide to the tune of $25 billion per year (Padilla and Williams 2004); the harmful impact of these species needs to be considered as part of the often-ignored cost of this trade. One such species is *Caulerpa taxifolia,* a highly invasive green algae used as a decorative plant in aquariums. This species is spreading in the northwestern Mediterranean, outcompeting native species of algae and reducing fish abundance. *Caulerpa* was discovered at many sites in California in 2000, and apparently, an aggressive eradication program involving the release of bleach has successfully eliminated this invader there. A ban on the most harmful aquarium species and the creation of a "white list" of noninvasive alternative species could reduce the harm done by invasive aquatic species.

Besides fish and plants, aggressive aquatic exotics can also include invertebrate animals. The deliberate introduction of the freshwater opossum shrimp into the Flathead catchment of Montana was supposed to provide food for salmon (Figure 10.8); instead, the shrimp directly competed with the fish for stocks of zooplankton and led

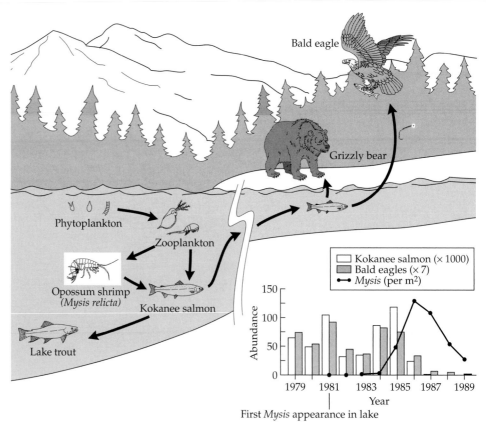

FIGURE 10.8 In Flathead Lake and its tributaries in Montana, the food web was disrupted by the deliberate introduction of opossum shrimp (*Mysis relicta*). The natural food chain consists of grizzly bears, bald eagles, and lake trout, which all eat kokanee salmon; kokanee eat zooplankton (cladocerans and copepods); and zooplankton eat phytoplankton (algae). Opossum shrimp, introduced as a food source for the kokanee salmon, ate so much zooplankton that there was far less food for the kokanee. Kokanee salmon numbers then declined radically, as did the eagle population that relied on the salmon. Eagle and salmon populations remain depressed as of 2005. (After Spencer et al. 1991 and Spencer, personal communication.)

FIGURE 10.9 (A) The zebra mussel (*Dreissena polymorpha*), a native of the Caspian Sea, was accidentally introduced into the Great Lakes and associated rivers in 1988. This shopping cart, which had been submerged in one of the Great Lakes, is thoroughly encrusted in zebra mussels. (B) The North American comb jelly (*Mnemiopsis leidyi*) may look delicate and beautiful, but it is an aggressive feeder on fish larvae in the Black Sea. (A, photograph courtesy of James F. Lubner, Ph.D., University of Wisconsin Sea Grant Institute; B, photograph © L. P. Madin.)

(A)

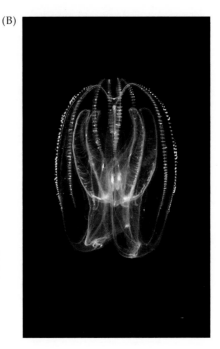

(B)

to a precipitous drop in salmon and bald eagle populations (Spencer et al. 1991). One of the most alarming recent invasions in North America was the arrival in 1988 of the zebra mussel (*Dreissena polymorpha*) in the Great Lakes (Drake and Bossenbroek 2004). This small, striped native of the Caspian Sea apparently was a stowaway in the ballast tanks of a European tanker. Within two years, zebra mussels had reached densities of 700,000 individuals per square meter in parts of Lake Erie, encrusting every hard surface and choking out native mussel species in the process (Figure 10.9A). This mussel has a prodigious capacity to reproduce: A single female can produce a million eggs per year, and the larval stage can disperse long distances in water currents. Zebra mussels are now spreading south throughout the entire Mississippi River drainage. As it spreads, this exotic species is causing enormous economic damage to fisheries, dams, power plants, water treatment facilities, and boats, as well as devastating the aquatic communities it encounters. Merely keeping water intake pipes clear of zebra mussels represents a huge new maintenance cost.

Whereas invasions in freshwater environments are often more readily noticed, invasions also can occur in marine ecosystems, as the case of the comb jelly (*Mnemiopsis leidyi*) demonstrates (Figure 10.9B). This species from North American coastal waters was first spotted in the Black Sea in Eastern Europe in 1982, where it had presumably been discharged in ship ballast water. The Black Sea has no predators or effective competitors of this fish-eating comb jelly. Only 7 years later, in 1989, this species constituted 95% of the biomass of the Black Sea. The voracious appetite of this jellyfish for fish larvae and for the zooplankton on which fish feed has led to the collapse of a $250 million fishing industry and disruption of the entire ecosystem. However, in 1997, a second exotic comb jellyfish appeared and began feeding on *Mnemiopsis* populations, leading to signs of recovery for the fish populations (Shiganova and Bulgakova 2000).

The Ability of Species to Become Invasive

The great majority of introduced species do not survive outside of their native range, and of those that do survive, only a small fraction (less than 1% of those arriving in new environments) are capable of increasing and spreading in their new location. Why are certain exotic species able to invade and dominate new habitats and displace native species so easily? One reason is the absence of their specialized natural predators and parasites in the new habitat to control their population growth (Torchin and Mitchell 2004). For example, in Australia, introduced rabbits spread uncontrollably, grazing native plants to the point of extinction, because there were no effective checks on their numbers. Australian control efforts have focused in part on introducing specific diseases that helped control rabbit populations elsewhere. In Hawaii, introduced Puerto Rican coqui frogs (*Eleutherdactylus coqui*) are reaching densities 100 times greater than in their native habitat, due in part to an absence of their predators, and in the process are decimating native insect populations and keeping people awake at night with their loud calls (Raloff 2005).

Exotic species also may be better suited to take advantage of disturbed conditions than native species (Facon et al. 2006). Human activity causes disturbances that may create unusual environmental conditions, such as higher mineral nutrient levels, increased incidence of fire, or enhanced light availability, to which exotic species sometimes are better adapted than are native species. In fact, the highest concentrations of invasive species are often found in the habitats that have been most altered by human activity. For example, in western North America, increased grazing (by cattle) and increased frequency of fire associated with humans, provided the opportunity for the establishment of exotic annual grasses in areas formerly dominated by native perennial grasses. In Southeast Asia, progressive degradation of forests results in a progressively smaller proportion of native species living in the habitat (Figure 10.10). When habitats are further altered by global climate change, they will become even more vulnerable to invasion. In one of the key generalizations of this field, we can say that of the enormous number of introduced species, the species most likely to become invasive in a new location are those species that have already been shown to be invasive someplace else.

"Invasive species" are generally defined as species that have proliferated outside their native range, but some native species dramatically flourish within their home ranges because they are suited to the ways in which humans have altered the environment and are therefore almost as much a source of concern as exotic invasive species (Soulé 1990). Within North America, fragmentation of forests, suburban development, and easy access to garbage have allowed the numbers of coyotes, red foxes, and certain seagull species to increase. Native jellyfish have become far more abundant in the Gulf of Mexico because they use oil rigs and artificial reefs

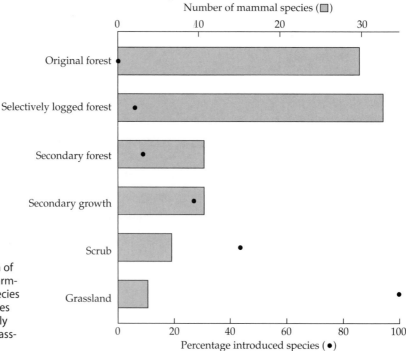

FIGURE 10.10 Progressive degradation of Southeast Asian forests by logging and farming not only decreases the number of species of nonflying native mammals, but increases the percentage of introduced species. Only introduced rats are present in the final grassland stage. (From Harrison 1968.)

for spawning and feed on plankton blooms stimulated by nitrogen pollution. As these aggressive species increase, they do so at the expense of other local native species, such as the juvenile stages of commercially harvested fish. These unnaturally abundant native species represent a further challenge to the management of vulnerable native species and protected areas.

A special class of invasive species is made up of those introduced exotic species that have close relatives in the native biota. When invasive species hybridize with the native species and varieties, unique genotypes may be eliminated from local populations and taxonomic boundaries become obscured (Campton and Kaeding 2005). This appears to be the fate of native trout species when confronted by commercial species. In the American Southwest, the Apache trout (*Oncorhynchus apache*) has had its range reduced by habitat destruction and competition with introduced species. The species has also hybridized extensively with rainbow trout (*O. mykiss*), an introduced sport fish. Studies of the Pecos pupfish (*Cyprinodon pecosensis*), a rare endemic species of western Texas and New Mexico, shows evidence of extensive hybridization with the introduced sheepshead minnow (*C. variegatus*), with hybrid individuals being more vigorous than genetically pure Pecos pupfish (Rosenfield et al. 2004).

Invasive species are considered to be the most serious threat facing the biota of the U.S. national park system. While the effects of habitat degradation, fragmentation, and pollution potentially can be corrected and reversed in a matter of years or decades as long as the original species are present, well-established exotic species may be impossible to remove from communities. They may have built up such large numbers and become so widely dispersed and so thoroughly integrated into the community that eliminating them may be extraordinarily difficult and expensive. Also, the general public may resist efforts to control the numbers of introduced mammals that overgraze native plant communities. Animal rights groups, in particular, have objected to attempts to reduce large populations of deer, wild horses, mountain sheep, and wild boar. Yet sometimes these populations must be reduced if rare native species are to be saved from extinction. When invasive plant species and non-native grazers are removed as part of a management plant, the native species may recover on their own. Recovery sometimes requires a comprehensive restoration program (see Chapters 13 and 19) (Samways et al. 2005; Campbell and Donlan 2005). As one example, native dune species were able to recover following the removal of an exotic grass species (Figure 10.11).

The threats posed by invasive species are so severe that reducing the rate of their introduction needs to become a greater priority for conservation efforts (Bax et al. 2001; McNeely et al. 2003; Simberloff 2003; Chornesky et al. 2005) (Figure 10.12). Governments must pass and enforce laws

FIGURE 10.11 Removal of exotic species can lead to the recovery of native species: in this case, dune vegetation at Lanphere Dunes Unit of the Humboldt Bay National Wildlife Refuge, California had become dominated by the exotic European beachgrass (*Ammophila arenarie*) (top photo). Following the removal of the beachgrass, native species recovered (bottom photo). (Photographs courtesy of Andrea Pickart.)

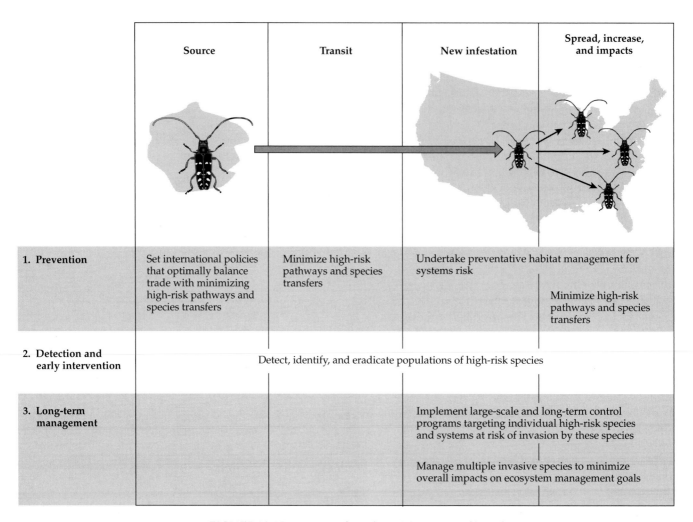

	Source	Transit	New infestation	Spread, increase, and impacts
1. Prevention	Set international policies that optimally balance trade with minimizing high-risk pathways and species transfers	Minimize high-risk pathways and species transfers	Undertake preventative habitat management for systems risk	Minimize high-risk pathways and species transfers
2. Detection and early intervention	Detect, identify, and eradicate populations of high-risk species			
3. Long-term management			Implement large-scale and long-term control programs targeting individual high-risk species and systems at risk of invasion by these species Manage multiple invasive species to minimize overall impacts on ecosystem management goals	

FIGURE 10.12 A strategy for reducing the impact of harmful invasive species involves a combination of prevention, detection and early intervention, and long-term management. This strategy is illustrated by the example of the Asian long-horned beetle (*Anoplophora glabripennis*). This species arrived in North America in wooden crates and other packing material from its native Asia. The beetle infects and kills a wide range of trees, especially maples. The only effective treatment is to cut down infected trees and destroy the wood. (After Chornesky et al. 2005.)

and customs restrictions prohibiting the transport and introduction of exotic species. In some cases this may require restrictions and inspections related to the movement of soil, wood, plants, animals, and other items across international borders and even checkpoints within countries. Better ecological information is required prior to deliberate introductions of species thought to be beneficial or potentially desirable. Currently, vast sums are spent controlling widespread outbreaks of exotics, but inexpensive, prompt control and eradication efforts at the time of first sighting can stop a species from getting established in the first place. Training citizens and protected-areas staff to monitor vulnerable habitats for the appearance of known invasive species and promptly implementing intensive control efforts can be an effective way to stop the establishment and early spread of a new exotic species. This may require a cooperative effort on the part of multiple levels of government and private land owners. A thoroughly researched, ecologically grounded program of biological control, using species from the exotic's original range, may be necessary in the overall strategy in severe cases (Hajek 2004; Louda et al. 2005). Such programs require careful testing to determine the host specificity and likely ecological interactions of the biological control species; they also require careful monitoring afterward to determine the effectiveness of the new species in controlling the invasive species as well as any nontarget effects on native species and communities. In some cases, land-use practices will need to be changed in ways that favor the restoration of native species.

Even though the impacts of invasive species are generally considered negative, they may provide some benefits as well. Invasive species can sometimes stabilize eroding lands, provide food for native insects such as bees, and supply nesting sites for birds and mammals (Schmidt et al. 2005). The trade-offs in such situations need to be evaluated to determine if the potential benefits will outweigh the overall costs.

Disease

Another major threat to species and biological communities is the increased transmission of disease resulting from human activities (such as habitat destruction, which may increase disease-carrying vectors) and interaction with humans (such as populations of wild animals that acquire diseases from nearby populations of domestic animals and people) (Haydon et al. 2002). Infections by disease organisms are common in both wild and captive populations and can reduce the size and density of vulnerable populations. Disease organisms can also have a major impact on the structure of an entire biological community. Infections may come from tiny microparasites, such as viruses, bacteria, fungi, and protozoa; or larger macroparasites, such as helminth worms and parasitic arthropods. While living inside or on the host, these parasites absorb nutrients and damage host tissue, weakening the host and lowering its chances of surviving and reproducing.

In some instances, human modifications to the environment have inadvertently increased the densities of disease-causing organisms (Cohn 1991; MacKenzie 2000). For example, biologists in Texas were puzzled by the increased winter deaths of sandhill cranes—the loss of 5000 birds over the winter of 1984 to 1985. Investigations revealed that the birds were eating unharvested, rotting peanuts on which a toxic fungus was growing. Thus, the increased cultivation of peanuts could be directly linked to increased crane mortality. To halt the spread of the fungus and save the cranes, farmers now plow under the unharvested peanuts left in their fields before the winter.

Within populations, individuals vary in their susceptibility to particular diseases. Conservation biologists may face this dilemma in practice: Either protect all individuals of a rare species from a potential disease in order to maintain population numbers and genetic variation or let natural selection take its course and allow the individuals that are genetically most susceptible to the disease die off. If the disease only kills a few individuals and the population is still large, the population may be more fit in the long term for having weathered the disease. However, if the disease kills large numbers of individuals and the population shrinks, then many potentially valuable alleles will be lost from the population and inbreeding depression may occur (see Chapter 11). It is often difficult to predict how virulent a disease will be in an isolated population of a rare species, especially if the environmental conditions and population have been altered by human activity.

The basic principles of epidemiology have three obvious practical implications for limiting disease in captive breeding and management of rare species (Scott 1988):

1. A high rate of contact between host and parasite encourages the spread of disease.

2. Indirect effects of habitat destruction increase susceptibility to disease.

3. Species in conservation programs may contract diseases from related species, and even from humans.

We'll examine each of these implications in turn, recognizing that increased levels of disease can be caused by the interactions of multiple factors. First, a high rate of contact between the host (such as a mountain sheep) and the parasite (such as an intestinal worm) is one factor that encourages the spread of disease. In general, as host population density increases, the parasite load also increases, as expressed by the percentage of hosts infected and the number of parasites per host. In addition, a high density of the infective stages of a parasite in the environment of the host population can lead to increased incidence of disease. In natural situations, the level of infection is typically reduced when animals migrate away from their droppings, saliva, old skin, dead animals, and other infection sources. However, in unnaturally confined situations, such as habitat fragments, zoos, or even parks, the animals remain in contact with the potential sources of infection, and disease transmission increases. At higher densities, animals have abnormally frequent contact, and, once one animal becomes infected, the parasite can rapidly spread throughout the entire population.

Second, indirect effects of habitat destruction can increase an organism's susceptibility to disease. When a host population is crowded into a smaller area because of habitat destruction, there will often be a deterioration in habitat quality and food availability, leading to high contact rates, lowered nutritional status, weaker animals, and less resistance to infection. Young, very old, and pregnant individuals may be particularly susceptible to disease in such a situation. Plant populations can be similarly affected by fragmentation and degradation. Changes in plant microenvironments caused by habitat destruction, fragmentation, stress caused by air pollution, and direct injury occurring during logging or other human activities directly lead to increased levels of disease in plant populations. Aquatic species, including marine mammals, sea turtles, fish, coral animals, shellfish, and sea grasses, also have exhibited increased levels of disease due to water pollution, injury, and unusual environmental perturbations (Epstein 1998; Aguirre et al. 2002; Harvell et al. 2004).

Third, in many conservation areas and zoos, species may come into contact with other species that they would rarely or never encounter in the wild, including humans, so that infections spread from one species to another (Figure 10.13). A species that is common and fairly resistant to a parasite can act as a reservoir for the disease, which can then infect a population of a highly susceptible species on contact. For example, apparently healthy African elephants can transmit a fatal herpes virus to related Asian elephants when kept together in zoos (Richman et al. 1999). Diseases can spread very rapidly between captive species kept in crowded conditions. An outbreak of herpes virus spread across the captive colony at the International Crane Federation, killing cranes belonging to several rare species. The outbreak was apparently related to a high density of birds in the colony (Docherty and Romaine 1983).

Infected humans have been responsible for directly transmitting tuberculosis, measles, and influenza to captive orangutans, chimpanzees, colobus monkeys, ferrets, and other animals (Thorne and Williams 1988). Certain emerging infectious disease vectors, such as human immunodeficiency virus (HIV) and Ebola virus, even appear to have spread from wildlife populations to both humans and domestic animals. Once infected with exotic diseases acquired from people or other species, such captive animals cannot be returned to the wild without threatening the entire wild population. Captive Arabian oryx infected with the bluetongue virus of domestic livestock and orangutans with human tuberculosis could not be reintroduced into the wild as planned for fear of infecting free-ranging animals.

Infectious disease also can spread from domestic animals into wild populations. A classic example from the late nineteenth century is that of rinderpest virus, which spread from domestic cattle to wild antelope, wildebeest, and other ungulates in eastern and southern Africa, killing off 75% of the animals. At Tanzania's Serengeti

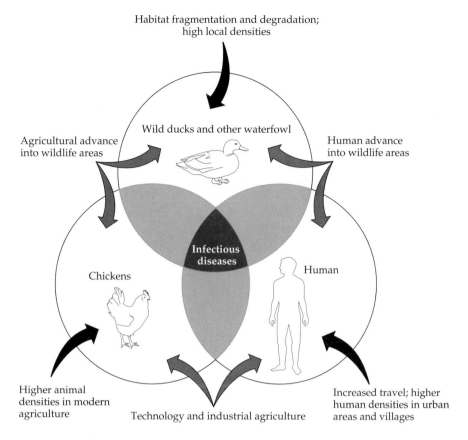

Habitat fragmentation and degradation;
high local densities

Agricultural advance
into wildlife areas

Wild ducks and other waterfowl

Human advance
into wildlife areas

Infectious
diseases

Chickens

Human

Higher animal
densities in modern
agriculture

Technology and industrial agriculture

Increased travel; higher
human densities in urban
areas and villages

FIGURE 10.13 Infectious diseases—such as rabies, lyme disease, influenza, bird flu, hantavirus, and canine distemper—spread among wildlife populations, domestic animals, and humans as a result of increasing population densities and the advance of agriculture and human settlements into wildlife areas. The figure illustrates the infection and transmission routes of the bird flu—wild waterfowl, chickens, and humans are all susceptible to the virus. The shaded areas of overlap indicate that diseases can be shared between the three groups. Black arrows indicate factors contributing to higher rates of infection; shaded arrows indicate factors contributing to the spread of disease among the three groups. (After Daszak et al. 2000.)

National Park, at least 25% of the lions were killed by canine distemper, a viral disease apparently contracted from one or more of the 30,000 domestic dogs living near the park (Packer 1997; Kissui and Packer 2004). For endangered species, such outbreaks can be the final blow: The last population of black-footed ferrets known to occur in the wild was destroyed by the canine distemper virus.

Diseases that spread to new regions of the world can decimate common species; the North American chestnut tree (*Castanea dentata*), once a prominent component of the hardwood forests throughout the eastern United States, has been virtually obliterated by an ascomycete fungus carried by Chinese chestnut trees imported to New York City. Fungal diseases are also eliminating elm trees (*Ulmus americana*) and flowering dogwoods (*Cornus florida*) from these forests (Figure 10.14). Reports of widespread oak tree deaths from fungal disease in the western United States are cause for serious concern due to their dominant role in many ecosystems (Rizzo et al. 2002). Introduced diseases have particularly powerful adverse effects on endemic island species (see Box 7.1) and frog species (see Box 8.1). An important factor in the decline and extinction of many endemic Hawaiian birds is the introduction of the mosquito *Culex quinquefasciatus* and the malaria protozoan *Plasmodium relictum capistranode*.

FIGURE 10.14 Populations of flowering dogwood (*Cornus florida*) are declining in eastern North American forests because of anthracnose disease, which is caused by the introduced fungus *Discula destructiva*. (Photograph by Jonathan P. Evans.)

A number of actions can be taken to reduce the spread of disease:

1. Plants, animals, soils, and other biological materials need to be inspected, tested, and, if needed, quarantined and appropriately treated before crossing borders. These procedures should include domestic and wild species.

2. Care must be taken to reduce the interaction of endangered species with humans, domesticated species, and closely related species. Such interactions can occur frequently in zoos, aquariums, and botanical gardens, or in small protected areas. For example, people working with endangered mammals may need to wear face masks and sterile clothing (see Figure 13.1).

3. Endangered species need to be monitored to detect outbreaks of disease. If necessary, diseased individuals may have to be treated or removed from the population.

4. Appropriate living conditions and population densities in both wild and captive situations will lower the susceptibility to disease vectors and reduce the rate of transmission.

Implications of Invasive Species and Diseases for Human Health

The presence of invasive species and disease-causing organisms also has serious, direct implications for humans. Invading killer bees (*Apis mellifera scutellata*) and fire ants (*Solenopis invicta*) that are spreading in the New World not only displace native insect species from their ecological niches, but they also can cause serious injuries to humans. Also, as people move into wild areas through suburban and exurban development and associated habitat fragmentation, there is greater potential for disease movement among people, domestic animals, and wild species (Daszak et al. 2000; Walters 2004). The potential for the spread of serious pests and disease-causing organisms also increases dramatically with the increasing movement of people, pets, wildlife, and materials from one part of the world to another. The dramatic upsurge in Lyme disease and Rocky Mountain spotted fever, spread by infected ticks, and West Nile virus, spread by mosquitoes, has caused near-panic in some regions of the United States. Hanta virus, HIV/AIDS, bubonic plague, mad cow disease, and bird flu are additional diseases that can move between wild species and people. Bird flu, for example, moves from wild birds to domestic birds such as chickens, with the potential to spread to people on a large scale. Bird flu might also eliminate the remaining populations of susceptible endangered animals.

Such examples are likely to become more common as a result of human-induced changes to the environment. Recent warm years linked to global climate change have allowed many disease-carrying insects and associated diseases, such as malaria and dengue fever, to expand their ranges to higher elevations in tropical countries and farther from the equator. If world temperatures increase as predicted by global climate change models (see Chapter 9), the stage will be set for major range expansions of diseases now confined primarily to tropical climates (Epstein 1998). Warmer and more polluted aquatic environments and unusually heavy rains are already allowing waterborne diseases, such as cholera, to ravage previously unaffected human and animal populations, and this range expansion will probably continue (Epstein 1999).

There is a serious potential for the environment of the developed world to become a more dangerous place as exotic stinging and disease-causing species arrive and thrive. In addition, if birdwatchers, hunters, swimmers, and hikers become frightened by and disenchanted with the outdoor experience, strong support for conservation efforts may be lost. Conservation biologists have an obligation to help prevent the spread of potentially invasive and dangerous species that threaten both people and biological diversity. Conservation biologists also need to keep the public engaged in conservation-related activities, in part to counter media reports that exaggerate the dangers of the outdoors.

Conclusion

As we've seen in Chapters 7–10, a combination of factors acting simultaneously or sequentially can overwhelm a species. Consider, for example, the large freshwater mussel *Margaritifera auricularia*. This species was formerly known from Western Europe to Morocco, but now it only occurs in one population of 2000 individuals in an old canal of the Ebro River basin of northern Spain (Araujo and Ramos 2000). Its attractive shell and pearls have been used as ornaments by humans as far back as the Neolithic Age. Overcollecting, the main reason for the decline of the mussel, led to its disappearance from rivers in Central Europe in the fifteenth and sixteenth centuries; pollution, destruction of freshwater habitats, and overcollecting continue to reduce its range and numbers in recent times. The mussel is also affected by the loss of other species, since its larval stage needs to attach to the gill filaments of salmonid fish to complete its life cycle. The lack of small individuals in the Spanish population indicates that the species is now unable to reproduce under present conditions. To save this species, a comprehensive conservation plan must be implemented, including preventing overcollecting, controlling water quality, maintaining fish stocks, and protecting the habitat.

Threats to biological diversity come from a number of different sources, but their underlying cause is the same: the magnitude of destructive human activity. It is often easy to blame a group of poor, rural people or a certain industry for the destruction of biological diversity, but the real challenge is to demonstrate that it is in people's best interest to establish and manage protected areas and to value biodiversity where ever it is found. In addition, we need to understand the economic conditions and national and international linkages that promote such destruction and to find viable alternatives. These alternatives must include stabilizing the size of the human population, finding a livelihood for rural people in developing countries that does not damage the environment, providing incentives and penalties that will convince people and industries to value and maintain the environment, restricting international trade in products that are obtained by damaging the environment, and persuading people in developed countries to reduce their consumption of the world's resources and to pay fair prices for products that are produced in a sustainable, nondestructive manner.

Summary

1. Overexploitation threatens about one-third of the endangered vertebrates in the world, as well as other groups of species. Poverty, more efficient methods of harvesting, and the globalization of the economy combine to encourage exploitation of species to the point of extinction; overharvesting of birds, mammals, and fish for food are of particular concern. Many traditional societies have customs to prevent overharvesting of resources, but these customs are breaking down.

2. Humans have deliberately and accidentally moved thousands of plant and animal species to new regions of the world. Some of these species have become invasive, increasing at the expense of native species. Island species are particularly vulnerable to invasive, exotic species. Aquatic communities throughout the world, as well as terrestrial ones, are often dramatically altered by the introduction of exotic species, such as sport and commercial fishes.

3. Human activities may increase the incidence of disease in wild species. The levels of disease and parasites often increase when animals are crowded together and under stress in a nature reserve or a habitat fragment rather than being able to disperse over a wide area. Animals held in captivity in zoos are prone to higher levels of disease, which sometimes spreads between related species of animals. Diseased captive animals cannot be returned to the wild, to prevent the spread of disease to the wild population.

4. Species may be threatened by a combination of factors, all of which must be addressed in a comprehensive conservation plan.

For Discussion

1. Learn about one endangered species in detail. What is the full range of immediate threats to this species? How do these immediate threats connect to larger social, economic, political, and legal issues?

2. Control of invasive species may involve searching for specialized natural enemies, parasites, or predators of that species within its original range and releasing such organisms in an attempt to control the invasive species at the new location. For example, an attempt is currently underway to control exotic purple loosestrife in North America by releasing several European beetle species that eat the plant in its home area. As another example, biologists are talking about introducing an exotic fungus into Hawaii to eliminate the invasive Puerto Rican coqui frog. What if these biological control agents begin to attack native species rather than their intended host? How might such a consequence be predicted and avoided? Consider the biological, economic, and ethical issues involved in a decision to institute a biological control program.

3. Why is it so difficult to regulate the fishing industry in many places and maintain a sustainable level of harvesting? Consider fishing, hunting, logging, and other harvesting activities in your region. Are these well managed? Try to calculate what the sustainable harvest levels of these resources would be and how such harvesting levels could best be monitored and enforced.

4. Develop a verbal or computer model of how disease spreads in a population. The rate of spread could be determined by the density of the host, the percentage of host individuals infected, the rate of transmission of the disease, and the effects of the disease on the host's survival and rate of reproduction. How will an increase in the density of the host—caused by crowding in zoos or nature reserves, or an inability to migrate due to habitat fragmentation—affect the percentage of individuals that are infected and the overall population size?

Suggested Readings

Bax, N., J. T. Carlton, A. Mathews-Amos, R. L. Haedrich, et al. 2001. The control of biological invasions in the world's oceans. *Conservation Biology* 15: 1234–1246. The problem of marine invasive species may be enormous, and scientists are now deciding how to deal with it.

Berkes, F., T. P. Hughes, R. S. Steneck, J. A. Wilson, D. R. Bellwood, B. Crona, et al. 2006. Globalization, roving bandits, and marine resources. *Science* 311: 1557–1558. Regulation of marine resources is not yet effective in keeping up with the rapid exploitation that is occurring.

Brashares, J. S., P. Arcese, M. K. Sam, P. B. Coppolillo, A. R. E. Sinclair, and A. Balmford. 2004. Bushmeat hunting, wildlife declines, and fish supply in West Africa. *Science* 306: 1180–1183. You will be surprised to learn about the linkages between bushmeat hunting in Africa and demand for fresh fish in developed countries.

Bushmeat Crisis Task Force 2004. *BCTF Phase I Report*. Washington D.C.: Bushmeat Crisis Task Force. Accessed 15 April 2005: www.bushmeat.org/cd. Extent of the crisis, recommendation for reducing hunting pressure, and new projects.

Daszak, P., A. A. Cunningham, and A. D. Hyatt. 2000. Emerging infectious diseases of wildlife—threats to biodiversity and human health. *Science* 287: 443–449. Review of new diseases that spread among wildlife, humans, and domestic animals.

Drake, J. M. and J. M. Brossenbroek. 2004. The potential distribution of zebra mussels in the United States. *Bioscience* 54: 931–940. Zebra mussels are a well-studied aquatic example of a devastating invasive species.

Facon, B., B. J. Genton, J. Shykoff, P. Jarne, A. Estoup, and P. David. 2006. A general eco-evolutionary framework for understanding bioinvasions. *Trends in Ecology and Evolution* 21: 130–135. Ecological factors can affect how susceptible a community is to invasion.

Gulbrandsen, L. H. 2005. Mark of stustainability? Challenges for fishery and forestry ecolabeling. *Environment* 47: 8–23. Ecolabeling has the potential to improve harvesting practices.

Hart, J. and T. Hart. 2003. Rules of engagement for conservation. *Conservation In Practice* 4: 14–22. First-person account of carrying out conservation programs in the midst of war.

Harvell, D., R. Aronson, N. Baron, J. Connell, A. Dobson, S. Ellner, et al. 2004. The rising tide of ocean diseases: unsolved problems and research priorities. *Frontiers in Ecology and the Environment* 2: 375–382. Diseases are a serious problem for marine species and appear to be increasing.

Li, Y. and D. S. Wilcove. 2005. Threats to vertebrate species in China and the United States. *BioScience* 55: 147–153. The dense, poor rural population of China poses different threats to wildlife than the more urbanized and affluent United States population.

Louda, S. M., A. E. Arnett, T. A. Rand, and F. L. Russell. 2003. Invasiveness of some biological control insects and adequacy of their ecological risk assessment and regulation. *Conservation Biology* 17: 73–82. Many biological control agents have hit the wrong target.

Mathiessen, P. 2000. *Tigers in the Snow*. North Point Press, New York. Account of heroic struggle to protect tigers from multiple threats, primarily in the Russian Far East.

Padilla, D. K. and S. L. Williams. 2004. Beyond ballast water: aquarium and ornamental trades as sources of invasive species in aquatic ecosystems. *Frontiers in Ecology and the Environment* 2: 131–138. Aquarium species are a major source of invasive species, and need to be more carefully regulated.

Parker, J. D., D. E. Burkepile, and M. E. Hay. 2006. Opposing effects of native and exotic herbivores on plant invasions. *Science* 311: 1459–1461. The introduction of exotic herbivores is a key factor in facilitating invasive plant species.

Pimental, D., L. Lach, R. Zuniga, and D. Morrison. 2000. Environmental and economic costs of nonindigenous species in the United States. *BioScience* 50: 53–65. Invasive species may cost the U.S. economy $137 billion per year.

Read, A. J., P. Drinker, and S. Northridge. 2006. Bycatch of marine mammals in U.S. and global fisheries. *Conservation Biology* 20: 163–169. Enormous numbers of marine mammals die accidentally during commercial fishing operations.

Simberloff, D. S., I. M. Parker, and P. N Windle. 2005. Introduced species policy, management, and future research needs. *Frontiers in Ecology and the Environment* 3: 12–20. Management and research can help deal with invasive species.

Simpson, S. 2001. Fishy business. *Scientific American* 285: 82–89. Cyanide and other poisons are used in the Philippines and Indonesia to capture live fish for the aquarium trade, damaging reefs in the process; a new program is teaching less destructive methods.

Snow, A. A., D. A. Andow, P. Gepts, E. M. Hallerman, A. Power, J. M. Tiedje, et al. 2005. Genetically engineered organisms and the environment: Current status and recommendations. *Ecological Applications* 15: 377–404. Balanced and authoritative treatment of the controversy regarding genetically modified organisms.

Vredenburg, V. T. 2004. Reversing introduced species effects: Experimental removal of introduced fish leads to rapid recovery of a declining frog. *Proceedings of the National Academy of Sciences* 101: 7646–7650. Case study showing that recovery is possible.

PART

IV

Conservation at the Population and Species Levels

Problems of Small Populations

No population lasts forever. Changing climate, succession, disease, and a range of rare events ultimately lead every population to the same fate: extinction. The real questions to consider are whether a population goes extinct sooner rather than later, what factors cause the extinction, and whether other populations of the same species will continue elsewhere. Will a population of African lions last for more than 1000 years and go extinct only after a change in climate, or will the population go extinct after 10 years because of hunting by humans and introduced disease? Will individual lions from the original population start new populations in currently unoccupied habitat, or has all potential lion habitat disappeared because of new human settlements?

As we discussed in Chapter 7, the extinction of species as a result of human activities is now occurring more than 100 times faster than the natural rate of extinction—far more rapidly than new species can evolve. Because an endangered species may consist of just a few populations, or even a single population, *protecting populations is the key to preserving species*; it is often the few remaining populations of a rare species that are targeted for conservation efforts. In order to successfully maintain species under the restricted conditions imposed by human activities, conservation biologists must determine the stability of populations under different circumstances. Will a population of an endangered species persist or even increase in a nature reserve? Is the species in rapid decline, and does it require special attention to prevent it from going extinct?

Many national parks and wildlife sanctuaries have been created to protect "charismatic" megafauna such as lions, tigers, rhinos, bison, and bears, which are important national symbols and attractions for the tourist industry. However, designating the habitats in which these species live as protected areas may not be enough to stop their decline and extinction, even when they are legally protected. Sanctuaries generally are created after most populations of the threatened species have been severely reduced by habitat loss, degradation, and fragmentation, or by overharvesting. Under such circumstances, a species tends to dwindle rapidly toward extinction (Young and Clarke 2001). Also, individuals outside park boundaries remain unprotected and at risk. What, then, is the best strategy for protecting the few remaining populations of an endangered species? Are there special concerns for protecting small populations?

Essential Concepts for Small Populations

An ideal conservation plan for an endangered species would protect as many individuals as possible within the greatest possible area of high-quality, protected habitat. In practical terms, the planners, land managers, politicians, and wildlife biologists often must attempt to achieve realistic goals, guided by general principles. For example, they need to know how much long-leaf pine habitat a red-cockaded woodpecker population requires to persist. Is it necessary to protect habitat containing 50, 500, 5000, 50,000, or more individuals to ensure the survival of the species? Furthermore, planners must reconcile conflicting demands on finite resources—somehow a compromise must be found that allows the economic development required by society while at the same time providing reasonable protection for biological diversity. This problem is vividly demonstrated by the current debate in the United States over the need to protect caribou and other wildlife in the vast Arctic National Wildlife Refuge and the equally compelling need to utilize the considerable oil resources of the area.

Minimum Viable Population (MVP)

In a groundbreaking paper, Shaffer (1981) defined the number of individuals necessary to ensure the long-term survival of a species as the **minimum viable population**, or **MVP**: "A minimum viable population for any given species in any given habitat is the smallest isolated population having a 99% chance of remaining extant for 1000 years despite the foreseeable effects of demographic, environmental, and genetic stochasticity, and natural catastrophes." In other words, MVP is the smallest population size that can be predicted to have a very high chance of persisting for the foreseeable future. Shaffer emphasized the tentative nature of this definition, saying that the survival probabilities could be set at 95%, 99%, or any other percentage, and that the time frame might similarly be adjusted, for example, to 100 or 500 years. The key point is that the MVP size allows a quantitative estimate to be made of how large a population must be to assure long-term survival.

Shaffer (1981) compares MVP protection efforts to flood control. It is not sufficient to use average annual rainfall as a guideline when planning flood control systems and developing regulations for building on wetlands; instead, we must plan for extreme situations of high rainfall and severe flooding, which may occur only once every 50 years. In protecting natural systems, we understand that certain catastrophic events, such as hurricanes, earthquakes, forest fires, volcanic eruptions, epidemics, and die-offs of food items, may occur at even greater intervals. To plan for the long-term protection of endangered species, we must provide for their survival not only in average years, but also in exceptionally harsh years. An accurate estimate of the MVP size for a particular species often requires a detailed demographic study of the

FIGURE 11.1 The relationship between initial population size (*N*) of bighorn sheep and the percentage of populations that persist over time. Almost all populations with more than 100 sheep persisted beyond 50 years, while populations with fewer than 50 individuals died out within 50 years. Not included are small populations that were actively managed and augmented by the release of additional animals. (After Berger 1990; photograph by Mark Primack.)

population and an analysis of its environment. This can be expensive and require months, or even years, of research. In a study of 102 vertebrate species for which adequate data were available, populations with around 7000 individuals were estimated to have a 99% chance of persistence for 40 generations (Reed et al. 2003). Another analysis of 11 perennial plant species indicates an MVP of 2000 individuals (Reed 2005). For species with extremely variable population sizes, such as certain invertebrates and annual plants, protecting a population of about 10,000 individuals might be an effective strategy.

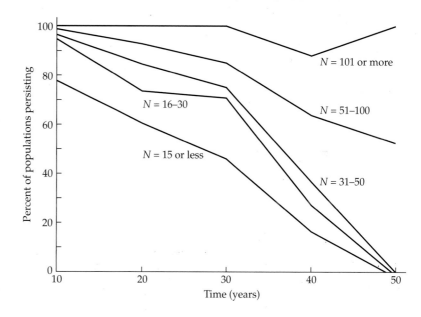

Unfortunately, many species, particularly endangered species, have population sizes smaller than these recommended minimums. For instance, a survey was done of two rare burrowing frog species in the genus *Geocrina*, which occur in swamps in southwestern Australia (Driscoll 1999). In one species, 4 of its 6 populations had fewer than 250 individuals, and in the other species, 48 of 51 populations had fewer than 50 individuals. For Carter's mustard (*Warea carteri*), a rare annual plant of south-central Florida, 9 of 13 populations had a population size of less than 20 individuals (Evans et al. 2000).

Small populations are especially threatened. One of the best-documented studies of MVP size tracked the persistence of 120 bighorn sheep (*Ovis canadensis*) populations (some of which have been followed for 70 years) in the deserts of the southwestern United States (Berger 1990, 1999). The striking observation is that 100% of the unmanaged populations with fewer than 50 individuals went extinct within 50 years, while virtually all of the populations with more than 100 individuals persisted within the same time period (Figure 11.1). No single cause was evident for most of the populations that died out; rather, a wide variety of factors appears responsible for the extinctions. For bighorn sheep, the minimum population size is at least 100 individuals. Unmanaged populations below 50 could not maintain their numbers, even in the short term. Additional research on bighorn sheep populations suggests that populations have a greater chance of persisting when they occupy large habitats (which allow populations to increase in size) that are more than 23 km from domestic sheep, a source of disease (Singer et al. 2001). However, despite the factors hindering the survival of small populations, habitat management by government agencies and the release of additional animals have allowed some other small populations to persist that might otherwise have gone extinct.

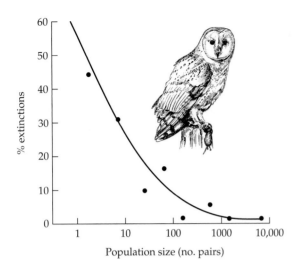

% extinctions

Population size (no. pairs)

FIGURE 11.2 Extinction rates of bird species on the Channel Islands. Each dot represents the extinction percentage of all the species in that population size class; extinction rate decreases as the size of the population increases. Populations with less than 10 breeding pairs had an overall 39% probability of extinction over 80 years, populations of between 10 to 100 pairs averaged around 10% probability of extinction, and populations of over 100 pairs had a very low probability of extinction. (From Jones and Diamond 1976.)

Field evidence from long-term studies of birds on the Channel Islands off the California coast supports the fact that large populations are needed to ensure population persistence; only bird populations with more than 100 breeding pairs had a greater than 90% chance of surviving for 80 years (Figure 11.2). In spite of most evidence to the contrary, however, small populations sometimes prevail: Many populations of birds apparently have survived for 80 years with 10 or fewer breeding pairs, and northern elephant seals have recovered to a population of 100,000 individuals after being reduced by hunting to only about 100 individuals in the late nineteenth century.

Once an MVP size has been established for a species, the **minimum dynamic area** (**MDA**)—the area of suitable habitat necessary for maintaining the minimum viable population—can be estimated by studying the home-range size of individuals and colonies of endangered species (Thiollay 1989). It has been estimated that reserves in Africa of 100 to 1000 km^2 are needed to maintain many small mammal populations (see Figure 16.2) (Schonewald-Cox et al. 1983). To preserve populations of large carnivores, such as lions, reserves of 10,000 km^2 are needed.

Exceptions notwithstanding, large populations are needed to protect most species, and species with small populations are in real danger of going extinct. Small populations are subject to rapid decline in numbers and local extinction for three main reasons:

1. Loss of genetic variability and related problems of inbreeding depression and genetic drift.

2. Demographic fluctuations due to random variations in birth and death rates.

3. Environmental fluctuations due to variation in predation, competition, disease, and food supply; and natural catastrophes that occur at irregular intervals, such as fires, floods, storms, or droughts.

We'll now examine in detail each of these causes for decline in small populations.

Loss of Genetic Variability

As was described in Chapter 2, a population's ability to adapt to a changing environment depends on genetic variability, which occurs as a result of individuals having different **alleles**—different forms of the same gene. Individuals with certain alleles or combinations of alleles may have just the characteristics needed to survive and reproduce under new conditions (Wayne and Morin 2004). Within a population, the frequency of a given allele can range from common to very rare. New alleles arise in a population either by random mutations or through the migration of individuals from other populations.

In small populations, allele frequencies may change from one generation to the next simply because of chance—based on which individuals survive to sexual maturity, mate, and leave offspring. This random process of allele frequency change is known as **genetic drift**, and is a separate process from changes in allele frequency caused by natural selection (Hedrick 2005). When an allele occurs at a low frequency in a small population, it has a significant probability of being lost in each generation. For example, if a rare allele occurs in 5% of all the genes present (the "gene pool") in a population of 1000 individuals, then 100 copies of the allele are present (1000 individuals × 2 copies per individual × 0.05 allele frequency), and the allele will probably remain in the population for many generations. However, in a population of 10 individuals, only 1 copy of the allele is present (10 individuals × 2 copies per individual × 0.05 allele frequency), and it is possible that the rare allele will be lost from the population in the next generation.

Considering the general case of an isolated population in which there are two alleles of each gene in the gene pool, Wright (1931) proposed a formula to express the proportion of original heterozygosity remaining after each generation (*H*) for a population of breeding adults, which constitutes the **effective population size**, (N_e)—the size of the population as estimated by the number of its breeding individuals:*

$$H = 1 - 1/[2\,N_e]$$

According to this equation, a population of 50 breeding individuals would retain 99% of its original heterozygosity after 1 generation:

$$H = 1 - 1/100 = 1.00 - 0.01 = 0.99$$

The proportion of heterozygosity remaining after *t* generations (H_t) is equal to:

$$H_t = H^t$$

For our population of 50 animals, then, the remaining heterozygosity would be 98% after 2 generations (0.99 × 0.99), 97% after 3 generations, and 90% after 10 generations. A population of 10 individuals would retain 95% of its original heterozygosity after 1 generation, 90% after 2 generations, 86% after 3 generations, and 60% after 10 generations (Figure 11.3).

This formula demonstrates that significant losses of genetic variability can occur in isolated small populations, particularly those on islands and fragmented landscapes. However, the amount of genetic variability within the population nevertheless will increase over time through two means: regular mutation of genes and migration of even a few individuals from distant populations. Mutation rates found in nature are about 1 in 10,000 to 1 in 1,000,000 per gene per generation; mutations therefore may make up for the random loss of alleles in large populations and, to a lesser extent, contribute to greater genetic diversity in small populations. However, mutations alone are not sufficient to counter genetic drift in populations of 100 individuals or less. Fortunately, even a low frequency of movement of individuals between populations minimizes the loss of genetic variability associated with small population size (Figure 11.4) (Wang 2004). If even one or two immigrants arrive each generation in an isolated population of about 100 individuals, the impact of genetic drift will be greatly reduced. With 4 to 10 migrants arriving per generation from nearby populations, the effects of genetic drift are negligible (Mills and Allendorf 1996). Gene flow from neighboring populations appears to be the major factor preventing the loss of genetic variability in small populations of Galápagos finches (Grant and Grant 1992) and Scandinavian wolves (Ingvarsson 2001). Notably, genetic variation that increases fitness will tend to be retained longer in a population, even when there is genetic drift (McKay and Latta 2002).

Field data also show that lower effective population size leads to a more rapid loss of alleles from the population. For example, the wind-pollinated dioecious conifer *Halocarpus bidwillii* of New Zealand naturally occurs in discrete populations in subalpine habitats. Protein electrophoresis was used to examine genetic variation in populations ranging from 10 to 400,000 individuals. There was a strong correlation between population size and genetic variation—large populations had the

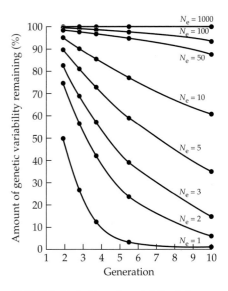

FIGURE 11.3 Genetic variability is lost randomly over time through genetic drift. This graph shows the average percentage of genetic variability remaining after 10 generations in theoretical populations of various effective population sizes (N_e). After 10 generations, there is a loss of genetic variability of approximately 40% with a population size of 10, 65% with a population size of 5, and 95% with a population size of 2. (From Meffe and Carroll 1997.)

---

*Factors affecting N_e, the effective population size, are discussed in detail beginning on page 255.

(A) **Immigration**

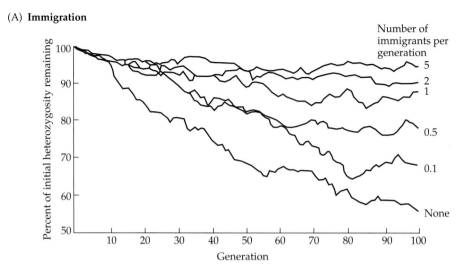

(B) **Mutation**

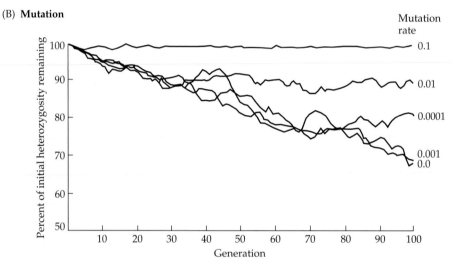

FIGURE 11.4 The effects of immigration and mutation on genetic variability in 25 simulated populations of size $N_e = 120$ individuals over 100 generations. (A) In an isolated population of 120 individuals, even low rates of immigration from a larger source population prevent the loss of heterozygosity from genetic drift. In the model, an immigration rate as low as 0.1 (1 immigrant per 10 generations) increases the level of heterozygosity, while genetic drift is negligible with an immigration rate of 1. (B) It is more difficult for mutation to counteract genetic drift. In the model, the mutation rate m must be 1% per gene per generation ($m = 0.01$) or greater to affect the level of heterozygosity. Because this mutation rate ($m = 0.01$) is far higher than what is observed in natural populations, mutation appears to play a minimal role in maintaining genetic variability in small populations. (From Lacy 1987.)

greatest levels of heterozygosity, percentage of polymorphic genes, and mean number of alleles per gene (Figure 11.5) (Billington 1991). Populations smaller than 8000 individuals appeared to suffer a loss of genetic variation, with the lowest variation in the smallest populations.

Unfortunately, rare and endangered species often have small, isolated populations, leading to a rapid loss of genetic variation. A meta-analysis of studies of genetic variation in plants and animals found that small populations had less genetic variation than large populations in 22 out of 23 species (Frankham 1996). Genetic variation was also lower for endangered species and species with narrow ranges

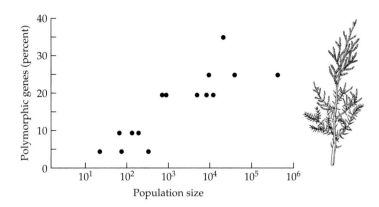

FIGURE 11.5 The level of genetic variability is directly correlated with population size in populations of *Halocarpus bidwillii*, a New Zealand coniferous shrub. This pattern holds true for the percentage of genes that are polymorphic as well as for the mean number of alleles per gene and the level of heterozygosity. Population size varies between 10 (10^1) and 1 million (10^6). (From Billington 1991.)

than for nonthreatened species and species with wide ranges. In some cases, entire species lacked genetic variation. In the recently discovered Wollemi pine (*Wollemia nobilis*) in Australia, only 40 plants occur in two nearby populations. As might be predicted, an extensive investigation has failed to find any genetic variation in this species (Peakall et al. 2003).

It seems safe to assume that to maintain genetic variability, conservation biologists should strive to preserve populations that are as large as possible. But how big should a given population be? How many individuals are needed to maintain genetic variability? Franklin (1980) suggested that 50 reproductive individuals might be the minimum number necessary to avoid short-term inbreeding depression, the lower fitness that results from matings between closely related individuals. This figure is based on the practical experience of animal breeders, and it indicates that animal stocks can be maintained with a loss of 2 to 3% of heterozygosity per generation. However, because this figure is based on work with domestic animals, its applicability to the wide range of wild species is uncertain.

Using data on mutation rates in *Drosophila* fruit flies, Franklin suggested that in populations of 500 reproductive individuals, the rate of new genetic variability arising through mutation might balance the variability being lost due to small population size. This range of values has been referred to as the **50/500 rule**: Isolated populations need to have at least 50 individuals, and preferably 500 individuals, to maintain genetic variability. This rule has been questioned by Lande (1995), who suggests that beneficial mutation rates may be lower than previously reported. Combining these lower mutation rates with the work on MVPs described earlier in this chapter, the best evidence suggests that at least several thousand reproductive individuals must be protected to maintain the genetic variability and long-term survival of a population. While this work on genetic variation and MVPs gives us some practical guidelines, the ideal is still to protect as many individuals of rare and endangered species as possible to maximize their chance of survival.

Consequences of Reduced Genetic Variability

Small populations subjected to genetic drift have greater susceptibility to a number of deleterious genetic effects such as inbreeding depression, loss of evolutionary flexibility, and outbreeding depression. These factors may contribute to a decline in population size, leading to an even greater loss of genetic variability, a loss of fitness, and a greater probability of extinction (Frankham et al. 2002; Stockwell et al. 2003; Frankham et al. 2004; Frankham 2005).

INBREEDING DEPRESSION   A variety of mechanisms prevents **inbreeding**, mating among close relatives, in most natural populations. In large populations of most animal species, individuals do not normally mate with close relatives; this tendency to mate with unrelated individuals of the same species is termed **out-breeding**. Individuals often disperse from their place of birth or are restrained from mating with relatives by behavioral inhibitions, unique individual odors, or other sensory cues. In many plants, a variety of morphological and physiological mechanisms encourage cross-pollination and prevent self-pollination. In some cases, particularly when population size is small and no other mates are available, these mechanisms fail to prevent inbreeding. Mating among parents and their offspring, siblings, and cousins, and self-fertilization in hermaphroditic species, may result in **inbreeding depression**, a condition that occurs when an individual receives two identical copies of a defective allele from each of its parents. Inbreeding depression is characterized by higher mortality of offspring, fewer offspring, or offspring that are weak, sterile, or have low mating success (Frankham et al. 2002; Keller and Waller 2002; Spielman et al. 2004). These factors result in even fewer individuals in the next generation, leading to more pronounced inbreeding depression.

Evidence for the existence of inbreeding depression comes from studies of human populations (in which there are records of marriages between close relatives for many generations), captive animal populations, and cultivated plants (Nieminen et al. 2001). In a wide range of captive mammal populations, matings among close relatives, such as parent–offspring matings and sibling–sibling matings, resulted on average in offspring with a 33% higher mortality rate than in noninbred animals (Figure 11.6) (Ralls et al. 1986, 1988). This lower fitness resulting from inbreeding is sometimes referred to as a "cost of inbreeding." Inbreeding depression can be a severe problem in small captive populations in zoos and domestic livestock breeding programs. Deleterious effects of inbreeding in the wild have also been demonstrated (Crnokrak and Roff 1999): Of over 150 valid data sets, 90% showed inbreeding to be detrimental. The scarlet gilia, *Ipomopis aggregata,* provides an example. Plants that come from populations with fewer than 100 individuals produce smaller seeds with a lower rate of seed germination and exhibit greater susceptibility to environmen-

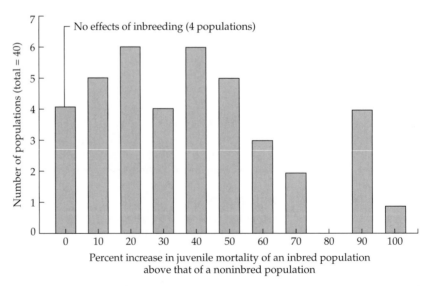

FIGURE 11.6 A high degree of inbreeding (such as matings between mother and son, father and daughter, brother and sister) results in a "cost of inbreeding." The data shown in the graph, based on a survey of 40 inbred mammal populations, express the cost as a percentage increase in juvenile mortality above the juvenile mortality rate of outbreeding animals of the same species. (From Ralls et al. 1988.)

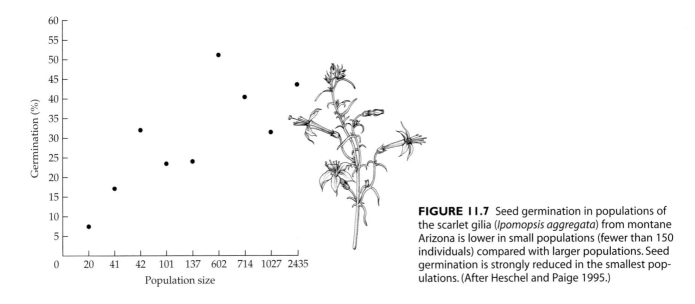

FIGURE 11.7 Seed germination in populations of the scarlet gilia (*Ipomopsis aggregata*) from montane Arizona is lower in small populations (fewer than 150 individuals) compared with larger populations. Seed germination is strongly reduced in the smallest populations. (After Heschel and Paige 1995.)

tal stress than do plants from larger populations (Figure 11.7) (Heschel and Paige 1995). In Illinois, isolated small populations of prairie chickens (*Tympanuchus cupido pinnatus*) were showing the effects of declining genetic variation and inbreeding depression, with lowered fertility and lowered rates of egg-hatching (Westemeier et al. 1998). When individuals from large, genetically diverse populations were released into the populations, egg viability was restored and the population grew, demonstrating the importance of maintaining genetic variation.

OUTBREEDING DEPRESSION Individuals of different species rarely mate in the wild; there are strong ecological, behavioral, physiological, and morphological isolating mechanisms that ensure mating occurs only between individuals of the same species. However, when a species is rare or its habitat is damaged, outbreeding—mating between individuals of different populations or species—may occur (Figure 11.8). Individuals unable to find mates within their own species may mate with an individual of a related species. The resulting offspring sometimes exhibit **outbreeding depression**, a condition that results in weakness, sterility, or lack of adaptability to the environment. Outbreeding depression may be caused by incompatibility of the chromosomes and enzyme systems that are inherited from the different parents (Montalvo and Ellstrand 2001). To use an example from artificial selection, domestic horses and donkeys are commonly bred to produce mules. Although mules are not physically weak (on the contrary, they are quite strong, which is why humans find them useful), they are almost always sterile.

Outbreeding depression can also result from matings between different subspecies, or even matings between divergent genotypes or populations of the same species. Such matings might occur in a captive breeding program or when individuals from different populations are kept together in captivity. In such cases, the offspring of such different genotypes are unlikely to have the precise mixture of genes that allows individuals to survive and reproduce successfully in a particular set of local conditions (Goldberg et al. 2005). For example, when the ibex (*Capra ibex*) population of Slovakia went extinct, ibex from Austria, Turkey, and the Sinai were brought in to start a new population. These different subspecies mated and produced hybrids that bore their young in the harsh conditions of winter rather than in the spring, and consequently had a low survival rate. Outbreeding depression caused by the pairing of individuals from the extremes of the species' geographical range meant failure for the experiment. However, many other studies of animals

FIGURE 11.8 Mating between unrelated individuals of the same species results in offspring with a high fitness as measured by survival or high reproduction (number of offspring produced). Mating among close relatives (sibling–sibling or parent–offspring matings) or self-fertilization in hermaphroditic species leads to low fitness. Mating between individuals from widely different populations or even different species sometimes, but not always, results in lowered fitness. (After Groom et al. 2006.)

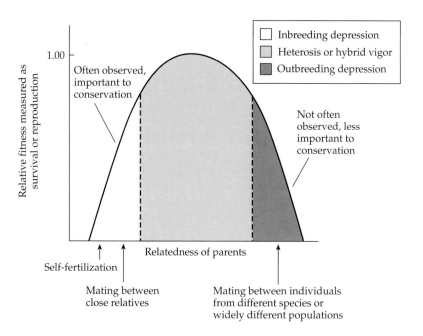

have failed to demonstrate outbreeding depression or have even observed hybrid vigor, suggesting that for animals, outbreeding depression is of less concern to conservation than inbreeding depression, the effects of which are well documented (Ralls et al. 2001).

Outbreeding depression may be considerably more significant in plants, where the arrival of pollen onto the receptive stigma of the flower is to some degree a matter of the chance movement of pollen by wind, insects, or another pollen vector. A rare plant species growing near a closely related common species may be overwhelmed by the pollen of the common species (Ellstrand 1992), and fail to produce seeds. Even when hybrids are produced by matings between a common and a rare species, the genetic identity of the rare species becomes lost as its small gene pool is mixed into the much larger gene pool of the common species. The seriousness of this threat is illustrated by the fact that more than 90% of California's threatened and endangered plants occur in close proximity to other species in the same genus with which the rare plants could possibly hybridize. Such a loss of identity can also take place in gardens when individuals from different parts of a species' range are grown next to each other and are cross-pollinated, producing hybrid seed.

LOSS OF EVOLUTIONARY FLEXIBILITY Rare alleles and unusual combinations of alleles that confer no immediate advantages may be uniquely suited for a future set of environmental conditions. Loss of genetic variability in a small population may limit its ability to respond to new conditions and long-term changes in the environment, such as pollution, new diseases, and global climate change (Falk and Holsinger 1991; Frankham et al. 2002). According to the Fundamental Theorem of Natural Selection, the rate of evolutionary change in a population is directly related to the amount of genetic variation in the population. A small population is less likely than a large population to possess the genetic variation necessary for adaptation to long-term environmental changes and so will be more likely to go extinct. For example, in many plant populations a small percentage of individuals have alleles that promote tolerance for high concentrations of toxic metals such as zinc and lead, even when these metals are not present. If toxic metals become abundant in the environment due to pollution, individuals with these alleles will be better able to adapt to them and to grow, survive, and reproduce better than typical individuals; consequently, frequency of these alleles in the population increases dramatically. However, if the population has become small and the genotypes for metal tolerance have been lost, the population could go extinct.

Factors That Determine Effective Population Size

In this section we will discuss the factors that determine the effective population size, the size of the population as estimated by the number of its breeding individuals. The factors limiting the estimated number of breeding individuals in a population include unequal sex ratio, variation in reproductive output, and population fluctuations and bottlenecks.

The effective population size is lower than the total population size because many individuals do not reproduce due to factors such as inability to find a mate, being too old or too young to mate, poor health, sterility, malnutrition, small body size, and social structures that restrict which individuals can mate. Many of the factors are initiated or aggravated by habitat degradation and fragmentation (Alò and Turner 2005). Furthermore, many plant, fungus, bacteria, and protist species have seeds, spores, or other structures in the soil that remain dormant unless stable conditions for germination appear. These individuals could be counted as members of the population, though they are obviously not part of the breeding population. Because of these factors, the effective population size (N_e) of breeding individuals is often substantially smaller than the actual population size (N). Because the rate of loss of genetic variability is based on the effective population size, the loss of genetic variability can be quite severe, even in a large population (Nunney and Elam 1994). For example, consider a population of 1000 alligators with 990 immature animals and only 10 mature breeding animals: 5 males and 5 females; in this case, the effective population size is 10, not 1000. For a rare oak species, there might be 20 mature trees, 500 saplings, and 2000 seedlings, resulting in a population size of 2520 but an effective population size of only 20.

A smaller than expected effective population size can also exist when there is an unequal sex ratio, variation in reproductive output, or population fluctuations and bottlenecks, as described below. The overall impact of these factors can be substantial. A review of a wide range of wildlife studies revealed that the average effective population size was only 11% of total population size; that is, a population of 300 animals, seemingly large enough to maintain the population, might only have an effective population size of 33, indicating that it is in serious danger of extinction (Frankham 1995). An effective population size that is smaller than might be expected based on an initial count of reproductive individuals can exist under any of the following circumstances:

UNEQUAL SEX RATIO   A population may consist of unequal numbers of males and females due to chance, selective mortality, or the harvesting of only one sex by people. If, for example, a population of a monogamous (one male and one female forming a long-lasting pair bond) goose species consists of 20 males and 6 females, only 12 individuals, 6 males and 6 females, will be mating. In this case, the effective population size is 12, not 26. In other animal species, social systems may prevent many individuals from mating even though they are physiologically capable of doing so. Among elephant seals, for example, a single dominant male usually mates with a large group of females and prevents other males from mating with them (Figure 11.9), whereas among African wild dogs, the dominant female in the pack often bears all of the pups.

The effect of unequal numbers of breeding males and females on N_e can be described by the formula:

$$N_e = [4(N_f \times N_m)]/(N_f + N_m)$$

FIGURE 11.9 A single male elephant seal (the larger animal with the extended snout, seen roaring in the center of the photograph) mates with large numbers of females; thus the effective population size is reduced because only one male is providing genetic input. (Photograph by Frank S. Balthis.)

where N_m and N_f are the numbers of adult (or potentially breeding) males and breeding females, respectively, in the population. In general, as the sex ratio of breeding individuals becomes increasingly unequal, the ratio of the effective population size to the number of breeding individuals (N_e/N) also goes down (Figure 11.10). This occurs because only a few individuals of one sex are making a disproportionately large contribution to the genetic makeup of the next generation, rather than the equal contribution found in monogamous mating systems. In the case of Asian elephants, for example, males are hunted by poachers for their tusks at the Periyar Tiger Reserve in India (Ramakrishnan et al. 1998). In 1997, there were 1166 elephants, of which 709 were adults. Of these adults, 704 were female and 5 were male, resulting in an effective population size of only 20, despite the large overall population size.

VARIATION IN REPRODUCTIVE OUTPUT In many species the number of offspring varies substantially among individuals. This phenomenon is particularly true in plants, where some individuals may produce a few seeds while others produce thousands. Unequal production of offspring leads to a substantial reduction in N_e because a few individuals in the present generation will be disproportionately represented in the gene pool of the next generation. In general, the greater the variation in reproductive output, the more the effective population size is lowered. For a variety of species in the wild, Frankham (1995) estimated that variation in offspring number reduces effective population size by a factor of 54%. In many annual plant populations that consist of large numbers of tiny plants producing one or a few seeds and a few gigantic individuals producing thousands of seeds, N_e could be reduced even more.

POPULATION FLUCTUATIONS AND BOTTLENECKS In some species, population size varies dramatically from generation to generation. Particularly good examples of this are butterflies, annual plants, and amphibians. In extreme fluctuations, the

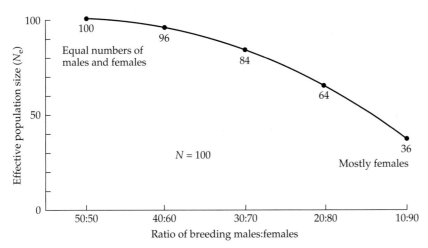

FIGURE 11.10 The effective population size (N_e) declines when the number of males and females in a breeding population (N) of 100 individuals is increasingly unequal. N_e is 100 when 50 males and 50 females breed, but only 36 when 10 males and 90 females breed.

effective population size is somewhere between the lowest and the highest numbers of individuals. This is often the most important factor reducing N_e below the census population size (Frankham 1995). The effective population size can be calculated over a period of t years using the number of individuals (N) breeding in any one year:

$$N_e = t/(1/N_1 + 1/N_2 + ... + 1/N_t)$$

Consider a butterfly population, monitored for five years, that has 10, 20, 100, 20, and 10 breeding individuals in the successive five years. In this case:

$$N_e = 5/(1/10 + 1/20 + 1/100 + 1/20 + 1/10) = 5/(31/100)$$
$$= 5(100/31) = 16.1$$

The effective population size over the course of 5 years is above the lowest population level of 10, but well below the maximum number of 100 and the arithmetic average, a population size of 32.

The effective population size tends to be determined by the years in which the population has the smallest numbers. A single year of drastically reduced population numbers will substantially lower the value of N_e. This principle applies to a phenomenon known as a **population bottleneck**, which occurs when a population is greatly reduced in size and rare alleles in the population are lost if no individuals possessing those alleles survive and reproduce (Frankham et al. 2002; Briskie and Mackintosh 2004; Jamieson et al. 2006). With fewer alleles present and a decline in heterozygosity, the overall fitness of the individuals in the population may decline. The effects of a population bottleneck are most severe when population size remains small (less than 10 individuals) for several generations. A special category of bottleneck, known as the **founder effect**, occurs when a few individuals leave one population to establish another new population. The new population often has less genetic variability than the larger, original population (Figure 11.11). Bottlenecks can also occur

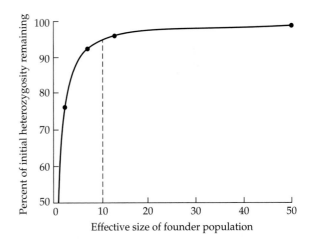

FIGURE 11.11 A new population started by only a few unrelated individuals is missing a substantial amount of the genetic variability of the source population. However, if the effective size of the founding population is more than 10 unrelated individuals, more than 90% of the genetic variability is preserved. If the population is started with a single breeding pair or just a pregnant female, giving an effective population size of two, 75% of the genetic variability is still preserved. This variability will be largely preserved if the population rapidly expands in size, but it will continue to be lost if population size remains very small. (From Foose 1983.)

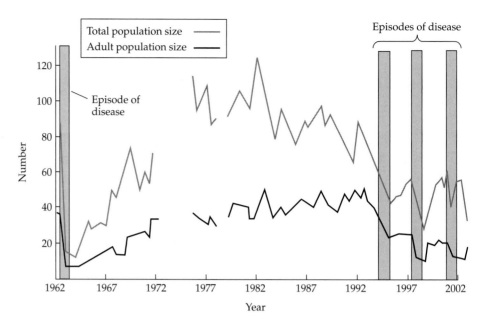

FIGURE 11.12 The Ngorongoro Crater lion population consisted of about 90 individuals in 1961 before crashing in 1962. Since that time the population reached a peak of 125 individuals in 1983 before collapsing to less than 40 total individuals with less than 20 adults in 2003. Small population size, an isolated location, lack of immigration since 1962, and the impact of disease have apparently resulted in the loss of genetic variation caused by a population bottleneck. The light line represents the total population size; the dark line represents just adults. A lack of census data for certain years is the cause of gaps in the lines. The four shaded bars represent episodes of disease outbreak. (From Kissui and Packer 2004.)

when captive populations are established using relatively few individuals. For example, the captive population of the Speke's gazelle in the United States was established from one male and three females. If a population is fragmented by human activities, each of the resulting small subpopulations may lose genetic variation and go extinct. Such is the fate of many fish populations fragmented by dams (Wofford et al. 2005).

The lions (*Panthera leo*) of Ngorongoro Crater in Tanzania provide a well-studied example of a population bottleneck (Kissui and Packer 2004). The lion population in the crater consisted of 60 to 75 individuals until an outbreak of biting flies in 1962 reduced the population to 9 females and 1 male (Figure 11.12). Two years later, 7 additional males immigrated to the crater; there has been no further immigration since that time. The small number of founders, the isolation of the population, and the variation in reproductive success among individuals have apparently created a population bottleneck, leading to inbreeding depression; in comparison with the large Serengeti lion population nearby, the Crater lions show reduced genetic variability, high levels of sperm abnormalities (Figure 11.13), reduced reproductive rates, and increased cub mortality. As a result, even though the population increased to a range of 75 to 125 animals in 1983, the population has since declined. By 2003, the population dropped to 34 animals following an outbreak of canine distemper virus that had spread from domestic dogs kept by people living just outside the Crater area.

Certain plant populations that show extreme fluctuations in size have lost genetic variation due to population bottlenecks. For example, a lack of allozyme genetic variation is apparent in four populations of the rare Furbish's lousewort (*Pedicularis furbishiae*), an endemic plant of Maine (Menges 1990). In this case, the lack of genetic variation is attributed to population bottlenecks resulting from a series of temporary populations established on riverbanks after colonization by a few seeds.

(A) 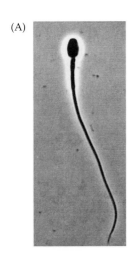 (B) 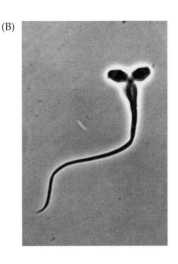 (C)

FIGURE 11.13 Males of the isolated and inbred population of lions at Ngorongoro Crater in Tanzania exhibit a high level of sperm abnormalities. (A) Normal lion sperm. (B) Bicephalic ("two-headed") sperm and (C) nonfunctional sperm with a coiled flagellum, both from lions of the Ngorongoro Crater population. (Photographs by D. Wildt.)

Population bottlenecks do not always lead to greatly reduced heterozygosity. The effects of population bottlenecks will be most evident when the breeding population is reduced below 10 individuals for several generations. If the population expands rapidly in size after a temporary bottleneck, average heterozygosity in the population may be restored even though the number of alleles present is severely reduced (Allendorf and Leary 1986). An example of this phenomenon is the high level of heterozygosity found in the greater one-horned rhinoceros (*Rhinoceros unicornis*) in Nepal, even after the population passed through a bottleneck (Figure 11.14; see also Box 11.1). Population size declined from 800 individuals in Chitwan National Park to less than 100 individuals; fewer than 30 were breeding. With an effective population size of 30 individuals for one generation, the population would have lost only 1.7% of its heterozygosity after one generation. As a result of strict protection of the species by park guards, the population recovered to 400 individuals (Dinerstein and McCracken 1990). The Mauritius kestrel (*Falco punctatus*) represents an even more extreme case, with a long population decline that result-

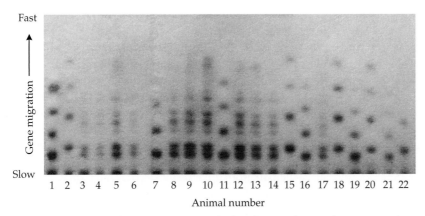

FIGURE 11.14 Starch gel electrophoresis reveals that the population of greater one-horned rhinoceroses (*Rhinoceros unicornis*) at Chitwan National Park in Nepal shows high levels of genetic variation. This technique is based on the fact that the proteins (in this case, an enzyme called LDH) produced by different alleles of a gene migrate at different rates across an electrically charged starch gel plate, appearing as bands at different distances from the starting point at the bottom of the gel. Each column represents one individual animal. Note that animals 10 and 11, for example, have bands at different positions, indicating that these two individuals are genetically different from each other for the enzyme LDH. While better technology now exists for this type of investigation, starch gel electrophoresis gives a particularly good visual demonstration of genetic variation. (From Dinerstein and McCracken 1990.)

ed in only one breeding pair remaining in 1974. An intensive conservation program has allowed the population to recover to over 200 pairs today. A study comparing the present birds with preserved museum specimens and kestrels living elsewhere has found that the Mauritius kestrel lost about only 50% of its genetic variation after passing through this bottleneck (Groombridge et al. 2000).

These examples demonstrate that effective population size is often substantially less than the total number of individuals in a population. Particularly where there is a combination of factors such as fluctuating population size, numerous nonreproductive individuals, and an unequal sex ratio, the effective population size may be far lower than the number of individuals alive in a good year. A review of a wide range of wildlife studies revealed that the effective population size averaged only 11% of the total population size (Frankham 1995), underscoring that simply maintaining large populations may not prevent the loss of genetic variation unless the effective population size is also large. In the case of captive populations, genetic variation may be effectively maintained by controlling breeding, perhaps by subdividing the population, periodically removing dominant males to allow subdominant males the opportunity to mate, and allowing limited migration of individuals among subpopulations.

BOX 11.1

Rhino species in Asia and Africa: Genetic Diversity and Habitat Loss

■ In recent decades, conservationists have focused extraordinary effort on protecting and restoring the numbers of rhinoceroses in parts of their original ranges. The task is monumental: The five species of rhinoceros that inhabit Asia and Africa, all critically endangered, represent ancient and unusual adaptations for survival. Habitat destruction and poaching represent serious threats to the three species of the Asian forests, while the illegal killing of rhinos for their horns is the main problem for the two African species.

Rhino losses are so severe that it is estimated that only 16,000 individuals of all five species survive today. These species only exist in a tiny fraction of their former range. The most numerous of the five is the white rhinoceros, *Ceratotherium simum*; this species numbers approximately 11,300 wild animals, although there are only 10 individuals of the distinctive northern subspecies (www.rhinos-irf.org). The rarest species—the elusive Javan rhinoceros, *Rhinoceros sondaicus*—is thought to number around 50 animals on the very western end of the island of Java, with another 2 to 7 individuals in Vietnam. These two populations are genetically very distant.

The overall decline of each species is alarming enough, but the problem is exacerbated by the fact that many of the remaining animals live in very small, isolated populations. The black rhino, *Diceros bicornis*, for example, numbers about 3600, but these individuals are in approximately 75 small, widely separated subgroups. The

existing populations of the Sumatran rhino (*Dicerorhinus sumatrensis*) each contain less than 100 individuals, with the total species count under 300. Some biologists fear that these small populations may not be viable over the long term as a result of loss of genetic variability, inbreeding depression, and genetic diseases resulting from mating among closely related individuals.

The question of genetic viability in rhino populations is not as simple as it first appears. Genetic diversity varies greatly among rhino species. Studies of the greater one-horned, or Indian, rhinoceros (*Rhinoceros unicornis*) in Nepal indicate that despite its small total population— an estimated 1500 animals—the genetic diversity in at least this population is relatively high (see Figure 11.14), contradicting the common assumption that small populations automatically have low heterozygosity. The combination of long generation times, high individual mobility, and the possibility that rhinos may have migrated into the park from great distances may have allowed the Indian rhino to maintain its genetic variability despite passing through a population bottleneck (Dinerstein and McCracken 1990; Melnick, personal communication). Considerable genetic variation is also present within each of the four recognized subspecies of the black rhinoceros (Harley et al. 2005). Furthermore, microsatellite DNA data shows that the four subspecies are genetically distinct, perhaps representing adaptations to local environmental conditions throughout the species' range.

BOX 11.1 *(continued)*

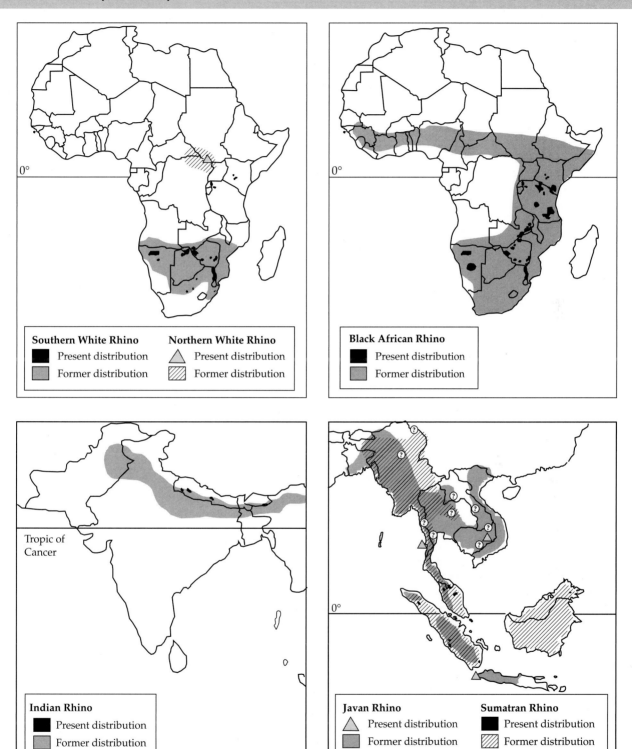

Each of the five rhinoceros species currently occupies only a tiny fraction of its former range, and their situations and levels of endangerment vary greatly. (After www.rhinos-irf.org.)

(continued)

BOX 11.1 *(continued)*

Despite the reduced population size of both the black rhino and the Indian rhino, the Indian rhino faces a different and possibly more deadly threat: habitat loss. Though no immediate threat of inbreeding exists for the Indian rhino, the critical pressure on this species' range since the nineteenth century has reduced its numbers dramatically, from possibly tens of thousands of animals to less than 1000 by the 1960s (Dinerstein and McCracken 1990). The geographical range of this animal, originally covering northern India, Pakistan, southern Nepal, Burma, and Bangladesh, has been almost completely taken over by human settlement. Indian rhino populations in parks and sanctuaries have increased dramatically and are genetically healthy; however, the species will always be limited to these small, heavily guarded remnant habitats, with no opportunity to return to its former range or numbers.

In contrast, much of the range of the black rhino in Africa is still open and is not likely to be subject to human encroachment at any time in the near future. Heterozygosity could be maintained in the species by moving individuals between populations (Harley et al. 2005). If the black rhino population is managed for genetic diversity in this manner, it is conceivable that this species could be fully restored to its original numbers and much of its range. Yet the problem of microenvironmental adaptations remains: by placing black rhinos from a number of different subspecies together in a sanctuary to increase genetic diversity in the species, would the rhinos risk losing adaptive differences that might prove crucial to the survival of local subspecies? Maintaining genetic diversity is contingent on controlling outside threats to the breeding population, including illegal poaching for their horns. Optimal park conditions must also be maintained to ensure that all adult individuals reproduce. Captive breeding of endangered rhinos presents special challenges; white rhinos in particular often will not breed in zoo programs.

Genetic analysis has also been useful for making decisions on the conservation of the Sumatran rhinoceros, numbering less than 300 individuals and found in scattered populations. Analysis of mitochondrial DNA from blood and hair samples from eastern Sumatra, western Sumatra, peninsular Malaysia, and Borneo populations showed that the Borneo population represented a distinct lineage from the other three populations, which were genetically similar. The recommendation is that the Borneo rhinos be treated as a separate population for breeding and conservation purposes, whereas the other three populations could be managed as one conservation unit (Morales et al. 1997).

As this research makes evident, rhino conservation must be tailored to the specific circumstances of particular species and populations. The different species face a number of challenges with a variety of possible solutions. For species threatened with habitat loss, such as the Indian rhino, sanctuaries and habitat preservation may be the most important methods of preserving the species. Others, such as the black rhino, may require management to maintain genetic diversity within populations and the genetic uniqueness of distinct subspecies, including breeding programs in the wild and protection of the remnant populations. The rarest species, the Sumatran and Javan rhinos, may require a combination of approaches, with the addition of captive breeding programs. They need habitat protection because both of these Asian species are under severe pressure from logging and conversion of forest to agricultural land, and they need breeding programs in the wild and in captivity to increase and maintain genetic diversity. For each of these rhinos, there is no single, all-encompassing answer; the problems and circumstances of conserving the species must be evaluated individually.

Other Factors That Affect the Persistence of Small Populations

In this section we discuss some other factors that affect small populations. Although small populations tend to go extinct over time because of the loss of genetic variation, in the short term, they are vulnerable to extinction due to random variations in demography and the environment. Demographic variations can produce a downward spiral of population numbers that increases in speed as numbers grow smaller; environmental factors, on the other hand, have the potential for causing extinction in one cataclysmic episode.

Demographic Variation

In an ideal, stable environment, a population would increase until it reached the carrying capacity (K) of the environment, at which point the average birth rate (b) per individual would equal the average death rate (d) and there would be no net change in population size. In any real population, individuals do not usually produce the average number of offspring: they might leave no offspring, somewhat fewer than the average, or more than the average. For example, in an ideal, stable giant panda population, each female would produce an average of two surviving offspring in her lifetime, but field studies show that rates of reproduction among individual females vary widely around that number. However, as long as population size is large, the average birth rate provides an accurate description of the population. Similarly, the average death rate in a population can be determined only by examining large numbers of individuals, because some individuals die young and other individuals live a relatively long time. This variation in population size due to random variation in reproduction and mortality rates is known as **demographic variation** or **demographic stochasticity**.

Population size may fluctuate over time due to changes in the environment or other factors without ever approaching a stable value. In general, once population size drops below about 50 individuals, individual variation in birth and death rates begins to cause the population size to fluctuate randomly up or down (Menges 1992). If population size fluctuates downward in any one year due to a higher than average number of deaths or a lower than average number of births, the resulting smaller population will be even more susceptible to demographic fluctuations in subsequent years. Random fluctuations upward in population size are eventually bounded by the carrying capacity of the environment, and the population may fluctuate downward again. Consequently, once a population decreases because of habitat destruction and fragmentation, demographic variation becomes important and the population has a higher probability of declining more and even going extinct due to chance alone (in a year with low reproduction and high mortality) (Lacy and Lindenmayer 1995). Species with highly variable birth and death rates, such as annual plants and short-lived insects, may be particularly susceptible to population extinction due to demographic stochasticity. The chance of extinction is also greater in species that have low birth rates, such as elephants, because these species take longer to recover from chance reductions in population size.

As a simple example, imagine a population of three hermaphroditic individuals that each live for one year, need to find a mate, reproduce, and then die. Assume that each individual has a 33% probability of producing 0, 1, or 2 offspring, resulting in an average birth rate of 1 per individual; in this instance, there is theoretically a stable population. However, when these individuals reproduce, there is a 1-in-27 chance ($0.33 \times 0.33 \times 0.33$) that no offspring will be produced in the next generation and the population will go extinct. Consider also that there is a 1-in-9 chance that only 1 offspring will be produced in the next generation ($0.33 \times 0.33 \times 0.33 \times 3$); because this individual will not be able to find a mate, the population will be doomed to extinction in the next generation. There is also a 22% chance that the population will decline to 2 individuals in the next generation. Thus, random variation in birth rates can lead to demographic stochasticity and extinction in small populations. Similarly, random fluctuations in the death rate can lead to fluctuations in population size. When populations are small, random high mortality in one year might eliminate the population altogether.

When populations drop below a critical number, deviations from an equal sex ratio may occur, leading to a declining birth rate and a further lowering of population size. For example, imagine a population of 4 birds that includes 2 mating pairs of males and females, in which each female produces an average of 2 surviving offspring in her lifetime. In the next generation, there is a 1-in-8 chance that only male or only female birds will be produced, in which case no eggs will be laid to produce the following generation. There is a 50% (8-in-16) chance that there will be either 3 males and 1 female or 3 females and 1 male in the next generation, in which case only 1 pair of birds will mate and the population will decline. This scenario is illustrated by the last 5 surviving individuals of the extinct dusky seaside sparrow (*Ammodramus maritimus nigrescens*); all individuals were males, so there was no opportunity to establish a captive breeding program. In Illinois, the last 3 individuals of the rare lakeside daisy (*Hymenoxys acaulis* var. *glabra*) remaining in the state were unable to produce viable seeds when cross-pollinated among themselves because they belong to the same self-infertile mating type (De Mauro 1993). Pollen had to be brought in from Ohio plants in order for the Illinois plants to produce seeds.

In many animal species, small populations may be unstable due to the inability of the social structure to function once the population falls below a certain size; this is known as the **Allee effect** (Keitt et al. 2001; Courchamp et al. 2002). Herds of grazing mammals and flocks of birds may be unable to find food and defend themselves against attack when numbers fall below a certain level. Animals that hunt in packs, such as wild dogs and lions, may need a certain number of individuals to hunt effectively. Many animal species that live in widely dispersed populations, such as bears, whales, spiders, and eagles, may be unable to find mates once the population density drops below a certain point. In this case, the average birth rate will decline, making the population density even lower and worsening the problem. In plant species, as population size decreases, the distance between plants increases; pollinating animals may not visit more than one of the isolated, scattered plants, resulting in the loss of seed production due to insufficient transfer of compatible pollen. This combination of random fluctuations in demographic characteristics, unequal sex ratios, disruption of social behavior, and decreased population density contributes to instabilities in population size, which often leads to local extinction.

Environmental Variation and Catastrophes

Random variation in the biological and physical environment, known as **environmental stochasticity**, can also cause variation in the population size of a species. For example, the population of an endangered rabbit species might be affected by fluctuations in the population of a deer species that eats the same types of plants, fluctuations in the population of a fox species that feeds on the rabbits, and fluctuations in the populations of parasites and disease-causing organisms that affect the rabbits. Variation in the physical environment might also strongly influence the rabbit populations—rainfall during an average year might encourage plant growth and allow the population to increase, while dry years might limit plant growth and cause rabbits to starve. Environmental stochasticity affects all individuals in the population, unlike demographic stochasticity, which causes variation among individuals within the population.

Natural catastrophes that occur at unpredictable intervals, such as droughts, storms, earthquakes, and fires, along with cyclical die-offs of the surrounding biological community, can cause dramatic fluctuations in population levels. Natural catastrophes can kill part of a population or even eliminate an entire population from an area. Numerous examples exist of die-offs in populations of large mammals; in many cases 70 to 90% of the population dies (Young 1994). For a wide range of vertebrates, the frequency of catastrophes is around 15% per generation (Reed et al. 2003). Even though the probability of a natural catastrophe in any one year is low, over the course of decades and centuries, natural catastrophes have a high likelihood of occurring.

As an example of environmental variation, imagine a rabbit population of 100 individuals in which the average birth rate is 0.2 and an average of 20 rabbits are eaten each year by foxes. On average, the population will maintain its numbers at exactly 100 individuals, with 20 rabbits born each year and 20 rabbits eaten each year. However, if there are three successive years in which the foxes eat 40 rabbits per year, the population size will decline to 80 rabbits, 56 rabbits, and 27 rabbits in years 1, 2, and 3, respectively. If there are then three years of no fox predation, the rabbit population will increase to 32, 38, and 46 individuals in years 4, 5, and 6. Even though the same average rate of predation (20 rabbits per year) occurred over this six-year period, by introducing variation in year-to-year predation rates the rabbit population size declined by more than 50%. At a population size of 46 individuals, the rabbit population will go extinct rapidly when subjected to the average rate of 20 rabbits eaten by foxes per year.

Modeling efforts by Menges (1992) and others have shown that random environmental variation is generally more important than random demographic variation in increasing the probability of extinction in populations of small to moderate size. Environmental variation can substantially increase the risk of extinction even in populations showing positive population growth under the assumption of a stable environment (Mangel and Tier 1994). In general, introducing environmental variation into population models, in effect making them more realistic, results in populations with lower growth rates, lower population sizes, and higher probabilities of extinction. Menges (1992) introduced environmental variation into models of plant populations that had been developed by field ecologists working with palms. Considering only demographic variation, and before the inclusion of environmental variation, these plant models suggested that the MVP size, the number of individuals needed to give the population a 95% probability of persisting for 100 years, was about 48 mature individuals (Figure 11.15). When moderate environmental variation was included, however, the MVP size increased to 380 individuals, meaning that populations larger in size need to be protected.

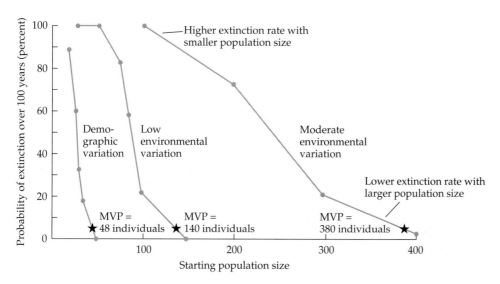

FIGURE 11.15 The effects of demographic variation, low environmental variation, and moderate environmental variation on the probability of extinction of a population of the Mexican palm, *Astrocaryum mexicanum*. In this study, the MVP size, indicated by a star, was defined as the population size at which there is a less than 5% chance of the population going extinct within 100 years. (From Menges 1992; data from Piñero et al. 1984.)

The interaction between population size and environmental variation was demonstrated using the biennial herb garlic mustard (*Alliaria petiolata*), an invasive plant in the United States, as an experimental subject (Drayton and Primack 1999). Populations of various sizes were assigned at random either to be left alone as controls or to be experimentally eradicated by removing every flowering plant in each of the four years of the study. Overall the probability of an experimental population going extinct over the four-year period was 43% for small populations (≤ 10 individuals initially), 9% for medium size populations (>10 and ≤ 50), and 7% for large populations (>50 individuals). For control populations, the probability of going extinct for small, medium, and large populations was 11%, 0%, and 0%. Large numbers of dormant seeds in the soil apparently allowed most experimental populations to persist even when every flowering plant was removed in four successive years. However, small populations were far more susceptible to extinction than large populations.

Extinction Vortices

The smaller a population becomes, the more vulnerable it is to further demographic variation, environmental variation, and genetic factors that tend to lower reproduction, increase mortality rates, and so reduce population size even more, driving the population to extinction. This tendency of small populations to decline toward extinction has been likened to a vortex, a whirling mass of gas or liquid spiraling inward—the closer an object gets to the center, the faster it moves. At the center of an **extinction vortex** is oblivion: the local extinction of the species. Once caught in such a vortex, it is difficult for a species to resist the pull toward extinction (Gilpin and Soulé 1986).

For example, a natural catastrophe, a new disease, or human disturbance could reduce a large population to a small size. This small population could then suffer from inbreeding depression with an associated lowered juvenile survival rate. This increased death rate could result in an even lower population size and more inbreeding. Similarly, demographic variation will often reduce population size, resulting in even greater demographic fluctuations and, once again, a greater probability of extinction.

These three forces—environmental variation, demographic variation, and loss of genetic variability—act together so that a decline in population size caused by one factor will increase the vulnerability of the population to the other two factors (Figure 11.16). For example, a decrease in orangutan population size caused by forest fragmentation may cause inbreeding depression, decreasing population size; decreased population size may then disrupt the social structure and the ability to find mates, leading to an even lower population size; the smaller population is then more vulnerable to further population reduction and eventual extinction caused by unusual environmental events.

It is also important to remember that as a population becomes smaller, it also tends towards ecological extinction. Once the orangutan population drops below a certain size, for example, the species would not be an effective seed disperser in the community.

An important implication of the extinction vortex is that addressing the original cause of population decline may not be sufficient to recover a threatened population. Such was the case with the greater prairie chicken population in Illinois described earlier (Westemeier et al. 1998). The original population of over 1 million prairie chickens declined following the arrival of Europeans to below 50, with a decline in fertility and hatchability. Habitat restoration reversing one of the major original causes of decline failed to help the population recover. The Illinois prairie chicken population only began to grow after it was outcrossed to populations from other states to reverse inbreeding depression.

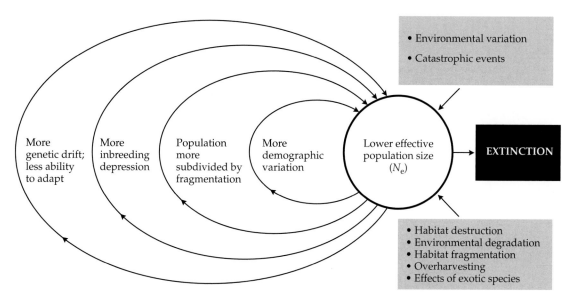

FIGURE 11.16 Extinction vortices progressively lower population size, leading to local extinctions of species. Once a population drops below a certain size, it enters a vortex, in which the factors that affect small populations tend to drive its size progressively lower. (After Gilpin and Soulé 1986 and Guerrant 1992.)

As the prairie chicken example illustrates, once a population has declined to a small size, it will probably go extinct unless unusual and highly favorable conditions allow the population size to increase (Schrott et al. 2005). Such populations often require a careful program of population and habitat management, as described in later chapters, to increase population growth rate and allow the population to escape from the harmful effects of small population size.

Summary

1. In many cases, protecting populations is the key to protecting species from extinction. The minimum viable population (MVP) size is the smallest population size that can be predicted to have a high chance of persisting for the forseeable future. The MVP for many species is at least several thousand individuals.

2. Biologists have observed that small populations have a greater tendency to go extinct than large populations. Small populations are subject to a more rapid rate of extinction for three main reasons: loss of genetic variability and related problems of inbreeding depression and genetic drift, demographic fluctuations, and environmental variation or natural catastrophes.

3. To protect small populations, we need to determine the effective population size, which is an estimate of the number of individuals that are actually producing offspring. The calculated effective population size is often much lower than simply the number of living individuals because (1) many individuals are not reproducing; (2) there may be an unequal sex ratio; (3) there may be variation among individuals in number of offspring produced; and (4) populations may show large fluctuations in size over time.

4. Variations in reproductive and mortality rates can cause small populations to fluctuate randomly in size, leading to extinction. Environmental variation can also cause random fluctuations in population size, with infrequent natural catastrophes sometimes causing major reductions.

5. Once a population's size has been reduced by habitat destruction, fragmentation, and other human activities, it is even more vulnerable to random fluctuations in size and eventual extinction. The combined effects of demographic variation, environmental variation, and loss of genetic variability on small populations create an extinction vortex that tends to accelerate the drive to extinction and may require population and habitat management to counteract.

For Discussion

1. Imagine a species that has four populations, consisting of 4, 10, 40, and 100 individuals. Using Wright's formula, calculate the loss in heterozygosity over 1, 2, 5, and 10 generations for each population. Calculate the effective population size for each population, assuming that there are equal numbers of males and females; then calculate it assuming different proportions of males and females. Allow the population size of each group to fluctuate at random around its average value. Calculate how this affects the loss of heterozygosity and the effective population size.

2. Construct a simple population model of a rabbit that has a stable population size (see page 265); then add environmental variation (such as severe winter storms or predation) and demographic variation (number of offspring produced per rabbit per year) and determine whether the population would be able to persist over time. Use the methods shown in the text, computer simulations (see Shultz et al. [1999] and Donovan and Welden [2002] for ideas), or random-number generators (flipping coins is the easiest).

3. Find out about species that are currently endangered in the wild. How are they or how might they be affected by the problems of small populations? Address genetic, physiological, behavioral, and ecological aspects, as appropriate.

Suggested Readings

Alò, D. and T. F. Turner. 2005. Effects of habitat fragmentation on effective population size in the endangered Rio Grande silvery minnow. *Conservation Biology* 19: 1138–1148. Case study of population size in a fish.

Briskie, J. V. and M. Mackintosh. 2004. Hatching failure increases with severity of population bottlenecks in New Zealand birds. *Proceedings of the National Academy of Science* 101: 558–561. Inbreeding depression can be seen in the wild.

Donovan, T. M. and C. W. Welden. 2002. *Spreadsheet Exercises in Conservation Biology and Landscape Ecology.* Sinauer Associates, Sunderland, MA. A straightforward method for building population models with some of the properties discussed in this chapter.

Falk, D. A. and K. E. Holsinger (eds.). 1991. *Genetics and Conservation of Rare Plants.* Oxford University Press, New York. Conservation efforts involving plants require some special considerations.

Frankham, R. 2005. Genetics and extinction (review article). *Biological Conservation* 126: 131–140. This important review article provides evidence that small populations in the wild suffer from negative genetic effects.

Frankham, R., J. D. Ballou, and D. A. Briscoe. 2002. *Introduction to Conservation Genetics.* Cambridge University Press, Cambridge. In a comprehensive treatment, the authors argue that genetic issues need to be addressed in the management of endangered species.

Frankham, R., J. D. Ballou, and D. A. Briscoe. 2004. *A Primer of Conservation Genetics.* Cambridge University Press, Cambridge, U.K. Good introduction to the relation of conservation and genetics.

Hedrick, P. W. 2005. *Genetics of Populations,* 3rd ed. Jones and Bartlett Publishers, Sudbury, MA. Excellent introduction to basic principles.

Jamieson, I. G., G. P. Wallis, and J. V. Briskie. 2006. Inbreeding and endangered species management: is New Zealand out of step with the rest of the world? *Conservation Biology* 20: 38–47. Population bottlenecks and inbreeding depression are factors to consider in rare species recovery.

Kissui, B. M. and C. Packer. 2004. Top-down population regulation of a top predator: lions in the Ngorongoro Crater. *Proceedings of the Royal Society of London: Biological Sciences* 271: 1867–1874. Long-term study of population censusing and inbreeding.

Ralls, K. S., R. Frankham, and J. Ballou. 2001. Inbreeding and outbreeding. *In* S. A. Levin (ed.), *Encyclopedia of Biodiversity*, Vol. 3, pp. 427–436. Academic Press, San Diego, CA. Short review of the genetic problems of small populations.

Reed, D. H. 2005. Relationship between population size and fitness. *Conservation Biology* 19: 563–568. Large populations often have healthier individuals than small populations.

Reed, D. H. and R. Frankham. 2003. Correlations between fitness and genetic diversity. *Conservation Biology* 17: 230–237. Higher genetic variability is associated with greater fitness.

Saccheri, I., M. Kuussaari, M. Kankare, P. Vikman, W. Fortelius, and I. Hanski. 1998. Inbreeding and extinction in a butterfly metapopulation. *Nature* 392: 491–494. Evaluates the importance of genetic factors in extinction risk in wild butterfly populations in Finland.

Schrott, G. R., K. A. With, and A. W. King. 2005. Demographic limitations on the ability of habitat restoration to rescue declining populations. *Conservation Biology* 19: 1181–1193. Intensive management is sometimes needed to rebuild small populations.

Wang, J. 2004. Application of the one migrant-per-generation rule to conservation management. *Conservation Biology.* 18: 332–343. Even low rates of migration can maintain genetic variation.

Wayne, R. K. and P. A. Morin. 2004. Conservation genetics in the new molecular age. *Frontiers in Ecology and the Environment.* 2: 89–97. Modern molecular techniques can be used to assess population characteristics and suggest management strategies.

Young, A. G. and G. M. Clarke (eds.). 2001. *Genetics, Demography, and Viability of Fragmented Populations.* Cambridge University Press, New York. Case studies of animals and plants are used to illustrate the impact of fragmentation on population viability.

Applied Population Biology

How can conservation biologists determine whether a specific plan to manage an endangered or rare species has a good chance of succeeding? Even without human disturbance, a population of any species can be stable, increasing, decreasing, or fluctuating in number. In general, widespread human disturbance destabilizes populations of many native species, often sending them into sharp decline. But how can this disturbance be measured, and what actions should be taken to prevent or reverse it? This chapter discusses applied population biology, which seeks to answer these and other questions by examining the factors affecting the abundance and distribution of rare and endangered species.

In protecting and managing a rare or endangered species, it is vital to have a firm grasp of the ecology of the species, its distinctive characteristics (sometimes called its **natural history**), and the status of its populations, particularly the dynamic processes that affect population size and distribution (its **population biology**). With more information concerning a rare species' natural history and population biology, land managers are able to more effectively maintain the species and identify factors that place it at risk of extinction. As will be discussed later in the chapter, this information can be used to make mathematical predictions of the ability of species to persist in a protected area and the impact of alternative management options.

To implement effective population-level conservation efforts, conservation biologists should try to answer as many questions as possible from the following categories. For most species, we're able to answer only a few of these questions without further investigation, yet management decisions may have to be made before this information is available or while it is being gathered:

- *Environment.* What are the habitat types where the species is found, and how much area is there of each? How variable is the environment in time and space? How frequently is the environment affected by catastrophic disturbance? How have human activities affected the environment?

- *Distribution.* Where is the species found in its habitat? Are individuals clustered together, distributed at random, or spaced out regularly? Do individuals of this species move and migrate among habitats or to different geographical areas over the course of a day or over a year? How efficient is the species at colonizing new habitats? How have human activities affected the distribution of the species?

- *Biotic interactions.* What types of food and other resources does the species need and how does it obtain them? What other species compete with it for these resources? What predators or parasites affect its population size? What mutualists (pollinators, dispersers, etc.) does it interact with? Do juvenile stages disperse by themselves or are they dispersed by other species? How have human activities altered the relationships among species in the community?

- *Morphology.* What does the species look like? What are the shape, size, color, surface texture, and function of its parts? How does the morphology of the species change over its geographical range? Do all of the individuals in the population look the same? How does the shape of its body parts relate to their function and help the species to survive in its environment? How large are new offspring, and are they different in appearance from adults?

- *Physiology.* How much food, water, minerals, and other necessities does an individual need to survive, grow, and reproduce? How efficient is an individual at using its resources? How vulnerable is the species to extremes of climate, such as heat, cold, wind, and rain? When does the species reproduce, and what are its special requirements during reproduction?

- *Demography.* What is the current population size, and what was it in the past? Are the numbers of individuals stable, increasing, or decreasing? Does the population have a mixture of adults and juveniles, indicating that recruitment of new individuals is occurring?

- *Behavior.* How do the actions of an individual allow it to survive in its environment? How do individuals in a population mate and produce offspring? In what ways do individuals of a species interact, cooperatively or competitively?

- *Genetics.* How much variation occurs in morphological, physiological, and behavioral characteristics? How much of this variation is genetically controlled? What percentage of the genes is variable? How many alleles does the population have for each variable gene?

- *Human Interaction.* How do human activities impact the species? Do people harvest or use this species in any way? What do local people know about this species?

Methods for Studying Populations

Methods for the study of populations have developed largely from the study of land plants and animals. Small organisms such as protists, bacteria, and fungi have not been investigated in comparable detail. Species that inhabit soil, freshwater, and marine habitats are particularly poorly investigated for population characteristics. In this section we will examine how conservation biologists undertake their studies of populations, recognizing that methods need to be modified for each species.

Gathering Ecological Information

The basic information needed for an effort to conserve a species or determine its status can be obtained from three major sources: published literature, unpublished literature, and fieldwork.

PUBLISHED LITERATURE   Other people may have studied the same rare species (or a related species) or have investigated a habitat type. Library indices such as *BioSys, Biological Abstracts,* and *The Zoological Record* are often accessible by computer and provide easy access to a variety of books, articles, and reports relating to a particular topic. This literature may contain records of previous population sizes and distributions that can be compared with the current status of the species. Some sections of the library will have related material shelved together, so finding one book often leads to others. The World Wide Web on the Internet provides ever-increasing access to databases, websites, electronic bulletin boards, journals, news articles, specialized discussion groups, and subscription databases such as the *ISI Web of Science*. Information on the Internet needs to be examined carefully to determine the accuracy and source of the data, because there is no control over what is posted. Asking biologists and naturalists for ideas on references is another way to locate published materials. Checking indices of newspapers, magazines, and popular journals is also an effective strategy because results of important scientific research often appear first in the popular news media and are sometimes more clearly summarized there than in the professional journals.

Once one key reference is obtained, the bibliography often can be used to discover useful earlier references. The *Science Citation Index* (available online via the subscription database the *ISI Web of Science*), available in many libraries, is a valuable tool for tracing the literature forward in time; for example, many recent scientific papers on the Hawaiian monk seal can be located by looking at the current *Science Citation Index* for the name T. Gerrodette, who wrote a key paper about the Hawaiian monk seal in 1990. Any recent paper citing Gerrodette will appear following a search of his name.

UNPUBLISHED LITERATURE   An enormous amount of information on conservation biology is contained in unpublished reports by individual scientists, enthusiastic citizens, government agencies, and conservation organizations such as national and regional forest and park departments, government fisheries and wildlife agencies, NatureServe, The Nature Conservancy, the IUCN, and the World Wildlife Fund. This so-called "gray literature" is sometimes cited in published literature or mentioned by leading authorities in conversations, lectures, or articles. For example, the unpublished series of Tropical Forest Action Plans contains some of the most comprehensive sources of information on conservation in tropical countries. Often a report known through word of mouth can be obtained through direct contact with the author. In addition, conservation organizations sometimes are able to supply additional reports not found in the published literature. People working at these agencies and organizations are sometimes willing to share a considerable amount of knowledge about species, conservation, and management efforts that is not contained in reports. (A list of environmental organizations and other information sources is found in the Appendix.)

FIELDWORK The natural history of species usually must be learned through careful observations in the field. Fieldwork is necessary because only a tiny percentage of the world's species have been studied, and the ecology of a species often changes from one place to another. Only in the field can the conservation status of a species be determined, as well as its relationships to the biological and physical environment. Fieldwork for species such as polar bears, humpback whales, tropical trees, or bog orchids can be time-consuming, expensive, and physically arduous, but it is crucial for developing conservation plans for endangered species, and it can be exhilarating and deeply satisfying as well. There is a long tradition, particularly in Britain, of dedicated amateurs conducting excellent studies of species in their immediate surroundings with minimal equipment or financial support. While much natural history information can be obtained through careful observation, many of the technical methods for investigating populations are very specialized and are best learned by studying under the supervision of an expert or by reading manuals (Wilson and Cole 1998; Feinsinger 2001). An important, and frequently neglected, part of fieldwork involves explaining the purpose of the study to people living in the area and listening to what they have to say about the project. In many cases, local people have surprising insights and observations that they are willing and eager to share with scientists (Smart et al. 2005).

The need for fieldwork is highlighted by recent work on Magellanic penguins in breeding colonies in Argentina that helped to define the foraging area that birds use when feeding their chicks (Boersma et al. 2002; Boersma 2005). It had previously been thought that the birds forage within only 30 km of their nests, but using radio telemetry, satellite tags attached to the penguins revealed that birds swim up to 600 km from their nesting sites (Figure 12.1). During the critical period when penguins are feeding their chicks, they forage primarily in a seasonal fishing exclusion zone where food is probably more abundant and they have reduced chances of getting caught in fishing nets. Based on this information, the Argentinian government

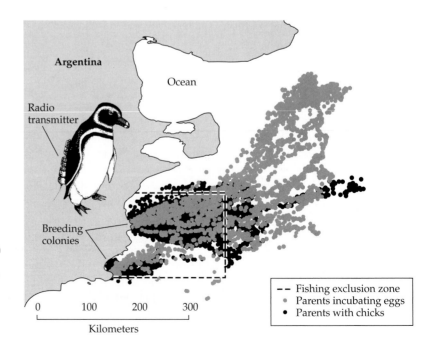

FIGURE 12.1 Satellite tracking of Magellanic penguins off the coast of Argentina shows that penguins incubating eggs forage up to 600 km from their breeding colonies. When penguins are feeding chicks, foraging takes place mainly within a seasonal fishing exclusion zone that was established to protect spawning fish. Fieldwork provided this vital information about the penguins' foraging habits, which led to the fishing zone remaining closed until the chicks left their nests. (After Boersma et al. 2005.)

agreed to extend the number of months of the fishing exclusion zone. The survival and growth of young penguins subsequently improved.

Monitoring Populations

To learn the status of a species of special concern, scientists must census its population in the field and monitor it over time (Figure 12.2). Census methods range from making a complete count of every individual to estimating population size using sampling methods. By repeatedly censusing a population on a regular basis, changes in the population can be determined (Schemske et al. 1994; Primack 1998; Laliberte and Ripple 2004; Arnold et al. 2006). Long-term census records can help to distinguish long-term population trends of increase or decrease (possibly caused by human disturbance) from short-term fluctuations caused by variations in weather or unpredictable natural events. Census records can also determine if a species is showing a positive response to conservation management.

Effective monitoring shows the response of a population to a change in its environment; for example, in a study discussed later in this chapter, a decline in an orchid species was shown to be connected with heavy cattle grazing in its habitat. Observing a long-term decline in the species they study often motivates biologists to take vigorous action to conserve it (Box 12.1). Monitoring can also follow char-

(A)

(B)

(C)

FIGURE 12.2 Monitoring populations requires specialized techniques suited to each species. (A) An ornithologist checks the health and weight of a piping plover on Cape Cod. Note the identification band on the bird's leg. (B) Botanists monitor tagged lady's slipper orchid plants (*Cypripedium acaule*) for their changes in leaf size and number of flowers over a ten-year period. As shown here, individual leaves are monitored for their rates of carbon dioxide uptake, a measure of photosynthetic rate and an index of plant health. Note the numbered aluminum tag, anchored to the ground by a wire. (C) Censusing fish populations on a tropical reef ecosystem. (A, photograph by Laurie McIvor; B, photograph by Richard Primack; C, photograph © Simon Jennings.)

BOX 12.1

Three Primatologists Who Became Activists

■ Human beings' closest living relatives are the great apes: chimpanzees, gorillas, and orangutans. Yet despite a fascination spanning centuries, most of what we know about them has been learned in the past 50 years. Much of our knowledge rests largely on the pioneering work of three primatologists: Jane Goodall, Dian Fossey, and Birute Galdikas, sometimes called the "trimates." Their contributions are all the more valuable because they came at a time when prominent female scientists were a rare breed. These women pioneered the long-term study of their respective subjects, and all three eventually came to devote much of their time to conservation efforts rather than to the sole pursuit of scientific knowledge.

The first of the trimates, Jane Goodall, began her study of chimpanzees in 1960 in Gombe, Tanzania. Her fieldwork quickly paid off. Within three months, she had witnessed activities no researcher had ever seen, including chimpanzees eating meat that they had killed and extracting termites from nests using plucked blades of grass. The latter finding caused a sensation: it was the first example of tool use in an animal other than humans (Morell 1993). Goodall's method of naming (rather than numbering) individual animals and focusing on each individual's unique characteristics in order to explain group dynamics was criticized by some primatologists, but in time it became the standard. By patiently following chimpanzee groups across generations, she gained new insights into their social structure. In her second decade of research, Goodall and her associates made more startling discoveries, including cannibalism within groups and elaborate, premeditated "warfare" between groups. Now entering its fifth decade, the work at Gombe is among the longest continuous field study of animal behavior ever undertaken.

The second trimate, Dian Fossey, studied mountain gorillas at Parc Nacional des Volcans in Rwanda, her research site and home for the next 18 years. She was the first researcher to note females transferring between groups and to document males killing infant gorillas to bring females into estrus: two important keys to gorilla social dynamics. Like Goodall at Gombe, Fossey developed her study site, Karisoke, into a major center for field research.

Birute Galdikas, the youngest of the trimates, embarked on her pioneering work among orangutans in Borneo in 1971. Unlike chimps and gorillas, orangutans are largely solitary and arboreal, making it difficult to study their social interactions or to habituate them to the presence of human observers. Nevertheless, over years of patient study, Galdikas uncovered basic information on the orangutan diet, documenting the sometimes lengthy courtships between males and females, maternal care-giving, and roving juvenile bands (Morell 1993). Like her fellow trimates, Galdikas' work led to the creation of a study center that has supported the work of new generations of scientists.

The scientific success of the trimates rested in part on the new study methods they developed, which allowed these researchers to study the effects of individual differences on group social dynamics. These new methods included long-term, multiyear observations of the same individuals, the habituation of primate groups to the presence of humans, much closer observation than had been attempted before, and an appreciation for the individuality of the animals being studied. Such methods, which led the researchers to develop empathy with the apes, ran counter to prevailing attitudes, which valued objectivity and emotional detachment as essential to "good science." For the work of the trimates, however, involvement with the study animals seemed less a barrier and more an aid to gaining scientific knowledge.

Empathy led the three researchers to fight for the conservation of the great ape species, all of which are endangered by poaching, habitat destruction, and human population growth. While her writings and well-publicized career helped increase popular knowledge about nature and support for its preservation, for many years Jane Goodall was content to concentrate on research and leave direct conservation work to others. Eventually her attitude changed as a result of the direct threats to chimpanzees in and around her study site (Goodall 1999). She remarked that "Gombe was still the best place in the world for me. But I came to realize the chimps needed me elsewhere… I knew I had to use the knowledge the chimps gave me in the fight to save them" (Miller 1995). Today Goodall devotes much of her time to conservation education and political advocacy, speaking out against habitat destruction, the illegal trade in chimpanzees, the hunting of chimpanzees for bushmeat, and the poor treatment of chimps in medical research.

Birute Galdikas also became actively involved in conservation issues. Throughout Borneo and Sumatra, forests are being cut down, leaving disoriented and isolated orangutans without any home. The Orangutan

BOX 12.1 *(continued)*

Foundation International, which she directs, has established rehabilitation centers to take care of homeless orangutans, and whenever possible, return them to the wild. (This approach has proved controversial, as it is uncertain if these reintroduced animals are still surviving in the wild.) Over time, more of her conservation work focused on habitat preservation, the key to preserving orangutans in the wild, and she was instrumental in halting logging within her study site, an area now designated as the Tanjung Puting National Park (Galdikas 1995).

Dian Fossey did not have the luxury of gradually developing into a conservationist. Like many other field scientists, she saw her study subjects being wiped out right before her eyes. The extremely rare mountain gorillas were being slaughtered to collect trophy heads and hands for sale to tourists and to capture infants for European zoos. Gorillas were also being killed accidentally by snares set by local villagers to catch antelope, and farmers and cattle were steadily reducing and degrading the habitat both inside and outside the park. In the face of lax enforcement of park rules, Fossey began to practice what she termed "active conservation"—destroying poachers' snares, shooting cattle pastured within the park, and leading armed antipoaching patrols (Fossey 1990). Her murder in 1985 was probably motivated by her antipoaching activities. Fossey's methods of personal confrontation and her dismissal of science were criticized by some, but others saw her efforts as essential, even heroic, steps in salvaging a population at the brink of extinction. Under such conditions, her supporters argued, detailed scientific study is beside the point. The well-known zoologist George Schaller believes Fossey had her priorities in order: "When you have any kind of rare species, the first priority is to work for its protection. Science is necessarily secondary" (Morell 1986).

"Trimates" Dian Fossey (left), Jane Goodall (center), and Birute Galdikas began by studying animal behavior but eventually devoted themselves to conservation activism. (Photograph courtesy of The Leakey Foundation.)

The contributions of these three scientists are, appropriately, threefold. First, they have created an astonishing body of knowledge on species that are our closest relatives. Second, they have made the international community aware of the dangerous plight of these species and have taken prominent, active, and self-sacrificing stands on behalf of the apes. Finally, they provide role models for young women, scientists, and students worldwide, inspiring them to enrich the scientific world with their own contributions.

acteristics of the community and ecosystem, such as the density and biomass of plants and the pattern of water release into nearby streams (Feinsinger 2001). Monitoring efforts can be targeted at particularly sensitive species, such as butterflies, using them as indicator species of the long-term stability of ecological communities (MacNally et al. 2004).

Monitoring has a long history in temperate countries, particularly in Britain, and it plays an important role in conservation biology; see for example Fitter and Fitter (2002). In North America, the Breeding Bird Survey has been censusing bird abundance at approximately 1000 transects over the past 35 years. This information has been used to determine the stability of migrant songbird populations over time (Sauer et al. 2003). Some of the most elaborate projects involve establishing permanent research plots in tropical forests, such as the 50-ha site at Barro Colorado Island in Panama, to monitor changes in species and communities (Hardesty et al. 2005). The Barro Colorado studies have shown that many tropical tree and bird species are more dynamic in numbers than had previously been suspected, suggesting that estimates of their minimum viable population sizes may need to be revised upward.

Monitoring studies are increasing dramatically as government agencies and conservation agencies have become more concerned with protecting rare and endangered species (Pérez-Arteaga and Gaston 2004). Some of these studies are mandated by law as part of management efforts. With some planning, monitoring can facilitate an estimate of the ability of a population to persist in the future, known as population viability analysis (PVA; discussed later in this chapter). The geographical range and intensity of monitoring has often been greatly extended through the use of volunteers. Training and educating citizens not only expands the data available to scientists, but often transforms these citizens into advocates for conservation. Examples of three programs that rely heavily on volunteers are the North American Amphibian Monitoring Program, Environment Canada, and Frogwatch USA (de Solla et al. 2005). Other programs target butterflies, birds, water quality, and endangered wildflowers. Journey North involves students in tracking the northward migration of birds and butterflies and other signs of spring (www.learner.org/jnorth).

The most common types of monitoring conducted are inventories, population demographic studies, and surveys.

INVENTORIES An **inventory** is a count of the number of individuals present in a population. It is an inexpensive and straightforward method. By repeating an inventory over successive time intervals, biologists can determine whether a population is stable, increasing, or decreasing in number. An inventory of southern sea lions (*Otaria flavescens*) in the Falkland Islands in the South Atlantic revealed that, as a result of hunting, annual births of pups declined from 80,550 in 1937 to 6000 in 1965, when hunting ended (Figure 12.3). Despite the cessation of hunting, the population continued to drop, to 2034 in 1995, perhaps due to more intense predation from killer whales. There has been some recovery, with 2747 pups recorded in 2003 (Thompson et al. 2005).

Inventories of a community can be conducted to determine what species are currently present in a locality; a comparison of current occurrences with past inventories can highlight species that have been lost. Inventories conducted over a wide area can help to determine the range of a species and its areas of local abundance. Inventories taken over time can highlight changes in the range of species.

The most extensive inventories have been carried out in the British Isles by a large number of local amateur naturalists supervised by professional societies. The most detailed mapping efforts have involved recording the presence or absence of plants, lichens, and birds in a mosaic of 10-km squares covering the British Isles. The Biological Records Centre (BRC) at Monks Wood Experimental Station maintains and analyzes the 4.5 million distribution records, which contain information on 16,000 species. One part

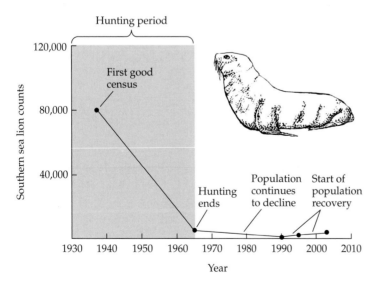

FIGURE 12.3 The number of pups of the Falkland Island sea lion has been periodically counted (as indicated by the black dots). The population underwent a severe decline due to hunting. Even when hunting ended in 1965, the population continued to decline. After 1990, the population has been recovering slowly. (After Thompson et al. 2005).

of these efforts involved the Botanical Society in the British Isles Monitoring Scheme, in which the British Isles were intensively surveyed from 1987 to 1988 by 1600 volunteers, who collected one million records of all plant species occurrences on a 10-km square grid (Rich and Woodruff 1996). When the 1987/1988 data were compared with a detailed survey from 1930 to 1960, it was found that numerous species of grasslands, heathlands, and aquatic and swamp habitats had declined in frequency, while introduced weed species had increased (Figure 12.4).

SURVEYS   A **survey** of a population involves using a repeatable sampling method to estimate the number of individuals or the density of a species in part of a community. An area can be divided into sampling segments and the number of individuals in certain segments counted. These counts can then be used to estimate the actual population size. For example, the number of trees of the rare Florida torreya (*Torreya taxifolia*) was estimated in five separate ravine populations along the Apalachicola River of northern Florida and southern Georgia (Schwartz et al. 2000). A total of 365 trees were counted in the 1825 ha surveyed, leading to estimated tree density of 0.2 trees per ha. Because the total area of ravines is 20,370 ha, the maximum number of trees in the whole region is estimated to be 4063 trees (20,370 ha × 0.2 trees/ha). This estimate is a maximum because the density of trees where the five surveys took place is probably higher than the

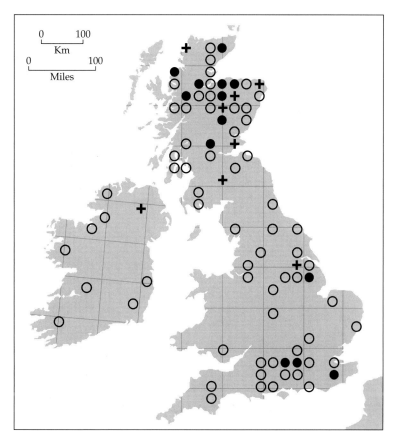

FIGURE 12.4   The British Isles Monitoring Scheme for *Gnaphalium sylvaticum*, the woodland cudweed. Large numbers of populations present from 1930 to 1960 were no longer present in the period from 1987 to 1988 (open circles), particularly in Ireland and England. Many populations in Scotland persisted during this interval (black dots), and there were few new populations (crosses). (From Rich and Woodruff 1996.)

density of the entire area. Similar methods can be used for different species in a variety of ecosystems; for instance, the number of crown-of-thorns starfish can be counted in a series of 10 m × 10 m quadrats (plots) to estimate the total starfish population on a coral reef. A survey might also count the number of bats caught in mist nets per hour or the density of a particular crustacean species per liter of seawater.

A variety of survey methods involving observing animals, their footprints, and dung and listening for animal calls has been used in Africa to document a sudden, widespread decline in wildlife populations, particularly large primates, as a result of hunting (Chapman and Peres 2001). A specialized type of survey, a mark-recapture survey, involves the capture, marking, releasing, and recapture of animals to estimate population size and individual movement (see Mousson et al. 1999 and Labonne and Gaudin 2005 for examples).

Survey methods are used when a population is very large or its range extensive. Although survey methods are time-consuming, they are a methodical and repeatable way to examine a population and determine whether it is changing in size. Such methods are particularly valuable when the species being studied has stages in its life cycle that are inconspicuous, tiny, or hidden, such as the seed and seedling stages of many plants or the larval stages of aquatic invertebrates. In the case of plants, the population may contain no adult individuals above ground but still may be present due to viable seeds in the ground (Adams et al. 2005). Soil samples could be taken at fixed survey points and examined in the laboratory to determine the density of seeds expressed as the number of seeds per cubic cm of soil. Disadvantages of survey methods are that they may be expensive (chartering a vessel to sample marine species), technically difficult (extracting seeds from the soil and identifying them), and inaccurate (sampling may miss or include infrequent aggregations of species). All of these disadvantages are present when conducting a survey in the deep-sea environment.

DEMOGRAPHIC STUDIES **Demographic studies** follow known individuals in a population to determine their rates of growth, reproduction, and survival (Dinsmore et al. 2003; Labonne and Gaudin 2005). Individuals of all ages and sizes must be included in such a study. Either the whole population or a subsample can be followed. In a complete population study, all individuals are counted, aged if possible, measured for size, sexed, and tagged or marked for future identification; their position on the site is mapped, and tissue samples sometimes are collected for genetic analysis. The techniques used to conduct a population study vary depending on the characteristics of the species and the purpose of the study. Each discipline has its own technique for following individuals over time; ornithologists band birds' legs, mammalogists often attach tags to an animal's ear, and botanists nail aluminum tags to trees (see Wilson and Cole 1998). Information from demographic studies can be used in life history formulae to calculate the rate of population change and to identify critical stages in the life cycle (Caswell 2001; Griffith and Forseth 2005).

An example of a specialized demographic study can be found in the work of researcher Katy Payne, who has pioneered new techniques in bioacoustic recording to monitor populations of forest elephants, which are difficult to observe in their forest habitat. Bioacoustic recording allows Payne to track individual animals by tracking the characteristic sonograms of their display calls, which are outside the range of human hearing. This technique can be used to give a precise estimate of population size and to track animal movements, information critical for a conservation strategy (Fox 2004).

Demographic studies provide the most information of any monitoring method and, when analyzed thoroughly, suggest ways in which a site can be managed to ensure population persistence. The disadvantages of demographic studies are that they are often time-consuming, expensive, require repeated visits, necessitate a knowledge of the species' life history, and can be quantitatively or statistically complex to analyze. Demographic data gathered over time can be used to predict whether the population will be present at different future dates and what the population size will be. If the population is predicted to go extinct, estimates can be made of the extent to which the survival and reproductive rates need to be increased through site management to maintain or enlarge the population. Populations showing a pattern of decline and populations predicted to decline in the future are cause for special concern and require action to prevent their extinction.

Demographic studies can provide information on the age structure of a population. A stable population typically has an age distribution with a characteristic ratio of juveniles, young adults, and older adults. The absence or low representation of any age class, particularly of juveniles, may indicate that the population is in danger of declining (Holmes and York 2003). Conversely, a large number of juveniles and young adults may indicate that the population is stable or even expanding. However, it is difficult to determine the age of individuals for species such as plants, fungi, and colonial invertebrates. A small individual may be either young or slow-growing and old; a large individual may be either old or unusually fast-growing and young. For these species, the distribution of size classes is often taken as an approximate indicator of population stability, but this needs to be confirmed by following individuals over time to determine rates of growth and mortality. It is significant that for many long-lived species, such as trees, the establishment of new individuals in the population is an episodic event, with many years of low reproduction and an occasional year with abundant reproduction. Careful analysis of long-term data on changes in the population over time is needed in order to distinguish short-term fluctuations from long-term trends.

In general, populations are stable when the growth rate is zero, that is, when the average birth rate equals the average death rate. While a population with an average growth rate of zero is expected to be stable over time, and a growth rate above zero should lead to an expanding population, random variation in population growth rates in different years can lead to population decline and extinction even with a positive average growth rate (see Chapter 11).

Demographic studies can also indicate the spatial characteristics of a species, which might be very important to maintaining the vitality of separate populations. The number of populations of the species, movement among populations, and the stability of these populations in space and time are all important considerations. This is particularly true for species that occur in an aggregate of temporary or fluctuating populations linked by migration, known as a metapopulation (discussed in detail later in this chapter). Demographic studies can identify the core sites that support large, fairly permanent populations and supply colonists to temporary satellite areas.

Reproductive characteristics of populations—such as sex ratio, mating structure, percentage of breeding adults, and monogamous or polygamous mating systems—will also affect the success of conservation strategies and should be thoroughly analyzed. For example, a strategy to increase genetic diversity in a highly inbred population such as the lions of Ngorongoro Crater (see Chapter 11) might include introducing individuals from outside this population to mate with the inbred animals. But if the "migrant" individuals do not fit into the social dynamics of the group, they may not breed and may even be driven out or killed by the native population.

Finally, demographic studies can supply clues to the maximum carrying capacity of the environment. These studies are important in determining how large a population the environment can support before it deteriorates and the population declines. Nature reserves may have abnormally large populations of certain species due to the recent loss of adjoining habitat or the inability of individuals to disperse from the nature reserve. Due to limited available space, many nature reserves are expected to support large populations over long periods of time. Data that help define the maximum carrying capacity of the reserves are crucial to preventing population and environmental stress, particularly in circumstances where natural population control mechanisms such as predators have been eliminated by humans.

MONITORING: SOME CASE STUDIES   A few case studies provide an overview of how the various monitoring techniques have been used in the field.

- *Butterflies.* In Britain, butterfly inventories have been carried out on a grid of 2 km × 2 km squares covering Hertfordshire County (Thomas and Abery 1995). This amazingly detailed study documents a surprisingly high rate of local extinction—67% of the 2-km squares occupied by particular species before 1970 had no current population of that species.

- *Hawaiian monk seals.* Population inventories of the Hawaiian monk seal (*Monachus schauinslandi*) on the beach at several islands in the Kure Atoll have documented a decline from almost 100 adults in the 1950s to less than 14 in the late 1960s (Figure 12.5) (Gerrodette and Gilmartin 1990). The number of pups similarly declined during this period. On the basis of these trends,

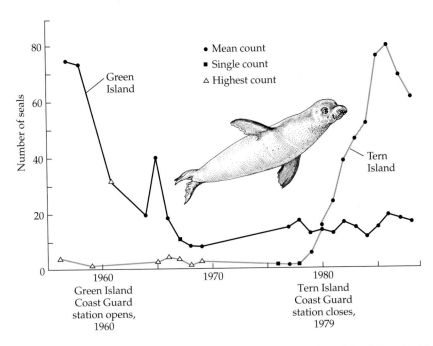

FIGURE 12.5 Inventories of Hawaiian monk seal populations on Green Island, Kure Atoll (black line) and on Tern Island, French Frigate shoals (shaded line) revealed that this species was in danger of extinction. Population counts were plotted from either a single count, the mean of several counts, or the maximum of several counts. Seal populations declined when a Coast Guard station was opened on Green Island in 1960; seal populations increased on Tern Island following the closing of a Coast Guard station in 1979. (After Gerrodette and Gilmartin 1990.)

the Hawaiian monk seal was declared an endangered species in 1976 under the U.S. Endangered Species Act, and conservation efforts were implemented that reversed the trend for some populations. The Tern Island population showed a substantial recovery following the closing of a Coast Guard station in 1979, but started to decline again in the 1990s due to high juvenile mortality (Baker and Johanos 2004). The Green Island population grew after its Coast Guard station was closed in 1994.

- Individuals of a rare fish species were studied at three sites in the Rhine River basin in France (Labonne and Gaudin 2005); 469 fish were implanted with transponder tags. Over a 2.5 year period, annual survival was very low (<1%), the individual fish were highly mobile, and recruitment was highly variable from year to year. The results show that the construction of dams would threaten this species by blocking the natural tendency of fish to move around and preventing the recolonization of habitat.

- *The early spider orchid.* This orchid (*Ophrys sphegodes*) has shown a substantial decline in range during the past 50 years in Britain. A nine-year demographic study showed that the plants were unusually short-lived for perennial orchids, with only half of the individuals surviving beyond two years (Hutchings 1987). This short half-life makes the species unusually vulnerable to unfavorable habitat changes. In one population in which the species was declining in numbers, demographic analysis highlighted soil damage by cattle grazing as the primary cause of decline. A change in land management to sheep grazing (sheep grazing causes less soil damage than cattle grazing) and restricting the sheep to graze only when the orchids are not flowering and fruiting has enabled the population to make a substantial recovery.

Population Viability Analysis

Predictions of whether a species has the ability to persist in an environment can be made using **population viability analysis** (**PVA**), an extension of demographic analysis (Beissinger and McCullough 2002; Morris and Doak 2002). PVA can be thought of as risk assessment—using mathematical and statistical methods to predict the probability that a population or a species will go extinct at some point in the future. By looking at the range of a species' requirements and the resources available in its environment, vulnerable stages in the natural history of the species can be identified. PVA can be useful in considering the effects of habitat loss, habitat fragmentation, and habitat deterioration on a rare species (Watson et al. 2005; Zabel et al. 2006). An important part of PVA is estimating how management efforts such as reducing (or increasing) hunting or increasing (or decreasing) the area of protected habitat will affect the probability of extinction (Akçakaya et al. 2005). PVA can model the effects of augmenting a population through the release of additional individuals caught in the wild elsewhere or raised in captivity (Kohlmann et al. 2005). PVA may be particularly useful when investigating species characterized by populations that fluctuate widely in size.

PVA begins by constructing a mathematical model of the population or species of concern using data on average mortality rates, average recruitment rates, and the current age (or size) distribution of the population (Possingham et al. 2001). The model can be readily constructed using a spreadsheet package, and it can be analyzed using the methods of matrix algebra. Because this initial model results in only one outcome—a population that is growing, declining, or stable—it is called a deterministic model. Environmental variability, as well as genetic and demographic variability, can then be added into the model by allowing model elements (such as the mortality rate) to vary at random between their observed range of annual values. Catastrophic events can be programmed to occur at random (Figure 12.6). Hundreds or thousands of simulations of individual populations can be run using this random variation to determine the probability of population extinction within a

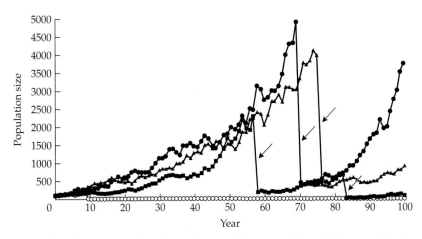

FIGURE 12.6 This PVA simulates the trajectory of four populations. Each population has an average growth rate of 5% per year, with fluctuations around this value due to demographic and environmental variation. In any one year, there is also a 2% chance of a catastrophe (indicated by arrows), in which 90% of the population dies. For example, one population (squares) experienced catastrophes in years 55 and 82. After a catastrophe strikes, population size is often so small that environmental and demographic variations cause the population to go extinct. All four populations have experienced at least one catastrophe. One population (open circles) went extinct after 10 years and a second population (squares) is on the verge of extinction after 100 years. (After Possingham et al. 2001.)

certain period of time or the mean time to extinction. Management regimes that affect population parameters can then be developed and analyzed (for example, a regime that increases adult survival by 10% and juvenile recruitment by 20%). Simulations of the impact of this management regime could be compared with the original population model to determine how it affects the probability that the population will persist in the future (Plissner and Haig 2000; Pfab and Witkowski 2000).

Existing computer-simulation packages such as VORTEX, ALEX, and RAMAS® can be used to run the models. Models can be tailored to include landscape information and a variety of independent environmental factors. The choice of models will depend on the goals of the analysis and the management options under consideration. A particularly useful feature of PVA is that the parameters of the model can be investigated using sensitivity analysis, a method that determines which parameter or combination of parameters most influences extinction probabilities. For example, sensitivity analysis might reveal that slight changes in adult mortality rates greatly affect the probability of extinction, whereas relatively large changes in juvenile mortality rates have minimal impact on the probability of extinction. Obviously, parameters that greatly influence the extinction rate should become the focus of conservation efforts, whereas parameters that have minimal effect on the extinction rate can be given less attention.

Such statistical models must be used with caution and a large dose of common sense (Brook et al. 2002; Coulson et al. 2003; Schultz and Hammond 2003). Generally, around ten years of data are needed to obtain a PVA with good predictive power (McCarthy et al. 2003). The results of some models can often change dramatically with different model assumptions and slight changes in parameters. Another problem is that models are still not sophisticated enough to include all possible parameters and cannot incorporate unanticipated future events, such as unusual weather events or the arrival of an invasive species. PVA does have value in demonstrating the possible impact of alternative management strategies. For this reason, attempts to utilize PVA as part of practical conservation efforts have already begun, as the following examples demonstrate. It will be valuable to revisit these studies in the future to determine if their predictions were accurate.

- *The Hawaiian stilt. Himantopus mexicanus knudseni* is an endangered, endemic bird of the Hawaiian islands (see photo in Box 18.1). Hunting and coastal development 70 years ago reduced the number of birds to 200, but protection has allowed recovery to the present population size of around 1400 individuals (Reed et al. 1998; Reed et al. in press). The goal of government protection efforts is to allow the population to increase to 2000 birds. A PVA was made of the species' ability to have a 95% chance of persisting for the next 100 years. Models treated the stilts as either one continuous population or six subpopulations inhabiting individual islands. Given the stilts' current positive growth under present conditions, the models predicted that stilt numbers will increase until they occupy all available habitat, but they will show a rapid decline if nesting failure and mortality rates of first-year birds exceed 70%, or if the mortality rate of adults increases above 30% per year. To keep mortality rates below these values will require the control of hunting and exotic predators and the restoration of wetland habitat. And most importantly, additional wetland needs to be protected in order for the goal of protecting 2000 stilts to be achieved.

- *Cowslip.* A study of the rare, declining cowslips (*Primula veris*) of Europe and Asia shows that nitrogen deposition from air pollution and agricultural fertilizers is negatively affecting populations. Population simulations show that population decline is most rapid with high rates of nitrogen deposi-

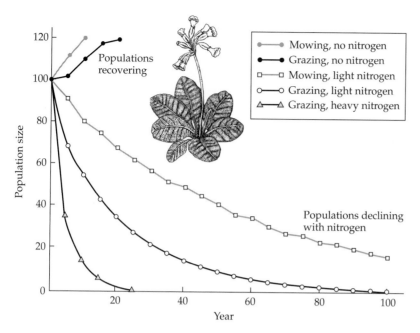

FIGURE 12.7 Simulations of future population size of populations of the cowslip, *Primula veris*, in nutrient-poor grasslands in Belgium, starting at an initial population size of 100 individuals. The population simulations were run for various levels of excess nitrogen deposition, combined with either mowing or grazing. Both light and heavy nitrogen deposition caused the population to decline. Nitrogen deposition stimulates tall plants to grow, shading out the cowslip plants. (After Brys et al. 2005.)

tion (Figure 12.7). Populations can be maintained only in low-nutrient environments with mowing or grazing only at the time of year when the plants are not flowering or fruiting (Brys et al. 2005).

• *Leadbeater's possum.* The most complete PVA ever undertaken is probably that of the Leadbeater's possum (*Gymnobelideus leadbeateri*), an endangered, arboreal marsupial inhabiting a rare type of eucalyptus forest in southeastern Australia (Lindenmayer 2000). Populations of this species are predicted to decline by more than 90% over the coming 20 to 30 years, due to habitat destruction caused by logging. Population models have been developed for the spatial distribution of habitat patches and dispersal corridors, den requirements, and forest dynamics. These models are based on extensive field research, and they have been used to estimate the impact of different logging management plans on the persistence of populations and the extinction of the species. The analyses all point to the need to manage the species at a landscape scale and over the entire present range of the species.

These examples illustrate the application of PVA to management situations. To be convincing, PVA must begin with a clear understanding of the ecology of the species, the threats it faces, and its demographic characteristics. In addition, the limitations of the model should be well understood (Morris and Doak 2002).

Metapopulations

Over time, populations of a species may become extinct on a local scale, while new populations may form nearby on other suitable sites. Many species of ephemeral habitats, such as streamside herbs, are characterized by a **metapopulation** (a "population of populations") that is made up of a shifting mosaic of populations linked by some degree of migration (Hanski and Simberloff 1997; Akçakaya et al. 2004; Harveson et al. 2004; Hoyle and James 2005). In some species, every population in the metapopulation is short-lived, and the distribution of the species changes dramatically with each generation. In other species, the metapopulation may be char-

(A)

Three independent
populations

(B)

Simple metapopulation of
three interacting populations

(C)

Metapopulation with a
large core population and
three satellite populations

(D)

Metapopulation with
complex interactions

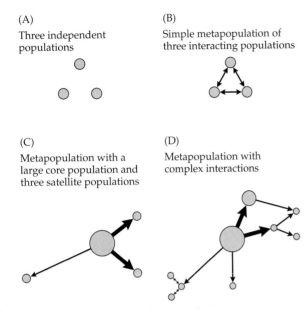

FIGURE 12.8 Possible metapopulation patterns, with the size of a population indicated by the size of the circle. The arrows indicate the direction and intensity of migration between populations. (After White 1996.)

acterized by one or more **source populations** (core populations) with fairly stable numbers, and several **sink populations** (satellite populations) that fluctuate with arrivals of immigrants. Populations in the satellite areas may become extinct in unfavorable years, but the areas are recolonized, or rescued, by migrants from the more permanent core population when conditions become more favorable (Figure 12.8). Metapopulations might also involve relatively permanent populations that individuals occasionally move between. Metapopulation structures have a further complexity in migratory species in which there are separate summer breeding grounds and overwintering areas, which may or may not be shared among populations (Esler 2000). Metapopulations also lend themselves to modeling efforts, and various programs have been developed for simulating them (Hokit et al. 2001; Donovan and Welden 2002). In one approach, metapopulation dynamics can be simulated by using PVA combined with spatial information on multiple populations.

The target of a population study is typically one or several populations, but a metapopulation may need to be studied to acquire a more accurate portrayal of the species. Metapopulation studies recognize that local populations are dynamic; that is, the locations of populations change over time, and individuals can move between populations and colonize new sites. Sites within the range of the species may be occupied only because they are repeatedly colonized after local extinction occurs; a reduction in migration rates between sites, perhaps caused by intervening roads and farms, would gradually result in the permanent extinction of local populations across the range of the metapopulation. Metapopulation models recognize that infrequent colonization events and migration occur, which allows biologists to consider the impact of founder effects, genetic drift, and gene flow on the species. Even infrequent movement of individuals between populations can restore much of the lost genetic variation, in effect genetically "rescuing" a small population otherwise headed toward extinction (Ingvarsson 2001). The following two examples demonstrate how evaluating species on the metapopulation level has proved to be more useful in understanding and managing many species than evaluating them on the single-population level.

- *California mountain sheep.* Mountain sheep (*Ovis canadensis*) in the desert of southeastern California exhibit the shifting mosaic of populations best described as a metapopulation. These sheep have been observed migrating between mountain ranges and occupying previously unpopulated sites, and mountains that previously had sheep populations are now unoccupied (Figure 12.9). Maintaining migration routes between known population areas and potentially suitable sites is important in managing this species.

- *Furbish's lousewort.* The endemic Furbish's lousewort (*Pedicularis furbishiae*) occurs along a 200-km stretch of the St. John's River in northern Maine and New Brunswick, Canada, that is subject to periodic flooding (Figure 12.10) (Menges 1990). Flooding often destroys some existing populations of this herb species but also creates exposed riverbank conditions suitable for establishing new populations. These populations eventually decline as the growth of shrubs and trees shade out the lousewort plants. Studies of any single population would give an incomplete picture of the species, because the current populations are short-lived. Dispersal of seeds from ex-

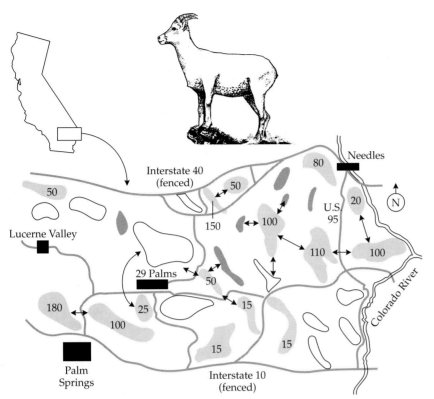

FIGURE 12.9 In 1990, mountain sheep in the southeastern California desert occupied the mountain ranges shown in light gray and had populations of the sizes indicated; open mountain ranges (the areas encircled by black lines) were unpopulated in 1990 but have had resident populations in the past. The mountains shown in dark gray have never had resident populations. Arrows indicate observed migrations of sheep. (After Bleich et al. 1990.)

isting populations to newly exposed soil suitable for colonization is a feature of the species. The metapopulation is really the appropriate unit of study for this species, and the watershed is the appropriate unit of management.

In metapopulations, destruction of the habitat of one central, core population might result in the extinction of numerous smaller populations that depend on the core population for periodic colonization (Gutiérrez 2005). Also, human disturbances that inhibit migration, such as fences, power lines, roads, and dams, might reduce the rate of migration among habitat patches and so reduce the probability of recolonization after local extinction. Habitat fragmentation resulting from these and other human activities sometimes has the effect of changing a large, continuous population into a metapopulation in which small, temporary populations occupy habitat fragments. When population size within each fragment is small and the rate of migration among fragments is low, populations within each fragment will gradually go extinct and recolonization will not occur.

Metapopulation models highlight the dynamic nature of population processes and show how eliminating a few core populations or reducing the potential for migration could lead to the local extinction of a species over a much wider area. This actually occurred with the California checkerspot butterfly (*Euphydryas* sp.): A large core population went extinct after an unmanaged grassland habitat underwent succession, followed soon after by the extinction of the satellite populations. Maintaining the butterfly would have required managing the site using periodic controlled fires or cattle grazing to keep the area in grassland. Effective management of a species often requires an understanding of these metapopulation dynamics and a restoration of lost habitat and dispersal routes.

FIGURE 12.10 The rare Furbish's lousewort occurs as a series of temporary populations that are best protected as a metapopulation.

Long-Term Monitoring of Species and Ecosystems

Monitoring of populations needs to be combined with monitoring of other parameters of the environment. The long-term monitoring of ecosystem processes (such as temperature, rainfall, humidity, soil acidity, water quality, discharge rates of streams, and soil erosion) and community characteristics (species present, percentage of vegetative cover, amount of biomass present at each trophic level, etc.) allows scientists to determine the health of the ecosystem and the status of species of special concern. Such monitoring is needed to distinguish normal year-to-year fluctuations from long-term trends (Magnuson 1990; Feinsinger 2001; Green et al. 2005; Steinbeck et al. 2005; Pereira and Cooper 2006). The Long-Term Ecological Research program in the United States focuses on changes that occur on time scales ranging from months and years to decades and centuries (Hobbie et al. 2003) (Figure 12.11).

For example, many amphibian, insect, and annual plant populations are highly variable from year to year, so many years of data are required to determine whether a particular species is actually declining in abundance over time or merely experiencing a number of low population years that are in accord with its regular pattern of variation. In one instance, a salamander species' low population numbers (based on several years of low breeding numbers) initially made it appear to be very rare. But in a subsequent favorable year for breeding, its population numbers turned out to be surprisingly large (Pechmann 2003). In another instance, 40 years of observation of populations of two flamingo species (*Phoenicopterus ruber,* the greater flamingo, and *Phoeniconaias minor,* the lesser flamingo) in southern Africa revealed that large numbers of chicks fledged only in years with high rainfall (Figure 12.12). However, the number of chicks fledging in the current populations is much lower than in the past, indicating that the species may be heading toward local extinction (Simmons 1996).

The fact that environmental effects may lag for many years behind their initial causes creates a challenge to understanding change in ecosystems. For example, acid rain, nitrogen deposition, and other components of air pollution may gradually change the water chemistry, algal community, and oxygen content of forest streams, ultimately making the aquatic environment unsuitable for the larvae of certain rare insect species. In this case, the cause (air pollution) may have occurred decades before the effect (insect decline) is detectable.

FIGURE 12.11 The Long-Term Ecological Research (LTER) program focuses on time scales ranging from years to centuries in order to understand changes in the structure, function, and processes of biological communities that are not apparent from short-term observations. (From Magnuson 1990.)

	Years	Research scales	Physical events	Biological phenomena
10^5	100 Millennia			Evolution of species
10^4	10 Millennia	Paleoecology and limnology	Continental glaciation	Bog succession Forest community migration
10^3	Millennium		Climate change	Species invasion Forest succession
10^2	Century		Forest fires CO_2-induced climate warming	Cultural eutrophication Population cycles
10^1	Decade			Prairie succession
10^0	Year		Sun spot cycle El Niño events Prairie fires Lake turnover	Annual plants Seasonal migration Plankton
10^{-1}	Month		Ocean upwelling	succession
10^{-2}	Day		Storms Daily light cycle Tides	Algal blooms Daily movements
10^{-3}	Hour	Most ecology		

LTER

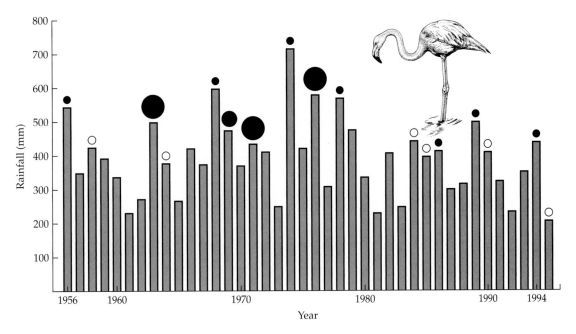

FIGURE 12.12 The bars show rainfall data from Etosha National Park for the years 1956 to 1995. The flamingo breeding events that occurred in those years are indicated by circles. Open circles indicate failed breeding events: Eggs were laid but no chicks hatched. The small, medium, and large black circles indicate, respectively, fewer than 100 chicks hatched, hundreds of chicks hatched, and thousands of chicks hatched. The last large hatching occurred in 1976. (From Simmons 1996.)

A major purpose of these monitoring programs is to gather essential data on ecosystem functions and biological communities that can be used to monitor changes in natural communities. Monitoring in these studies allows managers to determine if the goals of their projects are being achieved or if adjustments must be made in the management plans. Increasingly, monitoring of biological diversity is being combined with the monitoring of social and economic characteristics of the same area—tracking, for example, people's annual income, adequacy of diet, education level, and amount and value of plant and animal materials people obtain from nearby ecosystems—in recognition of the linkages between people and conservation (Bawa and Menon 1997). For example, the World Wildlife Fund's Biodiversity Conservation Network Program brings together biologists, social scientists, government officials, and local leaders to develop comprehensive monitoring programs for conservation projects. People who live in the local area are incorporated into the monitoring program because they know the area well and have the greatest interest in ensuring that the area is well-managed (Danielsen et al. 2000). Long-term monitoring provides an early-warning system for disruption or decline of ecosystem functions and the social systems of humans that depend on them. Magnuson (1990) expressed the need for long-term monitoring as follows:

> In the absence of the temporal context provided by long-term research, serious misjudgments can occur not only in our attempts to understand and predict change in the world around us, but also in our attempts to manage our environment. Although serious accidents in an instant of mismanagement can be envisioned that might cause the end of Spaceship Earth (sensu Fuller 1970), destruction is even more likely to occur at a ponderous pace in the secrecy of the invisible present.

Summary

1. Protecting and managing a rare or endangered species requires a firm grasp of its ecology and its distinctive characteristics, sometimes called its natural history. This essential knowledge covers the species' environment, distribution, biotic interactions, morphology, physiology, demography, behavior, genetics, and interactions with people. This information can be obtained from the published and unpublished literature, or from fieldwork. Long-term monitoring of a species in the field using inventories, surveys, and demographic studies can reveal temporal changes in population size and help to distinguish short-term fluctuations from long-term decline.

2. Population viability analysis (PVA) uses demographic, genetic, environmental, and natural-catastrophe data to estimate the probability of a population persisting in an environment to some future date. PVA can also be used to simulate the effects of various management actions.

3. Many species that reside in ephemeral habitats are characterized by metapopulations made up of a shifting mosaic of temporary populations that are linked by some degree of migration. In other species, the metapopulation may be characterized by one or more core populations with relatively stable numbers linked by dispersal to satellite areas with unstable, temporary populations.

4. Long-term monitoring efforts provide an early warning system for threats to species, communities, ecosystem functions, and human communities.

For Discussion

1. Read the paper on the Hawaiian stilt by Reed et al. (1998), the paper on the South African plant by Pfab and Witkowski (2000), or another PVA study. What are the strengths and weaknesses of PVA?

2. Construct models of various metapopulations using Figure 12.8 as a starting point. The simplest model would be an infinitely large core population that continuously sends out colonists to a satellite population, which is regularly destroyed by a catastrophic event such as a hurricane. Then include random variation in the frequency of hurricanes (destroying the population on average once every 4 years) and rate of colonization (sending out colonists on average once every 4 years). How realistic are your models?

3a. A construct your own PVA of an endangered toad species. This species formerly occupied many large islands, but now occupies only one small, isolated island in the middle of the Atlantic Ocean. There are presently 10 toads on the island, and the island can support a maximum of 20 toads. In the spring, males and females form mating pairs, and each pair can produce 0, 1, 2, 3, 4, or 5 offspring, all of which survive and reach maturity the following year (for example, flip 5 coins for each mated pair; the number of heads is the number of offspring). Individuals not mated because of uneven sex ratios do not breed. After the breeding season, the adult toads die. The sex of the offspring is assigned at random (for example, flip a coin for each animal with heads for males and tails for females, or use a random-number generator or simulation software such as VORTEX or RAMAS®).

3b. Run 10 population simulations of the island toad species for 10 generations each and chart population size over time. What percentage of populations go extinct? Try making the conditions more severe by lowering the island's carrying capacity to 15 (or even 10), or by imposing a 50% mortality on offspring every third year due to an introduced rat. Examine the impact of supplying extra food to the toads, which would allow more offspring to be produced per breeding pair. Make different variants of this basic model, corresponding to different ecological, genetic, and life history constraints. Use a computer program if possible.

Suggested Readings

Akçakaya, H. R., V. C. Radeloff, D. J. Mladenoff, and H. S. He. 2004. Integrating landscape and metapopulation modeling approaches: Vitality of the sharp-tailed grouse in a dynamic landscape. *Conservation Biology* 18: 526–547. The connections between populations need to be considered in determining whether a species can persist in a location.

Arnold, J. M., S. Brault, and J. P. Croxall. 2006. Albatross populations in peril: a population trajectory for black-browed albatrosses at South Georgia. *Ecological Applications* 16: 419–432. Monitoring demonstrates that intervention is needed to prevent the extinction of this species.

Chapman, C. A. and C. A. Peres. 2001. Primate conservation in the new millennium: The role of scientists. *Evolutionary Anthropology* 10: 16–33. Primate researchers need to become more actively involved in conservation efforts.

Donovan, T. M. and C. W. Welden. 2002. *Spreadsheet Exercises in Conservation Biology and Landscape Ecology.* Sinauer Associates, Sunderland, MA. A straightforward method for learning to build population models with some of the properties discussed in this chapter.

Feinsinger, P. 2001. *Designing Field Studies for Biodiversity Conservation.* Island Press, Washington, D.C. A guide to establishing a field research program for the conservation of species and communities.

Fossey, D. 1990. *Gorillas in the Mist.* Houghton Mifflin Company, Boston. Read the book, then watch the movie. Was she courageous or crazy?

Fox, D. 2004. The elephant listening project. *Conservation in Practice* 5: 30–37. Bioacoustics are a valuable new tool in monitoring animal populations.

Goodall, J. 1999. *Reason for Hope: A Spiritual Journey.* Warner Books, New York. This amazing woman explains her dedication to chimpanzees and people.

Gutiérrez, D. 2005. Effectiveness of existing reserves in the long-term protection of a regionally rare butterfly. *Conservation Biology* 19: 1586–1597. A metapopulation approach is needed to protect endangered butterflies.

Labonne, J. and P. Gaudin. 2005. Exploring population dynamics patterns in rare fish, *Zingel asper*, through capture-mark-recapture methods. *Conservation Biology* 19: 463–472. Fish present special challenges for population monitoring.

Laliberte, A. S. and W. J. Ripple. 2004. Range contractions of North American carnivores and ungulates. *BioScience* 54: 123–138. Census data shows changes—often dramatic declines—in population size.

Maschinski, J., J. E. Baggs, P. F. Quintana-Ascencio, and E. S. Menges. 2006. Using population viability analysis to predict the effects of climate change on the extinction risk of an endangered limestone endemic shrub, Arizona Cliffrose. *Conservation Biology* 20: 218–228. Models indicate that management efforts will be required to prevent the extinction of this species.

McCarthy, M. A., S. J. Andelman, and H. P. Possingham. 2003. Reliability of relative predictions in population viability analysis. *Conservation Biology* 17: 982–989. Good data and robust models are needed to predict future population sizes.

Morris, W. F. and D. F. Doak. 2002. *Quantitative Conservation Biology: Theory and Practice of Population Viability Analysis.* Sinauer Associates, Sunderland, MA. Introduction to PVA for conservation biology students.

Pereira, H. M. and H. D. Cooper. 2006. Towards the global monitoring of biodiversity change. *Trends in Ecology and Evolution* 21: 123–129. A large-scale program of monitoring could help to determine the effectiveness of efforts to protect biodiversity.

Pfab, M. F. and E. T. F. Witkowski. 2000. A simple PVA of the Critically Endangered *Euphorbia clivicola* R. A. Dyer under four management scenarios. *Biological Conservation* 96: 263–270. This article presents an application of PVA that is easy to understand.

Reed, J. M., C. S. Elphick, and L. W. Oring. 1998. Life-history and viability analysis of the endangered Hawaiian stilt. *Biological Conservation* 84: 35–45. Strategies of land management and land acquisition are analyzed for their impact on population size.

Steinbeck, J. R., D. R. Schiel, and M. S. Foster. 2005. Detecting long-term change in complex communities: a case study from the rocky intertidal zone. *Ecological Applications* 15: 1813–1832. Conservation biologists are learning that short-term changes are often deceptive; we need to be concerned with changes over longer time periods.

Zabel, R. W., M. D. Scheuerell, M. M. McClure, and J. G. Williams. 2006. The interplay between climate variability and density dependence in the population viability of Chinook salmon. *Conservation Biology* 20: 190–200. A variety of interacting factors determine the ability of these fish to persist in a changing world.

Establishing New Populations

In Chapters 11 and 12 we discussed the problems conservation biologists face in preserving naturally occurring populations of endangered species. This chapter discusses some exciting conservation methods to address those problems. These include establishing new wild and semi-wild populations of rare and endangered species and increasing the size of existing populations. These approaches allow species that have persisted only in captivity or in small, isolated populations to regain their ecological and evolutionary roles within the biological community.

Many species benefit from the complementary approaches of establishing new populations in the wild and developing captive breeding programs. Widely dispersed populations in the wild may be less likely to be destroyed by catastrophes (such as earthquakes, hurricanes, disease, epidemics, or war) than captive populations confined to a single facility or isolated wild populations occupying only a small area. Furthermore, increasing the number and size of populations for a species will generally reduce its probability of extinction.

Establishment programs are unlikely to be effective, however, unless the factors leading to the decline of the original wild populations are clearly understood and eliminated, or at least controlled. For example, the kakapo (*Strigops habroptilus*), a flightless parrot, has been eliminated from the New Zealand mainland because of predation by introduced domestic cats, weasels, stoats, and ferrets. In order for an establishment program to be successful, either these introduced predators would have to be removed from a large area, or the kakapo would have to be protected from predators in some way. Since neither of these options is possible at the present time, 56 birds have been established on five small islands where there are no introduced predators (Cockrem 2002). Therefore, a crucial initial step in establishing new populations is to locate suitable unoccupied sites for the species or to create new sites.

Three Approaches to Establishing New Populations

Three basic approaches have been used to establish new populations of animals and plants. A **reintroduction program*** involves releasing captive-bred or wild-collected individuals into an ecologically suitable site within their historical range where the species no longer occurs. The principal objective of a reintroduction program is to create a new population in its original environment. For example, a program initiated in 1995 to reintroduce gray wolves into Yellowstone National Park aims to restore the equilibrium of predators and herbivores that existed prior to intervention in the region by American wildlife managers (Box 13.1). Frequently, individuals are released near the site where they or their ancestors were collected to ensure genetic adaptation to their environment. Wild-collected individuals are also sometimes caught and later released elsewhere within the range of the species when a new protected area has been established, when an existing population is under a new threat and will no longer be able to survive in its present location, or when natural or artificial barriers to the normal dispersal tendencies of the species exist.

There are two other distinct types of release programs. An **augmentation program** involves releasing individuals into an existing population to increase its size and gene pool. These released individuals may be raised in captivity or may be wild individuals collected elsewhere. One special example of augmentation is "head-starting," an approach in which animals are raised in captivity during their vulnerable young stage and then are released into the wild. The release of sea turtle hatchlings produced from eggs collected from the wild and raised in nearby hatcheries is an example of an augmentation program. An **introduction program** involves moving captive-bred or wild-collected animals and plants to areas suitable for the species outside their historical range. This approach may be appropriate when the environment within the known range of a species has deteriorated to the point where the species can no longer survive there, or when reintroduction is impossible because the factor causing the original decline is still present.

The introduction of a species to new sites needs to be carefully considered and evaluated in order to ensure that the species does not damage its new ecosystem or harm populations of any local endangered species. Care must be taken that released individuals have not acquired any diseases while in captivity that could spread to and decimate wild populations. For example, captive, endangered black-footed ferrets must be carefully handled and quarantined so they do not acquire diseases from people and dogs that they might transfer into wild populations upon their release in North American grasslands (Figure 13.1). Also, a species may adapt genetically to the new environment where it is being released so that the original gene pool is not actually being preserved.

---

*Unfortunately, some confusion exists about the terms denoting the reintroduction of populations. These programs sometimes are called "reestablishments" or "restorations." Another term, "translocation," usually refers to moving individuals from a location where they are about to be destroyed to another site that often provides a greater degree of protection.

(A)

(B)

FIGURE 13.1 (A) A young black-footed ferret born at the captive colony in Sybille, Wyoming. (B) Cages within enclosures allow ferrets to experience the range where they will eventually be released. The ferrets' caretaker is wearing a mask to reduce the chance of exposing the ferrets to human disease. (Photographs by LuRay Parker, Wyoming Fish and Game Department.)

New populations can be established using different approaches and experimental treatments, which seek to help individuals make a successful transition to their new home—for example, giving supplemental food and water to the animals for a while as they learn about their new home; planting individual plants into a habitat from which competing plants have been removed. By carefully monitoring a variety of approaches, existing management techniques can be evaluated and new techniques developed (Falk et al. 1996; Goossens et al. 2005). These management techniques can then be applied to better manage existing natural populations of the species.

BOX 13.1

Wolves Return to A Cold Welcome

To the general public, "conservation" usually means saving endangered animal species on the verge of extinction—such as the California condor, with only around 120 remaining individuals, or the giant panda, estimated at fewer than 1100 in number. Although it is critical to try to prevent species extinctions, the ultimate goal of conservation is to restore damaged ecosystems to their previous balanced, functional state. Sometimes that involves reintroducing species into ecosystems to restore them—species that are abundant elsewhere and do not otherwise need reintroduction to protect them. An example of such a situation is the reintroduction of gray wolves into Yellowstone Park.

Until recently, Yellowstone National Park was an ecosystem out of balance, largely due to the systematic extermination of the Yellowstone gray wolf (*Canis lupus*) populations in the late 1800s and early 1900s. Wolves were believed to pose a threat to the herds of elk and other game animals inhabiting the park. The result of their extinction was a burgeoning population of elk and other herbivores that damaged vegetation and starved during times of scarcity. From a biological perspective, reintroducing wolves was necessary to restore ecological balance in the Yellowstone area through their effects on the populations of elk, deer, and other herbivores.

When the U.S. Fish and Wildlife Service proposed in 1987 that the gray wolf be reintroduced into Yellowstone National Park and surrounding government lands known as the Greater Yellowstone Area (GYA), opposition erupted

(continued)

BOX 13.1 *(continued)*

A gray wolf stalks an elk herd in Yellowstone National Park. As a result of the wolves' reintroduction to the park, elk have changed their behavior, congregating in dense herds and becoming more alert to danger. As a keystone predator, the activity of wolves has already altered the behavior and population numbers of many other species, including grizzly bears, coyotes, and carrion beetles. (Photograph by Bill Campbell.)

immediately. Ranchers in Montana, Wyoming, and Idaho argued that wolves would destroy livestock and possibly endanger humans as well (Smith et al. 2003). Hunters objected that wolves would reduce the supply of game animals, and logging and mining companies were concerned that the presence of a protected species would limit their ability to utilize resources on federal lands. Underpinning all these objections was the argument that the wolf, with an estimated population of 50,000 in Canada alone, is in no immediate danger of extinction. To accommodate these concerns, it was agreed that any wolf population at Yellowstone would be designated "experimental, nonessential," giving the wolves some degree of protection but allowing more flexible management to deal with wolves that left the park and attacked livestock.

In 1995 and 1996, elements of five wolf packs, as well as a few individuals, were transferred from Canada to the area (Smith 2005). The wolves were held in large pens for 10 weeks (to break their homing tendency) and then released. The wolves adapted well to the park, hunting prey and producing pups. As of 2005, a total of 300 free-ranging wolves have formed 33 packs, and most reside almost exclusively within the GYA (Smith et al. 2001;

Smith 2005). Because of the good health of the animals, there are large numbers of pups (71 surviving pups in 2000 alone) and an expanding wolf population.

The wolves' activities are reshaping the ecological structure of the park (Smith et al. 2003; Soulé et al. 2003; White and Garrott 2005). Elk are congregating in larger herds, and wolves are interacting with grizzly bears and coyotes. The availability of carrion from wolf kills is affecting the dynamics of scavengers, from grizzlies to carrion beetles. Some woody plant populations are recovering, due to reduced grazing pressure. Now one of the major attractions of Yellowstone National Park, wolves are having a positive economic impact as the featured subject of books and souvenirs sold to park visitors. The ecology and impact of wolves on the ecosystem have proved to be worthy of intensive study, with the participation of numerous scientists and student volunteers.

Fears that wolves would kill large numbers of livestock remain largely unfounded. Each year, wolves do kill some

The number of wolves in Wyoming, Idaho, and Montana has been increasing following the reintroduction of wolves to the Yellowstone area in 1995. There has also been an increase in domestic animals killed by wolves, primarily sheep, and an increase in the number of problem wolves killed by government authorities. (From Musiani et al. 2003.)

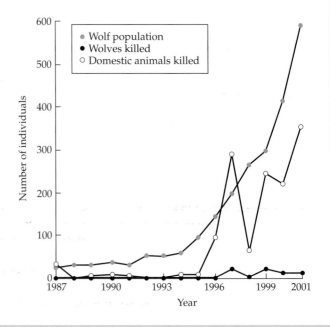

BOX 13.1 *(continued)*

cattle, sheep, and dogs, though these constitute a very small number compared with the 400,000 cattle alone living in the area. The number is also small in comparison with the millions of dollars invested in the project, its great ecological value to the Yellowstone area, and the tens of thousands of people who have visited the park or been exposed to the story of the Yellowstone wolves. These people may become supporters of the Yellowstone program or conservation programs like it as a result. In addition, an organization called Defenders of Wildlife has assumed responsibility for compensating ranchers for verified wolf kills, paying out $139,000 in 2004, but reactions by ranchers remain mixed. Wolves

that attack livestock on private land had previously been released onto government lands far away, but now they are killed by park officials because there is no land without wolves on which to release them (Musiani et al. 2003; Nyhus et al. 2003; Bradley et al. 2005). As the wolf population grows, so will the potential for depredations beyond park boundaries and for further conflict with ranchers.

Already the project has demonstrated that wolves can be reintroduced and the original ecosystem dynamics can be shifted back toward their original balance. But the success or failure of this project may rest on finding a compromise that moves ranchers and other private landowners from opposing the project to supporting it.

Considerations for Successful Programs

Establishing new populations is often expensive and difficult because it requires a serious, long-term commitment. The programs to capture, raise, monitor, and release California condors, peregrine falcons, and black-footed ferrets, for example, have cost millions of dollars and have required years of work. When the animals involved are long-lived, the program may have to continue for many years before its outcome is known.

Reintroduction programs can become highly emotional public issues, as demonstrated by the programs for the California condor, the black-footed ferret, the grizzly bear, and the gray wolf in the United States and comparable programs in Europe. Programs are often criticized on many different fronts. They may be attacked as a waste of money ("Millions of dollars for a few ugly birds!"), unnecessary ("Why do we need wolves here when there are so many elsewhere?"), intrusive ("We just want to go about our lives without the government telling us what to do!"), poorly run ("Look at all the ferrets that died of disease in captivity!"), or unethical ("Why can't the last animals just be allowed to live out their lives in peace without being captured and put into zoos?").

The answer to all of these criticisms is straightforward: Although reintroduction is not appropriate for every endangered species, a well-run, well-designed captive breeding and reintroduction program may be the best hope for preserving a species that is about to become extinct in the wild or is in severe decline. It is crucial to explain the need and the goals of the program to local people and to convince them to support the program or, at least, not to oppose it (Milton et al. 1999). Providing incentives to the local community as a part of the program often is more successful than imposing rigid restrictions and laws.

There is an important genetic component in selecting plants (Guerrant et al. 2004; Vilas et al. 2006) or animals for reintroduction programs. Captive populations may have lost much of their genetic variability. Genetic adaptations to the benign captive environment may occur in populations that have been raised for several generations in captive conditions, such as has occurred in the Pacific salmon (Waples et al. 2004), and may lower a species' ability to survive in the wild following release. Individuals have to be carefully selected to ensure against inbreeding depression and to produce the most genetically diverse release population (Vergeer et al. 2004). Also, to increase the chances that the individuals can survive, they must be selected from an environment and climate that are as similar as possible to the release site.

For some species, animals may require special care and assistance immediately to increase survival prospects (Kleiman 1989; Brightsmith et al. 2005). This approach is known as **soft release** (see Figure 13.1). Animals may have to be fed and sheltered at the release point until they are able to subsist on their own, or they may need to be caged temporarily at the release point and introduced gradually, until they become familiar with the area (Castro et al. 2003). Social groups abruptly released from captivity without assistance such as food supplementation (**hard release**) may disperse explosively from the protected area, resulting in a failed establishment effort. Intervention may be necessary if animals appear unable to survive, particularly during episodes of drought or low food abundance. Even when animals appear to have enough food to survive, supplemental feeding may lead to increased reproduction and allow the population to increase and persist. Outbreaks of diseases and pests may have to be monitored and dealt with. The impact of human activities in the area, such as farming and hunting, needs to be observed and possibly controlled. In every case, a decision has to be made whether it is better to give occasional temporary help to the species or to force the individuals to survive on their own.

Successful reintroduction programs often have considerable educational value. In Brazil, conservation and reintroduction efforts to protect golden lion tamarins have become a rallying point for the protection of the last remaining fragments of the Atlantic coastal forest. In the Middle East and North Africa, captive-bred Arabian oryx have been successfully reintroduced into many desert areas that they formerly occupied. In Oman, in particular, the reintroduction of the oryx created an important national symbol and a significant source of employment for the local Bedouins who ran the program (Stanley-Price 1989). However, despite almost two decades of successful management, the program in Oman was discontinued and all the animals brought back into captivity because of hunting and continuing thefts of animals to supply private collectors.

Establishment programs for common game species have always been widespread and have contributed a great deal of knowledge for the development of new programs for threatened and endangered species. A detailed study examined 198 bird and mammal establishment programs conducted between 1973 and 1986 that used both wild-caught and captive-reared animals. A number of significant generalizations were supported (Griffith et al. 1989):

1. Success was greater for releases in excellent quality habitat (84%) than in poor quality habitat (38%).

2. Success was greater in the core of the historical range (78%) than at the periphery of and outside the historical range (48%).

3. Success was greater with wild-caught (75%) than with captive-reared animals (38%).

4. Success was greater for herbivores (77%) than for carnivores (48%).

For these bird and mammal species studied, the probability of establishing a new population increased with the number of animals being released, up to about 100. Releasing more than 100 animals did not further enhance the probability of success. Certain of these results have been confirmed by a subsequent update and reanalysis (Wolf et al. 1996, 1998; Fischer and Lindenmayer 2000).

A second survey of reintroduction projects (Beck et al. 1994) analyzed a specific type of reintroduction: the release of captive-born animals within the historical range of the species. A program was judged a success if there was a self-maintaining population of 500 individuals. Using this narrower range of programs, only 16 out of 145 reintroduction projects were judged successful—a dramatically lower rate of success than the earlier survey, in which the majority of reintroductions were successful. An analysis consisting solely of ungulate reintroductions concluded that factors increasing the rate of success included: releasing at least 20 individuals, releasing a higher proportion of mature individuals, and having balanced sex ratios (Komers and Curman 2000). In many projects, success involves releasing large numbers of animals into suitable landscapes. A survey of more than 400 releases of short-lived fish species into wild habitats of the western United States showed a success rate of around 26%, though incomplete information on many species made compiling and evaluating the results extremely difficult (Hendrickson and Brooks 1991). Reintroductions and translocations of endangered amphibians, reptiles, and invertebrates appear to have an extremely low rate of success, perhaps due to their highly specialized habitat requirements (Platenberg and Griffiths 1999). The low success rate emphasizes the need to use many sites to increase the probability that the species establishes at least one population.

Clearly, monitoring ongoing programs is crucial in determining whether efforts to establish new populations are achieving their stated goals (e.g., see Hughes et al. 2003). Key elements of monitoring involve determining if released individuals survive and establish a breeding population, then following that population over time to see if it increases in numbers of individuals and geographical range. Monitoring of important ecosystem elements is also needed to determine the broader impact of a reintroduction; for example, when a predator is introduced, it will be crucial to determine its impact on prey species and competing species, and its indirect impact on vegetation (Berger et al. 2001). In an otter reintroduction program, for instance, the returned otter populations appealed to the general public, but the otters reduced populations of fish and crustaceans, which angered commercial fishermen (Fanshawe et al. 2003). Monitoring may need to be carried out over many years, even decades, because many reintroductions that initially appear successful eventually fail. For example, a reintroduction of topminnows into a stream in the western United States resulted in a large, viable population; however, a flood eliminated the population 10 years later (Minckley 1995). The costs of reintroduction need to be tracked and published to determine if reintroduction represents a cost-effective strategy. In the case of wild dogs in South Africa, reintroduction cost 20 times more than conserving existing packs in protected areas (Lindsey et al. 2005). Also, the results of monitoring need to be published in scientific journals so that successful methods can be incorporated into new reintroduction efforts (Fischer and Lindenmeyer 2000).

Social Behavior of Released Animals

To be successful, both introduction and reintroduction programs must often address the behaviors of animals that are being released (Festa-Bianchet and Apollonio 2003; Mathews et al. 2005). When social animals, including many mammals and some bird species, grow up in the wild they learn from other members of their population, particularly their parents, about their environment and how to interact with other members of their species. They learn how to search their environment for food and how to gather, capture, and consume it. For carnivores such as lions and wild dogs, hunting techniques are complex, subtle, and require considerable teamwork. To obtain the variety of food items necessary to stay alive and reproduce, frugivores such as hornbills and gibbons must learn seasonal migration patterns covering a wide area.

When mammals and birds are raised in captivity, their environment is limited to a cage or pen, so exploration is unnecessary. Searching for food and learning about

Introduce the concepts of learned & innate behaviors.

new food sources is not needed, since the same food items come day after day, on schedule. Social behavior may become highly distorted when animals are raised alone or in unnatural social groupings (i.e., in small groups or single-age groups). In such cases, animals may lack the skills to survive in their natural environment and the social skills necessary to cooperatively find food, sense danger, find mating partners, and raise young (McPhee 2003; Brightsmith et al. 2005).

To overcome these behavioral problems, captive-raised mammals and birds may require extensive training before and after release into the environment (Biggins et al. 1999). They must learn how to find food and shelter, avoid predators, and interact in social groups. Training techniques have been developed for several mammals and a few birds. Captive chimps, for instance, have been taught how to use twigs to feed on termites and how to build nests in captivity. Red wolves are taught how to kill live prey. Captive animals are taught to fear potential predators by pairing a frightening stimulus to a dummy predator when the dummy predator is shown.

Social interaction is one of the most difficult behaviors to teach captive-bred mammals and birds, because for most species the subtleties of social behavior are poorly understood. Nevertheless, some successful attempts have been made to socialize captive-bred animals (Valutis and Marzluff 1999). In one technique, humans mimic the appearance and behavior of the wild species. This method is particularly important when dealing with very young animals. For example, captive-bred condor hatchlings were originally unable to learn normal social bonds with other condors because they had imprinted on their human keepers. Newly hatched condors are now fed with condor puppets and kept from the sight of visitors so they learn to identify with their own species rather than a foster species or humans (Figure 13.2). However, even with such training, when captive-raised condors were released

FIGURE 13.2 California condor chicks raised in captivity are fed by researchers using puppets that look like adult birds. Conservation biologists hope that minimizing human contact with the birds will improve their chances of survival when they are returned to the wild. (Photograph by Mike Wallace, The Los Angeles Zoo.)

into the wild in protected areas, they often congregated around buildings, causing damage and frightening people. To break this association, condors are now being captive-reared in an enclosed outdoor area without any buildings.

When captive-bred animals are released into the wild as part of an augmentation program, developing social relationships with wild animals may be crucial to their success. Sometimes they join existing social groups or mate with wild animals and so gain some knowledge of their environment (Brightsmith et al. 2005). Failure to associate with wild birds during migration appears to be one of the reasons for the high mortality rate of captive-raised bald ibis (*Geronticus eremita*) (Akçakaya 1990). Eighty-eight chicks of the Mauritius kestrel (*Falco punctatus*) raised in captivity by humans and then given a soft release into the wild, however, did not have a significantly different survival rate from 284 chicks born in the wild (Powell and Cuthbert 1993; Nicoll et al. 2004).

Animal Reintroduction Case Studies

The following four case studies illustrate the various approaches to animal species reintroductions:

- *Red wolves.* Red wolves (*Canis rufus*) have been reestablished in the Alligator River National Wildlife Refuge in northeastern North Carolina through the release of 42 captive-born animals starting in 1987. Currently 100 animals occupy around 600,000 ha (1.5 million acres) of private and government land, including a military base. Animals in the program have produced pups, established packs, and survive by hunting deer, raccoons, rabbits, and rodents (Kelly and Phillips 2000; www.fws.gov/alligatorriver/redwolf.html). Even though the Red Wolf Recovery Program appears to be successful, many landowners remain unwilling to accept the presence of wolves on their land. Mating in the wild between red wolves and coyotes is probably the greatest threat to the species, because it obscures species differences.

- *Kemp's Ridley sea turtles.* Attempts have been made to stop the rapid decline of Kemp's Ridley sea turtles (*Lepidochelys kempii*) by collecting wild eggs from a Mexican beach, raising the hatchlings for one year in captivity, and releasing them in the wild on North Padre Island, Texas (Frazier 2000). Despite having released 22,000 "headstarted" hatchlings between 1978 and 1988, only 32 turtles have returned to breed on the beaches, with at least 6 having come from the headstarting program. Due to the low rate of success and high cost of the program, large-scale releases of turtles were discontinued. Modeling studies of sea turtle populations have subsequently shown that high mortality of turtles in commercial fishing operations is the cause of population decline and needs to be the primary target of conservation efforts (Lewison et al. 2003).

- *The kakapo.* The kakapo (*Strigops habraptilus*) is not only the largest parrot species in the world, it is also flightless, nocturnal, and solitary. The New Zealand kakapo was believed extinct because of introduced mammalian predators, but two small populations were discovered in the late 1970s. These populations were declining in numbers, requiring urgent action to save the species. Sixty-five kakapos were collected in the wild and released on three offshore islands that lacked most of their predators. Breeding success on the islands, while initially low, improved following supplemental feeding of adults with apples, sweet potatoes, and native seeds. Chick survival is gradually being improved by artificial incubation of eggs, raising chicks in captivity, and releasing young birds back into the wild. The current population size is 56 birds, which is expected to increase (www.kakaporecovery.org.nz).

- *Big Bend gambusia.* The Big Bend gambusia (*Gambusia gaigei*), also called the Big Bend mosquitofish, is a small fish originally known from two small springs in Texas. One population was eliminated when one spring dried up in 1954; at the same time, the second population began to decline rapidly when its spring was diverted to create an artificial fishing pond, and by 1960 it too had disappeared. In the interim, however, two females and one male had been taken from the artificial pond to establish a captive breeding program. A combination of captive breeding and releases into new artificial ponds in Big Bend National Park helped the species survive a series of droughts and invasions by exotic fish. In 1983 the species was reestablished in its original spring, and the natural flow of the spring is now mandated under the management plan for this protected species. A captive population is still maintained in a fish hatchery in New Mexico, however, in the event that the wild population declines again.

Establishing New Plant Populations

Methods used to establish new populations of rare and endangered plant species are fundamentally different from those used to establish terrestrial vertebrate animal species. (Falk et al. 1996; Primack and Drayton 1997; Montalvo and Ellstrand 2001). Animals can disperse to new locations and actively seek out the most suitable microsite conditions. In the case of plants, seeds are dispersed to new sites by agents such as wind, animals, water, or the actions of conservation biologists (Primack and Miao 1992); alternatively, either wild-collected or greenhouse-grown adults can be planted at the site to bypass the vulnerable seedling stage, a practice analogous to "headstarting." Once a seed lands on the ground or an adult is planted at a site, it is unable to move, even if a suitable microsite exists just a few meters away. The immediate microsite is crucial for plant survival—if the environmental conditions are in any way too sunny, too shady, too wet, or too dry, either the seed will not germinate or the resulting plant will not reproduce or will die.

Disturbance in the form of fire or tree falls may also be necessary for seedling establishment in many species; therefore, a site may be suitable for seedling establishment only once every several years. Careful site selection is thus critical in plant reintroductions. Plants and seeds need to be obtained from a site as similar as possible to the new site to ensure that they are genetically suited to the conditions of the new site (Montalvo and Ellstrand 2001; Vergeer et al. 2004). However, just as with animal reintroductions, identifying the factors that caused the original decline in the plant species is critical for success. In California, for example, many rare native plants are being outcompeted by introduced annual grasses. Developing management techniques to control or eliminate these grasses is an essential part of the reintroduction process (Guerrant and Pavlik 1998).

Plant populations typically fail to establish from introduced seeds at most sites that appear to be suitable for them. In one study, large numbers of seeds of six species of annual plants were planted at 48 apparently suitable sites (Primack 1996). Of these 48 attempts, new populations persisted for 2 years at only 5 sites, and for 6 years at only 1 site. At this single, apparently successful site, the population had increased to more than 10,000 individuals and had spread 30 m around the margins of a marshy pond (Figure 13.3). Subsequent attempts to establish new populations of 35 species of perennial herbs by sowing seeds at 173 apparently suitable sites had an even lower rate of success: no seedlings at all were seen at 167 of the 173 sites, and no individuals at all were seen for 32 of the 35 species.

To increase their chances of success, botanists often germinate seeds in controlled environments and grow the young plants in protected conditions (Figure 13.4). Only after the plants are past the fragile seedling stage are they transplanted into the wild. Planting must be executed using the techniques appropriate to the species (plant-

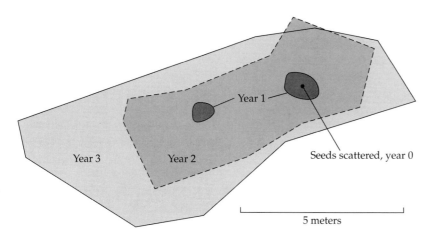

Year 1

Year 3

Year 2

Seeds scattered, year 0

5 meters

FIGURE 13.3 Sometimes a new plant population can be established by the introduction of seeds. In year 0, 100 seeds of *Impatiens capensis*, an annual species of jewelweed, were introduced into an unoccupied site in Hammond Woods, near Boston, Massachusetts. The seeds were scattered within 1 m of a stake (black dot). In year 1, two groups of plants separated by several meters had established themselves (darkest gray areas). The populations continued to expand in year 2 (as shown by the limits in dashed lines) and year 3 (solid lines). By year 7, population size had grown to more than 10,000 individuals and had spread 30 m. (After Primack 1996.)

ing depth, watering, time of day, time of year, site preparation, and so on) to ensure survival. Transplanted seedlings and adults often flower and fruit one or more years earlier than plants growing from seed sown directly into the wild, which increases the potential for seed dispersal and the formation of a second generation of plants (Guerrant et al. 2004).

While transplanting seedlings and adults may generally have a better chance of ensuring that the species survives at a new location, it does not perfectly mimic a natural process, and the new population may fail to produce seed and form the next generation. Plant ecologists are currently trying to work out new techniques to overcome these difficulties, such as fencing to exclude animals, removal of some of the existing vegetation to reduce competition, controlled burning, planting other species to provide shade and leaf litter in arid regions, and adding mineral nutrients to the soil (Figure 13.5). Keys to success seem to be using multiple sites, using as many seeds or transplants as possible, and reintroducing species over several successive years at the same site (Primack and Drayton 1997). Reintroductions require careful monitoring of the numbers of seedlings and adults to determine if the project is a success. A successful project (Guerrant et al. 2004) would have a self-maintaining—or even growing—population with subsequent generations of plants replacing the reintroduced individuals. In some cases, new populations that initially appeared to be well-established have died out in subsequent years. As research on this rapidly developing topic is published and synthesized, hopefully the chances for successful plant reintroductions will improve.

PLANT REINTRODUCTION CASE STUDIES The following two case studies illustrate experimental approaches to the reintroduction of plant species:

FIGURE 13.4 Seedlings of rare plant species being grown on a greenhouse bench; they were subsequently planted in the wild. Plant reintroductions from seed usually fail; they are often more successful when plants are grown from seeds or cuttings in a separate location and then transplanted into their new home site as seedlings or mature plants. (Photograph by R. Primack.)

FIGURE 13.5 A variety of methods are being investigated to create new populations of rare wildflower species on U.S. Forest Service land in South Carolina. Seeds are being planted in a pine forest from which the oak understory has been removed. Wire cages will be placed over some plantings to determine if excluding rabbits, deer, and other animals will help in plant establishment. (Photograph by R. Primack.)

- Mead's milkweed (*Asclepias meadii*) is a threatened perennial plant of tall-grass prairies in the midwestern United States. This species is a genetically diverse obligate outbreeder with low reproductive rates. Genetically heterogeneous populations have been restored using different establishment techniques in an experimental approach (Bowles et al. 1998; Bell et al. 2003). Survivorship has been greater for juvenile plants than for seedlings, and survival has been higher in burned habitat than in unburned habitat (Figure 13.6). Seedling survival was also higher in 1996 with greater than average rainfall. Using the information, burning is now being used to manage natural populations of this species.

- *Knowlton's cactus* (*Pediocactus knowltonii*) is a tiny, perennial cactus known only from one narrow hilltop location in northwestern New Mexico (Figure 13.7). Despite the fact that the site is now owned by The Nature Conservancy, this threatened species remains vulnerable to human disturbance from oil and gas exploration, livestock grazing, and removal of plants by col-

[handwritten margin note: Important point — "natural" plant survival is often very low — thus, should huge successes be expected?]

FIGURE 13.6 Planted seedling and juvenile Mead's milkweeds are evaluated in a reintroduction experiment. Survivorship is greater for juvenile plants than for seedlings, and greater in burned habitat than in unburned habitat. Seedling survivorship is greatest in 1996, a year with high rainfall. (From Bowles et al. 1998).

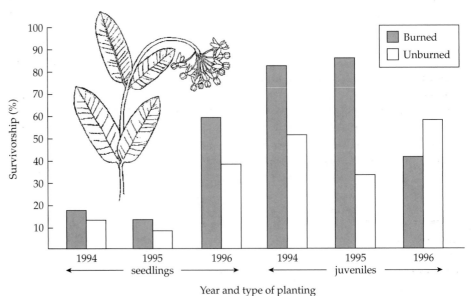

lectors. To reduce the possibility of extinction, two nearby, comparable sites were selected for introductions in 1985 (Cully 1996). At one site, 150 individuals grown from cuttings were planted and watered. As of 2002, 40% of the plants are still alive, with about half of them flowering and fruiting, but still no second generation has developed. Using a different approach, only 8 plants had been produced from 408 seeds sown at the same site.

The Status of New Populations

The establishment of new populations raises some novel issues at the intersection of scientific research, conservation efforts, government regulation, and ethics. These issues need to be addressed because reintroduction, introduction, and augmentation programs will increase in the coming years as the biological diversity crisis eliminates more species and populations from the wild, and many of the reintroduction programs for endangered species are mandated by official recovery plans set up by national governments.

Programs and research increasingly are being hampered by endangered species legislation that restricts the possession and use of endangered species (Reinartz 1995; Falk et al. 1996). If government officials rigidly apply these laws to scientific research programs, which was certainly not the original intent of the legislation, the programs will be blocked, and any possible creative insights and new approaches that could have come out of them will be lost. Projects to establish experimental populations sometimes have been delayed for more than five years while waiting for government approval. New scientific information is central to reintroduction programs and other conservation efforts. Government officials who block reasonable scientific projects may be doing a disservice to the organisms they are trying to protect. The potential harm to endangered species caused by carefully planned scientific research is relatively insignificant when compared with the actual massive loss of biological diversity being caused by habitat destruction and fragmentation, pollution, and overexploitation.

FIGURE 13.7 Knowlton's cactus (*Pediocactus knowltonii*) growing in New Mexico. The coin shown for scale is 1.9 cm (0.75 in) in diameter. (Photograph courtesy of The Nature Conservancy.)

Experimental populations of rare and endangered species—those that are successfully created by reintroduction and introduction programs—are given various degrees of legal protection. The U.S. Endangered Species Act recognizes two categories of experimental populations: "Experimental, essential" populations are regarded as critical to the survival of endangered species and are as rigidly protected as naturally occurring populations. "Experimental, nonessential" populations are not considered essential to the survival of a species and are not protected under the Act. Designating populations as nonessential, as was done for the gray wolf release in the Greater Yellowstone area, means that local landowners are not limited by the provisions of the Act and may be less inclined to oppose the creation of an experimental population. The disadvantage of this designation is that landowners can shoot or kill animals they perceive as a threat without any legal consequences.

Sometimes reintroduction programs are misused. In many cases, proposals are made by developers to create new habitat or new populations to compensate for the habitat damage or the eradication of populations of endangered species that occurred during a development project. This is generally referred to as **mitigation**. Mitigation is often directed at legally protected species and habitats. Proposals to establish new populations of endangered species merely for the convenience and profit of developers should be regarded with considerable skepticism. Claims that the loss of biodiversity can be mitigated are usually exaggerated. Given the poor success of most attempts to create new populations of rare species, protection of existing populations of rare species should be given the highest priority. While the replacement and restoration of damaged habitat such as wetlands may be beneficial, at least with respect to certain species and some ecosystem functions, artificially created wetlands are generally neither as biologically rich nor as functionally useful as natural wetlands in terms of water storage capacity and ability to break down sewage and other human pollutants (Zedler 1996). Legislators, environmental engineers, and scientists alike must understand that the establishment of new populations through reintroduction programs in no way reduces the need to protect the original populations of the endangered species. Original populations are more likely to have the most complete gene pool of the species and the most intact interactions with other members of the biological community. Reintroduction is not an alternative to the protection of existing populations and species, it is an additional tool to achieve a common end: increased survival probability in the wild. Finally, conservation biologists must be able to explain the benefits and limitations of reintroduction programs in a way that government officials and the general public can understand, and they must address the legitimate concerns of those groups (Musiani et al. 2003; Guerrant et al. 2004). One way this can be facilitated is by biologists incorporating citizen groups, in particular school groups, into reintroduction efforts. When people have the experience of working on reintroduction projects, they become more knowledgeable about the issues and often become advocates for conservation.

Summary

1. One approach to protect endangered species involves establishing new wild populations of those species. New populations of rare and endangered species can be established in the wild using either captive-raised or wild-caught animals. Reintroduction involves releasing individuals within the historical range of the species; introduction involves release of individuals at a site outside of the historical range of the species; augmentation involves releasing individuals into an existing population to increase population size and genetic variability.

2. Mammals and birds raised in captivity may lack the skills needed to survive in the wild. Some species require social and behavioral training before release, and some degree of maintenance after release ("soft release"). Establishment of a new population of a rare animal species is often not successful, but the potential for success is enhanced when the release occurs in excellent habitat within the historical range of the species and when large numbers of wild-caught animals are used.

3. Reintroductions of plant species require a different approach because of their specialized environmental requirements and inability to move. Current research focuses on improving site selection, habitat management and planting techniques.

4. Newly created populations of endangered species are sometimes given legal status as either "experimental, essential" or "experimental, nonessential" populations. Conservation biologists involved in establishing new populations of endangered species must be careful that their efforts do not weaken the legal protection currently given to natural populations of those species. Similarly, they must educate the public about the potential benefits and uncertainties of reintroduction efforts.

For Discussion

1. How do you judge whether a reintroduction project is successful? Develop simple and then increasingly detailed criteria to evaluate a project's success. Use demographic, environmental, and genetic factors in your evaluation.

2. Would it be a good idea to create new wild populations of African rhinos, elephants, and lions in Australia, South America, the southwestern United States, and other areas outside of their current range? What would be some of the legal, economic, and ecological issues?

3. Does our increasing ability to create new populations of rare and endangered species mean that we do not have to be concerned with protecting the known sites where these species occur? What are the costs and benefits of reintroduction programs?

4. Many endangered plant species are currently being propagated by commercial growers and botanical gardens and then sold (as both plants and seeds) to government agencies, conservation organizations, garden clubs, and the general public, who then in effect create new populations of these legally protected species (Reinartz 1995). There is little or no regulation of these sales or the subsequent plantings. What do you see as the advantages and disadvantages of this widespread activity? Should the propagation and planting of legally protected species be more closely regulated by the government?

5. What are the advantages and disadvantages of incorporating children into a local reintroduction project for wildflowers or butterflies? What concerns would their parents and teachers have?

Suggested Readings

Bowles, M. L. and C. J. Whelan (eds.). 1994. *Restoration of Endangered Species: Conceptual Issues, Planning, and Implementation.* Cambridge University Press, Cambridge. Good mixture of case studies, reviews, and analysis.

Clemmons, J. R. and R. Buchholz (eds.). 1997. *Behavioral Approaches to Conservation in the Wild.* Cambridge University Press, New York. Conservation projects need to pay careful attention to animal behavior and to adjust management practices accordingly.

Falk, D. A., C. I. Millar, and M. Olwell (eds.). 1996. *Restoring Diversity: Strategies for Reintroduction of Endangered Plants.* Island Press, Washington, D.C. Policy, biology, legal issues, case studies, and an appendix with practical guidelines.

Farnsworth, E. J. and J. Rosovsky. 1996. The ethics of ecological field experimentation. *Conservation Biology* 7: 463–472. Ecologists need to be able to justify their research to the government and the public and follow relevant regulations and laws.

Festa-Bianchet, M. and M. Apollonio (eds.). 2003. *Animal Behavior and Wildlife Conservation.* Island Press, Washington, D.C. A better understanding of animal behavior contributes to conservation efforts.

Fischer, J. and D. B. Lindenmayer. 2000. An assessment of published results of animal relocations. *Biological Conservation* 96: 1–11. A review of 180 relocation studies highlights factors leading to success: using wild-caught animals, releasing numerous animals, and removing the original cause of population decline.

Lindsey, P. A., R. Alexander, J. T. DuToit, and M. G. L. Mills. 2005. The cost efficiency of wild dog conservation in South Africa. *Conservation Biology* 19: 1205–1214. Correctly done reintroduction is often very expensive.

Mathews, F., M. Orros, G. Mclaren, M. Gelling, and R. Foster. 2005. Keeping fit on the ark: assessing the suitability of captive-bred animals for release. *Biological Conservation* 121: 569–577. Many animals raised in captivity have lost the behaviors needed to survive in the wild.

Milton, S. J., W. J. Bond, M. A. DuPleissis, D. Gibbs, et al. 1999. A protocol for plant conservation by translocation in threatened lowland Fynbos. *Conservation Biology* 13: 735–743. Describing the process of creating an organized program.

Minckley, W. L. 1995. Translocation as a tool for conserving imperiled fishes: Experiences in western United States. *Biological Conservation* 72: 297–309. Review of freshwater fish releases; also see other articles on fish conservation in this issue.

Nicoll, M. A. C., C. G. Jones, and K. Norris. 2004. Comparison of survival rates of captive-reared and wild-bred Mauritius kestrels (*Falco punctatus*) in a re-introduced population. *Biological Conservation* 118: 539–548. Case study of a species saved from the brink of extinction.

Primack, R. and B. Drayton. 1997. The experimental ecology of reintroduction. *Plant Talk* 11: 25–28. Investigation of the best methods for plant reintroduction in a beautiful magazine devoted to plant conservation.

Reinartz, J. A. 1995. Planting state-listed endangered and threatened plants. *Conservation Biology* 9: 771–781. Legal and moral issues involved in selling and planting endangered species.

Smith, D. W., R. O. Peterson, and D. B. Houston. 2003. Yellowstone after wolves. *BioScience* 53: 330–340. The Yellowstone ecosystem has been transformed by the reintroduction of wolves.

Snyder, N. and H. Snyder. 2000. *The California Condor: A Saga of Natural History and Conservation.* Academic Press, San Diego. People struggling to save the condor have to contend with difficult political, legal, and financial issues.

Tutin, C. E. G., M. Ancrenaz, J. Paredes, M. Vacher-Vallas, et al. 2001. Conservation biology framework for the release of wild-born orphaned chimpanzees into the Conkouati Reserve, Congo. *Conservation Biology* 15: 1247–1257. A model framework for a proposed release.

Vergeer, P., E. Sonderen, and N. J. Ouborg. 2004. Introduction strategies put to the test: Local adaptation versus heterosis. *Conservation Biology* 18: 812–821. Testing the importance of genetics in reintroductions.

Vilas, C., E. San Miguel, R. Amaro, and Carlos Garcia. 2006. Relative contribution of inbreeding depression and eroded adaptive diversity to extinction risk in small populations of Shore Campion. *Conservation Biology* 20: 229–238. Success in reintroduction is lowered if seeds resulting from inbreeding are used.

Ex Situ Conservation Strategies

The goal of conservation is to maintain biological diversity *in nature*, for the continued health of biological communities at all levels. For most species, the ideal strategy for the long-term protection of biological diversity would be the preservation of natural communities and populations in the wild, known as **in situ**, or on-site, **conservation**. Only in natural communities are such species able to continue their process of evolutionary adaptation to a changing environment. Community level interactions among species, as discussed in Chapter 2, are often crucial to rare species' continued survival; these interactions can be quite complex and probably cannot be replicated under captive conditions. Furthermore, captive animal populations are generally not large enough to prevent the loss of genetic variability through genetic drift; the same can also be true of plant species established in cultivation when they have special requirements for pollination that might make it difficult to ensure adequate cross-pollination among individuals. For such species, in situ conservation involving careful habitat protection and management would be the best solution.

In the face of increasing human activities, however, relying solely on in situ conservation is not currently a viable option for most rare species, and species that are under conservation management in situ may still decline and go extinct in the wild for any of the reasons already discussed: habitat destruction, loss of genetic variation and inbreeding depression, demographic and environmental variability, insufficient habitat, deteriorating habitat quality, habitat fragmentation, competition from invasive species, disease, and excessive hunting and collecting. If a remnant population is too small to maintain the species, if it is still declining despite conservation efforts, or if the remaining individuals are found outside of protected areas, then in situ preservation may not be adequate. It is likely that the only way species in such circumstances can be prevented from going extinct is to maintain individuals in artificial conditions under human supervision (Kleiman et al. 1996; Guerrant et al. 2004; Miller et al. 2004).

Ex situ (off-site) **conservation** used in place of or to complement in situ conservation can mean the difference between life and death for some species. For certain species, ex situ conservation can actually be superior to in situ conservation in terms of both its lower overall cost and its ability to rapidly augment small populations with captive-grown individuals drawn from a larger gene pool. Although it is always preferable to have a population in situ (the point of conservation, after all, is to maintain biological diversity in nature, not under glass or behind fences), ex situ methods are best viewed not as "second best" strategies but as complementary components of a larger, more comprehensive, integrated conservation strategy (Falk 1987, 1990). There are some species for which the original wild site or sites are so threatened or so badly degraded that attempting in situ conservation would be a death sentence for the species; ex situ methods are therefore more than simply a back-up plan, as they can mean the difference between a viable conservation plan and one that is unworkable.

Already a number of species that went extinct in the wild have survived because of propagation in captive colonies. Examples include Père David's deer (*Elaphurus davidianus*) and Przewalski's horse, or takhi (*Equus caballus przewalski*) (Figure 14.1). The beautiful Franklin tree (*Franklinia alatamaha*, see Figure 7.1) grows only in cul-

(A)

FIGURE 14.1 (A) Père David's deer (*Elaphurus davidinus*) has been extinct in the wild since about 1200 B.C. The species remained only in managed hunting reserves kept by Chinese royalty and is now kept in captive herds. (B) Przewalski's horse (*Equus caballus przewalski*) does well in captivity, but is now probably extinct in the wild. This species was once abundant in Central Asia and is the last living species of wild horse. Animals are now being reintroduced into grassland habitats in Mongolia. (Photographs by Jessie Cohen, National Zoological Park, Smithsonian Institution.)

(B)

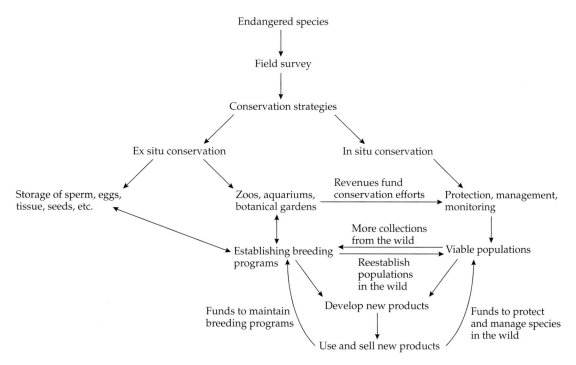

FIGURE 14.2 This model of biodiversity conservation shows the ways in which in situ (on-site) and ex situ (off-site) conservation efforts benefit each other and provide alternative conservation strategies. While no species exactly conforms to this somewhat idealized model, the giant panda program has many of its elements. (After Maxted 2001.)

tivation and is no longer found in the wild. In situations such as these, the long-term goal of many ex situ conservation programs is the eventual establishment of new populations in the wild, once sufficient numbers of individuals and a suitable habitat are available. In the case of Przewalski's horse, social groups were released in a national park in Mongolia starting in 1992. The population is showing steady growth, now numbering around 250 individuals (King and Gurnell 2005).

Ex situ facilities for animal preservation include zoos, aquariums, sanctuaries, game farms, and private breeders, while plants are maintained in botanical gardens, arboretums, and seed banks. An intermediate strategy that combines elements of both ex situ and in situ preservation is the monitoring and management of populations of rare and endangered species in small, protected areas; such populations are still somewhat wild, but human intervention may be necessary occasionally to prevent population decline.

As mentioned earlier, ex situ and in situ conservation are complementary strategies (Miller et al. 2004). Individuals from ex situ populations can be periodically released into the wild to augment in situ conservation efforts (Figure 14.2). Research on captive populations can provide insight into the basic biology of the species and suggest new conservation strategies for in situ populations. The ease of access to individual animals afforded in captivity allows scientists to develop and test relevant technologies (e.g., radio collars) that enhance the study and preservation of the species in the wild. Long-term, viable ex situ populations can also reduce the need to collect individuals from the wild for display and research. Captive-bred individuals on display can help to educate the public about the need to preserve the species and so protect other members of the species in the wild. The number of people visiting zoos is enormous; over 600 million people visit the world's zoos every year (Figure 14.3). Zoos, aquariums, and botanical gardens,

FIGURE 14.3 Modern zoos offer educational opportunities to the public in addition to serving as sanctuaries for animals. These zoo visitors are enjoying a close-up view of king penguins, a flightless bird that they would not normally see in the wild. (Photograph © Rough Guides/Alamy.)

and the people who visit them, regularly contribute money to in situ conservation programs. In addition, ex situ programs can be used to develop new products that potentially can generate funds from profits or licensing fees to protect species in the wild. In situ preservation of species, in turn, is vital to the survival of species that are difficult to maintain in captivity, as well as to the continued ability of zoos, aquariums, and botanical gardens to display species.

Limitations of Ex Situ Conservation

Ex situ conservation should not be regarded as the ideal solution for preserving all or even most species on the verge of extinction. Short- and long-term costs, limited population size, adaptation to artificial environments, inability to learn survival skills, and the potential for genetic drift are all significant concerns with ex situ preservation (Snyder et al. 1996). We will now address some of the limitations of ex situ conservation in detail.

• *Cost.* Particularly with respect to large animals, ex situ conservation is not cheap. Zoos are considerably more expensive to operate than many other conservation programs, and protecting individual species in this setting simply isn't cost effective as a single strategy; for example, the cost of maintaining African elephants and black rhinos in zoos is 50 times greater than protecting the same number of individuals in East African national parks (Leader-Williams 1990), so it is obvious that protecting these animals in the wild is a far better option. In such cases, an entire community consisting of thousands or tens of thousands of species is preserved, along with a range of ecosystem services. But it is also true that zoos and aquariums are able to attract money from visitors and donors that allows them to maintain populations of captive animals and use them as "ambassadors" to raise money for the protection of their wild counterparts. For smaller animal species, or for plant or animal species in which habitat preservation and management is prohibitively expensive, ex situ conservation can be more effective than attempting to sustain a wild population. The cost of maintaining each new captive chick of the endangered Puerto Rican parrot is $22,000; while this sounds expensive, it compares favorably with the $1 million spent per year to protect the declining wild population of 28 birds (Engeman et al. 2003).

• *Population size.* To prevent genetic drift, ex situ populations of at least several hundred and preferably several thousand individuals need to be maintained. Because of space limitations, no one zoo can maintain such large numbers of any of the larger animal species. Globally, only a few vertebrate species are maintained in captivity at such numbers, and these populations are distributed across tens and even hundreds of institutions. In botanical gardens, only one or a few individuals of most species typically are maintained, especially in the case of trees.

- *Adaptation.* Ex situ populations may undergo genetic adaptation to their artificial environment. For example, animal species conditioned to rapidly flee a predator will often not thrive in a fenced-in enclosure. The more docile, less reactive individuals are more likely to reproduce, and so the zoo population will change genetically over time. If the animals from this captive population are later returned to the wild, they may no longer be able to evade their natural enemies.

- *Learning skills.* Individuals in ex situ populations may be ignorant of their natural environment and unable to survive in the wild. For example, captive-bred animals released back into the wild may no longer recognize wild foods as edible or their predators as dangerous, or be able to locate water sources. This problem is most likely to occur among social mammals and birds, whose juveniles learn survival skills and locations of critical resources from adult members of the population. Migratory animals may not know where or when to migrate.

- *Genetic variability.* Ex situ populations may represent only a limited portion of the gene pool of the species. If a captive population was started using individuals collected from a warm lowland site, for example, these animals may be unable to adapt physiologically to colder highland sites formerly occupied by the species.

- *Continuity.* Ex situ conservation efforts require a continuous supply of funds and a steady institutional policy. While this is also true to some extent for in situ conservation efforts, interruption of care in a zoo, aquarium, or greenhouse lasting only days or weeks can result in considerable losses of both individuals and species. Frozen and chilled collections of sperm, eggs, tissues, and seeds are particularly vulnerable to the loss of electric power. The breakup of the former Soviet Union, deterioration of the Russian economy, and civil wars in its outlying states illustrate how rapidly conditions can shift in a country. Zoos will not be able to maintain their collections under such circumstances.

- *Concentration.* Because ex situ conservation efforts are sometimes concentrated in one relatively small place, there is a danger of an entire population of an endangered species being destroyed by a catastrophe such as a fire, hurricane, or epidemic.

- *Surplus animals.* Some species breed too easily in captivity. What should be done with these surplus animals that no other zoo wants and that have no chance of surviving in the wild? This ethical issue must be addressed: the welfare of any animal taken into human custody is the responsibility of its captors. It is often unacceptable to kill or sell an individual animal, particularly when each animal in a highly threatened species might represent a key component of the species' future survival.

In spite of these limitations, ex situ conservation strategies may prove to be the best—perhaps the only—alternative when in situ preservation of a species is difficult or impossible. As Michael Soulé says, "There are no hopeless cases, only people without hope and expensive cases" (Soulé 1987).

Ex Situ Conservation Facilities

The most common types of ex situ conservation facilities currently in use are zoos, aquariums, botanical gardens, and seed banks. In this section, we'll examine each of these facilities to determine their role in conservation programs.

Zoos

A current goal of most major zoos is to establish viable, long-term captive breeding populations of rare and endangered animals (Lyles 2001). Zoos have traditionally focused on maintaining large vertebrates—especially mammals—since these species are of greatest interest to the general public, whose entrance fees fund zoo budgets. In the past, these animals were typically displayed as curiosities in cages, without any relationship to a natural environment. The world's 2000 zoos and aquariums are increasingly incorporating ecological themes and information about the threats to endangered species in their public displays and their research programs as part of the World Zoo Conservation Strategy, which seeks to link zoo programs with conservation efforts in the wild (Ben-Ari 2001; Hancocks 2001; Praded 2002). The variety of species displayed has increased but the emphasis on "charismatic" megafauna such as pandas, giraffes, and elephants still holds because it helps to attract the general public and influence them favorably toward conservation. However, zoos must reach a better balance between displaying large animals to attract visitors and displaying smaller, lesser animals, such as insects, that comprise most of the world's animal species.

The potential educational and financial impact of zoos is enormous, considering that they receive approximately 600 million visitors per year. Educational programs at zoos, articles written about zoo programs, and zoo field projects all direct public attention to animals and habitats of conservation significance. If, for example, the general public becomes interested in protecting giant pandas after seeing them in zoos and reading about them, then money may be donated, pressure may be exerted on governments, and eventually appropriate habitat in China may be set aside as protected areas (Box 14.1). At the same time, thousands of other plant and animal species occupying these environments will be protected.

Zoos, along with affiliated universities, government wildlife departments, and conservation organizations, presently maintain over 400,000 individuals of terrestrial vertebrates, representing 7895 species and subspecies of mammals, birds, reptiles, and amphibians (Table 14.1). While this number of captive animals may seem

TABLE 14.1 *Number of terrestrial vertebrates currently maintained in zoos according to the International Species Inventory System (ISIS)*

Location	Mammals	Birds	Reptiles	Amphibians
Europe	72,789	82,292	21,826	7850
North America	50,651	57,019	28,870	16,679
Central America	5855	4082	1147	193
South America	2231	4014	1793	71
Asia	7314	16,044	2435	283
Australasia	5220	8754	3201	645
Africa	4265	8478	1549	129
Totals				
All species	148,325	180,683	60,821	25,850
Number of taxa[a]	2138	3563	1719	475
% wildborn[c]	7%	12%	18%	8%
Rare species[b]	34,743	95,670	31,613	2251
Number of taxa[a]	888	1292	485	26
% wildborn[c]	7%	13%	19%	7%

Source: Data from ISIS (2006, unpublished) and Laurie Bingaman Lackey (2006, personal communication).

[a]The number of taxa is not exactly equivalent to species because many species have more than one subspecies listed.

[b]Rare species are those covered by the Convention of International Trade in Endangered Species.

[c]The percentage of individuals born in the wild is only approximate (particularly for reptiles and amphibians), since the origin of the animals is often not given.

BOX 14.1

Love Alone Cannot Save The Giant Panda

The giant panda (*Ailuropoda melanoleuca*) is one of the most familiar endangered species in the world. It is so well known and so beloved by millions of people that its image is the symbol for the World Wide Fund for Nature (also known as the World Wildlife Fund), a prominent international conservation organization. Despite its popular appeal, the panda's future is in jeopardy. As with many endangered species, habitat destruction and fragmentation, a lack of knowledge about its behavior, and illegal hunting are the most significant threats to its survival (Loucks et al. 2003; Lindburg and Baragona 2004). Moreover, human pressure appears to exacerbate some of the unusual traits of the

A record 16 giant pandas were born in captivity in China in 2005 using the techniques of artificial insemination. The pandas are being raised as a group in a controlled nursery environment that is very different from their natural forest habitat. (Photograph © Li Wei/ChinaFotoPress.)

panda's physical and behavioral makeup that make this species particularly vulnerable to extinction.

One of the most unusual features of pandas is their diet of bamboo. However, bamboo species reproduce in long-term cycles of anywhere from 15 to over 100 years; typically, nearly all individuals in a given species within a certain area will flower and die in a single season. In the past, on those rare years when bamboos died off, pandas would travel to find remaining bamboo stands, especially in lowland areas. Now when agricultural areas, roads, and human settlements prevent them from migrating to lowland areas, pandas have nowhere to go during bamboo die-offs. In the 1970s, when several bamboo species flowered simultaneously over a large area, at least 138 pandas starved, and the population declined by more than 14%.

Following this catastrophe, the Chinese government tried to establish a self-sustaining captive breeding population. However, the success was low, as giant pandas are extremely selective in choosing mates while in captivity, and pandas paired by zoos and other breeding facilities often prove incompatible, or the zoos do not provide the pandas with enough time or enough mate choices. Also, pandas typically only give birth to one cub per season. Thus the rate of population growth is very slow even under the best conditions. Despite these problems, however, giant panda breeding has recently proved more suc-

cessful, due in part to a better understanding of nutrition, housing needs, and overall biology. Between 1963, when China first began to breed captive pandas, and 1989, only 90 cubs were born, of which only 37 survived for more than 6 months. After trying many methods, artificial insemination has emerged as the key to producing giant pandas in captivity. In 2005 alone, the Wolong Panda Protection and Breeding Center in Sichuan Provence, China carried out artificial insemination of 38 females, with 16 cubs born already and more soon to be born. However, a further issue is that captive-bred pandas lack the behavioral skills to ever be released into the wild. However, the captive breeding program is valuable in raising public interest and funds needed for in situ conservation. Currently, U.S. and European zoos with pairs of giant pandas on loan from China make large financial contributions for giant panda conservation programs in China. These contributions are required as part of the panda exchange program.

Fragmentation of habitat is another problem for the long-term survival of the species (Lindburg and Baragona 2004; Loucks et al. 2003). According to the last panda census released in 2004, there are around 1600 giant pandas occupying about 22,000 square kilometers of habitat scattered among more than 20 populations across 6 mountain ranges. As a result, the small populations, many

(continued)

BOX 14.1 *(continued)*

Pandas were once widely found in southern and eastern China, and even into Myanmar (Burma) and Vietnam. They are now restricted to a few areas along the eastern edge of the Tibetan Plateau. (After Schaller 1993.)

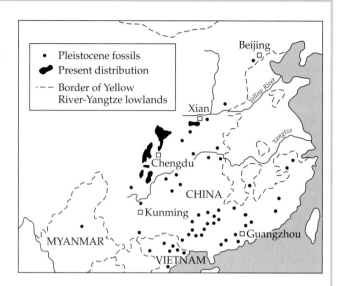

with less than 30 individuals, may eventually suffer from inbreeding depression. Many of the panda reserves are becoming more isolated over time due to habitat deterioration at the borders of the reserves by government projects and the activities of villagers (Li et al. 2003). Poaching pandas for their skins was formerly a serious problem that is now less common due to stiff penalties imposed by the Chinese government, but pandas still die in snares set by hunters for antelope, deer, and other game (Li et al. 2003).

The Chinese government has put significant financial resources into setting aside more habitat for the remaining wild pandas. Currently, there are 40 reserves covering 60% of the pandas' current habitat. However, it will not be easy for the reserves to withstand the pressure of China's immense human population. The pandas need more forest and bamboo, and protection from hunters—difficult resources to provide as people keep encroaching into their mountain refuges. Time will tell whether they will get what they need.

impressive, it is trivial in comparison to the numbers of domestic cats, dogs, and fish kept by people as pets. In the United States alone, about 50 million cats are kept as pets, over 100 times more than the world's total of zoo animals. Zoos could establish breeding colonies of even more species if they directed more of their efforts to smaller-bodied species such as insects, amphibians, and reptiles, which are less expensive to maintain in large numbers than large-bodied mammals such as giant pandas, elephants, and rhinos (Balmford et al. 1996). Many zoos are moving in this direction, with more displays of frogs and colorful butterflies that have popular appeal.

Zoos working with affiliated universities, government wildlife departments, and conservation organizations are the logical choices to develop captive populations of rare and endangered species because they have the needed knowledge and experience in animal care, veterinary medicine, animal behavior, reproductive biology, and genetics. Zoos and affiliated conservation organizations have embarked on a major effort to build facilities and develop the technology necessary to establish breeding colonies of these animals, and to develop the new methods and programs needed to reintroduce species in the wild (Conway et al. 2001). Some of these facilities are highly specialized, such as that run by the International Crane Foundation in Wisconsin, which is attempting to establish captive breeding colonies of all crane species. This effort has paid off. Currently, less than around only 7% of the terrestrial mammals kept in zoos have been collected in the wild, and this number is declining as zoos gain more experience (see Table 14.1). For endangered mammals, again, only around 7% of captive individuals were captured in the wild.

For common animals such as the raccoon and the white-tailed deer, there is no need to establish breeding colonies and conservation programs since individuals of these species can be readily obtained from the wild. The real need is for zoos to establish sustainable, captive populations of rare species that can no longer be readily captured in the wild, such as the orangutan, Chinese alligator, and snow leopard.

CAPTIVE BREEDING METHODS AND TARGETS   The success of captive breeding programs has been enhanced by efforts to collect and disseminate knowledge about the maintenance of rare and endangered species. The Species Survival Commission's Conservation Breeding Specialist Group, a division of the IUCN, and affiliated organizations, such as the American Zoo and Aquarium Association, the European Association of Zoos and Aquaria, and the Australasian Regional Association of Zoological Parks and Aquaria, provide zoos with the necessary information for proper care and handling of these species, as well as updates on the status and behavior of animals in the wild (www.aza.org). This includes data on nutritional requirements, anesthetic techniques to immobilize animals and reduce stress during transport and medical procedures, optimal housing conditions, vaccinations and antibiotics to prevent the spread of disease, and breeding records. This effort is being aided by a central database called ARKS, the Animal Record Keeping System, maintained by the International Species Inventory System (ISIS), which keeps track of all relevant information on 2 million animals belonging to 10,000 species at 650 member institutions in 70 countries. Such a database is an important tool in monitoring health trends in zoo populations.

Some rare animal species do not adapt or reproduce well in captivity. In many cases, better care of the animal's particular nutrition and housing needs has overcome these problems. In addition, new techniques are being developed to enhance the low reproductive rates of such species (Lanza et al. 2000; Holt et al. 2003). Some of these come directly from human and veterinary medicine, while others are novel methods developed at special research facilities such as the San Diego Zoo's Center for Reproduction of Endangered Species, the Audubon Institute Species Survival Center in New Orleans, and the Durrell Wildlife Conservation Trust at the Jersey Zoo. For example, foster parents from a common species can be used to raise the offspring of a rare species in an approach known as **cross-fostering**. Many bird species, such as the bald eagle, normally lay only one clutch of eggs per year, but if biologists remove this first clutch of eggs, the mother bird will lay and raise a second clutch. If the first clutch of eggs is given to another bird of a common related species, two clutches of eggs will be produced per year for each rare female. This technique, known informally as "double-clutching," potentially doubles the number of offspring one female of a rare species can produce.

Another aid to reproduction, similar to cross-fostering, is **artificial incubation**. If a mother does not adequately care for her offspring, or if the offspring are readily attacked by predators, parasites, or disease, humans may care for them during their vulnerable early stages. This approach has been tried extensively with egg-laying species such as sea turtles, birds, fishes, and amphibians: Eggs are collected and placed in ideal hatching conditions; the hatchlings are protected and fed during their vulnerable early stages; and the young are then released into the wild or raised in captivity. This approach is sometimes called "head-starting" (see Chapter 13).

Individuals of some animal species lose interest in mating while in captivity, or a zoo may have only one or a few individuals of a rare species such as the giant panda. In these circumstances, **artificial insemination** can be used when an isolated female animal comes into breeding condition, either on her own or after being chemically induced. Sperm is collected from suitable males, stored until needed at low temperatures, and then used for artificial insemination with a receptive female. While artificial insemination is performed routinely with many domesticated animal species, the exact techniques of sperm collection, sperm storage, recognition of female receptivity, and sperm delivery have to be worked out separately for each species in a conservation breeding program.

Embryo transfer has been accomplished successfully in a few rare animals such as the bongo, gaur, and Przewalski's horse. Superovulation, or production of multiple eggs, is induced using fertility drugs, and the extra eggs are surgically collect-

FIGURE 14.4 This bongo calf (*Tragelaphus euryceros*), an endangered species, was produced by embryo transfer using an eland (*Taurotagus oryxi*) as a surrogate mother at the Cincinnati Zoo Center for Reproduction of Endangered Wildlife. (Photograph © The Cincinnati Zoo.)

ed, fertilized with sperm, and surgically implanted into surrogate mothers, sometimes using related common species. The surrogate mother carries the offspring to term and then gives birth (Figure 14.4). In the future, this technology may be used to increase the reproductive output of rare species.

Cutting-edge medical and veterinary technologies have the potential to develop innovative approaches for some species that are difficult to breed in captivity (Lanza et al. 2000). These include cloning individuals from single cells (when only one or a few individuals remain), cross-species hybridization (when the remaining members of a species cannot breed among themselves), induced hibernation and induced dormancy as a way of maintaining dormant populations, biochemical and surgical sexing of animals that have no external sex differences, and biochemical tracking of hormonal levels in urine and feces to determine the timing of sexual receptivity in females. One of the most unusual and controversial techniques involves freezing purified DNA, eggs, sperm, embryos, and other tissue of species on the verge of extinction in the hope that these can be used to reestablish the species at some time in the future, or at least contribute to breeding programs and scientific research (Ryder et al. 2000). This technique has sparked controversy because it may be viewed by some as a "high-tech" solution to the problem of species extinction. However, many of these techniques are enormously expensive and may not actually be able to produce healthy animals for certain species. In any case, "frozen zoos" are no substitute for in situ and ex situ conservation programs that preserve ecological relationships and behaviors that are necessary for survival in the wild.

As we discussed in Chapter 11, genetic inbreeding is an important problem in small populations (such as those found in zoos). Traditionally, captive populations in zoos were usually extensively inbred (Figure 14.5), but zoo managers are more careful now to avoid potential genetic problems when assigning mates. Modern zoos now use global computerized databases provided by ISIS and special studbooks to carefully track the genetic lineages of endangered captive animals to prevent pairing of related animals and avoid inbreeding depression as part of a species survival plan. Hundreds of studbooks currently exist, detailing European, North American, Japanese, Australian, and other international captive animals. The international studbook of giraffes, for example, lists 7000 living and deceased animals, along with all available information on parentage and genetic relationships. This system of pedigree construction can also be used to create a breeding program to prevent the gradual loss of genetic diversity over time in small populations (see Chapter 11).

Ex situ conservation efforts have been increasingly directed at saving endangered species of invertebrates as well. One of the most striking examples are the partulid snails of the Pacific island of Moorea (Coote et al. 2004). All seven species of this snail family became extinct in the wild after a predatory snail was introduced to control an agricultural pest. Currently six of the seven partulid species survive

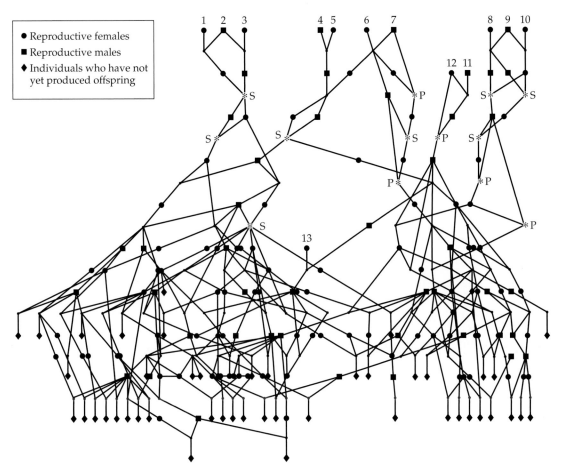

FIGURE 14.5 In the past, captive populations were often extensively inbred, as illustrated by this pedigree of a captive group of Przewalski's horses. The 13 "founder" individuals are indicated with numbers. Matings among close relatives become common; some sibling matings (S) and parent–offspring matings (P) are highlighted with asterisks. (After Thomas 1995.)

only in a captive breeding program. Attempts to reintroduce the native species on Moorea have failed due to attacks from the predatory snail.

Other important targets for captive breeding programs are the breeds of domestic animals on which human societies depend for animal protein, dairy products, leather, wool, agricultural labor, transportation, and recreation. Even though enormous populations of domestic animals exist (over 1 billion cattle and 1 billion sheep, for example), diverse and distinctive breeds of domestic animals adapted to local conditions are rapidly dying out as traditional agricultural practices are abandoned and intensive, high-yield agriculture is emphasized. For example, out of 3831 breeds of ass, water buffalo, cattle, goat, horse, pig, and sheep that existed during the last 100 years, 16% have already become extinct and an additional 23% are rare and in danger of extinction (Ruane 2000). Half of the breeds of domestic poultry are endangered. Preservation of the genetic variation from these local breeds for characteristics such as disease resistance, drought tolerance, general health, and meat production is crucial to animal breeding programs (Figure 14.6). Governments and conservation organizations are maintaining secure populations of some of these local breeds and developing frozen collections of sperm and embryos for later use. However, much more needs to be done to protect this global resource needed for healthy and productive domestic animals.

FIGURE 14.6 Soay sheep are a relict breed (a breed of an otherwise extinct group) of sheep living in the St. Kilda Islands, off the coast of Scotland. Soays retain characteristics of the first sheep brought to Britain more than 5000 years ago, and some of these characteristics may be valuable for low-maintenance animal husbandry in the future: small size (25–36 kg), robust health, and the ability to shed their fleece. (Photograph by Stephen J. G. Hall.)

ETHICAL ISSUES   Ex-situ techniques provide technological solutions to problems caused by human activities. Often the cheapest solution and the one most likely to succeed is protection of the species and its habitat in the wild so that it can recover naturally. Ex situ populations help support this solution through research and education programs and at the same time provide a safety net for those species that will become extinct without human intervention. When scientists consider ex situ methods for endangered species, they need to answer several ethical questions (Norton et al. 1995; Agoramoorthy 2004):

1. Will the ex situ population really benefit the wild population? Is it better for the last few individuals of a species to live out their days in the wild or to breed a captive population that may be unable to readapt to wild conditions?

2. Does a population of a rare species that has been raised in captivity and does not know how to survive in its natural environment really represent a victory for the species?

3. Are species held in captivity primarily for the benefit of these individuals or their entire species, the economic benefit of zoos, or the pleasure of zoo visitors?

4. Are the animals in captivity receiving appropriate care based on their biological needs? Does the benefit of the entire species outweigh any cost to the individual animals?

Even when the answers to these questions indicate a need for ex situ management, it is not always feasible to create ex situ populations of rare animal species. A species may have been so severely reduced in numbers that there is low breeding success and high infant mortality due to inbreeding depression. Certain animals, particularly marine mammals, are so large or require such specialized environments that there is no way to maintain population sizes large enough for long-term sustainability. Many invertebrates have complex life cycles in which their diet changes as they grow and in which their environmental needs vary in subtle ways. Many of these species are impossible to raise given our present knowledge. Finally, certain species are simply difficult to breed, despite the best efforts of scientists. Two prime examples of this are the giant panda (see Box 14.1) and the Sumatran rhino; neither species reproduces well in captivity, despite huge amounts of resources being directed at increasing the number of their offspring. As a result of these considerations, zoos are increasingly linking the animals in their exhibits to conservation projects in the wild.

Aquariums

Public aquariums have traditionally been oriented toward the display of unusual and attractive fish, sometimes supplemented with exhibits and performances of seals, dolphins, and other marine mammals. However, as concern for the environment has increased, aquariums have made conservation a major educational theme. The need is great, since thousands of fish species are threatened with extinction. In North America alone, 21 species are known to have gone extinct since the arrival of European settlers, and 154 species are now classified as endangered (Williams and Nowak 1993; Baillie et al. 2004). The rich fauna of the southern U.S. Gulf coastal plain, and the unique desert pupfish of the southwestern United States are in particular danger. Large-scale extinctions of fishes are occurring worldwide in places such as the African Great Lakes, the Andean lakes, Madagascar, and the Philippines. Freshwater mollusks in the United States and throughout the world are also a priority for protection because of their restricted distributions and vulnerability to changes caused by water pollution, dams, and invasive species.

In response to this threat to aquatic species, ichthyologists, marine mammalogists, and coral reef experts who work for public aquariums are increasingly linking up with colleagues in marine research institutes, government fisheries departments, and conservation organizations to develop programs for the conservation of rich natural communities and species of special concern. Currently approximately 600,000 individual fish are maintained in aquariums, with most of these obtained from the wild. Major efforts are being made to develop breeding techniques so that rare species can be maintained in aquariums without further collection in the wild and in the hope that some can be released back into the wild. These breeding programs utilize indoor aquarium facilities, semi-natural water bodies, and fish hatcheries and farms.

Many of the techniques for fish breeding were originally developed by fisheries biologists for large-scale stocking operations involving trout, bass, salmon, and other commercial species. Other techniques were discovered in the aquarium pet trade, when dealers attempted to propagate tropical fish for sale. These techniques are now being applied to endangered freshwater fauna. Programs for breeding endangered marine fishes and coral species are still in an early stage, but both public and private groups are making impressive efforts to unlock the secrets of propagating some of the more difficult species. Commercial production levels have been achieved for numerous species, and home aquarists can now expect fishes, corals, and other creatures to have been raised in captivity or certified as having been sustainably collected from the wild.

Aquariums have a particularly important role to play in the conservation of endangered cetaceans. Aquarium personnel often respond to public requests for assistance in handling whales stranded on beaches or disoriented in shallow waters. The lessons learned from working with common species may be used by the aquar-

FIGURE 14.7 Breeding bottle-nosed dolphins (*Tursiops truncatus*) in captivity has provided aquarium personnel with valuable experience that can be applied to endangered cetacean species. Shown here are a mother and calf. (Photograph courtesy of Sea World.)

ium community to develop programs to aid endangered species. Extensive experience with captive populations of the bottle-nosed dolphin, the most popular aquarium species, is being applied to other species (Figure 14.7): Researchers are able to maintain colonies, breed them naturally or perform artificial insemination, hand-raise calves, and release captive-born animals into the natural environment. Techniques learned with dolphins may eventually be applied to other endangered cetaceans such as the Chinese Yangtze River baiji, the Gulf of California vaquita, and the Mediterranean striped dolphin. A practical problem in establishing populations of captive marine mammals is the requirement of large volumes of water.

The ex situ preservation of aquatic biodiversity takes on additional significance due to the dramatic increase in aquaculture, which represents around 27% of fish and shellfish production worldwide. This aquaculture includes the extensive salmon, carp, and catfish farms of the temperate zones, the shrimp farms of the Tropics, and the 12 million tons of aquatic products grown in China and Japan. As fish, frogs, mollusks, and crustaceans increasingly become domesticated and are raised to meet human needs, it becomes necessary to preserve the genetic stocks needed to continue improvements in these species—and to protect them against disease and unforeseeable threats. Ironically, fishes and invertebrates that have escaped from aquaculture present major threats to the diversity of indigenous species because these exotic species can become invasive, spread disease, and hybridize with local species. A challenge for the future will involve balancing the need to increase human food production from aquaculture with the need to protect aquatic biodiversity from increasing human threats.

Botanical Gardens and Arboretums

Gardening is enjoyed by millions of people worldwide and has a history that dates back thousands of years. Kitchen gardens have long provided a source of vegetables and herbs for households. In ancient times, doctors and healers kept gardens of medicinal plants to treat their patients. In more recent centuries, royal families established large private gardens for their personal enjoyment, and governments established botanical gardens for the urban public. In recognition of the vital role plants play in the economic activity of society, many European countries set up botanical gardens throughout their colonial empires. An **arboretum** is a specialized botanical garden focusing on trees and other woody plants. While the major purpose of many of these large gardens was the display of beautiful plants, they also illustrate the diversity of the living world and assist in the dissemination and propagation of plants that can be used in horticulture, agriculture, forestry, landscaping, and industry.

The world's 1600 botanical gardens now contain major collections of living plants and represent a crucial resource for plant conservation; they currently contain around 4 million living plants, representing 80,000 species—approximately 30% of the world's flora (Guerrant et al. 2004; BGCI 2005). When we add in the species grown in greenhouses, subsistence gardens, and hobby gardens, the numbers are increased. One of the world's largest botanical gardens, the Royal Botanic Gardens, Kew, in England, has an estimated 25,000 species of plants under cultivation, about 10% of the world's total; 2700 of these are listed as threatened under the IUCN categories (Figure 14.8). One of the most exciting new botanical gardens is the Eden Project in southwest England, which focuses on displaying and explaining over 5000 species of economically important plants in a series of giant greenhouse domes (Figure 14.9). The Eden project currently receives about 1.4 million visitors per year (Readman 2004).

Botanical gardens increasingly focus their efforts on cultivating rare and endangered plant species, and many specialize in particular types of plants (Given 1995). The Arnold Arboretum of Harvard University grows thousands of different temperate tree species and the New England Wildflower Society has a collection of thousands of perennial temperate herbs at its Garden in the Woods location. South Africa's leading botanical garden has 25% of South Africa's plant species growing in cultivation. More than 250 botanical gardens maintain nature reserves that serve as important conservation areas in their own right. In addition, botanical gardens are able to educate an estimated 200 million visitors per year about conservation issues (BGCI 2005).

In many ways, plants are easier to maintain in controlled conditions than animals. Adequate population samples can often be established from seeds, shoot and

FIGURE 14.8 The Royal Botanic Gardens, Kew, is well known for its training courses and research in plant conservation and horticulture. Here a training session is being conducted around a collection of desert plants inside the Princess of Wales Conservatory. (Photograph courtesy of the Royal Botanic Gardens, Kew.)

FIGURE 14.9 The Eden Project in England has over 5000 plants of economic importance growing in giant greenhouses and also has an appealing public image. (Photograph from © Greenshoots Communication/Alamy.)

root cuttings, other plant parts, and by using tissue-culture techniques. Most plants have similar basic needs for light, water, and minerals, which can be readily supplied in greenhouses and gardens. Adjusting light, temperature, humidity levels, soil type, and soil moisture to suit species is the main concern, but this is often easily determined through knowledge of the plant's natural growing conditions. Since plants do not move, they often can be grown in high densities. If space is a limiting factor, plants can be pruned to a small size. Plants can often be maintained outdoors in gardens, where they need minimal care and weeding to survive. Some perennial plants, particularly shrubs and trees, are long-lived, so that individuals can be kept alive for decades or centuries once they grow beyond the seedling stage. Species that are primarily inbreeders (self-fertilizing), such as wheat, need fewer individuals to maintain genetic variability than primarily outcrossing species such as maize or corn. Many plant species readily produce seeds on their own, which can be collected and germinated to produce more plants. Wind, insects, and other animals cross-pollinate many plants in botanical gardens, while other species naturally self-pollinate. Simple hand pollination is used to produce seed in some plant species. In addition to living plants, botanical gardens and research institutes have developed collections of seeds, sometimes called **seed banks**, from both wild and cultivated plants that provide a crucial backup to their living collections. Many plants, particularly those found in the temperate zone, in dry climates, and those found growing in disturbed conditions, have seeds that can lie dormant for years—even decades—in cool, dry conditions.

Botanical gardens are in a unique position to contribute to conservation efforts because living collections in botanical gardens and their associated herbaria of dried plant collections represent the best sources of information we have on plant distribution and habitat requirements. The staff members of botanical gardens are often recognized authorities on plant identification, distribution, and conservation status. Expeditions sent out by botanical gardens discover new species and determine the distribution and status of known species.

The conservation of endangered species is becoming one of the major goals of botanical gardens as well as zoos. In the United States, conservation efforts by a network of 34 botanical gardens are being coordinated by the Center for Plant Conservation based at the Missouri Botanical Garden. These botanical gardens maintain joint collections of 600 rare plant species. While most plant species occur in the Tropics, the United States alone has 3000 species that are threatened in some way, and more than 450 of the threatened species are now being grown in cultivation in these botanical gardens. Their ultimate goal is to have adequate genetic material and expertise necessary to reintroduce a species back into the wild, should it become necessary to do so. Ex situ material can be thought of as an "insurance policy," and like all insurance policies, it is best not to have to redeem them.

The Botanical Gardens Conservation International (BGCI) of IUCN attempts to coordinate conservation efforts by the world's botanical gardens. Priorities of this program involve creating a worldwide database to coordinate collecting activity and identify important species that are underrepresented or absent from living collections. One project involves creating an online Plant Search Database that currently lists over 90,000 species and varieties growing in botanical gardens, of which 9000 are rare or threatened. The data identify which botanical gardens grow the plant and provide links to the IUCN lists of threatened plants, along with image-search services for pictures of the plant (Sharrock 2004).

Most botanical gardens are located in the temperate zone, even though most of the world's plant species are found in the Tropics. A number of major gardens do exist in places such as Singapore, Sri Lanka, Java, and Colombia, but establishing new botanical gardens in the Tropics should be a priority for the international community, along with training local plant taxonomists, geneticists, and horticulturalists to fill staff positions.

SEED BANKS Botanical gardens and research institutes have developed seed banks—collections of seeds from the wild and from cultivated plants (Guerrant et al. 2004). Seed banks have generally focused on the approximately 100 plant species that make up over 90% of human food consumption, but they are devoting more and more attention to a wider range of species that may be threatened with extinction or loss of genetic variability.

As mentioned earlier, seeds of most plant species can be stored in cold, dry conditions in seed banks for long periods of time and then later germinated to produce new plants (Figure 14.10) (Linington and Pritchard 2001; Guerrant et al. 2004). At low temperatures, a seed's metabolism slows down and the food reserves of the embryo are maintained. This property makes seeds extremely well-suited to ex situ conservation efforts, since seeds of large numbers of rare species can be stored in a small space with minimal supervision and at a low cost. The U.S. Department of Agriculture Agricultural Research Service (USDA ARS) National Center for Genetic Resources Preservation (NCGRP), formerly called the National Seed Storage Laboratory (NSSL), at Fort Collins, Colorado, stores some seeds in conditions as low as –196°C. The NCGRP stores 470,000 seed samples from 11,000 species. The Institute of Crop Germplasm Resources in Beijing, China, has over 370,000 seed collections. More than 50 other major seed banks exist in the world, many of them in developing countries, with another 1300 smaller regional collections. These seed banks collectively maintain around 6 million seed samples (Maunder 2001; BGCI 2005). The focus of most of these facilities is on preserving the genetic variation needed for breeding purposes in crop species.

At present, somewhere between 10,000 to 20,000 wild plant species are represented in seed banks, less than 10% of the world's total species. To deal with this collection gap, many botanical gardens have established seed banks to preserve genetic variation in wild species, particularly those in danger of extinction. These seed banks allow a greater range of genetic variation to be preserved than exists in their living collections. The most ambitious project is the Millennium Seed Bank Project of the Royal Botanic Gardens, Kew, which has a goal of conserving the seeds of 10% of the

FIGURE 14.10 (A) The National Center for Genetic Resources Preservation (NCGRP) in Fort Collins, Colorado. (B) Seeds of many plant varieties are sorted, cataloged, and stored. Detailed labels describe the plant's characteristics and the place and date of collection. (C) At the NCGRP facility, some seeds are stored in hermetically sealed packets at –20°C. (D) Seeds are also stored in liquid nitrogen at –196°C. (Photographs courtesy of the U.S. Department of Agriculture.)

world's estimated 250,000 species by the year 2010. The particular focus of the collection will be on species from dry climates of the world and the flora of the United Kingdom. As of 2005, over 23,700 seed samples of 11,870 species from 131 countries were in storage, including 96% of the U.K.'s flora. Another project is a collaboration among the botanical gardens of Spain to provide a comprehensive seed bank for that country's plants. Seed banks are also expanding their collections to include the pollen of seed plants and the spores of ferns, mosses, fungi, and microorganisms.

While seed banks have great potential for conserving species, they are limited by certain problems. If power supplies fail or equipment breaks down, an entire frozen collection may be damaged. Even seeds in storage gradually lose their ability to germinate after energetic reserves are exhausted and harmful mutations are accumulated. Old seed supplies simply may not germinate. To overcome the gradual deterioration of quality, samples must be regenerated periodically by germinating seeds, growing new plants to maturity, controlling pollination, and storing new samples. The testing and rejuvenation of seed samples can be a formidable task for seed banks with large collections. Renewing seed vigor in species that have large individual plants and delayed maturity, such as trees, may be extremely expensive and time-consuming.

Approximately 10% of the world's plant species have recalcitrant seeds that either lack dormancy or do not tolerate low-temperature storage conditions and consequently cannot be stored in seed banks. Seeds of these species must germinate right away or die. Species with recalcitrant seeds are much more common in tropical forests than in the temperate zone, and the seeds of many economically important tropical fruit trees, timber trees, and plantation crops such as cocoa and rubber cannot be stored. Intensive investigations are underway to find ways of storing recalcitrant seeds; one possibility may be storing just the embryo from inside the seed, or the young seedling (Figure 14.11). One of the ways to preserve genetic variation in these species is to establish special botanical gardens known as **clonal repositories**, or clonal orchards, which require considerable area and expense. In the past, root crops such as cassava (manioc), yams, and sweet potatoes have not been well represented in seed banks because they often do not form seeds. Genetic variation in these species is being preserved by vegetative propagation in special gardens such as the International Potato Centre in Peru and the International Center for Tropical Agriculture in Colombia. This undertaking is crucial, as these root crops are very important in the diets of people in developing tropical countries. An alternative method of conserving this genetic variability involves the in situ preservation of traditional agricultural practices (see Chapter 20). Vegetative propagation is also needed for plant species that have become so rare that in some cases only a single individual remains (Milinus 2003). For such species, parts of a single leaf can be grown in tissue culture and then used to propagate whole plants.

FIGURE 14.11 Cereal seedlings are checked for quality prior to their long-term cold storage. (Photograph courtesy of the U.S. Department of Agriculture.)

AGRICULTURAL SEED BANKS   Seed banks have been embraced by agricultural research institutes and the agricultural industry as an effective resource for preserving and using the genetic variability that exists in agricultural crops and their wild relatives. Often resistance to particular diseases and pests is found in only one variety of a crop, known as a **landrace**, that is grown in only one small area of the world, or in a wild relative. Preserving the genetic variability represented by landraces is crucial to the agricultural industry's interest in maintaining and increasing the high productivity of modern crops and their ability to respond to changing environmental conditions such as acid rain, global climate change, and soil erosion. Agricultural researchers have been combing the world for landraces of major food crops that can be stored and later hybridized with modern varieties in crop improvement programs. Many of the major food crops such as wheat, maize (corn), oats, potatoes, soybeans, and other legumes are well represented in seed banks, and other important crops such as rice, millet, and sorghum are being intensively collected. Researchers are in a race against time to preserve genetic variability because traditional farmers throughout the world, who only occupy 10 to 15% of the world's cultivated land (Altieri 2004), are abandoning their diverse local crop varieties in favor of standard, high-yielding varieties (Brush 2004) (Box 14.2). This worldwide phenomenon is illustrated by Sri Lankan farmers, who grew 2000 varieties of rice until the late 1950s, when they switched over to five high-yielding varieties (Rhoades 1991).

To better understand the value of agricultural seed banks, consider the following classic example. Rice crops in Africa were being devastated by a virus called grassy stunt virus strain 1. To find a solution to this problem, agricultural researchers grew wild and cultivated rice plants from thousands of seed samples obtained from collections around the world (Lin and Yuan 1980). One seed sample of wild rice

BOX 14.2

Seed Savers and Crop Varieties

▪ Preserving genetic diversity is a major concern for conservation biologists, with good reason: Even among populations that seem healthy, low genetic diversity can leave a population vulnerable to disease, which can wreak potentially disastrous consequences for a threatened species. Many common crop plants, including the fruits and vegetables that most people eat regularly, are potentially threatened by low genetic diversity. The reason for this is simple: Commercial farming tends to emphasize a few varieties that have high yield and appeal to consumer preferences for flavor, shape, size, and color. As such, many unique varieties of common crops have been ignored and are now relatively uncommon, even rare. Some varieties might have died out altogether, if not for the activities of ordinary gardeners and plant breeders belonging to a small Iowa-based organization, founded in 1975, called Seed Savers Exchange (SSE).

SSE concentrates on preserving many little-known "heirloom" varieties of crop plants that were brought to North America by immigrants (www.seedsavers.org). SSE accomplishes this task in an ingenious yet simple way: it makes these varieties available to individual gardeners and plant breeders—hobbyists who garden for their own pleasure or benefit, as well as various university agricultural programs and historic preservation societies—through newsletters and catalogs. In the 30 years of its existence, SSE has organized a group of some 750 individual gardeners and plant breeders responsible for preserving over 12,000 different varieties of crop plants, which are offered in the SSE catalog to other interested gardeners. More than 65% of these varieties are offered by only one grower, which shows just how unusual many of these varieties have become (Cherfas 1993).

The SSE produces the Garden Seed Inventory, an inventory of 245 seed catalogs and 6483 vegetable varieties. The headquarters of SSE is the Heritage Farm in Iowa, where many unusual and hard-to-find vegetable varieties are grown. The screened boxes enclose particular varieties and prevent cross-pollination between varieties.

BOX 14.2 *(continued)*

Many of these plants have long and fascinating histories, particularly the heirloom plants that can be traced back for centuries—even millennia—in their native habitat. Some are still linked to ongoing cultural traditions: Peruvian farmers in isolated Andean villages, for example, grow varieties of potatoes that may have been handed down from generation to generation since pre-Columbian times, yet remain completely unknown in nearby regions. Other plants may be interesting to look at, have medicinal properties, or be unusually colorful or flavorful. These reasons alone are sufficient rationale for most gardeners to obtain these varieties. For many gardeners, the opportunity to grow rare, unusual, and interesting plants is one of the great pleasures of gardening, and SSE is an excellent source of such plants.

SSE works on a unique system: Members pay a nominal fee in exchange for a catalog that describes the varieties available and provides the names of growers who will supply seeds. SSE founders Kent and Diane Whealy run a farm in Iowa (appropriately called Heritage Farm) at which many of the different varieties are grown. They have enlisted amateur and professional growers at other locations to act as curators for specific crops. These growers may produce hundreds of varieties of crops—melons, tomatoes, beans, or peppers, for example—for their own use, but they are specifically responsible for maintaining a smaller number of individual varieties and supplying seeds to others. To assure that no crop is left out because of habitat or climate limitations, growers are located in different parts of the United States and in different climatic zones.

SSE makes a phenomenal number of interesting and unique plants available to ordinary gardeners. One curator in Iowa offers almost 200 different types of squash and 53 varieties of watermelon. And for those growers seeking a particular variety—perhaps one they remember from childhood, but for which they have no name—the "Plant Finder Service," appearing annually in the *Seed Savers Harvest Edition*, publishes growers' descriptions of the plants they want and appeals to the general membership for help finding them.

Large national and international agricultural organizations have concentrated on preserving the genetic variation in major food crops, but have neglected less well-known crops. Private organizations such as the SSE—which recently went international in an attempt to preserve heirloom plants all over the world, especially in Eastern Europe—have filled in the gap to an extent. Turning the garden hobbyist's enthusiasm into a tool for conservation, this organization has managed to spread the word to an attentive worldwide audience of gardeners, breeders, and agricultural research and teaching institutions. Nevertheless, loss of crop varieties is a serious threat to world food supplies and should be given greater recognition by world food organizations such as the United Nations Food and Agriculture Organization, as well as by governments' agricultural departments and ministries. For all their valiant efforts, organizations such as Seed Savers Exchange/Seed Savers International have merely plugged the hole in the dike; unless the rest of the global village comes to their rescue, they will be unable to stop impending disaster.

from Gonda, Uttar Pradesh, India, was found to contain a gene for resistance to viral disease. These wild plants were immediately incorporated into a major breeding program to transfer the gene for viral resistance into high-yielding varieties of rice. If the sample of wild rice had not been collected or had died out before being discovered, the future of rice cultivation in Africa would have been uncertain.

Despite their obvious successes in collecting and storing material, agricultural seed banks have several important limitations. Collections are often poorly documented regarding the locality of collection and growing conditions. Many of the seeds are of unknown quality and may not germinate. Crops of regional significance as well as medicinal plants, fiber plants, and other useful plants are not as well represented, even though these are economically significant to tropical countries.

Many seed banks are coordinated by the Consultative Group on International Agricultural Research (CGIAR) and the International Board for Plant Genetic Resources (IBPGR) (Fuccilo et al. 1998; Linington and Pritchard 2001). One of the largest seed banks in the world, with around 80,000 separate collections of rice seeds, is maintained by the International Rice Research Institute (IRRI), an organization instrumental in the development of high-yielding, Green Revolution crop varieties.

Other specialized seed collections are held by the International Maize and Wheat Improvement Center (Centro Internacional de Mejoramiento de Maíz y Trigo, or CIMMYT) in Mexico, which holds 12,000 samples of maize and 100,000 samples of wheat, and by the Plant Genetic Resources Unit at the National Germplasm Repository in Geneva, New York. CGIAR is currently establishing a $250 million Global Crop Diversity Fund to help for the annual maintenance costs of these collections.

A major controversy in the development of agricultural seed banks is who owns and controls the genetic resources of crops (Brush and Stabinsky 1996; Guerrant et al. 2004). The genes of local landraces of crop plants and wild relatives of crop species represent the building blocks needed to develop elite, high-yielding varieties suitable for modern agriculture. Approximately 96% of the raw genetic variation necessary for modern agriculture comes from developing countries such as India, Ethiopia, Peru, Mexico, Indonesia, and China, yet the corporate breeding programs for elite strains frequently are located in the industrialized countries of North America and Europe (Figure 14.12). In the past, genetic material was perceived as free for the taking: The staffs of international seed banks freely collected seeds and plant tissue from developing countries and gave them to research stations and seed companies. Seed companies then developed new strains through sophisticated breeding programs and field trials and sold their seeds at high prices to maximize profits that often totaled hundreds of millions of dollars a year, but the countries from which the original seeds were collected saw no profit from this activity.

Developing countries now question why they should share their biological materials freely if they will have to pay for new seed varieties and cultivated plants based on those genetic resources. In fact, all countries of the world benefit from the free exchange of seeds and plant tissues. The modern varieties developed by international breeding centers and now grown throughout the world have the best

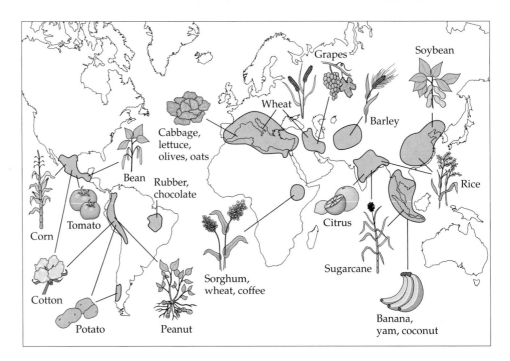

FIGURE 14.12 Crop species show high genetic diversity in certain areas of the world. These areas are often where the species was first domesticated or where the species is still grown in traditional agricultural settings. (Courtesy of Garrison Wilkes.)

qualities of the landraces that were originally found in many different countries. Many countries contribute genetic resources to international breeding efforts, but they also receive benefits in terms of higher agricultural productivity. Indeed, two-thirds of the agriculture of developing countries is grown in crops that were first domesticated in other regions of the world.

In 1993, a group of countries drew up the Convention on Biological Diversity in an effort to provide a fair way of dealing with the situation. The Convention, signed by 170 countries, sets forth a general framework for sharing the financial benefits of genetic resources more fairly and gives incentives for countries that preserve biological diversity. Among the important policy recommendations of the Convention are the following:

- Countries have the right to control access to their biological diversity and should be paid for its use.

- Countries have a responsibility to inventory their biological diversity and protect it.

- Collectors must have permission to collect samples from the host country, the local community, and the land owners.

- As much as possible, research, breeding, processing, and production of new varieties should take place in the countries where the biological resources occur.

- The financial benefits, new products, and new varieties should be shared fairly with countries that contributed genetic resources used in the final product.

Many countries, international agencies, conservation organizations, and corporations are presently developing the financial and legal mechanisms to carry out the provisions of the Convention. Disagreements among these groups have been difficult to resolve, which has impeded implementation of the Convention. However, a few contracts have been negotiated, such as the one between the Costa Rican government and the Merck Company for the development of products based on species collected in the wild (see Chapter 4), and these will be followed carefully to determine if they are mutually satisfactory and to see if they can serve as models for future contracts.

SEED SAMPLING STRATEGIES Botanical gardens and institutes are increasingly developing seed banks in addition to their collections of plants. Strategies for collecting seeds from endangered and rare wild plants for storage in seed banks are influenced by the distribution of genetic variability because species that are genetically variable may require more extensive sampling to acquire most of their alleles than species that are more genetically uniform.

The Center for Plant Conservation (Falk and Holsinger 1991) and other organizations have developed a list of five seed-sampling guidelines for conserving the genetic variability of endangered plant species both within and among populations (Guerrant et al. 2004). These guidelines could be modified for other groups of species such as animals, fungi, and microorganisms:

1. The highest priority for collecting should be species that (a) are in danger of extinction—that is, species showing a rapid decline in number of individuals or number of populations; (b) are evolutionarily or taxonomically unique; (c) can be reintroduced into the wild; (d) have the potential to be preserved in ex situ situations; (e) have potential economic value for agriculture, medicine, forestry, or industry.

2. Samples should be collected from up to five populations per species to ensure a sampling of the genetic variability contained among populations.

Where possible, populations should be selected to cover the geographical and environmental range of the species. For the 70% of endangered species that have five or fewer populations, all populations should be sampled.

3. Samples should be collected from 10 to 50 individuals per population. Sampling fewer than 10 individuals may miss alleles that are common in the population; sampling more than 50 may not result in enough new alleles to justify the effort.

4. The number of seeds (or cuttings, bulbs, etc.) collected per plant is determined by the viability of the species' seeds. If seed viability is high, then only a few seeds need to be collected per individual; if seed viability is low, then many seeds per individual have to be collected.

5. If individual plants of a species have a low reproductive output, collecting many seeds in one year may have a negative effect on the sampled populations. This is particularly true for annuals and other short-lived plants. In these cases, a better strategy would be to spread the collecting over several years.

These seed collections are not the final goal of conservation efforts, but rather the starting point in the establishment of living collections and eventual reintroduction of plants back into the wild.

CONSERVING THE GENETIC RESOURCES OF TREES   Forestry is a huge, global industry that depends on the genetic variation found in trees for its long-term success (Rogers and Ledig 1996). Relying on wild-collected seeds for establishing plantations has its drawbacks because selective logging often removes the superior trees and leaves the inferior ones behind. The results of poor initial seed sample will only be seen years and decades later in slow-growing, misshapen, disease-ridden trees with poor wood quality. To conserve genetic variation in tree species, foresters have used cuttings and families of closely related seeds taken from the best trees to establish plantations of superior genetic varieties, called **clone banks**, for long-term maintenance and research of commercially important tree species. For loblolly pine (*Pinus taeda*) alone, 8000 clones are being grown in clone banks in the southeastern United States. Selected trees are used to establish seed orchards for producing commercial seed. Storage of seeds is difficult for many important genera of trees such as oaks (*Quercus*) and poplars (*Populus*). Even pine seeds cannot be stored indefinitely and must eventually be grown as trees.

Preserving areas where commercial tree species occur naturally is an important way to protect genetic variability. International cooperation is needed in forestry research and conservation because commercial species are often grown far from their countries of origin. For example, loblolly pine (*Pinus taeda*) and Monterey pine (*Pinus radiata*) from North America are planted on 5.8 million ha of land outside that continent. In New Zealand, 1.3 million ha are planted in Monterey pine, making it a key element in the national economy. In Hungary, 19% of the forested area is planted in North American shipmast locust (*Robinia pseudoacacia* var. *rectissima*), because the species produces durable wood and grows on degraded, low-nutrient sites. These forest plantations far from home still depend on natural populations of the species to supply the genetic variability required for continued improvements and survival in a hostile environment.

Conclusion

As more of the environment is dominated by human activities, ex situ populations are playing an ever-greater role in contributing to the conservation of species in the wild. Species maintained in captivity and in cultivation can serve as ambassadors for their wild counterparts through a variety of conservation, research, and education programs. In the cases of highly endangered species, captive individuals can be used to establish new populations in the wild, once the threats to the species have been identified and controlled. Although ex situ programs can be expensive, they can also generate income—through the display of species in zoos, genetic improvements in domesticated species, and new products developed by the biotech and medical industries. Some of this income must be directed to support the protection of biodiversity in the wild by funding the creation and management of protected areas, which is the topic of Part Five.

Summary

1. Some species that are in danger of going extinct in the wild can be maintained in artificial conditions under human supervision; this is known as ex situ, or off-site, preservation. These captive colonies can sometimes be used later to reestablish species in the wild.

2. Zoos are developing self-maintaining populations of many rare terrestrial vertebrates, often using modern techniques of veterinary medicine to increase their reproductive rates. Currently zoos maintain over 400,000 individuals of 7895 species and subspecies, most of which were born in captivity. Collections are also being maintained of endangered breeds of domestic animals.

3. Marine mammalogists, ichthyologists, and coral reef experts who work for aquariums are using breeding techniques and conservation programs for the protection of endangered fishes, marine mammals, and aquatic invertebrates.

4. The world's 1600 botanical gardens and arboretums now make it one of their main priorities to collect and grow rare and endangered species. The seeds of most species of plants can be stored for long periods of time under cold conditions in seed banks. Seed banks often specialize in the collection of major crop species, commercial timber species, and their close relatives in order to preserve material for genetic improvement programs.

For Discussion

1. What are the similarities and differences among the ex situ conservation methods used for plants, terrestrial animals, and aquatic species?

2. Would biological diversity be adequately protected if every species were raised in captivity? Is this possible? Practical? How would freezing a tissue sample of every species help to protect biological diversity? Again, is this possible and is it practical?

3. Are the arguments for preserving the genetic variability in domesticated species of animals and plants (and their close relatives) the same arguments we would put forward for saving endangered wild species?

4. How much of an ex situ facility's resources should be devoted for conservation efforts in order for the institution to announce that it is a conservation organization? What sorts of conservation activities are appropriate for each institution? Visit such an institution and evaluate it for its conservation activities and efforts; use or modify some of the methods of Balmford et al. 1996.

Suggested Readings

Balmford, A., G. M. Mace, and N. Leader-Williams. 1996. Designing the Ark: Setting priorities for captive breeding. *Conservation Biology* 10: 719–727. Zoos should focus more on smaller-bodied species that breed well in captivity and are cheaper to maintain.

Conway, W. G., M. Hutchins, M. Souza, Y. Kapentanakos, and E. Paul. 2001. *The AZA Field Conservation Resource Guide.* Zoo Atlanta, Atlanta, GA. Information on hundreds of projects supported or directed by zoo and aquarium personnel.

Given, D. R. 1995. *Principles and Practice of Plant Conservation.* Timber Press, Portland, OR. Good summary of plant conservation approaches.

Guerrant, E. O. Jr., K. Havens, and M. Maunder. 2004. *Ex Situ Conservation: Supporting Species Survival in the Wild.* Island Press, Washington, D.C. Describes the linkages between botanical gardens and plant conservation.

Hancocks, D. 2001. *A Different Nature: The Paradoxical World of Zoos and their Uncertain Future.* University of California Press, Berkeley, CA. Criticism of traditional zoos, and a vision of zoos that are better for animals, people, and conservation.

Holt, W. V., A. R. Pickard, J. C. Rodger, D. E. Wildt, M. L. Gosling, G. Cowlishaw, et al. (eds.). 2003. *Reproductive Science and Integrated Conservation.* Conservation Biology Series, No. 8. Cambridge University Press, New York. Recent advances in reproductive technology are having a major impact on captive breeding programs.

Lanza, R. P., B. L. Dresser, and P. Damiani. 2000. Cloning Noah's Ark. *Scientific American* 283: 84–89. Biotechnology might be an effective way to propagate certain rare species, but is it really the answer to the problem?

Lyles, A. M. 2001. Zoos and zoological parks. *In* S. A. Levin (ed.), *Encyclopedia of Biodiversity*, Vol. 5, pp. 901–912. Academic Press, San Diego, CA. Explores the rise of the new zoo, which focuses on conservation.

Maunder, M. 2001. Plant conservation, overview. *In* S. A. Levin (ed.), *Encyclopedia of Biodiversity*, Vol. 4, pp. 645–658. Academic Press, San Diego, CA. Describes the importance of botanical gardens in plant conservation.

Miller, B., W. Conway, R. P. Reading, C. Wemmer, D. Wildt, D. Kleiman, et al. 2004. Evaluating the conservation mission of zoos, aquariums, botanical gardens, and natural history museums. *Conservation Biology* 18: 86–93. Eight tough questions are asked with hopes that these institutions can become more effective.

Norton, B. G., M. Hutchins, E. F. Stevens, and T. L. Maple. 1995. *Ethics on the Ark: Zoos, Animal Welfare, and Wildlife Conservation.* Smithsonian Institution Press, Washington, D.C. Vigorous examination of the ethical issues confronting modern zoos.

Praded, J. 2002. Reinventing the zoo. *E: The Environmental Magazine* 13: 24–31. Zoos are moving in new directions, especially towards conservation.

Readman, J. 2004. Conservation…connection…curiosity…conversation…communication. *Plant Talk*: 27–31. The Eden Project has emerged as one of the most exciting new botanical gardens with a conservation focus. Check out other articles in this beautiful magazine.

Ryder, O. A., A. McLaren, S. Brenner, Y. P. Zhang, and K. Benirschke. 2000. DNA banks for endangered animal species. *Science* 288: 275. Frozen tissue samples are presented as an alternative conservation strategy.

Practical Applications

Before

After

Establishing Protected Areas

Protecting habitats that contain healthy, intact biological communities is widely considered to be the most effective way to conserve biological diversity of wild species. One could argue that it is ultimately the only way, because we have the resources and knowledge to maintain only a small minority of the world's species in captivity. A **protected area** is "an area of land and/or sea especially dedicated to the protection and maintenance of biological diversity, and of natural and associated cultural resources, and managed through legal and other effective means" (IUCN 1994). Five approaches to preserving biological communities include the establishment of protected areas, creating networks of protected areas, the effective management of those areas, implementation of conservation measures outside protected areas, and the restoration of biological communities in degraded habitats.

In this chapter we will discuss the critical first step in protecting biological communities—establishing legally designated protected areas governed by laws and regulations that allow widely varying degrees of commercial resource use, traditional use by local people, and recreational use. We'll begin our discussion by examining existing protected areas and then will explore the steps involved in creating new ones.

The momentum to establish protected areas has been increasing throughout the twentieth century (Figure 15.1). Over 80% of the

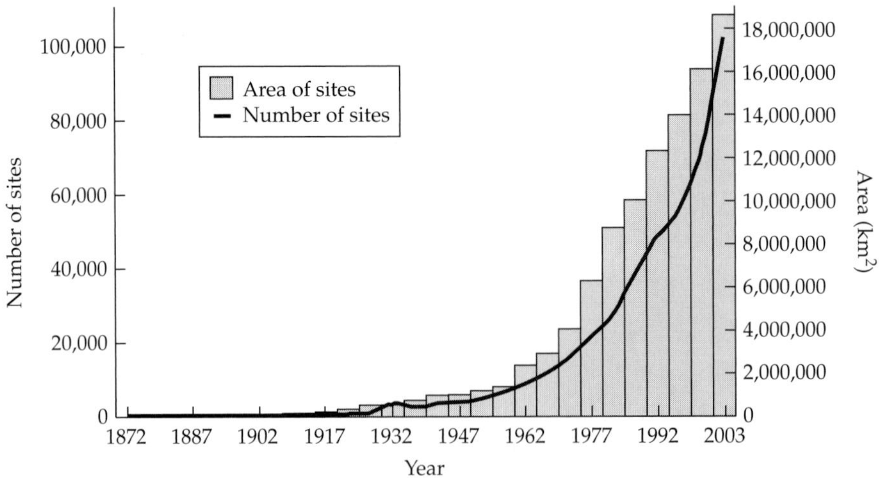

FIGURE 15.1 The solid line graphs the number of new protected areas worldwide since 1872, including both terrestrial and marine sites; the shaded bars indicate the total area encompassed in protected areas (in km²) of terrestrial sites alone at 15-year intervals. (After Chape et al. 2003.)

world's protected areas have been established since 1962, when the first World Parks Congress was held (Chape et al. 2003; World Data Base on Protected Areas Consortium 2004). Protected areas currently cover over 12.5% of the Earth's surface. This limited area of protected habitat emphasizes the biological significance of the 23% of the land that is managed for sustainable resource production, described in greater detail in Chapter 18.

The IUCN System of Classification

When a conservation area is established, a compromise must be struck between protecting biological diversity and ecosystem function and satisfying the immediate and long-term needs for resources of the local human community and its national government (MEA 2005b). At the outset, decisions must be made during the planning process regarding what human activities and how much human disturbance will be allowed. In general, when greater amounts of human disturbance are permitted, a narrower scope of biodiversity is preserved. However, some aspects of biodiversity depend on a certain level of habitat disturbance, especially where humans have a long historical presence.

The IUCN has developed a system of classifying protected areas that ranges from minimal to intensive use of the habitat by humans (IUCN 1994; Davey 1998; WRI 2000), with the following six categories:

I. *Strict nature reserves* and wilderness areas.* These areas protect natural organisms and natural processes in a relatively undisturbed state in order to have representative examples of biological diversity for scientific study, education, environmental monitoring, and maintenance of genetic variation. Included are two subcategories: (Ia) primarily includes nature reserves established for scientific research and monitoring; (Ib) primarily includes wilderness areas maintained for recreation, for subsistence economic activities, and to protect natural processes. This category currently includes approximately 5201 sites covering 1,922,831 km².

II. *National parks.* These are large areas of outstanding scenic and natural beauty of national or international importance that are maintained for sci-

---

*Protected areas that are managed primarily for biological diversity are often called nature reserves or nature sanctuaries.

entific, educational, and recreational use; they usually are not used for comercial extraction of resources. This category currently includes 3383 sites covering 4,001,463 km^2.

III. *National monuments and landmarks.* These are smaller areas designed to preserve unique natural areas of unique national interest. This category currently includes 2122 sites covering 193,022 km^2.

IV. *Managed wildlife sanctuaries and nature reserves.* These are similar to strict nature reserves, but some human manipulation may be necessary to maintain the characteristics of the community. Some controlled harvesting may be permitted. This category currently includes 11,169 sites covering 2,460,110 km^2.

V. *Protected landscapes and seascapes.* These are areas of land, with coast and sea as appropriate, where the interaction of people and nature over time has produced distinct character with significant esthetic, ecological, and/or cultural value, often with high biodiversity. Safeguarding the integrity of this traditional interaction is vital to the protection, maintenance, and evolution of such an area. This category currently includes 5578 sites covering 1,057,450 km^2.

VI. *Managed-resource protected areas.* These areas allow for the sustained production of natural resources, including water, wildlife, grazing for livestock, timber, tourism, and fishing, in a manner that ensures the preservation of some aspects of biological diversity. These areas are often large and may include both modern and traditional uses of natural resources. This category currently includes 30,350 sites covering 3,601,447 km^2 and is part of the 23% of the Earth's land surface that is managed for resource production.

Of these categories, the first five can be defined as true protected areas, because their habitat is managed primarily for biological diversity. (However, a stricter definition would include only the first three categories.) Areas in the sixth category, managed-resource protected areas, are administered to conserve biological diversity, but the production of natural resources may take higher priority. Managed-resource protected areas can be particularly significant because they are often much larger in area than other categories of protected areas, because they still may contain many or even most of their original species, and because protected areas are often embedded in a matrix of areas managed for production.

Existing Protected Areas

At least 180 countries—and perhaps more—currently have protected areas. Among the countries without protected areas as of the year 2005 are Syria, Yemen, Equatorial Guinea, and Guinea-Bissau. While it could be argued that virtually all countries should have at least one national park, large countries with rich biotas and a variety of ecosystem types would obviously benefit from having many protected areas. As of 2003, around 104,791 IUCN protected areas (IUCN categories I–VI) had been designated worldwide, covering some 18 million km^{2*} on land, and with a further 2 million km^2 at sea (WRI 2003). Although this may seem like an impressive amount, it represents only about 12.5% of the Earth's total land surface, and much

---

*Uncertainty about the number and size of protected areas stems from the different standards used throughout the world and the degree of protection actually given to a designated area, and when the data was gathered

of this protected land is not under pressure to be put to other uses. For example, the world's largest park is in Greenland and covers 970,000 km², accounting for about 5% of the global area protected. Only around 6% of the Earth's surface is *strictly protected* in scientific reserves and national parks (WRI 2005). The measurements of protected areas in individual countries and on continents are only approximate because sometimes the laws protecting national parks and wildlife sanctuaries are not strictly enforced; at the same time, there are sections of managed areas that, while not legally protected, are carefully protected in practice. Examples of this include the sections within U.S. national forests designated as wilderness areas. The coverage of strictly protected areas varies dramatically among countries: High proportions of land are protected in Germany (29%), Austria (28%), and the United Kingdom (15%), and surprisingly low proportions in Russia (5%), Greece (2%), and Turkey (0.7%). Even when a country has numerous protected areas, certain unique habitats of high economic value may remain unprotected (Dietz and Czech 2005).

Marine Protected Areas

Marine conservation has lagged behind terrestrial conservation efforts; even establishing priorities has proved difficult (Agardy 1997, 1999; Carr et al. 2003; Sobel and Dahlgren 2004; Zacharias and Gregr 2005). Priorities also need to be established to protect freshwater ecosystems, such as streams, rivers, and lakes (Higgins et al. 2005). Currently less than 1% of the marine environment is included in protected areas, yet as much as 20% of it may need to be protected in order to manage declining commercial fishing stocks (Costanza et al. 1998), and even more may be required to conserve the full range of coastal and marine biodiversity. Over 3400 marine and coastal protected areas have been established worldwide (WRI 2005), but most are small. Accounting for around half of the total are the three largest marine protected areas: the Great Barrier Reef Marine Park in Australia, the Galápagos Marine Park, and the Netherlands' North Sea Reserve. Unfortunately, many marine reserves exist only on the map and receive little protection from overharvesting and pollution. One survey found that less than 10% of marine protected areas achieved their management goals (IUCN 2004).

In the United States, only 14 marine sanctuaries have been designated, covering 46,548 km², in contrast to the 906 national forests, national parks, and wildlife refuges that total 1,657,084 km² (Lindholm and Barr 2001). Efforts to protect marine biological diversity have been hindered by the difficulty of identifying distinct biological communities and by the widespread migration and dispersal of marine species. In addition, opposition from fishing interests, the widespread impact of marine pollution, the challenge of demarcating boundaries, the difficulties of concluding international agreements, and the problems of policing large areas have also slowed efforts to establish effective marine reserves. Regulating the harvesting of fish that migrate in international waters has proven to be very difficult, and water pollution can damage extensive coastal areas, lagoons, and enclosed seas. These problems need to be seriously addressed. The conservation community has identified marine conservation as a high priority, and urgent efforts are currently underway to protect marine biological diversity by establishing marine parks that seek to protect the nursery grounds of commercial species and maintain high-quality areas for recreational activities such as diving, swimming, and fishing (Halpern 2003).

One approach to establishing marine protected areas involves protecting examples of each type of marine community. Determining biogeographical provinces for the marine environment is much more difficult than for the terrestrial environment because boundaries between realms are less sharp, dispersal of larval and adult stages is more widespread, and the marine environment is less well known

(Roberts et al. 2002; Lourie and Vincent 2004). Marine biogeographical provinces are being identified using a combination of the distribution of related marine animals (coastal, shelf, ocean) as well as physical properties that affect ecology and distribution (currents, temperature). Urgent efforts are being made throughout the world to protect marine biological diversity in each one of these biogeographical provinces by establishing marine parks comparable to terrestrial parks. One such example is the Hol Chan Marine Reserve in Belize, which is proving invaluable to the rapidly growing ecotourism industry. The El Nido Marine Reserve along the coast of Palawan Island in the Philippines provides protection for the sea cow (also called the dugong), the hawksbill sea turtle, and the Ridley sea turtle. In the Philippines, local communities are establishing many protected areas to ensure sustainable production of key fish species.

Size and Effectiveness

The value of protected areas in maintaining biological diversity is abundantly clear in many tropical countries; inside the park boundaries, forests and animal life abound, while outside the park, the land has been cleared and few animals are seen. Yet these protected areas still face threats from logging, hunting, and other human activities (Ervin 2003). It is also true that some national parks have become even more degraded than neighboring areas, due to management problems and conflicts with local people.

Two recent studies show that protected areas generally are effective in keeping land intact (Bruner et al. 2001; DeFries et al. 2005). In one study, land clearing in tropical forests in 86 national parks is far lower than in 88 control areas surrounding those parks (Figure 15.2). But if protected areas cover only a small percentage of the total area of the world, how effectively can they preserve the world's species and biological communities? Protected areas can be established where concentrations of species occur: along elevational gradients, at places where different geological formations are juxtaposed, in areas that are geologically old, and in places

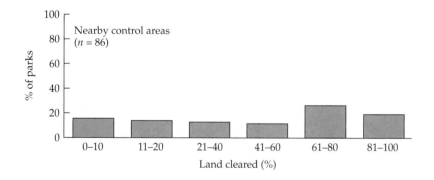

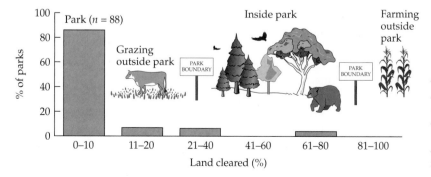

FIGURE 15.2 Land clearing of tropical forests in 85 national parks is far lower than in 88 control areas surrounding those parks. More than 80% of the parks have almost-intact vegetation (<10% cleared), whereas less than 20% of nearby control areas have almost-intact vegetation. National parks also have much lower-than-average levels of hunting, logging, and grazing than surrounding areas. (After Bruner et al. 2001.)

with an abundance of critical keystone resources (e.g., streams and water holes in otherwise dry habitats; caves and hollow tree trunks that can be used by birds, bats, and other animals for nesting; salt licks that provide essential mineral nutrients). New protected areas should also be sited along environmental gradients, so that a variety of biological communities are included. Such gradients could allow species dispersal as the global climate changes (T. B. Smith et al. 2001).

Often a landscape contains large expanses of a fairly uniform habitat type and only a few small areas of rare habitat types. Protecting biological diversity in such a case probably depends not so much on preserving large areas of the common habitat type as on including representatives of all the habitats in a system of protected areas (Shafer 1999). Even though a protected area may be within the geographical range of an endangered species, that species may be absent if the habitat and land use patterns are not suited to the species (Rondinini et al. 2005). The following examples illustrate the potential effectiveness of protected areas of limited extent:

- Parks and wildlife sanctuaries cover only about 8% of Thailand but include 88% of its resident forest bird species (Reid and Miller 1989); other categories of protected areas add another 5% to the total land conserved.

- The Indonesian government has designated 10% of Indonesia's land as protected area, with a goal of protecting populations of all native bird and primate species within its system of national parks and reserves.

- Santa Rosa Park in northwestern Costa Rica covers only 0.2% of the area of Costa Rica, yet it contains breeding populations of 55% of the country's 135 species of sphingid moth. Santa Rosa Park is included within the 82,500-ha Guanacaste National Park, which has populations of at least 90% of the sphingid moth species in the country (D. Janzen, personal communication).

While these examples clearly show that well-selected protected areas can include many if not most of the species in a country, the long-term future of many species in these reserves, and even of the biological communities themselves, remains in doubt. Populations of many species may be so reduced in size that their eventual fate is extinction. Similarly, catastrophic events like fires, outbreaks of disease, and episodes of poaching can rapidly eliminate particular species from isolated reserves. Consequently, although the number of species existing in a park is an important indicator of the park's potential in protecting biodiversity, the real value of the protected area lies in its ability to support viable long-term populations of species and maintain healthy biological communities.

Creating New Protected Areas

Protected areas can be established in a variety of ways, but the common mechanisms are: (1) by government action (usually at a national level, but often at regional or local levels as well); (2) through purchases of land by private individuals and conservation organizations such as the Audubon Society and The Nature Conservancy (see Box 16.1); (3) via the established customs of indigenous people; and (4) through the development of biological field stations (which combine biodiversity protection and research with conservation education) by many universities and other research organizations.

National governments are the most important force in establishing and managing protected areas today. The international conservation community can help to establish guidelines and find opportunities to protect biological diversity, but in the end national (and local) governments must determine their own priorities. Many countries are in the process of doing so or have recently prepared National Environmental Action Plans, National Biodiversity Action Plans, or Tropical Forest Action Plans. (National governments also determine the type of park management, a subject covered in detail in Chapters 17 and 18; park management is of central importance in ensuring that a protected area actually fulfills its goals and is not just a "paper park" that is soon destroyed and degraded.)

While legislation and land purchases alone do not ensure habitat preservation, they lay the groundwork for it. Partnerships among governments of developing countries in the Tropics, international and local conservation organizations, multi-national banks, and the governments of developed countries bring together funding, training, and scientific and management expertise to help establish new protected areas. Local people are often partners in these efforts (see Chapter 20). Traditional societies also have established protected areas to maintain their way of life or just to preserve their land. Many of these protected areas have been in existence for long periods and are linked to the religious beliefs of the people. Such "sacred sites" often have concentrations of rare plants and animals that have disappeared elsewhere, and often include keystone resources such as springs and forested watersheds. National governments in many countries, including the United States, Canada, Colombia, Brazil, Australia, and Malaysia, have recognized the rights of traditional societies to own and manage the land on which they live, hunt, and farm, although in some cases recognition of land rights only results following conflict in the courts, in the press, and on the land.

Creating new protected areas requires the following steps, which we'll examine in detail in the following sections:

1. Identifying those species and biological communities that are the highest priorities for conservation.

2. Determining those areas of each country that should be protected to meet conservation priorities.

3. Linking new protected areas to existing conservation networks using techniques such as gap analysis.

Identifying Priorities for Protecting Biodiversity

In a crowded world with limited natural resources and limited government funding, it is crucial to establish priorities for conserving biological diversity. Although some conservationists would argue that no biological community or any portion of its species should ever be lost, the reality is that numerous species are in danger of going extinct, and there are not enough resources available to save them all. The real challenge lies in finding ways to minimize the loss of biological diversity in an environment of limited financial and human resources. Conservation planners must address three interrelated questions (Johnson 1995; Rodrigues et al. 2004a; Shi et al. 2005): What needs to be protected? Where should it be protected? and How should it be protected? Three criteria can be used to answer these questions and set conservation priorities:

1. *Distinctiveness (or Irreplaceability)*. A biological community is given higher priority for conservation if it is composed primarily of rare endemic species than if it is composed primarily of common, widespread species. A species is often given more conservation value if it is taxonomically distinctive—that is, the only species in its genus or family—than if it is a member of a genus with many species. Similarly, a population of a species having unusual genetic characteristics that distinguish it from other populations of the species might be a greater priority for conservation than a more typical population.

2. *Endangerment (or Vulnerability).* Species in danger of extinction are of greater concern than species that are not; thus, the whooping crane, with about only 340 individuals, requires more protection than the sandhill crane, with approximately 500,000 individuals. Biological communities threatened with imminent destruction are also given priority, such as the rainforests of West Africa, the wetland ecosystems of the southeastern United States, and other biological communities with numerous endemic and restricted-range species. Endangerment of biological communities can be estimated by using past and current land uses to predict future impacts.

3. *Utility.* Species that have present or potential value to people are given more conservation priority than species of no obvious use to people. For example, wild relatives of wheat, which are potentially useful in developing new, improved cultivated varieties, are given greater priority than species of grass that are not known to be related to any economically important plant. Biological communities of major economic value, such as coastal wetlands, are usually given greater priority for protection than less valuable communities such as dry scrubland.

By applying these criteria, the Komodo dragon of Indonesia (Figure 15.3) is an example of a species that fits all three categories: it is the world's largest lizard (distinctive); it occurs on only a few small islands of a rapidly developing nation (endangered); and it has major potential as a tourist attraction in addition to being of great scientific interest (utility). Appropriately, Indonesian islands that provide its major habitat are now protected within the Komodo National Park. The Western Ghats, a series of hills paralleling the southwestern coast of India, contain tropical forests that are similarly a high priority for conservation: These forests contain many endemic species, including the ancestors of several cultivated species, such as black pepper (distinctive); many of the products from theses forests are necessary to the well-being of local villagers (utility); the forests perform vital watershed services that prevent flooding and provide hydroelectric power for the region (utility); and despite their importance, these forests are threatened by logging, by fires set by villagers to create forage for their animals, by the collection of fuelwood and other forest products, and by continuing fragmentation by human activities (endangered).

FIGURE 15.3 The carnivorous Komodo dragon (*Varanus komodoensis*) of Indonesia is the largest living monitor lizard. Many tourists want to see these animals in the wild. Protecting this endangered species was an important reason for establishing the Komodo National Park. (Photograph © Stephen Frink Collection/Alamy.)

Determining Which Areas Should Be Protected

Using these three criteria, several prioritization systems have been developed at both national and international levels to target both species and communities (Redford et al. 2003). These approaches are generally complementary; they differ more in their emphases than in fundamental principles.

SPECIES APPROACHES   One approach to establishing conservation priorities involves protecting particular species and in doing so protecting an entire biological community. Protected areas are often established to protect individual species of special concern, such as rare species, endangered species, keystone species, and culturally significant species; species that provide the impetus to protect an area and biological community are known as **focal species** (Noss et al. 2002). One type of focal species is an **indicator species**, a species that is associated with an endangered biological community or set of unique ecosystem processes, such as the endangered northern spotted owl in the U.S. Northwest (Figure 15.4) or the red-cockaded woodpecker in the U.S. Southeast. The goal of managing a site for indicator species is to protect the range of species and ecosystem processes with the same distribution (Lawton and Gaston 2001; Maes and Van Dyck 2005); for example, by protecting the red-cockaded woodpecker, the last remaining stands of old-growth, longleaf pine forest in the southeastern U.S. will also be protected. Of course, research must be conducted to establish that the designated indicator species is consistently associated with the full range of species and ecosystem processes, and in many cases, it might be more effective to designate a group of indicator species to ensure the protection of a biological community (Lawton and Gaston 2001).

FIGURE 15.4 The northern spotted owl (*Strix occidentalis caurina*) is an indicator species for old-growth forests in the Pacific northwest, a habitat coveted for its rich timber sources. Protecting the owl protects many other species in the same habitat. (Photograph courtesy of John and Karen Hollingsworth/U.S. Fish and Wildlife Service.)

Another type of focal species is **flagship species**, often known as the "charismatic megafauna." Many national parks have been created to protect flagship species, which capture public attention, have symbolic value, and are crucial to ecotourism. While protecting flagship and indicator species, whole communities that may consist of thousands of other species and their associated ecosystem processes are also protected. Flagship and indicator species, whose protection automatically extends protection to other species and the community, are therefore known as **umbrella species** (Roberge and Angelstam 2004). For example, Project Tiger in India was begun in 1973 after a census revealed that the Indian tiger was in imminent danger of extinction. The establishment of 18 Project Tiger reserves, combined with strict protection measures, has slowed the rapid decline in the number of tigers (despite some recent setbacks) and in so doing has also protected many important and endangered biological communities.

The species approach follows from developing survival plans for individual species, which also identifies areas of high conservation priority. In the Americas, Natural Heritage Programs and Conservation Data Centers are collecting data on rare and endangered species from all 50 U.S. states, 9 Canadian provinces, and 14 Latin American countries (Stein et al. 2000). This information is being used to target new localities for conservation that contain concentrations of endangered species or where the last populations of a declining species exist. Another important program is the IUCN Species Survival Commission Action Plans. Approximately 7000 scientists are organized in over 100 specialist groups to provide evaluations and recommendations for mammals, birds, invertebrates, reptiles, fishes, and plants.

APPROACHES USING BIOLOGICAL DIVERSITY INDICATORS Certain organisms are used as **biological diversity indicators** or **surrogate species** when specific data about whole communities are unavailable (Bani et al. 2006). For example, a site with a high diversity of flowering plants often has a higher diversity of mosses, snails, spiders, and fungi (Sætersdal et al. 2003) than areas with a low diversity of flowering plants. In another case, analysis of existing databases revealed that the protection of sites with endangered plants in the United States also would protect many endangered animal species—on a relatively small amount of the total U.S. land area (Dobson et al. 1997a).

This approach is now being expanded in a systematic way. The IUCN Plant Conservation Office in England is identifying and documenting about 250 global centers of plant diversity with large concentrations of species, with Important Plant Areas (IPAs) identified at a country level, starting in Europe (WWF 2000; Radford 2004). BirdLife International is identifying Important Bird Areas (IBAs): localities with large concentrations of birds that have restricted ranges (Tushabe et al. 2006; www.birdlife.org). To date, 218 localities containing 2451 restricted-range bird species have been identified. Many of these localities are islands and isolated mountain ranges that also have many endemic species of lizards, butterflies, and plants, and thus represent priorities for conservation. Further analysis has highlighted IBAs that contain no protected areas and thus require urgent conservation measures to prevent imminent extinctions. The biodiversity indicator approach may not work for all species in all places; for instance, vascular plant richness in protected areas in Italy was found not to be an effective surrogate for predicting the species richness of fungi (Chiarucci et al. 2005).

CENTERS OF BIODIVERSITY Using a similar approach, The World Conservation Monitoring Centre, BirdLife International, Conservation International, the World Wildlife Fund, and others have attempted to identify key areas of the world that have great biological diversity and high levels of endemism, and are under immediate threat of species extinctions and habitat destruction: so-called "hot spots" for preservation (Figure 15.5; Redford et al. 2003). Using these criteria, Mittermeier et al. (1999) identified 25 global hot spots that together encompass the entire ranges of 44% of the world's plant species, 28% of the bird species, 30% of the mammal species, 38% of the reptile species, and 54% of the amphibian species, on only 1.4% of the Earth's total land surface (Table 15.1). Because these hot spots also include more widespread species, they actually include about two-thirds of all nonfish vertebrates on the planet. These habitats originally covered 17 million km^2 but are now intact on only 2 million km^2, and protected on only 888,789 km^2, only 0.60% of the Earth's total surface.

Many of these hot spots are tropical rain forest areas, such as the Atlantic Coast of Brazil, the Chocó/Darien/Western Ecuador region, Mesoamerica, the Guinean forests of West Africa, the Western Ghats of India, and the Indo-Burma region. Island areas are also among these hot spots, including the Caribbean region, Madagascar, Sri Lanka, the Sundaland and Wallacea regions of Malaysia and Indonesia, the Philippines, New Caledonia, New Zealand, and the Polynesia region. Hot spots are also located in warm, seasonally dry areas in the temperate zone, such as the Mediterranean Basin, the California region, central Chile, the Cape region of South Africa, the Caucasus region, and southwest Australia. Remaining areas are the dry forests and savannahs of the Brazilian Cerrado, the eastern mountains of Kenya and Tanzania, the tropical Andes, and the mountains of south central China. One of the Earth's major centers of biodiversity is the tropical Andes, in which at least

(A)

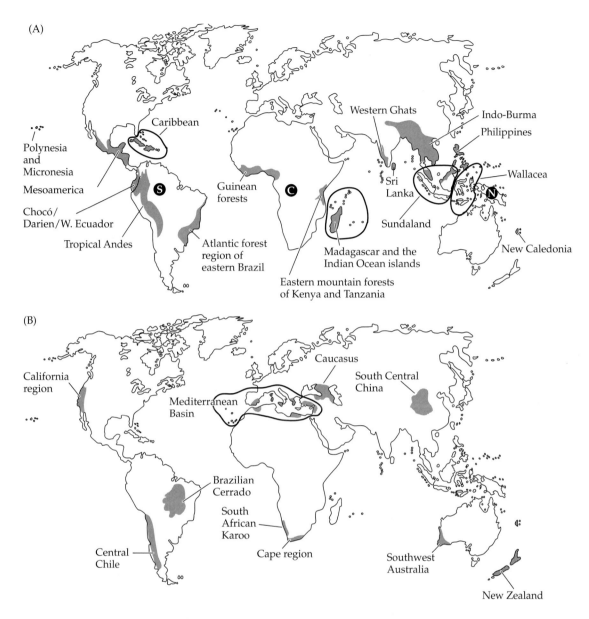

(B)

FIGURE 15.5 (A) Fifteen tropical rain forest hot spots of high endemism and significant threat of imminent extinctions. The circled areas enclose four island hot spots: Caribbean island, Madagascar, Indian Ocean islands, plus the Sundaland and Wallacea regions. The Polynesia/Micronesia region covers a large number of Pacific Ocean islands, including the Hawaiian Islands, Fiji, Samoa, French Polynesia, and the Marianas. Circled letters indicate the only three remaining tropical forest wilderness areas of any extent: S = South America, C = Congo Basin, N = New Guinea. (B) Ten hot spots in other ecosystems. The circled area encloses the Mediterranean Basin. (After Mittermeier et al. 1999.)

45,000 plant species, 1666 bird species, 414 mammal species, 479 reptile species, and 830 amphibian species persist in tropical forests and high-altitude grasslands on less than 00.25% of the Earth's total land surface. The hot spot approach has generated a considerable amount of enthusiasm and funding during the last seven years, and it will be worth watching to see how successful it is in advancing the goals of conservation in areas of intense human pressures on scarce and valuable biodiversity.

TABLE 15.1 *A comparison of twenty-five global hot spots*

	Original extent (× 1000 km²)	Percentage remaining	Percentage protected	Number of		
				Plants	Birds	Mammals
1. Tropical Andes	1258	25.0	6.3	45,000	1666	414
2. Central Chile	300	30.0	3.1	3429	198	56
3. Chocó/Darien/ Western Ecuador	261	24.2	6.3	9,000	830	235
4. Mesoamerica	1155	20.0	12.0	24,000	1193	521
5. California region	324	24.7	9.7	4426	341	145
6. Caribbean	264	11.3	15.6	12,000	668	164
7. Brazilian Cerrado	1783	20.0	1.2	10,000	837	161
8. Atlantic forest of Brazil	1227	7.5	2.7	20,000	620	261
9. Guinean forests of West Africa	1265	10.0	1.6	9000	514	551
10. South African Karoo	112	27.0	2.1	4849	269	78
11. Cape region of South Africa	74	24.3	19.0	8200	288	127
12. Eastern mountain forests of Kenya and Tanzania	30	6.7	16.9	4000	585	183
13. Madagascar and Indian Ocean islands	594	9.9	1.9	12,000	359	112
14. Mediterranean Basin	2362	4.7	1.8	25,000	345	184
15. Caucasus region east of the Black Sea	500	10.0	2.8	6,300	389	152
16. Western Ghats and Sri Lanka	182	6.8	10.4	4780	528	140
17. Indo-Burma	2060	4.9	7.8	13,500	1170	329
18. Mountains of south central China	800	8.0	2.1	12,000	686	300
19. Sundaland Island region	1600	7.8	5.6	25,000	815	328
20. Wallacea Island region	347	15.0	5.9	10,000	697	201
21. Philippines	301	8.0	1.3	7620	556	201
22. Polynesia/Micronesia	46	21.8	10.7	6557	254	16
23. New Caledonia	19	28.0	2.8	3332	116	9
24. New Zealand	271	22.0	19.2	2300	149	3
25. Southwest Australia	310	10.8	10.8	5469	181	54

Source: From Mittermeier et al. 1999.

The hot-spot approach can also be applied to individual countries (da Silva et al. 2005; Venevsky and Venevskaia 2005). In the United States, hot spots for rare and endangered species occur in the Hawaiian Islands, the southern Appalachians, the Florida Panhandle, the Death Valley region, the San Francisco Bay Area, and coastal and interior Southern California (Dobson et al. 1997; Flather et al. 1998; Figure 15.6). Despite the value of using the hot-spot approach, it is also important to continue protecting endangered biological communities and endemic species that lie outside of these high-profile areas (Kareiva and Marvier 2003; Stohlgren et al. 2005). This can be done by protecting representative examples of all the world's biomes (Olson et al. 2001), which is estimated to cost $90 to $330 billion over the next 30 years (Pimm et al. 2001).

Another valuable approach has been to identify 17 "megadiversity" countries (out of a global total of more than 230) that together contain 60 to 70% of the world's biological diversity: Mexico, Colombia, Brazil, Peru, Ecuador, Venezuela, the United States, the Democratic Republic of the Congo, South Africa, Madagascar, Indonesia,

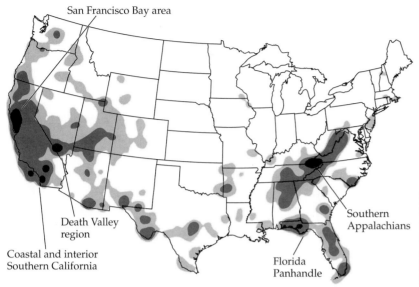

San Francisco Bay area

Death Valley region

Coastal and interior Southern California

Florida Panhandle

Southern Appalachians

FIGURE 15.6 Peaks of species richness in the United States, calculated by employing an index that gives extra weighting to rare species. The Hawaiian Islands, not shown here, have the greatest concentration of rare species. Darker shading indicates greater concentrations of rare species. (After Stein et al. 2000.)

Malaysia, the Philippines, India, China, Papua New Guinea, and Australia. At least some of these countries are possible targets for increased conservation attention and international funding (Mittermeier et al. 1997; Shi et al. 2005). A current priority is to establish comparable hot spot analyses for freshwater and marine ecosystems.

COMMUNITY AND ECOSYSTEM APPROACHES   A number of conservationists have argued that communities and ecosystems rather than species should be targeted for conservation (Possingham et al. 2002; Burgman 2002). They claim that spending $1 million on habitat protection and the management of a self-maintaining ecosystem, for example, might preserve more species in the long run than spending the same amount of money on an intensive effort to save just one conspicuous species (Box 15.1). Ecosystems benefit people by providing flood control, hydroelectric power, grazing for domestic animals, wood production, hunting and fishing, and recreation. Ecosystem conservation not only protects species as well as ecosystem services, it is often easy to demonstrate the economic value of ecosystem services to policy makers and the public (MEA 2005).

Using this approach, new protected areas should try to ensure that representative sites of as many types of biological communities as possible are protected. A **representative site** includes the species and environmental conditions characteristic of the biological community. While no site is perfectly representative, biologists working in the field can identify suitable sites for protection.

Biological communities vary from the few that are virtually unaffected by human influence (such as communities found on the ocean floor or in the most remote parts of the Amazon rain forest) to those that are heavily modified by human activity (such as agricultural land, forest plantations, cities, and reservoirs). Even in the most heavily modified human environments, though, remnants of the original biota may still exist and thrive, and habitats with intermediate levels of disturbance present some of the most interesting challenges and opportunities for conservation biology because they often cover large geographical areas. For instance, considerable biological diversity may remain in selectively logged forests, heavily fished oceans and seas, and grasslands grazed by domestic livestock (Chapman et al. 2000).

Determining which areas of the world urgently need additional protection is critical. Resources, research, and publicity must be directed to those areas (Nias 2001).

BOX 15.1

The Ivory-Billed Woodpecker and the Unexpected Value of Protected Areas

> "The reports of my demise are greatly exaggerated."
> *Mark Twain*

Establishing protected areas has the effect of preserving the full range of biological diversity, including thousands of species, the genetic variation of those species, and the range of ecosystem processes in biological communities. Given this range of biological diversity, it is not surprising that new discoveries keep being made in existing protected areas. One of the most astonishing discoveries in recent years occurred in the Cache River National Wildlife Refuge in the south-central United States. This protected area was established in 1982 when The Nature Conservancy purchased a 380-acre tract of swamp forest in hopes of conserving wetlands. This small piece of land became the first acquisition of a newly created wildlife refuge, and multiple land exchanges followed to create more than 50,000 ha (120,000 acres) of safeguarded land in the Big Woods of Arkansas.

More than 20 years later in February 2004, Gene Sparling, an amateur naturalist, was kayaking in the Cache River National Wildlife Refuge when he saw what he might have justifiably believed to be a ghost. It was a very large woodpecker with black and white plumage, a conspicuous crest, and, most notably, a large white bill. Sparling identified the bird as an ivory-billed woodpecker (*Campephilus principalis*), a species that hadn't been seen in 60 years and had long been considered extinct. Leading ornithologists confirmed that the initial identification was accurate (Fitzpatrick et al. 2005).

The rediscovery of the ivory-billed woodpecker, the world's second largest woodpecker, was a major media event, making headlines worldwide. People had been searching North America and Cuba for this conspicuous bird for more than half a century without success. To have finally discovered it alive after it had presumably gone extinct seemed nothing short of miraculous.

The decline of the ivory-billed woodpecker was due to the extensive logging of old-growth forests that took place in the southern United States during the 1870s. Each pair of these birds requires a territory of 6000 to 8000 ha, so huge blocks of forests are needed for an entire population to survive. And such large areas of forest were becoming rare as logging proceeded. In Cuba, the other part of the woodpecker's range, forests were cleared for sugar cane fields. In addition, during the late 1800s and

The ivory-billed woodpecker lives in remote swamp forests. This painting, created by an artist who has not seen the species in the wild, is being used as a stamp to generate popular support for conservation. (Courtesy of Larry Chandler, www.ivory-bill-woodpecker.com.)

early 1900s, many of these birds were shot, stuffed, and turned into trophies or specimens by collectors and naturalists. By 1939, the total number of ivory-billed woodpeckers remaining was estimated to be as few as 22. Its inclusion on the list of endangered species in 1967 was more an act of wishful thinking than a serious attempt to promote species management, as no one had reported sightings of the bird in the prior 23 years, and most biologists considered it extinct or nearly extinct even then.

We now know that the establishment of the Cache River National Wildlife Refuge had included, purely by chance, the last remaining population of this magnificent species, unknown to park managers until more than 20 years later. Without this protection, logging and habitat fragmentation would likely have resulted in the species' demise, the scenario that was assumed to have already occurred.

Since the rediscovery of the ivory-billed woodpecker, a recovery team with three working groups has been formed to oversee its conservation. The biology group focuses on performing natural history investigations, analyzing population viability, and assessing new monitoring techniques. One of their most important tasks is simply to determine how many woodpeckers there actually are in the population. The habitat management and conservation group evaluates and recommends management

BOX 15.1 (continued)

options for the refuge, and identifies current and potential future ivory-billed woodpecker habitats. The "corridor of hope" group is a partnership between public and private groups, including citizens and landowners, who support the recovery of the woodpeckers in the Big Woods of Arkansas. Part of this support includes $30 million in new conservation initiatives to benefit this species.

Decades after this species was presumed to be extinct, there is now hope for the ivory-billed woodpecker. While the current population is protected inside of the wildlife refuge, in coming years the species may be able to expand into nearby second growth forests that will soon be maturing into old-growth forests. It is now vital to protect these forests if the current population is to survive and expand. The rediscovery of the ivory-billed woodpecker shows the importance of establishing protected areas and validates decades of conservation work.

An analysis of 13 major terrestrial **biomes**—ecosystem types linked by the structure and characteristics of their vegetation, each of which supports unique biological communities—shows that the area of protected habitat and the percent of habitat converted to other uses can vary considerably (Figure 15.7). Based on the information in Figure 15.7, probably the greatest priority for conservation is increasing the area of protection for temperate grasslands, Mediterranean forests, and tropical dry forests because these communities are under significant threat and only a small percentage of their area is protected (Hoekstra et al. 2004). The lowest priority for new protected areas would be tundra, boreal forests, and montane grasslands.

ESTABLISHING PROTECTED AREAS WITH LIMITED DATA In general, new protected areas should encompass biological communities that are rich in endemic species of restricted range, that contain community types underrepresented in other protected areas, that support threatened species, and that contain resources of potential use to people, such as species of potential agricultural or medicinal use or ecosystem services that are easily understood by the public. The methods we have been describing for identifying areas of conservation assume knowledge of the areas in question. Sometimes taxonomists who collect plants, animals, and other species for museum specimens can provide data about species and the communities in which they live (van Gemerden et al. 2005). Unfortunately, such data typically do not exist or are incomplete. One approach to supplementing

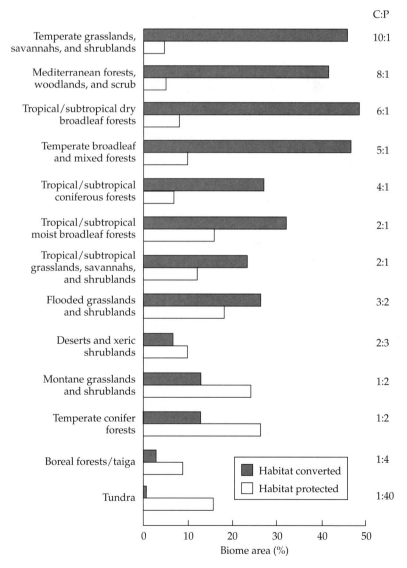

FIGURE 15.7 For 13 major biomes, the percent of the total area converted to other uses, and the percent of the total area that is protected from conversion. Also shown is the C:P ratio, the ratio of the percent converted to the percent protected. (After Hoekstra et al. 2004.)

the lack of data is to convene groups of biologists to pool their collective knowledge, identifying localities that should be protected (Groves 2003). Teams of biologists can also be dispatched to poorly known areas to make an inventory of species. Where decisions on park boundaries have to be made quickly, biologists are being trained to make **rapid biodiversity assessments**, also known as **RAPs** (Rapid Assessment Plans), that involve mapping vegetation, making lists of species, checking for species of special concern, estimating the total number of species, and looking out for new species and features of special interest.

Another way of circumventing the lack of data is to base decisions on general principles of ecology and conservation biology, as described more completely in Chapter 16. For example, a national park system could include elevational gradients that encompass diverse habitats, large parks to protect a large, charismatic species of significant public interest and tourist value, the need to protect representative habitats in different climatic zones, and individual biogeographical areas that have many endemic species.

WILDERNESS AREAS Wilderness areas are another high priority for establishing new protected areas. Large blocks of land that have been minimally affected by human activity, that have a low human population density, and are not likely to be developed in the near future are perhaps the only places on Earth where large mammals can survive in the wild. These wilderness areas potentially could serve as "controls," showing what natural communities are like with minimal human influence. For example, large protected areas of wilderness in the Chang Tang Reserve of the Tibetan Plateau will be needed to preserve the remaining declining populations of the wild yak (*Bos grunniens*) from hunting, habitat encroachment, and hybridization with domesticated yaks (Schaller and Wulin 1996). In the United States, proponents of the Wildlands Project, a private conservation policy group, are advocating the management of whole ecosystems to preserve viable populations of large carnivores such as grizzly bears, wolves, and large cats (Noss 2003). In Europe, efforts are being made to protect the Bialowieza Forest, a 1600-km² tract of primeval forest on the border between Poland and Belarus (part of the former Soviet Union) (Wesolowski 2005).

Three large tropical wilderness areas occupying 6.3% of the Earth's land surface have been identified and established as conservation priorities (see Figure 15.5A) (Mittermeier and Mittermeier 2003). It is important to emphasize that even these so-called "wilderness" areas have had a long history of human occupation and the structure of the forest and the densities of plants and animals have been affected by human activity. The following three large tropical forest wilderness areas are in danger of degradation:

- *South America.* One arc of wilderness containing rain forest, savannah, and mountains—but few people—runs through the southern Guianas, southern Venezuela, northern Brazil, Colombia, Ecuador, Peru, and Bolivia. The principal threat to this wilderness is the development of a modern road network, which will facilitate logging, migration, and agriculture (see Chapter 21). Experience has shown that this combination will in turn lead to widespread forest fires and other problems.

- *Africa.* A large area of equatorial Africa centered on the Congo River basin has a low population density and relatively undisturbed habitat, including large portions of Gabon, the Republic of the Congo, and the Democratic Republic of the Congo. Warfare and lack of government control prevent effective conservation activities in parts of the region, but also reduce development pressures.

- *New Guinea.* The island of New Guinea has the largest tracts of relatively undisturbed forest in the Asian Pacific region despite the impacts of logging, mining, and transmigration programs (especially in the Indonesian province of West Papua, the western half of the island). The eastern half of the island is the independent nation of Papua New Guinea, with 5.9 million people on 450,000 km² of land, while West Papua has a population of over 2 million people on 345,670 km². Large tracts of forest also occur on the island of Borneo, but logging, plantation agriculture, an expanding human population, and the development of a transportation network are rapidly reducing the area of undisturbed forest there.

A problem for conservation protection is that these wilderness areas act as a magnet for landless people living elsewhere. These areas currently have over 75 million people (1.3% of the world's total in 6.3% of the land area), but the population is rising at 3.1% per year, more than twice the global rate, due in large part to immigration (Cincotta et al. 2000).

Linking New Protected Areas to Reserve Networks

Once priorities are established, resources and personnel can be effectively directed to the most critical conservation areas. Prioritization should reduce the tendency of funding agencies, conservation organizations, and land trusts to cluster together in a few locations with high-profile projects. The decision of the MacArthur Foundation, one of the largest private sources of funds for conservation activities, to concentrate on different areas of the world for several years at a time—a "moving spotlight" approach—is a valuable counter to the tendency to concentrate resources on on a few well-known places such as Costa Rica, Panama, and Kenya.

An additional step is to link new protected areas with existing protected areas to create a reserve network, since biological diversity is protected most efficiently by ensuring that all major ecosystem types are included in such a system. These ecosystem types should include those that are unaffected by human activity as well as those managed and dominated by human activity such as plantation forests and pastures.

Gap Analysis

One way to determine the effectiveness of ecosystem and community conservation programs is to compare biodiversity priorities with existing and proposed protected areas (Figure 15.8). This comparison can identify gaps in biodiversity preservation that need to be filled in with new protected areas. In the past, this was done informally by establishing national parks in different regions with distinctive biological communities (Shafer 1999). At the present time, a more systematic conservation planning process, known as **gap analysis**, is sometimes used (Margules and Pressey 2000; Balmford 2003; Brooks et al. 2004; Dietz and Czech 2005; Riemann and Ezcurra 2005). Such complementary site selection increases the biodiversity of a network protected areas. Gap analysis consists of the following steps:

1. Data are compiled on the species, ecosystems, and physical features of the region, which are sometimes referred to as **conservation units**. Information on human densities and economic factors can also be included.

2. Conservation goals are identified, such as the amount of area to be protected for each ecosystem or the number of individuals of rare species to be protected.

3. Existing conservation areas are reviewed to determine what is protected already and what is not (known as "identifying gaps in coverage").

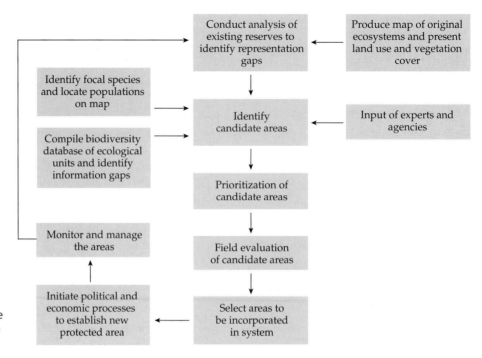

FIGURE 15.8 A model showing the process of gap analysis. (After Groom et al. 2006.)

4. Additional areas are identified to help meet the conservation goals ("filling the gaps").

5. These additional areas are acquired for conservation and a management plan is developed and implemented.

6. The new conservation areas are monitored to determine if they are meeting their stated goals. If not, the management plan can be changed or possibly additional areas can be acquired to meet the goals.

Gap analysis has been applied to the detailed bird census records in Britain to identify potential sites for new nature reserves (Williams et al. 1996). Using 170,098 documented breeding records of 218 species located within 2827 census grid cells (each 10 km × 10 km) that cover all of Britain, three possible reserve systems were analyzed for their ability to protect breeding sites for British birds; each network included only 5% of the grid cells—approximately 5% of Britain's land area. These three systems were created to: (1) protect "hot spots" of richness that contain the most species; (2) protect hot spots of rare species (narrowly distributed endemics); and (3) protect sets of **complementary areas**, areas in which each new cell added to the set includes one or more additional species. The results of the analysis show that while selecting species hot spots results in the greatest number of bird species per grid cell, it misses 11% of Britain's rare bird species. In contrast, selecting for complementary areas protects all of the bird species and is probably the most effective conservation strategy. In addition to using birds, this approach could also be implemented using mammals, plants, unique biological communities, or any other biodiversity component. The advantage of this approach is that each additional protected area adds to the total range of biological diversity protected (Cabeza and Moilanen 2001; Cowling and Pressey 2003). Despite their sophistication, such theoretical approaches are often regarded as impractical by land managers, who are preoccupied with nuts-and-bolts issues such as fund raising, public relations, the development of management plans, and dealing with competing demands for land resources.

On an international scale, scientists are comparing the distribution of endangered species and protected areas (Brooks et al. 2004). The Global Gap Analysis Project is helping to determine how effectively protected areas include populations of the world's vertebrate species (Rodrigues et al. 2004a,b; Brooks et al. 2004; Ricketts et al. 2005). The study compared the distribution of 11,633 species of mammals, birds, amphibians, turtles, and tortoises with the distribution of protected areas throughout the world to identify 1424 **gap species**: species not protected in any part of their range. The distressing result is that 804 of these gap species are threatened with extinction. Of all the groups, amphibians were the least well protected. Another study has mapped imminent extinctions of plant and animal species to highlight places urgently needing protection (Figure 15.9) (Ricketts et al. 2005).

Gap analysis can also be applied to major biome types (see Figure 15.7). On a global level, over 40% of major biomes such as temperate grasslands, Mediterranean-type forests and scrub, tropical dry forests, and temperate deciduous forests have been converted to other uses, such as agriculture and forestry; less than 10% of the area of these threatened habitats is currently protected (Hoekstra et al. 2004). Montane grasslands and temperate conifer forests are comparatively well protected, and thus are less threatened. Tropical rain forests are comparatively well protected on those areas that have not been converted to other uses.

At the national level, it is possible to compare maps of vegetation types and biological communities with maps showing lands under government protection (Wright et al. 2001). In the western United States, where 62% of the land is publicly owned, the gap analysis programs of individual states have developed a comprehensive system of ecosystem mapping. In the 148 million ha covered by this mapping system, the 73 distinct vegetation types can be compared to maps of the 8% of government land legally maintained in a natural state (such as national parks,

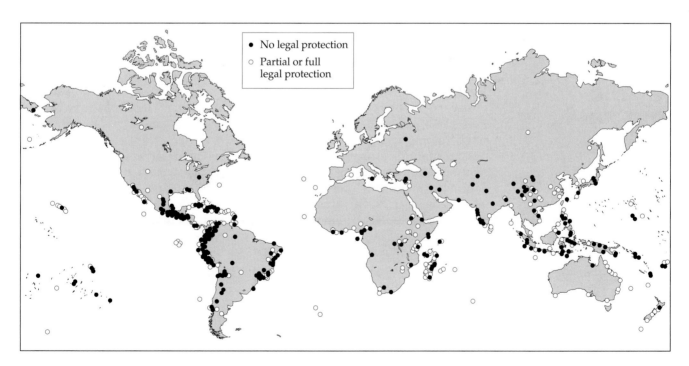

FIGURE 15.9 The imminent extinction of 794 animals and plant species is mapped at 595 sites around the world. Many of these species currently exist at sights with no legal protection, whereas others occur at sites with partial or full legal protection. (After Ricketts et al. 2005.)

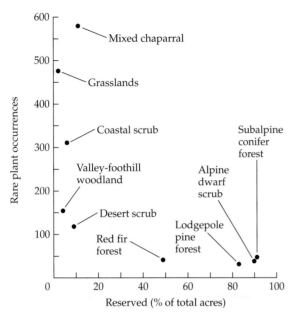

FIGURE 15.10 In California, most rare plants occur in low-elevation communities (such as mixed chaparral, grasslands, and coastal scrub), which are highly developed and are protected in less than 10% of their area. In contrast, high-elevation communities (subalpine and alpine communities and pine forests) are protected in more than 80% of their area, but few rare plants occur there. (After Szaro and Johnston 1996.)

wilderness areas, and wildlife refuges). Twenty-five vegetation types (34% of the total number of vegetation types) had at least 10% of their total area in protected areas; many of these vegetation types were high-elevation types that are well represented in mountainous national parks. Of the 48 vegetation types not currently having at least 10% of their area protected, 43 of them occur extensively on government land that is currently managed for resource extraction and could potentially be managed for conservation in the future. For the remaining vegetation types, negotiations with private landowners would be required to establish protection. It is important to note that no one federal agency has a complete representation of U.S. ecosystem types on its land; certain government agencies, such as the Department of Defense and the Bureau of Land Management, which have priorities other than conservation, may be important in efforts to preserve biological diversity. Cooperation among federal agencies, state and local governments, and private landowners is key to protecting biological communities.

Another example of gap analysis at a more local level (Szaro and Johnston 1996) compared California vegetation maps with protected areas. The result showed that more than 95% of the alpine and subalpine habitats were in reserves, even though these habitats had relatively few rare plant populations. In contrast, less than 10% of the biologically rich mixed chaparral, grasslands, and coastal scrub were protected (Figure 15.10). Preservation efforts had been successful at maintaining certain types of habitat, but others had been virtually ignored, especially where competing land uses led to conflict.

Amazonian Brazil has already lost about 10% of its original forest and continues to lose more each year (Fearnside and Ferraz 1995). Establishing new protected areas is an urgent priority because only 2.7% of the Amazon (13 million ha) is currently in reserves, and future plans call for increasing this to only 3.3%. A gap analysis of the Amazon reveals that 10 of the 38 distinct vegetation types of the region are not represented within protected areas. A series of reserves large enough to protect examples of each vegetation type and have viable populations of virtually all species has been proposed.

Geographic Information Systems (GIS) represent the latest development in gap analysis technology, using computers to integrate the wealth of data on the natural environment with information on species distributions (Stokes and Morrison 2003; Cantú et al. 2004). GIS analyses make it possible to highlight critical areas that need to be included within national parks and areas that should be avoided by development projects. The basic GIS approach involves storing, displaying, and manipulating many types of mapped data such as vegetation types, climate, soils, topography, geology, hydrology, species distributions, human settlements, and resource use (Figure 15.11). This approach can point out correlations among the abiotic and biotic elements of the landscape, help plan parks that include a diversity of biological communities, and even suggest sites that are likely to support rare and protected species. Aerial photographs and satellite imagery are additional sources of data for GIS analysis, and they can highlight patterns of vegetation structure and distribution over local and regional scales (Turner et al. 2003). In particular, a series of images taken over time can reveal patterns of habitat fragmentation and destruction that need prompt attention. These images can dramatically illustrate when current government policies are not working and need to be changed.

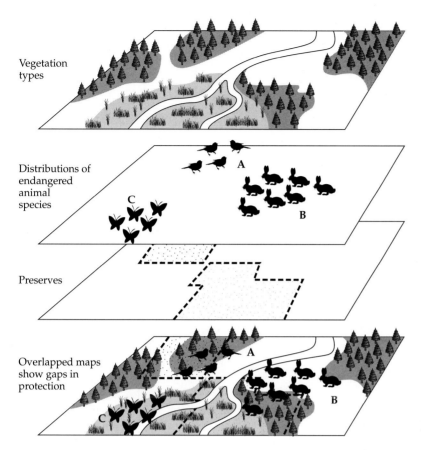

Vegetation types

Distributions of endangered animal species

Preserves

Overlapped maps show gaps in protection

FIGURE 15.11 Geographic Information Systems (GIS) provide a method for integrating a wide variety of data for analysis and display on maps. In this example, vegetation types, distributions of endangered animal species, and preserved areas are overlapped to highlight areas that need additional protection. The overlapped maps show that the distribution of Species A is predominantly in a preserve, Species B is only protected to a limited extent, and Species C is found entirely outside of the preserves. (After Scott et al. 1991.)

An ambitious attempt to apply GIS is the Interior Colombia Basin Ecosystem Management Project, which is charged with analyzing the ecosystem, biodiversity, and socioeconomic factors of the Columbia River Basin east of the Cascade Mountains (McLean 1995; www.icbemp.gov). One hundred specialists drawn from the U.S. Bureau of Land Management, the Forest Service, and other agencies have digitized 10,000 maps that cover 600,000 km² and included 100 layers of information. Completed in 2003, these GIS maps are used in the Interior Colombia Basin Strategy, a management plan that addresses the overall needs of the region: to preserve endangered species such as the northern spotted owl, to preserve salmon and trout fisheries, to maintain the timber industry, and to allow for local economic development.

Summary

1. Protecting habitat is the most effective method for preserving biological diversity. Land can be protected by governments, private conservation organizations, groups of local people, or private individuals. Protected areas include nature reserves, national parks, wildlife sanctuaries, national monuments, protected landscapes and seascapes, and managed-resource protected areas.

2. Over 12.5% of the Earth's surface is included in over 100,000 protected areas. Because of the real and perceived needs of human society for natural resources, strictly protected areas occupy only 6% of the Earth's surface. Therefore, the protection of biological diversity must be a priority on land and in water that is managed for resource production, including production forests, grazing lands, and fishing

grounds. Many new marine protected areas are currently being established, though their effectiveness needs to be evaluated.

3. Government agencies and conservation organizations have set priorities for establishing new protected areas based on the relative distinctiveness, endangerment, and utility of the species and biological communities that occur in an area. Many protected areas are established to safeguard focal species of special concern, often preserving an entire community with its associated ecosystem processes.

4. International conservation organizations are identifying "hot spots" of large concentrations of animal and plant species. If these areas can be protected, then most of the world's biological diversity will be protected. Another conservation priority is protecting wilderness areas so that ecological processes and evolution can continue with minimal human impact.

5. Gap analysis is an approach that identifies additional protected areas that need to be added to an existing network of protected areas. New computer mapping technologies, known as Geographical Information Systems, can facilitate this process.

For Discussion

1. Obtain a map of a town, state, or nation that shows protected areas (such as nature reserves and parks) and multiple-use managed areas. Who is responsible for each parcel of land, and what is their purpose in managing it?

   a. Consider aquatic habitats in this region (ponds, marshes, streams, rivers, lakes, estuaries, coastal zones, etc.). Who is responsible for managing these environments, and how do they balance the need for protecting biological diversity with the needs of society for natural resources?

   b. If you could add protected areas to this region, where would you place them and why? Show their exact location, size, and shape, and justify your choices.

2. Imagine that the only population of a rare and declining flamingo species lives along the shore of an isolated lake. This lake has numerous unique species of fish, crayfish, and insects. The lake and its shores are owned by a logging company that is planning to build a paper mill on the shore where the flamingos nest. This mill will seriously pollute the lake and destroy the food eaten by the flamingos. You have $1 million to spend on conservation in this area. The company is willing to sell the lake and its shores for $1 million. An effective flamingo management program involving captive breeding, release of new individuals into the population, habitat improvement, and natural history studies would cost $750,000. Is it better to buy the land and not devote resources to managing and researching the flamingo? Or would it be better to manage the flamingo and allow the lake to be destroyed? Can you suggest other alternatives or possibilities?

Suggested Readings

Bani, L., D. Massimino, L. Bottoni, and R. Massa. 2006. A multiscale method for selecting indicator species and priority conservation areas: a case study for broadleaved forests in Lombardy, Italy. *Conservation Biology* 20: 512–526. The use of indicator species is often more effective than using just information on vegetation structure and area.

DeFries, R., A. Hansen, A. C. Newton, and M. C. Hansen. 2005. Increasing isolation of protected areas in tropical forests of the past twenty years. *Ecological Applications* 15: 19–26. Protected areas are reasonably effective; however, the lands around them are often becoming degraded.

Dietz, R. W. and B. Czech. 2005. Conservation deficits for the continental United States: an ecosystem gap analysis. *Conservation Biology* 19: 1478–1487. Gap analysis can highlight what still needs to be protected.

Groves, C. R. 2003. *Drafting a Conservation Blueprint: A Practitioner's Guide to Planning for Biodiversity.* Island Press, Washington, D.C. Getting together experts to identify priority areas for conservation.

Higgins, J. V., M. T. Bryer, M. L. Khoury, and T. W. Fitzhugh. 2005. A freshwater classification approach for biodiversity conservation planning. *Conservation Biology* 19: 432–445. Freshwater systems have great economic value and need to have a higher priority in the establishment of new protected areas.

Kareiva, P. and M. Marvier. 2003. Conserving biodiversity coldspots: recent calls to direct conservation funding to the world's biodiversity hotspots may be bad investment advice. *American Scientist* 91: 344–351. Passionate argument that species outside the protected area system also need protection.

Lindholm, J. and B. Barr. 2001. Comparison of marine and terrestrial protected areas under federal jurisdiction in the United States. *Conservation Biology* 15: 1441–1444. Marine areas are not as well-protected as terrestrial areas.

Lourie, S. A. and A. C. J. Vincent. 2004. Using biogeography to help set priorities in marine conservation. *Conservation Biology* 18: 1004–1020. A challenge in establishing marine reserves is understanding the natural boundaries of ecosystems and populations.

Margules, C. R. and R. L. Pressey. 2000. Systematic conservation planning. *Nature* 405: 243–253. Review of principles for developing a comprehensive set of conservation areas.

Mittermeier, R. A., N. Myers, P. R. Gil, and C. G. Mittermeier. 1999. *Hotspots: Earth's Richest and Most Endangered Terrestrial Ecoregions.* Cemex/Conservation International and the University of Chicago Press, Chicago. Lavish, large-format book with pictures and information on each region.

Rabinowitz, A. 2000. *Jaguar. One Man's Struggle to Establish the World's First Jaguar Preserve.* Island Press, Covelo, CA. Sometimes one motivated individual makes a huge difference.

Redford, K. H., P. Coppolillo, E. W. Sanderson, G. A. B. Da Fonseca, E. Dinerstein, C. Groves, et al. 2003. Mapping the conservation landscape. *Conservation Biology* 17: 116–131. The challenges of getting international conservation organizations to agree on priorities for new protected areas.

Roberge, J. M. and P. Angelstam. 2004. Usefulness of the umbrella species concept as a conservation tool. *Conservation Biology.* 18: 76–85. Should the focus of conservation be on species or ecosystems?

Rodrigues, A. S. L., H. R. Akçakaya, S. J. Andelman, M. I. Bakarr, L. Boitani, T. M. Brooks, et al. 2004a. Global gap analysis: Priority regions for expanding the global protected-area network. *BioScience* 54:1092–1100. Numerous species are threatened with extinction and yet remain unprotected; urgent action is needed.

Shafer, C. L. 1999. History of selection and system planning for U.S. natural area national parks and monuments: beauty and biology. *Biodiversity and Conservation* 8: 189–204. Early efforts in U.S. park selection included attempts to protect species and special vegetation types.

Stein, B. A., L. S. Kutner, and J. S. Adams. 2000. *Precious Heritage: The Status of Biodiversity in the United States.* Oxford University Press, New York. Beautiful book with information on the status of U.S. biodiversity.

Stokes, D. and P. Morrison. 2003. GIS-based conservation planning. *Conservation in Practice* 4: 38–41. GIS is a powerful tool for conservation planning.

Tushabe, H., J. Kalema, A. Byaruhanga, J. Asasira, P. Ssegawa, A. Balmford, et al. 2006. A nationwide assessment of the biodiversity value of Uganda's Important Bird Areas network. *Conservation Biology* 20: 85–99. Protecting areas important for birds protects large numbers of other species.

Wesolowski, T. 2005. Virtual conservation: How the European Union is turning a blind eye to its vanishing primeval forests. *Conservation Biology* 19: 1349–1358. As Eastern European countries rush to modernize, in some places they are losing the opportunity to protect the remaining wild areas.

Designing Networks of Protected Areas

In this chapter we will examine some of the issues involved in designing effective protected areas. These issues are currently being investigated by conservation biologists, and they provide insight into the best methods for establishing new protected areas and reserve systems. Although networks of parks and conservation areas are often created in a haphazard fashion, dependent on the availability of money and land, a considerable body of ecological literature is now developing to address the most efficient way to design networks of conservation areas that protect the full range of biological diversity (Shafer 1990, 1997; Pressey et al. 1993, 2003; Poiani et al. 2000). Such networks are needed because many protected areas are required to protect examples of all species and biological communities. (These concepts were described briefly in Chapter 15.)

[handwritten margin note: Talk about conservation network.]

[handwritten margin note: TNC - CARL project.]

The size and placement of protected areas throughout the world are often determined by the distribution of people, potential land values, the political efforts of conservation-minded citizens, and historical factors (Newburn et al. 2005; Armsworth et al. 2006). In developed areas, the ability of private conservation groups and government departments to raise funds for land purchases is often the most important factor in determining what land is acquired.

In many cases, lands are set aside for conservation protection because they have no immediate commercial value—they are "the lands that nobody wants" (Pressey 1994; Scott et al. 2001).The largest parks usually occur in areas where few people live and where the land is considered unsuitable or too remote for agriculture, logging, urban development, or other human activities. Examples are the low heath forests on nutrient-poor soils at Bako National Park in Malaysia; the rugged, rocky mountain parks of Switzerland; the huge desert parks of the U.S. Southwest; and the one million km² of federal land in Alaska encompassing tundra and mountains. In other cases, small reserves are acquired in urban areas at great cost. Many of the conservation areas and parks in metropolitan areas of Europe and North America were formerly estates of wealthy citizens and royalty. In the U.S. Midwest, a number of the prairie nature reserves are former railroad rights-of-way and other oddly shaped pieces with unusual histories.

In contrast to haphazard and opportunistic approaches, models are now being developed that describe the most effective ways to use funds available to optimize biodiversity protection (Haight et al. 2002; Balmford 2003). In establishing new reserves, conservation biologists must consider the four "R's" of network design (Groves 2003):

- *Representation:* A reserve should contain as many aspects of biodiversity (species, populations, habitats, etc.) as possible.

- *Resiliency:* A reserve must be sufficiently large and well managed to maintain all aspects of biodiversity in a healthy condition for the foreseeable future.

- *Redundancy:* A network of protected areas must include enough examples of each aspect of biodiversity to ensure the long-term existence of the unit in the face of future uncertainties.

- *Reality:* There must be sufficient funds and political will to acquire and subsequently manage the protected areas.

Issues of Reserve Design

Issues of reserve design have proved to be of great interest to governments, corporations, and private landowners, who are being urged—and mandated—to manage their properties for both the commercial production of natural resources and for the protection of biological diversity. However, consideration of such issues does not necessarily produce universal design guidelines: Conservation biologists have been cautioned against providing simplistic, overly general guidelines for designing nature reserves, because every conservation situation requires special consideration (Ehrenfeld 1989). In addition, all would benefit from more communication between the academic scientists who are developing theories of nature reserve design and the managers, planners, and policy makers who are actually creating new nature reserves (Prendergast et al. 1999; Turner and Wilcove 2006). That said, the following topics in reserve design can provide a useful starting point for discussions about the best way to protect biodiversity and construct networks of protected areas.

In this chapter we'll review the following issues of reserve design, which attempt to provide guidance to conservation managers:

1. How large must nature reserves be to protect species?

2. Is it better to have a single large reserve or many smaller reserves?

3. How many individuals of an endangered species must be protected in a reserve to prevent extinction?

4. What is the best shape for a nature reserve?

5. When several reserves are created, should they be close together or far apart, and should they be isolated from one another or connected by corridors?

Some of these issues are being explored using the island biogeography model of MacArthur and Wilson (1967), described in Chapter 8. Many of them also have originated from the insights of wildlife and park managers (Shafer 2001; Tabarelli and Gascom 2005). The island biogeography approach makes the significant assumption, which is often invalid, that parks are habitat islands completely isolated by an unprotected matrix of inhospitable terrain. In fact, many species are capable of living in and dispersing through this habitat matrix. Researchers working with island biogeography models and data from protected areas have proposed some alterations to these models, but they are still being debated (Figure 16.1).

Also, all of these issues have been viewed mainly with land vertebrates, higher plants, and large invertebrates in mind. The applicability of these ideas to freshwater and marine nature reserves, where dispersal mechanisms are largely unknown, requires further investigation (Hastings and Botsford 2003; Roberts et al. 2003; Sobel and Dahlgren 2004; Cowen et al. 2006). Recent evidence suggests that many widespread marine species actually only disperse their offspring a short distance. If this proves true for many species, additional protected areas would have to be established to protect the genetic variation found in specific localities. Protecting marine nature reserves requires particular attention to pollution control because of its subtle and widespread destructive effects. Various countries in the Caribbean and Pacific regions have made steps in the right direction: Many individual islands have half or even more of their coastlines designated as marine parks, and the entire island of Bonaire is a protected marine park, with ecotourism emerging as the leading industry.

Protected Area Size and Characteristics

An early debate in conservation biology occurred over whether species richness is maximized in one large nature reserve or in several smaller ones of an equal total area (Soulé and Simberloff 1986; Wiersma and Urban 2005), known in the literature as the **SLOSS debate** (*single large or several small*). Is it better, for example, to set aside one reserve of 10,000 ha or four reserves of 2500 ha each? The proponents of large reserves argue that only large reserves have sufficient numbers of large, wide-ranging, low-density species (such as large carnivores) to maintain long-term populations (Figure 16.2). Large reserves also minimize the ratio of edge habitat to total habitat, encompass more species, and can have greater habitat diversity than small reserves.

The advantage of large parks is effectively demonstrated by an analysis of 299 mammal populations in 14 national parks in western North America (Figure 16.3) (Newmark 1995). Twenty-nine mammal species are now locally extinct and seven species have recolonized or newly colonized the parks. Extinction rates have been very low or zero in parks with area over 1000 km^2 and have been much higher in parks that are smaller than 1000 km^2. Extinction rates have been highest for species with low initial population numbers and small body size. It is also true that human population densities are lower on the edge of large reserves compared with human densities on the edge of small reserves, and this could contribute to the higher extinction rates in small parks (Parks and Harcourt 2002; Wiersma et al. 2004).

On the other hand, once a park reaches a certain size, the number of new species added with each increase in area starts to decline. At that point, creating a second large park, as well as a third or fourth park some distance away, may be an effective strategy for preserving additional species. The extreme proponents of large reserves argue that small reserves need not be maintained, because their inability to support long-term populations, ecosystem processes, and all successional stages gives them little value for conservation purposes. Other conservation biologists argue that well-placed small reserves are able to include a greater variety of habitat types and more populations of rare species than one large block of the same area

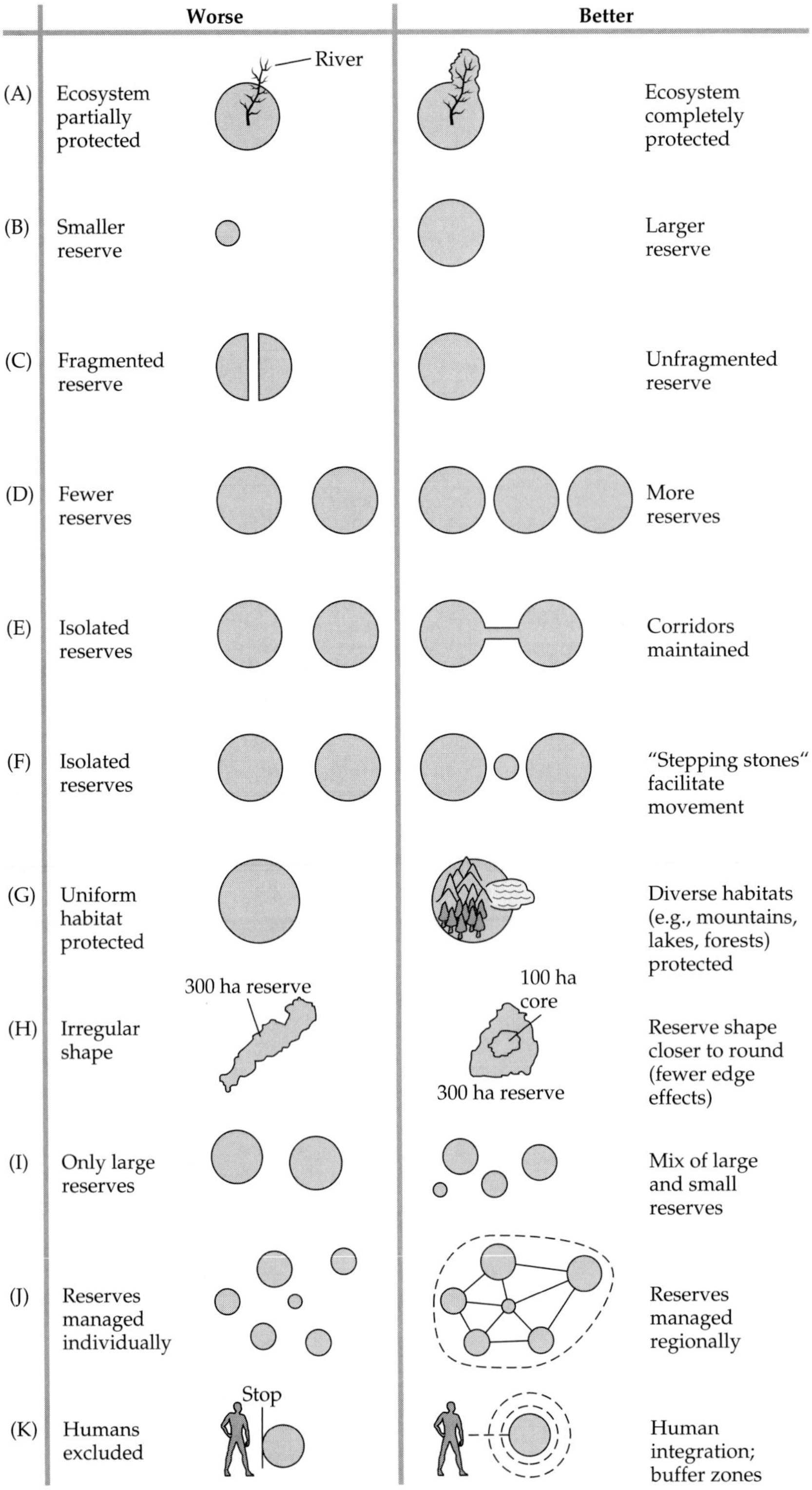

	Worse		Better
(A)	Ecosystem partially protected	River	Ecosystem completely protected
(B)	Smaller reserve		Larger reserve
(C)	Fragmented reserve		Unfragmented reserve
(D)	Fewer reserves		More reserves
(E)	Isolated reserves		Corridors maintained
(F)	Isolated reserves		"Stepping stones" facilitate movement
(G)	Uniform habitat protected		Diverse habitats (e.g., mountains, lakes, forests) protected
(H)	Irregular shape	300 ha reserve	100 ha core / 300 ha reserve / Reserve shape closer to round (fewer edge effects)
(I)	Only large reserves		Mix of large and small reserves
(J)	Reserves managed individually		Reserves managed regionally
(K)	Humans excluded	Stop	Human integration; buffer zones

FIGURE 16.1 Principles of reserve design that have been proposed based in part on theories of island biogeography. Imagine that the reserves are "islands" of the original ecosystem surrounded by land that has been made uninhabitable by human activities such as farming, ranching, or industrial development. The practical application of these principles is still being studied and debated, but in general the designs shown on the right are considered to be preferable to those on the left. (After Shafer 1997.)

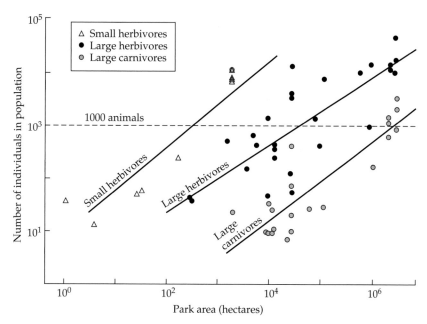

FIGURE 16.2 Population studies show that large parks and protected areas in Africa contain larger populations of each species than small parks; only the largest parks may contain long-term viable populations of many vertebrate species. Each symbol represents an animal population in a park. If the viable population size of a species is 1000 individuals (10^3; dashed line), parks of at least 100 ha (10^2) will be needed to protect small herbivores (e.g., rabbits, squirrels); parks of more than 10,000 ha will be needed to protect large herbivores (e.g., zebra, giraffes); and parks of at least 1 million ha will be needed to protect large carnivores (e.g., lions, hyenas). (From Schonewald-Cox 1983.)

(Simberloff and Gotelli 1984; Shafer 1995). The value of several well-placed reserves in different habitats is demonstrated by a comparison of four national parks in the United States. The total number of large mammalian species in three national parks located in contrasting habitats—Big Bend in Texas, North Cascades in Washington, and Redwoods in California—is greater than the number of species in the largest U.S. park, Yellowstone, even though the area of Yellowstone is larger than the combined area of the other three parks. Creating more reserves, even if they are small ones, decreases the possibility of a single catastrophic force—such as an exotic animal, a disease, or fire—destroying an entire species.

The consensus now seems to be that strategies for reserve size depend on the group of species under consideration as well as the scientific circumstances. It generally is accepted that large reserves are better able to maintain many species because they can support larger population sizes and include a greater variety of habitats. The research on extinction rates of populations in large parks has three practical implications:

1. When a new park is being established, it should be made as large as possible—to preserve as many species as possible, contain large populations of each species, and provide a diversity of habitats and natural resources (Wallis de Vries 2004). Keystone resources should be included, in addition to habitat features that promote biodiversity, such as elevational gradients.

2. Whenever possible, land adjacent to protected areas should be acquired in order to reduce external threats to existing parks and to maintain critical buffer zones. For example, terrestrial habitats adjacent to wetlands are often

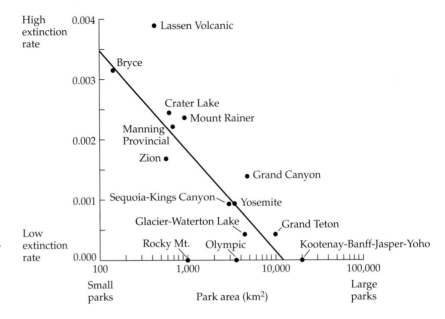

FIGURE 16.3 Each dot represents the extinction rate of animal populations for a particular U.S. national park, Canadian national park, or two or more adjacent parks. Mammals have higher extinction rates in smaller parks than in larger ones. (After Newmark 1995.)

necessary for semiaquatic species such as snakes, turtles, and amphibians (Semlitsch and Bodie 2003). The best protection may be provided when natural ecological units, such as entire watersheds or mountains, are encompassed within reserve borders as a means of reducing external threats (Possingham et al. 2005).

3. Even though large parks have many advantages, well managed small nature reserves also have value, particularly for the protection of many species of plants, invertebrates, and small vertebrates (Schwartz 1999). For example, woodland remnants in an Australian agricultural landscape retained some native insect species when they were as small as 50 m^2, an amazing demonstration of the conservation value of even extremely small habitat fragments (Abensperg-Traun and Smith 1999).

Often there is no choice but to accept the challenge of managing species and biological communities in small reserves (Schwartz 1997). Such small reserves often are surrounded by dense human populations and highly modified habitat (Wiersma et al. 2004). Small reserves may be effective at protecting isolated populations of rare species, particularly when they encompass a unique habitat type found nowhere else (Benes et al. 2003). Numerous countries have many more small protected areas (less than 100 ha) than medium and large ones, yet the combined area of these small reserves is only a tiny percentage of the total area under protection (IUCN 1994). This is particularly true in places that have been intensively cultivated for centuries, such as Europe, China, and Java. Bukit Timah Nature Reserve in Singapore is an excellent example of a small reserve that provides long-term protection for numerous species. This 50-ha forest reserve represents 0.2% of the original forested area on Singapore and has been isolated from other forests since 1860, yet it still protects 74% of the original flora, 72% of the original bird species, and 56% of the fish (Corlett and Turner 1996). In addition, small reserves located near populated areas make excellent conservation education and nature study centers that further the long-range goals of conservation biology by developing public awareness of important issues. By 2030, over 60% of the world's population will live in urban areas, thus there is a need to develop such reserves for the use and education of these people.

Reserve Design and Species Preservation

Because population size is the best predictor of extinction probability, reserves should be sufficient in area to preserve large populations of important species (rare and endangered species, keystone species, economically important species, etc.) (Noss et al. 2002). The best evidence to date suggests that populations of at least several hundred reproductive individuals are needed to ensure the long-term viability of most vertebrates, with several thousand individuals being a desirable goal (though it is also true that some small populations are able to persist for many decades; see Chapters 11 and 12). Having more than one population of a rare species within a protected area will increase the probability of survival for the species; if one population goes extinct, the species still remains in the reserve and can potentially recolonize its former range.

Several strategies exist to facilitate the survival of small populations of rare species in scattered, isolated nature reserves. They can be managed as one metapopulation, with efforts made to encourage natural migration between the nature reserves by maintaining connectivity among the reserves. Occasionally individuals can be collected from one nature reserve and added to the breeding population of another. Addressing the needs of wide-ranging species that cannot tolerate human disturbance is a more difficult aspect of ensuring viable populations in reserves. Ideally, a reserve should be large enough to include a viable population of the most wide-ranging species in it. Protection of the habitat of wide-ranging species, which are often large or conspicuous flagship or umbrella species, will often provide adequate protection for the other species in the community (see Chapter 15). Extensive areas of pine habitat surrounding the Savannah River nuclear processing plant in South Carolina are being protected to maintain the red-cockaded woodpecker (*Picoides borealis*), a species that needs large stands of mature longleaf pine trees (Figure 16.4). In the process, many endangered plant species are being protected as well.

(A)

(B)

FIGURE 16.4 Longleaf pine habitat in the southeastern United States, including areas of South Carolina, North Carolina, and Georgia, are being managed to protect the endangered red-cockaded woodpecker. (A) In Francis Marion National Forest, South Carolina, heavily logged areas lack older trees with the nesting holes that the woodpecker requires, so artificial nesting holes are drilled in the trees. (B) Here a young woodpecker leaves the nest for its first flight. (Photographs © Derrick Hamrick.)

The effective design of nature reserves requires a thorough knowledge of the natural history of important species and information on the distribution of biological communities. Knowledge about species' feeding requirements, nesting behavior, daily and seasonal movement patterns, potential predators and competitors, and susceptibility to disease and pests contributes to determining an effective conservation strategy. A balance must be struck between focusing on the needs of the indicator or flagship species to the exclusion of all other species and managing only for maximum species diversity and ecosystem processes, which could result in the loss of the flagship species that interest the general public.

Minimizing Edge and Fragmentation Effects

It is generally agreed that protected areas should be designed to minimize harmful edge effects (see Chapter 9). Conservation areas that are rounded in shape minimize the edge-to-area ratio, and the center is farther from the edge than in other park shapes. Long, linear parks have the most edge, and all points in the park are close to the edge. Consequently, for parks with four straight sides, a square park is a better design than an elongated rectangle of the same area. Unfortunately, these ideas have rarely, if ever, been implemented. Most parks have irregular shapes because land acquisition is typically a matter of opportunity rather than a matter of design.

As discussed in Chapter 9, internal fragmentation of reserves by roads, fences, farming, logging, and other human activities should be avoided as much as possible, because fragmentation often divides a large population into two or more smaller populations, each of which is more vulnerable to extinction than is the large population (Schonewald-Cox and Buechner 1992). Fragmentation alters the climate inside forest reserves, and it also provides entry points for invasive species that may harm native species, creates more undesirable edge effects, and creates barriers to dispersal that reduce the probability of colonization of new sites.

The forces promoting fragmentation are powerful, because protected areas are often the only undeveloped land available for new projects such as agriculture, dams, and residential areas. This has been particularly true in densely settled areas such as Western Europe, where undeveloped land is scarce and there is intense pressure for development. Undeveloped parkland near urban centers, for instance, may appear to be ideally positioned as a site for new industrial development, recreational facilities, schools, waste management sites, and government offices. In the eastern United States, many parks are crisscrossed by roads, railroad tracks, and power lines, which divide large areas of habitat like pieces of a roughly cut pie, in the process eliminating interior habitat needed by some species. Government planners often prefer to locate transportation networks and other infrastructure in protected areas because they assume there will be less political opposition to that than to locating the projects on privately owned, settled land. Indeed, park and forest supervisors are often rewarded for building infrastructure or increasing commodity production, regardless of whether it fragments their holdings and harms biodiversity. However, this situation is rapidly changing as conservation groups and some government officials become advocates for maintaining the integrity of protected areas.

Conservation Networks

Strategies do exist for aggregating small nature reserves into larger conservation networks (Balmford 2003; Bruinderink et al. 2003). Nature reserves are often embedded in a larger matrix of habitat managed for resource extraction (such as timber forest, grazing land, and farmland). If conservation biologists can make management for the protection of biological diversity a secondary priority of these areas, then larger habitat areas can be included in conservation plans and the effects of fragmentation can be reduced (Berry et al. 2005). Habitat managed for resource extraction can sometimes also be managed as an important secondary site for wildlife and as dispersal corridors between isolated nature reserves. Whenever possible, populations of rare species should be managed as a large metapopulation to facilitate gene flow and migration among populations (Nol et al. 2005). Cooperation among public and private landowners is particularly important in developed metropolitan areas, where there are often many small, isolated parks under the control of a variety of different government agencies and private organizations (Box 16.1) (Kohm and Franklin 1997).

BOX 16.1

Ecologists and Real Estate Experts Mingle at The Nature Conservancy

■ Of the many nonprofit organizations that now strive to protect biological diversity, the Nature Conservancy (TNC) is set apart by a unique approach that applies the methods of private business to accomplish the conservation of native species and their habitats around the world. Simply put, TNC works collaboratively with individual landowners, indigenous peoples, governments, the business community, and others to find creative ways to conserve ecologically important wildlife habitat for people *and* nature. In many situations, TNC either buys threatened habitat outright or shows landowners how managing their land for conservation may be as profitable as developing it.

Founded in 1951, TNC now has approximately one million members (Birchard 2005). TNC is not as widely known as some conservation organizations, nor is it as vocal. TNC advocates a nonconfrontational, businesslike, and results-oriented approach that contrasts with the methods of some high-profile, activist environmental groups such as Greenpeace and EarthFirst! (Groves 2003; McCormick 2004). Still, its methods have been quietly successful: In the United States alone, TNC has set aside more than 6 million ha; some parcels of land that TNC owned were so ecologically valuable that they have been sold or donated to local, state, or federal units of government and designated as public land, including state wildlife areas, national wildlife refuges, national parks, and national forests. Outside the U.S., the Conservancy has worked closely with local peoples, communities, nongovernmental organizations, and governments in 28 countries to conserve biologically important areas totaling around 50 million ha.

To achieve its goals, TNC maintains a revolving fund of over $160 million, created predominantly from private donations, with which TNC can make direct land purchases and fund high-leverage strategies such as debt-for-nature swaps (see Chapter 21) when necessary. Through these methods, the organization has created the largest system of private natural areas and wildlife sanctuaries in the world.

TNC, like other land trust organizations (see Chapter 20), uses creative approaches to accomplish its conservation mission. If TNC cannot purchase land outright for the protection of habitat, it seeks to offer alternatives to landowners that make conservation financially feasible. For example, 30 years ago, the U.S. Congress created tax incentives to encourage landowners to conserve ecologically important lands and waters by donating development rights to land trusts. These tax benefits provide landowners with valuable incentives to work with organizations such as TNC to conserve their lands.

When it is compatible with their biodiversity conservation mission, TNC also may pursue conservation strategies that allow some of the preserves it owns to be financially self-supporting. For example, the cost of maintaining one South Dakota prairie preserve is partially defrayed by maintaining a resident bison herd. Carefully managed bison grazing enhances biological diversity in these grasslands, provided the herd does not become too large. When the herd grows to a size at which overgrazing becomes a possibility, the excess animals are sold. The sale of bison brings roughly $25,000 annually to the preserve.

In addition, through its more than 400 staff scientists, TNC supports and encourages efforts to identify rare and at-risk species and habitats in the United States and in the 28 other countries in which the organization works (www.nature.org). In the U.S., TNC played a key leadership role by working jointly with every state government to create Natural Heritage Programs. Heritage staff inventory plant and animal populations in each state and add this information to a computerized database located in each state and at NatureServe, an

(continued)

BOX 16.1 *(continued)*

independent organization spun off from the Conservancy in 2001. With this database, biologists can monitor the status of species and populations throughout the nation. When Natural Heritage Program biologists identify populations of species that are rare, unique, declining, or threatened, state agencies and conservation organizations such as TNC have the information to make wise decisions.

In recent years, the Conservancy has designed portfolios of conservation areas within and across ecoregions. An ecoregion is a large unit of land and water typically defined by climate, geology, topography, and associations of plants and animals. Ecoregional portfolios represent the full distribution and diversity of native species, natural communities, and ecosystems.

The Conservancy's businesslike approach to conservation is successful largely because the organization's science-based, collaborative approach is appealing to many, including those, such as developers and large corporations, who sometimes have no great love for environmentalists. In general, TNC avoids lawsuits, preferring to use market-based approaches, financial incentives, and other creative solutions to achieve on-the-ground con-

Tina Buijs, a TNC park guard supervisor and operations manager, talks with Juan Antillanca, a farmer belonging to the Hurio indigenous community that borders The Nature Conservancy's Reserva Costera Valdiviana in Chile. The Reserve is a 147,500 acre site comprising temperate rainforest and 36 km of Pacific coastline. Keeping in close contact with their neighbors helps TNC officials realize their conservation goals. (Photograph by Mark Godfrey/ © The Nature Conservancy.)

servation results. The fundamental principle of TNC is, in essence, "Land and water conservation through private action"; so far, the idea has proved to be sound.

An excellent example of cooperation to achieve conservation goals is the Chicago Wilderness Project, which consists of 170 organizations collaborating to preserve more than 80,000 ha (200,000 acres) of tallgrass prairies, woodlands, rivers, streams, and other wetlands in metropolitan Chicago (Figure 16.5; www.chicagowilderness-mag.org). These cooperating organizations include museums, zoos, forest preserve districts, national and local government agencies, and private conservation organizations. This network of natural areas is critical to the quality of life of residents, since it is the only undeveloped land available for recreation between the densely developed urban core of Chicago and the highly developed agricultural landscape outside of the metropolitan area. The Chicago Wilderness Biodiversity Council coordinates conservation efforts, facilitates communication among members, develops policy and strategy, directs scientific research, and encourages volunteer participation. Among its many educational initiatives, the council has produced *The Atlas of Biodiversity* to publicize the diversity of habitats and species in the Chicago Wilderness network and has established the Mighty Acorns program to teach nature stewardship to schoolchildren.

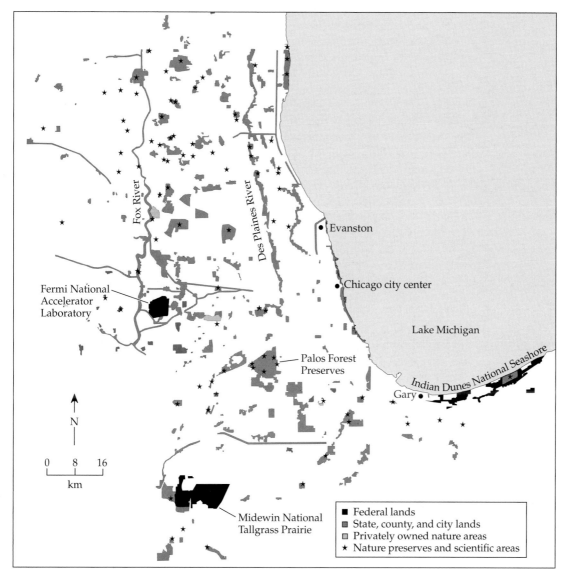

FIGURE 16.5 The Chicago Wilderness Project involves 143 organizations working together to preserve biodiversity and open space in the densely settled urban area, surrounded by agriculture. Many of the linear protected areas are trails and the banks of rivers. (After the Chicago Regional Biodiversity Council 2001.)

Linking Protected Areas with Habitat Corridors

One intriguing suggestion for designing a system of nature reserves has been to link isolated protected areas into one large system through the use of **habitat corridors**: strips of land running between the reserves (Simberloff et al.1992; Rosenberg et al. 1997; Wikramanayake et al. 2004). Such habitat corridors, also known as conservation corridors or movement corridors, can allow plants and animals to disperse from one reserve to another, facilitating gene flow and colonization of suitable sites. Corridors can potentially transform a set of isolated protected areas by establishing a linked network, with populations interacting as metapopulations. Corridors also might help to preserve animals that must migrate seasonally among a series of different habitats to obtain food; if these animals were confined to a single reserve, they could starve. Observations on Brazilian arboreal mammals suggest that corridors of 30 to 40 m in width may be adequate for migration of most species, and a corridor width of 200 m of primary forest will be adequate for all species (Laurance and Laurance 1999). In agricultural landscapes, increasing the connectivity of fragments allows native species to persist at higher densities (Steffan-Dewenter 2003; Hilty and Merenlender 2004).

The idea of corridors has been embraced with enthusiasm by some park managers as a strategy for managing wide-ranging species. In Riverside, California, the preservation of dispersal corridors was a key component in a plan to establish a 17,400-ha reserve to protect the endangered Stephen's kangaroo rat (*Dipodomys stephensi*). In Florida, millions of dollars have been spent to establish corridors between tracts of land occupied by the endangered Florida panther (*Felis concolor coryi*). In many areas, culverts, tunnels, and overpasses create passages under and over roads and railways that allow for dispersal between habitats for lizards, amphibians, and mammals (Forman et al. 2002; Clevenger et al. 2003; Ng et al. 2004). An added benefit of these passageways is that collisions between animals and vehicles are reduced, which saves lives and money. In Canada's Banff National Park, road collisions involving deer, elk, and other large mammals declined by 96% after fences, overpasses, and underpasses were installed along a road (Figure 16.6). These corridor projects all involved a large expenditure of public funds. An important question to ask is whether these corridors provided a greater benefit to the target species than using the same amount of money to acquire new blocks of conservation land elsewhere. The Wildlands Project has a detailed plan that would link all large protected areas in the United States by habitat corridors, creating a system that would allow large and currently declining mammals to coexist with human society (Soulé and Terborgh 1999). In eastern North America, there are over 2000 national, state, and provincial protected areas, but only 14 of them are over 2700 km^2, which is the approximate area needed to maintain populations of large mammals (Gurd et al. 2001). Linking the largest protected areas by corridors and managing them as single conservation systems would be an effective strategy to maintain rare species.

Corridors that facilitate natural patterns of migration will probably be the most successful at protecting species. For example, large grazing animals often migrate

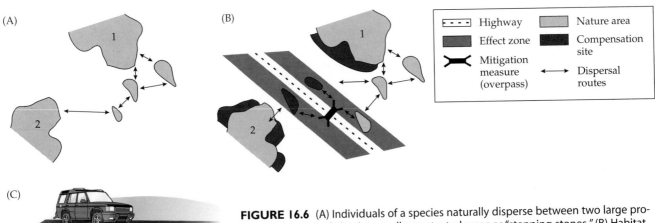

FIGURE 16.6 (A) Individuals of a species naturally disperse between two large protected areas (1 and 2) using smaller protected areas as "stepping stones." (B) Habitat destruction and a large edge-effect zone caused by a new road block the migration route. To offset the effects of the road, compensation sites are added to the system of protected areas, and an overpass is built over the highway to allow dispersal. (C) Wildlife can also use specially constructed underpasses to cross busy highways. When fences are built on the sides of highways, these crossing points are the only places for wildlife to cross. (B after Cuperus et al. 1999.)

in regular patterns across a rangeland in search of water and the best vegetation. In seasonally dry savannah habitats, animals often migrate along the riparian forests that grow along streams and rivers. In mountainous areas, many bird and mammal species regularly migrate to higher elevations during the warmer months of the year. To protect migrating birds, a corridor was established in Costa Rica to link two wildlife reserves, the Braulio Carillo National Park and La Selva Biological Station. A 7700-ha corridor of forest several kilometers wide and 18 km long, known as La Zona Protectora, was set aside to provide an elevational link that allows at least 75 species of birds to migrate between the two large conservation areas (Bennett 1999).

As the global climate changes in the coming decades, many species will begin to migrate to higher elevations and to higher latitudes. Creating corridors to protect expected migration routes—such as north–south river valleys, ridges, and coast-lines—would be a useful precaution. Extending existing protected areas in the direction of anticipated species movements would help to maintain long-term populations. Corridors that cross gradients of elevation, rainfall, and soils will also allow local migration of species to more favorable sites.

Although the idea of corridors is intuitively appealing, there are some possible drawbacks (Simberloff et al. 1992; Orrock and Damschen 2005). Corridors may facilitate the movement of pest species and disease; a single infestation could quickly spread to all of the connected nature reserves and cause the extinction of all populations of a rare species. Also, animals dispersing along corridors may be exposed to greater risks of predation, because human hunters as well as animal predators tend to concentrate on routes used by wildlife. Lastly, buying land to use as corridors and building overpasses and underpasses across existing roads are expensive solutions: Whenever a corridor project is being considered, the cost needs to be evaluated to determine whether this expenditure of money is the most effective way to reach the stated conservation objectives.

Some studies published to date support the conservation value of corridors, while other studies do not show any effect (Wallis de Vries 2004; Haddad and Tewksbury 2005; Pardini et al. 2005). In general, maintaining existing corridors is probably worthwhile, because many of them are along watercourses that may be biologically important habitats themselves. When new parks are being carved out of large blocks of undeveloped land, incorporating corridors by leaving small clumps of original habitat between large conservation areas may facilitate movement in a "stepping-stone" pattern. Similarly, forest species are more likely to disperse through a matrix of recovering secondary forest than through cleared farms and pastures (Castellón and Sieving 2006). Corridors are most obviously needed along known migration routes. Clearly, the abilities of different types of species to use corridors and intervening habitat areas to migrate between protected areas needs to be more thoroughly assessed.

Habitat Corridor Case Studies

Several case studies serve to illustrate the concept and practical applications of habitat corridors, and some of the difficulties involved in establishing and maintaining such protected pathways.

BANFF NATIONAL PARK In Banff National Park, the Canadian government has been building a variety of underpasses and overpasses across the four-lane Trans-Canadian highway to facilitate wildlife movement and at the same time to reduce the incidence of collision between vehicles and large mammals (Clevenger and Waltho 2005). Thirteen recent structures were evaluated for their use, which was measured as a function of animal tracks left in raked beds of soil. Certain mammals, such as grizzly bears, wolves, elk, and deer, used wide overpasses, whereas

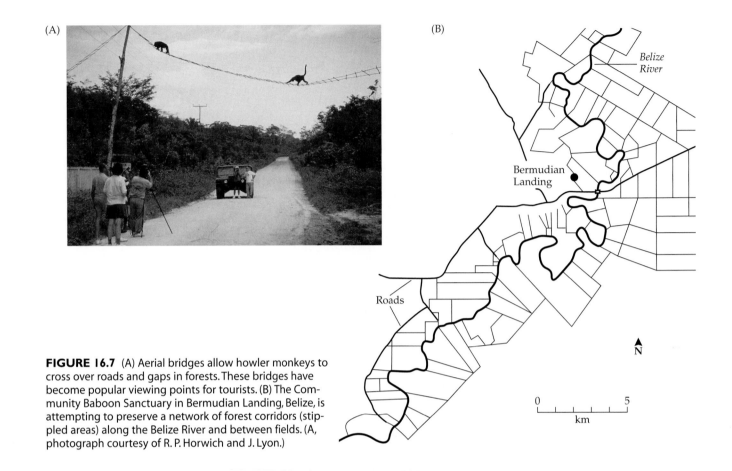

FIGURE 16.7 (A) Aerial bridges allow howler monkeys to cross over roads and gaps in forests. These bridges have become popular viewing points for tourists. (B) The Community Baboon Sanctuary in Bermudian Landing, Belize, is attempting to preserve a network of forest corridors (stippled areas) along the Belize River and between fields. (A, photograph courtesy of R. P. Horwich and J. Lyon.)

narrow underpasses were favored by black bears and cougars (see Figure 16.6C and the book cover). Cougars favored crossings with vegetation cover, but grizzly bear, elk, and deer preferred a more open landscape. The results demonstrate that a mixture of crossing types and associated vegetation covers are needed to allow connectivity across road barriers.

COMMUNITY BABOON SANCTUARY Corridors may be valuable on a small scale, linking isolated forest patches. Such an approach has been undertaken at the 47 km² Community Baboon Sanctuary (CBS) in the village of Bermudian Landing in Belize (Figure 16.7). Populations of black howler monkeys (*Alouatta pigra*) were declining because local landowners were clearing forest along the Belize River to create new agricultural land (Horwich and Lyon 1998), and the monkeys were unable to cross open fields between forest patches. As their food sources declined and their ability to move through the river forest became impaired, the monkey population underwent a serious decline. To reverse this trend, the 450 villagers living and owning land in the CBS agreed in 1985 to maintain corridors of forest approximately 20 m wide along the watercourses and property boundaries. Forest corridors also are being established across large fields and between forest patches. Other components of the plan include protecting trees that provide food for the monkeys and building aerial bridges over roads, so the monkeys can cross in safety. These measures appear to be successful, and the black howler monkey population has been steadily increasing as their habitat is reconnected. Ecotourism associated with the project provides significant income to villagers, as described in Chapter 20.

Landscape Ecology and Park Design

The interaction of actual land use patterns, conservation theory, and park design is evident in the discipline of **landscape ecology**, which investigates patterns of habitat types on a local and regional scale and their influence on species distribution and ecosystem processes (Turner et al. 2001; Poudevigne and Baudry 2003). A landscape is defined by Forman and Godron (1981) as an "area where a cluster of interacting stands or ecosystems is repeated in similar form" (Figure 16.8).

Landscape ecology has been more intensively studied in the human-dominated environments of Europe, where long-term practices of traditional agricultural and forest management determine the landscape pattern, than in North America, where research has emphasized single habitat types that were minimally affected by people. In the European countryside, cultivated fields, pastures, woodlots, and hedges alternate to create a mosaic that affects the distribution of wild species (Steffan-Dewentor 2003). In the traditional Japanese landscape, known as *satoyama*, flooded rice fields, fields, villages, and forests provide a rich diversity of habitat for wetland species, such as dragonflies, amphibians, and waterfowl (Kobori and Primack 2003) (Figure 16.9). In many areas of Europe and Asia, traditional patterns of farming, grazing, and forestry are being abandoned. In some places, rural people leave the land completely and migrate to urban areas, or their farming practices become more intensive, involving more machinery and inputs of fertilizer. In such cases, to protect biological communities, conservation biologists have to adopt strategies to maintain the traditional landscapes, in some cases by subsidizing traditional practices or having volunteers manage the land.

In such environments, many species are not confined to a single habitat; rather, they move between habitats or live on borders where two habitats meet. For these

(A) Scattered patch landscapes

 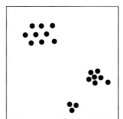

Open clearings in a forest | Groves of trees in a field

(B) Network landscapes

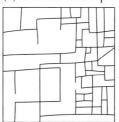 

Network of roads in a large plantation | Riparian network of rivers and tributaries in a forest

(C) Interdigitated landscapes

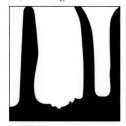 

Tributary streams running into a lake | Shifting forest–grassland borders

(D) Checkerboard landscapes

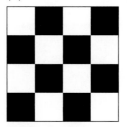 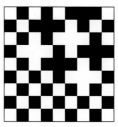

Farmland under cultivation for different crops | Lots in a residential development

FIGURE 16.8 Renditions of four different landscape types where interacting ecosystems or land uses form repetitive patterns. The discipline of landscape ecology focuses on such interactions rather than on a single habitat type. (After Zonneveld and Forman 1990.)

FIGURE 16.9 Traditional rural landscape near Tokyo, Japan, with an alternating pattern of villages (black); secondary forest (light gray shading); *padi*, or wet rice, fields (dark gray shading); and hay fields (white). Such landscapes were common in the past but are now becoming rare due to the increasing mechanization of Japanese agriculture, the movement of the population away from farms, and the urbanization of the Tokyo area. The area covered is approximately 4 km × 4 km. (After Yamaoko et al. 1977.)

species, the patterns of habitat types on a regional scale are of critical importance. The presence and density of many species may be affected by the size of habitat patches and their degree of linkage. For example, the population size of a rare animal species will be different in two 100-ha parks, one with an alternating checkerboard of 100 patches of field and forest, each 1 ha in area, the other with a checkerboard of four patches, each 25 ha in area (Figure 16.10). These alternative landscape patterns may have very different effects on the microclimate (wind, temperature, humidity, and light), pest outbreaks, and animal movement patterns, as described in Chapter 9. Different land uses often result in dramatically contrasting landscape patterns. Forest areas cleared for shifting agriculture, permanent subsistence agriculture, plantation agriculture, or suburban development have differing distributions and sizes of remnant forest patches and different kinds of species. The patterns of the landscape can strongly influence species distributions. For example, certain species of frogs are more abundant when there is greater forest cover around ponds (Mazerolle et al. 2005).

To increase the number and diversity of animals, wildlife managers sometimes create the greatest amount of landscape variation possible within the confines of their game management unit. Fields and meadows are created and maintained, small thickets are encouraged, groups of fruit trees and crops are planted, patches of forests are periodically cut, little ponds and dams are developed, and numerous trails and dirt roads meander across and along all of the patches. Such landscaping is often appealing to the public, who are the main visitors and financial contributors to the park. The result is a park transformed into a mass of edges where transition zones abound and animal life is abundant and easy to observe. However, the species in these landscapes are likely to be principally common species that depend on human disturbance—in some cases, invasive species. A reserve that contains the maximum amount of edge may lack many rare interior species that survive only in large blocks of undisturbed habitat (Horner-Devine et al. 2003; Crooks et al. 2004). The net result is that parks intensively managed for maximum wildlife and habitat diversity could be inhospitable to certain species of true conservation significance.

To remedy this localized approach, biological diversity needs to be managed on a regional landscape level, in which the size of the landscape units more closely approximates the natural size and migration patterns of the species. An alternative to creating a miniature landscape of a variety of habitats on a small scale is to link

FIGURE 16.10 Two square nature reserves, each 100 ha in area (1 km on a side). They have equal areas of forest (shaded) and pasture (unshaded) but in very differently sized patches. Which landscape pattern benefits which species? This is a question managers must endeavor to answer.

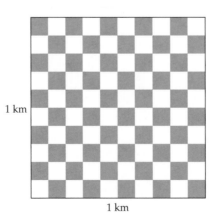

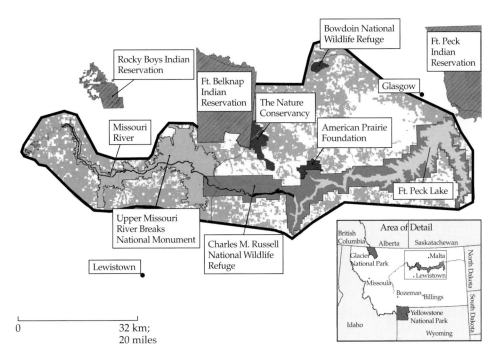

FIGURE 16.11 The American Prairie Foundation, with assistance from the World Wildlife Fund, is acquiring rangelands in the Missouri River area of Montana to connect government lands of high conservation value and Indian reservations. Their long-term goal is to restore a prairie ecosystem on a landscape scale (shown within the black-bordered area), including large mammals. The Nature Conservancy has also acquired a ranch for conservation purposes in this region. Within the black-bordered area some lands are privately owned (dark-shading) and other lands are publicly owned rangelands (white). (Map courtesy of World Wildlife Fund.)

all parks in an area in a regional plan, perhaps involving corridors, in which larger habitat units could be created (Figure 16.11). The Wildlands Project and the U.S. National Wildlife Refuge System are two examples of such an approach. Some of these larger habitat units would protect rare species, such as bears, wolves, and large cats, which are unable to tolerate human disturbance and need large areas to exist.

Conclusion

Within the field of conservation biology, there is ongoing discussion of the optimal procedures for designing networks of protected areas. The publication of new research results and vigorous discussion are helping to provide greater insight into the various issues. However, in describing the desire of conservation biologists to provide land managers with simplified general guidelines for designing networks of nature reserves, David Ehrenfeld (1989), a leading conservation scientist, states:

> I feel obliged to point out that there is a widespread obsession with a search for general rules of scientific conservation, the "genetic code of conservation" so to speak, and this finds expression in very general statements about extinction rates, viable population sizes, ideal reserve designs, and so forth. . . . Yet this kind of generality is easily abused, especially when would-be conservationists become bewitched by models of their own making. When this happens, the sight of otherwise intelligent people trying to extract non-obvious general rules about extinction from their own polished and highly simplified versions of reality becomes a spectacle that would have interested Lewis Carroll… We should not be surprised when different conservation problems call for qualitatively different solutions.

At present, the managers of protected areas still must approach each land acquisition decision on its individual merits. Managers need to be aware of the best examples and the appropriate models, but in the end the particular circumstances of a case, often involving such concerns as funding and politics, will determine the course of action. The greatest short-term challenge in designing systems of protected areas is to anticipate how the network will be managed to achieve its goals. In many cases, the management plan for the protected areas will be more important than the size and shape of the individual protected areas. In addition, people living nearby may help meet management objectives or come into conflict with park managers (as will be discussed in Chapter 17). The greatest long-term challenge is to anticipate how the current system of reserves will protect biodiversity in an uncertain world that is changing in terms of human population growth, land use patterns, climate, invasive species, and a host of other factors.

Summary

1. Conservation biologists are investigating the best way to design networks of protected areas. In some cases, investigations are based on the assumption that these areas have islandlike characteristics in a matrix of human-dominated landscape. The insight provided by these investigations can be combined with common sense and natural-history data to develop a useful approach.

2. Conservation biologists have debated whether it is better to create a single large park or several small parks comprising equivalent area; convincing arguments and evidence have been presented on both sides. In general, though, a large park will have more species than a small park of equivalent habitat.

3. Parks need to be designed to minimize harmful edge effects and, if possible, should contain an entire ecosystem. The tendency to fragment parks with roads, fences, and other human developments should be avoided, because they inhibit migration and facilitate the spread of exotic and other undesirable species and diseases. Whenever possible, government authorities and private landowners should coordinate their activities and manage adjoining parcels of land as one large unit.

4. Habitat corridors have been proposed to link isolated conservation areas. These corridors may allow the movement of animals between protected areas, which would facilitate gene flow as well as dispersal and colonization of new sites. Habitat corridors will be most effective when they protect existing routes of migratory animals.

5. In the past, wildlife biologists advocated creating a mosaic of habitats with abundant edges. While this landscape design often increases the number of species and the overall abundance of animals, it may not favor some species of greatest conservation concern, which often occupy large blocks of undisturbed habitat.

For Discussion

1. The only known population of a rare beetle species has 50 individuals and exists in a 10 m × 10 m area in a 1-ha (100 m × 100 m) patch of metropolitan woodland. Should this woodland be established as a protected area or is it too small to protect the species? How would you make this determination? What suggestions could you make for designing and managing a park that would increase the chances of survival for this beetle species?

2. Obtain a map of a national park or protected area. How does the shape and location of the protected area differ from the ideal designs discussed in this chapter? What would it take to improve the design of the park and/or coordinate its management with surrounding landholders, so that it had a greater likelihood of preserving biodiversity?

3. Obtain a map of protected areas for a country or region. Consider how these protected areas could be linked by a system of habitat corridors. What would it accomplish? How much land would have to be acquired? How much would it cost? Can you think of any other ways that the same funds could be spent more effectively to achieve the goals of conservation? To complete this exercise, you might have to make many assumptions.

Suggested Readings

Armsworth, P. R., G. C. Daily, P. Kareiva, and J. N. Sanchirico. 2006. Land market feedbacks can undermine biodiversity conservation. *Proceedings of the National Academy of Sciences U.S.A.* 103: 5403–5408. Creation of protected areas can have unintended consequences that are harmful to biodiversity.

Benes, J., P. Kepka, and M. Konvicka. 2003. Limestone quarries as refuges for European xerophilous butterflies. *Conservation Biology* 17: 1058–1069. Small, unique protected areas are the key to protecting certain rare species.

Berry, O., M. D. Tocher, D. M. Gleeson, and S. D. Sarre. 2005. Effect of vegetation matrix on animal dispersal: genetic evidence from a study of endangered skinks. *Conservation Biology* 19: 855–864. The pattern of populations and protected areas can affect the genetics of populations.

Birchard, B. 2005. *Nature's Keepers: The Remarkable Story of How the Nature Conservancy Became the Largest Environmental Group in the World.* Jossey-Bass, San Francisco. TNC is so large, wealthy, and influential, that you have to know about it.

Castellón, T. D. and K. E. Sieving. 2006. An experimental test of matrix permeability and corridor use by an endemic understory bird. *Conservation Biology* 20: 135–145. Habitats vary in their usefulness to birds as dispersal corridors.

Cowen, R. K., C. B. Paris, and A. Srinivasan. 2006. Scaling of connectivity in marine populations. *Science* 311: 522–527. The limited disperal ability of certain fish larvae is an important factor in marine reserve design.

Hilty, J. A. and A. M. Merenlendor. 2004. Use of riparian corridors and vineyards by mammalian predators in northern California. *Conservation Biology* 18: 126–135. Native predators are found at a much higher density in wide habitat corridors along rivers than in narrow corridors and agricultural lands.

Kobori, H. and R. Primack. 2003. Participatory conservation approaches for Satoyama: The traditional forest and agricultural landscape of Japan. *Ambio* 32: 307–311. Traditional agricultural landscape practices provide the habitat for numerous species.

Laurance, S. G. and W. F. Laurance. 1999. Tropical wildlife corridors: use of linear rainforest remnants by arboreal mammals. *Biological Conservation* 91: 231–239. This study from Australia shows that corridors 30 to 40m wide can be used by most arboreal mammals.

Mazerolle, M. J., A. Desrochers, and L. Rochefort. 2005. Landscape characteristics influence pond occupancy by frogs after accounting for detectability. *Ecological Applications* 15: 824–834. Landscape characteristics strongly influence frog distributions.

Ng, S. J., J. W. Dole, R. M. Sauvajot, S. P. D. Riley, and T. J. Valone. 2004. Use of highway undercrossings by wildlife in southern California. *Biological Conservation* 115: 499–507. Populations of certain species can be linked by underpasses.

Pardini, R., S. M. de Souza, R. Braga-Neto, and J. P. Metzger. 2005. The role of forest structure, fragment size and corridors in maintaining small mammal abundance and diversity in an Atlantic forest landscape. *Biological Conservation* 124: 253–266. Landscape patterns strongly affect animal distribution.

Pressey, R. L., C. J. Humphries, C. R. Margules, R. I. Vane-Wright, and P. H. Williams. 1993. Beyond opportunism: Key principles for systematic reserve selection. *Trends in Ecology and Evolution* 8: 124–128. An alternative to the current haphazard approach to land acquisition.

Rosenberg, D. K., B. R. Noon, and E. C. Meslow. 1997. Biological corridors: Form, function, and efficiency. *BioScience* 47: 677–687. Many experiments are evaluating corridors and will hopefully determine their value to conservation efforts.

Shafer, C. L. 1990. *Nature Reserves: Island Theory and Conservation Practice*. Smithsonian Institution Press, Washington, D.C. A comprehensive, well-illustrated review of the theories of reserve design, which presents evidence and counterevidence for particular theories.

Shafer, C. L. 2001. Conservation biology trailblazers: George Wright, Ben Thompson and Joseph Dixon. *Conservation Biology* 15: 332–344. Many of the modern principles of conservation biology, park design, and wildlife management were practiced by past field biologists.

Sobel, J. and C. Dahlgren. 2004. *Marine Reserves: A Guide to Science, Design and Use*. Island Press, Washington, D.C. Science can inform the establishment of marine protected areas.

Soulé, M. E. and J. Terborgh. 1999. *Continental Conservation: Scientific Foundations of Regional Reserve Networks*. Island Press, Washington, D.C. Planning for conservation on a really big scale.

Tabarelli, M. and C. Gascon. 2005. Lessons from fragmentation research: improving management and policy guidelines for biodiversity conservation. *Conservation Biology* 19: 734–739. Fragmented landscapes need to be reconnected.

Turner, W. R. and D. S. Wilcove. 2006. Adaptive decision rules for the acquisition of nature reserves. *Conservation Biology* 20: 527–537. Site availability, site condition and financial limitations are all important in establishing networks of protected areas.

Turner, M. G., R. H. Garner, and R. V. O'Neill. 2001. *Landscape Ecology in Theory and Practice: Pattern and Process*. Springer-Verlag, New York. Landscape ecology has strong links to conservation biology by helping to understand species distribution.

Wiersma, Y. F. and D. L. Urban. 2005. Beta diversity and nature reserve system design in the Yukon, Canada. *Conservation Biology* 19: 1262–1272. The distribution species across landscapes will determine the need for protected areas.

Wikramanayake, E., M. McKnight, E. Dinerstein, A. Josh, B. Gurung, and D. Smith. 2004. Designing a conservation landscape for tigers in human-dominated environments. *Conservation Biology* 18: 839–844. Connections need to be developed between tiger reserves to overcome the genetic problems of small populations.

Managing Protected Areas

Protected areas have different objectives depending on their legal status, establishment history, and individual characteristics. Some places are designated for biodiversity conservation and are managed to meet the needs of particular species while others protect whole ecosystems. Other types of protected areas are designated for recreational and cultural value. Regardless of their objective, most protected areas require active management, and it is important that the management be tailored to the goals of each individual protected area. This chapter examines some of the strategies employed in managing protected areas.

Although some people believe that "nature knows best" and that biodiversity is best served when humans do not intervene, the reality is often very different. In many cases, humans have already modified the environment so much that the remaining species and communities need human monitoring and intervention in order to survive.

Without human intervention, reserves exist in name only. The world is littered with paper parks that have been created by government decree and that exist only on maps. Although giving legal status to an area can help protect it from large-scale threats or development, without any real management on the ground, these paper parks, can, over time, lose all conservation value.

In some countries, particularly Asian and European countries such as Japan and the United Kingdom, the habitats of interest, such as woodlands, meadows, and hedges, have been formed from

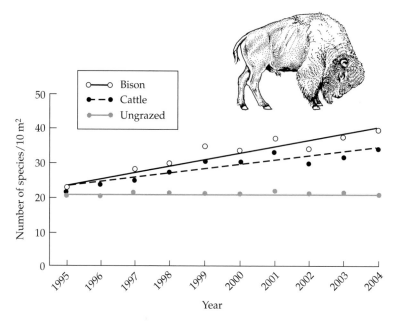

FIGURE 17.1 Large herbivores originally grazed the tallgrass prairies of the midwestern United States. The loss of these herbivores has altered the ecology of this ecosystem, with a resulting loss of plant species. Grazing by cattle and bison resulted in a gradual increase in plant species in prairie research plots over a 10-year period, compared with ungrazed control plots. (After Towne et al. 2005.)

hundreds and even thousands of years of human activity. These habitats support high species diversity as a result of traditional land-management practices, which must be maintained if the species are to persist. If these areas are not managed, they will undergo succession and lose many of their characteristic species; effective management then becomes necessary to restore the lost species. For example, in prairie grasslands, moderate grazing by cattle and bison results in more species than control areas that are ungrazed (Figure 17.1).

Many examples of successful park management come from the United Kingdom, where there is a history of scientists and volunteers successfully monitoring and managing small reserves such as the Monks Wood and Castle Hill Nature Reserves (Peterken 1996; Morris 2000). At these sites, the effects of different grazing methods (sheep vs. cattle, light vs. heavy grazing) on populations of wildflowers, butterflies, and birds are closely followed. For example, in montane grasslands at Ben Lawers National Nature Reserve in Scotland, the response of a rare alpine gentian plant has been studied in relation to the intensity of sheep grazing (Miller et al. 1999). Gentian populations initially increase when sheep are excluded, but decline after three years due to an inability to compete with taller plants and a lack of open sites for seedling establishment. Thus, the presence of moderate sheep grazing is critical to the maintenance of this rare wildflower. Livestock grazing may also be useful in reducing the abundance of certain invasive plant species (Marty 2005).

While such active management may be important in some places, in other places, management practices are ineffective or even detrimental. Often, this comes from a lack of understanding of biological interactions, or from unclear or conflicting management objectives. For example:

- Active management to promote the abundance of a game species such as deer to allow hunting and increase revenue for park management has frequently involved eliminating top predators such as wolves and cougars; without predators to control them, game populations (and, incidentally, rodents) sometimes increase far beyond expectations. The result is overgrazing, habitat degradation, and a collapse of the animal and plant communities.

- Overenthusiastic park managers who remove hollow trees, dead standing trees, rotting logs, and underbrush to "improve" a park's appearance and increase tourism may unwittingly remove critical resources needed by certain animal species for nesting and overwintering. Hollow trees, for instance, are the major nesting site for many birds, bats, and bears, and rotting logs are prime germination sites for the seeds of many orchids. Rotting wood and sprouting fallen trees are also important in the overall ecology of aquatic environments (Gurnell et al. 2005). In these instances, a "clean" park equals a biologically sterile park.

- In many parks, fire is part of the natural ecology of the area. Attempts to suppress fire completely are expensive and waste scarce management resources. They may eventually lead to loss of fire-dependent species and to massive, uncontrollable fires of unnatural intensity such as those that occurred in Yellowstone National Park in 1988.

Detrimental management practices aside, the crucial point is that parks often must be actively managed to prevent deterioration (Sutherland and Hill 1995; Halvorson and Davis 1996). The most effective parks are usually those whose managers have the benefit of information provided by research and monitoring programs and have funds available to implement management plans.

Small reserves, such as those found in long-settled areas and large cities, will generally require more active management than large reserves, because they often are surrounded by an altered environment, have less interior habitat, and are more easily affected by exotic species and human activities. Even in large reserves, active management may be required to control hunting and to regulate the frequency of fire and the number of visitors. Simply maintaining the park boundaries may not be sufficient except in the largest and most remote protected areas.

In a symposium volume entitled *The Scientific Management of Animal and Plant Communities for Conservation* (Duffey and Watts 1971), Michael Morris of Monks Wood emphasized the importance of designing management objectives for each individual reserve:

> There is no inherently right or wrong way to manage a nature reserve ... the aptness of any method of management must be related to the objects of management for any particular site... Only when objects of management have been formulated can results of scientific management be applied.

The level and type of management needed must be based on the ecological objectives of the reserve, but also on the social context of the area (Terborgh et al. 2002). Both can change over time. Protected areas in some countries may be extremely hard to manage. Different groups do not hesitate to farm, log, mine, hunt, and fish in protected areas because they feel that government land is owned by "everyone," "anybody" can take whatever they want, and "nobody" is willing to intervene. These protected areas have gradually—and sometimes rapidly—lost species, and their habitat quality has been degraded.

Management can break down in times of war when the central government ceases to function. In such situations there is often severe and rapid degradation of natural resources when trees are cut down and animals are hunted. Examples of such breakdowns have occurred in Afghanistan, the Democratic Republic of the Congo, and Rwanda, though in some cases park officials remained and continued to do their work, without proper security and without being paid (Zahler 2003; Hart and Hart 2003).

Monitoring as a Management Tool

An important aspect of park management involves monitoring components that are crucial for biological diversity, such as the water level of ponds; the amount of soil being washed into streams; the number of individuals of rare and endangered species; the density of herbs, shrubs, and trees; and the dates migratory animals arrive at and leave the park. This monitoring may also include tracking the amount of natural materials being removed by local people. Basic monitoring methods include recording standard observations, performing surveys of key elements, taking photographs from fixed points, and conducting interviews with park users (Danielsen et al. 2000) (see Chapter 12). The exact types of information gathered depend on the goals of park management (Feinsinger 2001). Not only does monitoring allow managers to determine the health of the park, it can suggest which management practices are working and which are not (Hockings 2003; Stem et al. 2005). Managers must continually refine the information they need on conditions inside, or sometimes outside, of protected areas and be ready to adjust park management practices in an adaptive manner to achieve conservation objectives (sometimes referred to as **adaptive management**) (Figure 17.2). In some protected areas, difficult choices may have to be made: for example, if protected seals are eating threatened seabirds, which species should be given priority in management practices (David et al. 2003)?

One species that has been intensively monitored for decades is the giant cactus, or saguaro (*Carnegiea gigantea*), an icon of the desert landscape (McAuliffe 1996). In 1933, the Saguaro National Park was established east of Tucson, Arizona, to protect this flagship species. Detailed observations, combined with precise photographic records (Figure 17.3), show that stands of large saguaro are declining within the park. Investigations over an 80-year period suggest that adult cacti are damaged or killed by periods of subfreezing weather that occur about once a decade. Also, cattle grazing, which occurred from the 1880s until 1979, prevented regeneration by trampling seedlings and compacting the soil. Now that cattle grazing has been stopped for over 20 years, permanent research plots within the park have recorded the establishment of large numbers of young saguaro plants (Drezner 2005). These will be closely watched to see if new cactus forests appear later this century.

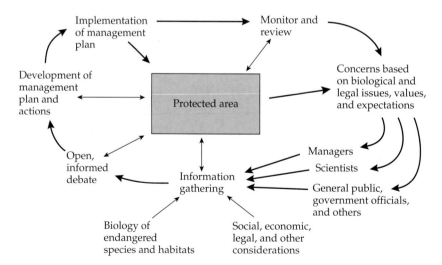

FIGURE 17.2 A model of an ideal adaptive management process for protected areas, emphasizing the stages of decision making. (After Cork et al. 2000.)

1935

1962

1986

FIGURE 17.3 The same landscape, photographed in 1935, 1962, and 1986, showing the decline of a saguaro cactus population in the Rincon Mountain District, Saguaro National Park. The photographs depict the same population—there are no new saguaro plants visible in the photos, though there are many young plants. (Photographs by H. L. Shantz, J. R. Hastings, and R. M. Turner.)

Identifying and Managing Threats

Management of protected areas must take into account factors that threaten the biological diversity and ecological health of the park. These include many of the threats detailed in Chapters 9 and 10, including exotic species; low population size among rare species; habitat destruction, fragmentation, or degradation; and human use. One such management approach that identifies these threats is the Rapid Assessment and Prioritization of Protected Areas Management methodology developed by the World Wide Fund for Nature International (Ervin 2003).

Even in a well-regulated park, air pollution, acid rain, water pollution, global climate change, and the changing composition of atmospheric gases influence natural communities and cause some species to increase and others to decrease or be eliminated. Unfortunately, natural history studies show that invasive exotic species are likely to be the main beneficiaries of an altered environment since they tend to be adaptable, efficient dispersers that are tolerant of disturbance. The ability of park managers to deal with these major, externally driven alterations in ecosystem processes is rather limited. In one approach to address such ecosystem changes, experiments are being conducted in which basic compounds such as lime are added to water bodies to prevent acidification. These measures, however, will never take the place of needed environmental reforms to limit human production and consumption patterns.

Managing Invasive Species

Invasion by exotic species is now recognized as a threat to many protected areas, particularly wetlands, grasslands, and island ecosystems. In many places, exotic species may already be present inside a park, and new exotic species may be invading along its boundaries. If these species are allowed to increase unchecked, native species and even entire communities might be eliminated from the park. Where an invasive species threatens native species, it should be removed or at least reduced in frequency (Myers et al. 2000). An exotic species that has just arrived and has known invasive tendencies should be aggressively removed while it is still at low densities. Removing invasive species each year is often highly cost effective compared with the expensive massive eradication programs that are required when the population of an exotic species explodes (Chen 2001). European purple loosestrife (*Lythrum salicaria*), which invades North American wetlands, is an example of an invasive species that can outcompete many native plants, often forming pure stands along river and pond edges and in marshes. This species has a detrimental effect on wildlife, because it is not eaten by most waterfowl and crowds out beneficial species that are.

Once such an exotic species becomes established in an area, it may be difficult (if not impossible) to eliminate it. The recovery of previously declining populations of native plants and animals has often been linked to the elimination of exotic animal species such as goats, rats, rabbits, and sea gulls from islands and other management areas. Common methods involve poisoning, shooting, capturing, and preventing reproduction. In such cases, a major effort in public relations is needed to explain the goal of the intervention and to respond to the concerns of the public. As an example of pest management, colonies of three rare species of terns on an island off the Maine coast were displaced by expanding common sea gull populations (Anderson and Devlin 1999). When the sea gulls were removed by poisoning and shooting, the terns returned to the island and their numbers appear to be recovering. Constant vigilance is required, as the sea gulls would quickly return to the island if park managers did not shoot at them.

Managing Habitat

A park may have to be carefully managed to ensure that the full range of original habitat types are maintained (Gram et al. 2003). Many species only occupy specif-

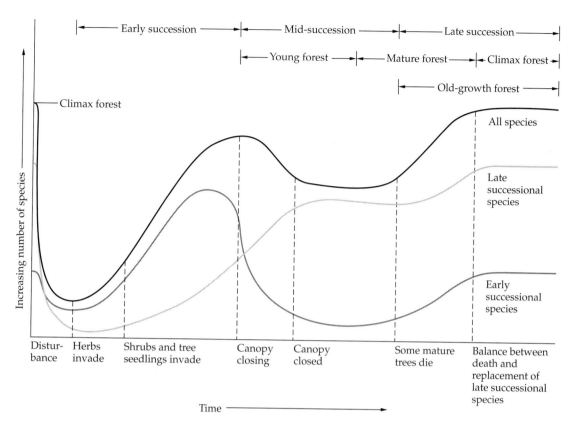

FIGURE 17.4 A general model of the change in species diversity during forest succession following a major disturbance such as a fire, hurricane, or clear-cut logging. Early successional species are generally fast-growing and intolerant of shade; late successional species grow more slowly and are shade-tolerant. The full successional time span covers many decades or centuries. (After Norse 1986.)

ic habitats and specific successional stages of habitat. When land is set aside as a protected area, often the pattern of disturbance and human usage changes so markedly that many species previously found on the site fail to persist. Natural disturbances, including fires, grazing, and tree falls, are key elements in the ecosystem required for the presence of certain rare species (Yates and Ladd 2005). In small parks, the full range of successional stages may not be present at a site, and many species may be missing for this reason. For example, in an isolated park dominated by old-growth trees, species characteristic of the early successional herb and shrub stage may be missing (Figure 17.4). If such a park is swept entirely by a fire or a windstorm, the species characteristic of old-growth forest may be eliminated. In many isolated protected areas in metropolitan locations, frequent human-caused fires and other human disturbances eliminate many of the late successional plant and animal species. However, early successional species may also be missing if they are not present in adjacent sites that serve as colonization sources.

Park managers sometimes must actively manage sites to ensure that all successional stages are present so that species characteristic of each stage have a place to persist and thrive (Box 17.1). One common way to do this is to set localized, controlled fires periodically in grassland, shrublands, and forests to reinitiate the successional process (Norton and DeLange 2003; Van Wilgen et al. 2004). In some wildlife sanctuaries, grasslands and fields are maintained by livestock grazing, burning, mowing, or shallow plowing in order to retain open habitat in the landscape. For example, many of the unique wildflowers of Nantucket Island off the coast of Massachusetts are found in the scenic heathland areas. These heathlands

BOX 17.1

Habitat Management:
The Key to Success in the Conservation of Endangered Butterflies

■ In 1980 the heath fritillary butterfly (*Mellicta athalia*) had the dubious honor of being closer to extinction than any other butterfly species in England. The distribution of the species had declined steadily for 70 years as its preferred habitat became overgrown or was converted to farmland. The larvae of the heath fritillary feed on plants found in unimproved grasslands or where woodland has recently been cleared to create sunny glades. These habitats are ephemeral and patchy by nature; they require regular cutting of trees or grazing to maintain populations of the butterflies' food plants. The decline of traditional forestry practices and intensive farming have interrupted the processes that provide the necessary butterfly habitat (Warren 1991). The problem faced by the heath fritillary is similar to that of a number of butterfly species that must colonize specialized, ephemeral habitats —they survive as a network of temporary populations linked by dispersal, which is best described as a metapopulation (Davies et al. 2005). The silver-studded blue butterfly (*Plebejus argus*), found in the heathlands of East Anglia, and the silver-spotted skipper (*Hesperis comma*), of short-turf grasslands in southern England, are two additional species that require habitat management to survive.

In the case of the silver-studded blue, the species is only found in young stands of bell heather and heath, where adults feed on nectar and larvae feed on leaves. The specialization goes even further because the larvae must be tended by a certain type of black ant (*Lasius* sp.) to survive, and the distribution of these ants is variable. When the butterflies' habitats are fragmented by human activities, these natural patterns may be interrupted. Species may be unable to locate new suitable habitat due to limited dispersal abilities. The silver-studded blue in particular seems to be unable to disperse more than 1 km from existing populations (Thomas 1995). Experimental attempts to establish new populations by carrying adults to unoccupied sites have had some degree of success.

Detailed ecological studies have provided the basis for species-specific management strategies. Areas with heath fritillary populations are now managed to encourage the habitat types that the species prefers, such as newly felled woodland and unimproved grasslands. Assessment of the fritillary's progress after nearly a decade of intervention to maintain early-succession food plants demonstrates that human intervention has been a significant factor in the success of the colonies. Where habitat management did not occur, the majority of colonies became extinct (Warren 1991). However, the practice of intensive management raises the disturbing issue of the extent to which endangered species depend on human action. The heath fritillary now appears to be utterly dependent on human intervention for survival; the fate of many other species probably rests entirely in our hands as well.

The rare silver-spotted skipper has shown a 10-fold increase in the area it occupies due to the deliberate development of a grazing policy to favor the species and two serendipitous circumstances: an increasing rabbit

Larvae of the heath fritillary butterfly (*Mellicta athalia*) feed on early succession plants and require the kind of patchy habitat that occurs when disturbances open up gaps in a forest. Intensive land use interrupts the natural processes that produce this habitat, endangering the survival of the species. (Photographs © Martin Warren.)

population that keeps the turf short, and global warming, which also helps this species survive through the winter (Davies et al. 2005).

In Iowa, roadsides dominated by exotic grasses are increasingly being replanted with native prairie wildflower species. The original purpose of the program was to reduce roadside maintenance costs and make the roadsides more attractive. An indirect benefit has been a substantial increase in the abundance and diversity of rare butterfly species, which benefit from the abundant nectar supply and whose catepillars feed on the diverse food plants (Ries et al. 2001).

Butterflies are important to most human societies as symbols of beauty and freedom. If we want to have butterflies in our world, we need to include maintaining habitat for butterflies as an important management goal. In many cases this will mean continuing traditional land use practices, particularly in European countries where the landscape has been strongly influenced by human activities, or even deliberately restoring habitat favored by butterflies. However, hard decisions must sometimes be made, as there are many types of butterflies, and the management that helps one species may harm another (Pöyre et al. 2005).

were previously maintained by grazing sheep; now they must be burned every few years to prevent scrub oak forest from taking over and shading out the wildflowers (Figure 17.5A). Obviously, such burning must be done in a legal and carefully controlled manner to prevent damage to nearby property. Also, prior to burning, land managers need to develop a program of public education to explain to local residents the role of fire in maintaining the balance of nature. In other situations, parts of protected areas must be carefully managed to minimize human disturbance and fire, providing the conditions required by old-growth species (Figure 17.5B).

The type of controlled management that provides optimal results can be determined through field experiments. For example, chalk grasslands in Britain require specific management measures to maintain a biologically rich community. Experiments have shown that the number, relative abundance, and type of species present are determined by the management regime: whether the grassland is grazed, mowed, or burned; the time of year of the management; the amount of fertilizer applied; and whether the management is carried out continuously, annually, or rotationally (Martorell and Peters 2005). Certain management regimes favor certain groups of species over others; for instance, biological communities can take on dramatically different appearances depending on how intensely they are grazed by domestic animals (Krueper et al. 2003; Figure 17.5C,D).

Managing Water

Rivers, lakes, swamps, estuaries, and all other types of wetlands must receive a sufficient supply of clean water to maintain their ecosystem processes. In particular, maintaining healthy wetlands is necessary for populations of waterbirds, fish, amphibians, aquatic plants, and a host of other species (Pringle 2000; Gaff et al. 2004; Greathouse et al. 2006). Yet protected areas may end up directly competing for water resources with irrigation projects, demands for residential and industrial water supplies, flood control schemes, and hydroelectric dams. Wetlands are often interconnected, so a decision affecting water levels and quality in one place has ramifications for other areas. One strategy for maintaining wetlands is to include an entire watershed within the protected area.

Biological reserves most likely to be affected by human alterations of hydrology are those located in the lower part of a watershed, whereas biological reserves located in the upper parts of a watershed are somewhat less likely to be affected.

FIGURE 17.5 Conservation management: intervention versus leave-it-alone. (A) Heathland in protected areas of Nantucket Island, Massachusetts, is burned on a regular basis in order to maintain the open vegetation habitat and protect wildflowers and other rare species. (B) Sometimes management involves keeping human disturbance to an absolute minimum. This old-growth stand in the Olympic National Forest in Washington is the result of many years of solitude. (C) The appearance of the San Pedro Riparian National Conservation Area in Arizona in 1987, with intensive cattle grazing, and four years later in 1991 (D) after the cattle had been removed; note the return of shrubs and herbs, which provide abundant cover for birds. (A, photograph by Jackie Sones, Massachusetts Audubon Society; B, photograph by Thomas Kitchin/Tom Stack & Associates; C,D, photographs courtesy of David Krueper.)

Such upland protected areas may protect water for thousands or even millions of people living downstream; in these cases, it is often possible to manage large areas for both biodiversity and watershed protection (Verhoeven et al. 2006). However, even remote sources of water may not be exempt from human demands. In the mountains of Puerto Rico, water intakes in the Caribbean National Forest divert stream water for use as drinking water and for power generation (Figure 17.6; Pringle 2000). Six hundred thousand people are dependent on this diverted stream water.

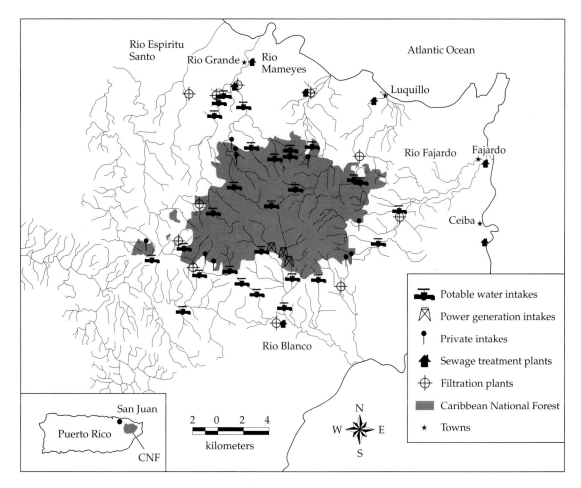

FIGURE 17.6 The Caribbean National Forest in the mountains of eastern Puerto Rico and its surroundings are the site of numerous intakes for drinking water, power generation, and private-use sewage treatment plants and water filtration plants. On an average day, these intakes divert more than half of the water in the streams, and as a result, some streams are typically dry. Note that water intakes are often in the mountains where the land is undeveloped and the water is clean, whereas the sewage treatment plants are near the coast, where the towns are located. (After Pringle 2000.)

However, this means that more than 50% of the water is diverted on an average day, and many streams are dry for most of the year, resulting in a major impact on populations of fish and other aquatic animals, as well as ecological processes.

The water in nature reserves can be contaminated from nearby agricultural, residential, and industrial areas. Such contamination can develop gradually over decades, as happened when the Everglades National Park in Florida was encircled by agricultural and urban development and its water source diverted and contaminated. An example of sudden contamination occurred in Spain in 1998 when a dam at a mine site collapsed, releasing approximately 150,000 m^3 of acid sludge with high concentrations of lead, zinc, and arsenic into the Doñana National Park wetlands. Huge numbers of fish and aquatic invertebrates died as a result. To deal with such situations, park managers may have to become politically sophisticated and effective at public relations to ensure that the wetlands under their supervision continue to receive the clean water they need to survive. A program of water-quality monitoring can help to document alterations in quality and quantity of water in ecosystems and to provide the information needed to convince government officials and the public of the seriousness of the problem.

FIGURE 17.7 Food must be supplied to Japanese cranes in order for them to survive through the winter. This picture shows a crane flying through a snow storm. (Photograph © Tim Laman.)

Managing Keystone Resources

In many parks, it may be necessary to preserve, maintain, and supplement keystone resources on which many species depend. These resources include sources of food, water, minerals, natural shelter, and so forth. For example, grains are supplied to rare Japanese cranes to replace a natural food source that was eliminated when wetlands were converted to rice paddies; without this additional food source, the cranes could not survive during the winter (Figure 17.7).

Keystone resources and keystone species can be enhanced in managed conservation areas to increase the populations of species whose numbers have declined. By planting areas with food plants and building an artificial pond, it might be possible to maintain vertebrate species in a smaller conservation area and at higher densities than would be predicted based on studies of species distribution in undisturbed habitat. Artificial ponds not only provide needed habitat for attractive insects such as dragonflies, they are important centers of public education in urban areas (Steytler and Samways 1995). Another example is providing nesting boxes or drilling nesting holes in trees for birds as a substitute resource when there are few dead trees with nesting cavities (see Figure 16.4; Poonswad et al. 2005). In this way, a viable population of a rare species could be established, whereas without such interventions the population size of the rare species might be too small to persist. In each case, a balance must be struck between establishing nature reserves free from human influence and creating seminatural gardens in which the plants and animals are dependent on people.

Managing Parks and People

In both developed and developing countries, a central part of any park's management plan must be a policy on the use of the park resources by different groups of people (Mascia 2003; Struhsaker et al. 2005). Different interest groups often try to sway how park systems or even individual parks are managed. In most countries, some of the greatest threats to parks come from the policies of those same governments responsible for managing them. Large development projects (e.g., roads, dams), concessions for extractive activities (logging forests) or for exploration (oil, gas, minerals), or policies that conflict with management objectives can all threaten biodiversity within protected areas. Local residents may resent any loss of access or use of resources: for example, ranchers used to grazing cattle and snowmobilers used to riding through roadless areas will not want to lose access. It is not surprising that people who have traditionally accessed a protected area but are then suddenly kept out, resent it. They will be understandably angry and frustrated and unlikely to support either conservation or the protected area (Wilkie et al. 2006).

Thus many parks flourish or are destroyed depending on the degree of support, or lack thereof, that they receive from the people who live in or near them. To encourage local people's support, the process of creating protected areas needs to involve many different stakeholders who should be given the opportunity to articulate what they want and why (see Figure 17.2). Such a process can combine "top-down" strategies, in which governments define conservation areas, with "bottom-up" programs, in which villages and other local groups formulate and identify their own development goals. This process will help make clear to local residents the purpose of the protected area, increasing the chances that they will support different components of park creation and management—from boundary demarcation, to ecological monitoring, to restoration activities. It is also likely to help the park meet and maintain its objectives.

In the most positive scenario, local people become involved in park management and planning, are trained and employed by the park authority, and benefit from the protection of biodiversity and regulation of activity within the park. Local residents often support protected areas when they see that such areas can help protect their livelihoods. But if there is a history of bad relations and mistrust between local people and the government, or if the purpose of the park is not explained adequately, local people may reject the park and ignore park regulations (Terborgh et al. 2002). In this case, the local people may conflict with park personnel (perhaps even violently) to the detriment of the park, and they may even destroy plants and animals in the park (Box 17.2).

In some cases, the people coming into conflict with park personnel are not "local." In many developing countries, recent migrants into areas who claim both land and resources can pose a huge threat to both local residents and protected areas. They may have little traditional knowledge of the area or its species, no experience being part of a community or working together, and are motivated only by the prospect of immediate economic gain.

Clear guidelines on who can use what resources within parks must be a central part of any management plan, both in developed and developing countries (Kothari et al. 1996; Terborgh et al. 2002). In some cases it is necessary to limit any extractive or consumptive uses of park resources by anyone, including local residents. This occurs most commonly when the integrity of the biological communities is being threatened; this strategy is sometimes referred to as "fences and fines." In Kenya, there has been an ongoing struggle between wildlife experts who advocate integrating local people into park management and others who favor excluding them from the parks. The result has been a shifting policy, which has left both wildlife officials and local people confused. Ideally, the benefits from tourism in a country like Kenya would be high enough to support park management, generate high levels of local employment, and provide revenue sharing with local communities (Brandon et al. 1998). In countries with high levels of nature-based tourism, it should be possible to structure benefits to compensate people for any real opportunity costs to them, such as food not grown, cattle not grazed, and natural products not harvested. The reality is that only a small portion of the revenue from the tourism is typically used to

BOX 17.2

Managing Leopards Together with People

■ The challenges of protected area management are illustrated dramatically by Sanjay Gandhi National Park, surrounded by Mumbai, one of India's largest and most densely settled cities and home to the Bollywood film industry. The park is home to an important leopard population numbering around 33 individuals, many of which were released in the park after they were caught in set-

tled areas by wildlife officials. Unfortunately, the 103-km^2 park is far too small for this number of leopards, because each leopard requires around 25 km of habitat for its territory and feeding ground. The current leopard population is around 8 times too big for the size of the park, forcing the leopards to leave the park to hunt for food. To make matters much worse, 65,000 impoverished people are also living illegally inside the park boundaries due to the lack of housing in Mumbai itself. Park officers are unable to evict these settlers, as it would be difficult to carry out, and unpopular with local politicians. Additionally, these people hunt the same wildlife that are the leopard's prey. When hungry leopards, with nothing else to eat, in turn prey upon dogs, cats, and other domestic animals both inside and outside the park, people in the way may be attacked and killed. At least 30 people were killed by leopards in 2004 and 2005.

Park officers have the unenviable task of protecting leopards from angry people who have had relatives, friends, and neighbors attacked, killed and eaten, and in turn protecting nearby people from hungry leopards. One short-term solution involves releasing pigs and rabbits in the park for the leopards to eat. A long-term solution is to move the people outside of the park and enforce the park boundaries; or to create a new park for the leopards far from the big city. A management decision is required, but no long-term decision is going to be universally popular.

Wildlife officials in India are struggling to find the right compromise between protecting leopards and providing for the basic needs of people. (Photograph © Dennis Sabo/Painet, Inc.)

benefit the people living around such protected areas. But this problem is beyond the scope of park management alone; it demonstrates the need for government policies and political will to share the financial benefits of tourism.

Zoning To Partition Resource Needs

A common solution to deal with a variety of conflicting demands on a protected area is **zoning**, which considers the overall management objectives for a park and sets aside designated areas that permit or give priority to certain activities. Some areas of a forest may be designated for timber production, hunting, wildlife protection, nature trails, or watershed maintenance. A marine reserve might allow fishing in certain areas and strictly prohibit it in others; certain areas might be designated for surfing, water-skiing, and recreational diving, but these sports may be prohibited elsewhere (Figure 17.8).

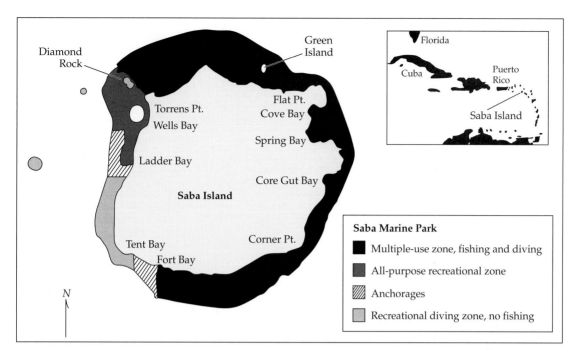

FIGURE 17.8 Saba, an island in the Caribbean under the jurisdiction of the Netherlands, has established a system of zoning to protect the marine environment and still allow fishing. The Saba Marine Park includes the entire coastal zone of the island. The designation of fishing exclusion zones is important to maintain the health of the coral reefs and fish populations that ecotourists come to see. (After Agardy 1997.)

Other commonly established zones are for the recovery of endangered species, restoration of degraded communities, and scientific research. For example, at the Cape Cod National Seashore in Massachusetts, protecting tern and piping plover nesting habitat on beaches has been given priority over the desire of people to drive off-road vehicles and to fish on the same beaches where birds are nesting (Figure 17.9). A hands-off policy by park managers that does not restrict beach access by fishermen and vehicles would result in the rapid destruction of the shorebird colonies. In this case, a compromise has been developed whereby prime nesting beaches are closed to human activities but other beaches remain open for recreational activities.

The challenge in zoning is to find a compromise that people are willing to accept that provides for the long-term, sustainable use of natural resources. Zoned marine reserves in the Philippines have proved an effective way to rebuild and maintain populations of fish and other marine organisms (Figure 17.10). These areas are also known as **marine protected areas (MPAs)**, marine parks, and no-fishing zones (Gell and Roberts 2003). In comparison with nearby unprotected sites, marine parks often have greater total weight of commercially important fish, greater numbers of individual fish, and greater coral reef cover (McClana-

FIGURE 17.9 Tern nesting habitat in the Cape Cod National Seashore and at nearby beaches is extremely vulnerable to the "wear and tear" that is inevitable in a heavily visited recreation area. Management is needed to reduce the impact on the birds from hikers, bicyclists, motorcyclists, dune-buggies, picnickers, and dog-walkers. (Photograph by David C. Twichell.)

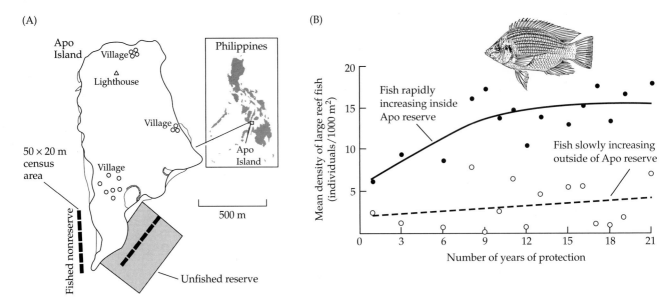

FIGURE 17.10 Large reef fish had been overharvested at Apo Island in the Philippines and were rarely seen. (A) In response to overharvesting, a reserve was set up (shaded area) on the eastern side of the island. Fishing continued at a nonreserve area on the western side of the island. A censusing study measured the number of large reef fish at each site (six underwater census areas are shown for each site). (B) Resulting data show that after the marine reserve was established, the number of fish observed in the unfished reserve increased substantially. Initially the number of fish in the unprotected area did not increase because the fish were still being intensively harvested; after about 8 years, though, an increase became detectable, originating from the spillover of fish from the reserve area. (After Abesamis and Russ 2005.)

han and Arthur 2001; Abesamis and Russ 2005). Evidence shows that fish from marine reserves spill over into adjacent unprotected areas, where they can help rebuild populations and also be caught by fishermen. Recently it has been demonstrated that MPAs also foster healthy populations of large herbivorous fishes that reduce fleshy algal cover, a process key to the survival of reef-building corals. Before we completely embrace zoning for the fishing industry, though, further research is needed to determine if concentrating fishing efforts into a few designated fishing zones will seriously damage that part of the ecosystem. Enforcement of zoning is often a major challenge in marine reserves because fishermen will tend to move toward and into the fishing-exclusion zones, because those are where fishing is best, which leads to overfishing at the margins of the marine reserve. Only a combination of local involvement, publicity, education, clear posting of warning signs, and visible enforcement can guarantee the success of a zoning plan, especially in the marine environment.

The Great Barrier Reef off the east coast of Australia provides an example of multiple use zoning to meet a variety of demands. The Great Barrier Reef Protected Area runs for 2300 km along the coast and is up to 400 km wide. A new management plan implemented in 2004 recognizes 70 distinct bioregions; within each bioregion, at least 20% of the area is off-limits to commercial fishing, though in some cases traditional fishing is allowed. Separate zones are designated for commercial fishing, research, and traditional fishing. The example set by the Great Barrier Reef Marine Park Authority is now slowly being emulated in other parts of the world.

The United Nations Educational, Scientific, and Cultural Organization (UNESCO) has pioneered approaches to balance human needs and conservation with its Man and the Biosphere (MAB) Program (Figure 17.11). This program has designated hundreds of Biosphere Reserves worldwide in an attempt to integrate ac-

FIGURE 17.11 Some parks try to protect natural areas by fencing them off from outside influences, which is impossible to do. This is analogous to preserving them in a bottle. Such policies may fail to recognize ecological and social forces that both maintain and threaten the ecosystem. UNESCO'S Man and the Biosphere (MAB) Program attempts to integrate the needs and cultures of local people in park planning and protection. (Poster from "Ecology in Action: An Exhibit," UNESCO, Paris, 1981.)

tivities of local people, research, protection of the natural environment, and often tourism at a single location (Batisse 1997). The MAB concept depends on a system of zoning that defines a core area in which biological communities and ecosystems are strictly protected with a surrounding buffer zone in which nondestructive research is conducted and traditional human activities, such as the collection of thatch, medicinal plants, and small fuelwood, are carefully monitored for their impact on biodiversity. Surrounding the buffer zone is a transitional zone in which some forms of sustainable development (such as small-scale farming) are allowed, along with some extraction of natural resources (such as selective logging) and experimental research. In many areas, additional income is generated by providing food, lodging, and guiding services to tourists visiting the area. While these zones are easy to draw on paper, in practice it has been difficult to inform and reach agreement with residents who live in or near biosphere reserves about where the zones are and what uses are allowed in them.

The general strategy of surrounding core conservation areas with buffer and transition zones is still being debated. The approach has benefits: local people may be more willing to support park activities if they are allowed zoned access to the park and certain desirable features of the landscape created by human use may be maintained (such as farms, gardens, and early stages of succession). Also, buffer zones may facilitate animal dispersal between highly protected core conservation areas and human-dominated transitional and protected areas (Figure 17.12). Yet zoning

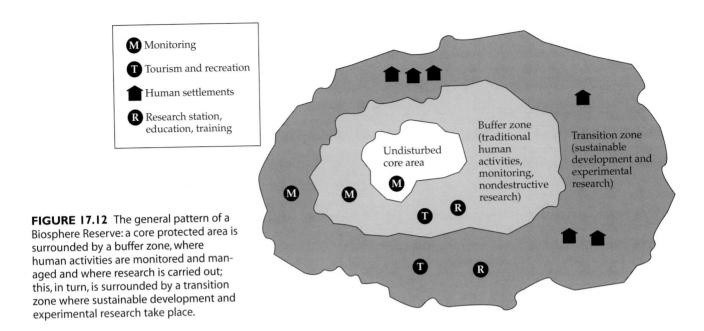

M Monitoring

T Tourism and recreation

⌂ Human settlements

R Research station, education, training

Undisturbed core area

Buffer zone (traditional human activities, monitoring, nondestructive research)

Transition zone (sustainable development and experimental research)

FIGURE 17.12 The general pattern of a Biosphere Reserve: a core protected area is surrounded by a buffer zone, where human activities are monitored and managed and where research is carried out; this, in turn, is surrounded by a transition zone where sustainable development and experimental research take place.

for multiple-use resource extraction including local residents may only work if the core area is large enough to protect viable populations of all key species and if people are willing to respect the zones and their designated uses. Respect for zones varies greatly in different parts of the world among different social situations. In places where park management, political will, and land tenure are weak, buffer zones often are seen as a commons or as unowned and unmanaged lands that are up for grabs. In many developing countries, one of the ironies of a well-managed park is that the economic benefits from the park will act as a magnet for poor people from neighboring areas, overwhelming the structure of the project and putting even more pressure on the protected areas. For this reason, greater attention is being given to protected areas as one unit in a mosaic of compatible land uses. Rather than trying to have parks conserve biodiversity *and* respond to development needs, broader planning is required that looks across large areas and considers the needs of both people and conservation.

Regulating Activities inside Protected Areas

Certain human activities are incompatible with maintaining biological diversity within a protected area. If these activities are allowed to continue, important elements of the biological communities eventually may be destroyed (Box 17.3) (Wells and McShane 2004). The following activities within protected areas must be regulated, or abolished altogether:

- *Commercial harvesting of game and fish.* Some regulated hunting and fishing may be acceptable for personal consumption and sport, as long as it is sustainable, but harvesting for commercial sale frequently leads to the elimination of species. Commercial hunting and fishing within a reserve, if it is allowed at all, must be carefully monitored by park officials to ensure that animal populations are not depleted. However, heavily armed local hunters operating in remote areas of parks at night are extremely difficult to monitor, and they frequently intimidate park officials. Regulating hunting is most effective when there are clear checkpoints that hunters must pass through, or when a village is so well organized and led that the community itself

BOX 17.3

Is Arctic Wildlife Management Compatible with Oil Drilling?

In the United States, there are over 500 national wildlife refuges protecting animals on 1 million km². In such places, one would imagine that the protection of biodiversity has the highest management priority. However, in 60% of the refuges, potentially harmful activities are allowed, such as fishing, hunting, grazing, logging, mining, or drilling. In the United States, a highly emotional struggle is being waged over the future management of the Arctic National Wildlife Refuge (ANWR), a pristine wilderness so remote that few humans have visited there, much less left any marks on the landscape. This area is sometimes referred to as "America's Serengeti" because of its abundant wildlife, consisting of herds of caribou and musk oxen, nesting sites of tundra swans and seabirds, and bowhead whales just offshore. The ANWR sits on top of up to 7 billion barrels of oil, considered vital by many to the strategic energy needs of the United States. Environmentalists describe the potential for oil spills, the ugliness of drilling platforms, damage to the tundra, and the loss of a national treasure, while the business community, the Bush White House, and certain government officials emphasize the need to give the country additional options for energy independence. In the end, a compromise might allow oil extraction in limited areas of the refuge using methods that minimize the impact on the environment, such as slant drilling to reduce the number of drilling platforms, and trucking in supplies only in winter when the tundra is frozen and roads can be made of ice. It is unclear how this situation will be resolved; it continues to be debated after many years. However, whenever strong conservation concerns come up against powerful business interests, any solution is bound to be imperfect.

Vast grasslands and herds of wildlife are a feature of the Arctic National Wildlife Refuge. Will the energy needs of the United States lead to oil explorations and extractions in this 60 million-ha wilderness? (Photograph courtesy of the U.S. Fish and Wildlife Service.)

can regulate the hunting. The difficulties of regulating harvesting in parks are illustrated by the ongoing conflicts in the Galápagos Islands of Ecuador, one of the world's premier national parks (Ferber 2000). Fishermen have refused to accept quotas on catches of lobster, sea cucumbers, sharks, and other marine species, and have directed their anger at the park and scientists, threatening research workers and holding them hostage, and destroying park offices, research labs, equipment, and data books. In less conflictive situations, establishment of marine protected areas with zones that regulate fishing has proved an effective way to rebuild and maintain populations of fish (see Figure 17.10) (Russ et al. 2004; Abesamis and Russ 2005).

- *Intensive harvesting of natural plant products.* As with hunting and fishing, collection of natural plant products such as fruits, fibers, resins, and mushrooms for personal use may be acceptable, but commercial harvesting may be detrimental. Even personal collecting can be unacceptable in national parks with tens of thousands of visitors per year and where the local human population is large in relation to the area of the park. Monitoring of plant populations is needed to ensure that overharvesting does not occur. A surprisingly large number of people are sometimes found in remote areas of parks illegally collecting forest products such as medicinal plants, ornamental plants, and mushrooms. Dealing with such a situation represents a great challenge for park managers, especially when there are links between illegal poaching or collection of high-value plants and organized criminal groups.

- *Logging and farming.* These activities sometimes degrade the habitat and eliminate species. Where these activities are large in scale, commercial in nature, and controlled by outside interests, they must be stopped whenever possible. However, when local people need to clear forests for income or farms to supply basic human needs, it is very difficult for managers to ban these activities. Changing the park zones, park type, or "swapping" transformed areas for intact places elsewhere have all been successful in some places. In certain contexts, some regulated harvesting and farming may even be useful to maintain successional stages and to preserve traditional agricultural systems. Such systems can often bring in needed revenue to protected areas and provide employment to local people.

- *Fire.* Widespread and highly destructive forest fires can result when fires are set to clear brush and open areas for farming. They are even more destructive when they follow selective logging. Occasional fires set accidentally or deliberately by local people can open up habitats, provide forage for livestock and wildlife, reduce undesirable species, and may help to create a variety of successional stages. Fires that are more frequent than would occur naturally can dry out a habitat, cause soil erosion, and eliminate many native species.

- *Recreational activities.* Popular recreational activities such as hiking off trails, camping outside designated areas, and riding motorcycles, off-road vehicles, and mountain bikes can eliminate sensitive plants and animals from protected lands and must be controlled and restricted to specified areas. Even such activities as birdwatching must sometimes be curtailed. In many heavily used parks, frequent traffic by hikers wearing heavy boots has degraded vegetation along trails and even killed trees. Redwood trees in California, for instance, are harmed when park visitors compress the soil too tightly by walking around the redwood trunks. In many parks, people are not allowed to bring dogs for walks, because the dogs frighten and chase animals. In tropical marine parks, swimmers and divers are often restricted to specific areas or trails to prevent widespread damage to delicate branching corals (Tratalos and Austin 2001).

Challenges in Park Management

Human populations will continue to increase dramatically in the coming decades, while resources such as fuelwood, medicinal plants, and wild meat will become harder to find. Managers of protected areas in the developing world need to anticipate ever-greater demand for use of the remaining patches of natural habitat. Seventy percent of the buffer zones around protected areas have lost forest cover over the last four decades due to this ever-increasing demand for natural resources (Mayaux et al. 2005). Conflict is inevitable as more people live and farm closer to high concentrations of wildlife that, when food is scarce, have nowhere to go but out of the park and into nearby agricultural fields and villages. Elephants, primates, and flocks of birds can all be significant crop raiders, while carnivores such as tigers pose a different set of challenges to nearby residents. For park management to be effective, there must be adequate funding for a sufficient number of well-equipped, properly trained, and motivated park personnel who are willing to carry out park policy. Buildings, communications equipment, and other appropriate elements of infrastructure are necessary to manage a park. In many areas of the world, particularly in developing, but also in developed, countries, protected areas are understaffed, and they lack the equipment to patrol remote areas of the reserve. In most developing countries, conservation programs receive less than 10% of the funds they need to carry out their goals (Balmford et al. 2003). Without enough radios and vehicles, the park staff may be restricted to the vicinity of headquarters, unaware of what is happening in their own park.

The importance of sufficient personnel and equipment should not be underestimated: In areas of Panama, for instance, the abundance of large mammals and the seed dispersal services they provide are directly related to the frequency of anti-poaching patrols by park guards (Wright et al. 2000). In another study of 86 tropical parks, the parks that were most effective at maintaining the vegetation of the park in good conditions had: (1) the greatest number of guards per unit area of the park, (2) clearly marked and maintained park borders, and (3) programs to compensate local people when park animals or other park activities damaged their crops (Bruner et al. 2001). (Interestingly, some parks were found to be effective at maintaining or even increasing the biological communities within their borders even with few park guards and poorly defined boundaries, because the legal designation of the national park prevented private land development.) A recent study of African rainforest protected areas shows that successful conservation is linked to a positive public attitude, effective enforcement of park regulations, large park size, low human populations, and the presence of conservation organizations at the park itself (Struhsaker et al. 2005).

The majority of the evidence shows that park personnel and equipment are integral to a park's success, but funding for these resources is often a problem (Bruner et al. 2004; Struhsaker et al. 2005). For instance, compare the national parks and biological reserves of the United States and the Brazilian Amazon (Table 17.1) (Peres and Terborgh 1995; Hockings et al. 2000; Peres and Lake 2003). The United States employs 4002 park rangers, while Brazil, due to inadequate funding, employs only

TABLE 17.1 *Comparison of personnel and resources available for protecting national parks and biological reserves in the Brazilian Amazon and the United States*

Feature	Brazilian Amazon	United States
Protected area (in km^2)	139,222	326,721
Number of park rangers	23	4002
Total number of park personnel[a]	65	19,000
Park ranger:km^2 ratio	1:6053	1:82
Park guard[b]	31	100
Administrative building[b]	45	100
Guard post[b]	52	100
Motor vehicle[b]	45	100

Source: After Peres and Terborgh 1995.

[a]Includes all office staff.

[b]Percentage of nature reserves with at least one.

23! That is a ratio of approximately one ranger per every 82 km^2 of park in the United States compared with one ranger for every 6053 km^2 of park in Brazil. Most of Brazil's parks lack even basic transportation, such as motorized boats, trucks, or jeeps; it is clearly impossible for Brazil's tiny park staff to adequately patrol large, rugged parks on foot or by canoe, and so protected areas remain unmanaged. The situation is even more disconcerting in the Democratic Republic of the Congo, in which the already inadequate budget for protected area management is actually declining due to war and a deteriorating economy (Inogwabini et al. 2005). To remedy the situation, international conservation organizations are trying to make up for the shortfall, spending around 20 times more on conservation in the Democratic Republic of the Congo than the hard-pressed government.

It is an irony of our world that vast sums are spent on captive breeding and conservation programs by zoos and conservation organizations in the developed countries of the world, while the biologically rich parks of so many developing countries languish for lack of resources. For instance, the San Diego Zoological Society, largely occupied with keeping exotic animals on display for the public, has an annual budget of $70 million, which is about the same as the combined wildlife conservation budgets of all African countries south of the Sahara. In many cases, the annual management costs for endangered species and habitats are a bargain compared to the large costs of conservation efforts to save species on the verge of extinction or ecosystems on the verge of collapse. And at the end of the day, conservation biologists need to account for whether their management of protected areas achieved stated goals and whether money was spent effectively (Salafsky et al. 2002; Christensen 2003).

Throughout this chapter the principles and practices of management have been discussed. To implement management, people must be trained as conservation managers, learning both academic and practical skills. Positions for managers need to be created which provide a secure and adequate salary. These managers will then be in a position to carry out their responsibilities of protecting biological diversity.

Summary

1. Protected areas often must be managed to maintain biological diversity because the original conditions of the area have been and continue to be altered by human activities. Effective management begins with a clearly articulated statement of priorities. Monitoring can be used to determine whether management practices are working or need to be adjusted.

2. Parts of protected areas may have to be periodically burned, dug up, or otherwise disturbed by people to create the openings and successional stages that certain species need. Such management is crucial, for example, to some endangered butterfly species that need early successional food plants to complete their life cycle.

3. Keystone resources such as nesting sites and water holes often need to be preserved, restored, or even added to protected areas in order to maintain populations of some species.

4. An effective management tool is zoning, allowing and prohibiting certain kinds of uses in different parts of a park. In Biosphere Reserves, a core area of strict protection is surrounded by buffer zones and transition zones in which various human activities are allowed.

5. For park management to be effective, protected areas must have an adequate staff and resources. In many cases, personnel and resources are insufficient to accomplish management objectives.

For Discussion

1. Think about a national park or nature reserve you have visited. In what ways was it well run or poorly run? What were the goals of the park or reserve, and how could they be achieved through better management?

2. Imagine a public nature preserve in a metropolitan area that protects a number of endangered species. Would the nature preserve be more effectively run by a government agency, a group of scientists, the local residents living near the reserve, an environmental nongovernmental organization (NGO), or by a council made up of all of them? What are the advantages and disadvantages of each of these possibilities?

3. Can you think of special challenges in the management of aquatic preserves such as coastal estuaries, islands, or freshwater lakes that would not be faced by managers of terrestrial protected areas?

4. Imagine you are a park ranger at Yellowstone National Park during the great fires of 1988. How would you explain the ecologically beneficial role of fire in mature lodgepole pine forests while reassuring park visitors that their park is not being destroyed?

Suggested Readings

Abesamis, R. A. and G. R. Russ. 2005. Density-dependent spillover from a marine reserve: Long-term evidence. *Ecological Applications* 15: 1798–1812. Marine protected areas appear to have great advantages; are there any disadvantages?

Critchley, C. N. R., M. J. W. Burke, and D. P. Stevens. 2003. Conservation of lowland semi-natural grasslands in the UK: a review of botanical monitoring results from agri-environment schemes. *Biological Conservation* 115: 263–278. Management is most effective when there are specific goals and long-term monitoring.

Cunningham, C. and J. Berger. 1997. *Horn of Darkness: Rhinos on the Edge.* Oxford University Press, New York. The emotional story of evaluating Namibia's rhino protection program and the resulting tangle with government officials.

Greathouse, E. A., C. M. Pringle, W. H. McDowell, and J. G. Holmquist. 2006. Indirect upstream effects of dams: consequences of migratory consumer extirpation in Puerto Rico. *Ecological Applications* 16: 339–352. Dams can have extensive impacts of aquatic ecosystems.

Hart, J. and T. Hart. 2003. Rules of engagement for conservation. *Conservation in Practice* 4: 14–22. Conservation can continue even in the middle of wars; see other articles in this special issue.

Inogwabini, B. I., O. Ilambu, and M. A. Gbanzi. 2005. Protected areas of the Democratic Republic of Congo. *Conservation Biology* 19: 15–22. Conservation organizations in many developing countries are spending more money than the government on protected area management.

Krueper, D., J. Bart, and T. D. Rich. 2003. Response of vegetation and breeding birds to the removal of cattle on the San Pedro River, Arizona (U.S.A.). *Conservation Biology* 17: 607–615. Amazing before-and-after pictures demonstrating how management affects biological communities.

MacDougall, A. S., B. R. Beckwith, and C. Y. Maslovat. 2004. Defining conservation strategies with historical perspectives: a case study from a degraded oak grassland system. *Conservation Biology* 18: 455–465. Management often needs clearly defined goals.

Mayaux, P., P. Holmgren, F. Achard, H. Eva, H-J Stibig, and A. Branthomme. 2005. Tropical forest cover change in the 1990s and options for future monitoring. *Phil. Trans. R. Soc. B.* 360: 373–384. Management is crucial as human settlements encircle protected areas.

Pringle, C. M. 2001. Hydrological connectivity and the management of biological reserves: A global perspective. *Ecological Applications* 11: 981–998. The integrity of protected areas is constantly threatened by external sources of water pollution, dam construction, and the diversion of water.

Redford, K. H. and S. E. Sanderson. 2000. Extracting humans from nature. *Conservation Biology* 2000: 1362–1364. Authors argue for the need to integrate local people in conservation strategies; other articles in the volume present the case for excluding local people or for giving local people greater rights.

Ries, L., D. M. Debinski, and M. L. Wieland. 2001. Conservation value of roadside prairie restoration to butterfly communities. *Conservation Biology* 15: 401–411. Restoring plant communities leads to an increase in native insects.

Salafsky, N., R. Margoluis, K. H. Redford, and J. G. Robinson. 2002. Improving the practice of conservation: A conceptual framework and research agenda for conservation science. *Conservation Biology* 16: 1469–1479. Conservation biologists need to demonstrate that they have achieved their management goals and used their funds effectively.

Semlitsch, R. D. and J. R. Bodie. 2003. Biological criteria for buffer zones around wetlands and riparian habitats for amphibians and reptiles. *Conservation Biology* 17: 1219–1228. Establishing buffer zones around wetlands enhances animal populations.

Terborgh, J., L. C. Davenport, and C. Van Schaik (eds.), *Making Parks Work: Identifying Key Factors to Implementing Parks in the Tropics*. Island Press, Covelo, CA. Managing national parks and biosphere reserves must be based on a clear understanding of ecological and social priorities.

Turner, W., S. Spector, N. Gardiner, M. Fladeland, E. Sterling, and M. Steininger. 2003. Remote sensing for biodiversity science and conservation. *Trends in Ecology and Evolution* 18: 306–314. Remote sensing provides a way to monitor biodiversity on large geographic scales.

Van Wilgen, B. W., N. Govender, H. C. Biggs, D. Ntsala, and X. N. Funda. 2004. Response of savanna fire regimes to changing fire-management policies in a large African national park. *Conservation Biology* 18: 1533–1540. Fire management will strongly affect the species composition and structure of a biological community.

Verhoeven, J. T. A., B. Arheimer, C. Yin, and M. M. Hefting. 2006. Regional and global concerns over wetlands and water quality. *Trends in Ecology and Evolution* 21: 96–103. Strategies are being considered by managers to improve water quality.

Wilkie, D. S., G. A., Morelli, J. Demmer, M. Starkey, P. Telfer, and M. Steil. 2006. Parks and people: assessing the human welfare effects of establishing protected areas for biodiversity conservation. *Conservation Biology* 20: 247–249. New national parks can have both positive and negative effects on localpeople.

Outside Protected Areas

A crucial component of conservation strategies must be the protection of biological diversity *outside* as well as inside protected areas. As David Western (1989), a leading conservation biologist based in Africa, says, "If we can't save nature outside protected areas, not much will survive inside." In the last chapter we discussed principles of managing protected areas. In this chapter, we explore strategies to include biodiversity protection as a management objective for both unprotected areas immediately outside protected areas and all other areas that are not protected. Protected and unprotected areas provide complementary roles in conserving nature. They each contribute to a matrix in which species live and ecosystem services are maintained. In the worst case, a devastated landscape polluting the air and water will strangle the protected area it surrounds. In the best case, unprotected areas surrounding protected areas will provide additional space for ecosystem processes and new populations.

Protecting these areas is essential because more than 80% of the world's land will remain outside of strictly protected areas, according to even the most optimistic predictions. Human use of ecosystems varies greatly in these unprotected lands, but significant portions are not used intensively by humans and still harbor some of their original biota (Figure 18.1). Strategies for reconciling human needs and conservation interests in unprotected areas are critical to the success of conservation plans (Lindenmayer and Franklin 2002; McNeely and Scherr 2003; Mayfield and Daily 2005). In almost

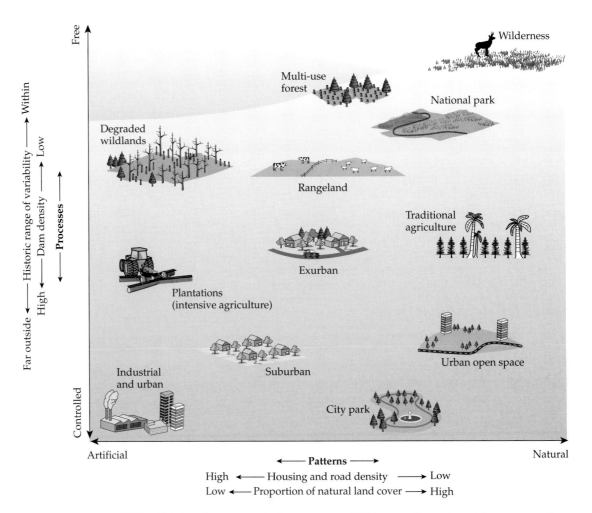

FIGURE 18.1 Landscapes vary in the extent to which humans have altered the patterns of species composition and natural vegetation cover through human activities such as agriculture, road construction, and housing; and ecosystem process, such as water flow and nutrient cycling, through activities such as control of fire, dam construction, and alteration of plant cover. Wilderness areas retain most of their original patterns and process, and urban areas retain the least, with other landscapes retaining intermediate amounts to various extents. (After Theobald 2004.)

every country, numerous rare species and biological communities will inevitably occur outside of protected areas. In the United States, 70% of the species listed under the U.S. Endangered Species Act occur on private land (Stein et al. 2000; Wilcove et al. 2004), and 10% occur exclusively on private lands. Even when endangered species occur on public land, it is often not land managed for biodiversity but rather managed primarily for timber harvesting, grazing, mining, or other economic uses. For many other countries as well, a gap exists in the protected-land system, with many rare and endangered ecosystems and species existing primarily or exclusively on private lands (Pressey et al. 2000; Deguise and Kerr 2006).

It is shortsighted to rely solely on parks and reserves to protect biological diversity. Such reliance can create a paradoxical situation in which the protections developed for species and habitats inside the parks become a rationale for continuing—or even expanding—behaviors and land uses that harm the same species and habitats outside park boundaries. Jeff McNeely (1989), an IUCN protected areas expert, suggests that the park boundary "is too often also a psychological boundary, suggesting that since nature is taken care of by the national park, we can abuse the surrounding lands, isolating the national park as an 'island' of habitat which is subject to the usual increased threats that go with insularity." Sharply demarcated borders between healthy and unhealthy ecosystems do little to preserve the overall welfare of either biological diversity or the human communities that, knowingly or not, rely on that biodiversity for food, materials, and ecosystem services; in many ways, conservation outside of protected areas should strive to blur the distinctions between protected and unprotected ecosystems as much as possible by maintaining unprotected areas in a state of reasonable ecological health. Such efforts will also help to keep the ecosystems within the park healthier.

Some countries such as Brazil and Malaysia are establishing new, large national parks to protect their biodiversity, to maintain ecosystem services, and to provide a destination for ecotourism. However, if the areas outside parks are degraded, then the biological diversity within the protected areas will decline as well. This decline is due, in part, to the fact that many species must migrate across park boundaries to access resources that the park itself cannot provide (Danby and Slocombe 2005). In general, the smaller a protected area is, the more dependent it is on neighboring unprotected lands for the long-term maintenance of biological diversity. For example, in India, tigers sometimes leave the nature sanctuary in which they live to hunt in the surrounding human-dominated landscape (Seidensticker et al. 1999). Also, the number of individuals of any one species contained within park boundaries may be lower than the minimum viable population size. New national parks that are meant to compensate for a country's intensive development outside parks are sometimes just attempts to mollify the international conservation community; they are not solutions to the long-term problem.

The Value of Unprotected Habitat

Strategies that encourage private landowners and government land managers to protect rare species and biological communities are obviously essential to the long-term survival of many species. In many countries, government programs inform road builders and developers of the locations of rare species or threatened communities and help them modify their plans to avoid damage to the sites. Public education programs and even financial subsidies may be needed to encourage conservation efforts. The following examples illustrate the importance of land outside protected areas.

- *Mountain sheep.* Mountain sheep (*Ovis canadensis*) often occur in isolated populations on steep, open terrain surrounded by large areas of unsuitable habitat (Bleich et al. 1990). Since mountain sheep had been considered to be slow colonizers of new habitat, past conservation efforts focused on protecting known mountain sheep habitat and releasing sheep into areas that they had previously occupied. However, studies using radio telemetry have revealed that mountain sheep often move well outside their normal territories and even show considerable ability to move across inhospitable terrain between mountain ranges. The isolated mountain sheep populations are really parts of a large metapopulation that occupies a much greater area (see Figure 12.8). Thus, not only the land occupied by mountain sheep must be protected but also the habitat between populations that acts as stepping-stones for dispersal, colonization, and gene flow.

- *The Florida panther.* The Florida panther (*Felis concolor coryi*) is an endangered subspecies of puma in South Florida with around only 87 individuals (Maehr et al. 2004). This panther was designated the Florida state animal in 1982 and has since received a tremendous amount of government and research attention. Half of the land in the present range of the panther is privately

(A)

(B)

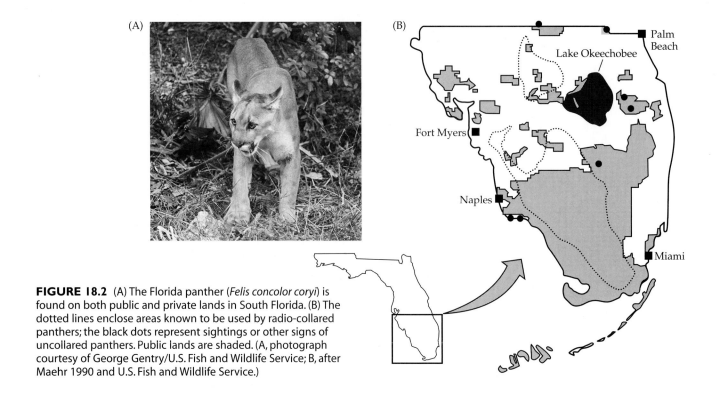

Palm Beach

Lake Okeechobee

Fort Myers

Naples

Miami

FIGURE 18.2 (A) The Florida panther (*Felis concolor coryi*) is found on both public and private lands in South Florida. (B) The dotted lines enclose areas known to be used by radio-collared panthers; the black dots represent sightings or other signs of uncollared panthers. Public lands are shaded. (A, photograph courtesy of George Gentry/U.S. Fish and Wildlife Service; B, after Maehr 1990 and U.S. Fish and Wildlife Service.)

owned, and animals tracked with radio collars have all spent at least some of their time on private lands (Figure 18.2). Private lands typically are on better soils that support more prey species. Panthers that spend most of their time on private lands have a better diet and are in better condition than panthers on public land.

Acquiring the 400,000 ha of private land occupied by the panther would cost around $2 billion, with management costs of around $30 million each year (Kautz and Cox 2001). Obviously, such a strategy would be financially and politically difficult. Even slowing down the pace of land development may be impractical. Two viable possibilities are educating private landowners on the value of conservation and paying willing landowners to practice management options that allow the continued existence of panthers—specifically, minimizing habitat fragmentation and maintaining preferred habitats of hardwood hammock forest, mixed hardwood swamp, and cypress swamp. In addition, special road underpasses have been built in the hopes of reducing panther deaths from collisions with motor vehicles.

Native species often can continue to live in unprotected areas, especially when those areas are set aside or managed for some other purpose that is not harmful to the ecosystem. Forests that are either selectively logged on a long cutting cycle or are cut down for farming using traditional shifting cultivation methods may still contain a considerable percentage of their original biota and maintain most of their ecosystem services (Dunn 2004; Scholes and Biggs 2004; Clarke et al. 2005). In Malaysia, most forest bird species are still found in rain forests 30 years after selective logging has occurred where undisturbed forest is available nearby to act as a source of colonists (Peh et al. 2005). Primate species also appear to tolerate selective logging involving low levels of disturbance (Chapman et al. 2000). However, more intensive logging can result in the loss of species such as woodpeckers that need large, older trees (Lammertink 2004).

The Forest Stewardship Council has been one of the leading organizations to promote the certification of timber produced from sustainably managed forests. Certification of forests is increasing rapidly, with demand especially in Europe, exceeding supply. For certification to be granted, the forests need to be managed and monitored for their long-term environmental benefits, and the rights and well-being of local people and workers need to be recognized. It should be noted, however, that industries for whom conservation is an impediment to continued economic growth (e.g., logging, mining, agriculture) continually lobby for acceptance of their own alternative certification programs, which have varying standards for what may be considered "sustainable" extraction and "acceptable" monitoring. The existing standards of these industries do little to ensure sustained biological monitoring of managed forests, nor do they support making adjustments to management systems in the event that the management practices in use don't sustain diversity adequately.

The mown edges of roadsides often provide an open grassland community that is a critical resource for many species such as butterflies (Saarinen et al. 2005). A surprisingly large amount of mown fields is occupied by power lines. In the United States, power line right-of-way corridors occupy over 2 million ha (5 million acres). Power line corridors maintained with infrequent mowing and without herbicides maintain high levels of bee density (Russell et al. 2005). If such management practices could be extended over a greater proportion of power line rights of way, these areas could become an important habitat for insects and a wide range of other species. Remnant prairies in the United States also represent an important habitat for many species, especially where they can be managed with grazing or burning. Even heavily altered ecosystems have some value for conservation. Although dams, reservoirs, canals, dredging operations, port facilities, and coastal development destroy and damage aquatic communities, some species are capable of adapting to altered conditions, particularly if the water is not polluted. Similarly, in estuaries and seas managed for commercial fisheries, many noncommercial native species can survive, though often at reduced densities.

Excellent examples of natural habitat occur on large tracts of government owned land; for instance, on watersheds adjacent to metropolitan water supplies such as the Quabbin Reservoir in Massachusetts. Security zones surrounding government installations and military reservations are some of the most outstanding natural areas in the world. The U.S. Department of Defense manages more than 10 million ha, much of it undeveloped, containing over 200 threatened and endangered species of plants and animals (Box 18.1). For example, the White Sands Missile Range in New Mexico is almost 1 million ha in area, about the same size as Yellowstone National Park. While certain sections of military reservations may be damaged by military activities, much of the habitat remains as an undeveloped buffer zone with restricted access.

Other areas that are not protected by law may retain species because the human population density and degree of utilization is typically very low. Border areas such as the demilitarized zone between North and South Korea often have an abundance of wildlife because they remain undeveloped and depopulated. Mountain areas, often too steep and inaccessible for development, are frequently managed by governments as valuable watersheds that produce a steady supply of water and prevent flooding; they also harbor important natural communities. Likewise, desert and tundra species and ecosystems may be at less risk than other unprotected communities because such regions are marginal for human habitation and use (MEA 2005).

In many parts of the world, wealthy individuals have acquired large tracts of land for their personal estates and for private hunting. These private estates are frequently, deliberately managed by the landowner to maintain large wildlife populations. Some estates in Europe, such as the Bialowieza Forest, have preserved unique

BOX 18.1

In Defense of Wildlife . . . Send in The Marines

■ The thump of mortar fire and the thudding of tank treads hardly seem compatible with wildlife conservation, yet some of the largest expanses of undeveloped land in the United States are on military reservations located throughout the nation. The U.S. Department of Defense controls more than 10 million ha of land, nearly one-third the size of the 35 million ha of national park lands owned by the National Park Service. Whereas national parks host millions of visitors a year, access to military bases is limited to military personnel and authorized visitors; because of these restrictions, much of the land remains in its natural state. Moreover, the land used for military exercises often is not used intensively; for instance, the Air Force uses only 1250 ha of its 44,000-ha base in Avon Park, Florida, and similar small fractions are used at other sites. In other cases, the impact of military training itself, including accidental fires, tank exercises, and artillery practice, provides the disturbance and open habitat required by certain species, such as the Karner Blue butterfly and its host plants at Fort McCoy in Wisconsin. As a result, many military bases have become de facto refuges for around 300 species of endangered plants and animals, many of which have their largest populations on military bases. Rare and endangered desert tortoises, manatees, red-cockaded woodpeckers, bald eagles, Atlantic white cedars, and the least Bell's vireo all have found safe havens on military lands.

Obviously, military reservations differ from true wildlife refuges in one important aspect: They are sites for significant disturbances caused by military exercises. While much of the land may be left undisturbed as a security zone, large parts of the otherwise undeveloped land may be used periodically for acclimating troops to potential combat environments. Many bases contain toxic waste dumps and high levels of chemical pollutants, and human disturbance in the form of bomb explosions, artillery practice, or the use of heavy vehicles can have a significant negative effect on the resident wildlife.

The passage of the Legacy Resource Management Program in 1991 by Congress allowed the military to place greater emphasis on environmentally sound practices by giving them funding for research and conservation programs (Jacobson and Marynowski 1997). Recent programs have ranged from helping individual species to restoring entire habitats (Burger 2000; McKee and Berrens 2001). In some cases, conservation efforts simply mean protecting the stands of old-growth forest at the Jim Creek Radio Station in the Pacific Northwest, or the largest chunk of ungrazed tallgrass prairie in the West at Fort Sill, or the pine habitat that houses endangered red-cockaded woodpeckers at Fort Bragg. At the Naval Weapons Station at Charleston, South Carolina, Navy biologists have installed nest boxes and drilled holes in trees to provide future nest sites for the red-cockaded woodpecker. Abandoned underground bunkers are being modified to provide habitat for bats. Construction of a pipeline in San Pedro, California, was halted when

The endangered Hawaiian stilt (*Himantopus mexicanus knudseni*) lives on exposed mud-flats in Nu'upia Wildlife Management Area of the Hawaii Marine Corps Base. The Marine Corps periodically uses amphibious assault vehicles to break up exotic woody plants that threaten to cover the mudflats and exclude the stilt. (Photographs courtesy of the Department of Defense.)

BOX 18.1 *(continued)*

workers found a population of the Palos Verdes blue butterfly, formerly thought to be extinct; Navy biologists are now monitoring the population and restoring its coastal scrub habitat. Habitat is also being restored at numerous bases around the country as trees are replanted and bulldozers reshape land that has been pitted with bomb craters and gouged with vehicle tracks. Personnel at the Barksdale Air Force Base in Shreveport, Louisiana, have reflooded drained wetlands along the Red River, restoring 830 ha of wetlands for thousands of wading birds. Contaminated sites are being cleaned up. The Army's Rocky Mountain Arsenal in Colorado is even being transformed into the Rocky Mountain Wildlife Refuge. Fences are being installed at Fort Irwin in California, to prevent

the endangered desert tortoises from getting run down during tank training activities, and hundreds of tortoises inside the training area will be used to augment a declining population elsewhere.

Habitat preservation on military lands isn't a perfect conservation solution: Conflict still arises when military commanders resist involvement in nonmilitary activities, when Congress questions funding such conservation activities, or when military activities appear to be incompatible with species protection. For the time being, though, military reservations are encouraging preservation. At Camp Pendleton in California, a clear message is being sent: A sign warns people away from a tern nesting site "by order of the base commander."

old-growth forests that have been owned and protected for hundreds of years by royal families. In recent decades, many such estates have been taken over by government agencies and conservation organizations.

Conservation in Urban Areas

Many native species can persist even in urban areas, in small protected areas, streams, ponds, and other less altered habitats (Rubbo and Kiesecker 2005). As suburban and urban communities expand at the margin of urban centers, this will become more common in the future (Theobold 2004). Protecting these remnants of biodiversity within a human-dominated matrix not only presents special challenges but provides unique opportunities to educate the public about biodiversity conservation. For example, a new species of salamander discovered at a popular swimming site in Austin, Texas, has required a change in how the site is managed to allow people and salamanders to coexist. In Europe, villages have erected special poles as stork nesting sites, now that the storks' natural nesting sites in forests are no longer available. Endangered raptors such as the peregrine falcon and bald eagle make nests and raise young in the skyscrapers of downtown Boston and New York, where the presence of small mammals in the inner city park systems (along with the ubiquitous pigeons and rats common to urban centers) provide abundant food sources.

As exciting as such examples of urban adaptations might be, we cannot assume that all species have the potential to live within human dominated landscapes. We have a lot to learn about just what habitat and disturbance features are important for various species and how to integrate those into our urban and suburban landscapes. Moreover, increasing the presence of wild animals in the urban landscape comes with fairly serious consequences for both animals and humans. Transmission of disease and other potentially harmful direct interactions among people, domestic animals, and wild animals is a major concern. For example, development of woodland areas and mountain canyons includes the creation of grassy lawns and gardens that attract deer. Deer may seem fairly innocuous to urbanites unused to wild animals, but they bring with them a host of problems: they can carry ticks that transmit illnesses to humans such as Lyme disease and Rocky Mountain spotted fever, are a significant potential road hazard, and males can become fairly aggressive toward humans during mating season. In some areas, deer that live within developments also attract predators such as cougars, increasing the potential for human–wildlife conflicts for a scarce and ecologically important top carnivore.

Conservation in Agricultural Areas

Considerable biological diversity can also be maintained in traditional agricultural systems and forest plantations (Imhoff 2003; McNeely and Scheer 2003; Van Buskirk and Willi 2006; Critchley et al. 2004; Laiolo et al. 2005) (see Chapter 20). Birds and other animal and plant species are often more abundant in traditional agricultural landscapes, characterized by a mixture of small fields, hedges, and woodlands. Some species are only found in such highly modified habitat. In comparison with more intensive "modern" agricultural practices, these landscapes experience less exposure to herbicides, fertilizers, and pesticides. Similarly, farmlands worked using organic methods have a greater abundance of birds than farmlands worked using nonorganic methods (Beecher et al. 2002). In European countries, farmers are sometimes paid by the government to maintain traditional agricultural landscapes and farming practice under a program called NATURA 2000. For example, farmers are paid to maintain the traditional wildflowers of farmland, such as corn marigold (*Chrysanthemum sagetum*) and corn cockle (*Agrostemona githago*), which are eliminated by the applications of fertilizer and herbicides associated with intensive agriculture (Figure 18.3; Shardlow and Harper 2000; Buner et al. 2005). These wildflowers sometimes are maintained by establishing hedges in fields and creating wildflower strips. However, not all of these programs are successful at increasing species richness (Kleijn et al. 2004).

Traditional tropical forest plantations often retain considerable species diversity. One notable example from tropical countries is traditional plantations of shade coffee, in which coffee is grown under a wide variety of shade trees, often as many as 40 tree species per farm (Figure 18.4A) (Perfecto et al. 2003; Armbrecht et al. 2005). In northern Latin America alone, shade coffee plantations cover 2.7 million ha. These plantations have structural complexity created by multiple vegetation layers and a diversity of birds and insects comparable to adjacent natural forest, and they represent a rich repository of biodiversity (Roberts et al. 2000; Daily et al. 2003). However, a concern remains as to whether native tree species can regenerate in these altered environments. In many areas, the spread of a fungal disease called coffee leaf rust has encouraged conversion of shade plantations to high-yielding sun coffee plantations without shade trees, which incorporate coffee varieties that require more pesticides and fertilizers (Figure 18.4B). These sun coffee plantations have only a tiny fraction of the species diversity found in shade coffee areas and are far more prone to water runoff and soil erosion. Therefore, maintaining species diversity in many tropical countries is being attempted by regulating and subsidizing shade coffee farmers to maintain practices that minimize forest clearing, monitoring the health of the forest species within shade-grown coffee plantations, and marketing their product at a premium price as "environmentally friendly," shade-grown

FIGURE 18.3 The traditional wildflowers of European cultivated fields can be maintained when farmers are paid to reduce applications of herbicides and fertilizer. This wheat field in Dorset, England, has an abundance of uninvited corn marigold and poppy plants, but many of the other wildflowers of farmlands are now rare or extinct in England. (Photograph by Bob Gibbons/Natural Image.)

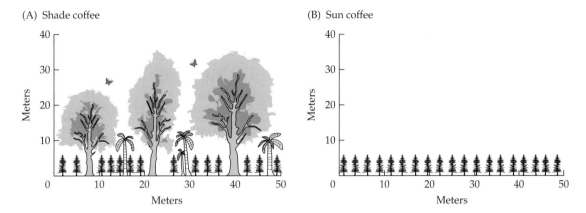

(A) Shade coffee

(B) Sun coffee

FIGURE 18.4 Two types of coffee management systems in the Central Valley of Costa Rica. (A) Shade coffee is grown under a diverse canopy of trees, providing a forest structure in which birds, insects, and other animals can live. (B) Sun coffee is grown as a monoculture, without shade trees. Animal life is greatly reduced. (After Fournier in Perfecto et al. 1996.)

coffee. A difficulty with this strategy is that the standards for shade coffee are not uniform, and some coffee marketed as "environmentally friendly, shade coffee" may actually be grown as sun coffee with a few small, interspersed trees.

Multiple-Use Habitat

In many countries, large parcels of government-owned land are designated for **multiple use**: They are managed to provide a variety of goods and services. The Bureau of Land Management in the United States oversees more than 110 million ha, including 83% of the state of Nevada and large amounts of Utah, Wyoming, Oregon, Idaho, and other western states (Figure 18.5). In the United States, national forests cover over 83 million ha including the Rocky Mountains, the Cascade Range, the Sierra Nevada, the Appalachian Mountains, and the southern coast of Alaska. In the past, these lands have been managed for logging, mining, grazing, wildlife, and recreation. Increasingly, multiple-use lands also are being valued and managed for their ability to protect species, biological communities, and ecosystem services (Hunter 1999; Dombeck et al. 2003). The U.S. Endangered Species Act of 1973 and other similar laws, such as the 1976 Forest Management Act, require landowners, including government agencies, to avoid activities that threaten listed species.

Laws and court systems are now being used by conservation biologists to halt government-approved activities on public lands that threaten the survival of endangered species. In the late 1980s in Wisconsin, for instance, conservation-oriented botanists questioned how the U.S. Forest Service was interpreting its multiple-use mandate in the Nicolet and Chequamegon National Forests. These forests had been managed for a wide variety of uses by the U.S. Forest Service, but timber production and deer hunting tended to predominate. In this part of the country, few threatened and endangered species exist, but many migrant songbirds and forest wildflowers have been declining for decades (Rooney et al. 2004). Many of these declines appeared attributable to the loss of forest interior conditions and an overabundance of white-tailed deer, responding to plentiful food in specially created "wildlife openings." The Wisconsin botanists argued that an effective way to protect this biodiversity would be to forego all logging, road construction, and wildlife openings in several large (200 to 400 km^2) blocks of land. The Chief of the U.S. Forest Service rejected proposals to establish these "diversity maintenance areas." This

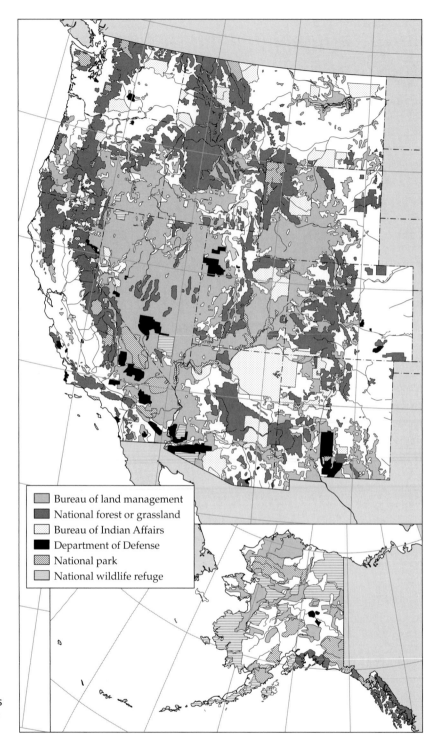

FIGURE 18.5 In Alaska and the western states, agencies of the U.S. government own the majority of the land including some truly enormous blocks of land. The management of this multiple-use land increasingly incorporates the protection of biodiversity as a major objective. (Data from National Geographic Society.)

prompted lawsuits involving not only the original scientists, but also conservation groups such as the Sierra Club. The U.S. Forest Service eventually agreed to increase the emphasis it placed on conserving biodiversity. However, new regulations recently issued by the U.S. Forest Service appear to restrict the role of scientists and the general public in influencing decisions on how to manage federal lands and place less emphasis on sustainable management (Noon et al. 2005). Thus, public forest management remains contentious in the United States.

Ecosystem Management

To achieve broad conservation objectives, governments are now encouraging the managers of protected areas to coordinate their conservation management activities with other government departments and private landowners. To achieve conservation objectives, many large blocks of land are being managed in an integrated manner, termed **ecosystem management**. While there is no standard definition of this term, ecosystem management can be considered enhanced multiple-use management at the landscape scale that involves many stakeholders. The concept is defined by Grumbine (1994) as follows: "Ecosystem management integrates scientific knowledge of ecological relationships within a complex sociopolitical and values framework toward the general goal of protecting native ecosystem integrity over the long term." Public and private resource managers are increasingly being urged to expand their traditional emphasis on the maximum production of goods (such as volume of timber harvested) and services (such as number of park visitors) and instead take a broader perspective that includes the conservation of biological diversity and the protection of ecosystem services (Yaffee 1999; Meffe et al. 2003; Guerry 2005).

Rather than each government agency, private conservation organization, business, or individual landowner acting in isolation, ecosystem management envisions them cooperating to achieve common conservation objectives (Machlis and Field 2000; Shepherd 2004). For example, in a large forested watershed along the coast, ecosystem management would link all owners and users from the tops of the hills to the seashore—including foresters, farmers, conservation biologists, business groups, townspeople, and the fishing industry (Figure 18.6)—into an interconnect-

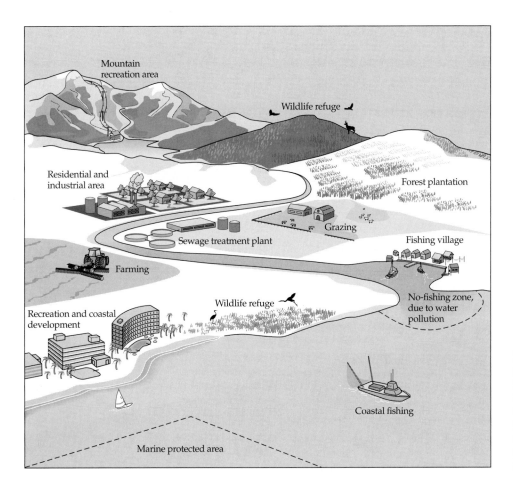

FIGURE 18.6 Ecosystem management involves linking all of the stakeholders that affect a large ecosystem and receive benefits from it. In this case, a watershed needs to be managed for a wide variety of purposes, many of which influence each other. (After Miller 1996.)

ed, cooperative force for conservation. While not all ecologists accept the ecosystem management paradigm (and others disagree with specific management practices), the concept of ecosystem management linked to the practice of conservation biology is being embraced by certain government agencies, businesses, and conservation groups—not all of whom are as enthusiastic about actual implementation as they are about persuading the general public that their organization is "green." Nonetheless, the fact that public relations benefits are on the side of ecosystem management for conservation is a significant factor in promoting the next important step of putting the paradigm into practice.

Important themes in ecosystem management include:

- Using the best science available to develop a coordinated plan for the area that is sustainable; that includes biological, economic, and social components; and that is shared by all levels of government, business interests, conservation organizations, and private citizens.

- Ensuring viable populations of all species, representative examples of all biological communities and successional stages, and healthy ecosystem functions.

- Seeking and understanding connections between all levels and scales in the ecosystem hierarchy—from the individual organism to the species, the community, the ecosystem, and even to regional and global scales.

- Monitoring significant components of the ecosystem (numbers of individuals of significant species, vegetation cover, water quality, etc.), gathering the needed data (Busch and Trexler 2003), and then using the results to adjust management in an adaptive manner (sometimes referred to as **adaptive management**) (Figure 18.7).

One example of ecosystem management is the Malpai Borderlands Group, a cooperative enterprise of ranchers and local landowners who promote collaboration between private landowners, government agencies, and conservation organizations such as The Nature Conservancy. The group is working to develop a network of cooperation across nearly 400,000 ha of unique, rugged mountain and desert habitat along the Arizona and New Mexico border (Curtin 2002). This country of isolated mountains, or "sky islands," includes the Animas and Peloncillo Mountains. This is one of the richest biological areas in the United States, supporting Mexican jaguars, 265 species of birds, and 90 species of mammals (Figure 18.8). It includes 19 listed threatened and endangered species, and dozens of other rare and

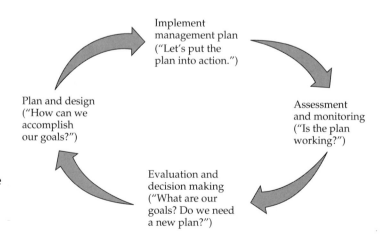

FIGURE 18.7 Adaptive management involves a cycle of planning and design, implementation, assessment and monitoring, and evaluation and decision making. (After Comiskey et al. 2001.)

FIGURE 18.8 The Malpai Borderlands Group encourages ecosystem management for 400,000 ha of desert and mountains in southern Arizona and New Mexico. Numerous rare and endangered species, including the Mexican jaguar (*Panthera onca*), are protected in the process. (Photograph by Warner Glenn, from *Eyes of Fire: Encounter with a Borderland Jaguar*.)

endemic species, such as the New Mexico ridge-nosed rattlesnake, the lesser long-nosed bat, and the Yaqui chub fish. The Malpai Borderlands Group is using controlled burning as a range management tool, reintroducing native grasses, applying innovative approaches to cattle grazing, incorporating scientific research into management plans, and taking action to avoid habitat fragmentation by using conservation easements (agreements not to develop land) to prevent residential development. Their goal is to create "a healthy, unfragmented landscape to support a diverse, flourishing community of human, plant and animal life in the Borderlands Region" (Yaffee 1996).

Most ecosystem management projects appear to be successful at improving cooperation among stakeholders and increasing public awareness of conservation issues (Brush et al. 2000; Zorn et al. 2001). However, many attempts at ecosystem management have not succeeded because of distrust among the participating groups (Rigg 2001). Certain groups, such as real-estate developers and conservation activists, often have fundamentally different objectives. Forcing conservation-minded groups into alliances might weaken their ability to lobby the government for conservation measures and prevent them from taking cases to court (Peterson et al. 2005).

A logical extension of ecosystem management is **bioregional management**, which often focuses on a single large ecosystem such as the Caribbean Sea, the Great Barrier Reef of Australia, or a series of linked ecosystems such as the protected areas of Central America. A bioregional approach is particularly appropriate where there is a single, continuous, large ecosystem that crosses international boundaries or when activity in one country or region will directly affect an ecosystem in another country. For the European Union and the 21 individual countries that participate in the Mediterranean Action Plan, for example, bioregional cooperation is absolutely necessary because the enclosed Mediterranean Sea has large human populations along the coasts, heavy oil tanker traffic, and weak tides that cannot quickly remove pollution resulting from cities, agriculture, and industry (Figure 18.9). This combi-

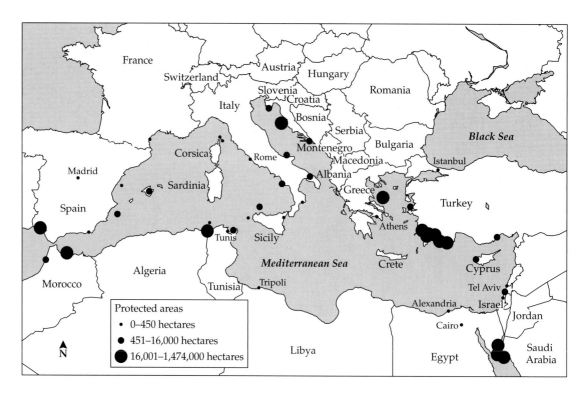

FIGURE 18.9 The countries participating in the Mediterranean Action Plan cooperate in monitoring and controlling pollution and coordinating their protected areas. Major protected areas along the coast are shown as dots. Note that there are no major protected areas on the coasts of France, Libya, and Egypt. (After Miller 1996.)

nation of problems threatens the health of the entire Mediterranean ecosystem, including the sea, its surrounding lands, and its associated tourist and fishing industries. Cross-boundary management is also necessary because pollution from one country can significantly damage the natural resources of neighboring countries. Participants in the plan agree to cooperate in monitoring and controlling pollution, carrying out research, and developing new pollution control methods.

Case Studies

Throughout the world, the protection of biological diversity is being incorporated as an important objective of land management. We conclude the chapter by examining three case studies—old-growth forests in the Pacific Northwest of the United States, Kenya's large wildlife populations outside its parks, and a successful community-based program in Namibia—that demonstrate the problems of managing biological diversity outside protected areas.

Managed Coniferous Forests

The coniferous forests of the Pacific Northwest of the United States are managed for a variety of natural resources, but timber production traditionally has been considered the most important (Franklin et al. 2002). In this ecosystem, the issue of timber production versus the conservation of unique species—the northern spotted owl (*Strix occidentalis caurina*), the marbled murrelet (*Brachyramphus marmoratus*), as well as the salmon—has been a highly emotional and political debate billed as "owls versus jobs." Some environmentalists want to stop all cutting in old-growth forests, while many local citizens want the logging industry to continue current practices without outside interference. A regional compromise has now emerged in which most federal lands have been made into forest reserves to protect biodiversity and ecosystem services, with a reduced level of logging on the remaining lands (Noon and Blakesley 2006; Molina et al. 2006). Logging has continued on state and private lands under Habitat Conservation Plans, but in a way that reduces impacts on rare and endangered species and maintains water quality and fish populations.

Research on forest management techniques has contributed to this compromise solution: Many of the species characteristic of old-growth forests over 200 years old, including cavity-nesting birds such as the northern spotted owl, are also found at lower densities in young forests following natural disturbances (because even very young forests have at least a few old, large trees; some dead, standing trees; and fallen trees that remain after fires and storms). These resources are sufficient to support a complex community of plants and animals. However, clear-cutting techniques that remove living and dead trees of all ages in order to maximize wood production eliminate the places and resources that certain animals and plants need to live. Further, clear-cutting damages the adjacent streams and rivers, leading to the loss of salmon and other aquatic animals. In managed forests of the Pacific Northwest, the past practice of clear-cut, staggered patches of timber produced a landscape pattern that was a mosaic of forest fragments, with different tree ages across fragments and uniform ages within them. These tree plantations lacked the old trees that certain animal species needed to live in.

Research has been used to develop an approach in which conifer forests could be managed to both produce timber and maintain the most important elements of biodiversity. These lessons have been incorporated into the "ecological forestry" now being practiced in the Pacific Northwest (Lindenmayer and Franklin 2002). This method essentially involves removing most trees in the areas that are designated for logging, but leaving a low density of medium to large live trees, standing dead trees, and some fallen trees to provide structural complexity (or what could be termed structural legacies) and to serve as habitat for animal species in the next forest cycle (Figure 18.10). Typically around 15% of the trees remain after this type of logging, but a greater percentage can remain, if necessary; this type of management is referred to as structural, or "green-tree," retention (Halpern et al. 2005). By avoiding logging near streams, water quality and other ecosystem services can also be protected.

This change in logging has had major economic consequences. Large areas of national forest are now off-limits to logging, and ecological forestry is now practiced in most areas of federal forests still being logged, and in some areas of state and private forests. Ecological forestry requires a reduced harvest of timber at the time of cutting and a somewhat longer cutting cycle, sometimes resulting in less short-term profit for the timber industry. Although strict environmentalists are still not satisfied because some old-growth "big trees" continue to be cut down, United States citizens and their government have reached a hard-won compromise on the use of these forests and the development of the entire region. Many other such examples of selective logging, including methods known as "low impact logging" and "light-touch logging" are being developed in other forested areas throughout the world.

African Wildlife Outside Parks

Many East African and Southern African countries such as Kenya are famous for the spectacular wildlife populations found in their national parks, which are the basis of a valuable ecotourist industry. Despite the fame of the parks, about three-fourths of Kenya's 2,000,000 large animals live outside the parks' boundaries in rangelands used by commercial ranches and as traditional grazing lands by local people (Western 1989; Young et al. 2005). The rangelands of Kenya occupy 700,000

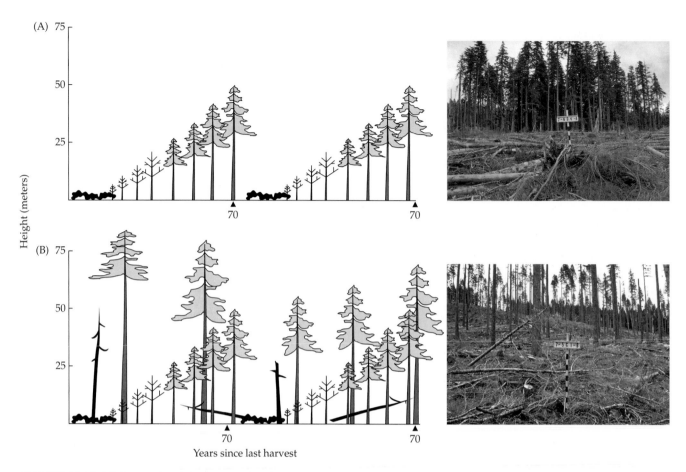

FIGURE 18.10 (A) Conventional clear-cutting involves removing all trees from an area on a 70-year cycle, thus reducing the structural diversity of the forest. The photo shows clear-cutting in the foreground, with some forest retained in the background.

(B) New practices better maintain structural diversity by leaving behind some old trees, standing dead trees, and fallen trees. The photo shows logging with "green-tree" retention. (Graphs after Hansen et al. 1991; photographs courtesy of David Phillips.)

km^2, or about 40% of the country. Among the well-known species found predominantly outside the parks are the giraffe (89%), impala (72%), Grevy's zebra (99%), oryx (73%), and ostrich (92%). Only the rhinoceros, elephant, and wildebeest are found predominantly inside the parks; rhinos and elephants are concentrated in parks because poachers seeking ivory, horn, and hides have virtually eliminated external populations of these animals. The large herbivores found in the parks often graze seasonally outside them. However, the rangelands outside the parks are increasingly unavailable to wildlife because of fences, poaching, and agricultural development. As a result, over the last 30 years, wildlife populations have declined by around 50% in the areas outside of Kenya's parks.

Even with these declines in wildlife populations, several factors contribute to the persistence of substantial populations of wildlife in unprotected areas of sub-Saharan Africa (Western 1989). Many wildlife species are valued for their meat, so their presence on rangeland is encouraged. Private ranching, in which wildlife and livestock are managed together, is often more profitable than managing livestock alone. Wildlife often eat different plants than cattle, are able to tolerate drought better, and are more resistant to certain diseases. Furthermore, many ranches have developed facilities for foreign tourists who want to view wildlife, creating an additional source of revenue. Some wildlife species are present in very low numbers; some are elusive and ignored by ranchers. Some areas containing wildlife are not used by people because they are inaccessible, have an inadequate water supply, or have chronic warfare or disease. In certain traditionally managed rangelands, human communities such as the Masai sometimes have prohibitions against hunting and eating wildlife. In these locations wildlife exists without interference. Some species such as elephants are tolerated since they open up woody vegetation for grassland and enhance the habitat for livestock. Some species are protected outside parks by laws against hunting and trading, which are enforced by wildlife officials. Finally, others persist simply because people enjoy them, fear them, or find them beautiful or amusing, and so encourage (or at least tolerate) their presence.

In Kenya, South Africa, Namibia, and other countries, a change in government policy is allowing rural communities and private landowners to profit directly from the presence of large game animals (Hulme and Murphree 2001; Virtanen 2003; King et al. 2005). With assistance from international donor agencies, local ecotourist businesses—geared toward hiking, photography, canoeing, and horseback safaris, for example—are being established. When the land is adequately stocked with animals, trophy hunting in certain countries is also allowed for high fees; sale of the meat and hide provides additional revenue. The hope is that people will protect wildlife when they can see that it is providing the community with income. Certain of these programs apparently are successful at combining conservation and community development, but they have been criticized by animal rights groups because they allow trophy hunting. Additionally, these programs often depend on continuing subsidies from outside donor agencies, and sometimes only a small percentage of funding actually reaches the village level. When outside subsidies cease, the programs often end, indicating the weakness of the local economy, the instability of the ecotourism industry, and ineffective government policies.

Community-Based Wildlife Management in Namibia

It has long been observed that conservation works best when local people are involved and have a strong investment in its success. Many countries in East and Southern Africa have tried to promote conservation by implementing Community Based Natural Resource Management (CBNRM), programs in which local landowners and communal groups are given the authority to manage and profit from the wildlife on their own property. Prior to this policy, wildlife was often managed by government officials, often with no input from the local people, who gained little or no economic benefit from the wildlife on their own land. By changing the management system to CBNRM, African countries hope to counterbalance pressures threatening local wildlife.

One of the most successful new programs for local communities managing wildlife is found in Namibia in Southern Africa (Hulme and Murphree 2001). In this country of 1.8 million people, 14% of the land is national parks and other protected areas, 44% is private land, and 41% is communal lands. Beginning in 1996, the Namibian government granted traditional communal groups the right to use and manage the wildlife on their own lands. To obtain these rights, the groups needed to form a management committee and determine the boundaries of their land. Once they did this, the government would designate them as a "community conservancy." The benefits of forming a conservancy and participating in wildlife management are fourfold:

1. The conservancy can form joint ventures with tour operators, with around 5 to 10% of the gross earnings paid to the conservancy. A certain number of the employees in the tourist operation are to be hired from among the communal group. Revenue from the joint ventures is used to train and pay game guards, again hired from the communal group, who monitor wildlife populations and prevent poaching.

2. Using funds from the joint ventures, the conservancy members build and operate campsites for tourist groups, providing direct revenue, employment, and experience for the communal group.

3. The conservancy can apply to the government for a trophy-hunting quota. The quota will be granted if wildlife populations are large enough, as indicated by monitoring. This quota can then be sold or auctioned off to professional hunters, who bring in wealthy foreign tourists willing to pay a high price for an African hunting experience. One hundred percent of the trophy fees go directly to the conservancy, regardless of whether the animals are actually killed. Payments to the conservancy for high-value animals such as lions and elephants can be as large as $11,000 per animal. Meat from the hunted animals is distributed to the group members as an added benefit.

4. Once the conservancy has formed a wildlife management plan, four species of wildlife—gemsbok, springbok, kudu, and warthog—can be hunted for subsistence. In practice, the hunting is often done by game guards and professional hunters, with the meat distributed to everyone in the community.

Over the last 10 years, 31 conservancies in Namibia have been established, with more in the process of forming (Figure 18.11). The total area covered is 80,000 square kilometers, or 9% of Namibia's area. Help in the initial establishment of the conservancies has come from external funding agencies, such as the United States Agency for International Development. Conservancy members have received further training in tourism, financial and marketing skills, and training in effective advocacy to gain support from the government and the private sector.

Certain conservancies are generating significant revenue from their wildlife operations. With this income they are able to build more tourist facilities, erect communal structures such as schools, distribute money to their members, and even establish bank accounts. However, the conservancies depend on international tourism as their main income, a source that might not be secure in times of local

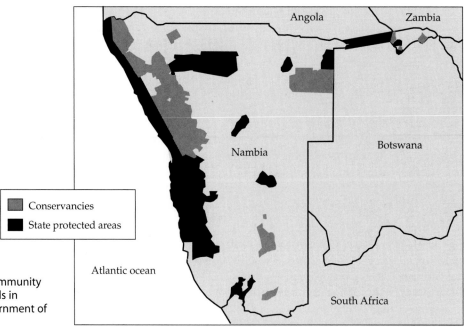

FIGURE 18.11 The distribution of community conservancies and state protected lands in Namibia. (After WRI 2005 and the Government of Namibia 2006.)

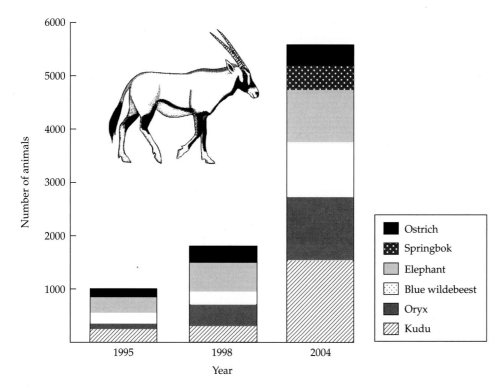

FIGURE 18.12 Number of animals observed in aerial censuses of the Nyae Nyae Community Conservancy in Namibia conducted in 1995, 1998, and 2004. (After Namibia Ministry of Environment and Tourism and WRI 2005.)

and global instability. In addition, conservancies in more remote areas have had difficulty gaining the interest of tour operators and negotiating joint ventures. As a result, their conservancies have generated little income and may not be profitable in the present system.

In general, the communal management system seems to be having positive effects. Wildlife populations in Namibia are showing strong increasing trends (Figure 18.12). While these trends began in the mid-1980s following the end of a severe drought, wildlife populations have continued to increase during this period of communal management in Namibia. Additionally, with the system of wildlife monitoring now in place, the trends in wildlife both inside and outside of protected areas can now be followed in much greater detail in the coming years.

Summary

1. Considerable biological diversity exists outside of protected areas, particularly in habitat managed for multiple-use resource extraction. Such unprotected habitats are vital for conservation because in almost all countries, protected areas account for only a small percentage of total area. Animal species living in protected areas often forage on or migrate to unprotected land where they are vulnerable to hunting, habitat loss, and other threats from humans. Governments are increasingly encouraging the protection of biological diversity as a priority on multiple-use land, including forests, grazing lands, agricultural areas, military reservations, and urban areas.

2. Government agencies, private conservation organizations, businesses, and private landowners are cooperating on large scale ecosystem management projects to achieve conservation objectives and to use natural resources sustainably. Bioregional management involves cooperation between countries to manage large ecosystems that cross international borders.

3. In temperate forest ecosystems, biological diversity can be enhanced if logging operations avoid damage to streams and minimize fragmentation, and if some late-successional components are left, including living trees, standing dead trees, and fallen trees.

4. In Africa, many of the characteristic large animals are found predominantly in rangeland outside the parks. Local people and landowners often maintain wildlife on their land for a variety of purposes. Local communities are now generating income by combining wildlife management and ecotourism, sometimes including trophy hunting.

For Discussion

1. Consider a national forest that has been used for decades for logging, hunting, and mining. If endangered plant species are discovered in this forest, should these activities be stopped? Can logging, hunting, and mining coexist with endangered species and, if so, how? If logging has to be stopped or scaled back, do logging companies or their employees deserve any compensation?

2. Imagine that you are informed by the government that the endangered Florida panther lives on a piece of land that you own and were planning to develop as a golf course. Are you happy, angry, confused, or proud? What are your options? What would be a fair compromise that would protect your rights, the rights of the public, and the rights of the panther?

3. Choose a large aquatic ecosystem that includes more than one country, such as the Black Sea, the Rhine River, the Caribbean, the St. Lawrence River, or the South China Sea. What agencies or organizations have responsibility for ensuring the long-term health of the ecosystem? In what ways do they, or could they, cooperate in managing the area?

Suggested Readings

Berkes, F. and C. Folke (eds.). 2000. *Linking Social and Ecological Systems: Management Practices and Social Mechanisms for Building Resilience.* Cambridge University Press, New York. Case studies of social responses to ecosystem changes.

Brooks, A., M. Zint, and R. DeYoung. 2003. Landowner's response to an Endangered Species Act listing and implications for encouraging conservation. *Conservation Biology* 17: 1638–1649. Landowners need to learn more before they will support conservation.

Buck, L. E., C. C. Geisler, J. Schelhas, and E. Wollenberg. 2001. *Biological Diversity: Balancing Interests through Adaptive Collaborative Management.* CRC Press, Tampa, Florida. Managers and scientists are developing flexible management approaches that reconcile local, regional, national, and global needs.

Critchley, C. N. R., M. J. W. Burke, and D. P. Stevens. 2004. Conservation of lowland semi-natural grasslands in the UK: A review of botanical monitoring results from agri-environment schemes. *Biological Conservation* 115: 263–278. Evaluation of the effectiveness of programs to enhance biodiversity.

Deguise, I. E. and J. T. Kerr. 2006. Protected areas and prospects for endangered species conservation in Canada. *Conservation Biology* 20: 48–55. Many threatened species and habitats remain outside of reserves.

Freemark, K. E. and D. A. Kirk. 2001. Birds on organic and conventional farms in Ontario: partitioning effects of habitat and practices on species composition and abundance. *Biological Conservation* 101: 337–350. Governments and conservation organizations are developing programs to directly pay farmers for maintaining bird species on their land.

Guerry, A. D. 2005. Icarus and Daedalus: conceptual and tactical lessons for marine ecosystem-based management. *Frontiers in Ecology and the Environment* 3: 202–211. Rapid progress is being made in the protection and management of marine systems.

Hunter, M. L., Jr. (ed.). 1999. *Maintaining Biodiversity in Forest Ecosystems*. Cambridge University Press, New York. Obtaining benefits from forests while maintaining biodiversity.

Imhoff, D. and R. Carra. 2003. *Farming with the Wild: Enhancing Biodiversity on Farms and Ranches*. Sierra Club Books, San Francisco, CA. Illustrated book of examples of how biodiversity can be integrated with agriculture in the United States.

Lindenmayer, D. B. and J. F. Franklin. 2002. *Conserving Forest Biodiversity: A Comprehensive Multiscaled Approach*. Island Press, Washington, D.C. Two leading experts try to reconcile multiple uses of forests.

Machlis, G. E. and D. R. Field. 2000. *National Parks and Rural Development: Practice and Policy in the United States*. Island Press, Washington, D.C. National parks and rural communities are intertwined in terms of their goals and economy, so cooperation is important.

Molina, R., B. G. Marcot, and R. Lesher. 2006. Protecting rare, old-growth, forest-associated species under the survey and manage program guidelines of the Northwest Forest Plan. *Conservation Biology* 20: 306–318. Intensive surveys have led to the location of numerous unknown populations of rare species, but controversy remains over how to balance resource use and conservation.

Noon, B. R. and J. A. Blakesley. 2006. Conservation of the Northern Spotted Owl under the Northwest Forest Plan. *Conservation Biology* 20: 288–296. Despite dramatic changes in forest management practices, this species still requires continued protection.

Putz, F. E., G. M. Blate, K. H. Redford, R. Fimel, and J. Robinson. 2001. Tropical forest management and conservation of biodiversity: An overview. *Conservation Biology* 15: 7–20. Leaders in the field argue that carefully managed selectively logged forests can help preserve biodiversity.

Rooney, T. P., S. M. Wiegmann, D. A. Rogers, and D. M. Waller. 2004. Biotic impoverishment and homogenization in unfragmented forest understory communities. *Conservation Biology* 18: 787–798. Management of forest areas for timber and deer can lead to the loss of plant species.

Rubbo, M. J. and J. M. Kiesecker. 2005. Amphibian breeding distribution in an urbanized landscape. *Conservation Biology* 19: 504–511. Species vary in their ability to adapt to the urban environment.

Wilcove, D. S., M. J. Bean, B. Long, et al. 2004. The private side of conservation. *Frontiers and Ecology and Environment* 2: 326–331. Private and public initiatives are both important in conservation.

Young T. P., T. M. Palmer, and M. E. Gadd. 2005. Competition and compensation among cattle, zebras, and elephants in a semi-arid savanna in Laikipia, Kenya. *Biological Conservation* 112: 251–259. How to protect African wildlife and still provide for the needs of people?

Zorn, P., W. Stephensen, and P. Grigoriev. 2001. An ecosystem management program and assessment process for Ontario National Parks. *Conservation Biology* 15: 353–362. Park lands and neighboring lands are being managed as large ecosystems.

Restoration Ecology

Damaged and degraded ecosystems provide important opportunities for conservation biologists to put research findings into practice by helping to restore historical species and communities (Allen et al. 2001; Perrow and Davy 2002; Suding et al. 2004). Rebuilding damaged ecosystems has great potential for enlarging, enhancing, and connecting the current system of protected areas. **Ecological restoration** is the process of assisting the recovery of degraded, damaged, or destroyed ecosystems (www.ser.org). **Restoration ecology** is the science of restoration and refers to research and scientific study of restored populations, communities, and ecosystems (Cairns and Heckman 1996). These are overlapping disciplines: ecological restoration provides useful scientific data in the process of its work, while restoration ecology interprets and evaluates restoration projects in a way that can lead to improved methods. In this chapter we examine these interconnected disciplines and the effects their practices are having on protecting biological diversity.

There are many different situations in which restoration ecology plays an important role (Clewell and Aronson 2006). For instance, in some cases, businesses are required by law to restore habitats they have degraded through activities such as strip mining or waste disposal. Governments sometimes must restore ecosystems damaged by their own activities, including the dumping of sewage into rivers and estuaries by municipalities or chemical pollution on military bases. Restoration efforts are often part of **compensatory**

(A)

(B)

FIGURE 19.1 Building a new railroad line through Glacier National Park in Canada created widespread habitat damage (A). As part of the project, these areas were restored using native plant species (B). (Photographs courtesy of David Polster, Polster Environmental Services; these and other pairs of restoration photographs can be viewed at www.ser.org.)

mitigation, in which a new site, often incorporating wetland communities, is created or rehabilitated in compensation for a site that would be destroyed elsewhere by development (Holl 2002; Zedler et al. 2001). At other times, ecological processes rather than ecosystems need to be restored; for example, annual floods disrupted by the construction of dams and levees and natural fires stopped by fire-suppression efforts may need to be reintroduced if the absence of these processes proves harmful to local and regional ecosystems and communities. The 2005 destruction of New Orleans and other Gulf Coast cities by Hurricane Katrina, and to a lesser extent by Hurricane Rita, was in part a result of the loss and overdevelopment of the region's wetlands. This event is fast becoming a "classic example" of the importance of such ecosystem services to biological and human communities alike (see Box 5.1). Ironically, the damage that followed these hurricanes had been predicted seven years earlier in an assessment of coastal wetlands by the Louisiana Coastal Wetlands Conservation and Restoration Task Force (1998), which had stressed the urgent need for immediate action to restore lost wetlands.

Ecological restoration has its origins in older applied technologies that attempted to restore ecosystem functions or species of known economic value, such as wetland replication (to prevent flooding), mine site reclamation (to prevent soil erosion), range management of overgrazed lands (to increase production of grasses), and tree planting on cleared land (for timber, recreational, and ecosystem values) (Figure 19.1). However, these technologies often produce only simplified biological communities or communities that cannot maintain themselves. As concern for biological diversity has grown, restoration plans have included as a major goal the reestablishment of original or historical species assemblages and communities. The input of conservation biologists is needed for these efforts to achieve their goals.

Damage and Restoration

Ecosystems can be damaged by natural phenomena such as volcanic eruptions, hurricanes, and fires triggered by lightning, but they typically recover their biomass, community structure, and even a similar species composition through the process of succession. However, some ecosystems have been so degraded by human activity that their ability to recover on their own is severely limited. For example, the original plant species will not be able to grow at a site if the soil has been washed away by erosion. Recovery is particularly unlikely when the damaging agent is still present in the ecosystem. Restoration of degraded savannah woodlands in the western United States, for instance, is not possible as long as the land continues to be overgrazed by introduced cattle; reduction of the grazing pressure is obviously the key starting point in these restoration efforts.

Once the damaging agent is removed or controlled, the original communities may reestablish themselves by natural successional processes from remnant populations. However, recovery is unlikely when many of the original species have been eliminated over a large area so that there is no source of colonists. Prairie species, for instance, were eliminated from huge areas of the United States when the land was converted to agriculture. Even when an isolated patch of land is no longer cultivated, the original community is unlikely to reestablish itself because there is no source of seeds and no potential colonizing animals of the original species. The site also may be dominated by invasive species, which often become established in disturbed areas; invasive species must be removed before native species can recover (D'Antonio and Meyerson 2002). Recovery also is unlikely when the physical environment has been so altered that the original species can no longer survive there; an example is mine sites, where the restoration of natural communities may be delayed by decades or even centuries because of soil erosion and the heavy-metal toxicity and low nutrient status of the remaining soil.

Restoration in such challenging habitats requires modification of the physical environment by adding soil, nutrients, and water; by removing invasive species; and by reintroducing native species to the point where the natural process of succession and recovery can begin. Because restoration efforts need to be customized for individual sites, an approach in which different methods are tested experimentally is often advisable (Zedler 2005) (Figure 19.2). These restored sites then

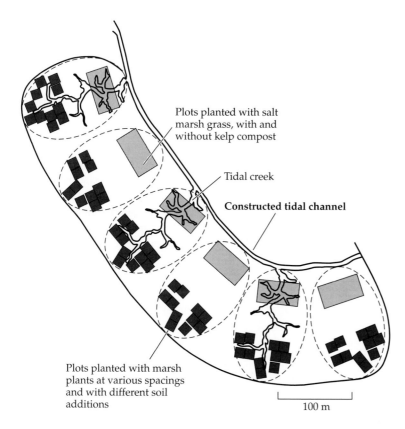

Plots planted with salt marsh grass, with and without kelp compost

Tidal creek

Constructed tidal channel

Plots planted with marsh plants at various spacings and with different soil additions

100 m

FIGURE 19.2 An experiment to test the effects of different treatments on the restoration at the "Friendship Marsh" in Tijuana Estuary, California. The marsh is divided into six experimental units, three with tidal channels and three without channels, to test the effects of drainage. Within each unit, restoration treatments in the small squares (dark squares) involve different species, different planting densities, and different soil additions. In the larger blocks (light shading), salt marsh grass was planted with or without kelp compost. The impact of these treatments on plants, fish and invertebrates, and algae are being evaluated. (From Zedler 2005.)

BOX 19.1

Can Many Small Projects Clean up the Chesapeake Bay?

▮ The Chesapeake Bay is one of the most important fishing grounds and recreational areas in the United States. However, pollution from residential, agricultural, and industrial lands enclosing the bay have been causing a dramatic decline in the quality of the marine environment, affecting all aspects of biodiversity. The immediate economic consequences of this pollution were also urgent: harvests of fish and shellfish were in decline, and the water was becoming unsafe for swimming. This type of general pollution from an entire landscape is referred to as "non-point source" pollution, and it requires a comprehensive restoration approach, as no single source of the pollution can be readily identified and contained. In 1987 the federal, state, and local government bodies responsible for the bay signed an agreement to reduce nutrient and sediment loads coming into the bay by 40%, to be achieved mainly through

improving the health of streams and watersheds feeding into the bay. Since that time, over 4700 individual restoration projects have been implemented, at a cost of over $400 million dollars (Hassett et al. 2005). The largest number of projects involve stream and river restorations that include regrading slopes and planting native vegetation. However, the most money has been spent on water treatment projects. A weakness of these projects is that only 5% of them have been monitored, mainly for vegetation structure, and even fewer have monitored water quality to determine if the project has been achieving the desired goals of reducing nutrient and sediment loads. The Chesapeake Bay project demonstrates that while society has accepted the need to restore large aquatic ecosystems, scientists need to do a better job of ensuring that the restoration jobs deliver the services as promised.

need to be monitored for years, even decades, to determine how well management goals are being achieved and if further intervention is required, an approach that is called **adaptive restoration** (Zedler and Calloway 2003; Zedler 2005). In particular, native species may have to be introduced again if they did not survive, and invasive species may have to be removed again if they are still abundant.

In certain cases entirely new environments have been created by human activity, such as reservoirs, canals, landfills, and industrial sites. If these sites are neglected, they often become dominated by invasive species, resulting in biological communities that are not useful to people, not typical of the surrounding areas, valueless or even damaging from a conservation perspective, and aesthetically unappealing (Suding et al. 2004). If these sites are properly prepared and native species are reintroduced, native communities possibly can be restored.

The goal of these and other restoration efforts often is to create new habitats that are comparable in ecosystem functions or species composition to existing **reference sites** (Kloor 2000; Egan and Howell 2001; Wolters et al. 2005). Reference sites provide explicit goals for restoration and supply quantitative measures of the success of a project. Indeed, reference sites act as control sites and are central to the very concept of restoration. Another goal of restoration sometimes is to recreate a historic landscape or assemblage, such as a traditional agricultural landscape, using old photographs and journals to establish restoration objectives. The use of reference sites does not mean restoration goals are set in stone: Since ecosystems change over time due to changing climate, plant succession, the varying abundance of common species, and other factors, the goals of restoration may have to change over time as well to remain realistic.

To determine whether the goals of restoration projects are being achieved, both the restoration and the reference sites need to be monitored over time (Box 19.1). In some cases, such as at arid and cold sites, ecosystem recovery might take decades or centuries. Monitoring is also needed to determine the efficacy of some methods

BOX 19.1 *(continued)*

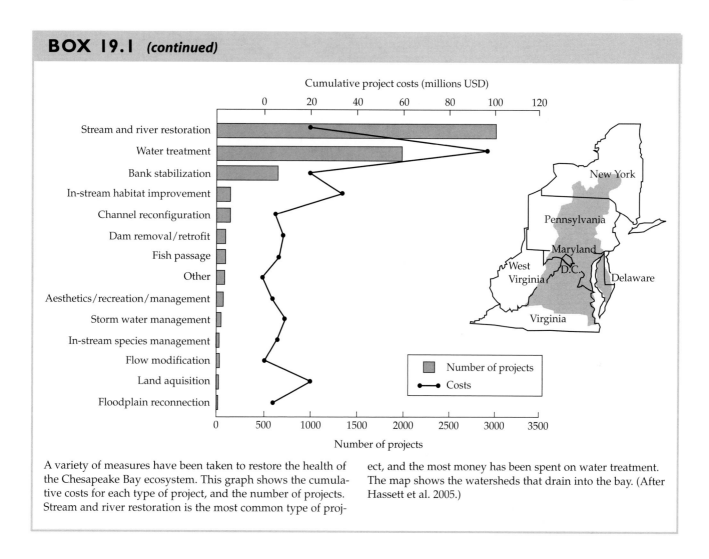

A variety of measures have been taken to restore the health of the Chesapeake Bay ecosystem. This graph shows the cumulative costs for each type of project, and the number of projects. Stream and river restoration is the most common type of project, and the most money has been spent on water treatment. The map shows the watersheds that drain into the bay. (After Hassett et al. 2005.)

versus their costs. For instance, roads are increasingly being removed in protected areas to restore ecosystem processes and reconnect fragmented landscapes; monitoring is needed to determine the effectiveness of this expensive activity (Switalski et al. 2004).

Ecological Restoration Techniques

Restoration ecology provides theory and techniques to restore various types of degraded ecosystems. Four main approaches are available in restoring biological communities and ecosystems (Figure 19.3) (Bradshaw 1990; Cairns and Heckman 1996; Whisenant 1999):

1. *No action:* Restoration is deemed too expensive, previous attempts have failed, or experience has shown that the ecosystem will recover on its own. Letting the ecosystem recover on its own, also known as passive restoration, is typical for old agricultural fields in eastern North America, which return to forest within a few decades after being abandoned.

2. *Rehabilitation:* Replacing a degraded ecosystem with another productive type, using just a few or many species. An example of this is replacing a degraded forest area with a productive pasture. Replacement at least establishes a biological community on a site and restores ecological functions such as flood

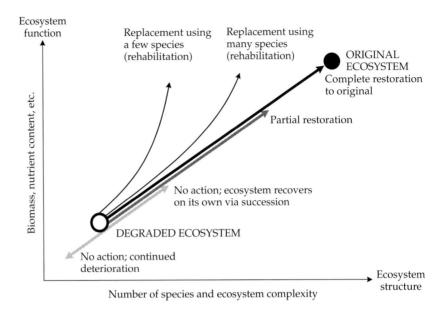

FIGURE 19.3 Degraded ecosystems have lost both their structure (in terms of number of species present and their interactions with the physical and biological environments) and their function (the accumulation of biomass and soil, water, and nutrient processes). In evaluating sites for restoration, scientists must decide whether the best course of action is to restore the site completely, partially restore the site, rehabilitate the site with different species, or take no action. (After Bradshaw 1990.)

control and soil retention. In the future, the new community might eventually come to incorporate a larger number of native species than its predecessor had.

3. *Partial restoration:* Restoring at least some of the ecosystem functions and some of the original, dominant species. An example is replacing a degraded forest with a tree plantation or replanting a degraded grassland with a few species that can survive. Partial restoration typically focuses on dominant species or particularly resilient species that are critical to ecosystem function, delaying action on the rare and less common species that are part of a complete restoration program.

4. *Complete restoration:* Restoring the area to its original species composition and structure by an active program of site modification and reintroduction of the original species. Restoration must first determine and reduce the source of ecological degradation. For example, a source of pollution must be controlled before a lake ecosystem can be restored. Natural ecological processes must be reestablished and allowed to heal the system.

Practical Considerations

Restoration ecology projects often involve professionals from other fields who lend their expertise. These practitioners often have different goals than conservation biologists. For instance, civil engineers involved in major projects seek to find economical ways to permanently stabilize land surfaces, prevent soil erosion, make the site look better to neighbors and the general public, and if possible, restore the productive value of the land. Sewage treatment plants must be built as part of the restoration of lakes, rivers, and estuaries. To restore wetland communities needed for flood control and wildlife habitat, dams and channels may need to be altered to reestablish the original water flow patterns. Ecologists contribute to these restoration efforts by developing ways to restore the communities in terms of species diversity, species composition, vegetation structure, and ecosystem function. To be practical, ecological restoration must also consider the speed of restoration, the cost, the reliability of results, and the ability of the target community to persist with little or no further maintenance. Practitioners of ecological restoration must have a clear grasp of how natural systems work and what methods of restoration are feasible (Allen et al. 2001; Zedler et al. 2001). Considerations of the cost and availability of seeds, when to water plants, how much fertilizer to add, how to remove invasive species, and how to prepare the surface soil may become paramount in determining a project's outcome. Permits will likely be needed, and all regulations must be followed. Dealing with such practical details generally has not been the focus of academic biologists in the past, but these details must be considered in ecological restoration.

Restoration ecology, the science of restoration, is valuable to the broader science of ecology because it provides a test of how well we understand a biological community, and the extent to which we can successfully reassemble a functioning community from its component parts demonstrates the depth of our knowledge and points out deficiencies. As Bradshaw (1990) has said, "Ecologists working in the field of ecosystem restoration are in the construction business, and like their engineering colleagues, can soon discover if their theory is correct by whether the airplane falls out of the sky, the bridge collapses, or the ecosystem fails to flourish." In this sense, restoration ecology can be viewed as an experimental methodology that complements existing basic research on intact systems. In addition to its role as a conservation strategy, restoration ecology provides opportunities to reassemble communities in different ways, to see how well they function, and to test ideas on a larger scale than would be possible otherwise (Holl et al. 2003; Temperton et al. 2004; Wallace et al. 2005). For example, it has been found that when more species are planted in restoration projects, there is subsequently more biomass accumulation, more plant cover, and a greater uptake of soil nutrients (Callaway et al. 2003).

Efforts to restore degraded terrestrial communities generally have emphasized the establishment of the original plant community. This emphasis is appropriate because the plant community typically contains the majority of the biomass and provides structure for the rest of the community. However, in the future, restoration ecology needs to devote more attention to the other major components of the community. Fungi and bacteria (see Box 5.2) play vital roles in soil decomposition and nutrient cycling; soil invertebrates are important in creating soil structure; herbivorous animals are important in reducing plant competition and maintaining species diversity; birds and insects are often essential pollinators; and many birds and mammals have vital functions as insect predators, soil diggers, and seed dispersers (Allen et al. 2003). Many of these nonplant species can be transferred to a restored site in sod samples. If an area is going to be destroyed and then restored later, as might occur during strip mining, the top layer of soil, which contains the majority of buried seeds, soil invertebrates, and other soil organisms, can be carefully removed and stored for later use in restoration efforts (Allen et al. 2001). Such efforts to use local biological materials avoid the problems of introducing foreign genotypes that may not be adapted to the site (Hufford and Mazer 2003). While these methods are a step in the right direction, many species will still be lost during this process and the community structure will be completely altered. Large animals and aboveground invertebrates may have to be caught deliberately in sufficient numbers and then released onto restored sites to establish new populations if they are unable to disperse to the site on their own.

Restoration ecology will play an increasingly important role in the conservation of biological communities if degraded lands and aquatic communities can be restored to their original species composition and added to the limited existing area under protection. Because degraded areas are unproductive and of little economic

FIGURE 19.4 Dr. Wangari Maathai won the Nobel Peace Prize for her leadership of the Green Belt Movement, which organizes rural women in Kenya to plant trees, protect forests, and participate in the political process. (Photograph © Peter Arnold, Inc./Alamy.)

value, governments may be willing to restore them to increase their productive and conservation value.

Many restoration efforts are supported and even initiated by local conservation groups because they can see the direct connection between a healthy environment and their own personal and economic well-being. People can understand that planting trees produces firewood, timber, and food; prevents soil from washing away; and cools off the surrounding area in hot weather. An excellent example of a restoration effort with strong local support is the Green Belt Movement, a grassroots effort involving mainly rural women in Kenya that has planted over 25 million trees in degraded sites. The movement also organizes rural people, especially poor women, to have a voice in the political process, to maintain access to public forests, and to resist illegal logging. For her leadership of this movement, Dr. Wangari Maathai was awarded the Nobel Peace Prize in 2004 (Figure 19.4).

Case Studies

The following case studies illustrate some of the problems and solutions of ecological restoration.

Wetlands Restoration in Japan

An informative example of wetlands restoration comes from Japan, where parents, teachers, and children have built over 500 small ponds next to schools and in public parks to provide habitat for dragonflies and other native aquatic species (Primack et al. 2000). Dragonflies are an important symbol in Japanese culture, and are useful as a starting point for teaching zoology, ecology, chemistry, and principles of conservation. These ponds provide a focus for an entire science and math curriculum. The ponds are planted with aquatic plants; many dragonflies colonize them on their own, and some species are carried in as nymphs from other ponds. The schoolchildren are responsible for the regular weeding and maintenance of

(A)

(B)

(C)

FIGURE 19.5 (A) Children in Yokohama, Japan, are building a dragonfly pond next to their school. Activities involved in its construction include excavating the site, packing the bottom with clay, and reinforcing the banks with wooden posts; later, when the pond is completed, the children will fill it with aquatic plants and release dragonfly larvae. (B) A group of children and adults uses butterfly nets to check for the diversity and abundance of dragonflies at a Yokohama city pond during a city-sponsored maintenance day. They will also remove excess aquatic plants and exotic fish species from the pond. (C) This publicity poster (which exclaims "Let's build a dragonfly pond!"), along with an extensive offering of brochures and practical manuals, is part of government efforts to interest schoolchildren and the general public to participate in programs to restore and enhance the environment. (Photographs courtesy of Seiwa Mori and Yokohama City Environmental Protection Bureau.)

these "living laboratories," which helps them to feel an ownership of the project and to develop environmental awareness (Figure 19.5).

The Grand Canyon–Colorado River Ecosystem

River damming has severe and extensive impacts on downstream ecosystems, and restoring river flow may allow these ecosystems to recover (Stanley and Doyle 2003; Bednarek and Hart 2005; Rood et al. 2005). One high-profile case of restoration in the United States involves the Colorado River where it flows through the Grand Canyon. The river had been drastically altered in 1963 by the construction of the Glen Canyon Dam and the filling-in of Lake Powell. While those projects did provide water and electricity throughout the region, there was a major reduction in the spring floods that once surged through the canyon creating new beaches and habitat for the unique Grand Canyon fish species. Without the flooding, beaches and banks were either worn away or became overgrown with woody vegetation, and introduced game fish began to replace native fish. To restore this crucial flooding event, the Bureau of Reclamation released an experimental flood of 900 million m^3 over the course of one week in March 1996 (Schmidt et al. 1998). The flood was effective in creating new beaches and habitat for native fish species, but by 2002 the river had mostly returned to its preflood condition. Currently, the government is experimenting with varying the rate of water release as a restoration technique.

Restoration in Urban Areas

Highly visible restoration efforts are also taking place in many urban areas, to reduce the intense human impact on ecosystems and enhance the quality of life for city dwellers (Higgs 2003; Jordan 2003). Local citizen groups often welcome the opportunity to work with government agencies and conservation groups to restore degraded urban areas. Unattractive drainage canals in concrete culverts can be replaced with winding streams bordered with large rocks and planted with native wetland species. Vacant lots and neglected lands can be replanted with native shrubs, trees, and wildflowers. Gravel pits can be packed with soil and restored as ponds. These efforts have the additional benefits of fostering neighborhood pride, creating a sense of community, and enhancing property value. However, such restorations are often only partially successful because of their small size and the fact that they are embedded in the highly modified urban environment (Moberg and Rönnbäck 2003). Developing urban places in which people and biodiversity can coexist has been termed "reconciliation ecology," and will increase in importance as urban areas expand (Rosenzweig 2003).

Restoring native communities on huge urban landfills presents one of the most unusual opportunities. In the United States, 150 million tons of trash are being buried in over 5000 active landfills each year. These eyesores can be the focus of conservation efforts. When they have reached their maximum capacity, these landfills are usually capped by sheets of plastic and layers of clay to prevent toxic chemicals and pollutants from seeping out. If these sites are left alone, they are often colonized by weedy, exotic species. However, planting native shrubs and trees attracts birds and mammals that will bring in and disperse the seeds of a wide range of native species.

Consider the ongoing restoration of the Fresh Kills landfill on Staten Island in New York city (Young 1995). The site occupies over 1000 ha, has a volume 25 times that of the Great Pyramid of Giza, and has garbage mounds as tall as the Statue of Liberty. The landfill was closed in 2001 and is now undergoing restoration to create native biological communities. The project began by using bulldozers to contour the site, creating an appearance and drainage similar to natural coastal dunes. Next, 52,000 individuals of 18 species of trees and shrubs were planted to create distinctive native plant communities: an oak scrub forest, a pine-oak forest, and a low shrubland. Herbs were planted within these communities. Right away, the trees provided perching places for fruit-eating birds that brought seeds of many new species to the site. After just one year, seedlings of 32 additional woody plant species had appeared on the site. The site appears to be on its way to establishing a native ecosystem, with a 50% survival rate of plants. Native birds of conservation interest such as ospreys, hawks, and egrets nest and feed there. The eventual goal is to create a new park with abundant wildlife, open to the citizens of this huge city.

Restoration of Some Major Communities

Many efforts to restore ecological communities have focused on wetlands, lakes, prairies, and forests. These environments have suffered severe alteration from human activities and are good candidates for restoration work, as described below.

Wetlands

Some of the most extensive restoration work has been done on wetlands, including swamps and marshes (Rood et al. 2003; DeWeedt 2004; Fang et al. 2005). Wetlands are often damaged or even filled in because their importance in flood control, maintenance of water quality, and preservation of biological communities is either not known or not appreciated. While the loss of a single wetland seems unimportant in most years, the cumulative loss of many wetlands over periods of years and decades can result in massive flood damage to low-lying properties following heavy rains and hurricanes. Because of wetland protection under the Clean Water Act and the U.S. government policy of "no net loss of wetlands," large development projects that damage wetlands must repair them or create new wetlands to compensate for those damaged beyond repair (Box 19.2). The focus of these efforts has been on

BOX 19.2

Easier Said than Done: Restoring the Kissimmee River

The Kissimmee River was formerly a long, meandering river that flowed from Lake Kissimmee to Lake Okeechobee in central Florida. Its loops and bends created a mosaic of wetlands and floodplains that supported a highly diverse community of waterfowl, wading birds, fish, and other wildlife. The hydrology of the Kissimmee River was unique. The large number of headwater lakes and streams that drain into the Kissimmee River, combined with flat floodplains, low riverbanks, and poor drainage, led to frequent, prolonged flooding, dense vegetation, and outstanding wildlife habitat.

But the annual floods that created such a unique ecosystem were not considered compatible with the rapid expansion of urban and agricultural development in the 1950s and 1960s. In response to the growing demand for flood protection, the Kissimmee River was channelized. The U.S. Army Corps of Engineers dug a 90-km long drainage canal down the center of the floodplain, built levees and other water control structures, and regulated water flow from the feeder lakes. Two-thirds of the wetlands were drained, one-third of the river's natu-

(continued)

The Kissimmee River Restoration project involves removing two water control structures (S-65B and S-65C) and backfilling the 37 km of canal between them. In the process, 72 km of continuous river channel will be restored, and floodwaters will cover the floodplain once again. In Phase 1, completed in 2001, control structure S-65B was removed, 24 km of the river channel was restored, and 15 km of channel was filled in. The map is not to scale. The distance from Lake Kissimmee to Lake Okeechobee is around 90 km. (Data from the South Florida Water Management District 2001.)

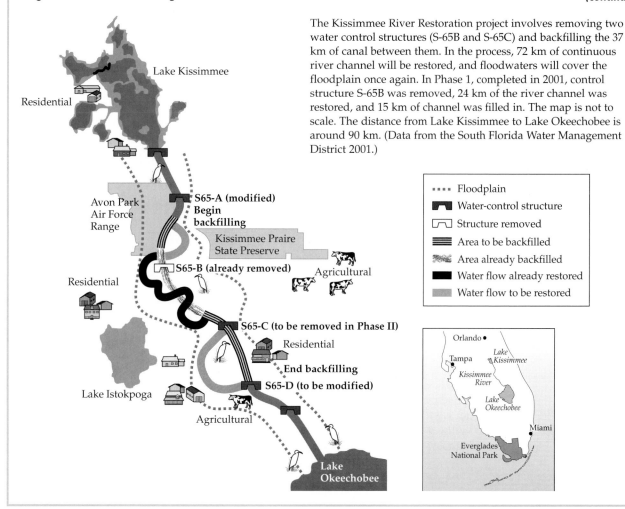

Legend:
- Floodplain
- Water-control structure
- Structure removed
- Area to be backfilled
- Area already backfilled
- Water flow already restored
- Water flow to be restored

BOX 19.2 *(continued)*

ral channel was destroyed, and much of the drained land was converted to rangeland for cattle. As the water flow was diverted through the canal, dissolved oxygen concentrations in the remaining sections of wetland declined. An ecosystem that had been characterized by highly variable water levels and patchy, diverse habitats became a stable, homogeneous environment. The impacts were immediate: The numbers of overwintering birds declined sharply, habitat for game fish was degraded, and a diverse natural community of wading birds and fish was replaced by a few dominant species such as cattle egrets, gar, and bowfin (Bousquin et al. 2005; Williams et al. 2005). As the impact of the channelization became apparent, public pressure from conservation groups mounted to restore the Kissimmee River to its original state. Initial plans focused on restoring certain target species or functions of the river. Fishermen lobbied for restoration of the largemouth bass fishery. Residents clamored for improving water quality by restoring the filtering function of the wetlands. Hunters and birdwatchers focused on improving conditions for waterfowl. Ultimately it became clear that efforts needed to focus on restoring the ecological integrity of the whole ecosystem, rather than on individual characteristics such as species abundance (Toth and Aumen 1994).

A demonstration project in 1984 used a dam across the canal to direct river water into the former wetland, recreating marshland and reestablishing old river channels. Within one year, wetland plant communities were reestablished and fish and bird populations increased dramatically in the reflooded areas. This demonstration project and other restoration studies and modeling efforts provided evidence that the restoration of the Kissimmee River was technically feasible.

In 1992, the U.S. Congress authorized the restoration of the Kissimmee River through backfilling 37 km of the flood-control canal, removing two water control structures, and recarving 15 km of old river channel. In the process, approximately 11,000 ha of wetlands and 72 continuous km of the twisting river channel will be restored. To accomplish this, approximately 40,000 ha of land are being acquired by the government. Important habitat will be provided for over 300 fish and wildlife species, including the threatened bald eagle, the endangered snail kite, and the endangered wood stork. The first phase of the reconstruction was completed between 1999 and 2001. It restored 24 km of river channel and approximately 4400 ha of floodplain. Key aspects of the biotic and abiotic environment are being evaluated and monitored before, during, and after each phase of the project to determine if project goals are being achieved. Results so far have been encouraging: densities of wading birds and ducks have increased more than fourfold, game fish populations have doubled, and dissolved oxygen levels have increased.

The next major phase of river restoration begins in 2006, with all work on the project scheduled to be completed by 2012. Monitoring will continue through 2017. The final project cost is estimated to be $578 million, shared equally between the federal government and the state of Florida. While this cost may seem enormous, the totality of ecosystem services provided by a healthy, restored Kissimmee River will be immensely valuable and will reestablish a significant part of Florida's natural heritage. The project might also serve as a tutorial for the far larger Comprehensive Everglades Restoration Plan—begun in 2001 and slated to cost $8 billion—which is designed to rebuild this degraded, world-famous wetland of south Florida (Schrope 2001; Polsenberg 2003; www.evergladesplan.org 2005).

recreating the natural hydrology of the area and then planting native species. Experience has shown that such efforts to restore wetlands often do not closely match the species composition or hydrologic characteristics of reference sites. The subtleties of species composition, water movement, and soils, as well as the site history, are too difficult to match. Often the restored wetlands are dominated by exotic, invasive species. However, the restored wetlands often do have some of the wetland plant species, or at least similar ones, and can provide some of the functions of the reference sites. The restored wetlands also have some of the beneficial ecosystem characteristics such as flood control and pollution reduction, and they are often valuable for wildlife habitat.

An example from Iraq illustrates the potential for restoration. An enormous marsh formerly covered southeastern Iraq; this wetland was home to 75,000 people with a unique culture and was a regional center for bird, fish, and plant biodiversity. The previous Iraqi government drained over 90% of the marshland, converting it to agricultural land and expelling the local people. With the fall of Saddam Hussein, local residents have opened the dikes, reflooding the area. Up to 30% of the marsh could be restored, returning former habitat and homes to the original wildlife and people (Richardson et al. 2005).

Lakes

Limnologists (scientists who study the chemistry, biology, and physics of freshwater bodies) involved in multibillion-dollar efforts to restore lakes are already gaining valuable insights into community ecology and trophic structure that otherwise would not be possible (Welch and Cooke 1990; MacKenzie 1996). One of the most common types of damage to lakes and ponds is **cultural eutrophication**, which occurs when there are excess mineral nutrients in the water resulting from human activity. Signs of eutrophication include increases in the algae population (particularly surface scums of blue-green algae), lowered water clarity, lowered oxygen content in the water, fish kills, and an eventual increase in the growth of floating plants and other water weeds.

Attempts to restore eutrophic lakes have not only provided practical management information, they have also provided insight into the basic science of limnology. In many lakes, the eutrophication process can be reversed by reducing amounts of mineral nutrients entering the water through better sewage treatment or by diverting polluted water. One of the most dramatic and expensive examples of lake restoration has been the effort to restore Lake Erie (Makarewicz and Bertram 1991). Lake Erie was the most polluted of the Great Lakes in the 1950s and 1960s, characterized by deteriorating water quality, extensive algal blooms, declining indigenous fish populations, the collapse of commercial fisheries, and oxygen depletion in deeper waters. To address this problem, the governments of the United States and Canada have invested more than $7.5 billion since 1972 in wastewater treatment facilities, reducing the annual discharge of phosphorus into the lake from 15,260 tons in 1972 to 2449 tons in 1985. The 1970s and 1980s saw improvement in Lake Erie water quality, as shown by lower concentrations of phosphorus, lower phytoplankton (algal) abundance, and an increase in native fish (Figure 19.6). There is even some evidence of increased oxygen levels at the lower depths of the lake. Even though the lake may never return to its historical condition because of altered water chemistry and the large number of exotic species present, the investment of billions of dollars has resulted in a significant degree of restoration in this large, highly managed ecosystem.

Prairies

Many small parcels of former agricultural land in central North America have been restored to prairies. Because they are species-rich, have many beautiful wildflowers, and can be established within a few years, prairies represent ideal subjects for restoration work (Samson and Knopf 1996; Packard and Mutel 1997). Some of the earliest research on the restoration of prairies was carried out in Wisconsin, starting in the 1930s. A wide variety of techniques was used in these prairie restora-

(A)

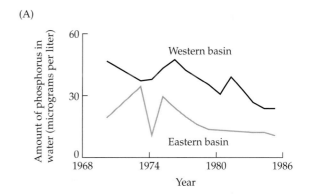

(B)

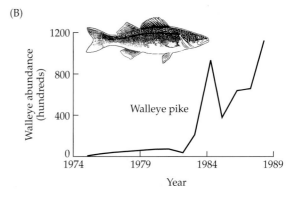

FIGURE 19.6 Signs of recovery in Lake Erie. (A) Levels of phosphorus at the eastern and western basins of the lake. Phosphorus levels were lowered during the 1970s and early 1980s by treating the sewage and other human effluents that entered the lake. (B) Walleye pike abundance, as measured by the sport fishermen catch, has increased once algal levels declined and water quality improved. Walleye are predatory fish that feed on zooplanktivorous fish such as alewife and spottail shiners; adding walleye to the lake is one way to increase the population of crustaceans and other zooplankton, which in turn feed on the algae. (After Makarewicz and Bertram 1991.)

(A)

(B)

FIGURE 19.7 (A) In the late 1930s, members of the Civilian Conservation Corps (one of the organizations created by President Franklin Roosevelt in order to boost employment during the Great Depression) participated in a University of Wisconsin project to restore the wild species of a Midwestern prairie. (B) The prairie as it looked 50 years later. (Photographs from the University of Wisconsin Arboretum and Archives.)

tion attempts, but the basic method involves a site preparation of shallow plowing, burning, and raking, if prairie species are present, or eliminating all vegetation by plowing or applying herbicides, if only exotics are present. Native plant species are then established by transplanting them in prairie sods obtained elsewhere, planting individuals grown from seed, or scattering prairie seed collected from the wild or from cultivated plants (Figure 19.7). The simplest method is gathering hay from a native prairie and spreading it on the prepared site. Of course, reestablishing the full range of plant species, soil structure, and invertebrates could take centuries or might never occur. In concluding his essay on five decades of Wisconsin experiments, Cottam (1990) says,

Prairie restoration is an exciting and rewarding enterprise. It is full of surprises, fantastic successes, and abysmal failures. You learn a lot—usually more about what not to do than what to do. Success is seldom high, but prairie plants are resilient, and even a poor beginning will in time result in a beautiful prairie.

Prairie restoration projects are also useful for their educational value and for their ability to excite urban dwellers eager to volunteer in conservation efforts. Because the techniques used for prairie restoration are similar to common gardening and agriculture, such restorations are well suited to volunteer labor. People who have the experience of working on restoration projects often become strong advocates for conservation. The Chicago metropolitan area is particularly well known for such projects; some involve creating prairie grasslands with native prairie species, rather than lawns, in suburban neighborhoods, while others involve converting forests back to their historical condition as prairies. However, some of the proposed prairie restorations on public land in Chicago have encountered fierce opposition from neighborhood groups, who preferred their parks to remain as forests. Both government officials and biologists were surprised by this reaction, which highlights the need to spend time talking with all stakeholders, especially local residents, before initiating restoration projects (Gobster and Bruce 2000). In this particular case, many of the neighborhood groups prevailed, and certain forests proposed for prairie restoration have remained intact.

One of the most ambitious proposed restorations involves re-creating a short-grass prairie ecosystem, or "buffalo commons," on about 380,000 km^2 of the Plains states, from the Dakotas to Texas and from Wyoming to Nebraska (Mathews and Worster 2003). This land is currently used for environmentally damaging and often unprofitable agriculture and grazing supported by government subsidies. The human population of this region is declining as farmers and townspeople go out of business and young people move away. From the ecological, sociological, and even economic perspectives, the best long-term use of much of the region might be as a restored prairie ecosystem. The human population of the region could stabilize around nondamaging core industries such as tourism, wildlife management, and low-level grazing by cattle and bison, leaving only the best lands in agriculture. The World Wildlife Fund has started to implement this concept with its American Prairie Restoration Project in Montana that will link government and private lands together in a regional conservation network (see Figure 16.11).

Tropical Dry Forest in Costa Rica

An exciting experiment in restoration ecology, begun in 1985, is ongoing in northwestern Costa Rica. The tropical dry forests of Central America have long suffered from large-scale conversion to cattle ranches and farms. Only a few fragments remain. Even in these fragments, logging and hunting threaten remaining species. This destruction has gone largely unnoticed as international scientific and public attention has focused on the more glamorous rain forests elsewhere. The American ecologist Daniel Janzen has been working with Costa Rica's National Park Service and resident staff to restore 110,000 ha of land and 43,000 hectares of marine habitat in the Area de Conservación Guanacaste (ACG) (Figure 19.8) (Allen 1988; Janzen 2000; Allen 2001).

Restoration of this area of marginal ranches, low-quality pastures, and forest fragments includes planting both native and exotic trees to shade out introduced invasive grasses, eliminating human-caused fires, and banning logging and hunting. Livestock grazing was initially used to lower the abundance of grasses and then was phased out as the forest invaded through natural animal- and windborne seed dispersal. In just 20 years, this process has converted 60,000 ha of pastures to a species-rich, dense young forest. This process reestablishes the dry forest ecosystem and benefits the adjacent rain forest to which animals of the dry forest season-

(A)

(B)

(C)

FIGURE 19.8 (A) The Area de Conservación Guanacaste is an experiment in restoration ecology—an attempt to restore the devastated and fragmented tropical dry forest of Costa Rica. (B) Eight years of fire suppression allowed native trees and other species to become established once again, turning a barren grassland (left) into a young forest (right). (C) Daniel Janzen, an ecologist from the United States, is a driving force behind the restoration project in Guanacaste. Here he inspects moth specimens from the study area. (A, B, photographs by C. R. Carroll; C, photograph by William H. Allen.)

ally migrate, but it will require an estimated 200 to 500 years to regain the original forest structure.

An innovative aspect of this restoration is that all 97 members of the staff and administration of the ACG are Costa Ricans and reside in the area. The ACG offers training and advancement for its staff, educational opportunities for their children, and the best economic use of these marginal lands, which were formerly ranch and farm lands. ACG employees are selected from the local community, rather than spending scarce resources on imported consultants. A key element in the restoration plan is what has been termed **biocultural restoration**, meaning that the ACG teaches basic biology in the field to all students in grades four through six in the neighboring schools and gives presentations to citizen groups. Janzen (quoted in Allen 1988) believes that, in rural areas such as Guanacaste, providing an opportunity for learning about nature can be one of the most valuable functions of national parks and restored areas:

> The public is starving for and responds immediately to presentations of complexity of all kinds—biology, music, literature, politics, education, et cetera.... The goal of biocultural restoration is to give back to people the understanding of the natural history around them that their grandparents had. These people are now just as culturally deprived as if they could no longer read, hear music, or see color.

This educational effort has created a community literate in conservation issues as well as a local viewpoint that the ACG offers something of value to all. Residents have begun to view the ACG as if it were a large ranch producing "wildland resources" for the community rather than an exclusionary "national park."

Funding for land purchases and park management for the ACG restoration project, totaling $51 million as of 2006, comes from the Costa Rican government and donations from over 6000 individuals, institutions, and private international foundations. Ecotourism is playing a significant part in the $1.2 million annual budget because of the proximity of the park to the Pan American Highway. Employment in the expanding research, ecotourist, and educational facilities is providing a significant source of income for the local community, particularly for those who are interested in nature and education. For continued success, the ACG must ensure that the plan for park development and management provides the proper integration of community needs and restoration needs in a way that satisfactorily fulfills both. Also, by having scientists involved in the design and implementation of the project, basic and applied information will be obtained that can be used to advance the science of restoration ecology.

This restoration effort has accomplished so many of its goals and has attracted so much media attention in large part because a highly articulate, well-known individual—Daniel Janzen—is committing all his time and resources to a cause in which he passionately believes. His enthusiasm and vision have inspired many other people to join his cause, and he is a classic example of how potent a force for conservation one individual can be.

The Future of Restoration Ecology

Restoration ecology is one of the major growth areas in conservation biology. It has its own scientific society, the Society for Ecological Restoration, and journals, *Restoration Ecology* and *Ecological Restoration*. Ecosystems are being restored using methods developed by the discipline, books are being written about the subject, and more courses are being taught at more universities. Of special importance, scientists are increasingly able to synthesize the growing range of published studies and suggest improvements in how to carry out restoration projects. However, conservation biologists in this field must take care to ensure that restoration efforts are legitimate, not just a public-relations cover by environmentally damaging corporations only interested in continuing business as usual (Zedler 1996; Young 2000). A 5-ha "demonstration" project in a highly visible location does not compensate for thousands or tens of thousands of hectares damaged elsewhere and should not be accepted as such by conservation biologists. Attempts to mitigate the destruction of an intact biological community by the building of a similar species assemblage at a new location is almost certainly not going to provide a home for the same species and provide similar ecosystem functions; therefore, conservation biologists need to be wary of such projects. The best long-term strategy still is to protect and manage biological communities where they are found naturally; only in these places can we be sure that the requirements for the long-term survival of all species are available.

Summary

1. Ecological restoration is the practice of reestablishing populations and whole communities in degraded, damaged, or even destroyed habitat. Restoration ecology is the scientific study of such restorations. Partial restoration of certain species or ecosystem functions may be an appropriate goal if complete restoration is impossible or too expensive.

2. Establishment of new communities such as wetlands, forests, and prairies on degraded or abandoned sites provides an opportunity to enhance biological diversity in habitats that have little other value and can improve the quality of life for people living in the area. Restoration ecology can also provide insight into community ecology by testing our ability to reassemble a biological community from its native species.

3. Restoration projects begin by eliminating or neutralizing factors that prevent the system from recovering. Then some combination of site preparation, habitat management, and reintroduction of original species gradually allows the community to regain the species and ecosystem characteristics of designated reference sites. Attempts to restore habitat need to be monitored to determine if they are reestablishing the historical species composition and ecosystem functions.

4. Creating new habitat in one place to replace lost habitat elsewhere, known as compensatory mitigation, has some value but is not an effective overall conservation strategy; the best strategy is still to protect populations and communities where they naturally occur.

For Discussion

1. Restoration ecologists are improving their ability to restore biological communities. Does this mean that biological communities can be moved around the landscape and positioned in convenient places that do not inhibit further expansion of human activities?

2. How would you evaluate the progress of a project that is currently restoring a biological community? What criteria and techniques would you use? How much time would you need to monitor the restored community?

3. What do you think are some of the easiest natural communities to restore? The most difficult? Why?

4. Conservation efforts are particularly difficult in areas of Africa where there is an increasing human population coupled with poverty, warfare, and environmental damage. Consider the plight of the mountain gorilla living in the Virunga Mountains of Africa. If it is not possible to protect this species in its native locality, why not use a range of African plants to restore a degraded site in a more stable place, such as the mountains of Costa Rica, Mexico, or Puerto Rico, and then release a population of gorillas onto the site? Is this feasible? What about extending the concept to create an entire African savanna ecosystem, complete with herds of grazing animals and predators, on degraded rangelands in Mexico? What are the advantages and disadvantages of such a restoration approach?

Suggested Readings

Allen, W. 2001. *Green Phoenix: Restoring the Tropical Forests of Guanacaste, Costa Rica*. Oxford University Press, Oxford. Vivid description of Dan Janzen's mission to restore Costa Rica's dry forest.

Allen, E., J. S. Brown, and M. Allen. 2001. Restoration of animal, plant, and microbial diversity. *In* S. A. Levin (ed.), *Encyclopedia of Biodiversity*, Vol. 5, pp. 185–202. Academic Press, San Diego, CA. Restoration projects can include animals and microbes.

Clewell, A. F. and J. Aronson. 2006. Motivations for the restoration of ecosystems. *Conservation Biology* 20: 420–428. Various reasons motivate the restoration of ecosystems, and conservation biologists need to contribute to the process.

Dobson, A. P., A. D. Bradshaw, and A. J. M. Baker. 1997. Hopes for the future: restoration ecology and conservation biology. *Science* 277: 515–522. Overview of the field in a special edition of *Science* devoted to human impact on the planet.

Gilbert, O. L. and P. Anderson. 1998. *Habitat Creation and Repair.* Oxford University Press, Oxford. Practical guide to restoration, with many examples from the United Kingdom.

Jordan, W. R., III. 2003. *The Sunflower Forest: Ecological Restoration and the New Communion with Nature.* The University of California Press, Berkeley, CA. The author urges us to create a place for biodiversity in the human-dominated landscape.

Mathews, A. and D. Worster. 2003. *Where the Buffalo Roam: Restoring America's Great Plains.* University of Chicago Press, Chicago. Superb popular account of the controversial "buffalo commons" proposal.

Perrow, M. R. and A. J. Davy (eds.). 2002. *Handbook of Ecological Restoration: Volume 1. Principles of Restoration.* Cambridge University Press, New York. Comprehensive treatment of principles and practices.

Restoration Ecology and *Ecological Restoration.* Check out these journals to see what is really happening in the field. Available from most college and university libraries and from the Society for Ecological Restoration, 285 W. 18th Street, Suite 1, Tucson AZ 85701 U.S.A.; or contact the society at www.ser.org.

Rood, S. B., G. M. Samuelson, J. H. Braatne, C. R. Gourley, F. M. R. Hughes, and J. M. Mahoney. 2005. Managing river flows to restore floodplain forests. *Frontiers in Ecology and the Environment* 3: 193–201. Removing dams and restoring river flows as a method for rebuilding ecosystems.

Suding, K. N., K. L. Gross, and G. R. Houseman. 2004. Alternative states and positive feedbacks in restoration ecology. *Trends in Ecology and Evolution* 19: 46–53. An attempt at restoration might end up with an expected endpoint.

Swetnam, T. W., C. D. Allen, and J. L. Betancourt. 1999. Applied historical ecology: using the past to manage the future. *Ecological Applications* 9: 1189–1206. A knowledge of the history of a site is important in a restoration project.

Switalski, T. A., J. A. Bissonette, T. H. DeLuca, C. H. Luce, and M. A. Madej. 2004. Benefits and impacts of road removal. *Frontiers in Ecology and the Environment* 2: 21–28. Roads can be removed, but it is expensive and difficult.

Temperton, V. M., R. J. Hobbs, T. Nuttle, and S. Hall. (eds.). 2004. *Assembly Rules and Restoration Ecology: Bridging The Gap Between Theory and Practice.* Island Press Book, Washington, D. C. Attempts to bridge the gap between theory and practice.

Van Andel, J. and J. Aronson. (eds.). 2005. *Restoration Ecology: The New Frontier.* Blackwell Publishing, Malden, MA. Strong presentation of European examples.

Wallace, K., J. Callaway, and J. Zedler. 2005. Evolution of tidal creek networks in a high sedimentation environment: A 5-year experiment at Tijuana Estuary, California. *Estuaries* 28: 795–811. A rigorous experiment allows researchers to identify the most effective restoration methods.

Whisenant, S. G. 1999. *Repairing Damaged Wildlands.* Cambridge University Press, Cambridge. Restoration emphasizing natural recovery processes.

White, P. S. and J. L. Walker. 1997. Approximating nature's variation: selecting and using reference information in restoration ecology. *Restoration Ecology* 5: 338–349. Selecting reference sites is difficult because no two sites are exactly the same; see other excellent articles in this special edition of the journal.

Zedler, J. B. 1996. Ecological issues in wetland mitigation: An introduction to the forum. *Ecological Applications* 6: 33–37. A special issue of *Ecological Applications* provides information on the creation of new wetlands.

Zedler, J. B. 2005. Restoring wetland plant diversity. A comparison of existing and adaptive approaches. *Wetlands Ecology and Management* 13: 5–14. Restorations need to be flexible.

Conservation and Human Societies

Conservation and Sustainable Development at the Local and National Levels

As we have seen, many problems in conservation biology require a multidisciplinary approach that addresses the need to protect biological diversity while simultaneously providing for the economic welfare of people (McShane and Wells 2004). The sea turtle conservation program described in Box 1.1 illustrates such an approach: Conservation biologists in Brazil are employing fisherfolk at the *local level* as conservation workers, developing tourist facilities and educational materials, providing medical care and aquaculture training for the local people, and supplying the information the national government needs to establish new protected areas and conservation protection laws. Conservation biologists throughout the world are actively working at the local and national levels to develop such innovative approaches. This chapter examines some of the strategies employed at the local and national levels to promote conservation, strategies that often involve action by combinations of government agencies, private conservation organizations, and local and indigenous peoples. The chapter also explores the efforts by traditional people to protect their lands, which is an important component of protecting biodiversity since many traditional peoples live in the most biologically diverse areas of the world. Finally, the chapter concludes with a brief evaluation of some of these initiatives and suggests possible improvements.

As has been discussed, efforts to preserve biological diversity sometimes conflict with both real and perceived human needs (Figure 20.1). Increasingly, many conservation biologists, policy

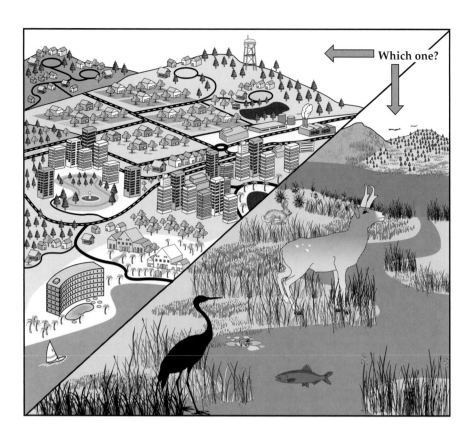

FIGURE 20.1 Sustainable development seeks to address the conflict that exists between development to meet human needs and the preservation of the natural world. (After Gersh and Pickert 1991.)

makers, and land managers are recognizing the need for **sustainable development**—economic development that satisfies both present and future needs for resources and employment while minimizing the impact on biological diversity (Lee 2001; Ehrenfeld 2005; Kates 2005). Sustainable development is needed because many current economic activities damage or deplete the environment in ways that cannot continue without causing irreparable harm to both natural and human communities. As defined by some environmental economists, **economic development** implies improvements in efficiency and organization but not necessarily increases in resource consumption. Economic development is clearly distinguished from **economic growth**, which is defined as material increases in the amount of resources used. Sustainable development is a useful and important concept in conservation biology because it emphasizes *improving current economic development and limiting economic growth.* By this definition, investing in national park infrastructure to improve protection of biological diversity and provide revenue opportunities for local communities would be an example of movement toward sustainable development, as would implementation of less destructive logging and fishing practices.

Unfortunately, the concept of sustainable development is often misappropriated. Many large corporations and the policy organizations that they fund have misused the concept of sustainable development to "greenwash" their industrial activities without any change in practice (Willers 1994; Peterson 2003). For instance, a plan to establish a huge mining complex in the middle of a forest wilderness cannot justifiably be called "sustainable development" simply because a small percentage of the land area is set aside as a park. Alternatively, some conservation biologists champion the opposite extreme, claiming that sustainable development means that vast areas of the world must be kept off limits to all development and should remain as or be allowed to return to wilderness. As with all such disputes, informed scientists and citizens must study the issues carefully, identify which groups are advocating which positions and why, and then make careful decisions that best meet the seemingly contradictory needs of human society and the protection of biological diversity. Such apparent contradiction necessitates compromise, and in most cases compromises form the basis of government policy and laws, with conflicts resolved by government agencies and courts.

Conservation at the Local Level

One of the most powerful strategies in protecting biological diversity at the local level is the designation of intact biological communities as nature reserves or land for conservation. Governments often set aside public lands for various conservation purposes and to preserve future options. Government bodies buy land as local parks for recreation, conservation areas to maintain biological diversity, forests for timber production and other uses, and watersheds to protect water supplies. In some cases, land is purchased outright, but often it is donated to conservation organizations by public-spirited citizens. Many of these citizens receive significant tax benefits from the government to encourage these donations.

Land Trusts

In many countries, private conservation organizations are among the leaders in acquiring land for conservation (Brewer 2003; Merenlender et al. 2004). In the Netherlands, about half of the protected areas are privately owned. In the United States alone, over 6 million ha of land are protected at the local level by land trusts, which are private, nonprofit corporations established to protect land and natural resources. There are around 3000 private conservation organizations in the United States, many of which have land protection, public education, and political lobbying as major objectives. At a national level, major organizations such as The Nature Conservancy and the Audubon Society have protected an additional 6 million ha in the United States (see Box 16.1).

Land trusts are particularly common in Europe. In Britain, the National Trust has more than 3.4 million members and owns around 250,000 ha of land, much of it farmland, including 57 National Nature Reserves, 500 Sites of Special Scientific Interest, 355 properties of Outstanding National Beauty, and 40,000 archaeological sites (Figure 20.2). Among the many private land trusts in Britain, one of the most notable is the Royal Society for the Protection of Birds (RSPB), which has

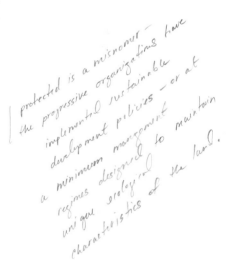

protected is a misnomer – the progressive organizations have implemented sustainable development policies – or at a minimum management regimes designed to maintain unique ecological characteristics of the land.

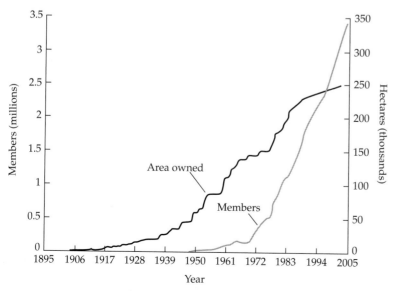

FIGURE 20.2 Membership in the British National Trust has been undergoing a dramatic increase since the 1960s, with a corresponding increase in land ownership; membership is more than 3.4 million as of 2005. (After Dwyer and Hodge 1996.)

more than one million members and manages 182 reserves with an area of 126,000 ha. A major emphasis of many of these reserves is nature conservation, often linked to school programs. The RSPB has an annual income of about $45 million and is active in bird conservation issues around the world. These private reserve networks are collectively referred to as CARTs—Conservation, Amenity, and Recreation Trusts, a name that reflects their varied objectives. Jean Hocker (in Elfring 1989), executive director of the Land Trust Exchange, an association of land trust organizations, explains:

> Different land trusts may save different types of land for different reasons. Some preserve farmland to maintain economic opportunities for local farmers. Some preserve wildlife habitat to ensure the existence of an endangered species. Some protect land in watersheds to improve or maintain water quality. Whether biologic, economic, productive, aesthetic, spiritual, educational, or ethical, the reasons for protecting land are as diverse as the landscape itself.

In addition to outright purchase of land, both governments and conservation organizations protect land through **conservation easements**, in which landowners give up the right to develop, build on, or subdivide their property in exchange for a sum of money, lower real-estate taxes, or some other tax benefit. Sometimes the government or conservation organization purchases the development rights to the land, compensating the landowner for not selling it to developers. For many landowners, accepting a conservation easement is an attractive option: They receive a financial advantage while still owning their land and are able to feel that they are assisting conservation objectives. Of course, the offer of lower taxes or money is not always necessary; many landowners will voluntarily accept conservation restrictions without compensation.

Another strategy that land trusts and governments use is **limited development**: A landowner, property developer, and a conservation organization reach a compromise that allows part of the land to be commercially developed while the remainder is protected by a conservation easement. Limited development projects are often successful because the value of the developed lands is usually enhanced by being adjacent to conservation land. Limited development also allows the construction of necessary buildings and other infrastructures for an expanding human society.

Governments and conservation organizations can further encourage conservation on private lands through other mechanisms, including compensating private landowners for desisting from some damaging activity and implementing some positive activity (Environmental Defense 2000; Ellison and Daily 2003; McQueen and McMahon 2003). **Conservation leasing** involves providing payments to private landowners who actively manage their land for biodiversity protection. Tax deductions and payments could also apply to any costs of restoration or management, including weeding, controlled burning, establishing nest holes, and planting native species. In some cases, private landowners may still be allowed to develop their land later, even if endangered species come to live on the land. A related idea is **conservation banking**, in which a landowner deliberately preserves an endangered species or a protected habitat type such as wetlands, or even restores degraded habitat and creates new habitat (Wilcove and Lee 2004; Fox and Nino-Murcia 2005). A developer can then pay the landowner or a conservation organization to protect this new habitat in compensation for a similar habitat that is being destroyed elsewhere by a construction project. The funds paid by the developer for such habitat mitigation can be used to pay for the management of the newly created, restored, or preserved habitat and endangered species living there. Utilities may also gain carbon credits by paying for such habitat protection and restoration; these carbon credits are then used to offset the carbon emissions produced through the burning of fossil fuels (Swingland 2003; Jenkins et al. 2004). **Conservation concessions** are a recent approach in which conservation organizations outbid logging companies or other extractive industries for the rights to use the land. The problem with all such conservation mechanisms is that they must be continuously monitored to make sure that the agreements are being carried out (Czech 2002).

Local efforts by land trusts to protect land are sometimes criticized as being elitist because they provide tax breaks only to those wealthy enough to take advantage of them, in addition to lowering the revenue collected from land and property taxes (Merenlender et al. 2004). Others argue that land used in other ways, such as for agriculture or to build shopping malls, is more productive. While land in trust may initially yield lower tax revenues, loss of tax revenue from land acquired by a land trust is often offset by the increased value and consequently increased property taxes of houses and land adjacent to the conservation area. In addition, by preserving important features of the landscape and natural communities, local nature reserves also preserve and enhance the cultural heritage of the local society, a consideration that must be valued for sustainable development to be achieved.

Local Legislation

Most efforts to find the right balance between the preservation of species and habitats and the needs of society rely on initiatives from concerned citizens, conservation organizations, and government officials. The result of these initiatives often end up codified into environmental regulations or laws. These efforts may take many forms, but they begin with individual and group decisions to prevent the destruction of habitats and species in order to preserve something of perceived economic, cultural, biological, scientific, or recreational value. One of the most significant developments of recent decades has been the rise of nongovernment organizations (NGOs), many of which mobilize people to protect the environment and promote the welfare of citizens. Many NGOs have a local focus, but there are already over 40,000 international NGOs (Figure 20.3). These NGOs help to organize and educate citizens to achieve conservation objectives.

In modern societies, local (city and town) and regional (county, state, and provincial) governments pass laws to provide effective protection for species and habitats

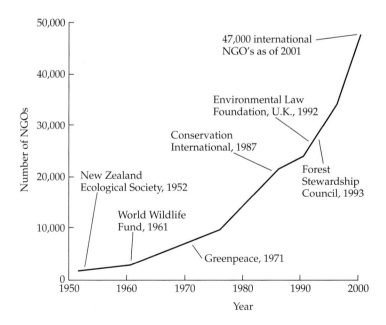

FIGURE 20.3 There has been enormous growth in the number of international nongovernment organizations since 1950; many of these organizations protect the environment, promote the welfare of people, and lobby the government to take actions relating to conservation. (Modified from WRI 2003.)

and at the same time provide development for the continued needs of society (Press et al. 1996; Saterson 2001). Often, but not always, these local and regional laws are comparable to or stricter than national laws. Such laws are passed because citizens and political leaders feel that they represent the will of the majority and provide long-term benefits to society. Conservation laws regulate activities that directly affect species and ecosystems. The most prominent of these laws governs when and where hunting and fishing can occur; the size, number, and species of animals that can be taken; and the types of weapons, traps, and other equipment that can be used. Restrictions are enforced through licensing requirements and patrols by game wardens and police. In some settled and protected areas, hunting and fishing are banned entirely. Similar laws affect the harvesting of plants, seaweed, and shellfish. Related legislation includes prohibitions on trade in wild-collected animals and plants. Certification of origin of biological products may be required to ensure that wild populations are not depleted by illegal collection or harvest. These restrictions have long applied to certain animals such as trout and deer and plants of horticultural interest such as orchids, azaleas, and cacti. New initiatives are being developed to certify the origin of additional products such as ornamental fish and wood.

Laws that control the ways in which land is used are another means of protecting biological diversity. These laws include restrictions on the extent of land use or access, type of land use, and generation of pollution. For example, vehicles and even people on foot may be restricted from habitats and resources that are sensitive to damage, such as bird-nesting areas, bogs, sand dunes, wildflower patches, and sources of drinking water. Uncontrolled fires may severely damage habitats, so practices such as campfires that contribute to accidental fires are often rigidly controlled. Zoning laws sometimes prevent construction in sensitive areas such as barrier beaches and floodplains. Wetlands are often strongly protected because of their recognized value for flood protection, preserving water quality and maintaining wildlife. Even where development is permitted, building permits are reviewed with increasing scrutiny to ensure that damage is not done to endangered species or ecosystems, particularly wetlands. For major regional and national projects, such as dams, canals, mining and smelting operations, oil extraction, and highway construction, environmental impact statements must be prepared describing the damage that such projects could cause so that these projects may be conducted in a more environmentally sensitive manner. To prevent inadvertent damage to natural resources and human health, it is essential to consider all the potential environmental impacts before projects are initiated.

The passage and enforcement of conservation-related laws on a local level can become an emotional experience that divides a community and even leads to violence. To avoid such counterproductive outcomes, conservationists must be able to convince the public that using resources in a thoughtful and sustainable manner creates the greatest long-term benefit for the community. The general public must be made to look beyond the immediate benefits that come with rapid and destructive exploitation of resources. For example, towns often need to restrict development in watershed areas to protect water supplies; this may mean that houses and businesses are not built in these sensitive areas and landowners may have to be compensated for these lost opportunities. It is essential that conservation biologists clearly communicate the reasons for these restrictions. Those affected by the restrictions can become allies in the protection of resources if they understand the importance and long-term benefits of reduced access. These people must be kept informed and consulted throughout the decision-making process. The ability to negotiate, compromise, and explain positions, regulations, and restrictions—often using the best scientific evidence available—are important skills for conservationists to develop. A fervent belief in one's cause is not enough.

Conservation at the National Level

Throughout much of the modern world, national governments play a leading role in conservation activities (Saterson 2001). Governments can use their revenues to buy new lands for conservation. Areas particularly targeted for conservation are the watersheds that protect drinking water, open lands near densely settled urban areas, areas occupied by endangered species, and lands adjacent to existing protected areas. In the United States, special funding mechanisms, such as the Land Legacy Initiative and the Land and Water Conservation Fund, have been established to purchase land for conservation purposes. National governments can also strongly influence conservation practices on private land through the payment of cash subsidies and the granting of tax deductions to landowners who manage their lands for biological diversity.

The establishment of national parks is a particularly important conservation strategy. National parks are the single largest source of protected lands in many countries. For example, Costa Rica's national parks protect around half a million hectares, or about 9% of the nation's land area (www.costarica-nationalparks.com). Outside the protected areas, deforestation is proceeding rapidly, and soon national parks may represent the only undisturbed habitat and source of natural products, such as timber, in the whole country. As of 2005, the U.S. National Park system, with 388 sites, protected around 34 million ha.

National Legislation

National legislatures and governing agencies are the principal bodies for developing policies that regulate environmental pollution. Laws are passed by legislature, and then implemented in the form of regulations by government agencies. Laws and regulations affecting aerial emissions, sewage treatment, waste dumping, and development of wetlands are often enacted to protect human health and property and resources such as drinking water, forests, and commercial and sport fisheries. The level of enforcement of these laws demonstrates a nation's determination to protect the health of its citizens and the integrity of its natural resources. At the same time, these laws protect biological communities that would otherwise be destroyed by pollution and other human activities. The air pollution that exacerbates human respiratory disease, for instance, also damages commercial forests and biological communities; pollution that ruins drinking water also kills terrestrial and aquatic species such as turtles and fish.

National governments can also have a substantial effect on the protection of biological diversity through the control of their borders, ports, and commerce. To protect forests and regulate their use, governments can ban logging, as was done in Thailand following disastrous flooding; they can restrict the export of logs, as was done in Indonesia; and they can penalize timber companies that damage the environment. Certain kinds of environmentally destructive mining can be banned. Methods of shipping oil and toxic chemicals can be regulated. Conservation biologists can provide government officials key information in developing the needed policy framework and then use the resulting laws and regulations to protect biodiversity.

To prevent the exploitation of rare species, governments can restrict the possession of certain species and control all imports and exports of the species through laws and agreements such as the Convention on International Trade in Endangered Species (CITES). For example, the U.S. government restricts trade in endangered tropical parrots through the enforcement of CITES and the Wild Bird Conservation Act. Persons caught violating these laws can be fined or imprisoned. National governments can also regulate the importation of all exotic species into their countries as a way of preventing the accidental or intentional introduction of invasive species.

FIGURE 20.4 Whooping cranes are protected by the U. S. Endangered Species Act and are intensively managed. Here captive-born juvenile whooping cranes are taught foraging and flying skills by a crane expert in a whooping crane costume. The birds will eventually join a flock in the wild without ever having seen an "unmasked" human. (Photograph courtesy of the International Crane Foundation.)

Finally, national governments can identify endangered species within their borders and take steps to conserve them, such as protecting and acquiring habitat for the species, controlling use of the species, developing research programs, and implementing in situ and ex situ recovery plans (Figure 20.4). In European countries, for example, endangered species conservation is accomplished through domestic enforcement of international agreements such as CITES and the Ramsar Wetlands Convention. International Red Lists of endangered species prepared by the International Union for the Conservation of Nature and national Red Data books also highlight priorities for conservation. In Europe, countries protect species and habitats through directives adopted by the European Union; these directives implement the earlier Bern Convention (Bouchet et al. 1999). Some countries may have additional laws, such as the National Parks and Access to the Countryside Act of 1981 in the United Kingdom, which protects habitat occupied by endangered species.

Many of the factors described so far come together to explain the recovery of green sea turtle (*Chelonia mydas*) populations at Tortuguero Beach, on the Caribbean coast of Costa Rica (Figure 20.5). Following decades of overcollection of sea turtle eggs and adult turtles, the Costa Rican government undertook a series of actions to protect this endangered species. First, the government banned the collecting of eggs and adults at Tortuguero Beach in 1963, then it stopped exports of turtle products in 1969; finally, the government established Tortuguero National Park in 1970 to protect the whole area. Protection has gradually been extended by the ban on turtle fishing and the recognition of how valuable nesting turtles are to the tourist industry. Nicaragua and neighboring countries have signed the CITES treaty and are also implementing protection measures. The overall result: The nesting population has more than tripled over the last 35 years (Troëng and Rankin 2005).

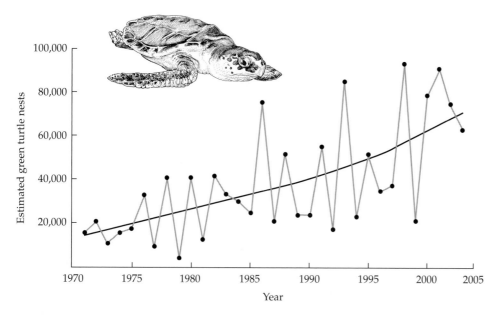

FIGURE 20.5 Greater numbers of green turtles have been nesting at Tortuguero Beach in Costa Rica following a series of protective measures implemented by the government starting in 1963. Nest counts (shown as dots) are variable from year to year. The solid line shows the general trend of increase in numbers. (After Troëng and Rankin 2005.)

It is interesting to note that national legal efforts to protect species are subject to cultural factors: Some species with cultural appeal receive extensive protection, while other species equally in danger may not get the protection they need. In the United Kingdom, for example, the beloved and relatively common hedgehog (*Erinaceous europaeus*) and the badger (*Meles meles*) receive far greater protection than many truly rare species of insects (Harrop 1999). Also, dilemmas may arise when conservation efforts for one endangered species would be detrimental to a second endangered species living in the same site. For example, one species may require protection from fires to survive, while another species may require frequent fires to maintain their populations. Despite the fact that many countries have enacted legislation to preserve biodiversity, it is also true that national governments are sometimes unresponsive to requests from conservation groups to protect the environment. In some cases national governments have acted to decentralize decision making, giving back control of natural resources and protected areas to local governments, village councils, and conservation organizations (WRI 2003). Because of the importance of laws and regulations in protecting biodiversity, conservation biologists need to have a thorough knowledge of this topic (Rohlf and Dobkin 2005).

The U.S. Endangered Species Act

Environmental laws are sometimes perceived as ineffective ("the law isn't going to help anyway"), unfair ("why should landowners be prevented from doing what they want?"), not feasible ("this law is too difficult to enforce") or too costly ("protecting the environment is just too expensive"). However, in many cases, environmental laws have made a huge impact in protecting biodiversity. In the United States, the principal conservation law protecting species is the Endangered Species Act (ESA), passed in 1973 and subsequently amended in 1978 and 1982. This legislation has been a model for other countries, though its implementation has often been controversial (Czech and Krausman 2001; Villa-Lobos 2003; Stem et al. 2005).

The ESA was created by the U.S. Congress to "provide a means whereby the ecosystems upon which endangered species and threatened species depend may be conserved [and] to provide a program for the conservation of such species." Species are protected under the ESA if they are on the official list of endangered and threatened species. In addition, a recovery plan is generally required for each listed species.

As defined by law, "endangered species" are those likely to become extinct as a result of human activities and/or natural causes in all or a significant portion of their range; "threatened species" are those likely to become endangered in the near future. The Secretary of the Interior, acting through the U.S. Fish and Wildlife Service (FWS), and the Secretary of Commerce, acting through the National Marine Fisheries Service (NMFS), can add and remove species from the list based on information available to them. Since 1973, more than 1270 U.S. species have been added to the list, including many well-known species, such as the bald eagle (*Haliaeetus leucocephalus*) and the gray wolf (*Canis lupus*), in addition to 566 endangered species from elsewhere in the world that may be imported into the United States.

The ESA requires all U.S. government agencies to consult with the FWS and the NMFS to determine whether their activities will affect listed species, and it prohibits activities that will harm these species and their habitat—a critical feature, since many of the threats to species comes from activities on federal lands, such as logging, cattle grazing, and mining. The ESA also prevents private individuals, businesses, and local governments from harming or "taking" listed species and damaging their habitat and prohibits all trade in listed species (Taylor et al. 2005). By protecting habitats, the ESA in effect uses listed species as indicator species to protect entire biological communities and the thousands of species that they contain. These restrictions on private land are important to species recovery because around 10% of endangered species are found exclusively on private land (Stein et al. 2000). Although the ESA provides legal recourse to protect species, obtaining the goodwill and cooperation of private landowners is important for recovery efforts (Brooks et al. 2003).

An analysis of the listing process for the U.S. Endangered Species Act shows a number of revealing trends. The great majority of U.S. species listed under the ESA are plants (745 species) and vertebrates (over 300 species), despite the fact that most of the world's species are insects and other invertebrates. If the same proportion of insects were protected as vertebrates, an estimated 29,000 species would be protected under the ESA, an awesome number to contemplate (Duan 2005). More than 40% of the 300 mussel species found in the United States are extinct or in danger of extinction, yet only 70 species are listed under the ESA. Clearly, greater efforts must be made to study the lesser known and underappreciated invertebrate groups and extend listing to those endangered species whenever necessary (Stankey and Shindler 2006). Another study of species covered by the ESA has shown that on average only about 1000 individuals remain at the time a given animal is listed, while plants have fewer than 120 individuals remaining when they are added to the list (Wilcove et al. 1993). Thirty-nine species were listed when they had 10 or fewer individuals remaining, and one freshwater mussel species was listed when it had only a single remaining population that was not reproducing. Species with dramatically reduced populations such as these may encounter genetic and demographic problems that can impede or prevent recovery. For the ESA to be most effective, endangered species must be given protection under the ESA before they decline to the point where recovery becomes virtually impossible. An early listing of a declining species might allow it to recover and thus become a candidate for removal from the list more quickly than if authorities were to wait for its status to worsen before adding it to the list.

The ESA has become a source of contention between conservation and some business interests in the United States. One common viewpoint of many private and business landowners is that the government should not be telling anyone what they can and cannot do on private property. The protection afforded to species listed under the ESA is so strong and the economic costs can be so staggering that business interests and landowners often lobby strenuously against the listing of species in their area. At the extreme are landowners who destroy endangered species on their property to evade the provisions of the ESA, a practice informally known as "shoot, shovel, and shut up." Such was the fate of a quarter of the sites that contained habitat suitable for the threatened Preble's jumping mouse (*Zapus hudsonius*) that lives in stream-side habitats in Colorado and Wyoming (Brook et al. 2003). Clearly, landowners need to be compensated in some way and encouraged publicly to get them to support the provisions of the ESA.

THE ESA AND RECOVERY At present over 280 species are candidates under consideration for listing; while awaiting official decision, numerous species have probably gone extinct. The reluctance of government agencies to put species on the list is caused primarily by the restrictions it places on economic activity, even though economic costs are not supposed to be a factor in listing. Another important obstacle to listing is the difficulty of species recovery—rehabilitating species or reducing the threats to species to the point where they can be removed from listing under the ESA, or "de-listed" (Doremus and Pagel 2001). So far, only 13 of more than 1200 listed U.S. species have been de-listed, and another 22 species have shown enough recovery to be changed from endangered to threatened (Scott et al. 2005). The most notable successes include the brown pelican, the American peregrine falcon, and the American alligator. In 1994, with great fanfare, the bald eagle was moved from the highly regulated "endangered" category to the less critical "threatened" category because its numbers in the lower 48 states had increased from 400 breeding pairs in the 1960s to the current 7000 pairs. Seven species have been de-listed because they went extinct, and eleven species were de-listed either because new populations were found or because biologists decided that they were not truly distinct species. Overall, just under half of the listed species are still declining in numbers, just under half are stable or increasing and, most surprisingly, the remaining approximately 100 species are of unknown status (Wilcove et al. 1996; Taylor et al. 2005). Due to their low numbers and consequent vulnerability, there is now recognition that even species that are candidates for de-listing will still require some degree of conservation management to maintain their populations (Figure 20.6; Scott et al. 2005).

The difficulty of implementing recovery plans for so many species is often not primarily biological but, rather, political, administrative, and ultimately financial (Hagen and Hodges 2006). For example, an endangered river clam species might need to be protected from pollution and the effects of an existing dam. Installing sewage treatment facilities and removing a dam are theoretically straightforward actions, but expensive and difficult to carry out in practice. The U.S. Fish and Wildlife Service annually spends only around $350 million per year on activities related to the ESA. Increasing funding to $650 million per year would be needed to create a truly effective program, one that would im-

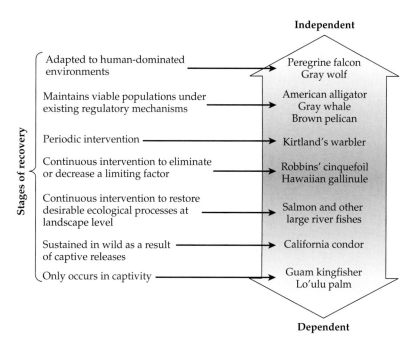

FIGURE 20.6 Endangered species will often require active management and intervention as part of the recovery process. There will be a continuum, with some species independent of humans and others dependent on human intervention. (After Scott et al. 2005.)

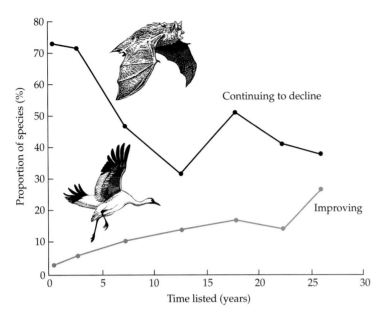

FIGURE 20.7 The longer species have been listed, protected, and managed under the Endangered Species Act, the greater probability they have of improving in status (as shown by the whooping crane), and the lower their probability of continuing to decline in status (with the Indiana bat as an example). The numbers do not add up to 100% because some species are not changing in status and others are of unknown status. (After Taylor et al. 2005.)

plement effective recovery programs for all listed species (Miller et al. 2002; Taylor et al. 2005). The cost eventually might be higher if the U.S. government grants private landowners financial compensation for ESA-imposed restrictions on the use of their property, an option that is periodically discussed in the U.S. Congress.

While funding for the ESA has been growing steadily over the past 20 years, the number of species protected under the ESA has been growing even faster. As a result, there is less money available per species in need of recovery now than ever before. The importance of adequate funding for species recovery is shown by a study demonstrating that species that receive a higher proportion of requested funding for their recovery plans have a higher probability of reaching a stable or improved status than species that receive a lower proportion of funding (Miller et al. 2002). The longer a species has been protected under the ESA, the higher the probability that it is improving (Figure 20.7) (Taylor et al. 2005). Also, species have a higher probability of improving if they have designated critical habitat and a recovery plan.

Even though funding is supposed to be allocated on a priority system according to the degree of threat a species faces, its potential for recovery, and its taxonomic distinctiveness, certain species often receive disproportionately large funding because they are widely recognizable bird and mammal species with strong public support (such as the bald eagle and the West Indian manatee) or because they are umbrella species whose protection is linked to the protection of economically valuable ecosystems (such as the red-cockaded woodpecker in Southeastern pine forests and the California gnatcatcher in California coastal sagebrush habitat). Other species are substantially underfunded because they are relatively unknown to the public, they have restricted distributions, they are not birds or mammals, and they are from geographical areas with weak or no political representation (Restani and Marzluff 2002).

CONFLICT AND THE ESA: COMPROMISE SOLUTIONS   An attempt was made to find compromises between the economic interests of the U.S.A. and conservation priorities during a controversy over whether the protection of the snail darter, a small endangered fish species, should block a major dam project. As a result, the ESA was amended in 1978 to allow a cabinet-level committee, the so-called "God Squad," to exclude certain endangered species from protection.

Despite the God-Squad amendment to the ESA, concerns about the implications of ESA protection have often forced business organizations, conservation groups, and governments to develop compromises that reconcile both conservation and business interests (James 1999). To provide a legal mechanism to achieve this goal, Congress amended the ESA in 1982 to allow the design of Habitat Conservation Plans (HCPs). HCPs are regional plans that allow development in designated areas but also protect remnants of biological communities or ecosystems that contain groups of actual and/or potentially endangered species. These plans are drawn up by the concerned parties—developers, conservation groups, citizen groups, and local governments—and given final approval by the U.S. Fish and Wildlife Service. An important feature of these plans is a "no surprises" clause, whereby developers have only limited financial responsibility if the conservation plan does not succeed in protecting the designated endangered species. Also, if any changes to the plan are subsequently needed, the government agrees to pay for them. Over 442 HCPs covering around 16 million ha and over 500 species have been approved as of 2005. In one case, an innovative program in Riverside County, California, allows developers to build within the historic range of the endangered Stephen's kangaroo rat (*Dipodomys stephensi*) if they contribute to a fund that will be used to buy wildlife sanctuaries. Already, more than $42 million has been used to secure 41,000 ha, with a long-term goal of raising $100 million. As a result of the HCP and the resulting new reserves, this species is being considered for removal from the endangered species list. In this case and others, the result is a compromise in which developers may proceed after paying additional fees into the fund to support conservation activities. Such plans need to be carefully monitored to determine if they are meeting their stated objectives.

In 1991 the state of California passed the Natural Community Conservation Planning Act, a law similar to that of Habitat Conservation Plans. One such plan addresses development in the coastal sage scrub habitat of southern California, which includes almost 100 rare, sensitive, threatened, or endangered plants and animals, most notably the coastal California gnatcatcher (*Polioptila californica californica*), protected under the U.S. Endangered Species Act (Figure 20.8). As a result of agricul-

(A)

(B)

FIGURE 20.8 (A) In southern California, a Natural Community Conservation Plan has been established to protect the California gnatcatcher, shown here at a nest with its chicks. (B) Protecting large blocks of coastal sage scrub community from uncontrolled development and fragmentation is key to the plan. (A, photograph by Robb Hirsch; B, photograph by Reed Noss.)

tural development and more recent urban development, less than 20% of the original coastal sage scrub habitat still exists, divided into small habitat fragments. Negotiating the plan has proved to be a challenge, since three-fourths of the habitat is privately owned and the planning area includes 50 cities and five counties. The plan that has been developed for the area involves protecting permanent reserves in high-quality habitat and allowing regions within the plan to develop up to 5% of their lower-quality habitat.

While HCPs are not perfect, they are at least attempts to create the next generation of conservation planning: approaches that seek to protect many species, entire ecosystems, or whole communities, and that extend over a wide geographical region that includes many projects, landowners, and jurisdictions. The difficulty with such an approach is that attempting to create a consensus among groups with clearly different goals prevents conservation biologists from pursuing their goals with single-minded intensity. Indeed, in some cases, conservation biologists have been incorporated into ineffective bureaucratic structures without having had a significant impact on protecting endangered species (Brower et al. 2001).

Traditional Societies, Conservation, and Sustainable Use

In this section of the chapter, we examine the attitudes held by traditional societies toward conservation, discuss how some traditional societies regulate their own resource use, and review some conservation projects that involve traditional societies (Timmer and Juma 2005). Human activities are sometimes compatible with the conservation of biological diversity. There are many highly diverse biological communities existing in places where people have practiced a traditional way of life for many generations, using the resources of their environment in a sustainable manner. But it is also true that many traditional societies have degraded their environment and driven species to extinction, both in the past and even more so in the present, once they acquire modern tools such as guns and chainsaws.

Local people practicing a traditional way of life in rural areas, with relatively little outside influence in terms of modern technology, are variously referred to as tribal people, indigenous people, native people, or traditional people (Dasmann 1991; Bayliss-Smith et al. 2003). These people regard themselves as the original inhabitants of the region and are often organized at the community or village level. Even remote regions of tropical rainforests, rugged mountains, and deserts designated as "wilderness" by governments and conservation groups often have sparse human populations. It is necessary to distinguish these established indigenous people from more recent settlers, who may not be as concerned with the health of surrounding biological communities or as knowledgeable about the species present and ecological limits of the land. In many countries, such as India and Mexico, there is a striking correspondence between areas occupied by local people and the areas of high conservation value and intact forest (Toledo 2001). Local people often have established local systems of rights to natural resources, which sometimes are recognized by their governments; they are potentially important partners in conservation efforts (Nepstad et al. 2006). Worldwide, there are approximately 300 million indigenous people living in more than 70 countries, occupying 12 to 19% of the Earth's land surface (Redford and Mansour 1996). However, indigenous people who practice their traditional culture are on the decline. In most areas of the world, local people are increasingly coming into contact with the modern world, resulting in changing belief systems (particularly among the younger members of society) and greater use of outside manufactured goods. Sometimes this shift can lead to a weakening of ties to the land and conservation ethics.

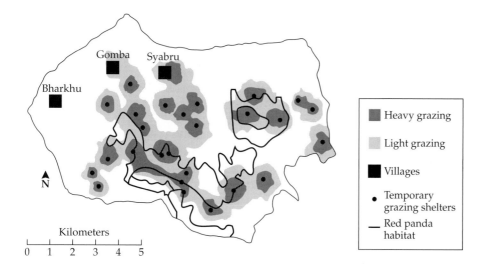

FIGURE 20.9 Red panda habitat in Langtang National Park, Nepal, overlaps areas grazed by cattle and frequented by herders and their dogs. A compromise needs to be developed so that people and wildlife can coexist, otherwise human needs will drive the red panda to extinction. (After Fox et al. 1996.)

Rather than being a threat to the "pristine" environment in which they live, in some cases traditional peoples have been an integral part of these environments for thousands of years (Bayliss-Smith et al. 2003). The present mixture and relative densities of plants and animals in many biological communities may reflect the historic activities—such as fishing, selective hunting of game animals, and planting or encouraging of useful plant species in fallow agricultural plots—of people in the area. However, as populations of local people increase and as they join the modern economy, their impact on biodiversity will similarly increase. The necessity to reconcile the needs of local people and conservation is illustrated by the example of Lantang National Park, which contains Nepal's largest population of the endangered red panda (*Ailurus fulgens*). Thousands of villagers live inside the park boundary and keep herds of livestock, including yak (a type of Asian ox) and cows. Most of the areas where red pandas live are grazed by livestock. Villagers are now increasing their herds to supply milk to the towns and the tourist industry (Figure 20.9). While people, livestock, and pandas currently coexist in the park, the increasing grazing pressure will eventually overtake the remaining habitat and eliminate red pandas from the area unless a compromise is found.

Conservation Beliefs

The conservation ethics of traditional societies have been viewed in a variety of perspectives by Western civilization. At one extreme, local people are viewed as destroyers of biological diversity who cut down forests and overharvest game. This destruction is accelerated when these people acquire guns, chainsaws, and outboard motors. At the other extreme, traditional peoples are viewed as "noble savages" living in harmony with nature and minimally disturbing the natural environment. A middle view is that traditional societies are highly varied, and there is no one simple description of their relationship to their environment that fits all groups (Redford and Sanderson 2000). In addition to the variation among traditional societies, these societies also vary from within; they are changing rapidly as they encounter outside influences, and there are often sharp differences between older and younger generations.

FIGURE 20.10 River fish are the main source of protein for the Tukano people of the Amazon Basin, who have a strong conservation ethic grounded in their cultural and religious beliefs. They do not cut the forest along the riverbanks because they believe that this forest belongs to the fish. (Photograph by Paul Patmore.)

Many traditional societies do have strong conservation ethics. These ethics are subtler and less clearly stated than Western conservation beliefs, but they tend to affect people's actions in their day-to-day lives, perhaps more than Western beliefs (Posey 1992; Folke and Colding 2001; Berkes 2004; Schwartzman and Zimmerman 2005). In such societies, people use their traditional ecological knowledge to create management practices that are linked to belief systems and enforced by village consent and the authority of leaders. These practices might include restricting harvesting seasons and methods of farming, restricting certain locations from harvesting, or restricting the ages, size, and sex of animals harvested. One well-documented example of such a conservation perspective is that of the Tukano Indians, who live in an indigenous reserve in northwest Brazil (Chernela 1987, 1999), subsisting on a diet of root crops and river fish (Figure 20.10). They have strong religious and cultural prohibitions against cutting the forest along the Upper Río Negro, which they recognize as important to the maintenance of fish populations: The Tukano believe that these forests belong to the fish and cannot be cut by people. They have also designated extensive refuges for fish and permit fishing along less than 40% of the river margin. Anthropologist Janet M. Chernela observes, "As fishermen dependent upon river systems, the Tukano are aware of the relationship between their environment and the life cycles of the fish, particularly the role played by the adjacent forest in providing nutrient sources that maintain vital fisheries."

In addition to coexisting with their environments without destroying them, local people can also manage the environment to maintain biological diversity, as shown by the traditional agroecosystems and forests of the Huastec Indians of northeastern Mexico (Alcorn 1984). In addition to their permanent agricultural fields and swidden agriculture, the Huastec maintain managed forests known as *te'lom,* on slopes, along watercourses, and in other areas that are either fragile or unsuitable for intensive agriculture. These forests contain more than 300 species of plants from which the people obtain food, wood, and other products. Species composition in the forest is altered in favor of useful species by planting and periodic selective weeding. Forest resources provide Huastec families with the means to survive the failure of their cultivated crops should they encounter a season of bad weather or an insect outbreak. Comparable examples of intensively managed village forests exist in traditional societies throughout the world (Stone and D'Andrea 2002).

Local people who support conservation as an integral part of their livelihoods and traditional values are often inspired to take the lead in protecting biological diversity. For instance, the destruction of communally owned forests by government-sanctioned logging operations has been a frequent target of protests by traditional people throughout the world. In India, followers of the Chipko movement hug trees to prevent logging. In Borneo, the Penans, a small tribe of hunter-gatherers, have attracted worldwide attention by blockading logging roads that enter their traditional forests. In Thailand, Buddhist priests are working with villagers to protect communal forests and sacred groves from commercial logging operations (Figure 20.11). As stated by a Tambon leader in Thailand:

This is our community forest that was just put inside the new national park. No one consulted us. We protected this forest before the roads were put in. We set up a roadblock on the new road to stop the illegal logging. We caught the district police chief and arrested him for logging. We warned him not to come again. (Alcorn 1991)

Empowering such local people and helping them to obtain **legal title**—right to ownership of the land that is recognized by the government—to their traditionally owned lands is often an important component of efforts to establish locally managed protected areas in developing countries (McSweeny 2005).

Conservation Efforts That Involve Traditional Societies

In the developing world and even in many developed countries such as Australia and Canada, it is often not possible to create a rigid separation between lands used by local people to obtain natural resources and those designated by governments as protected areas. Local people often live in and/or traditionally use the resources found in protected areas. Also, considerable biological diversity often occurs on traditionally managed land owned by local people. For example, indigenous communities own 97% of the land in Papua New Guinea, and Amerindian reserves in the Amazon Basin of Brazil occupy over 100 million ha (22% of the Brazilian Amazon) of incredibly diverse habitats. The Inuit people (formerly known as the Eskimos) govern one-fifth of Canada. In Australia, tribal people control 90 million ha, including many of the most important areas for conserva-

FIGURE 20.11 Buddhist priests in Thailand offer prayers and blessings to protect communal forests and sacred groves from commercial logging operations. (Photograph by Project for Ecological Recovery, Bangkok.)

tion. The challenge, then, is to develop strategies for incorporating these local people in conservation programs and policy development. Such new approaches have been developed in an effort to avoid **ecocolonialism**, the common practice by some governments and conservation organizations of disregarding the traditional rights and practices of local people in order to establish new conservation areas. This practiced is called ecolonialism because of its similarity to the historical abuses of native rights by colonial powers of past eras (Cox and Elmqvist 1997).

There are many examples of reserves with resident traditional peoples who were there before the reserves were established and reserves in which people are allowed to enter periodically to obtain natural products or are compensated for preserving and managing biological diversity. In Biosphere Reserves, an international land use designation, local people are allowed to use resources from designated buffer zones. For instance, agreements have been negotiated between local people and governments allowing cattle to graze inside certain African national parks in exchange for agreement from the local people not to harm wild animals outside the parks.

In some projects, the economic needs of local people are included in conservation management plans, to the benefit of both the people and the reserves. Such projects, known as **Integrated Conservation–Development Projects** (**ICDPs**) are now regarded as worthy of serious consideration, though in practice they are often problematic to implement, as described later in the chapter (Primack et al. 1998; Salafsky et al. 2001a; Sayer and Campbell 2003; Christensen 2004; McShane and Wells 2004). There are many possible strategies that could be classified as ICDPs, ranging from wildlife management projects to ecotourism. These projects normally attempt to combine the protection of biological diversity and the customs of traditional societies with aspects of economic development, including poverty reduction, job creation, health improvement, and food security (Timmer and Juma 2005). A large number of such programs have been initiated over the last 15 years, which have provided opportunities for evaluation and improvement. A critical component of these projects must be the ongoing monitoring of biological, social, and economic factors to determine how effective these programs are in meeting their goals. Involving local people in these monitoring efforts may be an important source of information and will also help to indicate how the people themselves perceive the benefits and problems of the project. The hope of such projects is that the local people will decide that sustainable use of their local resources is more valuable than destructive use of those resources, and these people will become involved in biodiversity conservation. The importance of these local people to ICDPs was emphasized at the 2002 United Nations World Summit on Sustainable Development. The following are some examples of the types of ICDPs currently in practice:

BIOSPHERE RESERVES   UNESCO's Man and the Biosphere Program (MAB), described in Chapter 17, includes among its goals the maintenance of "samples of varied and harmonious landscapes resulting from long-established land use patterns" (Batisse 1997). This program is a successful example of the ICDP approach, at least in terms of its adoption of land use zoning as a model of conservation; there are 482 Biosphere Reserves in 102 countries, covering over 260 million ha (Figure 20.12). The MAB Program recognizes the role of people in shaping the natural landscape, as well as the need to find ways in which people can sustainably use natural resources without degrading the environment. The research framework, applied in its worldwide network of designated Biosphere Reserves, integrates natural science and social science research. It includes investigations of how biological communities respond to different human activities, how humans respond to changes in their natural environment, and how degraded ecosystems can be restored to their former condition. A desirable feature of Biosphere Reserves is a system of land use zoning in which there are varying levels of use, from complete protection to areas where farming and logging are permitted (see Figure 17.12).

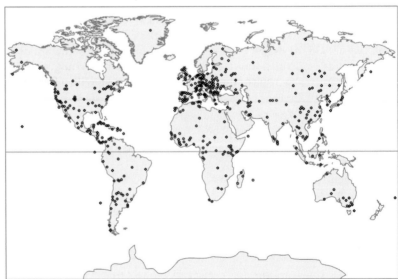

FIGURE 20.12 Locations of recognized Biosphere Reserves (dots). Although reserves are distributed throughout the world, there are still no reserves in New Guinea and only a few in the Amazon Basin. (Data from www.unesco.org/mab/wnbr.htm.)

One instructive example of a Biosphere Reserve is the Kuna Yala Indigenous Reserve on the northeast coast of Panama. In this protected area comprising 60,000 ha of tropical forest and coral islands, 50,000 Kuna people in 60 villages practice traditional medicine, agriculture, and forestry. Scientists from outside institutions carry out management research, in the process training and hiring local people as guides and research assistants (Figure 20.13). The Kuna have even tried to control the type and rate of economic development in the reserve. However, a change appears to be occurring in the Kuna: Traditional conservation beliefs are eroding in the face of outside influences, and younger Kuna are beginning to question the need to rigidly protect the reserve (Chapin 2000). Also, the Kuna people have had difficulties establishing a stable organization that can administer the reserve and work with external conservation and donor groups, and scientists working on marine studies have been ejected by the Kuna from the Biosphere Reserve. Furthermore, rising sea levels and declining marine resources are forcing village leaders to consider other options for their future (Guzmán et al. 2003). This example illustrates that empowering traditional people is no guarantee that biodiversity will be preserved. This is particularly true when traditions change or disappear, economic pressures for exploitation increase, and programs are mismanaged (Oates 1999).

FIGURE 20.13 Kuna park guards patrolling the boundary of the Kuna Yala Indigenous Reserve, a Biosphere Reserve in Panama. (Photograph courtesy of Mac Chapin.)

IN SITU AGRICULTURAL CONSERVATION The long-term health of modern agriculture depends on the preservation of the genetic variability maintained in local varieties of crops cultivated by traditional farmers (see Chapter 14). One innovative suggestion has been for an international agricultural body, such as the Consultative Group on International Agricultural Research, to subsidize villages as in situ (in place) landrace custodians (Figure 20.14) (Altieri 2004; Brush 2004). The cost of subsidizing villages to maintain the genetic variation of major crops such as wheat, maize, and potatoes would be a relatively modest investment in the long-term health of world agriculture. In China, the genetic variability of rice is maintained by a government program that involves interplanting high-quality traditional and high-yielding hybrid rice varieties (Zhu et al. 2003). Villages that participate in such programs have an opportunity to maintain their culture in the face of a rapidly changing world.

A different approach linking traditional agriculture and genetic conservation is being used in arid regions of the American Southwest, with a focus on dryland crops with drought tolerance (www.nativeseeds.org). A private organization, Native Seeds/SEARCH, collects the seeds of traditional crop cultivars for long-term preservation. The organization also encourages a network of 4600 farmers and other members to grow traditional crops, provides them with the seeds of traditional cultivars, and buys their unsold production.

Countries have also established special reserves to conserve areas containing wild relatives and ancient landraces of commercial crops (Miller and Hodgkin 2004). Species reserves have been created to protect the wild relatives of wheat, oats, and barley in Israel and citrus in India.

EXTRACTIVE RESERVES In many areas of the world, indigenous people have extracted products from natural communities for decades and even centuries. The sale and

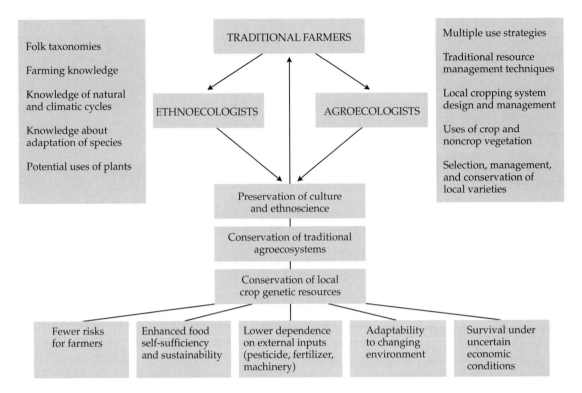

FIGURE 20.14 It is useful to view traditional agricultural practices both from a human cultural and an agricultural perspective. A synthesis of these viewpoints can lead to theoretical and methodological approaches that seek to conserve the environment, the culture, and the genetic variation found in these traditional agroecosystems. (After Altieri and Anderson 1992; Altieri 2004.)

barter of these natural products are a major part of people's livelihoods. Understandably, local people are very concerned about retaining their rights to continue collecting natural products from the surrounding countryside (Box 20.1). In areas where such collection represents an integral part of indigenous society, the establishment of a national park that excludes the traditional collection of products will meet with as much resistance from the local community as will a land-grab that involves exploitation of the natural resources and their conversion to other uses. A type of protected area known as an **extractive reserve** may present a sustainable solution to this problem. However, these programs need to be evaluated to determine if they are able to maintain a sustainable level of harvesting without damaging the underlying resource base.

The Brazilian government is trying to address the legitimate demands of local citizens through extractive reserves, from which settled people collect natural materials such as medicinal plants, edible seeds, rubber, resins, and Brazil nuts in ways that minimize damage to the forest ecosystem (Wunder 1999; Fagan et al. 2005). Such extractive areas in Brazil, which comprise about 3 million ha, guarantee the ability of local people to continue their way of life and guard against the possible conversion of the land to cattle ranching and farming. At the same time, the government protection afforded to the local population also serves to protect the biological diversity of the area because the ecosystem remains basically intact.

Extractive reserves appear to be appropriate for the Amazon rain forests, where about 68,000 rubber tapper families live. The rubber tappers live at a density of only about one family per 300 to 500 ha, of which they clear only a few hectares for grow-

BOX 20.1

People-Friendly Conservation in the Hills of Southwest India

▨ There is no question that human activities play an overwhelming role in the decline of many species and habitats. However, conservation activists often forget that human beings are among the potential victims of the worldwide biological diversity crisis. Some rural societies have already been affected by the decline of leaves, fruits, roots, and other nontimber forest products (NTFPs) traditionally harvested for household use and for sale in local markets. For these people, natural products represent a crucial subset of their income, and some may be essential for food preparation, medicines, or rituals. Now, in many cases, the social mechanisms that traditionally prevented overuse of a particular resource have broken down, and many NTFPs are becoming depleted. As forests shrink in size and become degraded, it is uncertain whether

Soliga villagers collect nontimber forest products from the nature sanctuary. (Photograph courtesy of Kamal Bawa.)

NTFP collection is sustainable in particular areas—if not, alternative sources of income and supplies must be found to support rural families. An important case study underway in the Biligiri Rangaswamy Temple (BRT) Sanctuary in southwestern India began by monitoring the amount of NTFPs taken from the BRT. But then the researchers took a huge step beyond the norm by training the local people to monitor the health of the forest and to process and sell the forest products themselves.

The inhabitants of these hilly forests, the Soliga people, are the remaining members of a tribe that has survived in this remote, species-rich area since ancient times (Bawa et al. 1998). The Soligas lived in the region for centuries as shifting cultivators but were forced by the Forest Department to become sedentary agriculturists in and around the reserve when the 540-km^2 BRT Sanctuary was established in 1974. Now, the 4500 Soligas farm small pieces of land (1 to 2 ha) and collect NTFPs for their own use and for sale through government-sponsored cooperatives.

A study of NTFP harvesting by the Soligas has been underway since 1993, involving researchers from both India and the United States. Although the primary goal of the study is the conservation of biological resources in the BRT forest, the study is uncommon in that it approaches the problem from a sociological and economic perspective rather than a strictly biological perspective

(Shankar et al. 2005). Most conservationists would agree that conservation efforts cannot succeed if they do not make some provision for the people who depend on a threatened resource, but it is unusual for the people to be the principal focus of a biological conservation project.

The project began by using extensive surveys to determine that nontimber forest products constitute as much as 50% of an average Soliga household's annual income (Hegde et al. 1996). The study also found that NTFP extraction practices are neither sustainable nor efficient, nor do they produce maximum benefits for the Soligas, even though many local products, such as medicinal and edible plants and honey, have great potential market value. Moreover, because there is open access to these unregulated resources, collection of NTFPs often occurs at the wrong time of year to promote regeneration, or is done using methods that damage the resource. In the case of honey collection, for instance, collection from a nest ideally should take place after bee larvae have matured to the point when they will not suffer from the loss of the honey. If the honey is collected too soon in the bees' growth cycle, the larvae may die, and fewer bees in the hive means that less honey is produced—and the resource begins a slow downward spiral of depletion. Similarly, medicinal plants have been overharvested near the villages so that people must go ever farther to find

(continued)

BOX 20.1 *(continued)*

A display of Soliga products in a village store. (Photograph courtesy of Kamal Bawa.)

plants to collect. Tree species with edible or medicinal fruits have few saplings or young trees to constitute the next generation when the older trees die. Another problem is that the Soligas sell raw materials through the government-controlled cooperatives, although the greatest amount of profit comes only after the product is processed and marketed. Thus, the Soligas do not receive the greatest possible return from the forest products they harvest and can only increase their income by collecting greater amounts of raw materials.

In response to these concerns, researchers developed a project with a simple concept: If the Soligas process the raw materials themselves and eliminate the middlemen, they can increase their income by marketing and selling the products directly in nearby towns and cities. By doing this, they can earn a much higher rate per unit of raw materials that they harvest and therefore will need to harvest less to make ends meet. Based on this concept, several enterprises are already

underway that generate employment for numerous individuals and profits for the entire community. The first involves collecting and processing honey from both wild and domestic apiaries. This honey is sold directly to consumers using the Soligas' own brand name (*Prakruti*, which means "nature"). The second project produces jams and pickles for sale, using the fruits of forest species. A third produces and markets herbal medicines using both wild herbs collected from the forest and herbs cultivated in gardens. The researchers have started to work with Soligas to establish plantations of these plants with the expectation that they would spend less time collecting products from forests. Simultaneously, the researchers are providing seedlings of native species to initiate the process. And finally, the Soligas and the researchers have joined forces to develop a participatory monitoring plan to regularly assess the state of the forests and the financial well-being of the enterprises. That is, the Soligas are assuming responsibility for the long-term maintenance of the resource base as well as the functioning of the enterprises. As the economic ventures started by this program gain momentum, hopefully more and more of the local residents will find that conserving forest resources is in their best interest. Those concerned with the conservation of species and habitat could ask for nothing more.

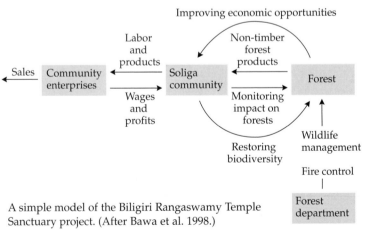

A simple model of the Biligiri Rangaswamy Temple Sanctuary project. (After Bawa et al. 1998.)

ing food and a few cattle. The efforts of Chico Mendes and his subsequent assassination in 1988 drew worldwide attention to the plight of the rubber tappers (see Box 22.2). In response to both local and international concern, the Brazilian government established extractive reserves in rubber-tapping areas, in some cases with support from international conservation organizations. To many people, establishing the reserves made sense because the rubber collection system was already in place and had been operating for over 100 years. The hope was that the rubber tappers themselves would have a strong vested interest against habitat destruction because it also would destroy their livelihood.

The Brazilian experiment has a number of major limitations (Wunder 1999). First, these reserves occupy only 4 to 7% of the Amazon area, so they do not address the farming and logging that are the major drivers of deforestation. Second, extractive reserves provide occupations for only a tiny percentage of the millions of Brazilians who need a livelihood. Third, populations of large animals in extractive reserves are often substantially reduced due to subsistence hunting; and fourth, the density of Brazil nut seedlings is reduced due to the intense collection of Brazil nuts (Peres et al. 2003). Fifth, the decade-long decline in prices paid for wild-collected rubber and Brazil nuts suggests that these reserves may not be economically viable. If they cannot make a living collecting rainforest products, local people may be forced out of economic desperation to cut down their forests for timber and subsistence agriculture.

These sorts of efforts are not limited to Latin America. Many countries in East and Southern Africa are aggressively applying community development and sustainable harvesting strategies in their efforts to preserve wildlife populations, as described in Chapter 18 for Namibia. The government of Zimbabwe in particular has developed a series of innovative programs for generating income from safari hunting and wildlife tourism that is used to run conservation programs and provide clear benefits to local people (Fischer et al. 2005). Much of the funding to support, develop, and administer these programs comes from foreign government agencies, such as the U.S. Agency for International Development.

It is unknown how long such programs would persist if the substantial subsidies provided by foreign governments were reduced or withdrawn. These programs are also expected to depend on tourism for much of their revenue, a prospect that is uncertain given political and economic instabilities within the countries themselves and internationally. Finally, it is unclear if wildlife populations could be maintained in the face of constant levels of harvesting. Future generations of conservation biologists will need to evaluate these programs to determine if they are meeting their stated short- and long-term goals of both conservation and economic development.

COMMUNITY-BASED INITIATIVES In many cases, local people already protect biological communities such as forests, wildlife, rivers, and coastal waters in the vicinity of their homes. Such protection is often enforced by village elders on the basis of religious and traditional beliefs. Governments and conservation organizations can assist local conservation initiatives by providing legal title to traditional lands, access to scientific expertise, and financial assistance to develop needed infrastructure. One example is the Baboon Sanctuary in eastern Belize, created by a collective agreement among a group of villages to maintain the forest habitat required by the local population of black howler monkeys (known locally as baboons) (see Figure 16.7) (Horwich and Lyon 1998; Alexander 2000). Ecotourists visiting the sanctuary pay a fee to the village organization and additional payments are made if they stay overnight and eat meals with a local family. Conservation biologists working at the site have provided training for local nature guides, a body of scientific information on the local wildlife, funds for a local natural history museum, and business training for the village leaders.

In the Pacific islands of Samoa, much of the rain forest land is under "customary ownership"—it is owned by communities of indigenous people (Cox 1997). Villagers are under increasing pressure to sell logs from their forests to pay for schools and other necessities. Despite this situation, the local people have a strong desire to preserve the land because of the forest's religious and cultural significance, as well as its value for medicinal plants and other products. A variety of solutions are being developed to meet these conflicting needs: In American (or Eastern) Samoa,

FIGURE 20.15 In Samoa, the U.S. Park Service leases communally owned land and marine habitat for a national park, while local families maintain their rights to collect traditional products. (Photograph © Debra Behr/Alamy.)

the U.S. government in 1988 leased forest and coastal land from the villages to establish a new national park. In this case, the villages retained ownership of the land and traditional hunting and collecting rights (Figure 20.15). Village elders were also assigned places on the park advisory board so they would have a voice in issues of governance and management. In Western Samoa, international conservation organizations and various donors agreed to build schools, medical clinics, and other public works projects that the villages needed in exchange for stopping all commercial logging. Thus, each dollar donated did double service, both protecting the forest and providing humanitarian aid to the villages.

PAYMENTS FOR ENVIRONMENTAL SERVICES A new creative strategy being developed involves direct payments to individual landowners and local communities that protect critical ecosystems, in effect paying the community to be good land stewards (Ellison 2003; du Toit et al. 2004). Such an approach has the advantage of greater simplicity than programs that attempt to link conservation with economic development. These types of programs are sometimes referred to as **Payments for Environmental Services (PES)**. Government and nongovernment conservation organizations develop markets in which local landowners can participate through protecting and restoring ecosystems (WRI 2005). One such example is the Cauca Valley in Colombia. Landowners in upland areas of the valley were cutting down trees and overgrazing the slopes with cattle, leading to flooding and erratic stream flows in the valley below. The downstream landowners had invested in establishing sugar plantations but recognized that they needed to protect their water supply. The downstream landowners organized into a Water Use Association, which established a series of initiatives targeted toward upland landowners, including a social program to provide education and training, a production program involving reforestation and intensive agriculture, and an infrastructure program to improve water quality and reduce erosion. From 1995 to 2000, $1.5 million was raised by the Water Use Association and spent on the upland areas.

Rural people can also be drawn into newly developing international markets for ecosystem services. In the Scolel Té project in Chiapas, Mexico, farmers agree to maintain their existing forest land and to restore degraded land. Farmers participating in the plan receive payments from large industrial companies seeking carbon credits to offset their own carbon dioxide emissions. Farmers gain additional income by planting high-value shade-grown coffee under the trees. So far, 700 farmers have agreed to participate in the program.

Evaluating Conservation Initiatives That Involve Traditional Societies

A key element in the success of many of the projects discussed in the preceding sections is the opportunity for conservation biologists to build on and work with stable, flexible, local communities with effective leaders and competent government agencies (Barrett et al. 2001; Salafsky et al. 2001b). Certain projects appear to be successful at combining biodiversity protection with sustainable development and poverty reduction. The Equator Initiative of the United Nations is cosponsored by many leading conservation organizations, businesses, and governments and is helping to fund and publicize such efforts. In 2006, the Initiative recognized six of the most outstanding projects in the world that received its Equator Prize (Timmer and Juna 2005).

However, in many other cases a local community may have internal conflicts and poor leadership, making it incapable of administering a successful conservation program. Also, conservation initiatives involving recent immigrants or impoverished, disorganized local people may be difficult to carry out. Additionally, government agencies working on the project may be ineffective or even corrupt (Ravenal et al. 2004). In such cases, conservation biologists, government officials, and local people may have difficulty establishing common objectives during the projects, leading to misunderstanding, mistrust, and miscommunication (Castillo et al. 2005). These factors will tend to prevent conservation programs from succeeding. An additional negative factor is the increasing population pressure that is generated not only by high local birth rates but by the tendency of successful programs to attract immigrants to the area (Strusaker et al. 2005). This increasing population leads to further environmental degradation and a breakdown of social structures. For example, newly established panda reserves in China have attracted additional people to the area because of the rapidly growing ecotourist activity, with deforestation resulting from the increased demand for timber to build and heat new tourist lodges. Consequently, while working with local people may be a desirable goal, in some cases this simply is not possible. Sometimes the only way to preserve biological diversity is to exclude people from protected areas and rigorously patrol their boundaries, although this may be politically difficult in many countries (Terborgh 2000; Peterson 2003).

In many cases, projects that initially appeared very promising were terminated when external funding and management ended, because the projected income stream never developed (Wells and McShane 2004). Even for projects that appear successful, there is often no monitoring of ecological and social parameters to determine if project goals are being achieved (Newmark and Hough 2000). It is essential for any conservation program design to include mechanisms for evaluating the progress and success of measures taken. Projects can also be undermined by external forces, such as political instability and economic downturns.

The catchphrase "think globally, act locally," is a true measure of how conservation must work. In the preceding examples, one factor is consistently true: Whether they are supporting conservation activities or opposing them, ordinary people with no strong feelings about conservation are more likely to respond to issues that affect their day-to-day lives. If people learn that a species or habitat to which they are accustomed to having access might be taken away from them because of pressures to develop the land (or to conserve a species), they may feel compelled to take direct action. This reaction can be a double-edged sword; when harm to the environment is viewed by local inhabitants as a threat to their well-being, it can be used to the advantage of conservation, but it is often the case that conservation activities are initially perceived as threatening the local way of life or obstructing the community from beneficial economic development. The challenge for conservation biologists is to energize local people in support of long-term conservation goals while recognizing and addressing the objections of those who oppose it. In many cases, improving the economic conditions of people's lives and helping them obtain secure rights to their land are essential to preserving biological diversity in developing countries.

Summary

1. Legal efforts to protect biodiversity occur at local, regional, and national levels, and regulate activities affecting both privately and publicly owned lands. Governments and private land trusts may buy land for conservation purposes or acquire conservation easements and development rights for future protection. Associated laws limit pollution, curtail or ban certain types of development, and set rules for hunting and other recreational activities—all with the aim of preserving biodiversity and protecting human health.

2. National governments protect biodiversity by establishing national parks, controlling imports and exports at their borders, and creating regulations for air and water pollution. The most effective law in the United States for protecting species is the Endangered Species Act. The protection afforded under the Act is so strong that pro-business and development groups are often forced to work with conservation organizations and government agencies to create compromises that protect species and allow some development.

3. Conservation biologists are collaborating with local people to achieve the combined objectives of protecting biological diversity, preserving cultural diversity, and providing new economic opportunities. Initiatives that allow people to use park resources in a sustainable manner without harming biological diversity are sometimes called Integrated Conservation–Development Projects. New programs called Payments for Environmental Services are now being explored for their feasibility.

For Discussion

1. Apply the concepts of development and growth to aspects of the economy that you know about. Are there industries practicing or at least approaching sustainable development? Are there industries or aspects of the economy that are clearly not sustainable? Are development and growth always linked, or can there be growth without development, or development without growth? Consider industries such as logging, mining, education, road construction, home construction, and nature tourism.

2. What are the roles of government agencies, private conservation organizations, businesses, community groups, and individuals in the conservation of biological diversity? Can they work together, or are their interests necessarily opposed to each other?

3. Imagine that a new tribe of hunting-and-gathering people is discovered in a remote area of the Amazon that has previously been designated for a logging and mining project. The area is also found to contain numerous species new to science. Should the project go forward as planned and the people be given whatever employment they are suited for? Should the area be closed to all outsiders and the people and new species allowed to live undisturbed? Should the tribe be contacted by social workers, educated in special schools, and eventually incorporated into modern society? Can you think of a possible compromise that would integrate conservation and development? In such a case, who should decide what actions should be taken?

4. Programs in Namibia, Zambia, and Zimbabwe have tried to generate rural income through safari hunting and wildlife tourism. Elephants and lions are hunted in these programs despite the fact that they are a protected species under the Convention on International Trade in Endangered Species. What ethical, economic, political, ecological, and social issues are raised by these programs?

Suggested Readings

Berkes, F., J. Colding, and C. Folke. 2000. Rediscovery of traditional ecological knowledge as adaptive management. *Ecological Applications* 10: 1251–1262. An article from a symposium on traditional ecological knowledge; describes how local people use their own observations to manage wildlife and other natural resources.

Castillo, A., A. Torres, A. Velázquez, and G. Bocco. 2005. The use of ecological science by rural producers: a case study in Mexico. *Ecological Applications* 15: 745–756. Local people and conservation biologists need to develop an understanding of each other's priorities.

Cox, P. A. 1997. *Nafanua: Saving the Samoan Rain Forest.* W. H. Freeman and Company, New York. Exciting and beautiful account of a scientist's efforts to save a forest and help a village.

du Toit, J. T., B. H. Walker, and B. M. Campbell. 2004. Conserving tropical nature: current challenges for ecologists. *Trends in Ecology and Evolution.* 19: 12–17. Direct payments for conservation are being tried as a new strategy.

Ehrenfeld, D. W. 2005. Sustainability: Living with the imperfections. *Conservation Biology* 19: 33–35. The concept has problems in practice, but seems to be the best compromise available.

Fox, J. and A Nino-Murcia. 2005. Status of species conservation banking in the United States. *Conservation Biology* 19: 996–1007. Innovative mechanisms are being developed to protect land.

Hagen, A. N. and K. E. Hodges. 2006. Resolving critical habitat designation failures: reconciling law, policy, and biology. *Conservation Biology* 20: 399–407. The government is often not willing to take the needed steps to protect species under the Endangered Species Act.

Kates, R. W., T. M. Parris, and A. A. Leiserowitz. 2005. What is sustainable development? Goals, indicators, values, and practice. *Environment* 47: 8–21. Ways to determine if sustainable development is working.

McShane, T. O. and M. P. Wells. 2004. *Getting Biodiversity Projects To Work: Towards More Effective Conservation and Development.* Columbia University Press, New York. Guides for effective conservation projects.

Merenlender, A. M., L. Huntsinger, G. Guthey, and S. K. Fairfax. 2004. Land trusts and conservation easement: Who is conserving what for whom? *Conservation Biology* 18: 66–75. Evaluation of land trusts is needed to determine how effective they are at achieving their stated goals.

Nepstad, D., S. Schwartzman, B. Bamberger, M. Santilli, D. Ray, P. Schlesinger, et al. 2006. Inhibition of Amazon deforestation and fire by parks and indigenous lands. *Conservation Biology* 20: 65–73. Reserves occupied by indigenous people are effective at slowing deforestation and fires.

Oates, J. F. 1999. *Myth and Reality in the Rainforest: How Conservation Strategies Are Failing in West Africa.* University of California Press, Berkeley. A skeptic argues that many sustainable development projects do not live up to expectations.

Redford, K. H. and S. E. Sanderson. 2000. Extracting humans from nature. *Conservation Biology* 14: 1362–1364. An article in a special issue debating the role of indigenous people in protected areas.

Schwartzman S. and B. Zimmerman. 2005. Conservation alliances with indigenous peoples of the Amazon. *Conservation Biology* 19: 721–727. Conservation biologists and local people have the potential to work together for common goals.

Scott, J. M., D. D. Goble, J. A. Wiens, D. S. Wilcove, M. Bean, and T. Male. 2005. Recovery of imperiled species under the Endangered Species Act: the need for a new approach. *Frontiers in Ecology and the Environment* 3: 383–389. Some species will always need a certain level of protection in order to survive.

Stankey, G. H. and B. Shindler. 2006. Formation of social acceptability judgments and their implications for management of rare and little-known species. *Conservation Biology* 20: 28–37. Conservation biologists need to be able to convince the public that little-known species may also deserve protection.

Stem, C., R. Margoluis, N. Salafsky, and M. Brown. 2005. Monitoring and evaluation in conservation: a review of trends and approaches. *Conservation Biology* 19: 295–309. Conservation projects need to be carefully monitored and evaluated to determine if they are meeting their goals.

Stone, R. D. and C. D'Andrea. 2002. *Tropical Forests and the Human Spirit*. University of California Press, Berkeley, CA. Strongly argues for the role of empowering local people to protect tropical forests.

Struhsaker, T. T., P. J. Struhsaker, and K. S. Siex. 2005. Conserving Africa's rain forests: problems in protected areas and possible solutions. *Biological Conservation* 123: 45–54. Excellent study of why certain projects succeed.

Taylor, M. F. J., K. F. Suckling, and J. J. Rachlinski. 2005. The effectiveness of the Endangered Species Act: A quantitative analysis. *BioScience* 55: 360–366. Is the ESA successful at protecting species?

Timmer. V. and C. Juma. 2005. Biodiversity conservation and poverty reduction come together in the tropics: Lessons learned from the Equator Initiative. *Environment* 47: 25–44. The Equator Initiative identifies and supports best practices that link conservation and community development.

Troëng, S and E. Rankin. 2005. Long-term conservation efforts contribute to positive green turtle *Chelonia mydas* nesting trend at Tortuguero, Costa Rica. *Biological Conservation* 121: 111–116. Excellent case study of the value of protection in aiding species recovery.

An International Approach to Conservation and Sustainable Development

Much biological diversity is concentrated in the countries of the developing world, many of which are relatively poor, suffer from political instability, and experience rapid rates of population growth, development, and habitat destruction. Despite these problems, developing countries are not averse to preserving biological diversity: many have established protected areas and have ratified the Convention on Biological Diversity (discussed in detail later in this chapter). Ultimately it is the responsibility of each country to protect its own natural environment, which is the source of products, ecosystem services, recreation, and culture—since many species and biological communities are a source of national pride and figure prominently in stories, songs, and art. However, given that many of the benefits of conservation accrue globally, until their economies are stronger, developing countries may require outside assistance to help pay for the habitat preservation, research, and management required for the task. It is appropriate for the developed countries of the world (including the United States, Canada, Japan, Australia, and many European nations) to provide such assistance, since industrialized nations rely on the biological diversity of the Tropics to supply genetic material and natural products for agriculture, medicine, and industry. And it is also true that many of the benefits of biological diversity have flowed back to developing countries. In this chapter, we examine the question of how countries can work together to preserve biological diversity.

The protection of biological diversity is a topic that must be addressed at multiple levels of government. Although the major control mechanisms that presently exist in the world are based within individual countries, international agreements among countries are increasingly being used to protect species and habitats. International cooperation is an absolute requirement for several reasons:

1. *Species migrate across international borders.* Conservation efforts must protect species at all points in their ranges; efforts in one country will be ineffective if critical habitats are destroyed in a second country to which an animal migrates. For example, efforts to protect migratory bird species in northern Europe will not work if the birds' overwintering habitat in Africa is destroyed. Efforts to protect whales in U.S. coastal waters will not be effective if these species are killed or harmed in international waters. Species are particularly vulnerable when they are migrating, as they may be more conspicuous, more tired, or more desperately in need of food and water.

2. *International trade in biological products is commonplace.* A strong demand for a product in one country can result in the overexploitation of the species by another country to supply this demand. When people are willing to pay high prices for exotic pets or plants and for esoteric wildlife products such as tiger bones and rhino horn, poachers looking for easy profits or poor, desperate people looking for any source of income they can find will take or kill even the very last animal to obtain this income. To prevent overexploitation, people involved in collection and trade of biological products need to be educated about the consequences of overuse of wild species. Where the source of the problem is a lack of economic alternatives, strategies to provide alternate income must be developed while strict control and management of the resource should discourage continued use. Where it is simply a question of greedy people seeking to make a profit by flouting the law, enforcement efforts and border checks should be strengthened (World Bank 2005).

3. *The benefits of biological diversity are of international importance.* The community of nations is helped by the species and varieties that can be used in agriculture, medicine, and industry; by the ecosystems that help regulate climate; and by the national parks and other protected areas of international scientific and tourist value. Biological diversity is also widely recognized to have intrinsic value, existence value, and option value. The countries of the world that use and rely on the value from biological diversity are already helping the less wealthy countries of the world preserve it. However, the funding is not adequate and needs to be increased (Balmford and Whitten 2003).

4. *Many problems of environmental pollution that threaten ecosystems are international in scope and require international cooperation.* Such threats include atmospheric pollution and acid rain; the pollution of lakes, rivers, and oceans; greenhouse gas production exchange and global climate change; and ozone depletion (Totten et al. 2003). Additionally, the costs of many of these phenomena do not fall on countries in proportion to their role in causing them. Consider the River Danube, which flows through Germany, Austria, Slovakia, Hungary, Croatia, Yugoslavia (Serbia and Montenegro), Bulgaria, Romania, and Ukraine, and carries the pollution of a vast agricultural and industrial region before emptying into the Black Sea—another international body of water, this one bordered by four additional countries. Only countries working together can solve problems such as these.

International Agreements to Protect Species

We begin by discussing the key international agreements that exist to protect species. To address the protection of biological diversity, countries of the world have signed international agreements, as described earlier in this book. International agreements have provided a framework for countries to cooperate in protecting species, habitats, ecosystem processes, and genetic variation. Treaties are negotiated at international conferences and come into force when they are ratified by a certain number of countries (Figure 21.1). One of the most important treaties protecting species at an international level is the **Convention on International Trade in Endangered Species** (**CITES**), established in 1973 in association with the United Nations Environmental Programme (UNEP) (Saterson 2001). The treaty has currently been ratified by 169 countries. CITES, headquartered in Switzerland, establishes lists (known as Appendices) of species for which international trade is to be controlled or monitored. Member countries agree to restrict trade in and destructive exploitation of these species. Appendix I includes 827 animals and plants for which commercial trade is prohibited. Appendix II includes about 4400 animals and 28,000 plants whose international trade is regulated and monitored. For plants, Appendices I and II cover important horticultural species such as orchids, cycads, cacti, carnivorous plants, and tree ferns; timber species and wild-collected seeds are increasingly being considered for regulation as well. For animals, closely regulated groups include parrots, large cat species, whales, sea turtles, birds of prey, rhinos, bears, and primates. Species collected for the pet, zoo, and aquarium trades and species harvested for their fur, skin, or other commercial products also are closely monitored.

International treaties such as CITES are implemented when a country signing the treaty passes laws to enforce it. Countries may also establish Red Data Books of endangered species, which are national versions of the international Red Lists prepared

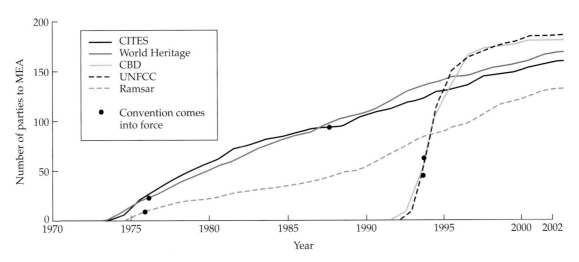

FIGURE 21.1 Major multinational environmental agreements (MEA) are negotiated and then ratified by the governments of individual countries, which become "parties," or participants, in the provisions of the agreement or treaty. The treaty comes into force (that is, countries begin to follow the provisions of the treaty) when a certain number of countries sign the treaty (indicated by a dot). The plot lines show the number of countries that have ratified various treaties that provide for biodiversity protection: those that protect habitat (the Ramsar Convention for the Protection of International Importance, the World Heritage Convention for the Protection of the World Cultural and Natural Heritage); species (Convention on International Trade in Endangered Species/CITES, the Convention on Biological Diversity/CBD); and the environment (United Nations Framework on Climate Change/UNFCC). (From WRI 2003.)

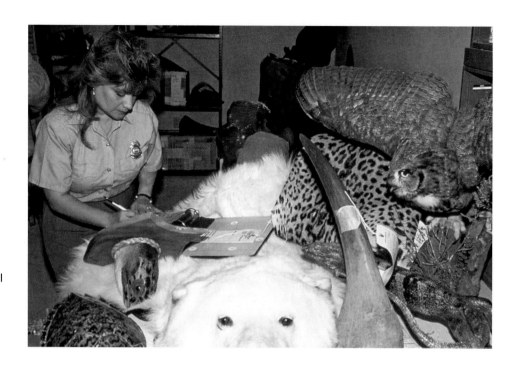

FIGURE 21.2 A customs official makes a list of illegal wildlife products seized at the border. (Photograph courtesy of John and Karen Hollingsworth/U.S. Fish and Wildlife Service.)

by the IUCN. Laws may protect both species listed by CITES and the national Red Data books. Once species protection laws are passed within a country, police, customs inspectors, wildlife officers, and other government agents can arrest and prosecute individuals possessing or trading in protected species and seize the products or organisms involved (Figure 21.2). In one case in Florida, an individual was sentenced to 13 months in jail for attempting to smuggle an orangutan into the United States. The CITES Secretariat periodically sends out bulletins aimed at publicizing specific illegal activities. In recent years, the CITES Secretariat has recommended to its member nations that they halt wildlife trade with the country of Vietnam because of its unwillingness to restrict the illegal export of wildlife from its territory.

Member countries are required to establish their own management and scientific authorities to implement their CITES obligations. Technical advice is provided by nongovernment organizations such as the World Conservation Union (IUCN) Wildlife Trade Specialist Group, the TRAFFIC network run by the World Wildlife Fund (WWF) and the IUCN, and the United Nations Environmental Programme's World Conservation Monitoring Centre (WCMC). CITES is particularly active in encouraging cooperation among countries in addition to fostering conservation efforts by development agencies. The treaty has been instrumental in restricting the trade in certain endangered wildlife species. Its most notable success was a global ban on the ivory trade when poaching was causing severe declines in African elephant populations (Box 21.1; Ginsberg 2002). Recently, countries in southern Africa with increasing elephant populations have been allowed to resume limited ivory sales.

Unfortunately, trade in wildlife remains a major problem; even compiling accurate data is a challenge (Blundell and Mascia 2005). A difficulty with enforcing CITES is that shipments of both living plants and animals and preserved parts of plants and animals are often mislabeled, due to either an ignorance of species names or a deliberate attempt to avoid the restrictions of the treaty. Also, sometimes countries fail to enforce the restrictions of the treaty due to a lack of trained staff or corruption. Finally, many restrictions are difficult to enforce because of remote bor-

BOX 21.1

The War for the Elephant: Is the Armistice Over?

■ Conservationists must occasionally take radical steps to save an overexploited species from extinction. For those concerned with the fate of the African elephant (*Loxodonta africana*) in the 1970s and 1980s, the measures employed to preserve the species sometimes amounted to actual warfare (Poole 1996). Park rangers who wanted to prevent the elephant's extinction had to protect the animals with drawn weapons. At the center of the conflict was the demand for elephant ivory, which grew rapidly during the 1970s and early 1980s because of the rising buying power of East Asian consumers. Over 800 tons of ivory were required annually to meet market demands. Most elephant poaching was not done by impoverished small-time hunters, but by organized bands of poachers carrying automatic weapons. In a few cases, the poachers were even the same people whose job it was to protect the animals: the game wardens themselves.

Under these circumstances it is hardly surprising that the total elephant population on the African continent dropped from 1.3 million in the late 1970s to under 600,000 by the late 1980s. Poaching accounted for 80% of elephant mortality in Kenya's Tsavo ecosystem in the 1980s as the price of ivory rose in world markets. East Africa's elephant populations were decimated: Kenya lost an estimated 85% of its elephant herd, Uganda nearly 90%—some 150,000 animals in less than a decade. In contrast, the large, well-protected herds of Zimbabwe, Botswana, South Africa, Malawi, and Namibia maintained their numbers. To deal with the threat, the wildlife service of Kenya and neighboring countries instituted a harsh policy toward poachers: Patrols of armed game wardens would aggressively search for and arrest poachers, shooting back if the poachers resisted arrest. This new policy, combined with other incentives, including higher pay, increased the commitment of game wardens to their job.

At the same time, the East African countries joined together to ask the member nations of CITES to halt ivory imports. Under the existing system, the ivory trade was officially regulated by the CITES treaty, and each country was allocated a specified maximum export quota. The reality was that countries that had reached their quota freely passed additional ivory to neighboring countries, where

Human settlements, farms, and poaching force large migratory animals, such as this elephant, to remain within the borders of Nairobi National Park in Kenya. As a result, overgrazing changes the savannah woodlands into a desert-like landscape with little plant life. (Photograph by Richard Primack.)

it was re-exported with official permits. It has been estimated that more than 80% of the ivory being exported from Africa in the late 1980s came from elephants killed by poachers. When the ban was finally instituted in 1989, the price of ivory dropped dramatically, and so did the rate of poaching.

The damage done to the East African elephant herds by three decades of unrestricted hunting is more than a matter of mere numbers. First, elephants are social animals with complex behaviors that are taught to younger elephants by their elders (Poole 1996). Because the poachers selectively killed the elephants with the largest tusks—in other words, the older elephants, generally between 25 and 60 years of age—the transmission of knowledge from mature animals to the next generation relating to sources of food and water has been disrupted.

Second, elephants have a profound impact on the development of microhabitats on which many other animals depend. Elephants strip leaves, knock down trees, and trample brush as they feed, opening up habitat for other kinds of vegetation. The elephants' foraging patterns initiate succession phases, opening up forest areas of East African bush for grazing animals such as gazelle, zebra, and wildebeest, and, in West and Central Africa, encourage the growth of vegetation favored by gorillas and other forest animals. With fewer elephants available

(continued)

BOX 21.1 *(continued)*

to perform this service, less open habitat is created, and the other species suffer as a consequence.

The efforts to save the elephant have had a significant, positive impact. The ivory ban and antipoaching patrols appear to have worked—the price of ivory has dropped precipitously, and elephant herds in many areas of Africa are increasing. Yet the elephant is not entirely safe; much of the increase is occurring inside national parks where excessive densities of elephants are changing savannah woodlands into desert-like landscapes with no trees and shrubs. The elephants are unable to leave the protected areas without coming into conflict with farmers and settlements building up along the park borders. Furthermore, countries in southern Africa with stable and even increas-

ing elephant herds have been granted permission to sell stockpiled ivory from savannah elephants, claiming that the sale of elephant products would provide financial support for their successful elephant management programs (Bulte et al. 2000, 2004; Fox 2004). But in other parts of Africa, wildlife officers and conservation biologists are concerned about the impact of this partially lifted ban. Will the measures designed to prevent poaching work? Or will the slaughter that has so badly damaged many elephant populations in East Africa be renewed—this time killing the remaining elephant families? Only time can tell for certain, but the eyes of many people concerned with the fate of these majestic animals will be watching closely.

ders; for example, those between Laos and Vietnam (Nooren and Claridge 2001). The result is the illegal wildlife trade continues to represent one of the most serious threats to biological diversity, particularly in Asia.

Another key treaty is the Convention on Conservation of Migratory Species of Wild Animals, often referred to as the Bonn Convention, signed in 1979, with a primary focus on bird species. This convention serves as an important complement to CITES by encouraging international efforts to conserve bird species that migrate across international borders and by emphasizing regional approaches to research, management, and hunting regulations. The convention now includes protection of bats and their habitats and cetaceans in the Baltic and North Seas. However, only 36 countries have signed this convention and its budget is very limited.

Other important international agreements that protect species include:

- Convention on Conservation of Antarctic Marine Living Resources

- International Convention for the Regulation of Whaling, which established the International Whaling Commission (see Box 10.1)

- International Convention for the Protection of Birds and the Benelux (Belgium/Netherlands/Luxembourg) Convention on the Hunting and Protection of Birds

- Convention on the Conservation and Management of Highly Migrating Fish Stocks in the Western and Central Pacific Oceans

- Additional agreements protecting specific groups of animals, such as prawns, lobsters, crabs, fur seals, Antarctic seals, salmon, and vicuña

A number of International Agreements with broader focuses are also increasingly seeking direct protection of endangered species. The Convention on Biological Diversity, described later in this chapter, for example, now includes recommendations for the protection of IUCN redlisted species (www.redlist.org).

A weakness of all these international treaties is that they operate through consensus, so strong, necessary measures often are not adopted if one or more countries are opposed to the measures. Also, any nation's participation is voluntary and countries can ignore these conventions to pursue their own interests when they find the conditions of compliance too difficult (DiMento 2003). This flaw was highlighted when several countries decided not to comply with the International Whaling Commission's 1986 ban on whale hunting. Persuasion and public pressure are the principal means used to induce countries to enforce treaty provisions and prosecute violators, though funding through treaty organizations can also help. A further problem is that many conventions are underfunded and consequently ineffective in achieving their goals. There is frequently no monitoring mechanism in place to determine if countries are even enforcing the treaties.

International Agreements to Protect Habitat

Habitat conventions at the international level complement species conventions by emphasizing unique biological communities and ecosystem features that need to be protected (and within these habitats, a multitude of individual species can be protected). Three of the most important are the **Ramsar Convention on Wetlands**, the **Convention Concerning the Protection of the World Cultural and Natural Heritage** (or the **World Heritage Convention**), and the awkwardly titled **UNESCO Man and the Biosphere Program** (also known as the **Biosphere Reserves Program**). Countries designating protected areas under these conventions voluntarily agree to administer them under the terms detailed in the conventions; countries do not give up sovereignty over these areas to an international body but retain full control over them. Such conventions have been found to be effective at protecting lands and meeting conservation goals (WWF International 2004).

The Ramsar Convention on Wetlands was established in 1971 to halt the continued destruction of wetlands, particularly those that support migratory waterfowl, and to recognize the ecological, scientific, economic, cultural, and recreational values of wetlands. The Ramsar Convention covers freshwater, estuarine, and coastal marine habitats, and includes 1524 sites with a total area of more than 129 million ha (Figure 21.3). The 147 countries that have signed the Ramsar Convention agree to conserve and protect their wetland resources and designate for conservation purposes at least one wetland site of international significance (WRI 2003). Twenty-eight Ramsar countries in the Mediterranean have joined together to form

FIGURE 21.3 Izunuma is a Ramsar-listed wetland in Japan. Rice paddies, roads, and buildings come right up to the edge of the lake. More than 25,000 geese overwinter on the lake and feed in the rice paddies. (Photograph by M. Kunimoto.)

a Wetlands Forum for regional cooperation. A comparable program, the Western Hemisphere Shorebird Reserve Network, focuses on protecting the declining wetland habitat of the Americas.

The World Heritage Convention is associated with UNESCO, IUCN, and the International Council on Monuments and Sites (von Droste et al. 1995; Sayer et al. 2000). This convention has received unusually wide support, with 170 countries participating. The goal of the convention is to protect cultural areas and natural areas of international significance through its World Heritage Site Program. The convention is unusual because it emphasizes the cultural as well as the biological significance of natural areas and recognizes that the world community has an obligation to support the sites financially. Limited funding for World Heritage Sites comes from the United Nations Foundation, which also supplies technical assistance. As with the Ramsar Convention, this convention seeks to give international recognition and support to protected areas that are established initially by national legislation. The 812 World Heritage Sites protecting natural areas cover around 142 million ha and include some of the world's premier conservation areas (Figure 21.4): Serengeti National Park in Tanzania, Sinharaja Forest Reserve in Sri Lanka, Iguaçu Falls in Brazil, Manu National Park in Peru, the Queensland Rain Forest of Australia, Komodo National Park in Indonesia, Ha Long Bay in Vietnam, and Great Smoky Mountains National Park in the United States, to name a few.

UNESCO's Man and the Biosphere Program (MAB) began in 1971. Biosphere reserves are designed to be models that demonstrate the compatibility of conservation efforts and sustainable development for the benefit of local people, as described in Chapter 20. As of 2003, a total of 482 biosphere reserves had been created in 102 countries, covering more than 263 million ha, and including 44 reserves in the United States, 20 in Russia, 17 in Bulgaria, 16 in China, 14 in Germany, and 11 in Mexico (see Figure 20.12). The largest designated biosphere is 70 million ha in area, located in Greenland.

These three conventions and provisions of the Convention on Biological Diversity establish an overarching consensus regarding appropriate conservation of protected areas and certain habitat types. More limited international agreements protect unique ecosystems and habitats in particular regions, including the Western Hemi-

(A)

(B)

FIGURE 21.4 World Heritage Sites include some of the most revered and well known conservation areas in the world. (A) Iguaçu Falls, Iguaçu National Park, Brazil. (B) Starfish thrive in the clear waters off Kanawa Island, one of the islands of Komodo National Park, Indonesia. (Photographs © Joshua Schachter of IUCN.)

sphere, the Antarctic biota, the South Pacific, Africa, the Caribbean, and the European Union (WRI 2003). Other international agreements have been ratified to prevent or limit pollution that poses regional and international threats to the environment. The Convention on Long-Range Trans-Boundary Air Pollution in the European Region recognizes the role that long-range transport of air pollution plays in acid rain, lake acidification, and forest dieback. The Convention on the Protection of the Ozone Layer was signed in 1985 to regulate and phase out the use of chlorofluorocarbons.

Conservation measures can also potentially provide for promoting cooperation between governments. Such is often the case when countries need to manage areas collectively. In many areas of the world, rugged, undeveloped border areas mark the boundaries between countries. Often, the region is managed by artificial units marked by political boundaries rather than as a single natural ecosystem. An alternative to this situation is to establish transfrontier parks that include larger areas (MacKinnon 2000; Pedymowski 2003). Park personnel from the countries involved can manage the park resources collectively and promote conservation on a larger scale (Godwin 2001). An early example of this collaboration was the decision to manage Glacier National Park in the United States and Waterton Lakes National Park in Canada as the Glacier International Peace Park. Today, intensive efforts are being made to link national parks and protected areas in Zimbabwe, Mozambique, and South Africa into larger management units (Figure 21.5). This joint man-

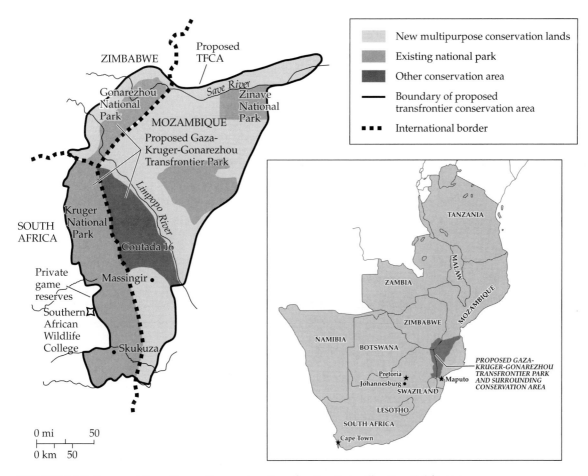

FIGURE 21.5 Proposed Gaza-Kruger-Gonarezhou Transfrontier Park will unite wildlife management activities in national parks and conservation areas of South Africa, Mozambique, and Zimbabwe. A larger conservation area will include national parks, private game reserves, and private farms and ranches. (After Godwin 2001.)

agement would have the added advantage of protecting the seasonal migratory routes of large animals. The establishment of the Red Sea Marine Peace Park between Israel and Jordan is important not only for conservation, but also for its potential for building trust in a war-ravaged region.

Marine pollution is another issue of vital concern because of the extensive areas of international waters not under national control and the ease with which pollutants released in one area can spread to another area. Agreements covering marine pollution include the Convention on the Prevention of Marine Pollution by Dumping of Wastes and Other Matters, the Convention on the Law of the Sea, and the Regional Seas Program of the United Nations Environmental Programme (UNEP). Regional agreements cover the northeastern Atlantic, the Baltic, and other specific locations, particularly in the North Atlantic region.

International Earth Summits

Progress can sometimes be made on conservation issues by bringing together leaders at international meetings. A significant step made in adopting a global approach to sound environmental management was the international conference held for 12 days in June, 1992, in Rio de Janeiro, Brazil. Known officially as the United Nations Conference on Environment and Development (UNCED), and unofficially as the Earth Summit, or the Rio Summit, the conference brought together representatives from 178 countries, including heads of state, leaders of the United Nations, major conservation organizations, and other groups representing religions and indigenous peoples. Their purpose was to discuss ways of combining increased protection of the environment with more effective economic development in less wealthy countries (United Nations 1993a,b). The conference successfully heightened awareness of the seriousness of the environmental crisis by placing the issue at the center of world attention. Also, the conference established a clear linkage between the protection of the environment and the need to alleviate poverty in the developing world through increased levels of financial assistance from developed countries (Figure 21.6). While the developed countries of the world potentially have the resources to provide for their citizens and protect the environment, for many of the poor countries, the immediate use of natural resources is often a prerequisite to raising the standard of living of an impoverished population. At the Earth Summit, the developed countries collectively agreed that they would assist the developing countries of the world in the long-term goal of protecting the global environment and biodiversity.

In addition to initiating many new projects, conference participants discussed, and most eventually signed, six major documents:

1. *The Rio Declaration.* This nonbinding declaration provides general principles to guide the actions of both wealthy and poor nations on issues of the environment and development. The right of nations to utilize their own resources for economic and social development is recognized, as long as the environments of other nations are not harmed in the process. The declaration affirms the "polluter pays" principle, in which companies and governments take financial responsibility for the environmental damage that they cause. As stated in the declaration, "States shall cooperate in a spirit of global partnership to conserve, protect, and restore the health and integrity of the earth's ecosystem. In view of the different contributions to global environmental degradation, states have common, but differentiated responsibilities."

2. *Convention on Climate Change.* This agreement requires industrialized countries to reduce their emissions of carbon dioxide and other greenhouse gases and to make regular reports on their progress. While specific emission lim-

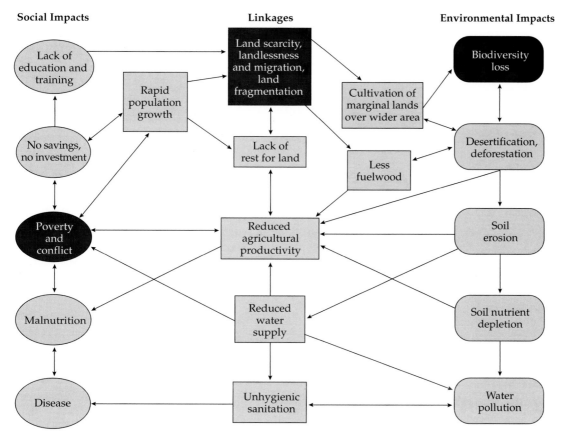

Social Impacts   Linkages   Environmental Impacts

FIGURE 21.6 Some linkages between poverty and environmental degradation. Breaking the linkages is a focus of national and international funding efforts by the World Bank and other donor organizations. (After Goodland 1994.)

its were not decided upon, the convention states that greenhouse gases should be stabilized at levels that will not interfere with the Earth's climate. The United States, the world's major user of fossil fuels, has continued to resist the provisions of this convention, along with Australia, Canada, China, and the oil-producing states of the Middle East.

3. *Convention on Biological Diversity.* The Convention on Biological Diversity has three objectives: protecting the various components of biological diversity, using them sustainably, and sharing the benefits of new products made with genetic resources of wild and domestic species (Tarasofsky 2002). The first two objectives recognize that countries have an obligation to protect their biological diversity and to use it in a responsible manner. While individual countries have the primary responsibility of protecting their own biological diversity, substantial international funding has been provided to assist developing countries in these efforts. The convention also recognizes that indigenous people should share in the benefits derived from biological diversity, particularly when they have contributed their own local knowledge about the species. Developing international intellectual property rights laws that fairly share the financial benefits of biological diversity among countries, biotechnology companies, and local people is proving to be a major challenge to the convention. Some progress has been made, but there are still some roadblocks to overcome. Because of concerns about how biological materials will be used or misused, certain developing countries have established

impossibly difficult procedures for granting permits to scientists who want to collect biological samples for their research. The effect has sometimes been to halt legitimate research on ecology, taxonomy, and biodiversity in general. In other cases, new research facilities have been built in developing countries and local people trained in scientific procedures so biological samples do not have to be exported.

4. *Agenda 21.* This 800-page document is an innovative attempt to describe in a comprehensive manner the policies needed by governments for environmentally sound development. Agenda 21 links the environment with other development issues that are often considered separately, such as child welfare, poverty, gender issues, technology transfer, and the unequal division of wealth. Plans of action are described to address problems of the atmosphere, land degradation and desertification, mountain development, agriculture and rural development, deforestation, aquatic environments, and pollution. Financial, institutional, technological, legal, and educational mechanisms that governments can use to implement these action plans are also described.

5. *Convention to Combat Desertification.* This convention has the goals of protecting dryland environments and improving the living standards of people. Specific activities involve land reform, improving agriculture and livestock management, better forestry practices, soil and water conservation, and wildlife protection. Over 130 countries have ratified the convention and many countries have submitted action plans describing how they would combat desertification and related land degradation. However, funding to implement these plans has not been forthcoming.

One of the most contentious issues resulting from the summit has been deciding how to fund the Earth Summit programs, particularly the Convention on Biological Diversity and Agenda 21. At the time, the cost of these programs was estimated to be about $600 billion per year, of which $125 billion was to come from the developed countries as overseas development assistance (ODA). Because the level of ODA from all countries in the early 1990s totaled approximately $60 billion per year, implementing these conventions would have required a severalfold increase of the aid commitment at that time. The developed countries did not agree to this increase in funding, and as an alternative proposal, the Group of 77 (a group of developing countries) had suggested that industrialized countries increase their level of foreign assistance to 0.7% of their Gross National Product (GNP) by the year 2000, which would have roughly doubled their level of assistance. While the major developed countries agreed in principle to this figure, no schedule was set to meet the target date. As of the year 2004, of 22 donor countries, only the foreign assistance from a few wealthy northern European countries has met the 0.7% of GNP target percentage, most notably Norway (0.87%), Denmark (0.85%), Sweden (0.78%) and the Netherlands (0.73%). Many of the larger developed countries, including the United States, at 0.17% of GNP, have actually lowered the percentage of GNP that they give as foreign assistance over the past 10 years (www.oecd.org).

The inability of the major industrial countries to allocate funds to implement the conference agreements has been disappointing. However, the fact remains that two important agreements—the Convention on Biological Diversity and the Convention on Climate—were ratified by many countries and have formed the basis for many specific actions on the part of governments and conservation organizations. Follow-up meetings indicated a willingness on the part of governments to continue the discussion (Figure 21.7). For example, the Convention on Biological Diversity Programme of Work on Protected Areas includes significant provisions on sustainable and sufficient finance, although again, targets are far from being met. The

FIGURE 21.7 World leaders met in 1997 for "Rio +5," a follow-up of the Earth Summit. At the meeting, Mikhail Gorbachev, the former president of the Soviet Union, addressed a forum that included prominent political and environmental leaders. (Photograph by Hiromi Kobori.)

most significant success is the international agreement, reached at Kyoto in December of 1997, to reduce global greenhouse gas emissions to below 1990 levels. The Kyoto Protocol was finally ratified in 2004, bringing it into force. However, many countries, most notably China, Japan, Australia, Canada, and Saudi Arabia, have not ratified the Kyoto treaty, and the United States, which also had not ratified the treaty, has withdrawn from it.

There have been related efforts to put the ideas of the Earth Summit into force. One example is the Aarhus Convention of 1998, signed by 40 countries, recognizing the right of all people to a healthy environment. The convention requires governments to make environmental data available, and gives citizens, organizations, and countries the right to investigate causes of pollution and to take action to reduce environmental damage. In August 2002, a second major environment summit was held: The World Summit on Sustainable Development in Johannesburg, South Africa, with representatives of 191 countries and 20,000 participants (WRI 2003). Although the conference emphasized the need to reduce the rate of biodiversity loss, the main focus was on achieving the social and economic goals of sustainability. This shift in focus from the Rio Summit highlights a significant, ongoing debate over conservation strategies. The sides of this debate can be broadly categorized into those in favor of focusing on protected areas and those in favor of focusing on sustainable use (Schwartzman et al. 2000; Lapham and Livermore 2003; Naughton-Treves et al. 2005). The major documents produced by the conference, including a Plan of Implementation, were guidelines for governments and do not have the binding force of treaties. Another positive development of recent years is international certification of products, such as timber, documenting that they have been produced sustainably, in a manner that does minimal damage to the environment and does not harm local people.

International Funding

Following the Earth Summit, international funding for conservation has increased, though not as much as originally promised. Much of this increase in funding has been channeled through the Global Environment Facility of the World Bank, as will be discussed later in the chapter. Funding priorities have also shifted significantly during this period (Lapham and Livermore 2003). What is the process that identifies projects for funding? Often it begins when a conservation biologist, conservation organization, or government identifies a conservation need, such as protecting a species, establishing a nature reserve, or training park personnel. This often initiates a lengthy process of analysis, discussion, planning, project design, proposal writing, fundraising, and implementation that involves different types of conservation organizations. Private foundations (e.g., the MacArthur Foundation), international organizations (e.g., the World Bank), and government agencies (e.g., the U.S. Agency for International Development) often provide money for conservation programs through direct grants to the institutions that implement the projects (e.g., nongovernment conservation organizations [NGOs], universities, museums, and national parks departments).

National governments and international banks provided 90% of the aid funding to Latin America, for instance, demonstrating the great importance of those institutions to funding international conservation (Castro et al. 2000). Although foundations and conservation organizations provided only 9.6% of the funding for Latin America, they are often able to fund innovative small projects and provide more intensive management. The growing importance of private funding throughout the world is illustrated by a $260 million donation given by the Moore Foundation to the NGO Conservation International. Conservation International in turn cooperated with the World Bank, the Global Environment Facility, the MacArthur Foundation, and the Japanese and French governments to establish the $150 million Critical Ecosystem Partnership Fund to protect threatened global hot spots and biological diversity. Such increased funding has allowed the development of large international conservation organizations that operate independently and have their own specific goals and policies (Halpern et al. 2006) (Figure 21.8).

Conservation work is carried out when foundations, development banks such as the World Bank, and government agencies give money to fund the activities of local and international conservation organizations. Major international conservation **NGOs** (nongovernmental organizations) (e.g., the World Wildlife Fund, Conservation International) implement conservation activities directly and also provide grants and technical assistance to local conservation organizations (Figure 21.9) (Romero and Andrade 2004; Pergams et al. 2004). The major international conservation organizations are often active in establishing, strengthening, and funding local NGOs as well as government programs in the developing world that run conservation programs; see the Appendix for a list of major conservation NGOs. From the perspective of an international conservation organization such as the World Wildlife Fund, working with local organizations in developing countries is an effective strategy because it relies on local knowledge and trains and supports groups of citizens within the country who can then be advocates for conservation for years to come. NGOs are often perceived to be more effective at carrying out conservation projects than government departments, but programs initiated by NGOs may end after a few years when funding runs out and often they do not achieve a lasting effect.

An unfortunate reality of the present method of funding projects is that conservation organizations compete intensively for a limited amount of funds (Redford et al. 2003). As a result, there is sometimes a duplication of conservation efforts and frequently a lack of coordination between organizations and projects that are very similar. In

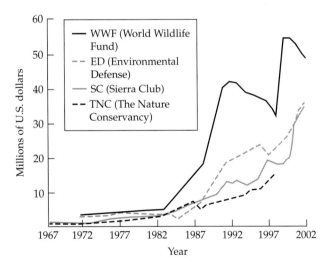

FIGURE 21.8 The contributions received by nongovernment organizations began to increase substantially from the 1980s onward, as illustrated by the contributions given to Environmental Defense (ED), the Sierra Club (SC), The World Wildlife Fund (WWF), and The Nature Conservancy (TNC). To keep the groups on the same scale, The Nature Conservancy values have been divided by 100. (After Pergams et al. 2004.)

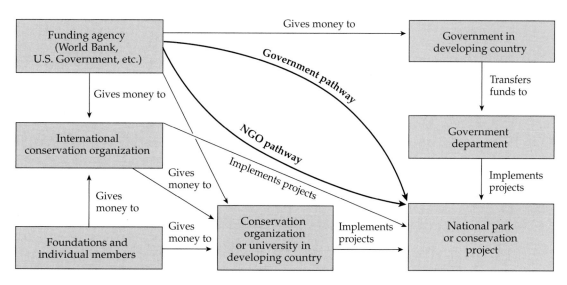

FIGURE 21.9 Conservation projects are funded by development banks, governments, foundations, and members of conservation organizations, and implemented by international and local nongovernmental conservation organizations and government departments in developing countries.

the drive for greater funding, conservation organizations have often emphasized the successful aspects of their projects and ignored their failures, missing the opportunity to learn from mistakes. Conservation organizations have begun to emphasize the need to cooperate to achieve shared, long-term goals, which is clearly a positive sign (Conservation Monitoring Partnership 2003; Stem et al. 2005).

An active local conservation program in a developing country often receives money from one or more conservation foundations and foreign governments, maintains scientific links to international conservation NGOs, and has affiliations with local and overseas research institutions (Romero and Andrade 2004; Rodrigues 2004). In such a manner, the world conservation community is knit together through networks of money, expertise, and mutual interests. The Program for Belize (PFB) is a good example of this (www.pfbelize.org/welcome.html). At first glance the PFB is a Belizean organization, staffed by Belizean personnel, with the main purpose of managing a Belizean conservation facility, the Rio Bravo Conservation and Management Area. However, the PFB has an extensive network of research, institutional, and financial connections to various government agencies in other countries (e.g., the U.S. Agency for International Development), major foundations (MacArthur Foundation), universities both in Belize and elsewhere (e.g., Boston University), international conservation NGOs (e.g., Conservation International) and even major industrial corporations (e.g., Suncor Energy). In such situations, there is a genuine concern that wealthy international organizations might be involved in an asymmetric power relationship with a local conservation organization struggling to survive; the fear is that the local NGO might wind up giving priority to international goals rather than local ones.

The World Bank and the Global Environment Facility

Increasingly, groups in the developed countries recognize that if they want to preserve biological diversity in species-rich but cash-poor countries, they cannot simply provide advice: a financial commitment is also required (Bruner et al. 2004). Approximately $5 billion is currently spent per year worldwide on biodiversity protection by governments and conservation organizations (Myers and Kent 2001). One of the single largest sources of funding for the protection of biological diver-

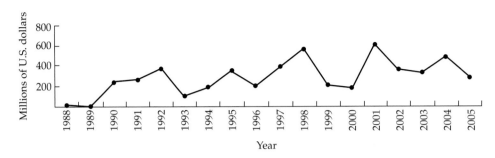

FIGURE 21.10 World Bank funding for biodiversity projects on an annual basis for the period 1988 to 2005. Annual fluctuations in funding are caused by the tendency to bunch large projects together. The total funding is $5.1 billion, of which 32% is loans, 23% is grants, and 45% is co-financing from other sources. (After World Bank 2006.)

sity is the World Bank and related banks (Figure 21.10). The largest program for biodiversity funding is the Global Environment Facility (GEF), based in Washington, D.C., created in 1991, and operating in cooperation with the World Bank, the United Nations Development Programme (UNDP) and the United Nations Environmental Programme (UNEP) (de Chazournes 2003). The World Bank has invested $5.1 billion in biodiversity from 1988 to 2005 (World Bank 2004, 2006). Much of the World Bank investment involved cofinancing from other sources, often national governments. Biodiversity activities funded by the World Bank include establishing protected areas, training people, developing infrastructure, addressing global climate change, protecting the ozone layer, managing and protecting forests, reducing the loss of biodiversity, and managing freshwater and marine resources (www.gefweb.org). It is relevant to note that the composition of the World Bank's portfolio of biodiversity projects is not static, with emphasis in recent years on projects outside protected areas (Lapham and Livermore 2003).

By the year 2004, the World Bank was managing 426 conservation programs in 102 countries and 17 regional multi-country programs (World Bank 2006). Currently, new biodiversity loans and grants worth an average of $330 million are funded each year by the GEF and the World Bank, though the amounts vary widely from year to year. The scale of World Bank activities is illustrated by its joint program with the World Wildlife Fund to establish 50 million ha of newly protected forest, to establish effective management for an additional 50 million ha currently protected, and to help in placing 200 million ha of production forest into management programs that are certified as sustainable. Examples of projects financed by the GEF and the World Bank are the following:

- *Zimbabwe.* The Wildlife Management and Environmental Conservation Project supports local communities in obtaining greater economic value from wildlife.

- *Ghana.* Conservation of coastal wetlands critical to birds migrating along the East Atlantic Flyway through better design of sewage treatment facilities and support of sustainable community projects.

- *Turkey.* Creating crop management zones and forest gene resource zones to conserve traditional varieties and wild ancestors of grain, legume, and fruit tree species that are vital to the maintenance of modern agriculture.

- *Indonesia*: Marine protected areas are being established in cooperation with 1500 coastal villages, with the goal of managing marine resources sustainably.

- *Mexico*: Highland forests in Mexico protect the quality of Mexico City's drinking water and provide habitat for overwintering monarch butterflies. An endowment fund has been established to compensate landowners for maintaining and restoring forest on their property.

National Environmental Funds

In addition to direct grants and loans for projects, another important mechanism used to provide secure, long-term support for conservation activities in developing countries is the **national environmental fund** (**NEF**). NEFs are typically set up as conservation trust funds or foundations in which a board of trustees—composed of representatives of the host government, conservation organizations, and donor agencies—allocates (GEF 1999) the annual income from an endowment to support inadequately funded government departments and nongovernment conservation organizations and activities. NEFs have been established in over 50 developing countries with funds contributed by developed countries and by major organizations such as the World Bank, the Global Environment Facility, and the World Wildlife Fund.

One important early example of an NEF, the Bhutan Trust Fund for Environmental Conservation (BTF), was established in 1991 by the government of Bhutan in cooperation with the World Bank and the World Wildlife Fund. The BTF has already received about $26 million (exceeding its goal of $20 million), with the Global Environment Facility its largest donor. The fund provides $1 million per year for surveying the rich biological resources of this eastern Himalayan country; training foresters, ecologists, and other environmental professionals; promoting environmental education; establishing and managing protected areas; and designing and implementing integrated conservation development projects.

NEFs have proliferated in recent years, with the Latin American and the Caribbean Network of Environmental Funds (REDLAC; http://www.redlac.org/english/default.asp) alone comprising funds in 21 countries that manage approximately $700 million.

Debt-For-Nature Swaps

Many countries in the developing world have accumulated huge international debts that they are unable to repay (Thapa 1998; Thapa and Thapa 2002). As a result, some developing countries have rescheduled their loan payments, unilaterally reduced them, or have stopped making them altogether. Because of the low expectation of repayment, the commercial banks that hold these debts are selling the debts at a steep discount on the international secondary debt market. For example, Costa Rican debt has traded for only 14 to 18% of its face value.

In a creative approach, debt from the developing world is being used as a vehicle for financing projects to protect biological diversity, so-called **debt-for-nature swaps** (Paddack 2003; WWF 2003). In one common type of debt-for-nature swap, an NGO in the developed world (such as The Nature Conservancy) buys up the debts of a developing country; the NGO agrees to forgive the debt in exchange for the country carrying out a conservation activity. This activity could involve land acquisition for conservation purposes, park management, development of park facilities, conservation education, or sustainable development projects.

In other swaps, governments of developed countries owed money directly by developing countries may decide to cancel a certain percentage of the debt if the developing country will agree to contribute to a national environmental fund or to some other conservation activity. Such programs have converted debt valued at $1.5 billion into conservation and sustainable development activities in Colombia, Poland, the Philippines, Madagascar, and a dozen other countries. Debt swaps are being incorporated into major foreign assistance programs such as the Enterprise for the Americas.

Costa Rica has taken the lead in debt swaps. Outside conservation organizations have spent $12 million to purchase more than $79 million of Costa Rican debt, which has then been exchanged for $42 million in bonds for use in conservation activities at La Amistad Biosphere Reserve, Braulio Carillo National Park, Corcovado National Park, Guanacaste National Park, Tortuguero National Park, and Monteverde Cloud Forest, a private reserve. The interest on the bonds is used to establish a fund administered by the Costa Rican government and several local NGOs, including the Costa Rican Parks Foundation.

While debt-for-nature swaps have great potential advantages, they present a number of potential limitations to both the donor and the recipient (Roodman 2001). Debt swaps will not change the underlying problems associated with poverty and mismanagement that led to environmental degradation in the first place. Also, spending money on conservation programs might divert money from other necessary domestic programs such as medical care, schools, and agricultural development.

Marine Environments

Innovative funding programs such as NEFs and debt-for-nature swaps are particularly needed for marine protected areas, which have lagged behind terrestrial protected areas in conservation efforts. The ease with which the marine environment can be polluted, the high value of seashore real estate, and the open access to marine resources mean that such protected areas will require special attention. Establishing low-impact ecotourism facilities and restricted fishing zones are among the types of activities being funded. Funding for marine conservation from the World Bank, conservation foundations, and government sources has greatly increased during the past decade, and remains a high priority.

Is the Funding Adequate and Effective?

Unfortunately, the amount of money being spent is still not sufficient to protect the great storehouse of biological riches needed for the long-term prosperity of human societies (Balmford and Whitten 2003). Compared with the $15 billion spent each year on the U.S. space program and the $451 million spent each year on the Human Genome Project, the approximately $100 million per year being spent by U.S. institutions on biological diversity in developing countries is meager indeed. Similarly, while the funds provided by the World Bank seem large, they are small compared with the other activities supported by the World Bank and related organizations.

Conservation organizations have developed a number of tools to evaluate the effectiveness of funded projects (Margoluis and Salafsky 1998; Woodhill 2000; Hockings et al. 2000). Evaluations of the GEF by the World Bank itself have judged the projects funded so far to be a mixture of positives and negatives (see various reports at: www.gefweb.org). On the positive side, the GEF provided increased funding for conservation and biodiversity projects, reviewed biodiversity-related legislation, transferred conservation information, planned national biodiversity strategies, identified and protected important ecosystems and habitats, and enhanced the capacity to carry out biodiversity projects. However, the lack of participation by community groups, local scientists, and government leaders; an overreliance on foreign consultants; an elaborate and time-consuming application procedure; and a lack of understanding of GEF objectives by people in the recipient countries were identified as major problems. An additional problem was the mismatch of funding over short periods with the long-term needs of poor countries.

Many of these problems apply to international conservation funding more broadly: a major shortcoming is that only a small fraction of available support ends up paying for what is arguably the foundation for conservation efforts worldwide—actual management of protected areas. Grant money is diverted for salaries, infrastructure, and overhead at administrative headquarters. Indeed, in countries from Peru to Ghana, even during periods of significant donor support, protected areas may still find themselves without funding to buy gas for vehicles, pay staff salaries, and meet other basic needs (Oates 1999).

It must be recognized that many environmental projects supported by international aid do not provide lasting solutions to the problems because of failure to deal with the "4 Cs"—concern, contracts, capacity, and causes (see Rabinowitz [1995] for an instructive case study). Environmental aid will be effective only when applied to situations in which both donors and recipients have a genuine *concern* to solve the problems (Do key people really want the project to be successful, or do they just want the money?); when mutually satisfactory and enforceable *contracts* for the project can be agreed on (Will the work actually be done once the money is given out?); where there is the *capacity* to undertake the project in terms of institutions, personnel, and infrastructure (Do people have the skills to do the work, and do they have the necessary resources, such as vehicles, research equipment, buildings, and libraries, to carry out the work?); and when the *causes* of the problem are addressed (Will the project treat the underlying causes of the problem or just provide temporary relief of the symptoms?). Despite these problems, international funding of conservation projects continues. Past experiences are informing new projects, which are more effective, but with the result that the application and accounting processes can be extremely cumbersome and time-consuming.

International Development Banks and Ecosystem Damage

The rates of deforestation, habitat destruction, and the loss of aquatic ecosystems have often been greatly accelerated by poorly conceived large-scale projects that are internationally financed, sometimes involving dams, roads, mines, and resettlements. These projects may be financed by the international development agencies of major industrial nations, as well as by the major **multilateral development banks (MDBs)** controlled by those nations. These MDBs include the World Bank, which lends to developing countries in all regions of the globe, and the Inter-American Development Bank (IDB), the Asian Development Bank (ADB), and the African Development Bank (AFDB).

Multilateral development banks annually loan more than $25 billion to 151 countries to finance development projects (Roessler 2000; Lee 2005). The impact of the MDBs is actually even greater than that yearly total suggests, however, because their funding is often linked to financing from donor countries, private banks, and other government agencies: the $25 billion in funding from the MDBs attracts about another $50 billion in loans, which makes the MDBs major players in the developing world. Related to the MDBs are international financial institutions, such as the International Monetary Fund (IMF) and the International Finance Corporation, and government-supported export credit agencies, such as the U.S. Export-Import Bank, Japan's Export-Import Bank, Germany's Hermes Guarantee, Britain's Export Credits and Guarantee Department, France's COFACE, and Italy's SACE. These international institutions collectively support $400 billion of foreign investments and exports each year, an amount equivalent to almost 8% of total world trade (Kapur et al. 1997; Rich 2000). These export credit agencies exist primarily to support the corporations of developed countries in selling manufactured goods and services to developing countries.

Even though the official goals of the MDBs include sustainable economic development and poverty alleviation, which are important and admirable goals, many of the projects they fund actually exploit natural resources to create exports for international markets (Becker 2003; Birn and Dmitrienko 2005). During the 1970s and 1980s, many of the MDB-funded projects resulted in the destruction of ecosystems over a wide area, involving soil erosion, flooding, water pollution, health problems, loss of income for local people, and loss of biological diversity (Rich 1994; Kapur et al. 1997; Janmanch 2004). Forestry, agriculture, mining, dam construction, power generation, and other components of economic development are certainly needed to supply human needs, but these activities need to be carried out in a way that minimizes the harm to the environment and the local people living in the area. Over the last 15 years, the World Bank has increasingly incorporated biodiversity protection into its large infrastructure projects, a practice they describe as "mainstreaming" (World Bank 2004), which is discussed in more detail later in this chapter. Such activities include providing grants for adding new protected areas into flood control projects, restoration of degraded habitats, and protection of endangered species.

Development Lending Case Studies

Among the most highly publicized examples of environmental destruction resulting from MDB and World Bank lending are the transmigration program in Indonesia; road construction, agricultural development, and industrialization projects in Brazilian Amazonia; and large dam construction in places such as Indonesia, India, China, Nepal, and Pakistan. While the MDBs now require careful review of the environmental impact of new projects, these case studies of past projects deserve to be remembered to illustrate what can go wrong if governments unexpectedly decide to ignore agreed upon environmental safeguards and break promises made to their own citizens.

INDONESIAN RESETTLEMENT   From the 1970s to the late 1980s, the World Bank loaned $560 million to the Indonesian government to resettle millions of people from the densely populated inner islands of Java, Bali, and Lombok to the sparsely inhabited, heavily forested outer islands of Borneo (Kalimantan), New Guinea (Irian Jaya), and Sulawesi. The relocated farm families were supposed to raise crops to feed themselves as well as cash crops for export, including rubber, oilpalm, and cacao; these exports would allow Indonesia to pay off the loans. Known as the transmigration program, this project has been an environmental and economic failure: The poor tropical forest soils on these outer islands are often unsuitable for the intensive agriculture practiced by the farmers. In addition, the infrastructure the farmers needed for their plantations did not develop, in part due to government corruption and mismanagement. As a result, many of the farmers have become impoverished and have been forced to practice shifting agriculture. The production of export crops to pay off the World Bank loans has not occurred. In addition, millions of ha of tropical rain forests have been destroyed by the transmigrating settlers, in combination with legal and illegal logging (CIFOR 2003). The presence of large numbers of new settlers in remote rural locations has contributed to political instability and ethnic violence. Having learned from past projects such as this one, the World Bank now requires countries to plan carefully for the social impacts of large projects and to allocate enough funds for this purpose.

BRAZILIAN HIGHWAYS   World Bank and Inter-American Development Bank projects in the Amazonian region of Brazil are classic examples of a development program gone awry—on a colossal scale. Hundreds of millions of dollars have been loaned to Brazil since 1981 to build roads and settlement areas as part of the Northwest Development Program, often without environmental impact studies and land use studies to determine their feasibility (Fearnside 1990; Kapur et al. 1997). Only 3% of the total budget of this project was allocated for biological and Amerindian reserves and only 0.5% for research. Once the highway was opened, the government encouraged poor, landless farmers from southern and northeastern Brazil to move to the region to receive free land. The farmers and ranchers who migrated to the region cut down huge areas of forest near the roads to establish new farms and ranches. At the peak of deforestation in 1987, 20 million ha—2.5% of Brazil's total land area—were burned in one of the world's most massive episodes of environmental devastation.

In its haste to develop the region, the Brazilian government built roads across Amerindian reserves and biological reserves that were supposed to be completely protected, effectively opening up even these areas to deforestation. The Ianomãmi Indians, for instance, were given legal rights to only 30% of the land that they occupied, and this holding was eventually fragmented into 19 separate pieces by roads and other developments. In general, the cattle ranches and tree plantations that were supposed to pay for the loans failed because the land was unsuitable for agriculture. The overall result has been environmental devastation with minor, fleeting economic benefits. Massive forest destruction in Brazil continued through the 1990s, with particularly high rates of clearing and forest fires in 1997 and 1998 (Nepstad et al. 1999, 2001). A massive new round of construction of 6245 km of roads funded by international development banks is just beginning, doubling the amount of forest area accessible by road, with the potential to substantially increase forest fragmentation and clearing (Figure 21.11; Laurance et al. 2001; Reid and De Sousa 2005; Soares-Filho et al. 2006). An alternative to spending billions of dollars on roads into the rain forest would be to intensify agriculture in existing cultivated regions; invest in education and health care, which are key to improving the quality of life for poor people; and take measures to reduce forest fires. Including environmental costs into economic analysis of road projects can also help ensure that the government only builds roads that actually benefit the country. Indeed, when environmental costs are included in the economic analysis of a project, many road projects may result in significantly reduced or even negative net economic gains (Reid 1999).

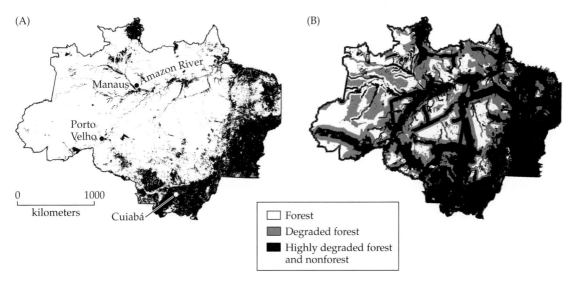

FIGURE 21.11 (A) A current map of the Brazilian Amazon showing forest (white) and deforested, degraded, and savannah areas (black). Note that deforestation occurs along rivers and roads and in eastern and southern populated areas. (B) When Brazil completes its proposed system of new roads by the year 2020, the amount of pristine forest cover (white) far from roads is predicted to be dramatically reduced, with much of the land lightly and moderately degraded (gray) and deforested, highly degraded, or converted to savannahs (black). If strong conservation measures are implemented by the government, the levels of degradation and deforestation could be somewhat reduced. (From Laurance et al. 2001.)

DAM PROJECTS A major class of projects financed by MDBs is the construction of dam and irrigation systems that provide water for agricultural activities and generate hydroelectric power (Janmanch 2004; McGirk and Buncombe 2005). While dams provide important benefits, these projects destroy free, wild rivers and often damage large aquatic ecosystems by changing water depth and current watershed patterns, increasing sedimentation, and creating barriers to animal dispersal. As a result of these changes, many species are no longer able to survive in the altered environment. In addition, all of the people living in the area to be flooded are displaced, which often forces them to move to cities and leads to impoverishment. China's Three Gorges Dam on the Yangtze River, which is financed by international lenders, including government-sponsored finance agencies and private banks, illustrates these issues (Box 21.2).

BOX 21.2

How Much Will the Three Gorges Dam Really Cost?

On the surface, it sounds like a great idea: build a dam to control flooding, improve navigation, and provide clean hydroelectric power to millions of people (Wu et al. 2004). The Yangtze River is one of the largest rivers in the world, running from the Tibetan plateau through China and emptying into the East China Sea. Flooding is a serious problem for the people living near the Yangtze: A series of floods in 1954 killed more than 30,000 people, and flooding in 1991 claimed at least another 3000 victims. The area is economically depressed and per capita income is low. In 1992, the Chinese government gave final approval to build a dam downriver of the Three Gorges area of the Yangtze River in central China, with the aims of improving navigation, protecting approximately 10 million people from floods, and generating electricity for industrial development. Construction of the main dams has already begun, with completion expected in 2009. It is estimated that the electricity

The waters of the Yangtze River already submerged many of the fields in this area, and will continue up these steep slopes almost reaching the houses. The village shown in this photograph is a new village, built to replace an old one across the river that is now almost under water. (Photograph © Tina Manley/Alamy.)

generated by the dam will reduce coal consumption (the primary source of electricity) by 30 to 50 million tons each year, which will significantly reduce air pollution (Wang and Bryant 2003). Slower currents and a more stable water flow would also improve navigability for shipping.

But the costs of building the dam are high—construction will cost over US$60 billion, and perhaps as much as $70 billion. In addition to funding by Chinese banks, substantial funding is coming from government-sponsored finance agencies such as Germany's Hermes Guarantee and Japan's Export-Import Bank, with private banks such as Cit-

igroup, Chase Manhattan Bank, Credit Suisse, First Boston, Merrill Lynch, Deutsche Bank, and Barclays Capital assisting with placing Chinese government bonds for the project. And as the reservoir behind the dam fills, it is flooding low-lying areas, necessitating the resettlement of entire villages, towns, and cities—eventually almost 2 million people in all (Chau 1995; Wang and Bryant 2003). The long, narrow reservoir will stretch across more than 400 km of the Yangtze Valley, from Yichang westward to Chongqing, one of China's largest cities. Temples, pagodas, and other important cultural sites are being submerged by up to 175 m of water. The Yangtze River Basin also contains a freshwater fishery

BOX 21.2 *(continued)*

that provides two-thirds of the country's catch, and agricultural lands that yield 40% of the country's crops—much of which will be affected by the dam. The dam's effect on natural communities and the environment is likely to be profound and detrimental. Previous water projects involving human resettlement have been less than successful. Often people are resettled in areas so far from their original homes that they have had trouble adjusting. To avoid this problem, the plan is to move one million people uphill from their current location. However, those uphill sites that are not already in use are typically steep, covered with thin, infertile soil, and lack sufficient water for agriculture. It is estimated that five times the present farmlands will be needed to yield the same amount of food. As steep hillsides are deforested, erosion will accelerate, increasing the buildup of silt behind the dam, and the likelihood of dangerous landslides (Liu et al. 2004).

Dams have a fairly predictable impact on the environment. They block the movement of nutrients downriver, slow water flow, and decrease variations in the water level. Slower currents decrease oxygen levels and decrease the ability of the river to flush out pollutants. As the hydrology changes, so will the composition of the plant and animal communities (Liu et al. 2003; Xie 2003). With the construction of the Three Gorges Dam, the rare Chinese sturgeon (*Acipenser sinensis*) probably will be unable to

swim up the Yangtze River to spawn. The endangered Chinese river dolphin (*Lipotes vexillifer*), a species with only about 300 individuals left, may also be unable to survive in the altered environment. Countless other species will be affected as well.

Some of these concerns have been addressed by the dam's planners. Millions of dollars have been spent to terrace steep slopes for agriculture, and large tracts of uncultivated land on the margins of the areas to be flooded have been set aside for relocation efforts. Electricity provided by the dam should reduce deforestation caused by collection of fuelwood. Reforestation efforts have been planned to reduce erosion and deposition of silt in the river. Little is known, however, about how suitable marginal lands are for farming, how fast silt will build-up behind the dam, or how endangered species in the drainage basin will adapt to the altered hydrology. Perhaps the best emblem of the Three Gorges Dam is the endangered Siberian crane (*Grus leucogeranus*), symbolic of well-being among the Chinese, that feeds in shallow waters along the Yangtze River Basin. Changing water levels may affect its survival—and the prosperity of the Chinese people as well. In coming years, we will be better able to determine if the clear benefits of the dam, in terms of electric power, flood control, and navigation, are balanced by the cost of construction, its environmental impacts, and the social disruption it will cause.

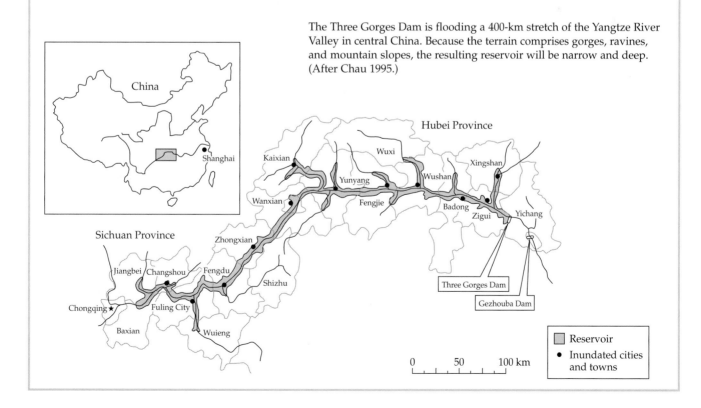

The Three Gorges Dam is flooding a 400-km stretch of the Yangtze River Valley in central China. Because the terrain comprises gorges, ravines, and mountain slopes, the resulting reservoir will be narrow and deep. (After Chau 1995.)

The Nam Theun 2 Dam in Laos that has recently been approved for funding by the World Bank and the Asian Development Bank, illustrates some of these issues. The dam will generate electrical power that will be sold to Thailand, and provide significant revenue to the government of Laos. As part of the project, 450 square kilometers of river forest habitat will be flooded and 4500 indigenous people will have to move. An estimated 100,000 people living downriver will be affected by an altered water regime once the dam is finished. To deal with these issues, the World Bank and the Laotian government have announced plans to establish, fund, and manage new protected areas and to compensate displaced people. However, environmental groups point out the failures of past agreements made for similar dam projects and the broken promises made to local people.

Ironically, research indicates that the long-term success of some of the large international dam projects that threaten aquatic ecosystems may depend on preserving the forest ecosystems that surround the project sites. The loss of plant cover on the slopes above water projects often results in soil erosion and siltation, with resulting loss of efficiency, higher maintenance costs, and damage to irrigation systems and dams. Protecting the forests and other natural vegetation in the watersheds is now widely recognized as an important and relatively inexpensive way to ensure the efficiency and longevity of these water projects, while at the same time preserving large areas of natural habitat. One such example is the $1.2 million loan by the World Bank to assist in the development and protection of a watershed in northern Sulawesi, Indonesia (McNeely et al. 1990). A 278,700-ha primary rain forest, which included the catchment area on the slopes above a $60 million irrigation project that was financed by the World Bank, was converted into the Bogani Nani Wartabone National Park (Figure 21.12). In this particular case, the World Bank was able to protect its original investment with less than 2% of the project's cost and create a significant new national park in the process. As is the case with evaluating road projects, economic analysis that considers changes to environmental services can be useful in assessing the economic value of a dam project before it begins.

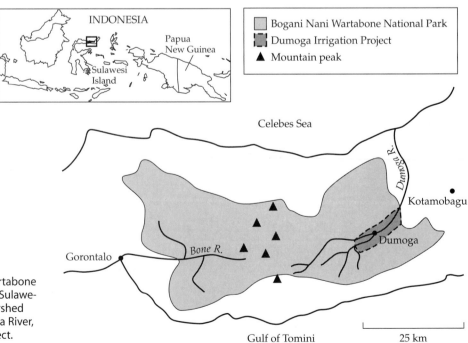

FIGURE 21.12 The Bogani Nani Wartabone National Park on the northern arm of Sulawesi Island, Indonesia, protects the watershed above the Bone River and the Dumoga River, including the Dumoga Irrigation Project. (After Wells and Brandon 1992.)

Reforming Development Lending

If many of the large international development projects in the past have been so environmentally harmful, why do host countries want them, and why do the MDBs agree to finance them? Why are such projects approved? One major reason is that there is often a real need for such development projects, and MDBs provide low-interest loans backed by considerable technical experience: To a poor country with no financial resources, large development projects have great value as a way to advance the national economy. However, projects are also often funded because economists, engineers, and government officials make overly optimistic predictions on construction schedules, costs, and prices of commodities while minimizing potential problems; surveys and pilot studies are not undertaken, or their results are disregarded; comparable projects elsewhere are not evaluated; and finally, the environmental and social costs of projects are often ignored or minimized, since these variables are considered external to economic analysis (see Chapter 4). It must be said, though, that many of the worst projects occurred in the past; current and future projects now have good environmental safeguards built into them.

Host governments often want large projects to proceed because the projects provide temporary jobs, temporary economic prosperity, and some release from social tensions for the duration of the project. Local business leaders, especially those with close links to the government, endorse the projects because they can make large profits on project contracts. Industrialized countries that support the banks often encourage these loans to stabilize governments in host countries—governments that are friendly to their interests, but which may lack popular support. And lastly, bank officials themselves want to make big loans because that is what they are trained to do.

In order to act more responsibly, for the last 15 years the World Bank and other MDBs have added environmental and social requirements to the projects that they are financing (Itano 2004; Vallette et al. 2004). As a result, many environmental NGOs now want the MDBs involved in lending so that environmental and social assessments are required. Additionally, the banks recognize the need for open public discussions from all interested parties before projects are implemented (Roessler 2000; Rosenberg and Korsmo 2001). The MDBs have moved in this direction by allowing public examination, independent evaluations, and discussion of environmental impact reports by local organizations that will be affected by projects being considered for funding (WRI 2003).

Because the MDBs are primarily financed by the governments of the major developed countries, their policies can be scrutinized by the elected representatives of the MDB member countries, the national media, and conservation organizations. Since past projects have been publicly criticized, the World Bank now requires new projects to be more environmentally responsible; they have hired ecological and environmental staff to review new and ongoing projects, conducted more thorough environmental analyses, and adopted a management policy that recognizes the linkages between economic development and environmental sustainability (World Bank 2000b; Bojö and Reddy 2003).

This new environmentalism recognizes that there is a high environmental cost for inappropriate economic policies, that reducing poverty is often crucial to protecting the environment, and that economic growth must incorporate environmental values. To implement this policy, the World Bank attempts to "mainstream" biodiversity conservation into many of its investments. On the positive side, this policy shift allows environmental costs and benefits to be included in policy decisions. On the negative side, more traditional biodiversity conservation activities, such as protected area management, are receiving decreased support. As a result of their increased concern with the environment, the World Bank and the other MDBs are now the greatest lending power globally for environmental projects, with much of the funding provided through the GEF. As of 2005, the World Bank has investments of $5.1 billion in hundreds of biodiversity projects in over 60 countries (World Bank 2005a). This increased biodiversity investment has attracted over $1 billion from other sources. Around 8% of its recent investments are for environmental projects, with a major focus on pollution abatement and control, but its investments also include funding for biodiversity conservation, forest management, and the conservation of natural resources. A recent trend is toward funding a larger number of smaller projects, which often have more specific goals and are managed on a local level.

For the remaining 92% of its recent investments, the World Bank requires environmental impact assessments as well as careful review by its environmental staff. Projects must include actions to mitigate their negative environmental impacts. Many conservation organizations remain skeptical that the World Bank will apply this new environmentalist policy to the bulk of its investments as time goes on (Vallette et al. 2004). Careful scrutiny of its actions in the future is required, particularly the lending done by the affiliated International Finance Corporation and import-export banks, which lend to the private sector. Conservation organizations must continue to monitor the funding decisions of the MDBs and the projects they undertake rather than only heeding their speeches and reports; the MDBs have proven to be extremely effective at public relations even as they continue with business as usual (Roessler 2000; www.globalpolicy.org). It should also be noted that the MDBs have no enforcement authority: Once they hand part of the money over for a project, countries can choose to ignore the environmental provisions in an agreement despite local and international protests. In such instances, one of the MDBs' few effective options is to cancel further stages of funding for these projects and delay new projects.

One important project to watch is the mammoth Hidrovia Project in South America, in which the Paraguay-Parana River is being dredged and channeled so that large ships can carry cargo from Buenos Aires on the Argentina coast 3000 km north into Bolivia, Paraguay, and Brazil, and then return carrying soybeans and other agricultural products from southern Brazil to world markets (Harris et al. 2005). This river system drains the Pantanal in South America, the world's largest wetland, covering nearly 200,000 km² in southwestern Brazil, eastern Bolivia, and northeastern Paraguay—an area larger than England, Wales, and the Netherlands combined (Figure 21.13). The wetland consists of a vast, unspoiled everglades, fabulously rich in endangered wildlife such as jaguars, tapirs, maned wolves, and giant otters. Environmentalists believe the Hidrovia Project will completely alter the hydrology of the area—submerging some areas, drying out others—and lead to an enormous loss of biological diversity. In Argentina, unprecedented flooding downriver could result, though maintenance of wetlands could minimize some of the adverse impacts. The final cost of the project is estimated to be $1 billion, with $3 billion in added maintenance costs over the next 25 years. As part of the total project, a natural gas pipeline from Bolivia to the coast of Brazil is currently being constructed, along with associated steel and petrochemical plants, with unknown environmental consequences to the region. Funding, publicity, and opposition to the project all go through cycles—the project moves forward, is stalled for a time, then starts again in a somewhat different form. On the positive side, the World Bank and conservation NGOs have been establishing Biosphere Reserves and new national parks in the area to protect some of the region's rich biodiversity.

The MDBs have shown some commitment to reducing environmental degradation. For example, in Papua New Guinea, the World Bank refused to provide development loans until the government carried out a number of measures that would ensure more prudent forest management practices, which led to a full review of forestry practices and a subsequent moratorium on opening additional areas for logging. Unfortunately, another trend is for the World Bank and the MDBs to finance "clean" projects that can be publicly justified on environmental and social

FIGURE 21.13 The Pantanal in South America is the world's largest wetland. This area is now being transformed by an enormous project involving improved river transportation, industrial development, and the expansion of soybean agriculture. (Photograph © Blickwinkel/Alamy.)

grounds, while the far larger import-export banks quietly support the huge projects that damage the environment and benefit large corporations. Given that the MDBs have funded some dubious projects, a vital role for conservation biologists is to track and report true environmental impacts. Improving transparency will help ensure that the MDBs pursue an environmentally responsible strategy in the future.

Increased Funding Is Necessary for the Future

The need for increased funding for biodiversity remains great at the local, national, and international levels. At present, about $6.5 billion is spent each year on budgets for terrestrial protected areas, yet $23 billion would be required for expanding and effectively managing global protected area systems to adequately protect the world's terrestrial biological diversity (James et al. 2001; Balmford and Whitten 2003). Simply managing the existing protected areas in developing countries alone would cost perhaps $2.1 billion, approximately 3 times the current expenditure (Bruner et al. 2004). While $23 billion is an enormous amount of money, it is small relative to the whopping $245 billion spent each year on agricultural subsidies in the United States and the $1 trillion spent on U.S. military defense. Certainly the world's priorities could be modestly adjusted to give more resources to the protection of biological diversity. Instead of countries rushing forward in a race to supply themselves with the next generation of fighter aircraft, missiles, and other weapons systems, what about spending what it takes to protect biological diversity? Instead of the world's affluent consumers buying the latest round of consumer luxuries and electronic gadgets to replace things that still work, what about contributing more money to conservation organizations and causes?

There is also a role to be played by conservation organizations and businesses working together to market "green products." Already the Forest Stewardship Council and similar organizations are certifying wood products from sustainably managed forests, and coffee companies are marketing shade-grown coffee. If consumers are educated to buy these products at a somewhat higher price, this could be a strong force in international conservation efforts.

Summary

1. International agreements and conventions that protect biological diversity are needed for the following reasons: species migrate across borders, there is an international trade in biological products, the benefits of biological diversity are of international importance, and the threats to diversity are often international in scope and require international cooperation. The Convention on International Trade in Endangered Species (CITES) regulates and monitors trade in endangered species; in some cases, all trade is prohibited. Other international agreements protect habitat, such as the Ramsar Convention on Wetlands, the World Heritage Convention, and the UNESCO Biosphere Reserves Program.

2. Six major environmental documents were signed at the 1992 Earth Summit, the most important of which are the Convention on Biological Diversity, which gives countries the rights to biological diversity within their borders, but the responsibility to protect it; and the Convention on Global Climate Change, which establishes targets for stabilizing and reducing emissions of CO_2 and other greenhouse gases. Park management and the rights of local people have been the subject of further meetings.

3. Multilateral development banks, such as the World Bank, and conservation groups and governments in developed countries are providing substantial funding to protect biological diversity in developing countries. While the increased levels of international funding are welcome, the amount of money is still not sufficient to deal with the loss of biological diversity that is taking place.

4. Innovative approaches are being developed to finance the preservation of biodiversity. One approach involves setting up national environmental funds (NEFs) in which the annual income from an endowment is used to finance conservation activities. A second approach involves debt-for-nature swaps, in which the foreign debt obligations of a government are canceled in exchange for the government providing increased conservation funding.

5. Major new development projects approved by the World Bank, and the closely associated Global Environment Facility, now include reviews and funding to address environmental and social issues. Due to the huge impact of World Bank funding, and past problems with some of their projects, environmental groups are closely monitoring their activities.

For Discussion

1. Imagine that Brazil, Indonesia, China, or India builds an expensive dam to provide electricity and water for irrigation. The project will take decades to pay back the costs of construction and lost ecosystem services—or it may never pay back those costs. Who are the winners with such a project, and who are the losers? Consider the local people who had to move, newly arrived settlers, construction companies, timber companies, local banks, international banks, the urban poor, government leaders, environmental organizations, and anyone else that you think will be affected. Consider also the animals and plants that lived in the watershed before the dam was built. Can they survive in the same region? Can they migrate to another place?

2. Are poverty and the conservation of biological diversity linked, and if so, how? Should these problems be attacked together or separately?

3. How do national governments decide on an acceptable amount of money to spend on protecting biological diversity? How much money should a particular country

spend on protecting biological diversity? Can you calculate an amount? What are the most cost-effective measures governments can take to protect biological diversity?

4. Suppose a species was discovered in Peru that could potentially cure a major disease affecting millions of people if it were grown on a large scale in cultivation and then widely marketed. If the government of Peru did not show interest in protecting this wonderful species, what could the international community do to protect the species and to fairly compensate the country for doing so? Come up with a variety of offers, suggestions, or alternatives that could be used to convince the government and people of Peru to protect the species and to become involved in its commercial development.

5. Do you think that the purchase of "green," environmentally responsible products is an effective way to promote the conservation of biodiversity? Would people be willing to spend more money for wood, coffee, and other products that have been produced in a sustainable manner, and if so, how much more? How could you determine if the purchase of such products was really making a difference?

Suggested Readings

Balmford, A., and T. Whitten. 2003. Who should pay for tropical conservation, and how could the costs be met? *Oryx* 37: 238–250. Developing countries need to pay more.

Blundell, A. G., and M. B. Mascia. 2005. Discrepancies in reported levels of international wildlife trade. *Conservation Biology* 19: 2020–2025. Illegal wildlife trade represents a huge challenge for conservation biologists.

Bruner, A. G., R. E. Gullison, and A. Balmford. 2004. Financial costs and shortfalls of managing and expanding protected-area systems in developing countries. *BioScience* 54: 1119–1126. Budgets for managing protected areas in developing countries are inadequate and need to be increased.

Godwin, P. 2001. Wildlife without borders. *National Geographic* 200: 2–31. Potential benefits and problems of establishing transfrontier protected areas.

Halpern, B. S., C. R. Pyke, H. E. Fox, J. C. Haney, M. A. Schlaepfer, and P. Zaradic. Gaps and mismatches between global conservation priorities and spending. *Conservation Biology* 20: 56–64. Conservation organizations are not yet able to present a coherent picture for their funding priorities.

Harris, M. B., W. Tomas, G. Mourao, C. J. Da Silva, E. Gumaraes, F. Sonoda, and E. Fachim. 2005. Safeguarding the Pantanal wetlands: Threats and conservation initiatives. *Conservation Biology* 19: 714–720. One of the world's great wetlands is being transformed by human activities.

Lapham, N. P., and R. J. Livermore. 2003. *Striking a Balance: Ensuring Conservation's Place on the International Biodiversity Agenda.* Conservation International, Washington, D.C. Money for conservation is needed for progress to be made.

Laurance, W. F., M. A. Cochrane, S. Bergen, P. M. Fearnside, et al. 2001. The future of the Brazilian Amazon. *Science* 291: 438–439. Road construction in the Amazon will lead to the rapid loss of forest cover.

Lee, R. 2005. Unholy trinity: The IMF, World Bank, and WTO. *Economic Geography* 81: 441–443. Many people are skeptical of the World Bank and its activities.

Naughton-Treves, L., M. B. Holland, and K. Brandon. 2005. The role of protected areas in conserving biodiversity and sustaining local livelihoods. *Annual Review of Environmental Resources* 30: 219–252. Discussion of a major controversy: Should protected areas exist for biodiversity or for the benefit of people?

Pedynowski, D. 2003. Prospects for ecosystem management in the Crown of the Continent ecosystem, Canada-United States: Survey and recommendations. *Conservation Biology* 17: 1261–1269. The Canadian government is now managing biodiversity at large spatial scales.

Pergams, O. R., B. Czech, J. C. Haney, and D. Nyberg. 2004. Linkage of conservation activity to trends in the U.S. economy. *Conservation Biology* 18: 1617–1623. Funding for conservation has increased dramatically over the last few decades.

Poole, A. 1996. *Coming of Age with Elephants: A Memoir.* Hyperion, New York. Personal account of how studies of elephants in Kenya led to involvement in their protection.

Sayer, J., N. Ishwaran, J. Thorsell, and T. Sigaty. 2000. Tropical forest biodiversity and the World Heritage Convention. *Ambio* 29: 302–309. The Convention provides a powerful international approach for protecting biodiversity.

Soares-Filho, B. S., D. C. Nepstad, L. M. Curran, G. C. Cerqueira, et al. 2006. Modelling conservation in the Amazon basin. *Nature* 440: 520–523. The rapid expansion of highways and agriculture will eliminate 40% of the Amazon basin's forests by the year 2050.

Stem, C., R. Margoluis, N. Salafsky, and M. Brown. 2005. Monitoring and evaluation in conservation: A review of trends and approaches. *Conservation Biology* 19: 295–309. Conservation organizations would benefit from cooperating in project evaluation to see what works best.

Totten, M., S. I. Pandya, and T. Janson-Smith. 2003. Biodiversity, climate, and the Kyoto Protocol: Risks and opportunities. *Frontiers in Ecology and the Environment* 1: 262–270. The United States and many other countries are ignoring the threats that climate change poses.

Valette, J., D. Wysham, and N. Martinez. 2004. *A Wrong Turn From Rio: The World Bank's Road to Climate Catastrophe.* Sustainable Energy & Economy Network, Washington, D. C. Many environmental groups are strongly critical of World Bank Activities.

World Bank. 2006. *Mountains to Coral Reefs. The World Bank and Biodiversity* 1988–2005. World Bank, Washington, D.C. An official statement of the World Bank's efforts on behalf of the environment; see earlier reports and related documents.

Wu, J., J. Huang, X. Han, X. Gao, F. He, M. Jiang, et al. 2004. The Three Gorges Dam: An ecological perspective. *Frontiers in Ecology and the Environment* 2: 241–248. A giant project with enormous environmental and social impacts.

An Agenda for the Future

As we have seen throughout this book, there is no mystery as to why biological diversity is showing a rapid, worldwide decline. Biological communities are destroyed and species are driven to extinction because of human resource use, which is propelled by the need of poor people to survive, by the excessive consumption of resources by affluent people and countries, and by the desire to make money (Myers and Kent 2004; Sachs 2005). The destruction may be caused by local people in the region, people recently arrived from outside the region, local business interests, large businesses in urban centers, suburban sprawl into rural areas, multinational corporations in other countries, military conflicts, or governments. People may also be unaware of the impact of human activities on the natural world, or they may be apathetic. In order for conservation policies to work, people at all levels of society must see that it is in their own interest to work for conservation (Cullen et al. 2005; Charnley 2006). If conservationists can demonstrate that the protection of biological diversity has more value than its destruction, people and their governments will be more willing to preserve biological diversity. This assessment should include not only immediate monetary value, but also less tangible aspects, including existence value, option value, and intrinsic value.

Ongoing Problems and Possible Solutions

There is a consensus among conservation biologists that there are a number of major problems involved in preserving biological diversity and that certain changes in policies and practices are needed. We list these problems, and suggested solutions, below. Note that, for the purposes of this text, the responses are simplified; they leave out many of the intricacies that would need to be addressed to provide comprehensive, real-world answers to these problems.

Problem: Protecting biological diversity is difficult when most of the world's species remain undescribed by scientists and are not known by the general public. Furthermore, most biological communities are not being monitored to determine how they are changing over time.

Solution: More scientists and enthusiastic nonscientists need to be trained to identify, classify, and monitor species and biological communities, and funding should be increased in this area (Raven and Wilson 1992; Goffredo et al. 2004; Main 2004; Evans et al. 2005). There is a particular need for training more scientists and establishing research institutes in developing countries. Enthusiastic nonscientists often can play an important role in protecting biodiversity once they are given some training and guidance by scientists. People interested in conservation biology should be taught basic skills, such as species identification and environmental monitoring techniques, and such people will often join and support local, national, and international conservation organizations (Box 22.1). Two particular groups that are especially responsive to conservation education are school children and senior citizens (Jacobson et al. 2005). Information on biological diversity must be made more accessible; this may be accomplished in part through the new Global Biodiversity Information Facility (Lane 2003; www.gbif.org), which is serving as a central clearinghouse for data from 47 countries and is accessible via the Internet.

BOX 22.1

Conservation Education: Shaping the Next Generation into Conservationists

Television, newspapers, and the Internet are filled with high-profile information regarding the importance of protecting the Earth on a daily basis, yet most people know relatively little about conservation. One of the best ways to educate people about conservation is to involve them in local conservation projects. Such efforts involving direct outreach to ordinary citizens require creativity and attention to popular concerns yet sometimes they can be successful (Jacobson et al. 2006).

For example, community residents in the Gulf of Saint Lawrence have traditionally lived by fishing and collecting seabird eggs for food. Unfortunately for the endangered birds in the area, community residents continued to feast on bird eggs even though it was no longer a necessary food source. As a result of human predation, seabird populations were in steep decline (Blanchard 2005). Between 1955 and 1978, populations of the Atlantic Puffin decreased from about 62,000 individuals to around 15,000.

The Quebec-Labrador Foundation, working with the Canadian Wildlife Service in their quest to save endangered seabirds, realized that the only way to save the seabirds was to convince the public to stop consuming birds and their eggs. Their plan included education programs for children, who participated in clubs and theatre productions that addressed the plight of the seabirds. Children aged 8 to 17 spent five days at Saint Mary Islands Sanctuary learning to appreciate seabirds through interactive activities. These children were crucial in convincing their parents to protect birds, reaching out to adults by performing a play about the importance of conservation. The foundation turned to the media in its education program, producing television specials and making posters and calendars. The Canadian Wildlife Service contributed by hiring local townspeople to work in the seabird conservation program.

A few years after this program commenced, it became clear that the Quebec-Labrador Foundation had been successful in educating the public about seabird conservation. While 54% of locals supported hunting the Atlantic Puffin in 1981, this number dropped to 27% as early as

BOX 22.1 *(continued)*

1988. Due in part to reduced hunting and egg collecting, the population of Atlantic Puffins in the Gulf of St. Lawrence more than doubled from 1977 to 1988.

Another water bird, the West Indian Whistling-Duck, is an example of how a species can become a flagship for wetlands conservation. These ducks have become rare in their native Caribbean island habitats due to combined effects of wetland habitat loss, overhunting, and predation by introduced rats and mongoose (Sorenson et al. 2004). Because wetlands have long been regarded as marginal land to be filled in and developed, conservationists with the Society for the Conservation and Study of Caribbean Birds recognized that the first step to saving this species was changing perceptions of the duck's habitat. With support from local and international NGOs and the U.S. Fish and Wildlife Service, a region-wide public education and awareness program was developed to train local teachers and educators to raise awareness of and appreciation for the value of local wetlands. The project developed and distributed a teacher's manual called the *Wondrous West Indian Wetlands: Teachers' Resource Book* that contains comprehensive information and educational activities relating to the ecology and conservation of Caribbean wetlands. Companion materials include a slide show, puppet show, poster, coloring book, conservation buttons, postcard, wetland field trip notebook, mangrove identification booklet, and wetland and seabird identification cards. These materials provided teachers with the essential tools needed to incorporate conservation themes into their classrooms and reach an enormous number of schoolchildren and their parents. One teacher's comment conveys the reaction of many: "This wetland workshop was a very interesting experience for me. Prior to the workshop I viewed wetlands as murky, stagnant, mosquito-infested areas to be avoided. Now I am fully aware of their importance to the environment." The educational materials and associated workshops have helped to raise the profile of the duck, which now has increased species and habitat protection in many Caribbean islands; this has, in turn, positively affected the duck's populations, which on several islands are now stable or increasing (Sorenson et al. 2004).

Education in the schools should include learning about the local environment, but too often, academic demands preclude the chance to study the natural world outside the

Bahamian schoolteachers try out a plant sampling technique during the wetlands field trip portion of the Wetlands Education Training Workshop. (Photograph courtesy of Lisa Sorenson, West Indies Whistling-Duck and Wetlands Conservation Project.)

classroom door. When conservation education links academic demands to the study of the natural and social systems and their interactions, the winners include students, teachers, administrators, and conservation. To implement conservation education within schools, a variety of approaches are available, such as environment-based education, service learning, and action projects (Jacobson 2006). The Global Rivers Environmental Education Network (GREEN) exemplifies an effective action project that demonstrates the importance of a practical, hands-on approach to teach environmental messages. This program has allowed children in over 60 countries to learn about pollution, with an emphasis on water quality, and to help protect local water reserves. GREEN began when students at Huron High School in Michigan contracted hepatitis A after participating in water sports in the Huron River. To investigate the source of the disease, students tested the river water and found large amounts of fecal coliform bacteria that indicate the presence of untreated sewage. The city identified defective storm drains as the cause of the problem, and these were subsequently repaired.

Many other schools enthusiastically adopted this program, eventually expanding GREEN into a global environmental network in which parents and teachers are con-

(continued)

BOX 22.1 *(continued)*

nected through the Internet (Earth Force 2005). Through the GREEN website, teachers can access resources on teaching students about water quality research and schools can post data they have collected from local watersheds. The program urges students to think critically about the possible causes of water pollution and to "take action" by urging the community to stop pollution (Earth Force 2005). GREEN not only teaches children about science, it shapes a new generation of children into activists. At a middle school in Denver, Colorado, for

instance, students identified the diesel fuel used by school buses as a major local air pollutant and petitioned the school district to switch to a safer form of fuel such as biodiesel (Earth Force 2005).

Public education programs such as those described here have proven to be effective in teaching children about science and encouraging people to protect environmental resources. These programs would greatly benefit from increased participation from conservation biologists.

Problem: Many conservation issues are global in scope, and involve many countries.

Solution: Countries are increasingly willing to discuss international conservation issues, as shown by the 1992 Earth Summit, the 1997 Climate Change Conference in Kyoto, and the 2002 Sustainability Conference in South Africa. Nations are also more willing to sign and implement treaties such as the Convention on Biological Diversity, the Convention on Global Climate Change, and the Convention on International Trade in Endangered Species. International conservation efforts are expanding, and further participation in these activities by conservation biologists and the general public should be encouraged. One positive development is the trend toward establishing transfrontier parks that straddle borders; these parks are good for wildlife and encourage cooperation between countries. Citizens and governments of developed countries must also become aware that they bear a direct responsibility for the destruction of biological diversity through their overconsumption of the world's resources and the specific products that they purchase (Figure 22.1). Conservation professionals need to demonstrate how changes in the actions and lifestyles of individuals on the local level can have a positive influence far beyond their immediate community.

Problem: Developing countries often want to protect their biological diversity but are under pressure to develop their natural resources.

Solution: Conservation organizations, zoos, aquariums, botanical gardens, and governments in developed countries and international organizations such as the United Nations and the World Bank should continue to provide technical and financial support to developing countries for conservation activities, in particular establishing and maintaining national parks and other protected areas. This support should continue until countries are able to protect biodiversity with their own resources. This is fair and reasonable since developed countries have the funds to support these parks and make use of the protected biological resources in their agriculture, industry, research programs, zoos, aquariums, botanical gardens, and educational systems. Economic and social problems in developing countries must be addressed at the same time, particularly those relating to poverty and war. Reducing or forgiving foreign debt payments, debt-for-nature swaps, and environmental trust funds may be additional mechanisms to achieve these goals. Individual citizens can donate money and participate in organizations that further advance these conservation goals. Educational programs need to be developed to train conservation biologists in developing countries (Bonine et al. 2003).

FIGURE 22.1 In one year, an average U.S. family of four with a typical American lifestyle consumes approximately 3785 liters (1000 gallons) of oil, shown here in barrels, for fueling its two cars and heating its home. The same family burns about 2270 kg (5000 pounds) of coal, shown here in a pile in the right foreground, to generate the electricity to power lights, refrigerators, air conditioners, and other home appliances. The air and water pollution that results from this consumption of resources directly harms biological diversity, and creates an "ecological footprint" that extends far beyond their home. Regulating such consumption must be addressed in a comprehensive conservation strategy at individual, local, regional, national, and global scales. (Photograph by Robert Schoen/ Northeast Sustainable Energy Association.)

Problem: Economic analyses often paint a falsely encouraging picture of development projects that are environmentally damaging.

Solution: Development projects must be evaluated using comprehensive cost–benefit analyses that compare potential project benefits with environmental and human costs such as soil erosion, loss of natural products, loss of tourist potential, and loss of places for people to live. Better analyses of development options and alternatives are needed; these can be pursued by conservation organizations and financial institutions such as the World Bank within their policy dialogues with countries. Local communities and the general public should be presented with this information and asked to provide input into the decision process.

Problem: Ecosystem services are often not assigned value in economic decision-making.

Solution: Economic activities that affect the environment should be linked to the maintenance of ecosystem services through payment of fees, penalties, and the establishment of nearby protected areas. Industry and human communities must become morally and financially responsible for the resources that they use and the pollution that they cause. The "polluter pays" principle must be adopted, in which industries, governments, and individual citizens pay for cleaning up the environmental damage their activities have caused (Wolbarts 2001). Steps in this direction are the increased rates utilities are now charging customers for water and sewer use, rates that better reflect the actual costs of providing these services. Agricultural practices should be encouraged that reduce nitrogen run-off, improve water use efficiency, maintain soil quality, and encourage wildlife, while at the same time increasing yield (Green et al. 2005). Financial subsidies to industries that damage the environment—such as the pesticide, transportation, petrochemical, logging, fishing, and tobacco industries—should end, particularly to the industries that damage human health as well. Those funds should be redirected to activities that enhance the environment and human well-being, in particular to people whose lands are providing ecosystem services to the public.

Problem: Poor people who are simply trying to survive are frequently blamed for the destruction of the world's biological diversity.

Solution: Changing the government policies that act as the "root causes of biodiversity loss" can improve conservation and the lives of local people. In many cases, this involves better zoning of land uses and enforcement of environmental laws. In places where local actions are leading to losses, conservationists can help bring in the development and humanitarian organizations with the skills to assist local people in organizing and developing sustainable economic activities that do not damage biological diversity. Conservation biologists and conservation organizations are increasing their participation in programs for poor rural areas that promote smaller families, a more reliable food supply, and more training in economically useful skills. These programs should be closely linked to efforts aimed at improving economic opportunities, recognizing basic human rights, and halting environmental degradation (Hollander 2003; Picolotti and Taillant 2003; Sachs 2005).

There is also a role to be played by conservation organizations and businesses working together to market "green products," with some of the profits shared by rural communities. Already the Forest Stewardship Council and similar organizations are certifying wood products that derive from sustainably managed forests, and coffee companies are marketing shade-grown coffee (TransFair U.S.A. 2004; Bacon 2005; Gulbrandsen 2005). Aquariums and ocean conservation organizations are developing lists of seafood that are harvested unsustainably and should be avoided (Kaiser and Edward-Jones 2006). Collectively this is sometimes termed Fairtrade Labeling and includes 400 organizations (WRI 2005). If consumers are educated to buy these certified products (even if they are somewhat higher in price than noncertified products), their purchases could be a strong force in local and international conservation efforts and provide tangible benefits to poor people in rural areas.

Problem: Decisions about land conservation and the establishment of protected areas are often made by central governments with little input from people and local organizations in the region being affected. Consequently, local people sometimes feel alienated from conservation projects and do not support them.

Solution: In order for a conservation project to be successful, it is imperative that local people believe that they will benefit from it and that their involvement is important. To achieve this goal, environmental impact statements and other project information should be publicly available to encourage open discussion at all steps of a project. Local people should be provided with whatever assistance they may need in order to understand and evaluate the implications of the project being presented to them. Local people often want to protect biodiversity and associated ecosystem services because they know that their own survival depends on the protection of the natural environment (MEA 2005b). Mechanisms should be established to ensure that the rights, responsibilities, and if possible, the decisions for management are shared between government agencies, conservation organizations, and local communities and businesses (Salafsky et al. 2001b). Conservation biologists working in national parks should periodically explain the purpose and results of their work to nearby communities and school groups and listen to what the local people have to say. In some cases, a regional strategy such as a habitat conservation plan or a natural community conservation plan may have to be developed to reconcile the need for some development (and resulting loss of habitat) with the need to protect species and biological communities.

Problem: Revenues, business activities, and scientific research associated with national parks and other protected areas do not directly benefit the surrounding communities.

Solution: Whenever possible, local people should be trained and employed in parks as a way of utilizing local knowledge and providing income. A portion of park revenues should be used to fund local community projects such as schools, clinics, roads, cultural activities, sports programs and facilities, and community businesses—infrastructure that benefits a whole village, town, or region; this establishes a link between conservation programs and the improvement of local lives.

Problem: National parks and conservation areas often have inadequate budgets to pay for conservation activities.

Solution: It is often possible to increase funds for park management by raising rates for admission, lodging, or meals so that rates reflect the actual cost of maintaining the area. Concessions selling goods and services may be required to contribute a percentage of their income to the park's operation. Also, zoos and conservation organizations in the developed world should continue to make direct financial contributions to conservation efforts in developing countries. For example, members of the American Zoo and Aquarium Association and their partners participate in over 700 in situ conservation projects in 80 countries worldwide.

Problem: Many endangered species and biological communities are on private land and on government land that is managed for timber production, grazing, mining, and other activities. Timber companies that lease forests and ranchers that rent rangeland from the government often damage biological diversity and reduce the productive capacity of the land in pursuit of short-term profits. Private landowners often regard endangered species on their land as restrictions on the use of it.

Solution: Change the laws so that people can obtain leases to harvest trees and use rangelands only as long as the health of the biological community is maintained (Davis and Wali 1994). Eliminate tax subsidies that encourage the overexploitation of natural resources, and establish payments for land management, especially on private land, that enhances conservation efforts (Losos et al. 1995; Environmental Defense 2000). Alternatively, educate landowners to protect endangered species and praise them publicly for their efforts. Develop connections among farmers, ranchers, conservation biologists, and perhaps even hunting groups, because biodiversity, wildlife, and the rural way of life are all threatened by the process of economic growth.

Problem: In many countries, governments are inefficient and are bound by excessive regulation. Consequently, governments are often slow and ineffective at protecting biological communities.

Solution: Local NGOs (nongovernment organizations) and citizen groups are often the most effective agents for promoting conservation. Accordingly, these groups should be encouraged and supported politically, scientifically, and financially. Conservation biologists need to educate citizens about local environmental issues and encourage them to take action when necessary. Building the capacity of universities, the national media, and NGOs to evaluate, propose, and implement policies is also an effective way to encourage national-level action. New foundations should be started by individuals, organizations, and businesses to financially support conservation efforts (WRI 2003). One of the most important trends in conservation funding and policy is the increased strength of international NGOs, such as the World Wide Fund for Nature (with 4.5 million members) and the Royal Society for the Protection of Birds (with a membership of 1 million). The number of NGOs has risen dramatically in past decades, and the ability of NGOs to influence local conservation programs and environmental policy at the national and international levels is often substantial (WRI 2003).

Problem: Many businesses, banks, and governments are uninterested in and unresponsive to conservation issues.

Solution: Leaders may become more willing to support conservation efforts once they receive additional information. In countries with fairly open societies, lobbying and similar efforts may also be effective in changing the policies of unresponsive institutions, because most will want to avoid bad publicity. Petitions, rallies, letter-writing campaigns, and economic boycotts all have their place when requests for change are ignored (Box 22.2). In many situations, radical environmental groups such as Greenpeace and EarthFirst! dominate media attention with dramatic, publicity-grabbing actions, while mainstream conservation organizations follow behind to negotiate a compromise. In closed societies, identifying and educating key leaders is usually a better strategy.

BOX 22.2

Environmental Activism Confronts the Opposition

The past two decades have witnessed a tremendous increase in popular awareness of environmental issues (Gore 1992; Rohrman 2004). Many conservation organizations such as the Sierra Club, the World Wildlife Fund, and The Nature Conservancy, to name only a few, have gained hundreds of thousands of new members while attempting to achieve conservation goals within the current political and social systems. Other organizations have tried to take a more direct approach: Greenpeace International, with approximately 2.8 million members and an annual budget of around $100 million, actively protects environmental destruction. The surge in environmental activism, however, has triggered a disturbing backlash from those industries, business interests, labor organizations, and even some governments that resent and fear any restrictions on the exploitation of natural resources (Motavelli 1995; Ehrlich and Ehrlich 1996; Rohrman 2004). Conservation of natural resources may be linked, in some peoples' minds, to a loss in profits and job opportunities. When people fear losing their jobs or businesses because of conservation measures, they direct their anger

Greenpeace ships have attracted global media attention during high-profile confrontations with ships involved in illegal fishing and whaling operations or other activities considered by them to be immoral. (Photograph courtesy of Greenpeace.)

at environmental activists. This tends to be more prevalent in a slow economy. Incidents of intimidation, threats, and physical harassment, sometimes frighteningly

BOX 22.2 *(continued)*

violent, have been reported worldwide by environmental activists.

Perhaps the best-known violent incident occurred in 1988, when Chico Mendes, a Brazilian activist organizing rubber tappers to resist the encroachment of cattle ranching and logging in the Amazon rain forest, was assassinated by ranchers. Mendes's martyrdom created a worldwide uproar and focused global attention on the destruction of the rain forest. Many other environmental and social activists in Brazil have been beaten or killed, both before and since Mendes's death. Most recently, in February 2005, Dorothy Stang, a 74-year-old nun working selflessly on behalf of poor rural workers and forest protection, was assassinated in the state of Pará after receiving death threats and no government protection.

In many countries, people who protest destructive activities have been branded as subversives, traitors, or foreign agents by their own governments for fighting government policies that promote unrestricted development at the expense of the environment. In 1995, nine environmental activists were hanged in Nigeria after a secret trial; they were members of the Ogoni tribe, whose land is being destroyed by a massive oil production operation sanctioned by the Nigerian government. Such incidents occur even in countries considered progressive with regard to conservation.

Individual activists fighting industrial pollution and the destruction of important biological communities in North America, Europe, and other developed countries have also been victims of persecution, ranging from arson to assault to attempted murder. On occasion, authorities responsible for investigating the crimes have responded with either indifference or overt antagonism toward the victims. In a famous incident, French government agents were convicted in the 1985 bombing in New Zealand of the Greenpeace flagship *Rainbow Warrior,* in which a crew member died. The ship was being readied to leave for the South Pacific to protest the French nuclear weapons testing program.

In Northern California, members of Earth First! have staged many nonviolent protests against logging in a 24,000-ha region known as the Headwaters Forest. This area is one of the last remaining unprotected old-growth redwood forests and is a home for the federally endangered marbled murrelet. Clear-cutting of trees on steep

Demonstrations such as this protest led by Julia "Butterfly" Hill against the extensive logging of old-growth forests in northern California can focus media attention on environmental problems that society must not ignore. This demonstration is peaceful, but other environmental demonstrations have been confrontational and even violent. (Photograph by Shaun Walker.)

slopes has led to massive landslides, destroying homes and silting up streams. Protesters from Earth First! and other groups have been arrested for trespassing, have had their eyes dabbed with painful pepper spray by police, and have been threatened with violence by area residents. In 1997, national media attention was drawn to a young, articulate woman, Julia "Butterfly" Hill, who decided to protest the logging by sitting and living in a tall, 1000-year-old redwood tree she named "Luna" until the logging company agreed to end cutting in the Headwaters region. After two years in the tree and ever-increasing levels of publicity and tension, Hill finally descended from her tree perch when the logging company agreed to stop logging in some of the old-growth forests (Hill 2001). Earth First! regards this as only a partial victory on the way to complete conservation protection for the Headwaters Forest, and protests and tree-sits continue.

The publicity created by her tree-sitting allowed Hill to establish an environmental group, the Circle of Life, which promotes an outlook on life that could be described as a variation of Deep Ecology. Their activities include environmental festivals, tours, campaigns, and social justice. The goal of the group is to "transform the way humans interact with the Earth and all living beings" (www.circleoflife-foundation.org).

(continued)

BOX 22.2 *(continued)*

Environmental activists work to persuade or force society to accept the limitations that must be imposed on human consumption if a healthy biosphere is to survive. Activists interested in protecting the environment and biological diversity are joining the entire spectrum of organizations, from mainstream political parties that work within the system, including newly formed Green Parties, to hard-line confrontational groups. In some cases, this has meant undertaking acts of civil disobedience, such as blocking trucks and occupying trees to stop the chain saw. This is sometimes referred to as "passionate activism" by its proponents, and "ecoterrorism" by its opponents. In a few extreme cases, protestors have engaged in ecosabotage, de-

stroying vehicles and buildings (Rohrman 2004). Business organizations and conservative elements in society are increasingly lobbying and forming action groups to counter conservation groups. In one such development, a law has been proposed in the U.S. called Stop Terrorism of Property (STOP) to prevent the destruction of property for environmental purposes. In an interesting twist, these prodevelopment groups often use environmental rhetoric to argue for the "wise use" of natural resources. "Wise use" in this case often refers to unlimited grazing, logging, mining, oil and natural gas drilling, and other unrestricted resource utilization that degrades the environment.

The Role of Conservation Biologists

The problems and solutions we just discussed underscore the importance of conservation biologists—they will be the primary participants in solving these problems. Conservation biology differs from many other scientific disciplines in that it plays an active role in the preservation of biological diversity in all its forms: species, genetic variability, biological communities, and ecosystem functions. Members of the diverse disciplines that contribute to conservation biology share the common goal of protecting biological diversity in practice, rather than simply investigating it and talking about it (Barry and Oelschlaeger 1996; Robertson and Hull 2001). However, they must work together to provide practical solutions that can be used to deal with real-world situations (Fazey et al. 2005).

Challenges for Conservation Biologists

The ideas and theories of conservation biology are increasingly being incorporated into decisions about park management and species protection. At the same time, botanical gardens, museums, nature centers, zoos, national parks, and aquariums are reorienting their programs to meet the challenges of protecting biological diversity. The need for large parks and the need to protect large populations of endangered species are two particular topics that have received widespread attention in both academic and popular literature. The vulnerability of small populations to local extinction, even when they are carefully protected and managed, and the alarming rates of species extinction and destruction of unique biological communities worldwide have also been highly publicized. As a result of this publicity, the need to protect biological diversity is entering political debate and has been targeted as a priority for government conservation programs. What is ultimately required, however, is to get the principles of conservation biology into the broader domestic policy arena and the economic planning process (Box 22.3) (Czech 2002; Soulé and Orians 2002). Incorporating conservation biology into economic policy or re-prioritizing domestic policy goals will take substantial public education and political effort.

One of the most serious challenges facing conservation biology is reconciling the needs of local people and the need to preserve biological diversity. How can poor people—particularly in the developing world but also in rural areas of developed countries—be convinced to forego the exploitation of nature reserves and biological diversity when they are desperate to obtain the food, wood, and other natural products that they need for their daily survival? Park managers in particular need

BOX 22.3

What Will Our World be Like in 2050?

Most environmental studies analyze a particular project, industry, place, or region. However, scientists have recently initiated large efforts to assess environmental changes on a global scale. For example, the Intergovernmental Panel on Climate Change (IPCC), which produced its first report in 1990, considers the full range of causes and consequences of climate change worldwide. Designed in a similar mold, the Millennium Ecosystem Assessment (MEA) was conceived as a multi-year, international effort to document changes in ecosystem services, how they are affecting and will continue to affect people, and how people might mitigate detrimental changes (MEA 2005). Thousands of scientists, economists, and social scientists participated. As a part of its effort to examine how ecosystem services will continue to change and how people might respond, the MEA developed four scenarios for how societies, economies, and the environment might plausibly change over the next 50 years (MEA 2005a). These scenarios are not predictions; instead, they allow scientists and decision-makers to explore the likely environmental and human consequences of plausible changes in various driving forces such as population and economic growth, advances in technology, and changes in governance. The scenarios explore how global trade, industry and agriculture, human welfare, and international cooperation might reasonably be expected to behave over time, and outline various approaches that might be used to address resulting environmental problems.

(A) Order from Strength

(B) Global Orchestration

(C) Adapting Mosaic

(D) TechnoGarden

Four potential scenarios for the future and how they will affect the world's ecosystems and people. (Drawings courtesy of Millenium Ecosystem Assessment 2005.)

The Order from Strength scenario depicts a fragmented world concerned with security and regional markets that fix environmental problems after they occur.

The Global Orchestration scenario describes a global society with reduced world trade barriers coupled with strong investments to reduce poverty and promote social well-being. As in the Order from Strength scenario, this society fixes environmental problems after they happen.

The Adaptive Mosaic scenario portrays a strongly regionalized society that emphasizes regional eco-system management and economic activity, with an emphasis on maintaining ecosystem health.

The TechnoGarden scenario describes a highly managed, globally connected world that uses technology to maintain ecosystem health.

To many observers, the Order from Strength scenario appears most similar to the trajectory of our current modern world, although each scenario begins with similar conditions around the year 2000. It is also the most detrimental to both environmental health and human well-being. The Global Orchestration scenario represents what many conservation organizations and development agencies view as an improvement over our current situation and an attainable goal. The Adaptive Mosaic and the Techno-Garden scenarios portray societies that protect ecosystems best. However, the TechnoGarden society reduces

(continued)

BOX 22.3 *(continued)*

personal freedoms. In addition, many people regard the Adaptive Mosaic and TechnoGarden as unattainable given society's present emphasis on security and economic growth.

International conservation organizations and policy makers, particularly those in the European Union, are currently discussing these four scenarios. While these discussions have not produced any tangible results so far, the scenarios describe clear alternatives to business as usual and present possible outcomes for the world's ecosystems and people. The scenarios show that immediate measures to protect the environment will have minimal effects initially, but will result in better outcomes over a 50-year pe-

riod than if we take no action and allow environmental destruction to continue. One surprising result of the analysis highlighted that reductions in agricultural subsidies in developed countries could benefit the environment by allowing marginal farmland to return to a more natural condition. The scenarios also showed that technologies and practices that increase water use efficiency and reduce the need for nitrogen fertilizer could also significantly benefit the environment. The MEA scenarios provide a practical tool for policy makers by clearly illustrating the future costs and benefits to people and ecosystems of policy decisions being made today.

to find compromises, such as those exemplified by biosphere reserves and integrated conservation–development projects, that allow people to obtain the natural resources that they need to support their families yet not damage the park's natural communities. In each instance, a balance must be achieved between excluding people to protect vulnerable species and encouraging people to freely use park resources. At national and international levels, the world's resources must be distributed more fairly to end the inequalities that exist today. Effective programs must be established to stabilize the world's human population. At the same time, the destruction of natural resources by industries must be halted, so that the short-term quest for profits does not lead to a long-term ecological catastrophe (Johns 2003). Management strategies to preserve biological diversity also need to be developed for the 85% of the terrestrial environment that will remain outside of protected areas, as well as for the vast, largely unexplored marine environment.

Achieving the Agenda

If these challenges are to be met successfully, conservation biologists must take on several active roles. They must become more effective *educators* in the public forum as well as in the classroom (Figure 22.2). Conservation biologists need to educate as broad a range of people as possible about the problems that stem from loss of biological diversity (Collett and Karakashain 1996; Sutherland 2000; Primack 2002; Broberg 2003; Main 2004; Evans et al. 2005). The Society of Conservation Biology has even made the dissemination of knowledge the first item in its new Code of Ethics. Conservation biologists need to convey a positive message about what has been accomplished and what can be accomplished to protect biological diversity by delivering a sense of realistic optimism to counter the pessimism and passivity so frequently encountered in modern society.

Conservation biologists often teach college students and write technical papers addressing these issues, but they reach only a limited audience in this way: Remember that only a few hundred or a few thousand people read most scientific papers. In contrast, millions of adults watch nature programs on television, especially ones produced by the National Geographic Society, the Public Broadcasting Service, and the British Broadcasting Corporation, and tens of millions of children watch the television channel Animal Planet and movies such as *Finding Nemo*, which often have powerful conservation themes. Conservation biologists need to reach a wider range of people through speaking in villages, towns, cities, elementary and secondary

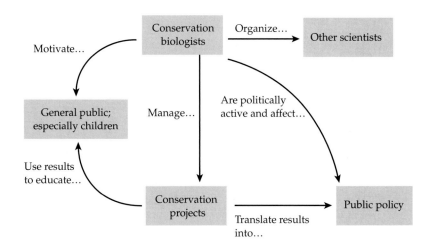

FIGURE 22.2 Conservation biologists need to be active in various ways to achieve the goals of conservation biology and the protection of biological diversity. Not every conservation biologist can be active in each role, but all of the roles are important.

schools, parks, neighborhood gatherings, and religious organizations (Nadkarni 2004; Jacobson et al. 2005). Also, the themes of conservation need to be even more widely incorporated into public discussions. Conservation biologists must spend more of their time writing articles and editorials for newspapers and magazines, as well as speaking on radio, television, and other mass media. Conservation biologists need to make a special effort to talk to children's groups and to write versions of their work that children can read. Hundreds of millions of people visit zoos, aquariums, and botanical gardens, making these another prime venue for communicating conservation messages to the public. Conservation biologists must continue to seek out creative ways to reach wider audiences and avoid repeatedly "preaching to the converted."

The efforts of Merlin Tuttle and Bat Conservation International (BCI) illustrate how public attitudes toward even unpopular species can be changed. BCI has campaigned throughout the United States and the world to educate people on the importance of bats in ecosystem health, emphasizing their roles as insect eaters, pollinators, and seed dispersers. A valuable part of this effort has involved producing bat photographs and films of exceptional beauty. In Austin, Texas, Tuttle intervened when citizens petitioned the city government to exterminate the hundreds of thousands of Mexican freetail bats (*Tadarida brasiliensis*) that lived under a downtown bridge. He and his colleagues were able to convince people that the bats are both fun to watch and critical in controlling noxious insect populations over a wide area. The situation has changed so drastically that now the government protects the bats as a matter of civic pride and practical pest control, and citizens and tourists gather every night to watch the bats emerge from under the bridge on their nightly expeditions (Figure 22.3).

Conservation biologists must also become *politically active* and influence public policy. Involvement in the political process allows conservation biologists to influence the passage of new laws to support the preservation of biological diversity or to argue against legislation that would prove harmful to species or ecosystems (Brown 2000; Clark 2001; Alpert 2003; Chhatre and Saberwal 2005). An important first step in this process is joining conservation organizations or mainstream political parties to gain strength by working in a group and to learn more about the issues. It is important to note that there is also room for people who prefer to work by themselves. Recent difficulties in getting the U.S. Congress to reauthorize the Endangered Species Act and to ratify the Convention on Biological Diversity and the Convention on Global Climate Change dramatically illustrate the need for greater political activism on the part of scientists who understand the implications of not taking action now. Though much of the political process is time-consuming

FIGURE 22.3 Citizens and tourists gather in the evening to watch bats emerge from their roosts on the underside of a bridge in Austin, Texas. Merlin Tuttle and his organization Bat Conservation International have successfully changed many people's opinions about bats, animals that are generally unpopular with the public. (Photograph by Merlin Tuttle, Bat Conservation International.)

and tedious, it is often the only way to accomplish major conservation goals such as acquiring new land for reserves or preventing overexploitation of old-growth forests. Conservation biologists need to master the language and methods of the legal process and form effective alliances with environmental lawyers, citizen groups, and politicians. They also must be clear about when they are presenting objective scientific evidence and when they are expressing personal opinions.

A key role is for conservation biologists to become *translational scientists* that is, scientists who can take the data and results of conservation science and translate them into legislation and other public policy (Brosnan 2000; Soberón 2004). To be effective, conservation biologists have to demonstrate the relevance of their research and show that their findings are unbiased and respectful of the values and concerns of all stakeholders (Cash et al. 2002, 2003; Robertson and Hull 2003). Conservation scientists have to be aware of the full range of issues that may affect their programs and be able to speak to a general audience in terms that they can understand.

Conservation biologists need to become *organizers* within the scientific community. Many professional biologists in universities, colleges, museums, high schools, and government agencies concentrate their energies on the specialized needs of their professional niche. They may feel that their institutions want them to concentrate on "pure science" and "not get involved in politics." These biologists may not realize that the world's biological diversity is under imminent threat of destruction and that their contributions are urgently needed to save it (Blockstein 2002). Or they may feel that they are too busy with career goals or too unimportant to get involved in the struggle. By stimulating interest among their colleagues, conservation biologists can increase the ranks of trained professional advocates fighting the destruction of natural resources. These professional biologists may also find their involvement to be personally and professionally beneficial, as their new interests may result in heightened scientific creativity and more inspired teaching.

Conservation biologists need to become *motivators,* convincing a range of people to support conservation efforts. At a local level, conservation programs have to be created and presented in ways that provide incentives for local people to support them. Local people need to be shown that protecting the environment not only saves species and biological communities but also improves the long-term health of their families, their own economic well-being, and their quality of life

(WRI 1998; McMichael et al. 1999). Public discussions, education, and publicity need to be a major part of any such program. The scientists may present their knowledge as expert witnesses at public panels and in testimony. Careful attention must be devoted in particular to convincing business leaders and politicians to support conservation efforts. Many of these people will support conservation efforts when they are presented in the right way. Sometimes conservation is perceived to have good publicity value, or supporting it is perceived to be better than a confrontation that may otherwise result. National leaders may be among the most difficult people to convince, since they must respond to a diversity of interests. However, whether it is due to reason, sentiment, or professional self-interest, once converted to the conservation cause, these leaders may be in a position to make major contributions.

Finally, and most important, conservation biologists need to become effective *managers* and *practitioners* of conservation projects (Sutherland 1998; Rabinowitz 2001). They must be willing to walk on the land and go out on the water to find out what is really happening, to get dirty, to talk with local people, to knock on doors, and to take risks. Conservation biologists must learn everything they can about the species and communities that they are trying to protect and then make that knowledge available to others in a form that can be readily understood and can affect decision-making (Latta 2000; Poff et al. 2003). If conservation biologists are willing to put their ideas into practice, and to work with park managers, land-use planners, politicians, and local people, then progress will follow. Getting the right mix of models, new theories, innovative approaches, and practical examples is necessary for the success of the discipline. Once this balance is found, conservation biologists working with an energized citizenry will be in a position to protect the world's biological diversity during this unprecedented era of change.

Summary

1. There are major problems involved in protecting biological diversity; to address these problems, many changes must be made in policies and practices. These changes must occur at local, national, and international levels and require action on the part of individuals, conservation organizations, and governments.

2. Conservation biologists must demonstrate the practical value of the theories and approaches of their new discipline and actively work with all components of society to protect biological diversity and restore the degraded elements of the environment.

3. To achieve the long-term goals of conservation biology, practitioners need to become involved in conservation education and the political process.

For Discussion

1. Is conservation biology fundamentally different from other branches of biology such as physiology, genetics, or cell biology? Does conservation biology have underlying assumptions that are distinct from other fields of biology?

2. As a result of studying conservation biology, have you decided to change your lifestyle or your level of political activity? Do you think you can make a difference in the world, and if so, in what way?

3. Go to the library or search online to find articles that interest you in journals such as *Conservation Biology, Biological Diversity, BioScience, Biodiversity and Conservation, Ecological Applications,* and *National Geographic.* What is appealing about the articles you selected?

4. Read more about the four alternative scenarios presented by the Millennium Ecosystem Assessment (2005). Are these scenarios realistic? Select aspects of each scenario that you could or could not accept.

Suggested Readings

Alpert, P., A. Keller, S. Airame, W. K. Lauenroth, R. V. Pouyat, H. A. Mooney, et al. 2003. The ecology-policy interface. *Frontiers in Ecology and the Environment* 1: 45–50. Discusses the role scientists play in directing governments' environmental policy.

Brown, K. 2000. Transforming a discipline: A new breed of scientist-advocate emerges. *Science* 287: 1192–1193. Several articles in this issue describe how conservation biologists and ecologists are working with the government to affect policy.

Caro, T., B. Mulder, and M. Moore. 2003. Effects of conservation education on reasons to conserve biological diversity. *Biological Conservation* 114: 143–152. Not surprisingly, conservation education makes students more informed and motivated about conservation issues.

Charnley, S. 2006. The Northwest Forest Plan as a model for broad-scale ecosystem management: a social perspective. *Conservation Biology* 20: 330–340. Challenges remain in finding ways to balance the economic needs of society with the conservation of biodiversity.

Chhatre A. and V. Saberwal. 2005. Political incentives for biodiversity conservation. *Conservation Biology* 19: 310–317. Involvement in the political process is sometimes necessary to achieve conservation goals.

Christensen, J. 2003. Auditing conservation in an age of accountability. *Conservation in Practice* 4: 12–19. Careful evaluations of conservation projects can help identify what works and what does not.

Collett, J. and S. Karakashain (eds.). 1996. Greening the College Curriculum: A Guide to Environmental Teaching in the Liberal Arts. Island Press. Washington, D.C. Environmental and conservation issues can be a theme unifying many university courses and programs of study.

Cullen Jr., L., K. Alger, and D. M. Rambaldi. 2005. Land reform and biodiversity conservation in Brazil in the 1990's: conflict and the articulation of mutual interests. *Conservation Biology* 19: 747–755. Conservation biologists need to find common ground with other advocacy groups.

Evans, C., E. Abrams, R. Reitsma, K. Roux, L. Salmonsen, and P. P. Marra. 2005. The Neighborhood Nestwatch Program: Participant outcomes of a citizen-science ecological research project. *Conservation Biology* 19: 589–594. Conservation biologists can accomplish multiple objectives by working with volunteers.

Fazey, I., J. Fischer, and D. B. Lindenmayer. 2005. What do conservation biologists publish? *Conservation Biology* 124: 63–73. Conservation biologists need to get involved in real-world management questions rather than academic debates.

Groom, M. J., G. K. Meffe, and C. R. Carroll (eds.). 2005. *Principles of Conservation Biology,* 3rd ed. Sinauer Associates, Sunderland, MA. Excellent advanced textbook with numerous guest essays.

Gulbrandsen, L. H. 2005. Mark of stustainability? Challenges for fishery and forestry ecolabeling. *Environment* 47: 8–23. Environmental labeling can potentially contribute to conservation.

Jacobson, S. K., M. McDuff, and M. Monroe. 2006. *Conservation Education and Outreach Techniques.* Oxford University Press, U.K. Practical ways for enlarging public support for conservation.

Johns, D. M. 2003. Growth, conservation, and the necessity of new alliances. *Conservation Biology* 17: 1229–1237. Conservation biologists need to establish connections to others concerned with environmental issues.

Kaiser, M. J. and G. Edwards-Jones. 2006. The role of ecolabeling in fisheries management and conservation. *Conservation Biology* 20: 392–398. The Marine Stewardship Council is developing the labeling of fish as a way to promote sustainable fishing.

Millennium Ecosystem Assessment (MEA). 2005b. *Ecosystems and Human Well-being: Biodiversity Synthesis*. World Resources Institute, Washington, D.C. Huge set of reports on the status and value of the world's ecosystems.

Nadkarni, N. M. 2004. Not preaching to the choir: communicating the importance of forest conservation to non-traditional audiences. *Conservation Biology* 18: 606–609. Communicating with new audiences, such as religious organizations and school groups, can help spread the conservation message.

Rabinowitz, A. 2001. *Beyond the Last Village. A Journey of Asia's Forbidden Wilderness*. Island Press, Washington, D.C. A personal account of wildlife research and conservation in a remote area of Burma.

Sachs, J. 2005. *The End of Poverty: Economic Possibilities for Our Time*. Penguin Group, East Rutherford, N.J. Innovative ideas for eliminating poverty.

Stearns, B. P. and S. C. Stearns. 1999. *Watching, from the Edge of Extinction*. Yale University Press, New Haven, CT. Captures the drama, excitement, and frustrations of conservation biologists involved in last-ditch efforts to save species.

World Resources Institute (WRI) in collaboration with United Nations Development Programme, United nations Environment Programme, and World Bank. 2005. *World Resources 2005: The Wealth of the Poor—Managing Ecosystems to Fight Poverty*. Washington, DC: WRI. A special issue focuses on the importance of ecosystems in alleviating poverty.

Selected Environmental Organizations and Sources of Information

The best single reference on conservation activities is the *Conservation Directory 2005-2006*, (www.nwf.org/conservationdirectory). This directory lists over 4000 local, national, and international conservation organizations; conservation publications; and more than 18,000 leaders and officials in the field of conservation; available online or through Island Press. Another publication of interest is: *The Eco Guide to Careers that Make a Difference; Environmental Work for a Sustainable World* (2004); also published by Island Press. Online searches, especially using Google, provide a powerful way to search for information concerning people, organizations, places, and topics.

The following is a list of some major organizations and resources:

American Zoo and Aquarium Association
8403 Colesville Road, Suite 710
Silver Spring, MD 20910-3314 U.S.A.
www.aza.org
Preservation and propagation of captive wildlife.

BirdLife International
Wellbrook Court
Girton Road
Cambridge, CB3 0NA, U.K.
www.birdlife.org.uk
Determines status, priorities, and conservation plans for birds throughout the world.

Convention on Biological Diversity Secretariat
413 Rue Saint-Jacques, Suite 800
Montreal, Quebec, Canada H2Y 1N9
www.biodiv.org
Promotes the goals of the CBD: sustainable development, biodiversity conservation, and equitable sharing of genetic resources.

CITES Secretariat of Wild Fauna and Flora
International Environment House
15 Chemin des Anémones
CH-1219 Châtelaine-Geneva, Switzerland
www.cites.org
Regulates trade in endangered species.

Conservation International (CI)
1919 M Street N.W., Suite 600
Washington, D.C. 20036 U.S.A.
www.conservation.org; www.biodiversityscience.org
Active in international conservation efforts and developing conservation strategies; home of Center for Biodiversity Science.

Earthwatch Institute
3 Clock Tower Place, Suite 100
P.O. Box 75
Maynard, MA 01754 U.S.A.
www.earthwatch.org
Clearinghouse for international conservation projects in which volunteers can work with scientists.

Environmental Defense
257 Park Avenue South
New York, N.Y. 10010 U.S.A.
www.environmentaldefense.org
Involved in scientific, legal, and economic issues.

Conservation Employment Opportunities
Various organizations have websites with environmental and conservation opportunities and internships throughout the world: www.webdirectory.com/Employment, www.eco.org, www.ecojobs.com, etc.

European Center for Nature Conservation
P.O. Box 90154
5000 LG Tilburg
The Netherlands
www.ecnc.nl
Provides the scientific expertise that is required for making conservation policy.

Fauna & Flora International
Great Eastern House
Tenison Road
Cambridge CB1 2TT U.K.
www.fauna-flora.org
Long-established international conservation body acting to protect species and ecosystems.

Food and Agriculture Organization of the United Nations (FAO)
Viale delle Terme di Caracalla
00100 Rome, Italy
www.fao.org
A UN agency supporting sustainable agriculture, rural development, and resource management.

Friends of the Earth
1025 Vermont Avenue N.W.
Washington, D.C. 20005-6303 U.S.A.
www.foe.org
Attention-grabbing organization working to improve and expand environmental policy.

Global Environment Facility Secretariat (GEF)
1818 H Street N.W.
Washington, D.C. 20433 U.S.A.
www.gefweb.org
Funds international biodiversity and environmental projects.

Greenpeace International
Ottho Heldringstraat 5
1006 AZ Amsterdam
The Netherlands
www.greenpeace.org
Activist organization, known for grassroots efforts and dramatic protests against environmental damage.

Missouri Botanical Garden/Center for Plant Conservation
4344 Shaw Boulevard
St. Louis, MO, 63110 U.S.A.
www.mobot.org
Major center for worldwide plant conservation activities.

National Audubon Society
700 Broadway
New York, N.Y. 10003 U.S.A.
www.audubon.org
Wildlife conservation, public education, research, and political lobbying, with emphasis on birds.

National Council for Science and the Environment
1707 H Street N.W., Suite 200
Washington, D.C. 20006-3918 U.S.A.
www.cnie.org
Formerly the Committee for the National Institute for the Environment. Works to improve the scientific basis for environmental decision making; their website provides extensive environmental information.

National Wildlife Federation
11100 Wildlife Center Drive
Reston, VA 20190-5362 U.S.A.
www.nwf.org
Advocates for wildlife conservation. Publishes the *Conservation Directory 2005-2006,* as well as the outstanding children's publications *Ranger Rick* and *Your Big Backyard.*

Natural Resources Defense Council
40 West 20th Street
New York, N.Y. 10011 U.S.A.
www.nrdc.org
Uses legal and scientific methods to monitor and influence government actions and legislation.

The Nature Conservancy (TNC)
International Headquarters
4245 North Fairfax Drive, Suite 100
Arlington, VA 22203-1606 U.S.A.
www.nature.org
Emphasizes land preservation. Maintains extensive records on rare species distribution in the Americas, particularly North America.

New York Botanical Garden/Institute for Economic Botany
200th Street and Kazimiroff Boulevard
Bronx, N.Y. 10458 U.S.A.
www.nybg.org
Conducts research and conservation programs involving plants that are useful to people.

NatureServe
1101 Wilson Boulevard, 15th floor
Arlington, VA 22209 U.S.A
www.natureserve.org
Maintains databases of endangered species for North America

Rainforest Action Network
221 Pine Street, Suite 500
San Francisco, CA 94104 U.S.A.
www.ran.org
Works for rain forest conservation and human rights.

Ocean Conservancy
2029 K Street, N.W.
Washington, D.C. 20006 U.S.A.
www.oceanconservancy.org
Focuses on marine wildlife and ocean and coastal habitats.

Royal Botanic Gardens, Kew
Richmond Surrey TW9 3AB, United Kingdom
www.rbgkew.org.uk
The famous "Kew Gardens" are home to a leading botanical research institute and an enormous plant collection.

Sierra Club
85 Second Street, Second Floor
San Francisco, CA 94105-3441 U.S.A.
www.sierraclub.org
Leading advocate for the preservation of wilderness and open space.

Smithsonian Institution/National Zoological Park
3001 Connecticut Ave., N.W.
Washington, D.C. 20008 U.S.A.
www.natzoo.si.edu
The National Zoo and the nearby U.S. National Museum of Natural History represent a vast resource of literature, biological materials, and skilled professionals.

Society for Conservation Biology
4245 N Fairfax Drive
Arlington, VA 22203 U.S.A.
www.conbio.net/scb
Leading scientific society for the field. Develops and publicizes new ideas and scientific results through the journal *Conservation Biology* and annual meetings.

Student Conservation Association (SCA)
689 River Road P.O. Box 550
Charlestown, NH 03603 U.S.A.
www.sca-inc.org
Places volunteers and interns with conservation organizations and public agencies.

United Nations Development Programme (UNDP)
One United Nations Plaza
New York, NY 10017 U.S.A.
www.undp.org
Funds and coordinates international economic development activities, particularly those that use natural resources in a responsible way.

United Nations Environment Programme (UNEP)
United Nations Avenue, Gigiri
P.O. Box 30552, Nairobi, Kenya
www.unep.org
International program of research and management relating to major environmental problems.

United States Fish and Wildlife Service
Department of the Interior
1849 C Street N.W.
Washington, D.C. 20240 U.S.A.
www.fws.gov
The leading U.S. government agency concerned with conservation research and management; with connections to state governments, other government units, including the National Marine Fisheries Service, U.S. Forest Service, and the Agency for International Development, which is active in developing nations. The *Conservation Directory 2005-2006*, mentioned above, shows how these units are organized.

Wetlands International
Droevendaalsesteeg 3
6708 PB Wageningen
The Netherlands
www.wetlands.org
Focus on the conservation and sustainable management of wetlands.

Wilderness Society
1615 M Street N.W.
Washington D.C. 20036 U.S.A.
www.tws.org
Organization devoted to preserving wilderness and wildlife.

Wildlife Conservation Society/New York Zoological Society (WCS)
2300 Southern Boulevard
Bronx, N.Y. 10460-1099 U.S.A.
www.wcs.org
Leaders in wildlife conservation and research.

World Bank
1818 H Street N.W.
Washington, D.C. 20433 U.S.A.
www.worldbank.org
A multinational bank involved in economic development; increasingly concerned with environmental issues.

World Conservation Monitoring Centre (WCMC)
219 Huntingdon Road
Cambridge CB3 0DL, United Kingdom
www.unep-wcmc.org
Monitors global wildlife trade, the status of endangered species, natural resource use, and protected areas.

World Conservation Union (IUCN)
Rue Mauverney 28
CH-1196, Gland, Switzerland
www.iucn.org
The premier coordinating body for international conservation efforts. Produces directories of specialists and the Red Lists of endangered species.

World Resources Institute (WRI)
10 G Street N.E., Suite 800
Washington, D.C. 20002 U.S.A.
www.wri.org
Research center producing excellent papers on environmental, conservation, and development topics.

World Wildlife Fund (WWF)
1250 Twenty-Fourth Street N.W.
P.O. Box 97180
Washington, D.C. 20077-7180 U.S.A.
www.worldwildlife.org or www.wwf.org
Major conservation organization, with branches throughout the world. Active both in research and in the management of national parks.

Xerces Society
4828 Southeast Hawthorne Boulevard
Portland, OR 97215-3252 U.S.A.
www.xerces.org
Focuses on the conservation of insects and other invertebrates.

Zoological Society of London
Regent's Park
London NW1 4RY, U.K.
www.zsl.org
Center for worldwide activities to preserve nature.

Glossary

A

adaptive management implementing a management plan, monitoring how well it works, then using the results to adjust the management plan.

adaptive radiation different populations of a species adapting to local conditions, followed by subsequent speciation.

adaptive restoration using monitoring data to adjust management plans to achieve restoration goals.

Allee effect inability of the social structure to function once a population falls below a certain number of individuals or density.

alleles different forms of the same gene.

alpha diversity the number of species in a community or specific place.

amenity value recreational value of biodiversity, including ecotourism.

arboretum specialized botanical garden focusing on trees and other woody plants.

artificial incubation conservation strategy that involves humans caring for eggs or newborn animals.

artificial insemination introduction of sperm into a receptive female animal by humans; used to increase the reproductive output of endangered species.

artificial selection selective breeding by humans to produce desired and useful characteristics in domesticated plants and animals.

augmentation program releasing additional individuals into an existing population to increase population size and genetic variability.

B

bequest (or beneficiary) value how much people are willing to pay to protect something of value for their own children, descendants, or future generations.

beta diversity rate of change of species composition along a gradient or transect.

binomial nomenclature system of scientific names in which each species has a two-part name consisting of a genus name and a species name.

biocultural restoration restoring lost ecological knowledge to people and giving them an appreciation of the natural world.

biodiversity shortened form of biological diversity.

biological community group of species that occupy a particular locality.

biological control method of controlling an invasive species by releasing a second species that will reduce the population size of the invasive species.

biological definition of a species group of individuals that can potentially breed among themselves in the wild and that do not breed with individuals of other groups.

biological diversity complete range of species, biological communities, and their ecosystem interactions and genetic variation within species.

biological diversity indicators (or surrogate species) species or group of species that provide an estimate of biological diversity in an area when data on the whole community is unavailable.

biomagnification process whereby toxins become concentrated at higher levels in the food chain.

biome ecosystem characterized by the structure and characteristics of its vegetation, which supports unique biological communities.

biophilia a predisposition in humans to like biological diversity.

bioregional management a management system that focuses on a single large ecosystem or a series of linked ecosystems, particularly where these cross political boundaries.

Biosphere Reserve protected area established as part of a United Nations program to demonstrate the compatibility of biodiversity conservation and sustainable development to benefit local people.

biota a region's plants and animals.

Blue List list of threatened species that have positively responded to conservation efforts.

bushmeat crisis the sharp decline in animal populations caused by intensive hunting for food.

by-catch animals caught by accident during a fishing operation.

C

carnivore (or secondary consumer or predator) an animal species that consumes other animals to survive.

carrying capacity the number of individuals or biomass of a species that an ecosystem can support.

census a count of the number of individuals in a population.

clonal repository (or clonal orchard) special botanical garden or facility that preserves genetic variation for plants with seeds that cannot be stored, or plants that are long-lived.

commodity value value assigned to products, such as timber and animals, harvested by people.

common property or open access resources natural resources that are not controlled by individuals but are collectively owned by society.

compensatory mitigation when a new site is created or rehabilitated in compensation for a site damaged or destroyed elsewhere.

competition interaction involving two or more individuals or species using the same limited environmental resources.

complementary areas conservation strategy in which each new protected area adds additional species or other aspects of biodiversity to an existing system of protected areas.

conservation banking preservation of an endangered species or protected habitat type (or even restoration of a degraded habitat) by landowners to compensate for a species or habitat that is destroyed as the result of a development project.

conservation biology scientific discipline that carries out research on biological diversity, identifies threats to biological diversity, and plays an active role in the preservation of biological diversity.

conservation concession method of protecting land whereby a conservation organization pays a government or other landowner to preserve habitat rather than allow an extractive industry to damage the habitat.

conservation easement method of protecting land in which landowners give up the right to develop or build on their property, often in exchange for financial or tax benefit.

conservation leasing providing payments to private landowners who actively manage their land for biodiversity protection.

conservation network system of protected areas established and managed to maximize the protection of biological diversity at larger scales.

conservation units species, ecosystems, and physical features of a region; data about them are gathered and stored by conservation organizations.

consumptive use value values assigned to goods that are collected and consumed locally.

Convention on Biological Diversity (CBD) a treaty that obligates countries to protect the biological diversity within their borders, and gives them the right to receive economic benefits from the use of that biological diversity.

Convention on International Trade in Endangered Species (CITES) international treaty that establishes lists (known as Appendices) of species for which international trade is to be prohibited, regulated, or monitored.

cost–benefit analysis comprehensive analysis that compares values gained against the costs of a project or resource use.

cross-fostering conservation strategy in which individuals from a common species raise the offspring of a rare, related species.

cultural eutrophication algal booms and associated impacts caused by excess mineral nutrients released into the water from human activity.

D

debt-for-nature swap an agreement in which a developing country agrees to fund additional conservation activities in exchange for a conservation organization canceling some of its discounted debt.

decomposer (or detritivore) species that feeds or grows on dead plant and animal material.

deep ecology philosophy emphasizing biodiversity protection, personal lifestyle changes, and working towards political change.

demographic study study in which individuals and populations are monitored over time to determine rates of growth, reproduction, and survival.

demographic variation (or demographic stochasticity) random variation in birth, death, and reproductive rates in small populations, sometimes causing further decline in population size.

desertification process by which ecosystems are degraded by human activities into man-made deserts.

direct use values (or private goods or commodity values) values assigned to products, such as timber and animals, that are harvested by people.

discount rate method for reducing the current value of a resource that is going to be used at some point in the future.

E

Earth Summit international conference held in 1992 in Rio de Janeiro that resulted in new environmental agreements.

ecocolonialism practice of governments and conservation organizations disregarding the land rights and traditions of local people in order to establish new conservation areas.

ecological economics discipline that includes valuations of biological diversity in economic analyses.

ecological footprint the influence that people's patterns of consumption and lifestyle have on the surrounding ecosystem and across the globe.

ecological restoration altering a site to establish an indigenous ecosystem.

ecologically extinct a species that has been so reduced in numbers that it no longer has a significant ecological impact on the biological community.

ecologically functional a species that is sufficiently abundant to have a significant impact on other species in a community.

ecology relationship of a species to its biological and physical environment.

economic development economic activity focused on improvements in efficiency and organization but not necessarily on increases in resource consumption.

economic growth economic activity characterized by increases in the amount of resources used.

ecosystem a biological community together with its associated physical and chemical environment.

ecosystem health property of an ecosystem in which all processes are functioning normally.

ecosystem integrity condition in which an ecosystem is complete and functional and has not been damaged by human activity.

ecosystem management large-scale management that often involves multiple stakeholders, the primary goal of which is the preservation of ecosystem components and processes.

ecosystem services range of benefits provided to people from ecosystems, including flood control, clean water, and reduction of pollution.

ecotourism tourism focused on viewing unusual biological communities and species.

edge effects altered environmental and biological conditions at the edge of a fragmented habitat.

effective population size number of breeding individuals in a population.

embryo transfer surgically implanting embryos into a surrogate mother; used to increase the number of individuals of a rare species, with a common species used as the surrogate mother.

endangered species species that has a high risk of extinction in the wild in the near future.

Endangered Species Act important law in the U.S.A. protecting endangered species and the habitats in which they live.

endemic occurring in a place naturally, without the influence of people; i.e., gray wolves are endemic to Canada.

endemic species species found in one place and nowhere else.

environmental and economic impact assessment evaluation of a project which considers its possible present and future impacts on the environment and the economy.

environmental ethics discipline of philosophy that articulates the intrinsic value of the natural world and people's responsibility to protect the environment.

environmental stochasticity random variation in the biological and physical environment; can increase the risk of extinction in small populations.

eutrophication process of degradation in aquatic environments caused by pollution and characterized by algal blooms and oxygen depletion.

evolutionary biologist scientist who studies the processes of evolution and speciation.

evolutionary–ecological land ethic Aldo Leopold's philosophy advocating human use of natural resources that is compatible with, or even enhances ecosystem health.

ex situ conservation preservation of species under artificial conditions, such as zoos, aquariums, and botanical gardens.

existence value amount of money that people are willing to pay to protect biological diversity for the sole purpose of its continued existence.

exotic species species that occurs outside of its natural range due to human activity.

extant still presently alive; not extinct.

externalities hidden costs or benefits that result from an economic activity to individuals or a society not directly involved in that activity.

extinct absence of any living members of a species.

extinct in the wild species is no longer found in the wild, but individuals may remain alive in zoos, botanical gardens, or other artificial environments.

extinction cascade series of linked extinctions whereby the extinction of one species leads to the extinction of one or more other species.

extinction debt future extinction of species caused by current human activities.

extinction vortex tendency of small populations to decline toward extinction.

extirpation local extinction of a population, even though the species may still exist elsewhere.

extractive reserve protected area in which sustainable extraction of certain natural products is allowed.

F

50/500 rule proposed rule that at least 50 and up to 500 reproductive individuals are needed to prevent the loss of genetic variability in a population; larger numbers are now considered necessary for wild populations.

fitness an individual's ability to grow, survive, and reproduce.

flagship species species that captures public attention, aids in conservation efforts, such as establishing a protected area, and may be crucial to ecotourism.

focal species species that provides a reason for establishing a protected area.

food chains specific feeding relationships between species at different trophic levels.

food web network of feeding relationships among species.

founder effect reduced genetic variability when a new population is established by a small number of individuals.

frontier forest intact block of forest large enough to support all aspects of biodiversity.

G

gamma diversity number of species in a large geographic area.

gap analysis comparing the distribution of endangered species and biological communities with existing and proposed protected areas to determine gaps in protection.

gap species species not protected in any part of its range.

gene unit of a chromosome that codes for a specific protein.

gene flow transfer of new alleles and genetic combinations between populations, resulting from the movement of individuals.

gene frequency percentage of different allele forms within a population.

gene pool total array of genes and alleles in a population.

genetic drift loss of genetic variation and change in gene frequencies that occur by chance in small populations.

genotype particular combination of alleles that an individual possesses.

genus unit of classification that includes one or more species.

geographic information systems (GIS) computer analyses that integrate and display spatial data; relating in particular to the natural environment, biological communities, species, protected areas, and human activities.

global climate change climate characteristics that are changing now and will continue to change in the future, in part resulting from human activity.

Global Environment Facility large program associated with the World Bank, involved in funding conservation activities in developing countries.

global warming current and future increases in temperatures caused by higher atmospheric concentrations of carbon dioxide and other greenhouse gases produced by human activities.

globally extinct no individuals of a species are presently alive anywhere.

greenhouse effect warming of the Earth caused by carbon dioxide and other atmospheric gases.

greenhouse gases gases in the atmosphere, primarily carbon dioxide, that are transparent to sunlight but trap heat near the Earth's surface.

guild group of species at the same trophic level that use approximately the same environmental resources.

H

habitat conservation plans regional plans that allow development in designated areas while protecting biological diversity in other areas.

habitat corridors connections between protected areas that allow for dispersal.

habitat fragmentation process whereby a continuous area of habitat is both reduced in area and divided into two or more fragments.

hard release occurs in the establishment of a new population when individuals are released in a new location without assistance.

healthy ecosystem ecosystem in which processes are functioning normally, whether or not there are human influences.

herbivore (or primary consumer) species that eat plants and other photosynthetic organisms.

heterozygous condition of an individual having two different allele forms of the same gene.

hybrid intermediate offspring resulting from mating between individuals of two related but distinct species.

hybrid vigor (or heterosis) increased fitness of individuals resulting from outbreeding.

I

in situ conservation preservation of natural communities and populations of endangered species in the wild.

inbreeding depression lowered reproduction or production of weak offspring following mating among close relatives or self-fertilization.

indicator species species used in a conservation plan to identify and often protect a biological community or set of ecosystem processes.

indirect use values (or public goods) values provided by biological diversity that do not involve harvesting or destroying the resource (such as water quality, soil protection, recreation, and education).

integrated conservation and development project (ICDP) conservation project that also provides for the economic needs and welfare of local people.

intrinsic value value of a species and other aspects of biodiversity for their own sake, unrelated to human needs.

introduced species a species established outside of its natural range due to human activities or intervention.

introduction release of a species outside of its natural range either accidentally or as a deliberate part of a conservation plan.

introduction program moving individuals to areas outside their historical range in order to create a new population of an endangered species.

invasive species introduced species that increases in abundance at the expense of native species.

inventory a count of the number of individuals in a population.

island biogeography model relationship between island size and the number of species living on the island; now used to predict the impact of habitat destruction on species extinction.

IUCN The World Conservation Union, a major international conservation organization; previously known as the International Union for the Conservation of Nature.

K

keystone resource resource in an ecosystem that is crucial to the survival of many species; for example, a water hole.

keystone species species that has a disproportionate impact on the organization of a biological community, the loss of which may have far reaching consequences.

L

land trust conservation organization that protects and manages land.

landscape ecology discipline that investigates patterns of habitat types and their influence on species distribution and ecosystem processes.

legal title to land right to ownership of land that is recognized by a government; traditional people often struggle to achieve this recognition.

limited development compromise involving a landowner, a property developer, and a conservation organization that combines some commercial development with protection of the remaining land.

limiting resource any requirement that limits population size.

locally extinct a species no longer exists in a place where it used to occur, but still exists elsewhere.

locus part of a chromosome that codes for a particular protein.

M

marine protected area protected area established to rebuild and maintain marine biodiversity.

market failure misallocation of resources in which individuals or businesses benefit from using a common resource, such as water, the atmosphere, or a forest, but the society at large bears the cost.

maximum sustainable yield greatest amount of a resource that can be harvested each year and replaced through population growth without detriment to the population.

metapopulation shifting mosaic of populations linked by some degree of migration.

minimum dynamic area (MDA) area needed for a population to have a high probability of surviving into the future.

minimum viable population (MVP) number of individuals necessary to ensure a high probability that a population will survive a certain number of years into the future.

mitigation process by which a new population or habitat is created to compensate for a habitat damaged or destroyed elsewhere.

monitoring observation of species and ecosystems over time; often done to determine if management activities are achieving their objectives.

morphological definition of a species group of individuals, recognized as a species, that is morphologically, physiologically, or biochemically distinct from other groups.

morpho-species individuals that are probably a distinct species based on their appearance, but do not currently have a scientific name.

multilateral development banks World Bank and other regional banks established by developed countries to provide money for economic development in developing countries.

multiple-use habitat area managed to provide a variety of goods and services.

mutalistic relationship when two species benefit each other by their relationship.

mutations changes that occur in genes and chromosomes, resulting in new allele forms and genetic variation.

N

national environmental fund trust fund or foundation that uses its annual income to support conservation activities.

natural history ecology and distinctive characteristics of a species.

natural selection genetic changes that occur in a population as it adapts over time to its environment.

neoendemic species that occupies a small area because it has only recently evolved from a closely related species.

nonconsumptive use value value assigned to benefits provided by some aspect of biological diversity that does not involve harvesting or destroying the resource (such as water quality, soil protection, recreation, and education).

nongovernmental organization (NGO) private organization that acts to benefit society in some way; many conservation organizations are NGOs.

O

omnivore species that eats both plants and animals.

option value value of biodiversity in providing possible future benefits for human society (such as new medicines).

outbreeding mating and production of offspring between individuals that are not closely related; i.e., individuals of different populations within a species or individuals of two closely related but distinct species.

outbreeding depression lowered fitness that sometimes occurs when individuals of different species or widely different populations mate and produce offspring.

overexploitation harvesting a resource or species at a high level, resulting in a decline or loss in that resource or species.

P

paleoendemic ancient species with a narrow geographical range and no closely related species still alive.

parasite predator that grows and feeds on or in a host individual without immediately killing it.

payment for environmental services (PES) direct payment to individual landowners and local communities that protect critical ecosystem characteristics.

phenotype morphological, physiological, anatomical, and biochemical characteristics of an individual that result from the expression of its genotype in a particular environment.

photosynthetic species (or primary producers) species that obtains its energy directly from the sun.

phyletic evolution gradual transformation of one species into another over time.

polymorphic gene gene that has more than one form or allele.

polyploid individual with an extra set of chromosomes; in plants, important in the evolution of new species.

population group of individuals in a species that mate with one another and produce offspring.

population biology study of the ecology and genetics of populations, often with a focus on population numbers.

population bottleneck radical reduction in population size, sometimes leading to the loss of genetic variation.

population viability analysis (PVA) demographic analysis that predicts the probability of a population persisting in an environment for a certain period of time; sometimes linked to various management scenarios.

precautionary principle principle stating that it may be better to avoid taking a particular action due to the possibility of causing unexpected harm.

predation act of killing and consuming another organism for food.

preservationist ethic belief in the need to preserve wilderness areas for their intrinsic value.

productive use value values assigned to products that are sold in markets.

protected areas habitats managed primarily or in part for biological diversity.

R

Ramsar Convention on Wetlands treaty that promotes the protection of wetlands of international importance.

rapid biodiversity assessments (or rapid assessment plans [RAPs]) species inventories and vegetation maps made by teams of biologists when urgent decisions must be made on where to establish new protected areas.

recombination mixing of genes from two parents that occurs during sexual reproduction.

Red Data Books lists of endangered species prepared by the IUCN and other conservation organizations.

reference site control site that provides goals for restoration in terms of species composition, community structure, and ecosystem processes.

regionally extinct a species is no longer found in part of its former range, but still lives elsewhere.

reintroduction program releasing of captive-bred or wild-collected individuals at a site within their historical range where the species does not presently occur.

relaxation loss of species over time in a degraded or fragmented habitat.

representative site protected area which includes species and ecosystem properties characteristic of a larger area.

resilience ability of an ecosystem to return to its original state following disturbance.

resistance ability of an ecosystem to remain in the same state even with ongoing disturbance.

resource conservation ethic natural resources should be used for the greatest good for the largest number of people.

restoration ecology scientific study of restored populations, communities, and ecosystems.

restoration management management that reestablishes some or all of the original species, community structure, and ecosystem processes.

S

seed bank collection of seeds, collected from the wild and from cultivated plants; used in conservation and agricultural programs.

shifting cultivation farming method, also called "slash-and-burn" agriculture, in which farmers cut down trees, burn them, plant crops for a few years, and then abandon the site when soil fertility declines.

sink population population which receives new individuals from a source population.

SLOSS debate controversy concerning the relative advantages of a *single large or several small* conservation areas.

soft release when animals are given additional assistance at a site following release back into the wild.

source population population from which individuals disperse to new locations.

speciation process whereby one species is transformed into one or more new species.

species group of individuals that could potentially interbreed among themselves in the wild, or are similar in appearance, or are genetically similar.

species–area relationship number of species found in an area increases with the size of the area; i.e., more species are found on large islands than small islands.

species richness number of species found in a community.

stable ecosystem ecosystem that is able to remain in the same state.

substitute cost approach valuing a resource by estimating how much people would have to pay for an equivalent product in the marketplace if their local supply was no longer available.

succession gradual process of change in species composition, vegetation structure, and ecosystem characteristics following natural and human caused disturbance.

survey repeatable sampling method to estimate population size or density, or some other aspect of biodiversity.

sustainable development economic development that meets present and future human needs without damaging the environment and biological diversity.

symbiotic relationship mutualistic relationship in which the two species involved cannot survive without each other.

T

taxonomist scientist involved in the classification and identification of species.

taxonomy science of identifying and classifying living things.

traditional people people who regard themselves as the original inhabitants of a region; often organized by social groups and villages. (Also known as local people, indigenous people, native people, or tribal people.)

tragedy of the commons unregulated use of a public resource that results in its degradation.

trophic levels levels of biological communities representing ways in which energy is captured and moves through the ecosystem.

tropical rainforest tropical forest that has leaves throughout the year and rain in most months, characterized by a great species richness.

U

umbrella species protecting this species results in the protection of other species.

V

vulnerable species species that has a high risk of extinction in the medium-term future and may become endangered.

W

wilderness area large area with minimal human impact.

World Bank international bank established to support economic development in developing countries.

World Heritage Convention treaty to protect cultural and natural areas of international significance.

Z

zoning method of managing protected areas that allows or prohibits certain activities in designated places.

Bibliography

Abensperg-Traun, M. and G. T. Smith. 1999. How small is too small for small animals? Four terrestrial arthropod species in different-sized remnant woodlands in agricultural Western Australia. *Biodiversity and Conservation* 8: 709–726.

Abesamis, R. A. and G. R. Russ. 2005. Density-dependent spillover from a marine reserve: Long-term evidence. *Ecological Applications* 15: 1798–1812.

Adams, C. A., J. M. Baskin, and C. C. Baskin. 2005. Comparative morphology of seeds of four closely related species of *Aristolochia* subgenus *Siphisia* (Aristolochiaceae, Piperales). *Botanical Journal of the Linnean Society* 148: 433–436.

Adams, D. and M. Carwardine. 1990. *Last Chance to See*. Harmony Books, New York.

Agar, N. 2001. *Life's Intrinsic Value: Science, Ethics, and Nature*. Columbia University Press, New York.

Agardy, T. S. 1997. *Marine Protected Areas and Ocean Conservation*. R. G. Landes Company, Austin, TX.

Agardy, T. S. 1999. Creating havens for marine life. *Issues in Science and Technology* 16: 37–44.

Agoramoorthy, G. 2004. Ethics and welfare in Southeast Asian Zoos. *Journal of Applied Animal Welfare Science* 7: 189–195.

Aguirre, A. A., R. S. Ostfeld, G. M. Tabor, C. House, and M. C. Pearl (eds.). 2002. *Conservation Medicine: Ecological Health in Practice*. Oxford University Press, New York.

Akçakaya, H. R. 1990. Bald ibis *Geronticus eremita* population in Turkey: An evaluation of the captive breeding project for reintroduction. *Biological Conservation* 51: 225–237.

Akçakaya, H. R., J. Franklin, A. D. Syphard, and J. R. Stephenson. 2005. Viability of Bell's Sage Sparrow (*Amphispiza belli* ssp. *Belli*): altered fire regimes. *Ecological Applications* 15: 521–531.

Akçakaya, H. R., V. C. Radeloff, D. J. Mladenoff, and H. S. He. 2004. Integrating landscape and metapopulation modeling approaches: Viability of the sharp-tailed grouse in a dynamic landscape. *Conservation Biology* 18: 526–547.

Alcock, J. 1993. *Animal Behavior: An Evolutionary Approach*. Sinauer Associates, Sunderland, MA.

Alcorn, J. B. 1984. Development policy, forests and peasant farms: Reflections on Huastec-managed forests' contributions to commercial production and resource conservation. *Economic Botany* 38: 389–406.

Alcorn, J. B. 1991. Ethics, economies and conservation. *In* M. L. Oldfield and J. B. Alcorn (eds.), *Biodiversity: Culture, Conservation and Ecodevelopment*, pp. 317–349. Westview Press, Boulder, CO.

Alexander, S. E. 2000. Resident attitudes towards conservation and black howler monkeys in Belize: the Community Baboon Sanctuary. *Environmental Conservation* 27: 341–350.

Alford, R. A. and S. J. Richards. 1999. Global amphibian declines: A problem in applied ecology. *Annual Review of Ecology and Systematics* 30: 133–165.

Allan, B. F., F. Keesing, and R. S. Ostfeld. 2003. Effects of forest fragmentation on Lyme disease risk. *Conservation Biology* 17: 267–272.

Allan, T. and A. Warren (eds.). 1993. *Deserts, the Encroaching Wilderness: A World Conservation Atlas*. Oxford University Press, London.

Allen, C., R. S. Lutz, and S. Demarais. 1995. Red imported fire ant impacts on Northern bobwhite populations. *Ecological Applications* 5: 632–638.

Allen, E., M. F. Allen, L. Egerton-Warburton, L. Corkidi, and A. Gómez-Pompa. 2003. Impacts of early- and late- seral mycorrhizae during restoration in seasonal tropical forest, Mexico. *Ecological Applications* 13: 1701–1717.

Allen, E. B., J. S. Brown, and M. F. Allen. 2001. Restoration of animal, plant, and microbial diversity. *In* S. A. Levin (ed.), *Encyclopedia of Biodiversity*, vol. 5, pp. 185–202. Academic Press, San Diego, CA.

Allen, W. H. 1988. Biocultural restoration of a tropical forest: Architects of Costa Rica's emerging Guanacaste National Park plan to make it an integral part of local culture. *BioScience* 38: 156–161.

Allen, W. H. 2001. *Green Phoenix: Restoring the Tropical Forests of Guanacaste, Costa Rica*. Oxford University Press, Oxford.

Allendorf, F. W. and R. F. Leary. 1986. Heterozygosity and fitness in natural populations of animals. *In* M. E. Soulé (ed.), *Conservation Biology: The Science of Scarcity and Diversity*, pp. 57–76. Sinauer Associates, Sunderland, MA.

Alò, D. and T. F. Turner. 2005. Effects of habitat fragmentation on effective population size in the endangered Rio Grande silvery minnow. *Conservation Biology* 19: 1138–1148.

Alpert, P., A. Keller, S. Airame, W. K. Lauenroth, R. V. Pouyat, H. Mooney, K. H. Rogers, and C. M. Breen. 2003. The ecology-policy interface. *Frontiers in Ecology and the Environment* 1: 45–50.

Altieri, M. A. 2004. Linking ecologists and traditional farmers in the search for sustainable agriculture. *Frontiers in Ecology and the Environment* 2: 35–42.

Altieri, M. A. and M. K. Anderson. 1992. Peasant farming systems, agricultural modernization and the conservation of crop genetic resources in Latin America. *In* P. L. Fiedler and S. K. Jain (eds.), *Conservation Biology: The Theory and Practice of Nature Conservation, Preservation and Management*, pp. 49–64. Chapman and Hall, New York.

Anderson, J. G. T. and C. M. Devlin. 1999. Restoration of a multi-species seabird colony. *Biological Conservation* 90: 175–181.

Antongiovanni, M. and J. P. Metzger. 2005. Influence of matrix habitats on the occurrence of insectivorous bird species in Amazonian forest. *Biological Conservation* 122: 441–451.

Araujo, R. and M. A. Ramos. 2000. Status and conservation of the giant European freshwater pearl mussel (*Margaritifera auricularia*) (Spengler, 1793) (*Bivalvia: Unionoidea*). *Biological Conservation* 96: 233–239.

Armbrecht, I., L. Rivera, and I. Perfecto. 2005. Reduced diversity and complexity in the leaf-litter ant assemblage of Colombian coffee plantations. *Conservation Biology* 19: 897–907.

Armstrong, S. and R. Botzler (eds.). 2004. *Environmental Ethics: Divergence and Convergence*. McGraw-Hill, New York.

Armsworth, P. R., G. C. Daily, P. Kareiva, and J. N. Sanchirico. 2006. Land market feedbacks can undermine biodiversity conservation. *Proceedings of the National Academy of Sciences U.S.A.* 103: 5403–5408.

Arnold, A. E. and L. C. Lewis. 2005. Evolution of fungal endophytes, and their roles against insects. *Ecological and Evolutionary Advances in Insect-Fungus Associations*, pp. 74–96. Oxford University Press, Oxford.

Arnold, A. E., L. C. Mejia, D. Kyllo, E. I. Rojas, Z. Maynard, N. Robbins, et al. 2003. Fungal endophytes limit pathogen damage in a tropical tree. *Proceedings of the National Academy of Sciences U.S.A.* 100: 15649–15654.

Arnold, J. M., S. Brault, and J. P. Croxall. 2006. Albatross populations in peril: a population trajectory for black-browed albatrosses at South Georgia. *Ecological Applications* 16: 419–432.

Aron, J. L. and J. A. Patz (eds.). 2001. *Ecosystem Change and Public Health: A Global Perspective*. John Hopkins University Press, Baltimore, MD.

Arrow, K., B. Bolin, R. Costanza, P. Dasgupta, C. Folke, et al. 1995. Economic growth, carrying capacity and the environment. *Science* 268: 520–522.

Azam, F. and A. Z. Worden. 2004. Oceanography: Microbes, molecules, and marine ecosystems. *Science* 303: 1622–1624.

Bacon, C. 2005. Confronting the coffee crisis: can fair trade, organic, and specialty coffees reduce small-scale farmer vulnerability in northern Nicaragua? *World Development* 33: 497–511.

Baillie, J. E. M., C. Hilton-Taylor, and S. N. Stuart. 2004. *2004 IUCN Red List of Threatened Species: A Global Assessment*. IUCN, Gland, Switzerland.

Baker, J. D. and T. C. Johanos. 2004. Abundance of the Hawaiian monk seal in the main Hawaiian Islands. *Biological Conservation* 116: 103–110.

Balick, M. J. and P. A. Cox. 1996. *Plants, People and Culture: The Science of Ethnobotany*. Scientific American Library, New York.

Balmford, A. 1996. Extinction filters and current resilience: The significance of past selection pressures for conservation biology. *Trends in Ecology and Evolution* 11: 193–196.

Balmford, A. 2003. Conservation planning in the real world: South Africa shows the way. *Trends in Ecology and Evolution* 18: 435–438.

Balmford, A. and T. Whitten. 2003. Who should pay for tropical conservation, and how could the costs be met? *Oryx* 37: 238–250.

Balmford, A., R. E. Green, and M. Jenkins. 2003. Measuring the changing state of nature. *Trends in Ecology and Evolution* 18: 326–330.

Balmford, A., G. M. Mace, and N. Leader-Williams. 1996. Designing the ark: Setting priorities for captive breeding. *Conservation Biology* 10: 719–727.

Balmford, A., L. Bennun, B. ten Brink, D. Cooper, I. M. Côté, P. Crane, et al. 2005. The Convention on Biological Diversity's 2010 target. *Science* 307: 212–213.

Balmford, A., A. Bruner, P. Cooper, R. Costanza, S. Farber, R. E. Green, et al. 2002. Economic reasons for conserving wild nature. *Science* 297: 950–953.

Bani, L., D. Massimino, L. Bottoni, and R. Massa. 2006. A multiscale method for selecting indicator species and priority conservation areas: a case study for broadleaved forests in Lombardy, Italy. *Conservation Biology* 20: 512–526.

Banks, S. C., G. R. Finlayson, S. J. Lawson, D. B. Lindenmayer, D. Paetkau, S. J. Ward, and A. C. Taylor. 2005. The effects of habitat fragmentation due to forestry plantation establishment on the demography and genetic variation of a marsupial carnivore, *Antechinus agilis*. *Biological Conservation* 122: 581–597.

Barbier, E. B. 1993. Valuation of environmental resources and impacts in developing countries. *In* R. K. Turner (ed.), *Sustainable Environmental Economics and Management*, pp. 319–337. Belhaven Press, New York.

Barbier, E. B., J. C. Burgess, and C. Folke. 1994. *Paradise Lost? The Ecological Economics of Biodiversity*. Earthscan Publications, London.

Barnhill, D. S. and R. S. Gottlieb. (eds.) 2001. *Deep Ecology and World Religions: New Essays on Sacred Ground*. Albany, State University of New York Press.

Barnosky, A. D., P. L. Koch, R. S. Feranec, S. L. Wing, and A. B. Shabel. 2004. Assessing the causes of Late Pleistocene extinctions on the continents. *Science* 306: 70–75.

Barrett, C. B., K. Brandon, C. Gibson, and H. Gjertsen. 2001. Conserving tropical biodiversity amid weak institutions. *BioScience* 51: 497–502.

Barry, D. and M. Oelschlager. 1996. A science for survival: Values for conservation biology. *Conservation Biology* 10: 905–911.

Baskin, Y. 1997. *The Work of Nature: How the Diversity of Life Sustains Us*. Island Press, Washington, D.C.

Bassett, L. (ed.). 2000. *Faith and Earth: A Book of Reflection for Action*. United Nations Environment Programme, New York.

Batisse, M. 1997. A challenge for biodiversity conservation and regional development. *Environment* 39: 7–33.

Baum, J. K. and R. A. Myers. 2004. Shifting baselines and decline of pelagic sharks in the Gulf of Mexico. *Ecology Letters* 7: 135–145.

Baum, J. K., R. A. Myers, D. G. Kehler, B. Worm, S. J. Harley, and P. A. Doherty. 2003. Collapse and conservation of shark populations in the Northwest Atlantic. *Science* 299: 389–392.

Baur, B., A. Coray, N. Minoretti, and S. Zschokke. 2005. Dispersal of the endangered flightless beetle *Dorcadion fuliginator* (Coleoptera: Cerambycidae) in spatially realistic landscapes. *Conservation Biology* 124: 49–61.

Bawa, K. S. and S. Menon. 1997. Biodiversity monitoring: The missing ingredients. *Trends in Ecology and Evolution* 12: 42.

Bawa, K. S., S. Lele, K. S. Murali, and B. Ganesan. 1998. Extraction of non-timber forest products in Biligiri Rangan Hills, India: Monitoring of a community-based project. *In* K. Saterson, R. Margolis, and N. Salafsky (eds.), *Measuring Conservation Impact: Proceedings from a Symposium at the 1996 Joint Meeting of the Society for Conservation Biology and the Ecological Society of America, Providence, RI*. Biodiversity Support Program, Washington, D.C.

Bax, N., J. T. Carlton, A. Mathews-Amos, R. L. Haedrich, F. G. Howarth, E. Purcell, et al. 2001. The control of biological invasions in the world's oceans. *Conservation Biology* 15: 1234–1246.

Bayliss-Smith, T., E. Hviding, and T. Whitmore. 2003. Rainforest composition and histories of human disturbance in Solomon Islands. *A Journal of the Human Environment* 32: 346–352.

Bazilchuk, N. 2004. Living the good life. *Conservation in Practice* 5: 38–39.

Beck, B. B., L. G. Rapport, M. R. Stanley Price, and A. C. Wilson. 1994. Reintroduction of captive-born animals. *In* P. J. Olney,

G. M. Mace, and A. T. C. Feistner (eds.), *Creative Conservation: Interactive Management of Wild and Captive Animals*, pp. 265–286. Chapman and Hall, London.

Becker, B. H. and S. R. Beissinger. 2006. Centennial decline in the trophic level of an endangered seabird after fisheries decline. *Conservation Biology* 20: 470–479.

Becker, E. 2003. *World Bank inaugurates oil pipeline in Africa.* New York Times, October 2, 2003.

Bednarek, A. T. and D. D. Hart. 2005. Modifying dam operations to restore rivers: ecological responses to Tennessee River dam mitigation. *Ecological Applications* 15: 997–1008.

Beecher, N. A., R. J. Johnson, J. R. Brandle, R. M. Case, and L. J. Young. 2002. Agroecology of birds in organic and nonorganic farmland. *Conservation Biology* 16: 1620–1631.

Beedlow, P. A., D. T. Tingey, D. L. Phillips, W. E. Hogsett, and D. M. Olszyk. 2004. Rising atmosphere CO_2 and carbon sequestration in forests. *Frontiers in Ecology and the Environment* 2: 315–322.

Beier, P., M. van Drielen, and B. O. Kankam. 2002. Avifaunal collapse in West African forest fragments. *Conservation Biology* 16: 1097–1111.

Beissinger, S. R. and D. R. McCullough (eds.). 2002. *Population Viability Analysis.* University of Chicago Press, Chicago.

Beland, P. 1996. The beluga whales of the St. Lawrence River. *Scientific American* 274: 74–81.

Bell, T. J., M. L. Bowles, and K. A. McEachern. 2003. Projecting the success of plant population restoration with viability analysis. *In* C. A. Brigham and M. M. Schwartz (eds.), *Population Viability in Plants*, pp. 313–348. Springer-Verlag, Heidelberg.

Beman, J. M., K. R. Arrigo, and P. A. Matson. 2005. Agricultural runoff fuels large phytoplankton blooms in vulnerable areas of the ocean. *Nature* 434: 211–214.

Ben-Ari, E. T. 2001. What's new at the zoo? *BioScience* 51: 172–177.

Benes, J., P. Kepka, and M. Konvicka. 2003. Limestone quarries as refuges for European xerophilous butterflies. *Conservation Biology* 17: 1058–1069.

Bennear, L. S. and C. Coglianese. 2005. Measuring progress: Program evaluation of environmental policies. *Environment* 47: 22–39.

Bennett, A. F. 1999. *Linkages in the Landscape: The Role of Corridors and Connectivity in Wildlife Conservation.* IUCN, Gland, Switzerland.

Bennett, E., H. Eves, J. Robinson, and D. Wilkie. 2002. Why is eating bushmeat a biodiversity crisis? *Conservation in Practice* 3: 28–29.

Benton, M. J. and R. J. Twitchett. 2003. How to kill (almost) all life: The end-Permian extinction event. *Trends in Ecology and Evolution* 18: 358–365.

Berger, J. 1990. Persistence of different-sized populations: An empirical assessment of rapid extinctions in bighorn sheep. *Conservation Biology* 4: 91–98.

Berger, J. 1999. Intervention and persistence in small populations of bighorn sheep. *Conservation Biology* 13: 432–435.

Berger, J. 2004. The last mile: How to sustain long-distance migration in animals. *Conservation Biology* 18: 320–331.

Berger, J., P. B. Stacey, L. Bellis, and M. P. Johnson. 2001. A mammalian predator-prey imbalance: Grizzly bear and wolf extinction affect Neotropical migrants. *Ecological Applications* 11: 947–960.

Berglund, H. and B. G. Jonsson. 2005. Verifying an extinction debt among lichens and fungi in northern Swedish boreal forests. *Conservation Biology* 19: 338–348.

Berkes, F. 1999. Sacred Ecology: *Traditional Ecological Knowledge and Resource Management.* Taylor and Francis, Philadelphia and London.

Berkes, F. 2001. Religious traditions and biodiversity. *In* S. A. Levin (ed.), *Encyclopedia of Biodiversity*, vol. 5, pp. 109–120. Academic Press, San Diego, CA.

Berkes, F. 2004. *From Community-Based Resource Management to Complex Systems: The Scale Issue and Marine Commons.* From www.millenniumassessment.org.

Berkes, F., J. Colding, and C. Folke. 2000. Rediscovery of traditional ecological knowledge as adaptive management. *Ecological Applications* 10: 1251–1262.

Berkes, F., T. P. Hughes, R. S. Steneck, J. A. Wilson, D. R. Bellwood, B. Crona, et al. 2006. Globalization, roving bandits, and marine resources. *Science* 311: 1557–1558.

Berry, O., M. D. Tocher, D. M. Gleeson, and S. D. Sarre. 2005. Effect of vegetation matrix on animal dispersal: genetic evidence from a study of endangered skinks. *Conservation Biology* 19: 855–864.

Bezemer, T. M. and T. H. Jones. 1998. Plant-insect herbivore interactions in elevated atmospheric CO_2: Quantitative analyses and guild effects. *Oikos* 82: 212–222.

Bhattacharya, M., R. B. Primack, and J. Gerwein. 2003. Are roads and railroads barriers to bumblebee movement in a temperate suburban conservation area? *Biological Conservation* 109: 37–45.

Bibby, C. J., N .J. Collar, M. J. Crosby, M. F. Heath, C. Imboden, T. H. Johnson et al. 1992. *Putting Biodiversity on the Map: Priority Areas for Global Conservation.* International Council for Bird Preservation, Cambridge.

Bierregaard, R. O., T. E. Lovejoy, V. Kapos, A. A. Dos Santos, and R. W. Hutchings. 1992. The biological dynamics of tropical rainforest fragments. *BioScience* 42: 859–866.

Biggins, D. E., A. Vargas, J. L. Godbey, and S. H. Anderson. 1999. Influence of prerelease experience on reintroduced black-footed ferrets (*Mustela nigripes*). *Biological Conservation* 89: 121–129.

Billington, H. L. 1991. Effect of population size on genetic variation in a dioecious conifer. *Conservation Biology* 5: 115–119.

Birchard, B. 2005. *Nature's Keepers: The Remarkable Story of How the Nature Conservancy Became the Largest Environmental Group in the World.* Jossey-Bass, San Francisco.

Birkeland, C. (ed.). 1997. *The Life and Death of Coral Reefs.* Chapman and Hall, New York.

Birn, A. E. and K. Dmitrienko. 2005. The World Bank: Global health or global alarm? *American Journal of Public Health* 95: 1091–1092.

Bisby, F. A. 2000. The quiet revolution: Biodiversity informatics and the internet. *Science* 289: 2309–2314.

Blanchard, K. A. 2005. Seabird populations of the North Shore of the Gulf of St. Lawrence. *In* Natural Resources As Community Assets: Lessons From Two Continents. From: http://www.sand-county.net/assets/chapters/assets_chapter_8.pdf.

Blaustein, A. R., J. M. Romansic, J. M. Kiesecker, and A. C. Hatch. 2003. Ultraviolet radiation, toxic chemicals and amphibian population declines. *Diversity and Distribution* 9: 123–140.

Bleich, V. C., J. D. Wehausen, and S. A. Holl. 1990. Desert-dwelling mountain sheep: Conservation implications of a naturally fragmented distribution. *Conservation Biology* 4: 383–389.

Blockstein, D. E. 2002. How to lose your political virginity while keeping your scientific credibility. *BioScience* 52: 91–96.

Blundell, A. G. and M. B. Mascia. 2005. Discrepancies in reported levels of international wildlife trade. *Conservation Biology* 19: 2020–2025.

Boersma, D. 2006. Landscape-level conservation for the sea. *In* In M. J. Groom, G. K. Meffe, and C. R. Carroll (eds.). *Principles of Conservation Biology*, 3rd ed, pp. 447–448. Sinauer Associates, Sunderland, MA.

Boersma, P. D., D. L. Stokes, and I. Strange. 2002. Applying ecology to conservation: Tracking breeding penguins at New Island South Reserve, Falkland Islands. *Aquatic Conservation* 12: 1–11.

Bohlen, J. B., S. Scheu, C. M. Hale, M. A. McLean, S. Migge, P. M. Groffman, and D. Parkinson. 2004. Non-native invasive earthworms as agents of change in northern temperate forests. *Frontiers in Ecology and the Environment* 2: 427–435.

Bojö, J. and R. C. Reddy. 2003. *Status and Evolution of Environmental Priorities in the Poverty Reduction Strategies.* The World Bank Environmental Department, Washington, D.C.

Bonine, K., J. Reid, and R. Dalzen. 2003. Training and education for tropical conservation. *Conservation Biology* 17: 1209–1218.

Botanic Gardens Conservation International (BGCI). 2005. www.bgci.org.

Boucher, G. and P. J. D. Lambshead. 1995. Ecological biodiversity of marine nematodes in samples from temperate, tropical and deep-sea regions. *Conservation Biology* 9: 1594–1605.

Bouchet, P., G. Falkner, and M. B. Seddon. 1999. Lists of protected land and freshwater molluscs in the Bern Convention and European Habitats Directive: Are they relevant to conservation? *Biological Conservation* 90: 21–31.

Bourne, J. K. 2004. Gone with the Water (Louisiana's wetlands). *National Geographic* 206: 88–105.

Bousquin, S. G., D. H. Anderson, G. E. Williams, and D. J. Colangelo (eds). 2005. Establishing a baseline: pre-restoration studies of the channelized Kissimmee River. Technical Publication ERA #432. South Florida Water Management District, West Palm Beach, FL.

Bouton, S. N. and P. C. Frederick. 2003. Stakeholders' perceptions of a wading bird colony as a community resource in the Brazilian pantanal. *Conservation Biology* 17: 297–306.

Bowles, M. L., J. L. McBride, and R. F. Betz. 1998. Management and restoration ecology of Mead's milkweed. *Annals of the Missouri Botanical Garden* 85: 110–125.

Bradley, E. H., D. H. Pletscher, E. E. Bangs, K. E. Kunkel, D. W. Smith, C. M. Mack, et al. 2005. Evaluating wolf translocation as a nonlethal method to reduce livestock conflicts in the northwestern United States. *Conservation Biology* 19: 1498–1508.

Bradshaw, A. D. 1990. The reclamation of derelict land and the ecology of ecosystems. *In* W. R. Jordan III, M. E. Gilpin, and J. D. Aber (eds.), *Restoration Ecology: A Synthetic Approach to Ecological Research*, pp. 53–74. Cambridge University Press, Cambridge.

Braithwaite, R. W. 2001. Tourism, role of. *In* S. A. Levin (ed.), *Encyclopedia of Biodiversity*, Vol. 5, pp. 667–679. Academic Press, San Diego, CA.

Brandon, K., K. H. Redford, and S. E. Sanderson (eds.). 1998. *Parks in Peril: People, Politics and Protected Areas*. Island Press, Washington, D.C.

Brashares, J. S. 2003. Ecological, behavioral, and life-history correlates of mammal extinctions in West Africa. *Conservation Biology* 17: 733–743.

Brashares, J. S., P. Arcese, M. K. Sam, P. B. Coppolillo, A. R. E. Sinclair, and A. Balmford. 2004. Bushmeat hunting, wildlife declines, and fish supply in West Africa. *Science* 306: 1180–1183.

Brewer, R. 2003. *Conservancy: The Land Trust Movement in America*. University Press of New England, Hanover, NH.

Briggs, J. C. 1995. *Global Biogeography*. Elsevier, Amsterdam.

Brightsmith, D., J. Hilburn, A. del Campo, J. Boyd, M. Frisius, R. Frisius, et al. 2005. The use of hand-raised psittacines for reintroduction: a case study of scarlet macaws (*Ara macao*) in Peru and Costa Rica. *Biological Conservation* 121: 465–472.

Briskie, J. V. and M. Mackintosh. 2004. Hatching failure increases with severity of population bottlenecks in New Zealand birds. *Proceedings of the National Academy of Sciences U.S.A.* 101: 558–561.

Broberg, L. 2003. Conserving ecosystems locally: A role for ecologists in land-use planning. *BioScience* 53: 670–673.

Brook, A., M. Zint, and R. DeYoung. 2003. Landowner's response to an Endangered Species Act listing and implications for encouraging conservation. *Conservation Biology* 17: 1638–1649.

Brook, B. W., M. A. Burgman, H. R. Akçakaya, J. J. O'Grady, and R. Frankham. 2002. Critiques of PVA ask the wrong questions: Throwing the heuristic baby out with the numerical bath water. *Conservation Biology* 16: 262–263.

Brooks, T. M., S. L. Pimm, and J. O. Oyugi. 1999. Time lag between deforestation and bird extinction in tropical forest fragments. *Conservation Biology* 13: 1140–1150.

Brooks, T. M., M. I. Bakarr, T. Boucher, G. A. B. Da Fonseca, C. Hilton-Taylor, J. M. Hoekstra, et al. 2004. Coverage provided by the global protected-area system: Is it enough? *BioScience* 54: 1081–1091.

Brooks, T. M., R. A. Mittermeier, C. G. Mittermeier, G. A. B. daFonseca, A. B. Rylands, W. R. Konstant, et al. 2002. Habitat loss and extinction in the hotspots of biodiversity. *Conservation Biology* 16: 909–923.

Brosnan, D. M. 2000. Can peer review help resolve natural resource conflicts? *Issues in Science and Technology* XVI: 32–36.

Brower, A., C. Reedy, and J. Yelin-Kefers. 2001. Consensus versus conservation in the Upper Colorado River Basin recovery implementation program. *Conservation Biology* 15: 1001–1007.

Brown, D. A. 2002. *American Heat: the Ethical Problem with the United States' Response to Global Warming*. Lanham, MD, Rowman and Littlefield.

Brown, K. S. 2000. Transforming a discipline: A new breed of scientist-advocate emerges. *Science* 287: 1192–1193.

Brown, R. M. and D. N. Laband. 2006. Species imperilment and spatial patterns of development in the United States. *Conservation Biology* 20: 239–244.

Brown, V. 2003. *Causes for Concern: Chemicals and Wildlife*. World Wildlife Fund, London.

Brownlow, C. A. 1996. Molecular taxonomy and the conservation of the red wolf and other endangered carnivores. *Conservation Biology* 10: 390–396.

Bruinderink, G. G., T. Van Der Sluis, D. Lammertsma, P. Opdam, and R. Pouwels. 2003. Designing a coherent ecological network for large mammals in Northwest Europe. *Conservation Biology* 17: 549–557.

Bruner, A. G., R. E. Gullison, and A. Balmford. 2004. Financial costs and shortfalls of managing and expanding protected-area systems in developing countries. *BioScience* 54: 1119–1126.

Bruner, A. G., R. E. Gullison, R. E. Rice, and G. A. B. da Fonseca. 2001. Effectiveness of parks in protecting tropical biodiversity. *Science* 291: 125–128.

Brush, S. B. 2004. Growing biodiversity. *Nature* 430: 967–968.

Brush, S. B. and D. Stabinsky (eds.). 1996. *Valuing Local Knowledge: Indigenous People and Intellectual Property Rights*. Island Press, Washington, D.C.

Brush, M. T., A. S. Hance, K. S. Judd, and E. A. Rettenmaier. 2000. *Recent Trends in Ecosystem Management*. School of Natural Resources, University of Michigan.

Bryant, D., D. Nelson, and L. Tangley. 1997. *The Last Frontier Forests: Ecosystems and Economies on the Edge*. World Resources Institute, Washington, D.C.

Bryant, D., L. Burke, J. McManus, and M. Spalding. 1998. *Reefs at Risk: A Map-Based Indicator of Threats to the World's Coral Reefs*. World Resources Institute, Washington, D.C.

Brys, R., H. Jacquemyn, P. Endels, G. De Blust, and M. Hermy. 2005. Effect of habitat deterioration on population dynamics and extinction risks in a previously common perennial. *Conservation Biology* 19: 1633–1643.

Buchmann, S. L. and G. P. Nabhan. 1996. *The Forgotten Pollinators*. Island Press, Washington, D.C.

Buddemeier, R. W., J. A. Kleypas, and R. Aronson. 2004. *Coral Reefs and Global Climate Change: Potential Contributions of Climate Change to Stresses on Coral Reef Ecosystems*. Pew Center on Global Climate Change.

Bulte, E. H. and G. C. van Kooten. 2000. Economic science, endangered species, and biodiversity loss. *Conservation Biology* 14: 113–119.

Bulte, E. H. and G. C. van Kooten. 2001. State intervention to protect endangered species: Why history and bad luck matter. *Conservation Biology* 15: 1799–1803.

Bulte, E., R. Damania, G. Lindsey, and K. Lindsay. 2004. Enhanced: space—the final frontier for economists and elephants. *Science* 306: 420–421.

Buner, F., M. Jenny, N. Zbinden, and B. Naef-Daenzer. 2005. Ecologically enhanced areas—a key habitat structure for re-introduced grey partidges *Perdix perdix*. *Biological Conservation* 124: 373–381.

Burbidge, A. A. and N. L. McKenzie. 1989. Patterns in the modern decline of Western Australia's vertebrate fauna: Causes and conservation implications. *Biological Conservation* 50: 143–198.

Burger, J. 2000. Integrating environmental restoration: Long-term stewardship at the Department of Energy. *Environmental Management* 26: 469–478.

Burgman, M. A. 2002. Are listed threatened plant species actually at risk? *Australian Journal of Botany* 50: 1–13.

Burke L. and J. Maidens. 2004. *Reefs at Risk in the Caribbean*. World Resources Institute, Washington, D.C.

Burke, L., Y. Kura, K. Kassem, C. Revenga, M. Spalding, and D. McAllister. 2000. *Pilot Assessment of Global Ecosystems:Coastal Ecosystems*. World Resources Institute, Washington, D.C.

Burks, D. C. (ed.). 1994. *Place of the Wild: A Wildlands Anthology*. Island Press/Shearwater, Washington, D.C.

Burton, A. 2005. Microbes muster pollution power. *Frontiers in Ecology and the Environment* 3: 182.

Busch, D. E. and J. C. Trexler (eds.). 2003. *Monitoring Ecosystems: Interdisciplinary Approaches for Evaluating Ecoregional Initiatives*. Island Press, Washington, D.C.

Bush, G. L. 2001. Speciation, process of. *In* S. A. Levin (ed.), *Encyclopedia of Biodiversity*, vol. 5, pp. 371–382. Academic Press, San Diego, CA.

Bushmeat Crisis Task Force. 2004. *BCTF Phase I Report*. Bushmeat Crisis Task Force, Washington D.C. http://www.bushmeat.org/cd.

Bustnes, J. O., K. E. Erikstad, J. U. Skaare, V. Bakken, and F. Mehlum. 2003. Ecological effects of organochlorine pollutants in the Arctic: A study of the Glaucous Gull. *Ecological Applications* 13: 504–515.

Butchart, S. H. M., A. J. Sattersfield, L. A. Bennun, S. M. Shutes, H. R. Akçakaya, J. E. M. Baillie, et al. 2004. Measuring global trends in the status of biodiversity: Red List Indices for birds. *Public Library of Science Biology* 2: 2294–2304.

Cabeza, M. and A. Moilanen. 2001. Design of reserve networks and the persistence of biodiversity. *Trends in Ecology and Evolution* 16: 242–248.

Cade, T. J. and W. Burnham (eds.). 2003. *Return of the Peregrine, a North American Saga of Tenacity and Teamwork*. The Peregrine Fund, Boise, ID.

Cairns, J. and J. R. Heckman. 1996. Restoration ecology: The state of an emerging field. *Annual Review of Energy and the Environment* 21: 167–189.

Caldecott, J. 1988. *Hunting and Wildlife Management in Sarawak*. IUCN, Gland, Switzerland.

Callaway, J. C., G. Sullivan, and J. B. Zedler. 2003. Species-rich plantings increase biomass and nitrogen accumulation in a wetland restoration experiment. *Ecological Applications* 13: 1626–1639.

Callaway, R. M., G. C. Thelen, A. Rodriguez, and W. E. Holben. 2004. Soil biota and exotic plant invasion. *Nature* 427: 731–733.

Callicott, J. B. 1990. Whither conservation ethics? *Conservation Biology* 4: 15–20.

Callicott, J. B. 1994. Earth's Insights: A Multicultural Survey of Ecological Ethics from the Mediterranean Basin to the Australian Outback. University of California Press, Berkeley, CA.

Campana, S., L. Marks, and W. Joyce. 2005. The biology and fishery of shortfin mako sharks (*Isurus oxyrinchus*) in Atlantic Canadian waters. *Fisheries Research* 73: 341–352.

Campbell K. and C. J. Donlan. 2005. Feral goat eradications on islands. *Conservation Biology* 19: 1362–1374.

Campton, D. E. and L. R. Kaeding. 2005. Westslope cutthroat trout, hybridization, and the U.S. Endangered Species Act. *Conservation Biology* 19: 1323–1325.

Cantú, C., R. G. Wright, J. M. Scott, and E. Strand. 2004. Assessment of current and proposed nature reserves of Mexico based on their capacity to protect geophysical features and biodiversity. *Biological Conservation* 115: 411–417.

Cardillo, M., G. M. Mace, K. E. Jones, J. Bielby, O. R. P. Bininda-Emonds, W. Sechrest, et al. 2005. Multiple causes of high extinction risk in large mammal species. *Science* 309: 1239–1241.

Carlton, J. T. 2001. Endangered marine invertebrates. *In* S. A. Levin (ed.), *Encyclopedia of Biodiversity*, vol. 2, pp. 455–464. Academic Press, San Diego, CA.

Carlton, J. T. and J. B. Geller. 1993. Ecological roulette: The global transport of nonindigenous marine organisms. *Science* 261: 78–82.

Carlton, J. T., J. B. Geller, M. L. Reaka-Kudla, and E. A. Norse. 1999. Historical extinction in the sea. *Annual Review of Ecology and Systematics* 30: 515–538.

Caro, T. M., M. B. Mulder, and M. Moore. 2003. Effects of conservation education on reasons to conserve biological diversity. *Biological Conservation* 114: 143–152.

Carr, M. H., J. E. Neigel, J. A. Estes, S. Andelman, R. R. Warner, and J. L. Largier. 2003. Comparing marine and terrestrial ecosystems: Implications for the design of coastal marine reserves. *Ecological Applications* 13: S90–S107.

Carrier, J. G. and D. V. L. Macleod. 2005. Bursting the bubble: The socio-cultural context of ecotourism. *Journal of the Royal Anthropological Institute* 11: 315.

Carroll, C., R. F. Noss, P. C. Paquet, and N. H. Schumaker. 2004. Extinction debt of protected areas in developing landscapes. *Conservation Biology* 18: 1110–1120.

Carson, R. 1982. *Silent Spring*. Reprint, Penguin, Harmondsworth, England.

Carson, R. L. 1998. *A Sense of Wonder*. New York, HarperCollins.

Carte, B. K. 1996. Biomedical potential of marine natural products: Marine organisms are yielding novel molecules for use in basic research and medical applications. *BioScience* 46: 271–286.

Cash, D., W. Clark, F. Alcock, N. Dickson, N. Eckley, and J. Jager. 2002. *Salience, Credibility, Legitimacy, and Boundaries: Linking Research, Scientific Assessment and Decision-Making*. John F. Kennedy School of Government, Harvard University, Faculty Working Papers Series, RWP02–046.

Cash, D. W., W. C. Clark, F. Alcock., N. M. Dickson, N. Eckley, D. H. Guston, et al. 2003. Knowledge systems for sustainable devlopment. *Proceedings of the National Academy of Sciences USA* 100: 8086–8091.

Castelletta, M., N. S. Sodhi, and R. Subaraj. 2000. Heavy extinctions of forest avifauna in Singapore: Lessons for biodiversity conservation in Southeast Asia. *Conservation Biology* 14: 1870–1880.

Castellón, T. D. and K. E. Sieving. 2006. An experimental test of matrix permeability and corridor use by an endemic understory bird. *Conservation Biology* 20: 135–145.

Castillo, A., A. Torres, A. Velázquez, and G. Bocco. 2005. The use of ecological science by rural producers: a case study in Mexico. *Ecological Applications* 15: 745–756.

Castree, N. 2003. Bioprospecting: from theory to practice (and back again). *Transactions of the Institute of British Geographers* 28: 35–55.

Castro, G., I. Locker, V. Russell, L. Cornwell, and E. Fajer. 2000. *Mapping Conservation Investments: An Assessment of Biodiversity Funding in Latin America and the Caribbean*. World Wildlife Fund, Washington, D.C.

Castro, I, D. H. Brunton, K. M. Mason, B. Ebert, and R. Griffith. 2003. Life history traits and food supplementation affect productivity in a translocated population of the endangered Hihi (Stitchbird, *Notiomystis cincta*). *Biological Conservation* 114: 271–280.

Caswell, H. 2001. *Matrix Population Models*, 2nd ed. Sinauer Associates, Sunderland, MA.

Caughley, G. and A. Gunn. 1996. *Conservation Biology in Theory and Practice*. Blackwell Science, Malden, MA.

Caulfield, C. 1985. *In the Rainforest*. Alfred A. Knopf, New York.

Chandrashekara, U. M. and S. Sankar. 1998. Ecology and management of sacred groves in Kerala, India. *Forest Ecological Management* 112: 165–177.

Chape, S., S. Blyth, L. Fish, P. Fox, and M. Spaulding. 2003. *2003 United Nations List of Protected Areas*. IUCN and UNEP-WCMC, Gland, Switzerland.

Chapin, F. S. III, O. E. Sala, I. C. Burke, J. P. Grime, D. U. Hooper, W. K. Lauenroth, et al. 1998. Ecosystem consequences of changing biodiversity. *BioScience* 48: 45–52.

Chapin, F. S. III, E. S. Zavaleta, V. T. Eviner, R. L. Naylor, P. M. Vitousek, H. L. Reynolds, et al. 2000. Consequences of changing biodiversity. *Nature* 405: 234–242.

Chapin, M. 2000. *Defending Kuna Yala: PEMASKY, The Study Project for the Management of Wildlands of Kuna Yala, Panama—A Case Study For Shifting The Power: Decentralization And Biodiversity Conservation*. Biodiversity Support Program, Washington, D.C.

Chapman, C. A. and C. A. Peres. 2001. Primate conservation in the new millennium: The role of scientists. *Evolutionary Anthropology* 10: 16–33.

Chapman, C. A., S. R. Balcomb, T. R. Gillespie, J. P. Skorupa, and T. T. Struhsaker. 2000. Long-term effects of logging on African primate communities: A 28-year comparison from Kibale National Park, Uganda. *Conservation Biology* 14: 207–217.

Chapman, J. W., T. W. Miller, and E. V. Coan. 2003. Live seafood species as recipes for invasion. *Conservation Biology* 17: 1386–1395.

Chapple, C. K. and M. E. Tucker (eds.), 2000. *Hinduism and Ecology: The Intersection of Earth, Sky, and Water*. Cambridge, Harvard Divinity School.

Charnley, S. 2006. The Northwest Forest Plan as a model for broad-scale ecosystem management: a social perspective. *Conservation Biology* 20: 330–340.

Chau, K. 1995. The Three Gorges Project of China: Resettlement prospects and problems. *Ambio* 24: 98–102.

Chen, L. Y. 2001. Cost savings from properly managing endangered species habitats. *Natural Areas Journal* 21: 197–203.

Cherfas, J. 1993. Backgarden biodiversity. *Conservation Biology* 7: 6–7.

Chernela, J. 1987. Endangered ideologies: Tukano fishing taboos. *Cultural Survival Quarterly* 11: 50–52.

Chernela, J. 1999. Indigenous knowledge and Amazonian blackwaters of hunger. *In* D. Posey (ed.), *Cultural and Spiritual Values of Biodiversity*, pp 423–426. United Nations Environment Programme (UNEP), London.

Chhatre A. and V. Saberwal. 2005. Political incentives for biodiversity conservation. *Conservation Biology* 19: 310–317.

Chiarucci, A., F. D'auria, V. De Dominicis, A. Laganà, C. Perini, and E. Salerni. 2005. Using vascular plants as a surrogate taxon to maximize fungal species richness in reserve design. *Conservation Biology* 19: 1644–1652.

Chicago Regional Biodiversity Council. 2001. *Chicago Wilderness, An Atlas of Biodiversity*. Chicago Regional Biodiversity Council, Chicago, IL.

Chicago Wilderness Magazine. 2004. chicagowildernessmag.org.

Chornesky, E. A., A. M. Bartuska, G. H. Aplet, K. O. Britton, J. Cummings-Carlson, F. W. Davis, et al. 2005. Science priorities for reducing the threat of invasive species to sustainable forestry. *BioScience* 55: 335–348.

Chown, S. L. and K. J. Gaston. 2000. Areas, cradles and museums: the latitudinal gradient in species richness. *Trends in Ecology and Evolution* 15: 311–315.

Christensen, J. 2003. Auditing conservation in an age of accountability. *Conservation in Practice* 4: 12–19.

Christensen, J. 2004. Over the past two decades, efforts to heal the rift between poor people and protected areas have foundered. So what next? Win-win illusions. *Conservation in Practice* 5: 12–19.

Chu, E. W. and J. R. Karr. 2001. Environmental impact, concept and measurement of. *In* S. A. Levin (ed.), *Encyclopedia of Biodiversity*, vol. 2, pp. 557–577. Academic Press, San Diego, CA.

Chuenpagdee, R., L. E. Morgan, S. M. Maxwell, E. A. Norse, and D. Pauly. 2003. Shifting gears: Assessing collateral impacts of fishing methods in U.S. waters. *Frontiers in Ecology and the Environment* 1: 517–524.

CIFOR. 2003. *Fires in Indonesia: Causes, costs and policy implications*. Center for International Forestry Research. Bogor Barat, Indonesia.

Cincotta, R. P. and R. Engelman. 2000. *Nature's Place: Human Population and the Future of Biological Diversity*. Population Action International, Washington, D.C.

Cincotta, R. P., J. Wisnewski, and R. Engelman. 2000. Human population in biodiversity hotspots. *Nature* 404: 990–992.

Cinner, J. E., M. J. Marnane, T. R. McClanahan, T. H. Clark, and J. Ben. 2005. Trade, tenure, and tradition: influence of sociocultural factors on resource use in Melanesia. *Conservation Biology* 19: 1469–1477.

Circle of Life Foundation. 2005. circleoflifefoundation.org.

Clapham, P. J., P. Berggren, S. Childerhouse, N. A. Friday, T. Kasuya, L. Kell, et al. 2003. Whaling as science. *BioScience* 53: 210–212.

Clark, T. W. 2001. Developing policy-oriented curricula for conservation biology: Professional and leadership education in the public interest. *Conservation Biology* 15: 31–39.

Clarke, F. M., D. V. Pio, and P. A. Racey. 2005. A comparison of logging systems and bat diversity in the Neotropics. *Conservation Biology* 19: 1194–1204.

Clarke, S. C., J. E. Magnussen, D. L. Abercrombie, M. K. Mcallister, and M. S. Shivji. 2006. Identification of shark species composition and proportion in the Hong Kong shark fin market based on molecular genetics and trade records. *Conservation Biology* 20: 201–211.

Clevenger, A. P. and N. Waltho. 2005. Performance indices to identify attributes of highway crossing structures facilitating movement of large mammals. *Biological Conservation* 121: 453–464.

Clevenger, A. P., B. Chruszcz, and K. E Gunson. 2003. Spatial patterns and factors influencing small vertebrate fauna road-kill aggregations. *Biological Conservation* 109: 15–26.

Clewell, A. F. and J. Aronson. 2006. Motivations for the restoration of ecosystems. *Conservation Biology* 20: 420–428.

Clewell, A. F. and J. Rieger. 1997. What practitioners need from restoration ecologists. *Restoration Ecology* 5: 350–354.

Cobb, C., T. Halstead, and J. Rowe. 1995. If the GDP is up, why is America down? *Atlantic Monthly*, October 1995.

Cochrane, M. A., A. Alencar, M. D. Schulze, C. M. Souza, D. C. Nepstad, P. Lefebvre, et al. 1999. Positive feedbacks in the fire dynamics of closed canopy tropical forests. *Science* 284: 1832–1835.

Cockrem, J. F. 2002. Reproductive biology and conservation of the endangered kakapo (*Strigops habroptilus*) in New Zealand. *Avian and Poultry Biological Review* 13: 139–144.

Cohen, M. L. 2004. Silence on the issue of our time. *The Environmentalist* 24: 255–261.

Cohn, J. P. 1991. New focus on wildlife health. *BioScience* 41: 448–450.

Colding, J. and C. Folke. 2001. Social taboos: "Invisible" systems of local resource management and biological conservation. *Ecological Applications* 11: 584–600.

Coleman, D. C. 2001. Soil biota, soil systems, and processes. *In* S. A. Levin (ed.), *Encyclopedia of Biodiversity*, vol. 5, pp. 305–314. Academic Press, San Diego, CA.

Coley, P. D., M. V. Heller, R. Aizpúra, B. Araúz, N. Flores, M. Correa, et al. 2003. Using ecological criteria to design plant collection strategies for drug discovery. *Frontiers in Ecology and the Environment* 1: 421–428.

Collett, J. and S. Karakashian (eds.). 1996. *Greening the College Curriculum: A Guide to Environmental Teaching in the Liberal Arts*. Island Press, Washington, D.C.

Comiskey, J. A., F. Dallmeier, and A. Alonso. 2001. Framework for assessment and monitoring of biodiversity. *In* S. A. Levin (ed.), *Encyclopedia of Biodiversity*, vol. 3, pp. 63–74. Academic Press, San Diego, CA.

Common, M. and S. Stagl. 2005. *Ecological Economics: An Introduction*. Cambridge University Press, New York.

Connor, E. F. and E. D. McCoy. 2001. Species-area relationships. *In* S. A. Levin (ed.), *Encyclopedia of Biodiversity*, vol. 5, pp. 397–412.

Conservation Monitoring Partnership. 2003. *Open standards for the practice of conservation*. Conservation Monitoring Partnership, Washington, D.C.

Conway, W. G., M. Hutchins, M. Souza, Y. Kapentanakos, and E. Paul. 2001. *The AZA Field Conservation Resource Guide.* Zoo Atlanta, Atlanta, Georgia.

Cook, E. A. and N. H. van Lier (eds.). 1994. *Landscape Planning and Ecological Networks.* Elsevier, Amsterdam.

Cooper, N. S. 2000. How natural is a nature reserve?: An ideological study of British nature conservation landscapes. *Biological Conservation* 9: 1131–1152.

Coote, T., D. Clarke, C. S. Hickman, J. Murray, and P. Pearce-Kelly. 2004. Experimental release of endemic Partula species, extinct in the wild, into a protected area of natural habitat on Moorea. *Pacific Science* 58: 429–424.

Cork, S. J., T. W. Clark, and N. Mazur. 2000. Introduction: An interdisciplinary effort for koala conservation. *Conservation Biology* 14: 606–609.

Corlett, R. T. and I. M. Turner. 1996. The conservation value of small, isolated fragments of lowland tropical rain forest. *Trends in Ecology and Evolution* 11: 330–333.

Costa Rica National Parks. 2005. www.costarica-nationalparks.com.

Costanza, R., O. Segurea, and J. Martinez-Alier. 1996. *Getting Down to Earth: Practical Applications of Ecological Economics.* Island Press, Washington, D.C.

Costanza, R., F. Andrade, P. Antunes, M. van den Belt, D. Boersma, D. F. Boesch, et al. 1998. Principles for sustainable governance of the oceans. *Science* 281: 198–199.

Costanza, R., R. d'Arge, R. de Groot, S. Farber, M. Grasso, B. Hannon, et al. 1997. The value of the world's ecosystem services and natural capital. *Nature* 387: 253–260.

Cottam, G. 1990. Community dynamics on an artificial prairie. *In* W. R. Jordan III, M. E. Gilpin, and J. D. Aber (eds.), *Restoration Ecology: A Synthetic Approach to Ecological Research*, pp. 257–270. Cambridge University Press, Cambridge.

Coulson, T., G. M. Mace, E. Hudson, and H. Possingham. 2003. The use and abuse of population viability analysis. *Trends in Ecology and Evolution* 16: 219–221.

Courchamp, F., G. S. A. Rasmussen, and D. W. Macdonald. 2002. Small pack size imposes a trade-off between hunting and pup-guarding in the painted hunting dog *Lycaon pictus. Behavioral Ecology* 13: 20–27.

Couzin, J. 1999. Landscape changes make regional climate run hot and cold. *Science* 283: 317–318.

Cowen, R. K., C. B. Paris, and A. Srinivasan. 2006. Scaling of connectivity in marine populations. *Science* 311: 522 – 527.

Cowling, R. M. and R. L. Pressey. 2003. Introduction to systematic conservation planning in the Cape Floristic Region. *Biological Conservation* 112: 1–13.

Cowling, R. M., P. W. Rundel, B. B. Lamont, M. K. Arroyo, and M. Arianoutsou. 1996. Plant diversity in mediterranean-climate regions. *Trends in Ecology and Evolution* 11: 362–366.

Cox, G. W. 1993. *Conservation Ecology.* W. C. Brown, Dubuque, IA.

Cox, P. A. 1997. *Nafanua: Saving the Samoan Rain Forest.* W. H. Freeman, New York.

Cox, P. A. 2001. Pharmacology, biodiversity and. *In* S. A. Levin (ed.), *Encyclopedia of Biodiversity*, vol. 4, pp. 523–536. Academic Press, San Diego, CA.

Cox, P. A. and T. Elmqvist. 1997. Ecocolonialism and indigenous-controlled rainforest preserves in Samoa. *Ambio* 26: 84–89.

Critchley, C. N. R., M. J. W. Burke, and D. P. Stevens. 2004. Conservation of lowland semi-natural grasslands in the UK: A review of botanical monitoring results from agri-environment schemes. *Biological Conservation* 115: 263–278.

Crnokrak, P. and D. A. Roff. 1999. Inbreeding depression in the wild. *Heredity* 83: 260–270.

Crooks, K. R., A. V. Suarez, and D. T. Bolger. 2004. Avian assemblages along a gradient of urbanization in a highly fragmented landscape. *Biological Conservation* 115: 451–462.

Cruz, F., C. J. Donlan, K. Campbell, and V. Carrion. 2004. Conservation action in the Galapagos: feral pig (*Sus scrofa*) eradication from Santiago Island. *Biological Conservation* 121: 473–478.

Cullen Jr., L., K. Alger, and D. M. Rambaldi. 2005. Land reform and biodiversity conservation in Brazil in the 1990's: conflict and the articulation of mutual interests. *Conservation Biology* 19: 747–755.

Cully, A. 1996. Knowlton's cactus (*Pediocactus knowltonii*) reintroduction. *In* D. A. Falk, C. Miller, and M. Olwell (eds.), *Restoring Diversity: Strategies for Reintroduction of Endangered Plants*, pp. 403–410. Island Press, Washington, D.C.

Cunningham, C. and J. Berger. 1997. *Horn of Darkness: Rhinos on the Edge.* Oxford University Press, New York.

Cuperus, R., K. J. Canters, H. A. V. de Hars, and D. S. Friedman. 1999. Guidelines for ecological compensation associated with highways. *Biological Conservation* 90: 41–51.

Curtin, C. G. 2002. Integration of science and community-based conservation in the Mexico/U.S. borderlands. *Conservation Biology* 16: 880–886.

Czech, B. 2002. A transdisciplinary approach to conservation land acquisition. *Conservation Biology* 16: 1488–1497.

Czech, B. and P. R. Krausman. 2001. *Endangered Species Act: History, Conservation Biology, and Public Policy.* Johns Hopkins University Press, Baltimore, MD.

Dahles, H. 2005. A trip too far: Ecotourism, politics, and exploitation. *Development Change* 36: 969–971.

Daily, G. C. (ed.). 1997. *Nature's Services: Societal Dependence on Ecosystem Services.* Island Press, Washington, D.C.

Daily, G. C. and K. E. Ellison. 2002. *New Economy of Nature: The Quest to Make Conservation Profitable.* Island Press, Washington, D.C.

Daily, G. C., T. Soderqvist, S. Aniyar, K. Arrow, P. Dasgupta, P. R. Ehrlich, et al. 2003. The value of nature and the nature of value. *Science* 289: 395.

Danby, R. K. and D. S. Slocombe. 2005. Regional ecology, ecosystem geography, and transboundary protected areas in the St. Elias Mountains. *Ecological Applications* 15: 405–422.

Danielsen, F., D. S. Balete, M. K. Poulsen, M. Enghoff, C. M. Nozawa, and A. E. Jensen. 2000. A simple system for monitoring biodiversity in protected areas of a developing country. *Biodiversity and Conservation* 9: 1671–1705.

D'Antonio, C. and L. A. Meyerson. 2002. Exotic plant species as problems and solutions in ecological restoration: a synthesis. *Restoration Ecology* 10: 703–713.

Darling, J. D. 1988. Working with whales. *National Geographic* 174: 886–908.

Darwin, C. R. 1859. *On the Origin of Species.* John Murray, London.

Dasgupta, P. 2001. Economic value of biodiversity, overview. *In* S. A. Levin (ed.), *Encyclopedia of Biodiversity*, vol. 2, pp. 291–304. Academic Press, San Diego, CA.

da Silva, J. M. C., A. B. Rylands, and G. A. B. Da Fonseca. 2005. The fate of the Amazonian areas of endemism. *Conservation Biology* 19: 689–694.

Dasmann, R. F. 1991. The importance of cultural and biological diversity. *In* M. L. Oldfield and J. B. Alcorn (eds.), *Biodiversity: Culture, Conservation and Ecodevelopment*, pp. 7–15. Westview Press, Boulder, CO.

Daszak, P., A. A. Cunningham, and A. D. Hyatt. 2000. Emerging infectious diseases of wildlife—threats to biodiversity and human health. *Science* 287: 443–449.

Davey, A. G. 1998. *National System Planning for Protected Areas.* IUCN, World Conservation Union, Gland, Switzerland.

David, J. H. M., P. Cury, R. J. M. Crawford, R. M. Randall, L. G. Underhill, and M. A. Meÿer. 2003. Assessing conservation priorities in the Benguela ecosystem, South Africa: Analysing predation by seals on threatened seabirds. *Biological Conservation* 114: 289–292.

Davidson, C., H. B. Shaffer, and M. R. Jennings. 2002. Spatial tests of the pesticide drift, habitat destruction, UV-B, and climate-change hypotheses for California amphibian declines. *Conservation Biology* 16: 1588–1601.

Davidson, E. W., M. Parris, J. P. Collins, J. E. Longcore, A. P. Pessier, and J. Brunner. 2003. Pathogenicity and transmission of chytridiomycosis in tiger salamanders (*Ambystoma tigrinum*). *Copeia* 2003: 601–607.

Davies, Z. G., R. J. Wilson, T. M. Brereton, and C. D. Thomas. 2005. The re-expansion and improving status of the silver-spotted skipper butterfly (*Hesperia comma*) in Britain: a metapopulation success story. *Biological Conservation* 124: 189–198.

Davis, S. H. and A. Wali. 1994. Indigenous land tenure and tropical forest management in Latin America. *Ambio* 23: 485–490.

Davradou, M. and G. Namkoong. 2001. Science, ethical arguments, and management in the preservation of land for grizzly bear conservation. *Conservation Biology* 15: 570–577.

de Chazournes, L. B. 2003. *The Global Environment Facility as a Pioneering Institution.* The Global Environment Facility, Washington, D. C.

Decker, D. J., M. E. Krasny, G. R. Goff, C. R. Smith, and D. W. Gross (eds.). 1991. *Challenges in the Conservation of Biological Resources: A Practitioner's Guide.* Westview Press, Boulder, CO.

DeFries, R. S., J. A. Foley, and G. P. Asner. 2004. Land-use choices: Balancing human needs and ecosystem function. *Frontiers in Ecology and the Environment* 2: 249–257.

DeFries, R. S., A. Hansen, A. C. Newton, and M. C. Hansen. 2005. Increasing isolation of protected areas in tropical forests of the past twenty years. *Ecological Applications* 15: 19–26.

De Grammont, P. C. and A. D. Cuarón. 2006. An evaluation of threatened species categorization systems used on the American continent. *Conservation Biology* 20: 14–27.

Deguise, I. E. and J. T. Kerr. 2006. Protected areas and prospects for endangered species conservation in Canada. *Conservation Biology* 20: 48–55.

De Marco, P. and F. Coelho. 2004. Services performed by the ecosystem: forest remnants influence agricultural cultures' pollination and production. *Biodiversity and Conservation* 13: 1245–1255.

De Mauro, M. M. 1993. Relationship of breeding system to rarity in the lakeside daisy (*Hymenoxys acaulis* var. *glabra*). *Conservation Biology* 7: 542–550.

Derraik, J. G. B., G. P. Closs, K. J. M. Dickinson, P. Sirvid, B. I. P. Barratt, and B. H. Patrick. 2002. Arthropod morphospecies versus taxonomic species: A case study with Araneae, Coleoptera and Lepidoptera. *Conservation Biology* 16: 1015–1023.

de Solla, S. R., K. J. Fernie, G. C. Barrett, and C. A. Bishop. 2005. Population trends and calling phenology of anuran populations surveyed in Ontario estimated using acoustic surveys. *Biodiversity and Conservation* (online).

Devall, B. and G. Sessions. 1985. *Deep Ecology.* Gibbs Smith Publisher, Salt Lake City, Utah.

Diamond, J. 1999. *Guns, Germs and Steel: The Fates of Human Societies.* W. W. Norton & Company, New York.

Diamond, J. 2005. *Collapse: How Societies Choose to Fail or Succeed.* Viking Books, New York.

Diamond, J., K. D. Bishop, and S. van Balen. 1987. Bird survival in an isolated Java woodland: Island or mirror? *Conservation Biology* 4: 417–422.

Diaz, J. A., J. Perez-tris, J. L. Telleria, R. Carbonell, and T. Santos. 2005. Reproductive investment of a lacertid lizard in fragmented habitat. *Conservation Biology* 19: 1578–1585.

Diaz, S. 2001. Ecosystem function measurement, terrestrial communities. *In* S. A. Levin (ed.), *Encyclopedia of Biodiversity*, vol. 2, pp. 321–344. Academic Press, San Diego, CA.

Díaz, S., F. S. Chapin III, A. J. Symstad, D. A. Wardle, and L. F. Huenneke. 2003. Functional diversity revealed by removal experiments. *Trends in Ecology and Evolution* 18: 140–146.

Dietz, R. W. and B. Czech. 2005. Conservation deficits for the continental United States: an ecosystem gap analysis. *Conservation Biology* 19: 1478–1487.

DiMento, J. F. C. 2003. *The Global Environment and International Law.* University of Texas Press, Austin, TX.

Dinerstein, E. and G. F. McCracken. 1990. Endangered greater one-horned rhinoceros carry high levels of genetic variation. *Conservation Biology* 4: 417–422.

Dinsmore, S. J., G. C. White, and F. L. Knopf. 2003. Annual survival and population estimates of Mountain Plovers in southern Phillips County, Montana. *Ecological Applications* 13: 1013–1026.

Dobson, A. 1995. Biodiversity and human health. *Trends in Ecology and Evolution* 10: 390–392.

Dobson, A. 1998. *Conservation and Biodiversity.* Scientific American Library, no. 59. W. H. Freeman, New York.

Dobson, A. 2005. Monitoring global rates of biodiversity change: challenges that arise in meeting the Convention on Biological Diversity (CBD) 2010 goals. *Philosophical Transactions of the Royal Society of London. Series B.* 360: 229–241.

Dobson, A. P., A. D. Bradshaw, and A. J. M. Baker. 1997b. Hopes for the future: Restoration ecology and conservation biology. *Science* 277: 515–522.

Dobson, A. P., J. P. Rodriguez, W. M. Roberts, and D. S. Wilcove. 1997a. Geographic distribution of endangered species in the United States. *Science* 275: 550–554.

Docherty, D. E. and R. I. Romaine. 1983. Inclusion body disease of cranes: A serological follow-up to the 1978 die-off. *Avian Diseases* 27: 830–835.

Dombeck, M. P., C. A Wood, and J. E. Williams. 2003. *From Conquest to Conservation: Our Public Lands Legacy.* Island Press, Washington, D.C.

Donoghue, M. J. and W. S. Alverson. 2000. A new age of discovery. *Annals of the Missouri Botanical Garden* 87: 110–126.

Donoso, D. S., A. A. Grez, and J. A. Simonetti. 2004. Effects of forest fragmentation on the granivory of differently sized seeds. *Biological Conservation* 115: 63–70.

Donovan, T. M. and C. W. Welden. 2002. *Spreadsheet Exercises in Conservation Biology and Landscape Ecology.* Sinauer Associates, Sunderland, MA.

Doremus, H. and J. E. Pagel. 2001. Why listing may be forever: Perspectives on delisting under the U.S. Endangered Species Act. *Conservation Biology* 15: 1258–1268.

Drake, J. M. and J. M. Bossenbroek. 2004. The potential distribution of zebra mussels in the United States. *BioScience* 54: 931–940.

Drayton, B. and R. B. Primack. 1996. Plant species lost in an isolated conservation area in metropolitan Boston from 1894 to 1993. *Conservation Biology* 10: 30–40.

Drayton, B. and R. B. Primack. 1999. Experimental extinction of garlic mustard (*Alliaria petiolata*) populations: Implications for weed science and conservation biology. *Biological Invasions* 1: 159–167.

Drezner, T. D. 2005. Saguaro (*Carnegiea gigantea*, Cactaceae) growth rate over its American range and the link to summer precipitation. *Southwestern Naturalist* 50: 65–68.

Driscoll, D. A. 1999. Genetic neighbourhood and effective population size for two endangered frogs. *Biological Conservation* 88: 221–229.

Driscoll, D. A. 2004. Extinction and outbreaks accompany fragmentation of a reptile community. *Ecological Applications* 14: 220–240.

Duffus, D. A. and P. Dearden. 1990. Non-consumptive wildlife-oriented recreation: A conceptual framework. *Biological Conservation* 53: 213–231.

Duffy, E. and A. S. Watts (eds.). 1971. *The Scientific Management of Animal and Plant Communities for Conservation.* Blackwell Scientific Publications, Oxford.

Duncan, J. R. and J. L. Lockwood. 2001. Extinction in a field of bullets: A search for causes in the decline of the world's freshwater fishes. *Biological Conservation* 102: 97–105.

Dunlap, P. V. 2001. Microbial diversity. *In* S. A. Levin (ed.), *Encyclopedia of Biodiversity*, vol. 4, pp. 191–206. Academic Press, San Diego, CA.

Dunn, R. R. 2004. Recovery of faunal communities during tropical forest regeneration. *Conservation Biology* 18: 302–309.

Dunn, R. R. 2005. Modern insect extinctions, the neglected majority. *Conservation Biology* 19: 1030–1036.

du Toit, J. T., B. H. Walker, and B. M. Campbell. 2004. Conserving tropical nature: current challenges for ecologists. *Trends in Ecology and Evolution*. 19: 12–17.

Dwyer, J. C. and I. D. Hodge. 1996. *Countryside in Trust: Land Management by Conservation, Recreation and Amenity Organizations*. John Wiley and Sons, Chichester, UK.

Earth Force. 2005. http://www.earthforce.org.

Eaton M. A., R. D. Gregory, D. G. Noble, J. A. Robinson, J. Hughes, D. Proctor, et al. 2005. Regional IUCN red listing: the process as applied to birds in the United Kingdom. *Conservation Biology* 19: 1557–1570.

Edgar, G. J., C. R. Samson, and N. S. Barrett. 2005. Species extinction in the marine environment: Tasmania as a regional example of overlooked losses in biodiversity. *Conservation Biology* 19: 1294–1300.

Edwards, J. L., M. A. Lane, and E. S. Nielsen. 2000. Interoperability of biodiversity databases: Biodiversity information on every desktop. *Science* 289: 2312–2314.

Edwards-Jones, G., B. B. Davies, and S. Hussein. 2000. *Ecological Economics: An Introduction*. Blackwell Scientific, Oxford.

Egan, D. and E. Howell (eds.). 2001. *The Historical Ecology Handbook: A Restorationist's Guide to Reference Ecosystems*. Island Press, Washington, D.C.

Ehrenfeld, D. W. 1970. *Biological Conservation*. Holt, Rinehart and Winston, New York.

Ehrenfeld, D. W. 1989. Hard times for diversity. *In* D. Western and M. Pearl (eds.), *Conservation for the Twenty-first Century*, pp. 247–250. Oxford University Press, New York.

Ehrenfeld, D. W. 2005. Sustainability: Living with the imperfections. *Conservation Biology* 19: 33–35.

Ehrlich, A. H. and P. R. Ehrlich. 1996. *Betrayal of Science and Reason: How Anti-Environmental Rhetoric Threatens Our Future*. Island Press, Washington, D.C.

Ehrlich, P. R. and A. H. Ehrlich. 1981. *Extinction: The Causes and Consequences of the Disappearance of Species*. Random House, New York.

Elfring, C. 1989. Preserving land through local land trusts. *BioScience* 39: 71–74.

Elliott, J. E., M. J. Miller, and L. K. Wilson. 2005. Assessing breeding potential of peregrine falcons based on chlorinated hydrocarbon concentrations in prey. *Environmental Pollution* 134: 353–361.

Elliot, R. 1992. Intrinsic value, environmental obligation and naturalness. *The Monist* 75: 138–160.

Ellison, K. 2003a. A question of faith: *Frontiers in Ecology and the Environment* 1: 56.

Ellison, K. 2003b. Renting biodiversity: The conservation concessions approach. *Conservation in Practice* 4: 20–29.

Ellison, K. 2004. Mercury rising. *Frontiers in Ecology and the Environment* 2: 56.

Ellison, K. and G. C. Daily. 2003. Making conservation profitable. *Conservation in Practice* 4: 12–19.

Ellstrand, N. C. 1992. Gene flow by pollen: Implications for plant conservation genetics. *Oikos* 63: 77–86.

Emerson, R. W. 1836. *Nature*. James Monroe and Co., Boston, MA.

Enderson, J. H., W. Heinrich, L. Kiff, and C. M. White. 1995. Population changes in North American peregrines. *Transactions of the 60th North American Wildlife and Natural Resource Conference*, pp. 142–161. Wildlife Management Institute, Washington, D.C.

Engeman, R. M., S. A. Shwiff, F. Cano, and B. Constantin. 2003. An economic assessment of the potential for predator management to benefit Puerto Rican parrots. *Ecological Economics* 46: 283–292.

Environmental Defense. 2000. Progress on the Back Forty: An Analysis of the Incentive-Based Approaches to Endangered Species Conservation on Private Land. Washington, D.C.

Epstein, P. R. 1998. *Marine Ecosystems: Emerging Diseases as Indicators of Change: Health of the Ocean from Labrador to Venezuela*. Harvard Medical School, Boston.

Epstein, P. R. (ed.). 1999. *Extreme Weather Events: The Health and Economic Consequences of the 1997/98 El Niño and La Niña*. Harvard Medical School, Boston.

Erdelen, W. 1988. Forest ecosystems and nature conservation in Sri Lanka. *Biological Conservation* 43: 115–135.

Ervin, J. 2003. Rapid assessment of protected area management effectiveness in four countries. *BioScience* 53: 833–841.

Esler, D. 2000. Applying metapopulation theory to conservation of migratory birds. *Conservation Biology* 14: 366–372.

Essington, T. E. 2001. The precautionary approach in fisheries management: The devil is in the details. *Trends in Ecology and Evolution* 16: 121–122.

Estes, J. A., K. Crooks, and R. Holt. 2001. Predators, ecological role of. *In* S. A. Levin (ed.), *Encyclopedia of Biodiversity*, vol. 4, pp. 857–878. Academic Press, San Diego, CA.

Esty, D. C., M. Levy, T. Srebotnjak, and A. de Sherbinin. 2005. *2005 Environmental Sustainability Index: Benchmarking National Environmental Stewardship*. Yale Center for Environmental Law & Policy, New Haven, CT.

Evans, C., E. Abrams, R. Reitsma, K. Roux, L. Salmonsen, and P. P. Marra. 2005. The Neighborhood Nestwatch Program: Participant outcomes of a citizen-science ecological research project. *Conservation Biology* 19: 589–594.

Evans, M. E. K., R. W. Dolan, E. S. Menges, and D. R. Gordon. 2000. Genetic diversity and reproductive biology in *Warea carteri* (Brassicaceae), a narrowly endemic Florida scrub annual. *American Journal of Botany* 87: 372–381.

Eyles, J. and N. Consitt. 2004. What's at risk? Environmental influences on human health. *Environment* 46: 25–39.

Fa, J. E, C. A. Peres, and J. Meeuwig. 2001. Bushmeat exploitation in tropical forests: An intercontinental comparison. *Conservation Biology* 16: 232–237.

Facon, B., B. J. Genton, J. Shykoff, P. Jarne, A. Estoup, and P. David. 2006. A general eco-evolutionary framework for understanding bioinvasions. *Trends in Ecology and Evolution* 21: 130–135.

Faeth, S. H., P. S. Warren, E. Shochat, and W. A. Marussich. 2005. Trophic dynamics in urban communities. *BioScience* 55: 399–407.

Fagan, C., C. A. Peres, and J. Terborgh. 2005. Tropical forests: A protected area strategy for the 21st Century. *In* W. F. Laurance and C.A. Peres (eds.), *Emerging Threats to Tropical Forests*. University of Chicago Press, Chicago.

Falk, D. A. 1987. Integrated conservation strategies for endangered plants. *Natural Areas Journal* 7: 118–123.

Falk, D. A. 1990. Endangered forest resources in the United States—integrated strategies for conservation of rare species and genetic diversity. *Forest Ecology and Management* 35: 91–117.

Falk, D. A. and K. E. Holsinger (eds.). 1991. *Genetics and Conservation of Rare Plants*. Oxford University Press, New York.

Falk, D. A., C. I. Millar, and M. Olwell (eds.). 1996. *Restoring Diversity: Strategies for Reintroduction of Endangered Plants*. Island Press, Washington, D.C.

Fang, J., S. Rao, and S. Zhao. 2005. Human-induced long-term changes in the lakes of the Jianghan Plain, Central Yangtze. *Frontiers in Ecology and the Environment* 3: 186–192.

Fanshawe, S., G. R. Vanblaricom, and A. A. Shelly. 2003. Restored top carnivores as detriments to the performance of marine protected areas intended for fishery sustainability: A case study with red abalones and sea otters. *Conservation Biology* 17: 273–283.

Fazey, I., J. Fischer, and D. B. Lindenmayer. 2005. What do conservation biologists publish? *Conservation Biology* 124: 63–73.

Fearnside, P. M. 1990. Predominant land uses in Brazilian Amazonia. *In* A. Anderson (ed.), *Alternatives to Deforestation: Steps Toward Sustainable Use of the Amazon Rain Forest*, pp. 233–251. Columbia University Press, Irvington, NY.

Fearnside, P. M. 2001. Saving tropical forests as a global warming countermeasure: An issue that divides the environmental movement. *Ecological Economics* 39: 167–184.

Fearnside P. M. 2005. Deforestation in Brazilian Amazonia: History, rates, and consequences. *Conservation Biology* 19: 680–688.

Fearnside, P. M. and J. Ferraz. 1995. A conservation gap analysis of Brazil's Amazonian vegetation. *Conservation Biology* 9: 1134–1148.

Feinsinger, P. 2001. *Designing Field Studies for Biodiversity Conservation*. Island Press, Washington, D.C.

Ferber, D. 2000. Galápagos station survives latest attack by fishers. *Science* 290: 2059–2060.

Ferraz, G., G. J. Russell, P. C. Stouffer, R. O. Bierregaard, S. L. Pimm, and T. E. Lovejoy. 2003. Rates of species loss from Amazonian forest fragments. *Proceedings of the National Academy of Sciences U.S.A.* 100: 14069–14073.

Ferry, L. 1995. *The New Ecological Order*. University of Chicago Press, Chicago.

Festa-Bianchet, M. and M. Apollonio (eds.). 2003. *Animal Behavior and Wildlife Conservation*. Island Press, Washington, D.C.

Field, D. B., T. R. Baumgartner, C. D. Charles, V. Ferreira-Bartrina, and M. D. Ohman. Planktonic foraminifera of the California current reflect 20th-century warming. *Science* 311: 63–66.

Fischer, C., E. Muchapondwa, and T. Sterner. 2005. Shall we gather 'round the campfire? Zimbabwe's approach to conserving indigenous wildlife. *Resources* 158: 12–15.

Fischer, J. and D. B. Lindenmayer. 2000. An assessment of published results of animal relocations. *Biological Conservation* 96: 1–11.

Fish, M. R., I. M. Cote, J. A. Gill, A. P. Jones, S. Renshoff, and A. R. Watkinson. 2005. Predicting the impact of sea-level rise on Caribbean sea turtle nesting habitat. *Conservation Biology* 19: 482–491.

Fisk, M. R., S. J. Giovannoni, and I. H. Thorseth. 1998. Alteration of oceanic volcanic glass: Textural evidence of microbial activity. *Science* 281: 978–980.

Fitter, A. H. and R. S. R. Fitter. 2002. Rapid changes in flowering time in British plants. *Science* 296: 1689–1691.

Fitzpatrick, J. W., M. Lammertink, M. D. Luneau, T. W. Gallagher, B. R. Harrison, G. M. Sparling, et al. 2005. Ivory-billed woodpecker (*Campephilus principalis*) persists in continental North America. *Science* 308: 1460–1462.

Flather, C. H., M. S. Knowles, and I. A. Kendall. 1998. Threatened and endangered species geography. *BioScience* 48: 365–376.

Foley, J. A., R. DeFries, G. P. Asner, C. Barford, G. Bonan, S. R. Carpenter, et al. 2005. Global consequences of land use. *Science* 309: 570–574.

Folke, C. and J. Colding. 2001. Traditional conservation practices. *In* S. A. Levin (ed.), *Encyclopedia of Biodiversity*, vol. 5, pp. 681–694. Academic Press, San Diego, CA.

Foltz, R., F. M. Denny, and A. Baharuddin (eds), 2003. *Islam and Ecology: A Bestowed Trust*. Cambridge, Harvard Divinity School.

Foose, T. J. 1983. The relevance of captive populations to the conservation of biotic diversity. *In* C. M. Schonewald-Cox, S. M. Chambers, B. MacBryde, and L. Thomas (eds.). *Genetics and Conservation*, pp. 374–401. Benjamin/Cummings, Menlo Park, CA.

Forkner, R. E., R. J. Marquis, J. T. Lill, and J. Le Corff. 2006. Impacts of alternative timber harvest practices on leaf-chewing herbivores of oak. *Conservation Biology* 20: 429–440.

Forman, R. T. 1995. *Land Mosaics: The Ecology of Landscapes and Regions*. Cambridge University Press, New York.

Forman, R. T. 2004. Road ecology's promise: What's around the bend? *Environment* 46: 9–21.

Forman, R. T. and M. Godron. 1981. Patches and structural components for a landscape ecology. *BioScience* 31: 733–740.

Forman, R. T., D. Sperling, J. H. Bissonette, A. P. Clevenger, C. D. Cutshall, V. H. Dale, et al. 2003. *Road Ecology: Scienceand Solutions*. Island Press, Washington, D.C.

Fossey, D. 1990. *Gorillas in the Mist*. Houghton Mifflin, Boston.

Foster, S. J. and A. C. J. Vincent. 2005. Enhancing sustainability of the international trade in seahorses with a single minimum size limit. *Conservation Biology* 19: 1044–1050.

Fowler, S. L. 2000. Basking shark (*Cetorhinus maximus*). *In* R. P. Reading and B. Miller (eds.), *Endangered Animals*, pp. 49–53. Greenwood Press, Westport, CT.

Fox, D. 2004. The elephant listening project. *Conservation in Practice* 5: 30–37.

Fox, J. and A Nino-Murcia. 2005. Status of species conservation banking in the United States. *Conservation Biology* 19: 996–1007.

Fox, J., P. Yonzon, and N. Podger. 1996. Mapping conflicts between biodiversity and human needs in Langtang National Park. *Conservation Biology* 10: 562–569.

Frankham, R. 1995. Inbreeding and conservation: A threshold effect. *Conservation Biology* 9: 792–799.

Frankham, R. 1996. Relationships of genetic variation to population size in wildlife. *Conservation Biology* 10: 1500–1508.

Frankham, R. 2005. Genetics and extinction (review article). *Biological Conservation* 126: 131–140.

Frankham, R., J. D. Ballou, and D. A. Briscoe. 2002. *Introduction to Conservation Genetics*. Cambridge University Press, New York.

Frankham, R., J. D. Ballou, and D. A. Briscoe. 2004. *A Primer of Conservation Genetics*. Cambridge University Press, Cambridge, U.K.

Franklin, I. R. 1980. Evolutionary change in small populations. *In* M. E. Soulé and B. A. Wilcox (eds.), *Conservation Biology: An Evolutionary-Ecological Perspective*, pp. 135–149. Sinauer Associates, Sunderland, MA.

Franklin, J. F., T. A. Spies, R. Van Pelt, A. B. Carey, D. A. Thornburgh, D. R. Berg, et al. 2002. Disturbances and structural development of natural forest ecosystems with silvicutural implications, using Douglas-fir forests as an example. *Forest Ecology and Management* 155: 399–423.

Frazier, J. 2000. Kemp's Ridley sea turtle (*Lepidochelys kempii*). *In* R. P. Reading and B. Miller (eds.), *Endangered Animals*, pp. 164–170. Greenwood Press, Westport, CT.

Fredrickson, J. K. and T. C. Onstott. 1996. Microbes deep inside Earth. *Scientific American* 275: 68–73.

Fricke, H. and K. Hissmann. 1990. Natural habitat of the coelocanths. *Nature* 346: 323–324.

Friedman, G. M., P. K. Mukhopadhyay, A. Moch, and M. Ahmed. 2000. Waters and organic-rich waste near dumping grounds in the New York Bight. *International Journal of Coal Geology* 43: 325–355.

Frisvold, G., J. Sillivan, and A. Raneses. 2001. Who gains from genetic improvements in US crops? *AgBioForum* 2: 237–246.

Frohlich, J. and K. D. Hyde. 1999. Biodiversity of palm fungi in the tropics: are global fungal diversity estimates realistic? *Biodiversity and Conservation* 8: 977–1004.

Fuccilo, D., L. Sears, and P. Stapleton. 1998. *Biodiversity in Trust: Conservation and Use of Plant Genetic Resources in CGIAR Centres*. Cambridge University Press, New York.

Fujita, M. S. and M. D. Tuttle. 1991. Flying foxes (*Chiroptera: Pteropodidae*): Threatened animals of key ecological and economic importance. *Conservation Biology* 5: 455–463.

Fuller, D. O., T. C. Jessup, and A. Salim. 2004. Loss of forest cover in Kalimantan, Indonesia since the 1997–1998 El Niño. *Conservation Biology* 18: 249–254.

Fuller, R. J., R. D. Gregory, D. W. Gibbons, J. H. Marchant, J. D. Wilson, S. R. Baillie, et al. 1995. Population declines and range contractions among lowland farmland birds in Britain. *Conservation Biology* 9: 1425–1441.

Funch, P. and R. Kristensen. 1995. Cycliophora is a new phylum with affinities to Entoprocta and Ectoprocta (*Symbion pandora*). *Nature* 378: 711–714.

Futuyma, D. J. 1998. *Evolutionary Biology*, 3rd ed. Sinauer Associates, Sunderland, MA.

Gadgil, M. and R. Guha. 1992. *This Fissured Land: An Ecological History of India*. Oxford University Press, Oxford.

Gaff, H., J. Chick, J. Trexler, D. DeAngelis, L. Gross, and R. Salinas. 2004. Evaluation of and insights from ALFISH: A spatially explicit, landscape-level simulation of fish populations in the Everglades. *Hydrobiologia* 520: 73–87.

Galbraith, C. A., P. V. Grice, G. P. Mudge, S. Parr, and M. W. Pienkowski. 1998. The role of statutory bodies in ornithological conservation. *Ibis* 137: S224–S231.

Galdikas, B. 1995. *Reflections of Eden: My Years with the Orangutans of Borneo*. Little Brown, Boston.

Gärdenfors, U. 2001. Classifying threatened species at national versus global levels. *Trends in Ecology and Evolution* 16: 511–516.

Gärdenfors, U., C. Hilton-Taylor, G. Mace, and J. P. Rodriguez. 2001. The application of IUCN red list criteria at regional levels. *Conservation Biology* 15: 1206–1212.

Gaston, K. J. 2000. Global patterns in biodiversity. *Nature* 405: 220–227.

Gaston, K. J. and J. I. Spicer. 2004. *Biodiversity: An Introduction*, 2nd ed. Blackwell, Oxford.

Gates, D. M. 1993. *Climate Change and Its Biological Consequences*. Sinauer Associates, Sunderland, MA.

Gelbard, J. L. and J. Belnap. 2003. Roads as conduits for exotic plant invasions in a semiarid landscape. *Conservation Biology* 17: 420–432.

Gell, F. R. and C. M. Roberts. 2003. Benefits beyond boundaries: The fishery effects of marine reserves. *Trends in Ecology and Evolution* 18: 448–455.

Gentry, A. H. 1986. Endemism in tropical versus temperate plant communities. *In* M. E. Soulé (ed.), *Conservation Biology: The Science of Scarcity and Diversity*, pp. 153–181. Sinauer Associates, Sunderland, MA.

Gerrodette, T. and W. G. Gilmartin. 1990. Demographic consequences of changing pupping and hauling sites of the Hawaiian monk seal. *Conservation Biology* 4: 423–430.

Gersh, J. and R. Pickert. 1991. Land-use modeling: Accommodating growth while conserving biological resources in Dutchess County, New York. *In* D. J. Decker, M. E. Krasnyk, G. R. Goff, C. R. Smith, and D. W. Gross (eds.), *Challenges in the Conservation of Biological Resources: A Practitioner's Guide*, pp. 233–242. Westview Press, Boulder, CO.

Gerwick, W. H., B. Marquez, K. Milligan, L. Tong Tan, and T. Williamson. 2001. Plant sources of drugs and chemicals. *In* S. A. Levin (ed.), *Encyclopedia of Biodiversity*, vol. 4, pp. 711–722. Academic Press, San Diego, CA.

Ghimire, S. K., D. McKey, and Y. Aumeeruddy-Thomas. 2005. Conservation of Himalayan medicinal plants: Harvesting patterns and ecology of two threatened species, *Nardostachys grandiflora* DC. and *Neopicrorhiza scrophulariiflora* (Pennell) Hong. *Biological Conservation* 124: 463–475.

Gibbs, W. W. 2001. The Arctic oil and wildlife refuge. *Scientific American* 284: 63–69.

Giese, M. 1996. Effects of human activity on adelie penguin *Pygoscelis adeliae* breeding success. *Biological Conservation* 75: 157–164.

Gigon, A., R. Langenauer, C. Meier, and B. Nievergelt. 2000. Blue Lists of threatened species with stabilized or increasing abundance: A new instrument for conservation. *Conservation Biology* 14: 402–413.

Gilbert, O. L. and P. Anderson. 1998. *Habitat Creation and Repair*. Oxford University Press, Oxford.

Gillespie, G. R. 2001. The role of introduced trout in the decline of the spotted tree frog (*Litoria spenceri*) in south-eastern Australia. *Conservation Biology*. 100: 187–198.

Gillett, N. P., F. W. Zwiers, A. J. Weaver, and P. A. Stott. 2003. Detection of human influence on sea-level pressure. *Nature* 422: 292–294.

Gilpin, M. E. and M. E. Soulé. 1986. Minimum viable populations: Processes of species extinction. *In* M. E. Soulé (ed.), *Conservation Biology: The Science of Scarcity and Diversity*, pp. 19–34. Sinauer Associates, Sunderland, MA.

Ginsberg, J. 2002. CITES at 30, or 40. *Conservation Biology* 16: 1184–1191.

Gittleman, J. L. 1994. Are the pandas successful specialists or evolutionary failures? *BioScience* 44: 456–464.

Gittleman, J. L., S. M. Funk, D. McDonald, and R. K. Wayne (eds.). 2000. *Carnivore Conservation*. Cambridge University Press, Cambridge.

Given, D. R. 1995. *Principles and Practice of Plant Conservation*. Timber Press, Portland, OR.

Global Biodiversity Information Facility. 2005. www.gbif.org.

Global Environment Facility. 1999. *Experience with Conservation Trusts*. World Bank, New York.

Global Environment Facility. 2005. www.gefweb.org.

Gobster, P. H. and R. B. Hull (eds.). 2000. *Restoring Nature: Perspectives from the Social Science and Humanities*. Island Press, Washington, D.C.

Godoy, R. A. 2001. *Indians, Markets and Rainforests: Theoretical, Comparative, and Quantitative Explorations in the Neotropics*. Columbia University Press, New York.

Godwin, P. 2001. Wildlife without borders. *National Geographic* 200: 2–31.

Goerck, J. M. 1997. Patterns of rarity in the birds of the Atlantic forest of Brazil. *Conservation Biology* 11: 112–118.

Goffredo, S., C. Piccinetti, and F. Zaccanti. 2004. Volunteers in marine conservation monitoring: a study of the distribution of seahorses carried out in collaboration with recreational scuba divers. *Conservation Biology* 18: 1492–1503.

Goldammer, J. G. 1999. Forests on fire. *Science* 284: 1782–1783.

Goldberg, T. L., E. C. Grant, K. R. Inendino, T. W. Kassler, J. E. Claussen, and D. P. Philipp. 2005. Increased infectious disease susceptibility resulting from outbreeding depression. *Conservation Biology* 19: 455–462.

Goldburg, R. and N. Naylor. 2005. Future seascapes, fishing, and fish farming. *Frontiers in Ecology and the Environment* 3: 21–28.

Goodall, J. 1999. *Reason for Hope: A Spiritual Journey*. Warner Books, New York.

Goodland, R. J. A. 1990. The World Bank's new environmental policy for dams and reservoirs. *Water Resources Development* 6: 226–239.

Goossens, B., J. M. Setchell, E. Tchidongo, E. Dilambaka, C. Vidal, M. Ancrenaz, et al. 2005. Survival, interactions with conspecifics and reproduction in 37 chimpanzees released into the wild. *Biological Conservation* 123: 461–475.

Gore, A. 1992. *Earth in the Balance: Ecology and the Human Spirit*. Houghton Mifflin, New York.

Gössling, S. 1999. Ecotourism: a means to safeguard biodiversity and ecosystem functions? *Ecological Economics* 29: 303–320.

Gotelli, N. J. 2001. *A Primer of Ecology*, 3rd ed. Sinauer Associates, Sunderland, MA.

Goulder, L. H. and R. N. Stavins. 2002. Discounting: An eye on the future. *Nature* 419: 673–674.

Gram, W. K., P. A. Porneluzi, R. L. Clawson, J. Faaborg, and S. C. Richter. 2003. Effects of experimental forest management on density and nesting success of bird species in Missouri Ozark Forests. *Conservation Biology* 17: 1324–1337.

Granek, E. F., C. J. Lundquist, and R. H. Bustamante. 2005. Special Section: Implementation and management of marine protected areas. *Conservation Biology* 19: 1699–1700.

Grant, P. R. and B. R. Grant. 1992. Darwin's finches: Genetically effective population sizes. *Ecology* 73: 766–784.

Grant, P. R. and B. R. Grant. 1997. The rarest of Darwin's finches. *Conservation Biology* 11: 119–126.

Grant, P. R., B. R. Grant, K. Petren, and L. F. Keller. 2005. Extinction behind our backs: the possible fate of one of the Darwin's finch species on Isla Floreana, Galapagos. *Biological Conservation* 122: 499–503.

Grassle, J. F. 2001. Marine ecosystems. *In* S. A. Levin (ed.), *Encyclopedia of Biodiversity*, vol. 4, pp. 13–26. Academic Press, San Diego, CA.

Greathouse, E. A., C. M. Pringle, W. H. McDowell, and J. G. Holmquist. 2006. Indirect upstream effects of dams: consequences of migratory consumer extirpation in Puerto Rico. *Ecological Applications* 16: 339–352.

Grebmeier, J. M., J. E. Overland, S. E. Moore, E. V. Farley, E. C. Carmack, L. W. Cooper, et al. 2006. A major ecosystem shift in the northern Bering Sea. *Science* 311: 1461–1464.

Green, R. E., S. J. Cornell, J. P. W. Scharlemann, and A. Balmford. 2005. Farming and the fate of wild nature. *Science* 307: 550–555.

Gregg, W. P., Jr. 1991. MAB Biosphere reserves and conservation of traditional land use systems. *In* M. L. Oldfield and J. B. Alcorn (eds.), *Biodiversity: Culture, Conservation and Ecodevelopment*, pp. 274–294. Westview Press, Boulder, CO.

Greuter, W. 1995. Extinction in Mediterranean areas. *In* J. H. Lawton and R. M. May. *Extinction Rates*, pp. 88–97. Oxford University Press, Oxford.

Griffith, A. B. and I. N. Forseth. 2005. Population matrix models of *Aeschynomene virginica*, a rare annual plant: implications for conservation. *Ecological Applications* 15: 222–233.

Griffith, B., J. M. Scott, J. W. Carpenter, and C. Reed. 1989. Translocation as a species conservation tool: Status and strategy. *Science* 245: 477–480.

Grifo, F. and J. Rosenthal (eds.). 1997. *Biodiversity and Human Health*. Island Press, Washington, D.C.

Grigg, R. W. and D. Epp. 1989. Critical depth for the survival of coral islands: Effects on the Hawaiian archipelago. *Science* 243: 638–641.

Groom, M. J., G. K. Meffe, and C. R. Carroll (eds.). 2006. *Principles of Conservation Biology*, 3rd ed. Sinauer Associates, Inc. Sunderland, MA.

Groombridge, B. and M. D. Jenkins. 2002. *World Atlas of Biodiversity: Earth's Living Resources in the 21st Century*. University of California Press, Berkeley, CA.

Groombridge, J. J., C. G. Jones, M. W. Bruford, and R. A. Nichols. 2000. Conservation biology—"Ghost" alleles of the Mauritius kestrel. *Nature* 403: 616.

Grove, A. T. and O. Rackham. 2001. *The Nature of Mediterranean Europe: An Ecological History*. Yale University Press, New Haven, CT.

Grove, R. H. 1992. Origins of Western environmentalism. *Scientific American* 267: 42–47.

Groves, C. R. 2003. *Drafting a Conservation Blueprint: A Practitioner's Guide to Planning for Biodiversity*. Island Press, Washington, D.C.

Grumbine, E. R. 1994. What is ecosystem management? *Conservation Biology* 8: 27–38.

Gude, P. H., A. J. Hansen, R. Rasker, and B. Maxwell. 2005. Rates and drivers of rural residential development in the Greater Yellowstone. *Landscape and Urban Planning*, in press.

Guerrant, E. O. 1992. Genetic and demographic considerations in the sampling and reintroduction of rare plants. *In* P. L. Fiedler and S. K. Jain (eds.), *Conservation Biology: The Theory and Practice of Nature Conservation, Preservation and Management*, pp. 321–344. Chapman and Hall, New York.

Guerrant, E. O. and B. M. Pavlik. 1998. Reintroduction of rare plants: Genetics, demography and the role of *ex-situ* conservation methods. *In* P. L. Fiedler and P. M. Kareiva (eds.), *Conservation Biology for the Coming Decade*, pp. 80–108. Chapman and Hall, New York.

Guerrant, E. O. Jr., K. Havens, and M. Maunder. 2004. *Ex Situ Conservation. Supporting Species Survival in the Wild*. Island Press, Washington, D.C.

Guerry, A. D. 2005. Icarus and Daedalus: conceptual and tactical lessons for marine ecosystem-based management. *Frontiers in Ecology and the Environment* 3: 202–211.

Gulbrandsen, L. H. 2005. Mark of stustainability? Challenges for fishery and forestry eco-labeling. *Environment* 47: 8–23.

Gundale, M. J., W. M. Jolly, and T. H. Deluca. 2005. Susceptibility of a northern hardwood forest to exotic earthworm invasion. *Conservation Biology* 19: 1075–1083.

Gurd, D. B. 2006. Variation in species losses from islands: artifacts, extirpation rates, or pre-fragmentation diversity? *Ecological Applications* 16: 176–185.

Gurd, D. B., T. D. Nudds, and D. H. Rivard. 2001. Conservation of mammals in eastern North American wildlife reserves: How small is too small? *Conservation Biology* 15: 1355–1363.

Gurnell, A., K. Tockner, P. Edwards, and G. Petts. 2005. Effects of deposited wood on biocomplexity of river corridors. *Frontiers in Ecology and the Environment* 3: 377–382.

Guzmán, H. M., C. Guevara, and A. Castillo. 2003. Natural disturbances and mining of Panamanian coral reefs by indigenous people. *Conservation Biology* 17: 1396–1401.

Haberl, H., F. Kransmann, K, Erb, N. B. Schulz, S. Rojstaczer, S. M. Sterling, et al. 2002. Human appropriation of NPP. *Science* 296: 1968–1969.

Haddad, N. M. and J. J. Tewksbury. 2005. Low-quality habitat corridors as movement conduits for two butterfly species. *Ecological Applications* 15: 250–257.

Haddad, N. M., J. Haarstad, and D. Tilman. 2000. The effects of long-term nitrogen loading on grassland insect communities. *Oecologia* 124: 73–84.

Hagen, A. N. and K. E. Hodges. 2006. Resolving critical habitat designation failures: reconciling law, policy, and biology. *Conservation Biology* 20: 399–407.

Haight, R. G., B. Cypher, P. A. Kelly, S. Phillips, H. P. Possingham, K. Ralls, et al. 2002. Optimizing habitat protection using demographic models of population viability. *Conservation Biology* 16: 1386–1397.

Hajek, A. 2004. *Natural Enemies: An Introduction to Biological Control*. Cambridge University Press, Cambridge.

Halpern, B. S. 2003. The impact of marine reserves: Do reserves work and does reserve size matter? *Ecological Applications* 13: S117–S137.

Halpern, B. S., C. R. Pyke, H. E. Fox, J. C. Haney, M. A. Schlaepfer, and P. Zaradic. 2006. Gaps and mismatches between global conservation priorities and spending. *Conservation Biology* 20: 56–64.

Halpern, C. B., D. McKenzie, S. A. Evans, and D. A. Maguire. 2005. Initial responses of forest understories to varying levels and patterns of green-tree retention. *Ecological Applications* 15: 175–195.

Halvorson, W. L. and G. E. Davis (eds.). 1996. *Science and Ecosystem Management in the National Parks*. University of Arizona, Tucson.

Hammond, P. M. 1992. Species inventory. *In* B. Groombridge (ed.), *Global Diversity: Status of the Earth's Living Resources*, pp. 17–39. Chapman and Hall, London.

Hancocks, D. 2001. *A Different Nature: The Paradoxical World of Zoos and Their Uncertain Future*. University of California Press, Berkeley, CA.

Hanley, N. and C. Splash. 1994. *Cost-Benefit Analysis and the Environment*. Edward Elgar Publishing, Cheltenham, UK.

Hannah, L., G. F. Midgley, G. O. Hughes, and B. Bomhard. 2005. The view from the Cape: extinction risk, protected areas and climate change. *BioScience* 55: 231–242.

Hansen, A. J., T. A. Spies, F. J. Swanson, and J. L. Ohmann. 1991. Conserving biodiversity in managed forests. *BioScience* 41: 382–392.

Hansen, A. J., R. P. Neilson, V. H. Dale, C. H. Flather, L. R. Iverson, D. J. Currie, et al. 2001. Global change in forests: Responses of species, communities, and biomes. *BioScience* 51: 765–779.

Hanski, I. and D. Simberloff (eds.). 1997. *Metapopulation Biology*. Academic Press, San Diego, CA.

Hardesty, B. D., C. W. Dick, A. Kremer, S. Hubbell, and E. Bermingham. 2005. Spatial genetic structure of *Simarouba amara* Aubl. (Simaroubaceae), a dioecious, animal-dispersed Neotropical tree, on Barro Colorado Island, Panama. *Heredity* 95: 290–297.

Hardin, G. 1985. *Filters against Folly: How to Survive Despite Economists, Ecologists and the Merely Eloquent*. Viking Press, New York.

Hardin, G. 1993. *Living within Limits: Ecology, Economics and Population Taboos*. Oxford University Press, New York.

Harley, E. H., I. Baumgarten, J. Cunningham, and C. O'Ryan. 2005. Genetic variation and population structure in remnant populations of black rhinoceros, *Diceros bicornis*, in Africa. *Molecular Ecology* 14: 2981–2990.

Harmon, D. and A. Putney (eds.). 2003. *The Full Value of Parks: From Economics to the Intangible*. Rowman & Littlefield Publishers, Lanham, MD.

Harms, K. E., S. J. Wright, O. Calderón, A. Hernández, and E. A. Herre. 2000. Pervasive density-dependent recruitment enhances seedling diversity in a tropical forest. *Nature* 404: 493–495.

Harper, K. A., S. E. Macdonald, P. J. Burton, J. Chen, K. D. Brosofske, S. C. Saunders, et al. 2005. Edge influence on forest structure and composition in fragmented landscapes. *Conservation Biology* 19: 768–782.

Harris, M. B., W. Tomas, G. Mourao, C. J. Da Silva, E. Gumaraes, F. Sonoda, et al. 2005. Safeguarding the Pantanal wetlands: Threats and conservation initiatives. *Conservation Biology* 19: 714–720.

Harrison, I. J. and M. L. J. Stiassny. 1999. The quiet crisis: A preliminary listing of the freshwater fishes of the world that are extinct or "missing in action." *In* R. D. E MacPhee (ed.), *Extinctions in Near Time*, pp. 271–329. Kluwer Academic/Plenum Publishers, New York.

Harrison, J. L. 1968. The effect of forest clearance on small mammals. *Conservation in Tropical Southeast Asia*. IUCN, Morges, Switzerland.

Harrop, S. R. 1999. Conservation regulation: A backward step for biodiversity? *Biodiversity and Conservation* 8: 679–707.

Hart, J. and T. Hart. 2003. Rules of engagement for conservation. *Conservation in Practice* 4: 14–22.

Hart, M. M. and J. T. Trevors. 2005. Microbe management: application of mycorrhizal fungi in sustainable agriculture. *Frontiers in Ecology and the Environment* 10: 533–539.

Harvell, D., R. Aronson, N. Baron, J. Connell, A. Dobson, S. Ellner, et al. 2004. The rising tide of ocean diseases: unsolved problems and research priorities. *Frontiers in Ecology and the Environment* 2: 375–382.

Harveson, P. M., R. R. Lopez, N. J. Silvy, and P. A. Frank. 2004. Source-sink dynamics of Florida Key deer on Big Pine Key, Florida. *Journal of Wildlife Managment* 68: 909–915.

Hassan, H. and H. E. Dregne. 1997. *Natural Habitats and Ecosystems Management in Drylands: An Overview*. Environment Department Paper no. 51. The World Bank, Washington, D.C.

Hassett, B, M. Palmer, E. Bernhardt, S. Smith, J. Carr, and D. Hart. 2005. Restoring watersheds project by project: trends in Chesapeake Bay tributary restoration. *Frontiers in Ecology and Environment* 3: 259–267.

Hastings, A. and L. W. Botsford. 2003. Comparing designs of marine reserves for fisheries and for biodiversity. *Ecological Applications* 13: S65–S70.

Hay, J. M., C. H. Daughtery, A. Cree, and L. R. Maxson. 2003. Low genetic divergence obscures phylogeny among populations of *Sphenodon*, remnant of an ancient reptile lineage. *Molecular Phylogenetics and Evolution* 29: 1–19.

Haydon, D. T., M. K. Laurenson, and C. Sillero-Zubiri. 2002. Integrating epidemiology into population viability analysis: Managing the risk posed by rabies and canine distemper to the Ethiopian wolf. *Conservation Biology* 16: 1372–1385.

Hedges, S., M. J. Tyson, A. F. Sitompul, M. F. Kinnaird, D. Gunaryadi, and Aslan. 2005. Distribution, status, and conservation needs of Asian elephants (*Elephas maximus*) in Lampung Province, Sumatra, Indonesia. *Biological Conservation* 124: 35–48.

Hedrick, P. W. 2005. *Genetics of Populations*, 3rd ed. Jones and Bartlett Publishers, Sudbury, MA.

Hegde, R., S. Suryaprakash, L. Achoth, and K. S. Bawa. 1996. Extraction of non-timber forest products in the forests of Biligiri Rangan Hills, India. *Economic Botany* 50: 243–251.

Hemley, G. (ed.). 1994. *International Wildlife Trade: A CITES Sourcebook*. Island Press, Washington, D.C.

Hendrey G. 2001. Acid rain and deposition. *In* S. A. Levin (ed.), *Encyclopedia of Biodiversity*, vol. 1, pp. 1–16. Academic Press, San Diego, CA.

Hendrickson, D. A. and J. E. Brooks. 1991. Transplanting short-lived fishes in North American deserts: Review, assessment and recommendations. *In* W. L. Minckley and J. E. Deacon (eds.), *Battle against Extinction: Native Fish Management in the American West*, pp. 283–302. University of Arizona Press, Tucson.

Heschel, M. S. and K. N. Paige. 1995. Inbreeding depression, environmental stress and population size variation in Scarlet Gilia (*Ipomopsis aggregata*). *Conservation Biology* 9: 126–133.

Heywood, V. H. (ed.). 1995. *Global Biodiversity Assessment*. Cambridge University Press, Cambridge.

Higgins, J. V., M. T. Bryer, M. L. Khoury, and T. W. Fitzhugh. 2005. A freshwater classification approach for biodiversity conservation planning. *Conservation Biology* 19: 432–445.

Higgs, E. 2003. *Nature by Design: People, Natural Process, and Ecological Restoration*. MIT Press, Cambridge, MA.

Hilborn, R., F. Micheli, and G. A. De Leo. 2006. Integrating marine protected areas with catch regulation. *Canadian Journal of Fisheries and Aquatic Sciences* 63: 642–649.

Hill, J. 2001. *The Legacy of Luna: The Story of a Tree, a Woman, and the Struggle to Save the Redwoods*. Harper, San Francisco.

Hilty, J. A. and A. M. Merenlender. 2004. Use of riparian corridors and vineyards by mammalian predators in northern California. *Conservation Biology* 18: 126–135.

Hobbie, J. E., S. R. Carpenter, N. B. Grimm, J. R. Gosz, and T. R. Seastedt. 2003. The U.S. Long Term Ecological Research Program. *BioScience* 53: 21–32.

Hockings, M. 2003. Systems for assessing the effectiveness of management in protected areas. *BioScience* 53: 823–832.

Hockings, M., S. Stolton, and N. Dudley. 2000. *Evaluating Effectiveness: A Framework for Assessing the Management of Protected Areas*. IUCN, Gland, Switzerland and Cambridge, U.K.

Hodgson, G. and J. A. Dixon 1988. Logging versus fisheries and tourism in Palawan. *East-West Environmental Policy Institute Occasional Paper No. 7*. East-West Center, Honolulu, Hawaii.

Hoekstra, J. M., T. M. Boucher, T. H. Ricketts, and C. Roberts. 2004. Are we losing ground? *Conservation in Practice* 5: 28–29.

Hoffman, S. W. and J. P. Smith. 2003. Population trends of migratory raptors in western North America, 1977–2001. *Condor* 105: 397–419.

Hokit, D. G. and L. C. Branch. 2003. Associations between patch area and vital rates: Consequences for local and regional populations. *Ecological Applications* 13: 1060–1068.

Hokit, D. G., B. M. Stith, and L. C. Branch. 2001. Comparison of two types of metapopulation models in real and artificial landscapes. *Conservation Biology* 15: 1102–1113.

Holbrook, S. J., R. J. Schmitt, and J. S. Stephens, Jr. 1997. Changes in an assemblage of temperate reef fishes associated with a climatic shift. *Ecological Applications*. 7: 1299–1310.

Holden, E. and K. G. Hoyer. 2005. The ecological footprints of fuels. *Transportation Research Part D: Transport and Environment*, 10: 395–403.

Holl, K. D. 2002. Long-term vegetation recovery on reclaimed coal surface mines in the eastern USA. *Journal of Applied Ecology* 39: 960–970.

Holl, K. D., E. E. Crone, and C. B. Schultz. 2003. Landscape restoration: moving from generalities to methodologies. *BioScience* 53: 491–502.

Hollander, J. M. 2003. *The Real Environment Crisis: Why Poverty, Not Affluence, Is the Environment's Number One Enemy*. University of California Press, Berkeley, CA.

Holmes, E. E. and A. E. York. 2003. Using age structure to detect impacts on threatened populations: a case study with Steller sea lions. *Conservation Biology* 17: 1794–1806.

Holt, W. V., A. R. Pickard, J. C. Rodger, D. E. Wildt, M. L. Gosling, G. Cowlishaw, et al. (eds.). 2003. *Reproductive Science and Integrated Conservation.* Conservation Biology Series, No. 8. Cambridge University Press, New York.

Horner-Devine, M. C., G. C. Daily, P. R. Ehrlich, and C. L. Boggs. 2003. Countryside biogeography of tropical butterflies. *Conservation Biology* 17: 168–177.

Horwich, R. H. and J. Lyon. 1998. Community-based development as a conservation tool: The Community Baboon Sanctuary and the Gales Point Manatee Reserve. *In* R. B. Primack, D. Bray, H. A. Galletti, and I. Ponciano (eds.), *Timber, Tourists, and Temples: Conservation and Development in the Maya Forest of Belize, Guatemala, and Mexico,* pp. 343–364. Island Press, Washington, D.C.

Howarth, F. G. 1990. Hawaiian terrestrial arthropods: An overview. *Bishop Museum Occasional Papers* 30: 4–26.

Howarth, W. 2001. Literary perspectives on biodiversity. *In* S. A. Levin (ed.), *Encyclopedia of Biodiversity,* vol. 3, pp. 739–746. Academic Press, San Diego, CA.

Hoyle, M. and M. James. 2005. Global warming, human population pressure, and viability of the world's smallest butterfly. *Conservation Biology* 19: 1113–1124.

Hubbell, S. P. 2001. *The Unified Neutral Theory of Biodiversity and Biogeography.* Princeton University Press, Princeton, NJ.

Hufford, K. M. and S. J. Mazer. 2003. Plant ecotypes: Genetic differentiation in the age of ecological restoration. *Trends in Ecology and Evolution* 18: 147–155.

Hughes, J. B. and J. Roughgarden. 2000. Species diversity and biomass stability. *American Naturalist* 155: 618–627.

Hughes, J., K. Goudkamp, D. Hurwood, M. Hancock, and S. Bunn. 2003. Translocation causes extinction of a local population of the freshwater shrimp *Paratya australiensis. Conservation Biology* 17: 1007–1012.

Hughes, T. P. 1994. Catastrophes, phase shifts and large-scale degradation of a Caribbean coral reef. *Science* 265: 1547–1551.

Hulme, D. and M. Murphree. 2001. *African Wildlife and Livelihood: The Promise and Performance of Community Conservation.* James Currey, Oxford.

Hulse, D. and R. Ribe. 2000. Land conversion and the production of wealth. *Ecological Applications* 10: 679–682.

Hunter, J. T. 2005. Geographic variation in plant species richness patterns within temperate eucalypt woodlands of eastern Australia. *Ecography* 28: 505.

Hunter, M. L., Jr. (ed.). 1999. *Maintaining Biodiversity in Forested Ecosystems.* Cambridge University Press, New York.

Huston, M. A. 1994. *Biological Diversity: The Coexistence of Species on Changing Landscapes.* Cambridge University Press, Cambridge.

Hutchings, M. J. 1987. The population biology of the early spider orchid, *Ophrys sphegodes* Mill. 1. A demographic study from 1975–1984. *Journal of Ecology* 75: 711–727.

Huxel, G. R. and G. Polis. 2001. Food webs. *In* S.A. Levin (ed.), *Encyclopedia of Biodiversity,* vol. 3, pp. 1–18. Academic Press, San Diego, CA.

Imhof, A. 2001. *An Analysis of Nam Theum 2 Compliance with World Commission on Dam Guidelines.* International Rivers Network, Berkeley.

Imhoff, D. 2003. *Farming with the Wild: Enhancing Biodiversity on Farms and Ranches.* Sierra Club Books, San Francisco.

Ingvarsson, P. K. 2001. Restoration of genetic variation lost: The genetic rescue hypothesis. *Trends in Ecology and Evolution* 16: 62–63.

Inogwabini, B. I., O. Ilambu, and M. A. Gbanzi. 2005. Protected areas of the Democratic Republic of Congo. *Conservation Biology* 19: 15–22.

Inoue, J. G., M. Miya, B. Venkatesh, and M. Nishida. 2005. The mitochondrial genome of Indonesian coelacanth *Latimeria menadoensis* (*Sarcopterygii: Coelacanthiformes*) and divergence time estimation between the two coelacanths. *Gene* 11: 227–235.

Intergovernmental Panel on Climate Change (IPCC). 2001. *Climate Change 2001: Synthesis Report.* Cambridge University Press, Cambridge.

Isaac, N. J. B. and G. Cowlishaw. 2004. How species respond to multiple extinction threats. *Proceedings of the Royal Society of London Series B* 271: 1135–1141.

Itano, N. 2004. Proposal to limit oil and coal projects draw fire. *New York Times,* March 24, 2004.

Ito, T. Y., N. Miura, B. Lhagvasuren, D. Enkhbileg, S. Takatsuki, A. Atsushi, et al. 2005. Preliminary evidence of a barrier effect of a railroad on the migration of Mongolian gazelles. *Conservation Biology* 19: 945–948.

IUCN. 1994. *Guidelines for Protected Area Management Categories.* IUCN, Gland, Switzerland.

IUCN. 2001. *IUCN Red List Categories and Criteria: Version 3.1.* IUCN Species Survival Commission. IUCN, Gland, Switzerland.

IUCN. 2003. *Recommendation 29: Poverty and Protected Areas.* World Parks Congress, Durban, South Africa.

IUCN. 2004. *2004 IUCN Red List of Threatened Species.* www.redlist.org.

IUCN/Conservation International/NatureServe. 2004. *Global Amphibian Assessment Summary of Key Findings.* IUCN. Data from http://www.globalamphibians.org/summary.htm.

IUCN (World Conservation Union) Species Survival Commission. 2004. *IUCN Global Amphibian Assessment.* Conservation International Center for Applied Biodiversity Science, NatureServe. www.globalamphibians.org.

Jacobson, S. K. 2006. The importance of public education for biological conservation. *In* M. J. Groom, G. K. Meffe, and C. R. Carroll (eds.), *Principles of Conservation Biology,* 3rd ed., pp. 681–683. Sinauer Associates, Sunderland.

Jacobson, S. K. and S. Marynowski. 1997. Public attitudes and knowledge about ecosystem management of Department of Defense lands in Florida. *Conservation Biology* 11: 770–778.

Jacobson, S. K., M. D. McDuff, and M. C. Monroe. 2006. *Conservation Education and Outreach Techniques.* Oxford University Press, Oxford.

Jaffe, M. 1994. *And No Birds Sing: A True Ecological Thriller Set in a Tropical Paradise.* Simon and Schuster, New York.

James, A., K. Gaston, and A. Balmford. 2001. Can we afford to conserve biodiversity? *BioScience* 51: 43–52.

James, F. C. 1999. Lessons learned from a study of habitat conservation planning. *BioScience* 49: 871–874.

James, F. C., C. E. McCulloch, and D. A. Wiedenfeld. 1996. New approaches to the analysis of population trends in land birds. *Ecology* 77: 13–27.

Jamieson, I. G., G. P. Wallis, and J. V. Briskie. 2006. Inbreeding and endangered species management: is New Zealand out of step with the rest of the world? *Conservation Biology* 20: 38–47.

Janmanch. 2004. World Bank resumes lending for big dams in India. *Janmanch,* April 22, 2004.

Janzen, D. H. 1986. The eternal external threat. *In* M. Soulé (ed.), *Conservation Biology: The Science of Scarcity and Diversity,* pp. 286–303. Sinauer Associates, Sunderland, MA.

Janzen, D. H. 2000. How to grow a wildland: The gardenification of nature. *In* P. H. Raven and T. Williams (eds.), *Nature and Human Society,* pp. 521–529. National Academy Press, Washington, D.C.

Janzen, D. H. 2001. Latent extinctions—the living dead. *In* S. A. Levin (ed.), *Encyclopedia of Biodiversity,* vol. 3, pp. 689–700. Academic Press, San Diego, CA.

Jenkins, M., R. E. Green, and J. Madden. 2003. The challenge of measuring global change in wild nature: Are things getting better or worse? *Conservation Biology* 17: 20–23.

Jenkins, M., S. J. Scherr, and M. Inbar. 2004. Markets for biodiversity services: Potential roles and challenges. *Environment:* 33–42.

Jennings, S., M. J. Kaiser, and J. D. Reynolds. 2001. *Marine Fisheries Ecology.* Blackwell Science, Oxford.

Johns, D. M. 2003. Growth, conservation, and the necessity of new alliances. *Conservation Biology* 17: 1229–1237.

Johnson, C. N. 2002. Determinants of loss of mammal species during the Late Quaternary "megafauna" extinctions: Life history and ecology, but not body size. *Proceedings of the Royal Society of London Series B* 269: 2221–2227.

Johnson, N. 1995. *Biodiversity in the Balance: Approaches to Setting Geographic Conservation Priorities.* Biodiversity Support Program, World Wildlife Fund, Washington, D.C.

Jones, G. A., K. E. Sieving, and S. K. Jacobson. 2005. Avian diversity and functional insectivory on north-central Florida farmlands. *Conservation Biology* 19: 1234–1245.

Jones, H. L. and J. M. Diamond. 1976. Short-time-base studies of turnover in breeding birds of the California Channel Islands. *Condor* 76: 526–549.

Jordan, W. R. III. 2003. *The Sunflower Forest: Ecological Restoration and the New Communion with Nature.* University of California Press, Berkeley, CA.

Jovan, S. and B. McCune. 2005. Air-quality bioindication in the greater central valley of California, with epiphytic macrolichen communities. *Ecological Applications* 15: 1712–1726.

Kahn, P. H., Jr. and S. R. Kellert (eds.). 2002. *Children and Nature: Psychological, Sociocultural, and Evolutionary Investigations.* MIT Press, Cambridge, MA.

Kaiser, M. J. and G. Edwards-Jones. 2006. The role of ecolabeling in fisheries management and conservation. *Conservation Biology* 20: 392–398.

Kappel, C. V. 2005. Losing pieces of the puzzle: threats to marine, estuarine, and diadromous species. *Frontiers in Ecology and the Environment* 3: 275–282.

Kappelle, M., M. M. I. van Vuuren, and P. Baas. 1999. Effects of climate change on biodiversity: a review and identification of key research issues. *Biodiversity and Conservation* 8: 1383–1397.

Kapur, D., J. P. Lewis, and R. Webb (eds.). 1997. *The World Bank: Its First Half-Century.* The Brookings Institute, Washington, D.C.

Kareiva, P. and S. A. Levin (eds.). 2003. *The Importance of Species: Perspectives on Expendability and Triage.* Princeton University Press, Princeton, NJ.

Kareiva, P. and M. Marvier. 2003. Conserving biodiversity coldspots: recent calls to direct conservation funding to the world's biodiversity hotspots may be bad investment advice. *American Scientist* 91: 344–351.

Karl, T. R. and K. E. Trenberth. 2003. Modern global climate change. *Science* 302: 1719–1723.

Karoly, D. J., K. Braganza, P. A. Stott, J. M. Arblaster, G. A. Meehl, A. J. Broccoli, et al. 2003. Detection of a human influence on North American climate. *Science* 302: 1200–1203.

Kates, R. W., T. M. Parris, and A. A. Leiserowitz. 2005. What is sustainable development? Goals, indicators, values, and practice. *Environment* 47: 8–21.

Kauffman, J. B. and D. A. Pyke. 2001. Range ecology, global livestock influences. *In* S. A. Levin (ed.), *Encyclopedia of Biodiversity,* vol. 5, pp. 33–52. Academic Press, San Diego, CA.

Kautz, R. S. and J. A. Cox. 2001. Strategic habitats for biodiversity conservation in Florida. *Conservation Biology* 15: 55–77.

Keitt, T. H., M. A. Lewis, and R. D. Holt. 2001. Allee effects, invasion pinning, and species' borders. *American Naturalist* 157: 203–216.

Keller, L. F. and D. M. Waller. 2002. Inbreeding effects in wild populations. *Trends in Ecology and Evolution* 17: 230–241.

Keller, V. and K. Bollman. 2004. From Red Lists to species conservation concern. *Conservation Biology* 18: 1712–1717.

Kellert, S. R. 1996. *The Value of Life: Biological Diversity and Human Society.* Island Press/Shearwater Books, Washington, D.C.

Kellert, S. R. 1997. *Kinship to Mastery: Biophilia in Human Evolution and Development.* Island Press, Washington, D.C.

Kellert, S. R. and T. J. Farnham. 2002. *The Good in Nature and Humanity: Connecting Science, Religion, and Spirituality with the Natural World.* Island Press, Washington, D.C.

Kellert, S. R. and E. O. Wilson (eds.). 1993. *The Biophilia Hypothesis.* Island Press, Washington, D.C.

Kelly, B. T. and M. K. Phillips. 2000. Red wolf (*Canis rufus*). *In* R. P. Reading and B. Miller (eds.), *Endangered Animals,* pp. 247–252. Greenwood Press, Westport, CT.

Kelly, J. F., K. C. Ruegg, and T. B. Smith. 2005. Combining isotopic and genetic markers to identify breeding origins of migrant birds. *Ecological Applications* 15: 1487–1494.

Kelly, P. K. 1994. *Thinking Green: Essays on Environmentalism, Feminism and Nonviolence.* Parallax Press, Berkeley, CA.

Kindvall, O. and U. Gärdenfors. 2003. Temporal extrapolation of PVA results in relation to the IUCN Red List criterion E. *Conservation Biology* 17: 316–321.

King, R. J. H. 2005. The ethics of hunting. *Frontiers in Ecology and the Environment* 3: 392–393.

King, S. R. B. and J. Gurnell. 2005. Habitat use and spatial dynamics of takhi introduced to Hustai National Park, Mongolia. *Biological Conservation* 124: 277–290.

Kissui, B. M. and C. Packer. 2004. Top-down population regulation of a top predator: lions in the Ngorongoro Crater. *Proceedings of the Royal Society of London: Biological Sciences* 271: 1867–1874.

Klass, K. D., O. Zompro, N. P. Kristensen, and J. Adis. 2002. Mantophasmatodea: A new insect order with extant members in the Afrotropics. *Science* 296: 1456–1459.

Kleijn, D., F. Berendse, R. Smit, N. Gilissen, J. Smit, B. Brak, et al. 2004. Ecological effectiveness of agri-environment schemes in different agricultural landscapes in the Netherlands. *Conservation Biology* 18: 775–786.

Kleiman, D. G. 1989. Reintroduction of captive mammals for conservation. *BioScience* 39: 152–161.

Kleiman, D. G., M. E. Allen, K. V. Thompson, and S. Lumpkin. 1996. *Wild Mammals in Captivity: Principles and Techniques.* University of Chicago Press, Chicago.

Klein, B. C. 1989. Effects of forest fragmentation on dung and carrion beetle communities in central Amazonia. *Ecology* 70: 1715–1725.

Kloor, K. 2000. Ecology—Everglades restoration plan hits rough waters. *Science* 288: 1166–1167.

Knapp, R. A., C. P. Hawkins, J. Ladau, and J. G. McClory. 2005. Fauna of Yosemite National Park lakes has low resistance but high resilience to fish introductions. *Ecological Applications* 15: 835–847.

Knight, R. L., E. A. Odell, and J. D. Maetas. 2006. Subdividing the West. *In* M. J. Groom, G. K. Meffe, and C. R. Carroll (eds.), *Principles of Conservation Biology,* 3rd ed., pp. 241–243. Sinauer Associates, Sunderland, MA.

Kobori, H. and R. Primack. 2003. Participatory conservation approaches for Satoyama: The traditional forest and agricultural landscape of Japan. *Ambio* 32: 307–311.

Koh, L. P., R. R. Dunn, N. S. Sodhi, R. K. Colwell, H. C. Proctor, and V. S. Smith. 2004. Species coextinctions and the biodiversity crisis. *Science* 305: 1632–1634.

Kohlmann, S. G., G. A. Schmidt, and D. K. Garcelon. 2005. A population viability analysis for the Island Fox on Santa Catalina Island, California. *Ecological Modeling* 183: 77–94.

Kohm, K. and J. F. Franklin (eds.). 1997. *Creating a Forestry for the 21st Century: The Science of Ecosystem Management.* Island Press, Washington, D.C.

Kolb, A. and M. Diekmann. 2005. Effects of life-history traits on responses of plant species to forest fragmentation. *Conservation Biology* 19: 929–938.

Komdeur, J. and M. D. Pels. 2005. Rescue of the Seychelles warbler on Cousin Island, Seychelles: The role of habitat restoration. *Biological Conservation* 124: 15–26.

Komers, P. E. and G. P. Curman. 2000. The effect of demographic characteristics on the success of ungulate re-introductions. *Biological Conservation* 93: 187–193.

Koopowitz, H., A. D. Thornhill, and M. Andersen. 1994. A general stochastic model for the prediction of biodiversity losses based on habitat conversion. *Conservation Biology* 8: 425–438.

Kothari, A., N. Singh, and S. Suri (eds.). 1996. *People and Protected Areas: Toward Participatory Conservation in India.* Sage Publications, New Delhi.

Kratochwil, A. (ed.). 2000. *Biodiversity in Ecosystems.* Kluwer Academic Publishers, Dordrecht, Netherlands.

Kraus, S. D., M. W. Brown, H. Caswell, C. W. Clark, M. Fujiwara, P. K. Hamilton, et al. 2005. North Atlantic right whales in crisis. *Science* 309: 561–562.

Kremen, C. and R. S. Ostefeld. 2005. A call to ecologists: measuring, analyzing and managing ecosystem services. *Frontiers in Ecology and the Environment* 10: 539–548.

Kremen, C., N. M. Williams, R. L. Bugg, J. P. Fay, and R. W. Thorp. 2004. The area requirements of an ecosystem service: Crop pollination by native bee communities in California. *Ecology Letters* 7: 1109–1119.

Kristensen, R. M. 1983. Loricifera, a new phylum with Aschelminthes characters from the meiobenthos. *Zeitschrift für Zoologische Systematik* 21: 163–180.

Krueper, D., J. Bart, and T. D. Rich. 2003. Response of vegetation and breeding birds to the removal of cattle on the San Pedro River, Arizona (U.S.A.). *Conservation Biology* 17: 607–615.

Kruger, O. 2005. The role of ecotourism in conservation: Panacea or Pandora's Box? *Biodiversity and Conservation* 14: 579–600.

Kuylenstierna, J. C. I., H. Rodhe, S. Cinderby, and K. Hicks. 2001. Acidification in developing countries: Ecosystem sensitivity and the critical load approach on a global scale. *Ambio* 30: 20–28.

Labonne, J. and P. Gaudin. 2005. Exploring population dynamics patterns in a rare fish, *Zingel asper*, through capture-mark-recapture methods. *Conservation Biology* 19: 463–472.

Lacy, R. C. 1987. Loss of genetic diversity from managed populations: Interacting effects of drift, mutation, immigration, selection and population subdivision. *Conservation Biology* 1: 143–158.

Lacy, R. C. and D. B. Lindenmayer. 1995. A simulation study of the impacts of population subdivision on the mountain brushtail possum *Trichosurus caninus* Ogilby (Phalangeridae: Marsupialia), in south-eastern Australia: Loss of genetic variation within and between subpopulations. *Biological Conservation* 73: 131–142.

Laiolo, P. 2004. Diversity and structure of the bird community overwintering in the Himalayan subalpine zone: Is conservation compatible with tourism? *Biological Conservation* 115: 251–262.

Laiolo, P. 2005. Spatial and seasonal patterns of bird communities in Italian agroecosystems. *Conservation Biology* 19: 1547–1556.

Laliberte, A. S. and W. J. Ripple. 2004. Range contractions of North American carnivores and ungulates. *BioScience* 54: 123–138.

Lambshead, J. and P. Schalk. 2001. Invertebrates, marine, overview. *In* S. A. Levin (ed.), *Encyclopedia of Biodiversity,* vol. 3, pp. 543–560. Academic Press, San Diego, CA.

Lammertink, M. 2004. A multiple-site comparison of woodpecker communities in Bornean lowland and hill forests. *Conservation Biology* 18: 746–757.

Lamoreux, J. F., J. C. Morrison, T. H. Ricketts, D. M. Olson, E. Dinerstein, M. W. McKnight, et al. 2006. Global tests of biodiversity concordance and the importance of endemism. *Nature* 440: 212–214.

Lampila, P., M. Monkkonen, and A. Desrochers. 2005. Demographic responses by birds to forest fragmentation. *Conservation Biology* 19: 1537–1546.

Lande, R. 1995. Mutation and conservation. *Conservation Biology* 9: 782–792.

Lane, M. A. 2003. *The Global Biodiversity Information Facility.* Bulletin of the American Society for Information Science and Technology 22–25.

Lane, R. E. 2000. *The Loss of Happiness in Market Democracies.* Yale University Press, New Haven.

Lanza, R. P., B. L. Dresser, and P. Damiani. 2000. Cloning Noah's Ark. *Scientific American* 283: 84–89.

Lapham, N. P. and R. J. Livermore. 2003. *Striking a Balance: Ensuring Conservation's Place on the International Biodiversity Agenda.* Conservation International, Washington, D.C.

Latta, S. C. 2000. Making the leap from researcher to planner: Lessons from avian conservation planning in the Dominican Republic. *Conservation Biology* 14: 132–139.

Laurance, S. G. 2004. Responses of understory rain forest birds to road edges in central Amazonia. *Ecological Applications* 14: 1344–1357.

Laurance, S. G. and W. F. Laurance. 1999. Tropical wildlife corridors: Use of linear rainforest remnants by arboreal mammals. *Biological Conservation* 91: 231–239.

Laurance, S. G., P. C. Stouffer, and W. F. Laurance. 2004. Effects of road clearings on movement patterns of understory rainforest birds in central Amazonia. *Conservation Biology* 18: 1099–1109.

Laurance, W. F. 1991. Ecological correlates of extinction proneness in Australian tropical rain forest mammals. *Conservation Biology* 5: 79–89.

Laurance, W. F. 1999. Reflections on the tropical deforestation crisis. *Biological Conservation* 91: 109–117.

Laurance, W. F. 2000. Do edge effects occur over large spatial scales? *Trends in Ecology and Evolution* 15: 134–135.

Laurance, W. F. and R. O. Bierregaard, Jr. (eds.). 1997. *Tropical Forest Remnants: Ecology, Management, and Conservation of Fragmented Communities.* University of Chicago Press, Chicago.

Laurance, W. F. and M. A. Cochrane. 2001. Synergistic effects in fragmented landscapes. *Conservation Biology* 15: 1488–1489.

Laurance, W. F. and G. B. Williamson. 2001. Positive feedback among forest fragmentation, drought and climate change in the Amazon. *Conservation Biology* 15: 1529–1535.

Laurance, W. F., L. V. Ferreira, J. M. Rankin-de Merona, and S. G. Laurance. 1998. Rain forest fragmentation and the dynamics of Amazonian tree communities. *Ecology* 79: 2032–2040.

Laurance, W. F., M. A. Cochrane, S. Bergen, P. M. Fearnside, P. Delamônica, C. Barber, et al. 2001. The future of the Brazilian Amazon. *Science* 291: 438–439.

Laurance, W. F., T. E. Lovejoy, H. L. Vasconcelos, E. M. Bruna, R. K. Didham, P. C. Stouffer, et al. 2002. Ecosystem decay of Amazonian forest fragments: A 22-year investigation. *Conservation Biology* 16: 605–618.

Lawton, J. H. and K. Gaston. 2001. Indicator species. *In* S. A. Levin (ed.), *Encyclopedia of Biodiversity,* vol. 3, pp. 437–450. Academic Press, San Diego, CA.

Leader-Williams, N. 1990. Black rhinos and African elephants: Lessons for conservation funding. *Oryx* 24: 23–29.

Leakey, R. and R. Lewin. 1996. *The Sixth Extinction: Patterns of Life and the Future of Humankind.* Doubleday, New York.

Lee, K. 1996. The source and locus of intrinsic value. *Environmental Ethics* 18: 297–308.

Lee, K. N. 2001. Sustainability, concept and practice of. *In* S. A. Levin (ed.), *Encyclopedia of Biodiversity,* vol. 5, pp. 553–568. Academic Press, San Diego, CA.

Lee, R. 2005. Unholy Trinity: The IMF, World Bank, and WTO. *Economic Geography* 81: 441–443.

Legendre P., D. Borcard, and P. R. Peres-Neto. 2005. Analyzing beta diversity: Partitioning the spatial variation of community composition data. *Ecological Monographs* 75: 435–450.

Lemonick, M. D. 1997. Under attack: It's humans, not sharks, who are nature's most fearsome predators. *Time* 150: 59–64.

Leopold, A. 1939a. A biotic view of land. *Journal of Forestry* 37: 113–116.

Leopold, A. 1939b. The farmer as a conservationist. *American Forests* 45: 294–299, 316, 323.

Leopold, A. 1949. *A Sand County Almanac and Sketches Here and There*. Oxford University Press, New York.

Leopold, A. C. 2004. Living with the land ethic. *BioScience* 54: 149–154.

Lepczyk, C. A., A. G. Mertig, and J. Liu. 2003. Landowners and cat predation across rural-to-urban landscapes. *Biological Conservation* 115: 191–201.

Letourneau, D. K., L. A. Dyer, and G. C. Vega. 2004. Indirect effects of a top predator on a rainforest understory plant community. *Ecology* 85: 2144–2152.

Levin, S. A. (ed.). 2001. *Encyclopedia of Biodiversity*. Academic Press, San Diego, CA.

Lewis, D. M. 2004. *Snares vs. Hoes: Why Food Security is Fundamental to Wildlife Conservation*. Presentation to the Africa Biodiversity Collaborative Group, Food Security and Wildlife Conservation in Africa Meeting, 29 October 2004, Washington, D.C.: http://www.frameweb.org/ev.php; accessed 14 April 2005

Lewison, R. L., L. B. Crowder, and D. J. Shaver. 2003. The impact of turtle excluder devices and fisheries closures on loggerhead and Kemp's Ridley strandings in the western Gulf of Mexico. *Conservation Biology* 17: 1089–1097.

Li, L., C. Kato, and K. Horikoshi. 1999. Bacterial diversity in deep-sea sediments from different depths. *Biodiversity and Conservation* 8: 659–677.

Li, Y. and M. Norland. 2001. The role of soil fertility in invasion of Brazilian pepper (*Schinus terebinthifolius*) in Everglades National Park, Florida. *Soil Science* 166: 400–405.

Li, Y and D. S. Wilcove. 2005. Threats to vertebrate species in China and the United States. *BioScience* 55: 147–153.

Li, Y., G. Zhongwei, Y. Qisen, W. Yushan, and J. Niemela. 2003. The implications of poaching for giant panda conservation. *Biological Conservation* 111: 125–136.

Lin, S. C. and L. P. Yuan. 1980. Hybrid rice breeding in China. *In Innovative Approaches to Rice Breeding*, pp. 35–51. International Rice Research Institute, Manila, Philippines.

Lindburg, D. and K. Baragona (eds.). 2004. *Giant Pandas: Biology and Conservation*. University of California Press, Berkeley

Lindenmayer, D. B. 2000. Factors at multiple scales affecting distribution patterns and their implications for animal conservation: Leadbeater's Possum as a case study. *Biodiversity and Conservation* 9: 15–35.

Lindenmayer, D. B. and J. F. Franklin. 2002. *Conserving Forest Biodiversity: A Comprehensive Multiscaled Approach*. Island Press, Washington, D.C.

Lindholm, J. and B. Barr. 2001. Comparison of marine and terrestrial protected areas under federal jurisdiction in the United States. *Conservation Biology* 15: 1441–1444.

Lindsey, P. A., R. Alexander, J. T. duToit, and M. G. L. Mills. 2005. The cost efficiency of wild dog conservation in South Africa. *Conservation Biology* 19: 1205–1214.

Linington, S. and H. Pritchard. 2001. Gene banks. *In* S.A. Levin (ed.), *Encyclopedia of Biodiversity*, vol. 3, pp. 165–182. Academic Press, San Diego, CA.

Liu, J., Z. Ouyang, S. L. Pimm, P. H. Raven, X. Wang, H. Miao, and N. Han. 2003. Protecting China's biodiversity. *Science* 300: 1240–1241.

Liu, J. G., P. J. Mason, N. Clerici, S. Chen, A. Davis, F. Miao, et al. 2004. Landslide hazard assessment in the Three Gorges area of the Yangtze River using ASTER imagery: Zigui-Badong. *Geomorphology* 61: 171–187.

Lloyd, P., T. E. Martin, R. L. Redmond, U. Langer, and M. M. Hart. 2005. Linking demographic effects of habitat fragmentation across landscapes to continental source-sink dynamics. *Ecological Applications* 15: 1504–1514.

Loehle, C. and B. Li. 1996. Habitat destruction and the extinction debt revisited. *Ecological Applications* 6: 665–692.

Loh, J., R. E. Green, T. Ricketts, J. Lamoreaux, M. Jenkins, V. Kapos, and J. Randers. 2005. The Living Planet Index: Using species population time series to track trends in biodiversity. *Philosophical Transactions of the Royal Society Biological Sciences* 360: 289–295.

Loope, L. L. 1995. Strategies for long-term protection of biological diversity in rainforests of Haleakala National Park and East Maui, Hawaii. *Endangered Species Update* 12: 1–5.

Loope, L. L., O. Hamann, and C. P. Stone. 1988. Comparative conservation biology of oceanic archipelagoes: Hawaii and the Galápagos. *BioScience* 38: 272–282.

Loreau, M., S. Naeem, and P. Inchausti (eds.). 2002. *Biodiversity and Ecosystem Functioning: Synthesis and Perspectives*. Oxford University Press, Oxford.

Losos, E., J. Haynes, A. Phillips, and C. Alkiere. 1995. Taxpayer-subsidized resource extraction harms species. *BioScience* 45: 446–455.

Loucks, C. J., Z. Lu., E. Dinerstein, D. Wang, D. Fu, and H. Wang. 2003. The giant pandas of the Qinling Mountains, China: a case study in designing conservation landscapes for elevation migrants. *Conservation Biology* 17: 558–565.

Loucks, C. L. and R. F. Gorman. 2004. Regional ecosystem services and the rating of investment opportunities. *Frontiers in Ecology and the Environment* 2: 207–216.

Louda, S. M., A. E. Arnett, T. A. Rand, and F. L. Russell. 2003. Invasiveness of some biological control insects and adequacy of their ecological risk assessment and regulation. *Conservation Biology* 17: 73–82.

Louda, S. M., T. A. Rand, A. E. Arnett, A. S. McClay, K. Shea, and A. K. McEachern. 2005. Evaluation of ecological risk to populations of a threatened plant from an invasive biocontrol insect. *Ecological Applications* 15: 234–249.

Louisiana Coastal Wetlands Conservation and Restoration Task Force and the Wetlands Conservation and Restoration Authority. 1998. *Coast 2050: Toward a Sustainable Coastal Louisiana. Louisiana Department of Natural Resources*. Baton Rouge, La. 161 p. http://www.lacoast.gov/Programs/2050/MainReport/report1.pdf; accessed January 22, 2006.

Lourie, S. A. and A. C. J. Vincent. 2004. Using biogeography to help set priorities in marine conservation. *Conservation Biology* 18: 1004–1020.

Lövei, G. 2001. Extinctions, modern examples of. 2001. *In* S. A. Levin (ed.), *Encyclopedia of Biodiversity*, vol. 2, pp. 731–744. Academic Press, San Diego, CA.

Lowman, M. D. 1999. *Life in the Treetops: Adventures of a Woman in Field Biology*. Yale University Press, New London, CT.

Lubchenco, J., A. M. Olson, L. B. Brubaker, S. R. Carpenter, M. M. Holland, S. B. Hubbell, et al. 1991. The Sustainable Biosphere Initiative: An ecological research agenda. *Ecology* 72: 371–412.

Luck, G. W., T. H. Ricketts, G. C. Daily, and M. Imhoff. 2004. Alleviating spatial conflict between people and biodiversity. *Proceedings of the National Academy of Sciences U.S.A.* 101: 182–186.

Lyles, A. M. 2001. Zoos and zoological parks. *In* S. A. Levin (ed.), *Encyclopedia of Biodiversity*, vol. 5, pp. 901–912. Academic Press, San Diego, CA.

Lynch, J. A., V. C. Bowersox, and J. W. Grimm. 2000. Acid rain reduced in eastern United States. *Environmental Science and Technology* 6: 940–949.

Lyons K. G., C. A. Brigham, B. H. Traut, and M. W. Schwartz. 2005. Rare species and ecosystem functioning. *Conservation Biology* 19: 1019–1024.

MacArthur, R. H. and E. O. Wilson. 1967. *The Theory of Island Biogeography*. Princeton University Press, Princeton, NJ.

MacDougall, A. S., B. R. Beckwith, and C. Y. Maslovat. 2004. Defining conservation strategies with historical perspectives: a case study from a degraded oak grassland system. *Conservation Biology* 18: 455–465.

Mace, G. M. 1995. Classification of threatened species and its role in conservation planning. *In* J. H. Lawton and R. M. May (eds.), *Extinction Rates*, pp. 131–146. Oxford University Press, Oxford.

Mace, G. M., H. Masundire, J. Baillie, T. Ricketts, T. Brooks, M. Hoffmann, et al. 2005. Biodiversity. *In* R. Hassan, R. Scholes, and N. Ash (eds.). *Ecosystems and Human Well-being: Current State and Trends*, vol. 1, pp. 77–122. Island Press, Washington D.C.

Machlis, G. E. and D. R. Field. 2000. *National Parks and Rural Development: Practice and Policy in the United States.* Island Press, Washington, D.C.

MacIsaac, H. J., J. Borbely, J. Muirhead, and P. Graniero. 2004. Backcasting and forecasting biological invasion of inland lakes. *Ecological Applications* 14: 773–783.

MacKenzie, D. 2000. Sick to death. *New Scientist* 167: 32–35.

MacKenzie, S. H. 1996. *Integrated Resource Planning and Management: The Resource Approach in the Great Lakes Basin.* Island Press, Washington, D.C.

MacKinnon, K. 2000. *Transboundary Reserves: World Bank Implementation of the Ecosystem Approach.* World Bank, New York.

MacNally, R., E. Fleishman, L. P. Bulluck, and C. J. Betrus. 2004. Comparative influence of spatial scale on beta diversity within regional assemblages of birds and butterflies. *Journal of Biogeography* 31: 917–929.

Mader, H. J. 1984. Animal habitat isolation by roads and agricultural fields. *Biological Conservation* 29: 81–96.

Maehr, D. S. 1990. The Florida panther and private lands. *Conservation Biology* 4: 167–170.

Maehr, D. S., J. L. Larkin, and J. J. Cox. 2004. Shopping centers as panther habitat: Inferring animal locations from models. *Ecology and Society* 9: 9.

Maes, D. and H. Van Dyck. 2005. Habitat quality and biodiversity indicator performances of a threatened butterfly versus a multispecies group for wet heathlands in Belgium. *Biological Conservation* 123: 177–187.

Maezono, Y., R. Kobayashi, M. Kusahara, and T. Miyashita. 2005. Direct and indirect effects of exotic bass and bluegill on exotic and native organisms in farm ponds. *Ecological Applications* 15: 638–650.

Magnuson, J. J. 1990. Long-term ecological research and the invisible present. *BioScience* 40: 495–501.

Main, M. B. 2004. Mobilizing grass-roots conservation education: the Florida master naturalist program. *Conservation Biology.* 18: 11–16.

Makarewicz, J. C. and P. Bertram. 1991. Evidence for the restoration of the Lake Erie ecosystem. *BioScience* 41: 216–223.

Malcolm, J. R., C. Liu, R. P. Neilson, L. Hansen, and L. Hannah. 2006. Global warming and extinctions of endemic species from biodiversity hotspots. *Conservation Biology* 20: 538–548.

Mangel, M. and C. Tier. 1994. Four facts every conservation biologist should know about persistence. *Ecology* 75: 607–614.

Manne, L. L., T. M. Brooks, and S. L. Pimm. 1999. Relative risk of extinction of passerine birds on continents and islands. *Nature* 399: 258–261.

Marcovaldi, M. Â. and G. G. Marcovaldi. 1999. Marine turtles of Brazil: The history and structure of Projeto TAMAR-IBAMA. *Biological Conservation* 91: 35–41.

Marcovaldi, M. Â., V. Patiri, and J. C. Thomé. 2005. Projeto Tamar-Ibama: Twenty-five years protecting Brazilian sea turtles through a community-based conservation programme. *Mast 3 and 4:* 39–62.

Mares, M. A. 1992. Neotropical mammals and the myth of Amazonian biodiversity. *Science* 255: 976–979.

Margoluis, R. and N. Salafsky. 1998. *Measures of Success: Designing, Managing, and Monitoring Conservation and Development Projects.* Island Press, Washington, D.C.

Margules, C. R. and R. L. Pressey. 2000. Systematic conservation planning. *Nature* 405: 243–253.

Marrell, A. 2005. Ecotourism: Impacts, potentials, and possibilities. *The Geography Journal* 171: 275.

Martin, P. S. 2001. Mammals (late Quaternary), extinctions of. *In* S. A. Levin (ed.), *Encyclopedia of Biodiversity*, vol. 3, pp. 825–840. Academic Press, San Diego, CA.

Martorell, C. and E. M. Peters. 2005. The measurement of chronic disturbance and its effects on the threatened cactus *Mammillaria pectinifera. Biological Conservation* 124: 199–207.

Marty, J. T. 2005. Effects of cattle grazing on diversity in ephemeral wetlands. *Conservation Biology* 19: 1626–1632.

Marvell, A. 2005. Literature review. *Tourism Geographies* 7: 228–231.

Maschinski, J., J. E. Baggs, P. F. Quintana-Ascencio, and E. S. Menges. 2006. Using population viability analysis to predict the effects of climate change on the extinction risk of an endangered limestone endemic shrub, Arizona Cliffrose. *Conservation Biology* 20: 218–228.

Mascia, M. B. 2003. The human dimension of coral reef marine protected areas: Recent social science research and its policy implications. *Conservation Biology* 17: 630–632.

Mateo, N., W. Nader, and G. Tamayo. 2001. Bioprospecting. *In* S. A. Levin (ed.), *Encyclopedia of Biodiversity*, vol. 1, pp. 471–488. Academic Press, San Diego, CA.

Mathews, F., M. Orros, G. Mclaren, M. Gelling, and R. Foster. 2005. Keeping fit on the ark: assessing the suitability of captive-bred animals for release. *Biological Conservation* 121: 569–577.

Mathiessen, P. 2000. *Tigers in the Snow.* North Point Press, New York.

Matsuda, H. 2003. Challenges posed by the precautionary principle and accountability in ecological risk assessment. *Environmetrics* 14: 245–254.

Matthews, A. and D. Worster. 2003. *Where the Buffalo Roam: Restoring America's Great Plains*, 2nd ed. University of Chicago Press, Chicago.

Mauchamp, A. 1997. Threats from alien plant species in the Galapagos Islands. *Conservation Biology* 11: 260–263.

Maunder, M. 2001. Plant conservation, overview. *In* S. A. Levin (ed.), *Encyclopedia of Biodiversity*, vol. 4, pp. 645–658. Academic Press, San Diego, CA.

Maxted, N. 2001. *Ex Situ, In Situ* conservation. *In* S. A. Levin (ed.), *Encyclopedia of Biodiversity*, vol. 2, pp. 683–696. Academic Press, San Diego, CA.

May, R. M. 1992. How many species inhabit the Earth? *Scientific American* 267: 42–48.

Mayaux, P., P. Holmgren, F. Achard, H. Eva, H-J Stibig, and A. Branthomme. 2005. Tropical forest cover change in the 1990s and options for future monitoring. *Philosphy Transactions of the Royal Society of London B.* 360: 373–384.

Mayfield, M. and G. C. Daily. 2005. Countryside biogeography of Neotropical herbaceous and shrubby plants. *Ecological Applications* 15:423–439.

Mazerolle, M. J., A. Desrochers, and L. Rochefort. 2005. Landscape characteristics influence pond occupancy by frogs after accounting for detectability. *Ecological Applications* 15: 824–834.

McAuliffe, J. R. 1996. Saguaro cactus dynamics. *In* W. Halvorson and G. Davis (eds.), *Science and Ecosystem Management in the National Parks*, pp. 96–131. University of Arizona Press, Tucson.

McCallum, H. 2005. Inconclusiveness of chytridiomycosis as the agent in widespread frog declines. *Conservation Biology* 19: 1421–1430.

McCallum, H. and A. Dobson. 1995. Detecting disease and parasite threats to endangered species and ecosystems. *Trends in Ecology and Evolution* 10: 190–194.

McCarthy, M. A., S. J. Andelman, and H. P. Possingham. 2003. Reliability of relative predictions in population viability analysis. *Conservation Biology* 17: 982–989.

McClanahan, T. R. and R. Arthur. 2001. The effect of marine reserves and habitat on populations of East African coral reef fishes. *Ecological Applications* 11: 559–569.

McCormick, S. 2004. *Conservation by Design: A Framework for Mission Success.* The Nature Conservancy. Washington, D.C.

McGirk, J. and A. Buncombe. 2005. *Rare Habitat Dammed to Oblivion by World Bank.* April 4, The Independent, UK.

McKay, J. K. and R. G. Latta. 2002. Adaptive population divergence: Markers, TL and traits. *Trends in Ecology and Evolution* 17: 285–291.

McKee, J. K., P. W. Sciulli, C. D. Fooce, and T. A. Waite. 2003. Forecasting global biodiversity threats associated with human population growth. *Biological Conservation* 115: 161–164.

McKee, M. and R. P. Berrens. 2001. Balancing army and endangered species concerns: Green vs. Green. *Environmental Management* 27: 123–133.

McKibben, B. 1996. What good is a forest? *Audubon* 98: 54–65.

McLachlan, J. A. and S. F. Arnold. 1996. Environmental estrogens. *American Scientist* 84: 452–461.

McLaughlin, A. 1993. *Regarding Nature: Industrialism and Deep Ecology.* State University of New York Press, Albany.

McLaren, B. E. and R. O. Peterson. 1994. Wolves, moose and tree rings on Isle Royale. *Science* 266: 1555–1558.

McLean, H. E. 1995. Smart maps: Forestry's newest frontier. *American Forests* (March/April): 13–21.

McMichael, A. J., B. Bolin, R. Costanza, G. C. Daily, C. Folke, K. Lindahl-Kiessling, et al. 1999. Globalization and the sustainability of human health. *BioScience* 49: 205–210.

McNeely, J. A. 1989. Protected areas and human ecology: How national parks can contribute to sustaining societies of the twenty-first century. *In* D. Western and M. Pearl (eds.), *Conservation for the Twenty-first Century*, pp. 150–165. Oxford University Press, New York.

McNeely, J. A. 2001. Social and cultural factors. *In* S. A. Levin (ed.), *Encyclopedia of Biodiversity*, vol. 5, pp. 285–294. Academic Press, San Diego, CA.

McNeely, J. A. 2004. The problem of invasive alien species. *Environment* 46: 16–29.

McNeely, J. A. and W. S. Keeton. 1995. The interaction between biological and cultural diversity. *In* B. von Droste, H. Plachter, G. Fisher, and M. Rossler (eds.), *Cultural Landscapes of Universal Value*, pp. 25–37. Gustav Fischer Verlag, New York.

McNeely, J. A. and S. J. Scherr. 2003. *Ecoagriculture: Strategies to Feed the World and Save Wild Biodiversity.* Island Press, Washington, D.C.

McNeely, J. A., J. Harrison, and P. Dingwall (eds.). 1994. *Protecting Nature: Regiona l Reviews of Protected Areas.* IUCN, Cambridge.

McNeely, J. A., L. E. Neville, and M. Rejmánek. 2003. When is eradication a sound investment? *Conservation in Practice* 4: 30–31.

McNeely, J. A., K. R. Miller, W. Reid, R. Mittermeier, and T. B. Werner. 1990. *Conserving the World's Biological Diversity.* IUCN, World Resources Institute, CI, WWF-US, the World Bank, Gland, Switzerland and Washington, D.C.

McPhee, J. 1971. *Encounters with the Archdruid.* Farrar, Straus and Giroux, New York.

McPhee, M. E. 2003. Generations in captivity increases behavioral variance: Considerations for captive breeding and reintroduction programs. *Biological Conservation* 115: 71–77.

McQueen, M. and E. McMahon. 2005. *Land Conservation Financing.* Island Press, Washington, D.C.

McShane, T. O. and M. P. Wells. 2004. *Getting Biodiversity Projects to Work: Towards More Effective Conservation and Development.* Columbia University Press, New York.

McSweeney, K. 2005. Indigenous population growth in the lowland Neotropics: social science insights for biodiversity conservation. *Conservation Biology* 19: 1375–1384.

Meffe, G. C., C. R. Carroll, and contributers. 1997. *Principles of Conservation Biology*, 2nd ed. Sinauer Associates, Sunderland, MA.

Meffe, G. C., L. Nielson, R. L. Knight, and D. Schenborn (eds.). 2003. *Ecosystem Management: Adaptive, Community-Based Conservation.* Island Press, Washington, D.C.

Meine, C. 2001. Conservation movement, historical. *In* S. A. Levin (ed.), *Encyclopedia of Biodiversity*, vol. 1, pp. 883–896. Academic Press, San Diego, CA.

Menges, E. S. 1990. Population viability analysis for an endangered plant. *Conservation Biology* 4: 52–62.

Menges, E. S. 1992. Stochastic modeling of extinction in plant populations. *In* P. L. Fiedler and S. K. Jain (eds.), *Conservation Biology:*

The Theory and Practice of Nature Conservation, Preservation and Management, pp. 253–275. Chapman and Hall, New York.

Menz, F. C. and H. M. Seip. 2004. Acid rain in Europe and the United States: an update. *Environmental Science and Policy* 7: 253–265.

Merenlender, A. M., L. Huntsinger, G. Guthey, and S. K. Fairfax. 2004. Land trusts and conservation easement: Who is conserving what for whom? *Conservation Biology.* 18: 66–75.

Michalski, F. and C. A. Peres. 2005. Anthropogenic determinants of primate and carnivore local extinctions in a fragmented forest landscape of southern Amazonia. *Biological Conservation* 124: 383–396.

Milius, S. 2003. Emergency gardening: Labs step in to help conserve the rarest plants on Earth. *Science News* 164: 88–90.

Milius, S. 2005. Bushmeat on the menu: Untangling the influences of hunger, wealth, and international commerce. *Science News* 167: 138–140.

Millennium Ecosystem Assessment (MEA). 2005. *Ecosystems and Human Well-being.* 4 Volumes. Island Press, Covelo, CA.

Millennium Ecosystem Assessment (MEA). 2005b. *Ecosystems and Human Well-being: Biodiversity Synthesis.* World Resources Institute, Washington, D.C.

Miller, B. and T. Hodgkin. 2004. *In situ* conservation of wild crop relatives: status and trends. *Biodiversity and Conservation* 13: 663–684.

Miller, B., W. Conway, R. P. Reading, C. Wemmer, D. Wildt, D. Kleiman, et al. 2004. Evaluating the conservation mission of zoos, aquariums, botanical gardens, and natural history museums. *Conservation Biology* 18: 86–93.

Miller, G. R., C. Geddes, and D. K. Mardon. 1999. Response of the alpine gentian *Gentiana nivalis* L. to protection from grazing by sheep. *Biological Conservation* 87: 311–318.

Miller, J. K., J. M. Scott, C. R. Miller, and L. P Waits. 2002. The Endangered Species Act: Dollars and sense? *BioScience* 52: 163–168.

Miller, K. R. 1996. *Balancing the Scales: Guidelines for Increasing Biodiversity's Chances through Bioregional Management.* World Resources Institute, Washington, D.C.

Miller, P. 1995. Crusading for chimps and humans: Jane Goodall. *National Geographic* 188(December): 102.

Miller-Rushing, A. and R. Primack. 2004. Climate change and plant conservation. *Plant Talk* 35: 34–38.

Mills, E. L., H. H. Leach, J. T. Carlton, and C. L. Secor. 1994. Exotic species and the integrity of the Great Lakes. *BioScience* 44: 666–676.

Mills, L. S. and F. W. Allendorf. 1996. The one-migrant-per-generation rule in conservation and management. *Conservation Biology* 10: 1509–1518.

Milner-Gulland, E. J. and E. L. Bennett. 2003. Wild meat: The bigger picture. *Trends in Ecology and Evolution* 18: 351–357.

Milner-Gulland, E. J., E. Kreuzberg-Mukhina, B. Grebot, S. Ling, E. Bykova, I. Abdusalamov, et al. 2006. Application of IUCN red listing criteria at the regional and national levels: A case study from Central Asia. *Biodiversity and Conservation* (in press).

Milton, S. J., W. J. Bond, M. A. DuPleiss, D. Gibbs C. Hilton-Taylor, and H. P. Linder. 1999. A protocol for plant conservation by translocation in threatened lowlands fynbos. *Conservation Biology* 13: 735–743.

Minckley, W. L. 1995. Translocation as a tool for conserving imperiled fishes: Experiences in western United States. *Biological Conservation* 72: 297–309.

Minteer, B. A. and J. P. Collins. 2005. Ecological ethics: Building a new tool kit for ecologists and biodiversity managers. *Conservation Biology* 1803–1812.

Mittermeier, C. G. and R. A. Mittermeier (eds.). 2003. *Wilderness: Earth's Last Wild Places.* University of Chicago Press, Chicago.

Mittermeier, R. A., P. R. Gil, and C. G. Mittermeier. 1997. *Megadiversity: Earth's Biologically Wealthiest Nations.* Conservation International, Washington, D.C.

Mittermeier, R. A., N. Myers, P. R. Gil, and C. G. Mittermeier. 1999. *Hotspots: Earth's Richest and Most Endangered Terrestrial Ecoregions.* Agrupacion Sierra Madre, S. C., Mexico City.

Mittermeier, R. A., P. R. Gil, M. Hoffmann, J. D. Pilgrim, T. M. Brooks, C. G. Mittermeier, et al. 2004. *Hotspots Revisited: Earth's Biologically Richest and Most Endangered Ecoregions.* CEMEX, Mexico.

Moberg, F. and P. Rönnbäck. 2003. Ecosystem services of the tropical seascape: interactions, substitutions and restoration. *Ocean and Coastal Management* 46: 27–46.

Moffat, M. W. 1994. *The High Frontier: Exploring the Tropical Rainforest Canopy.* Harvard University Press, Cambridge.

Molina, R., B. G. Marcot, and R. Lesher. 2006. Protecting rare, old-growth, forest- associated species under the survey and manage program guidelines of the Northwest Forest Plan. *Conservation Biology* 20: 306–318.

Montalvo, A. M. and N. C. Ellstrand. 2001. Nonlocal transplantation and outbreeding depression in the subshrub *Lotus scoparius* (Fabaceae). *American Journal of Botany* 88: 28–269.

Moore, D., M. M. Nauta, S. E. Evans, and M. Rotheroe (eds.). 2001. *Fungal Conservation: Issues and Solutions.* Cambridge University Press, Cambridge.

Morales, J. C., P. M. Andau, J. Supriatna, Z. Z. Zainuddin, and D. J. Melnick. 1997. Mitochondrial DNA variability and conservation genetics of the Sumatran rhinoceros. *Conservation Biology* 11: 539–543.

Morell, V. 1986. Dian Fossey: Field science and death in Africa. *Science* 86: 17–21.

Morell, V. 1993. Primatology: Called 'trimates,' three bold women shaped their field (Dian Fossey, Jane Goodall and Birute Galdikas). *Science* 260: 420–425.

Morell, V. 1996. New mammals discovered by biology's new explorers. *Science* 273: 1491.

Morell, V. 1999. The variety of life. *National Geographic* 195(February): 6–32.

Morris, M. G. 2000. The effects of structure and its dynamics on the ecology and conservation of arthropods in British grasslands. *Biological Conservation* 95: 129–142.

Morris, W. F. and D. F. Doak. 2002. *Quantitative Conservation Biology: Theory and Practice of Population Viability Analysis.* Sinauer Associates, Sunderland, MA.

Morrissey, J. P., J. M. Dow, G. L. Mark, and F. O'Gara. 2004. Are microbes at the root of a solution to world food production? Rational exploitation of interactions between microbes and plants can help tranform agriculture. *European Molecular Biology Organization Reports* 5: 922–926.

Moser, S. C. and L. Dilling. 2004. Making climate hot: Communicating the urgency and challenge of global climate change. *Environment* 46: 33–46.

Motavelli, J. 1995. In harms' way. *E: The Environmental Magazine* 6: 28–37.

Mousson, L., G. Nève, and M. Baguette. 1999. Metapopulation structure and conservation of the cranberry fritillary *Boloria aquilonaris* (Lepidoptera, Nymphalidae) in Belgium. *Biological Conservation* 87: 285–293.

Moyle, P. B. 1995. Conservation of native freshwater fishes in the Mediterranean-type climate of California, USA: A review. *Biological Conservation* 72: 271–279.

Muir, J. 1901. *Our National Parks.* Houghton Mifflin, Boston, MA.

Muir, J. 1916. *A Thousand Mile Walk to the Gulf.* Houghton Mifflin, Boston, MA.

Mumby, P. J., C. P. Dahlgren, A. R. Harborne, C. V. Kappel, F. Micheli, D. R. Brumbaugh, et al. 2006. Fishing, trophic cascades, and the process of grazing on coral reefs. *Science* 311: 98–101.

Musiani, M., C. Mamo, L. Boitani, C. Callaghan, C. C. Gates, L. Mattei, et al. 2003. Wolf depredation trends and the use of fladry barriers to protect livestock in western North America. *Conservation Biology* 17: 1538–1547.

Muths, E. and M. P. Scott. 2000. American burying beetle (*Nicrophorus americanus*). *In* R. P. Reading and B. Miller (eds.), *Endangered Animals*, pp. 10–15. Greenwood Press, Westport, CT.

Myers, J. H., D. Simberloff, A. M. Kuris, and J. R. Carey. 2000. Eradication revisited: dealing with exotic species. *Trends in Ecology and Evolution* 15: 316–320.

Myers, N. 1983. *A Wealth of Wild Species.* Westview Press, Boulder, CO.

Myers, N. 1987. The extinction spasm impending: Synergisms at work. *Conservation Biology* 1: 14–21.

Myers, N. 1993. Sharing the earth with whales. *In* L. Kaufman and K. Mallory (eds.), *The Last Extinction*, pp. 179–194. MIT Press, Cambridge, MA.

Myers, N. and J. Kent. 2001. *Perverse Subsidies: How Tax Dollars Can Undercut the Environment and the Economy.* Island Press, Washington, D.C.

Myers, N. and J. Kent. 2004. *New Consumers: The Influence of Affluence on the Environment.* Island Press, Washington, D.C.

Myers, N. and A. Knoll. 2001. The biotic crisis and the future of evolution. *Proceedings of the National Academy of Sciences U.S.A.* 98: 5389–5392.

Myneni, R. B., C. D. Keeling, C. J. Tucker, G. Asrar, and R. R. Nemani. 1997. Increased plant growth in the northern high latitudes from 1981 to 1991. *Nature* 386: 698–702.

Nadkarni, N. M. 2004. Not preaching to the choir: communicating the importance of forest conservation to non-traditional audiences. *Conservation Biology* 18: 606–609.

Naess, A. 1986. Intrinsic value: Will the defenders of nature please rise? *In* M. E. Soulé (ed.), *Conservation Biology: The Science of Scarcity and Diversity*, pp. 153–181. Sinauer Associates, Sunderland, MA.

Naess, A. 1989. *Ecology, Community and Lifestyle.* Cambridge University Press, Cambridge.

Naidoo, R. and W. L. Adamowicz. 2006. Modeling opportunity costs of conservation in transitional landscapes. *Conservation Biology* 20: 490–500.

Naiman, R. J., J. J. Magnuson, D. M. McKnight, J. A. Stanford, and J. R. Karr. 1995. Fresh-water ecosystems and their management—A national initiative. *Science* 270: 584–585.

Nash, R. 1990. *American Environmentalism: Readings in Conservation Biology*, 3rd ed. McGraw-Hill, New York.

National Park Service. 2005. www.nps.gov.

Native Seeds. 2005. www.nativeseeds.com.

NatureServe. 2005. www.natureserve.org.

Naughton-Treves, L. M. B. Holland, and K. Brandon. 2005. The role of protected areas in conserving biodiversity and sustaining local livelihoods. *Annual Review of Envrionmental Resources* 30: 219–252.

Naylor, R. L., R. J. Goldburg, H. Mooney, M. Beveridge, J. Clay, C. Folke, et al. 1998. Nature's subsidies to shrimp and salmon farming. *Science* 282: 883–884.

Nee, S. 2003. Unveiling prokaryotic diversity. *Trends in Ecology and Evolution* 18: 62–63.

Neff, J. C., R. L. Reynolds, J. Belnap, and P. Lamothe. 2005. Multi-decadal impacts of grazing on soil physical and biogeochemical properties in southeast Utah. *Ecological Applications* 15: 87–95.

Nellemann, C., I. Vistnes, P. Jordhoy, and O. Strand. 2001. Winter distribution of wild reindeer in relation to power lines, roads, and resorts. *Biological Conservation* 101: 351–360.

Nepstad, D., G. Carvalho, A. C. Barros, A. Alencar, J. P. Capobianco, J. Bishop, et al. 2001. Road paving, fire regime feedbacks, and the future of Amazon forests. *Forest Ecology and Management* 5524: 1–13.

Nepstad, D., S. Schwartzman, B. Bamberger, M. Santilli, D. Ray, P. Schlesinger, et al. 2006. Inhibition of Amazon deforestation and fire by parks and indigenous lands. *Conservation Biology* 20: 65–73.

Nepstad, D. C., A. Verissimo, A. Alencar, C. Nobre, E. Lima, P. Lefebvre, et al. 1999. Large-scale impoverishment of Amazonian forests by logging and fire. *Nature* 398: 505–508.

Newburn, D., S. Reed, P. Berck, and A. Merenlender. 2005. Economics and land-use change in prioritizing private land conservation. *Conservation Biology* 19: 1411–1420.

Newmark, W. D. 1995. Extinction of mammal populations in western North American national parks. *Conservation Biology* 9: 512–527.

Newmark, W. D. and J. L. Hough. 2000. Conserving wildlife in Africa: Integrated conservation and development projects and beyond. *BioScience* 50: 585–592.

Ng, S. J., J. W. Dole, R. M. Sauvajot, S. P. D. Riley, and T. J. Valone. 2004. Use of highway undercrossings by wildlife in southern California. *Biological Conservation* 115: 499–507.

Nias, R. C. 2001. Endangered ecosystems. *In* S. A. Levin (ed.), *Encyclopedia of Biodiversity*, vol. 2, pp. 407–424. Academic Press, San Diego, CA.

Nicoll, M.A.C., Jones, C.G., and K. Norris. 2004. Comparison of survival rates of captive-reared and wild-bred Mauritius kestrels (*Falco punctatus*) in a re-introduced population. *Biological Conservation* 118: 539–548.

Niemi, G. J. and M. E. McDonald. 2004. Application of ecological indicators. *Annual Review of Ecology and Systematics* 35: 89–111.

Nieminen, M., M. C. Singer, W. Fortelius, K. Schops, and I. Hanski. 2001. Experimental confirmation that inbreeding depression increases extinction risk in butterfly populations. *American Naturalist* 157: 237–244.

Noble, I. and S. Roxburgh. 2001. Terrestrial ecosystems. *In* S. A. Levin (ed.), *Encyclopedia of Biodiversity*, vol. 5, pp. 637–646. Academic Press, San Diego, CA.

Nol, E., C. M. Francis, and D. M. Burke. 2005. Using distance from putative source woodlots to predict occurrence of forest birds in putative sinks. *Conservation Biology* 19: 836–844.

Noon, B. R. and J. A. Blakesley. 2006. Conservation of the Northern Spotted Owl under the Northwest Forest Plan. *Conservation Biology* 20: 288–296.

Noon, B. R., P. Parenteau, and S. C. Trombulak. 2005. Conservation science, biodiversity, and the 2005 U.S. forest service regulations. *Conservation Biology* 19: 1359–1361.

Nooren, H. and G. Claridge. 2001. *Wildlife Trade in Laos: the End of the Game*. Netherlands Committee for IUCN. Amsterdam.

Norse, E. A. 1986. *Conserving Biological Diversity in Our National Forests*. The Wilderness Society, Washington, D.C.

Norton, B. G. 1991. *Toward Unity Among Environmentalists*. Oxford University Press, New York.

Norton, B. G. 2003. *Searching For Sustainability: Interdisciplinary Essays in the Philosophy of Conservation Biology*. Cambridge University Press, New York.

Norton, B. G., M. Hutchins, E. F. Stevens, and T. L. Maple. 1995. *Ethics on the Ark: Zoos, Animal Welfare and Wildlife Conservation*. Smithsonian Institution Press, Washington, D.C.

Norton, D. A. and P. J. De Lange. 2003. Fire and vegetation in a temperate peat bog: Implications for the management of threatened species. *Conservation Biology* 17: 138–148.

Noss, R. F. 1992. Essay: Issues of scale in conservation biology. *In* P. L. Fiedler and S. K. Jain (eds.), *Conservation Biology: The Theory and Practice of Nature Conservation, Preservation and Management*, pp. 239–250. Chapman and Hall, New York.

Noss, R. F. 2003. A checklist for wildlands network design. *Conservation Biology* 17: 1270–1275.

Noss, R. F., C. Carroll, K. Vance-Borland, and G. Wuerthner. 2002. A multicriteria assessment of the irreplaceability and vulnerability of sites in the Greater Yellowstone ecosystem. *Conservation Biology* 16: 895–908.

Noss, R. F., E. T. La Roe III, and J. M. Scott. 1995. *Endangered Ecosystems of the United States: A Preliminary Assessment of Loss and Degradation*. Biological Report 28. U.S. Department of Interior, National Biological Service, Washington, D.C.

Novotny, V., Y. Basset, S. E. Miller, G. D. Weiblen, B. Bremer, L. Cizek, et al. 2002. Low host specificity of herbivorous insects in a tropical forest. *Nature* 416: 841–844.

Nunes, P., J. Van Den Bergh, and P. Nijkamp. 2003. *The Ecological Economics of Biodiversity*. Edward Elgar, UK.

Nunney, L. and D. R. Elam. 1994. Estimating the effective population size of conserved populations. *Conservation Biology* 8: 175–184.

Nyhagen, D. F., S. D. Turnbull, J. M. Olesen, and C. G. Jones. 2005. An investigation into the role of the Mauritian flying fox, *Pteropus niger*, in forest regeneration. *Biological Conservation* 122: 491–497.

Nyhus, P., H. Fischer, F. Madden, and S. Osofsky. 2003. Taking the bite out of wildlife damage: The challenges of wildlife compensation schemes. *Conservation in Practice* 4: 37–40.

Nyssen, J., J. Poesen, J. Moeyersons, J. Deckers, M. Haile, and A. Land. 2004. Human impact on the environment in the Ethiopian and Eritrean highlands—a state of the art. *Earth-Science Reviews* 64: 273–320.

Oates, J. F. 1999. *Myth and Reality in the Rainforest: How Conservation Strategies Are Failing in West Africa*. University of California Press, Berkeley, CA.

Oates, J. F., M. Abedi-Lartey, W. S. McGraw, T. T. Struhsaker, and G. H. Whitesides. 2000. Extinction of a West African red colobus monkey. *Conservation Biology* 14: 1526–1532.

Ødegaard, F. 2000. How many species of arthropods? Erwin's estimate revised. *Biological Journal of the Linnean Society* 71: 583–597.

Odell, J., M. E. Mather, and R. M. Muth. 2005. A biosocial approach for analyzing environmental conflicts: a case study of horseshoe crab allocation. *BioScience* 55: 735–748.

Oelschlaeger, M. 1994. *Caring for Creation: An Ecumenical Approach to the Environmental Crisis*. Yale University Press, New Haven, CT.

Office of Technology Assessment of the U.S. Congress (OTA). 1993. *Harmful Non-Indigenous Species in the United States. OTA-F-565*. U.S. Government Printing Office, Washington D.C.

O'Grady, J. J., D. H. Reed, B. W. Brook, and R. Frankham. 2004. What are the best correlates of predicted extinction risk? *Biological Conservation* 118: 513–520.

Olson, D. M., E. Dinerstein, E. D. Wikramanayake, N. D. Burgess, G. V. N. Powell, E. C. Underwood, et al. 2001. Terrestrial ecoregions of the world: A new map of life on Earth. *BioScience* 51: 933–938.

Organisation for Economic Co-operation and Development (OECD). 2005. http://www.oced.org/statsportal/.

Orr, D. W. 1994. *Ecological Literacy: Education and the Transition to a Postmodern World*. State University of New York Press, Albany.

Orr, D. W. 2004. *The Last Refuge: Patriotism, Politics, and the Environment in an Age of Terror*. Island Press, Washington.

Orrock, J. L. and E. I. Damschen. 2005. Corridors cause differential seed predation. *Ecological Applications* 15: 793–798.

Osterlind, K. 2005. Concept formation in environmental education: 14-Year olds' work on the intensified greenhouse. *International Journal of Science Education* 27: 891–908.

Otway, N. M., C. J. A. Bradshaw, and R. G. Harcourt. 2004. Estimating the rate of quasi-extinction of the Australian grey nurse shark (*Carcharias taurus*) population using deterministic age- and stage-classified models. *Biological Conservation* 119: 341–350.

Pacific Whale Foundation. 2003. *Exploring Hawaii's Coral Reefs*. http://www.pacificwhale.org/printouts/coral_reef_guide.pdf.

Packard, S. and C. Mutel (eds.). 1997. *Tallgrass Prairie Restoration Handbook*. Island Press, Washington, D.C.

Packer, C. 1997. Viruses of the Serengeti: Patterns of infection and mortality in African lions. *Journal of Animal Ecology* 68: 1161–1178.

Paddack, J.-P. 2003. *Mobilizing Funding For Biodiversity Conservation: A User-Friendly Training Guide*. www.worldwildlife.org/conservationfinance.

Paddack, M. J. and J. A. Estes. 2000. Kelp forest fish populations in marine reserves and adjacent exploited areas of central California. *Ecological Applications* 10: 855–870.

Padilla, D. K. and S. L. Williams. 2004. Beyond ballast water: aquarium and ornamental trades as sources of invasive species in aquatic ecosystems. *Frontiers in Ecology and the Environment* 2: 131–138.

Paine, R. T. 1966. Food web complexity and species diversity. *American Naturalist* 100: 65–75.

Palumbi, S. R. 2004. Marine reserves and ocean neighborhoods: The spatial scale of marine populations and their management. *Annual Review of Environmental Resources* 29: 31–68.

Pardini, R., S. M. de Souza, R. Braga-Neto, and J. P. Metzger. 2005. The role of forest structure, fragment size and corridors in maintaining small mammal abundance and diversity in an Atlantic forest landscape. *Biological Conservation* 12: 253–266.

Parfit, M. 1995. Diminishing returns: Exploiting the ocean's bounty. *National Geographic* 188(May): 2–56.

Parker, J. D., D. E. Burkepile, and M. E. Hay. 2006. Opposing effects of native and exotic herbivores on plant invasions. *Science* 311: 1459–1461.

Parker, T. H., B. M. Stansberry, C. D. Becker, and P. S. Gipson. 2005. Edge and area effects on the occurrence of migrant forest songbirds. *Conservation Biology* 19: 1157–1167.

Parks, S. A. and A. H. Harcourt. 2002. Reserve size, local human density, and mammalian extinctions in U.S. protected areas. *Conservation Biology* 16: 800–808.

Parmesan, C. and G. Yohe. 2003. A globally coherent fingerprint of climate change impacts across natural systems. *Nature* 421: 37–42.

Pärtel, M., R. Kalamees, Ü. Reier, E. Tuvi, E. Roosaluste, A. Vellak, et al. 2005. Grouping and prioritization of vascular plant species for conservation: combining natural rarity and management need. *Biological Conservation* 123: 271–278.

Pauly, D. and J. Maclean. 2003. *In a Perfect Ocean: The State of Fisheries and Ecosystems in the North Atlantic.* Island Press, Washington, D.C.

Peakall, R., D. Ebert, L. J. Scott, P. F. Meagher, and C. A. Offord. 2003. Comparative genetic study confirms exceptionally low genetic variation in the ancient and endangered relictual conifer, *Wollemia nobilis* (Araucariaceae). *Molecular Ecology* 12: 2331–2343.

Pearce, F. 2005. Pipe dreams. *Conservation in Practice* 6: 20–27.

Pearce, J. B. 2000. The New York Bight. *Marine Pollution Bulletin* 41(1–6): 44–45.

Pearman, P. B., M. R. Penskar, E. H. Schools, and H. D. Enander. 2006. Identifying potential indicators of conservation value using Natural Heritage occurrence data. *Ecological Applications* 16: 186–201.

Pearson, R. G. 2006. Climate change and the migration capacity of species. *Trends in Ecology and Evolution* 21: 111–113.

Pechmann, J. H. K. 2003. Natural population fluctuations and human influences: Null models and interactions. *In* R. D. Semlitsch (ed.), *Amphibian Conservation,* pp. 85–93. Smithsonian Institution Press, Washington, D.C.

Pedersen, B. S. and A. M. Wallis. 2004. Effects of white-tailed deer herbivory on forest gap dynamics in a wildlife preserve, Pennsylvania, USA. *Natural Areas Journal* 24: 82–94.

Pedynowski, D. 2003. Prospects for ecosystem management in the Crown of the Continent ecosystem, Canada-United States: Survey and recommendations. *Conservation Biology* 17: 1261–1269.

Peery, M. Z., S. R. Beissinger, S. H. Newman, E. B. Burkett, and T. D. Williams. 2004. Applying the declining population paradigm: Diagnosing causes of poor reproduction in the marbled murrelet. *Conservation Biology* 18: 1088–1098.

Peh, K. S. H., J. de Jong, N. S. Sodhi, S. L. H. Lim, and C. A. M. Lap. 2005. Lowland rainforest avifauna and human disturbance: persistence of primary forest birds in selectively logged forests and mixed-rural habitats of southern Peninsular Malaysia. *Biological Conservation* 123: 489–505.

Pereira, H. M. and H. D. Cooper. 2006. Towards the global monitoring of biodiversity change. *Trends in Ecology and Evolution* 21: 123–129.

Peres, C. A. 2000a. Effects of subsistence hunting on vertebrate community structure in Amazonian forests. *Conservation Biology* 14: 240–253.

Peres, C. A. 2000b. Evaluating the impact and sustainability of subsistence hunting at multiple Amazonian forest sites. *In* J. G. Robinson and E. L. Bennett (eds.), *Hunting for Sustainability in Tropical Forests,* pp. 31–57. Columbia University Press, New York.

Peres, C. A. 2005. Why we need megareserves in Amazonia. *Conservation Biology* 19: 728–733.

Peres, C. A. and I. R. Lake. 2003. Extent of nontimber resource extraction in tropical forests: Accessibility to game vertebrates by hunters in the Amazon Basin. *Conservation Biology* 17: 521–535.

Peres, C. A. and J. W. Terborgh. 1995. Amazonian nature reserves: An analysis of the defensibility status of existing conservation units and design criteria for the future. *Conservation Biology* 9: 34–46.

Peres, C. A., C. Baider, P. A. Zuidema, L. H. O. Wadt, K. A. Kainer, D. A. P. Gomes-Silva, et al. 2003. Demographic threats to the sustainability of Brazil nut exploitation. *Science* 302: 2112–2114.

Pérez-Arteaga, A. and K. J. Gaston. 2004. Wildfowl population trends in Mexico, 1961–2000: A basis for conservation planning. *Biological Conservation* 115: 343–355.

Perfecto, I., A. Mas, T. Dietsch, and J. Vandermeer. 2003. Conservation of biodiversity in coffee agroecosystems: a tri-taxa comparison in southern Mexico. *Biodiversity Conservation* 12: 1239–1252.

Perfecto, I., R. A. Rice, R. Greenberg, and M. E. Van der Voort. 1996. Shade coffee: A disappearing refuge for biodiversity. *BioScience* 46: 598–608.

Pergams, O. R., B. Czech, J. C. Haney, and D. Nyberg. 2004. Linkage of conservation activity to trends in the U.S. economy. *Conservation Biology* 18: 1617–1623.

Perrings, C. 1995. Economic values of biodiversity. *In* V. H. Heywood (ed.), *Global Biodiversity Assessment,* pp. 823–914. Cambridge University Press, Cambridge.

Perrow, M. R. and A. J. Davy (eds.). 2002. *Handbook of Ecological Restoration.* Volume 1. *Principles of Restoration.* Cambridge University Press, New York.

Persson, N. J., J. Axelman, and D. Broman. 2000. Validating possible effects of eutrophication using PCB concentrations in bivalves and sediment of the U.S. Musselwatch and benthic surveillance programs. *Ambio* 29: 246–251.

Peterken, G. F. 1996. *Natural Woodland, Ecology and Conservation in Northern Temperate Regions.* Cambridge University Press, Cambridge.

Peters, R. L. and T. E. Lovejoy (eds.). 1992. *Global Warming and Biological Diversity.* Yale University Press, Boulder, CO.

Peterson, D. 2003. *Eating Apes.* University of California Press, Berkeley, CA.

Peterson, M. N., M. J. Peterson, and T. R. Peterson. 2005. Conservation and the myth of consensus. *Conservation Biology* 19: 762–767.

Pfab, M. F. and E. T. F. Witkowski. 2000. A simple population viability analysis of the critically endangered *Euphorbia clivicola* R. A. Dyer under four management scenarios. *Biological Conservation* 96: 263–270.

Phillips, K. 1990. Where have all the frogs and toads gone? *BioScience* 40: 422–424.

Picolotti, R. and J. D. Taillant (eds.). 2003. *Linking Human Rights and the Environment.* University of Arizona Press, Tucson.

Piessens, K., O. Honnay, and M. Hermy. 2005. The role of fragment area and isolation in the conservation of heathland species. *Biological Conservation* 122: 61–69.

Pimentel, D., L. Westra, and R. F. Noss (eds.). 2000a. *Ecological Integrity: Integrating Environment, Conservation, and Health.* Island Press, Washington, D.C.

Pimentel, D., L. Lach, R. Zuniga, and D. Morrison. 2000b. Environmental and economic costs of nonindigenous species in the United States. *BioScience* 50: 53–65.

Pimentel, D., C. Harvey, P. Resosudarmo, K. Sinclair, D. Kurtz, M. McNair, et al. 1995. Environmental and economic costs of soil erosion and conservation benefits. *Science* 267: 1117–1121.

Pimentel, D., C. Wilson, C. McCullum, R. Huang, P. Dwen, J. Flack, et al. 1997. Economic and environmental benefits of diversity. *BioScience* 47: 747–757.

Pimm, S. L. and J. H. Brown. 2004. Domains of diversity. *Science* 304: 831–833.

Pimm, S. L. and C. Jenkins. 2005. Sustaining the variety of life. *Scientific American* 293: 66–73.

Pimm, S. L. and P. Raven. 2000. Biodiversity: Extinction by numbers. *Nature* 403: 843–845.

Pimm, S. L., H. L. Jones, and J. Diamond. 1988. On the risk of extinction. *American Naturalist* 132: 757–785.

Pimm, S. L., M. P. Moulton, and L. J. Justice. 1995. Bird extinction in the Central Pacific. *In* J. H. Lawton and R. M. May (eds.), *Extinction Rates*, pp. 75–87. Oxford University Press, Oxford.

Pimm, S. L., M. Ayres, A. Balmford, G. Branch, K. Brandon, T. Brooks, et al. 2001. Can we defy nature's end? *Science* 293: 2207–2208.

Pinchot, G. 1947. *Breaking New Ground*. Harcourt, Brace, New York.

Piñero, D., M. Martinez-Ramos, and J. Sarukhan. 1984. A population model of *Astrocaryum mexicanum* and a sensitivity analysis of its finite rate of increase. *Journal of Ecology* 72: 977–991.

Pinto, M., P. Rocha, and F. Moreira. 2005. Long-term trends in great bustard (*Otis tarda*) populations in Portugal suggest concentration in single high quality area. *Biological Conservation* 124: 415–423.

Pitman, N. C. A., P. M. Jørgensen, R. S. R. Williams, S. León-Yánez, and R. Valencia. 2002. Extinction-rate estimates for a modern Neotropical flora. *Conservation Biology* 16: 1427–1431.

Platenberg, R. J. and R. A. Griffiths. 1999. Translocation of slowworms (*Anguis fragilis*) as a mitigation strategy: A case-study from south-east England. *Biological Conservation* 90: 125–132.

Plissner, J. H. and S. M. Haig. 2000. Viability of piping plover *Charadrius melodus* metapopulations. *Biological Conservation* 92: 163–173.

Plotkin, M. J. 1993. *Tales of a Shaman's Apprentice*. Viking/Penguin, New York.

Poff, N. L., J. D. Allan, M. A. Palmer, D. D. Hart, B. D. Richter, A. H. Arthington, et al. 2003. River flows and water wards: emerging science for environmental decision making. *Frontiers in Ecology and the Environment* 1: 298–306.

Poffenberger, M. (ed.). 1990. *Keepers of the Forest*. Kumarian, West Hartford, CT.

Poiani, K. A., B. D. Richter, M. G. Anderson, and H. E. Richter. 2000. Biodiversity conservation at multiple scales: Functional sites, landscapes and networks. *BioScience* 50: 133–146.

Polsenberg, J. 2003. Replumbing the Everglades. *Frontiers in Ecology and the Environment* 1: 232.

Poole, A. 1996. *Coming of Age with Elephants: A Memoir*. Hyperion, New York.

Poonswad, P., C. Sukkasem, S. Phataramata, S. Hayeemuida, K. Plongmai, and P. Chuailua, et al. 2005. Comparison of cavity modification and community involvement as strategies for hornbill conservation in Thailand. *Biological Conservation* 122: 385–393.

Porter, J. and J. Tougas. 2001. Reef ecosystems: Threats to their biodiversity. *In* S. A. Levin (ed.), *Encyclopedia of Biodiversity*, vol. 5, pp. 73–96. Academic Press, San Diego, CA.

Porter, S. D. and D. A. Savignano. 1990. Invasion of polygyne fire ants decimates native ants and disrupts arthropod communities. *Ecology* 71: 2095–2106.

Posey, D. A. 1992. Traditional knowledge, conservation and "the rain forest harvest." *In* M. Plotkin and L. Famolare (eds.), *Sustainable Harvest and Marketing of Rain Forest Products*, pp. 46–50. Island Press, Washington, D.C.

Possingham, H., D. B. Lindenmayer, and M. A. McCarthy. 2001. Population viability analysis. *In* S. A. Levin (ed.), *Encyclopedia of Biodiversity*, vol. 4, pp. 831–844. Academic Press, San Diego, CA.

Possingham, H. P., J. Franklin, K. Wilson, and T. J. Regan. 2005. The roles of spatial heterogeneity and ecological processes in conservation planning. *In* G. M. Lovett, C. G. Jones, M. G. Turner, and K. C. Weathers, (eds.), *Ecosystem Function in Heterogeneous Landscapes*. Springer-Verlag, New York.

Possingham, H. P., S. J. Andelman, M.A. Burgman, R. A. Medellin, L. L. Masters, and D. A. Keith. 2002. Limits to the use of threatened species lists. *Trends in Ecology and Evolution* 17: 503–507.

Poudevigne, I. and J. Baudry. 2003. *Landscape Ecology*. Springer Netherlands.

Pounds, J. A. and R. Puschendorf. 2004. Clouded futures. *Nature* 427: 107–109.

Pounds, J. A., M. R. Bustamante, L. A. Coloma, J. A. Consuegra, et al. 2006. Widespread amphibian extinctions from epidemic disease driven by global warming. *Nature* 439: 161–167.

Powell, A. N. and F. J. Cuthbert. 1993. Augmenting small populations of plovers: An assessment of cross-fostering and captive-rearing. *Conservation Biology* 7: 160–168.

Powell, J. R. and J. P. Gibbs. 1995. A report from Galapagos. *Trends in Ecology and Evolution* 10: 351–354.

Power, M. E., D. Tilman, J. A. Estes, B. A. Menge, W. J. Bond, L. S. Mills, et al. 1996. Challenges in the quest for keystones. *BioScience* 46: 609–620.

Power, T. M. 1991. Ecosystem preservation and the economy in the Greater Yellowstone area. *Conservation Biology* 5: 395–404.

Power, T. M. and R. N. Barret. 2001. *Post-Cowboy Economics: Pay and Prosperity in the New American West*. Island Press, Washington, D.C.

Praded, J. 2002. Reinventing the zoo. *E: The Environmental Magazine* 13: 24–31.

Prance, G. T., W. Balée, B. M. Boom, and R. L. Carneiro. 1987. Quantitative ethnobotany and the case for conservation in Amazonia. *Conservation Biology* 1: 296–310.

Prato, T. 2005. Accounting for uncertainty in making species protection decisions. *Conservation Biology* 19: 806–814.

Precht, W. F. and R. B. Aronson. 2004. Climate flickers and range shifts of reef corals. *Frontiers in Ecology and the Environment* 2: 307–314.

Prendergast, J. R., R. M. Quinn, and J. H. Lawton. 1999. The gap between theory and practice in selecting nature reserves. *Conservation Biology* 13: 484–492.

Prescott-Allen, C. and R. Prescott-Allen. 1986. *The First Resource: Wild Species in the North American Economy*. Yale University Press, New Haven, CT.

Press, D., D. F. Doak, and P. Steinberg. 1996. The role of local government in the conservation of rare species. *Conservation Biology* 10: 1538–1548.

Pressey, R. L. 1994. Ad hoc reservations: Forward or backward steps in developing representative reserve systems? *Conservation Biology* 8: 662–668.

Pressey, R. L., R. M. Cowling, and M. Rouget. 2003. Formulating conservation targets for biodiversity pattern and process in the Cape Floristic Region, South Africa. *Biological Conservation* 112: 99–127.

Pressey, R. L., T. C. Hager, K. M. Ryan, J. Schwarz, S. Walls, S. Ferrier, et al. 2000. Using abiotic data for conservation assessments over extensive regions: Quantitative methods applied across New South Wales, Australia. *Biological Conservation* 96: 55–82.

Pressey, R. L., C. J. Humphries, C. R. Margules, R. I. Vane-Wright, and P. H. Williams. 1993. Beyond opportunism: Key principles for systematic reserve selection. *Trends in Ecology and Evolution* 8: 124–128.

Primack, D., C. Imbres, R. B. Primack, A. J. Miller-Rushing, and P. Del Tredici. 2004. Herbarium specimens demonstrate earlier flowering times in response to warming in Boston. *American Journal of Botany* 91: 1260–1264.

Primack, R. B. 1988. Forestry in Fujian province (People's Republic of China) during the Cultural Revolution. *Arnoldia* 48: 26–29.

Primack, R. B. 1996. Lessons from ecological theory: Dispersal, establishment and population structure. *In* D. A. Falk, C. I. Millar, and M. Olwell (eds.), *Restoring Diversity: Strategies for Reintroduction of Endangered Plants*. Island Press, Washington, D.C.

Primack, R. B. 1998. Monitoring rare plants. *Plant Talk* 15: 29–35.

Primack, R. B. 2002. *Essentials of Conservation Biology*, 3rd ed. Sinauer Associates, Sunderland, MA.

Primack, R. B. 2004. *A Primer of Conservation Biology*, 3rd ed. Sinauer Associates, Sunderland, MA.

Primack, R. B. and P. Cafaro. 2001. Environmental ethics. *In* S. A. Levin (ed.), *Encyclopedia of Biodiversity*, vol. 2, pp. 545– 556. Academic Press, San Diego, CA.

Primack, R. B. and R. Corlett. 2005. *Tropical Rainforests: An Ecological and Biogeographical Comparison*. Blackwell Publishing, Malden, MA.

Primack, R. B. and B. Drayton. 1997. The experimental ecology of reintroduction. *Plant Talk* 11 (October): 25–28.

Primack, R. B. and T. Lovejoy (eds.). 1995. *Ecology, Conservation and Management of Southeast Asian Rainforests*. Yale University Press, New Haven, CT.

Primack, R. B. and S. L. Miao. 1992. Dispersal can limit local plant distribution. *Conservation Biology* 6: 513–519.

Primack, R. B., E. Hendry, and P. Del Tredici. 1986. Current status of *Magnolia virginiana* in Massachusetts. *Rhodora* 88: 357–365.

Primack, R. B., H. Kobori, and S. Mori. 2000. Dragonfly pond restoration promotes conservation awareness in Japan. *Conservation Biology* 14: 1553–1554.

Primack, R. B., D. Bray, H. Galetti, and J. Ponciano (eds.). 1998. *Timber, Tourists and Temples: Conservation and Development in the Maya Forest of Belize, Guatemala and Mexico*. Island Press, Washington, D.C.

Primack, R., R. Rozzi, P. Feinsinger, R. Dirzo, and F. Massardo. 2001. *Elementos de Conservacion Biologica: Perspectivas Latin Americanas*. Fundo de Cultura Economica, Mexico City.

Pringle, C. M. 2000. Threats to U.S. public lands from cumulative hydrologic alterations outside of their boundaries. *Ecological Applications* 10: 971–989.

Pringle, C. M. 2001. Hydrological connectivity and the management of biological reserves: A global perspective. *Ecological Applications* 11: 981–998.

Pringle, C. M. 2006. The fragmentation of aquatic ecosystems and the alteration of hydrologic connectivity: neglected dimensions of conservation ecology. *In* M. J. Groom, G. K. Meffe, and C. R. Carroll (eds.), *Principles of Conservation Biology*, 3rd ed., pp. 243–246. Sinauer Associates, Sunderland, MA.

Purvis, A. and A. Hector. 2000. Getting the measure of biodiversity. *Nature* 405: 212–219.

Pykala, J. 2004. Effects of new forestry practices on rare epiphytic macrolichens. *Conservation Biology* 18: 831–838.

Pyke, C. R. 2004. Habitat loss confounds climate change impacts. *Frontiers in Ecology and Environment* 4: 178–182.

Pyke, C. R. and D. T. Fischer. 2005. Selection of bioclimatically representative biological reserve systems under climate change. *Biological Conservation* 121: 429-441.

Quammen, D. 1996. *The Song of the Dodo: Island Biogeography in an Age of Extinctions*. Scribner, New York.

Quinn, R. M., J. H. Lawton, B. C. Eversham, and S. N. Wood. 1994. The biogeography of scarce vascular plants in Britain with respect to habitat preference, dispersal ability and reproductive biology. *Biological Conservation* 70: 149–157.

Quist, M. C., P. A. Fay, C. S. Guy, A. K. Knapp, and B. N. Rubenstein. 2003. Military training effects on terrestrial and aquatic communities on a grassland military installation. *Ecological Applications* 13: 432–442.

Rabinowitz, A. 1995. Helping a species go extinct: The Sumatran rhino in Borneo. *Conservation Biology* 9: 482–488.

Rabinowitz, A. 2000. Jaguar. *One Man's Struggle to Establish the World's First Jaguar Preserve*. Island Press, Covelo, CA.

Rabinowitz, A. 2001. *Beyond the Last Village: A Journey of Discovery in Asia's Forbidden Wilderness*. Island Press, Washington, D.C.

Rabinowitz, D., S. Cairns, and T. Dillon. 1986. Seven forms of rarity and their frequency in the flora of the British Isles. *In* M. E. Soulé (ed.), *Conservation Biology: The Science of Scarcity and Diversity*, pp. 182–204. Sinauer Associates, Sunderland, MA.

Radeloff, V. C., R. B. Hammer, S. I. Stewart, J. S. Fried, S. S. Holcomb, and J. F. McKeffry. 2005. The wildland-urban interface in the United States. *Ecological Applications* 15: 799–805.

Radford, E. 2004. Important plant areas: a practical route to target 5. *Plant Talk* : 32–33.

Radmer, R. J. 1996. Algal diversity and commercial algal products: New and valuable products from diverse algae may soon increase the already large market for algal products. *BioScience* 46: 263–270.

Ralls, K., J. D. Ballou, and A. Templeton. 1988. Estimates of lethal equivalents and the cost of inbreeding in mammals. *Conservation Biology* 2: 185–193.

Ralls, K., P. H. Harvey, and A. M. Lyles. 1986. Inbreeding in natural populations of birds and mammals. *In* M. Soulé (ed.), *Conservation Biology: The Science of Scarcity and Diversity*, pp. 35–56. Sinauer Associates, Sunderland, MA.

Ralls, K. S., R. Frankham, and J. Ballou. 2001. Inbreeding and outbreeding. *In* S. A. Levin (ed.), *Encyclopedia of Biodiversity*, vol. 3, pp. 427–436. Academic Press, San Diego, CA.

Raloff, J. 2003. Hawaii's hated frogs: Tiny invaders raise a big rukus. *Science News* 163: 11–13.

Raloff, J. 2005. Empty nets: Fisheries may be crippling themselves by targeting the big ones. *Science News* 167: 360–362.

Ramakrishnan, U., J. A. Santosh, U. Ramakrishnan, and R. Sukumar. 1998. The population and conservation status of Asian elephants in the Periyar Tiger Reserve, southern India. *Current Science India* 74: 110–113.

Rao, M. and P. McGowan. 2002. Wild-meat use, food security, livelihoods, and conservation. *Conservation Biology* 16: 580–583.

Raup, D. M. 1979. Size of the Permo-Triassic bottleneck and its evolutionary implications. *Science* 206: 217–218.

Raup, D. M. 1992. *Extinction: Bad Genes or Bad Luck?* W. W. Norton & Company, New York.

Raven, P. H. and E. O. Wilson. 1992. A fifty-year plan for biodiversity surveys. *Science* 258: 1099–1100.

Ravenal, R. M., I. M. E. Granoff, and C. A. Magee (eds.). 2004. *Illegal Logging in the Tropics: Strategies for Cutting Crime*. Haworth Press, Binghamton, NY.

Ravenga, C., J. Brunner, N. Henninger, K. Kassem, and R. Payne. 2000. *Pilot Analysis of Global Ecosystems*. World Resources Institute, Washington, D.C.

Read, A. J., P. Drinker, and S. Northridge. 2006. Bycatch of marine mammals in U.S. and global fisheries. *Conservation Biology* 20: 163–169.

Readman, J. 2004. Conservation… connection… curiosity… conversation… communication. *Plant Talk* : 27–31.

Red de Fondos Ambientales de Latino America y el Caribe (RED-LAC). 2005. http://www.redlac.org/english.asp.

Red Wolf Coalition. 2004. www.redwolves.com.

Redford, K. H. 1992. The empty forest. *BioScience* 42: 412–422.

Redford, K. H. and J. A. Mansour (eds.). 1996. *Traditional Peoples and Biodiversity Conservation in Large Tropical Landscapes*. The Nature Conservancy, Arlington, VA.

Redford, K. H. and S. E. Sanderson. 2000. Extracting humans from nature. *Conservation Biology* 14: 1362–1364.

Redford, K. H. and M. A. Sanjayan. 2003. Retiring Cassandra. *Conservation Biology* 17: 1473–1474.

Redford, K. H., P. Coppolillo, E. W. Sanderson, G. A. B. Da Fonseca, E. Dinerstein, C. Groves, et al. 2003. Mapping the conservation landscape. *Conservation Biology* 17: 116–131.

Reed, D. H. 2005. Relationship between population size and fitness. *Conservation Biology* 19: 563–568.

Reed, D. H. and R. Frankham. 2003. Correlations between fitness and genetic diversity. *Conservation Biology* 17: 230–237.

Reed, D. H., E. H. Lowe, D. A. Briscoe, and R. Frankham. 2003. Fitness and adaptability in a novel environment: Effect of inbreeding, prior environment, and lineage. *Evolution* 57: 1822–1828.

Reed, J. M. 1999. The role of behavior in recent avian extinctions and endangerments. *Conservation Biology* 13: 232–241.

Reed, J. M., C. S. Elphick, and L. W. Oring. 1998. Life-history and viability analysis of the endangered Hawaiian stilt. *Biological Conservation* 84: 35–45.

Reed, J. M., C. S. Elphick, A. F. Zuur, E. N. Ieno, and G. M. Smith. 2006. Time series analysis of Hawaiian waterbirds. *In* A. F. Zuur, E. N. Ieno, and G. Smith (eds.), *Analysis of Ecological Data.* Springer-Verlag.

Rees, W. 2001. Ecological footprint, concept of. *In* S. A. Levin (ed.), *Encyclopedia of Biodiversity*, vol. 2, pp. 229–244. Academic Press, San Diego, CA.

Regan, H. M., R. Lupia, A. N. Drinan, and M. A. Burgman. 2001. The currency and tempo of extinction. *American Naturalist* 157: 1–10.

Regan, T. 2004. *The Case for Animal Rights*, 2nd ed. Berkeley, University of California Press.

Reid, D. J. 2005. Conservation on the right track. *Conservation Biology* 19: 981–982.

Reid, J. 1999. *Two Roads and a Lake: An Economic Analysis of Infrastructure Development in the Beni River Watershed.* Conservation Straegy Fund, Philo, California.

Reid, J. and W. C. De Sousa Jr. 2005. Infrastructure and conservation policy in Brazil. *Conservation Biology* 19: 740–746.

Reid, W. R. 1992. How many species will there be? *In* T. C. Whitmore and J. A. Sayer (eds.), *Tropical Deforestation and Species Extinction.* Chapman and Hall, London.

Reid, W. V. and K. R. Miller. 1989. *Keeping Options Alive: The Scientific Basis for Conserving Biodiversity.* World Resources Institute, Washington, D.C.

Reid, W. V., S. A. Laird, R. Gamez, A. Sittenfeld, et al. 1993. *Biodiversity Prospecting.* World Resources Institute, Washington, D.C.

Reinartz, J. A. 1995. Planting state-listed endangered and threatened plants. *Conservation Biology* 9: 771–781.

Relyea, R. A. 2005. The impact of insecticides and herbicides on the biodiversity and productivity of aquatic communities. *Ecological Applications* 15: 618–627.

Restani, M. and M. Marzluff. 2002. Funding extinction? Biological needs and political realities in the allocation of resources to endangered species recovery. *Bioscience* 52: 169–177.

Rhoades, R. E. 1991. World's food supply at risk. *National Geographic* 179 (April): 74–105.

Rich, B. 1994. *Mortgaging the Earth.* Beacon Press, Boston.

Rich, B. 2000. Trading in dubious practices: OECD countries must stop export credit agencies funding environmentally damaging and immoral projects. *Financial Times*, February 24, 2000, p. 15.

Rich, T. C. G. and E. R. Woodruff. 1996. Changes in the vascular plant floras of England and Scotland between 1930–1960 and 1987–1988: The BSBI monitoring scheme. *Biological Conservation* 75: 217–229.

Richardson, C. J., P. Reiss, N. A. Hussain, A. J. Alwash, and D. J. Pool 2005. The restoration potential of the Mesopotamian marshes of Iraq. *Science* 307: 1307–1311.

Richardson, J. E., F. M. Weitz, M. F. Fay, Q. C. B. Cronk, H. P. Linder, G. Reeves, et al. 2001. Rapid and recent origin of species richness in the Cape flora of South Africa. *Nature* 412: 181–183.

Richman, L. K., K. J. Montali, R. L. Garber, M. A. Kennedy, J. Lehnhardt, T. B. Hildebrandt, et al. 1999. Novel endotheliotropic herpes viruses fatal for Asian and African elephants. *Science* 283: 1171–1176.

Ricketts, T. H., E. Dinerstein, T. Boucher, T. M. Brooks, S. H. M. Butchart, M. Hoffmann, et al. 2005. Pinpointing and preventing imminent extinctions. *Proceedings of the National Academy of Sciences U.S.A.* 102: 18497–18501.

Ricketts, T. H., E. Dinerstein, D. M. Olson, C. J. Loucks, W. Eichbaum, C. J. Loucks, et al. 1999. *Terrestrial Ecoregions of North America: A Conservation Assessment.* Island Press, Washington, D.C.

Ricklefs, R. E. 2001. *The Economy of Nature*, 5th ed. W. H. Freeman, New York.

Riemann, H. and E. Ezcurra. 2005. Plant endemism and natural protected areas in the peninsula of Baja California, Mexico. *Biological Conservation* 122: 141–150.

Ries, L., D. M. Debinski, and M. L. Wieland. 2001. Conservation value of roadside prairie restoration to butterfly communities. *Conservation Biology* 15: 401–411.

Rigg, C. M. 2001. Orchestrating ecosystem management: Challenges and lessons from Sequoia National Forest. *Conservation Biology* 15: 78–90.

Ripple, W. J. and R. L. Beschta. 2004. Wolves and the ecology of fear: Can predation risk structure ecosystems? *BioScience* 54: 755–766.

Rizzo, D. M., M. Garbelotto, J. M. Davidson, G. W. Slaughter, and S. T. Koike. 2002. *Phytophthora ramorum* as the cause of extensive mortality of *Quercus* spp. and *Lithocarpus densiflorus* in California. *Plant Disease* 86: 205–214.

Roberge, J. M. and P. Angelstam. 2004. Usefulness of the umbrella species concept as a conservation tool. *Conservation Biology.* 18: 76–85.

Roberts, C., G. Branch, R. H. Bustanamte, J. C. Castilla, J. Dugan, B. S. Halpern, et al. 2003. Application of ecological criteria in selecting marine reserves and developing reserve networks. *Ecological Applications* 13: S125–S228.

Roberts, C., C. McLean, J. E. N. Veron, J. P. Hawkins, G. R. Allen, D. E. McAllister, et al. 2002. Marine biodiversity hotspots and conservation priorities for tropical reefs. *Science* 295: 1280–1284.

Roberts, D. L, R. J. Cooper, and L. J. Petit. 2000. Use of premontane moist forest and shade coffee agrosystems by army ants in Western Panama. *Conservation Biology* 15: 192–199.

Roberts, S. and M. Hirshfield. 2004. Deep-sea corals: Out of sight, but no longer out of mind. *Frontiers in Ecology and the Environment* 2: 123–130.

Robertson, D. P. and R. B. Hull. 2001. Beyond biology: Toward a more public ecology for conservation. *Conservation Biology* 15: 970–979.

Robertson, D. P. and R. B. Hull. 2003. Public ecology: an environmental science and policy for global society. *Environmental Science and Policy* 6:399–410.

Robertson, G. P. and S. M. Swinton. 2005. Reconciling agricultural productivity and environmental integrity: a grand challenge for agriculture. *Frontiers in Ecology and the Environment*: 3: 38–46.

Rodrigues, A. S., H. R. Akçakaya, S. J. Andelman, M. I. Bakarr, L. Boitani, T. M. Brooks, et al. 2004a. Global gap analysis: Priority regions for expanding the global protected-area network. *BioScience* 54: 1092–1100.

Rodrigues, A. S. L., J. D. Pilgrim, J. F. Lemeroux, M. Hoffman, and T. M. Brooks. 2006. The value of the IUCN Red List for conservation. *Trends in Ecology and Evolution* 21: 71–76.

Rodrigues, A. S. L., S. J. Andelman, M. I. Bakarr, L. Boitani, T. M. Brooks, R. M. Cowling, et al. 2004b. Effectiveness of the global protected area network in representing species diversity. *Nature* 428: 640–643.

Rodrigues, M. G. M. 2004. Advocating for the environment: Local dimensions of transnational networks. *Environment* 46: 15–25.

Roessler, T. 2000. The World Bank's lending policy and environmental standards. *North Carolina Journal of International Law and Commercial Regulation* 26: 105–137.

Rogers, D. L. and F. T. Ledig. 1996. *The Status of Temperate North American Forest Genetic Resources.* U. S. Department of Agriculture Forest Service and Genetic Resources Conservaton Program, University of California, Davis.

Rohlf, D. J. and D. S. Dobkin. 2005. Legal ecology: ecosystem function and the law. *Conservation Biology* 19: 1344–1348.

Rohrman, D. F. 2004. Environmental terrorism. *Frontiers in Ecology and the Environment* 2: 332.

Roldán, G. 1988. Guía para el Estudio de los Macroinvertebrados Acuáticos del Departamento de Antioquia. Fondo-FEN Colombia, Editorial Presencia, Santa fe de Bogotá.

Rolston, H., III. 1988. *Environmental Ethics: Values In and Duties To the Natural World*. Temple University Press, Philadelphia.

Rolston, H., III. 1989. *Philosophy Gone Wild: Essays on Environmental Ethics*. Prometheus Books, Buffalo, NY.

Rolston, H., III. 1994. *Conserving Natural Value*. Columbia University Press, New York.

Rolston, H., III. 1995. Duties to endangered species. *In* W. A. Nierenberg (ed.), *Encyclopedia of Environmental Biology*, 1: 517–528. Harcourt/Academic Press, San Diego.

Rolston, H., III. 2000. The land ethic at the turn of the millennium. *Biodiversity and Conservation* 9: 1045–1058.

Roman, J. and S. R. Palumbi. 2003. Whales before whaling in the North Atlantic. *Science* 301: 508–510.

Romero, C. and G. I. Andrade. 2004. International conservation organizations and the fate of local tropical forest conservation initiatives. *Conservation Biology* 18: 578–580.

Rommens, C. M. and J. M. Humara. 2004. Crop improvement through modification of the plant's own genome. *Plant Physiology* 135: 421–431.

Rondinini, C., S. Stuart, and L. Boitani. 2005. Habitat sustainability models and the shortfall in conservation planning for African vertebrates. *Conservation Biology* 19: 1488–1497.

Rood, S. B., C. R. Gourley, E. M. Ammon, L. G. Heki, J. R. Klotz, M. L. Morrison, et al. 2003. Flows for floodplain forests: A successful riparian restoration. *BioScience* 53: 330–340.

Rood, S. B., G. M. Samuelson, J. H. Braatne, C. R. Gourley, F. M. R. Hughes, and J. M. Mahoney. 2005. Managing river flows to restore floodplain forests. *Frontiers in Ecology and the Environment* 3: 193–201.

Roodman, D. M. 2001. *Still Waiting for the Jubilee: Pragmatic Solutions for the Third World Debt Crisis*. Worldwatch Paper 155, Worldwatch Institute, Washington, D.C.

Rooney, T. P., S. M. Wiegmann, D. A. Rogers, and D. M. Waller. 2004. Biotic impoverishment and homogenization in unfragmented forest understory communities. *Conservation Biology* 18: 787–798.

Rosenberg, D. K., B. R. Noon, and E. C. Meslow. 1997. Biological corridors: Form, function, and efficacy. *BioScience* 47: 677–687.

Rosenberg, J. and F. L. Korsmo. 2001. Local participation, international politics, and the environment: The World Bank and the Grenada Dove. *Journal of Environmental Management* 62: 283–300.

Rosenfield, J. A., S. Nolasco, S. Lindauer, C. Sandoval, and A. Kodric-Brown. 2004. The role of hybrid vigor in the replacement of Pecos pupfish by its hybrids with sheepshead minnow. *Conservation Biology* 18: 1589–1598.

Rosenzweig, M. L. 2003. *Win-Win Ecology: How the Earth's Species Can Survive in the Midst of Human Enterprise*. Oxford University Press, Oxford.

Ruane, J. 2000. A framework for prioritizing domestic animal breeds for conservation purposes at the national level: A Norwegian case study. *Conservation Biology* 14: 1385–1393.

Rubbo, M. J. and J. M. Kiesecker. 2005. Amphibian breeding distribution in an urbanized landscape. *Conservation Biology* 19: 504–511.

Rubin, D. M., D. J. Topping, J. C. Schmidt, J. Hazel, M. Kaplinski, and T. S. Melis. 2002. Recent sediment studies refute Glen Canyon dam hypothesis. *American Geophysical Union Transactions* 85: 273.

Ruiz, G. M., T. K. Rawlings, F. C. Dobbs, L. A. Drake, T. Mullady, A. Huq, et al. 2000. Global spread of microorganisms by ships. *Nature* 408: 49.

Rundel, P. W. 2001. Mediterranean-climate ecosystems. *In* S. A. Levin (ed.), *Encyclopedia of Biodiversity*, vol. 4, pp. 145–160. Academic Press, San Diego, CA.

Russ, G. R., A. C. Alcala, A. P. Maypa, H. P. Calumpong, and A. T. White. 2004. Marine reserve benefits local fisheries. *Ecological Applications* 14: 597–606.

Russell, K. N., H. Ikerd, and S. Droege. 2005. The potential conservation value of unmowed powerline strips for native bees. *Biological Conservation* 124: 133–148.

Ryder, O. A., A. McLaren, S. Brenner, Y. P. Zhang, and K. Benirschke. 2000. Ecology: DNA banks for endangered animal species. *Science* 288: 275.

Saarinen, K., A. Valtonen, J. Jantunen, and S. Saarino. 2005. Butterflies and diurnal moths along road verges: Does road type affect diversity and abundance? *Biological Conservation* 123: 403–412.

Sachs, J. 2005. *The End of Poverty: Economic Possibilities for Our Time*. Penguin Group, East Rutherford, N.J.

Sætersdal, M., I. Gjerde, H. H. Blom, P. G. Ihlen, E. W. Myrseth, R. Pommeresche, et al. 2003. Vascular plants as a surrogate species group in complementary site selection for bryophytes, macrolichens, spiders, carabids, staphylinids, snails, and wood living polypore fungi in a northern forest. *Biological Conservation* 115: 21–31.

Safina, C. 1993. Bluefin tuna in the West Atlantic: Negligent management and the making of an endangered species. *Conservation Biology* 7: 229–234.

Safina, C. 2001. Fish conservation. *In* S. A. Levin (ed.), *Encyclopedia of Biodiversity*, vol. 2, pp. 783–800. Academic Press, San Diego, CA.

Sagoff, M. 2004. *Price, Principle and the Environment*. Cambridge University Press, New York, NY.

Sairam, R., S. Chennareddy, and M. Parani. 2005. OBPC Symposium: Maize 2004 & Beyond—Plant regeneration, gene discovery, and genetic engineering of plants for crop improvement. *In Vitro Cellular and Developmental Biology-Plant* 41: 411.

Salafsky, N., H. Cauley, G. Balachander, B. Cordes, J. Parks, C. Margoluis, et al. 2001a. A systematic test of an enterprise strategy for community-based biodiversity conservation. *Conservation Biology* 15: 1585–1595.

Salafsky, N., R. Margoluis, and K. H. Redford. 2001b. *Adaptive Management: A Tool for Conservation Practitioners*. Biodiversity Support Program, Washington, D.C.

Salafsky, N., R. Margoluis, K. H. Redford, and J. G. Robinson. 2002. Improving the practice of conservation: A conceptual framework and research agenda for conservation science. *Conservation Biology* 16: 1469–1479.

Saltz, D. 2001. Wildlife management. *In* S. A. Levin (ed.), *Encyclopedia of Biodiversity*, vol. 5, pp. 823–830. Academic Press, San Diego, CA.

Samson, F. B. and F. L. Knopf (eds.). 1996. *Prairie Conservation: Preserving America's Most Endangered Ecosystem*. Island Press, Washington, D.C.

Samways, M. J., S. Taylor, and W. Tarboton. 2005. Extinction reprieve following alien removal. *Conservation Biology* 19: 1329–1330.

Sánchez-Velásquez, L. R., E. Ezcurra, M. Martínez-Ramos, E. Álvarez-Buylla, and R. Lorente. 2002. Population dynamics of *Zea diploperennis*, an endangered perennial herb: effect of slash and burn practice. *Journal of Ecology* 90: 684–692.

Sanderson, E., M. Jaiteh, M. A. Levy, K. H. Redford, A. V. Wannebo, and G. Woolmer. 2002. The human footprint and the last of the wild. *BioScience* 52: 891–904.

Sandler, R and P. J. Cafaro, 2005. *Environmental Virtue Ethics*. Lanham, MD, Rowman and Littlefield.

Sapozhnikova, Y., N. Zubcov, S. Hungerford, L. A. Roy, N. Boicenco, E. Zubcov, et al. 2005. Evaluation of pesticides and metals in fish of the Dniester River, Moldova. *Chemosphere* 60: 196–205.

Saterson, K. 2001. Government legislation and regulation. *In* S. A. Levin (ed.), *Encyclopedia of Biodiversity*, vol. 3, pp. 233–246. Academic Press, San Diego, CA.

Sauer, J. R., J. E. Fallon, and R. Johnson. 2003. Use of North American Breeding Bird Survey data to estimate population change for bird conservation regions. *Journal of Wildlife Management* 67: 372–389.

Sayer, J. A. and B. M. Campbell. 2003. *The Science of Sustainable Development: Local Livelihoods and the Global Environment*. Cambridge University Press, New York.

Sayer, J. A., N. Ishwaran, J. Thorsell, and T. Sigaty. 2000. Tropical forest biodiversity and the World Heritage Convention. *Ambio* 29: 302–309.

Schaller, G. B. 1993. *The Last Panda*. University of Chicago Press, Chicago.

Schaller, G. B. and L. Wulin. 1996. Distribution, status and conservation of wild yak *Bos grunniens*. *Biological Conservation* 76: 1–8.

Scharlemann, J. P. W., A. Balmford, and R. E. Green. 2005. The level of threat to restricted-range bird species can be predicted from mapped data on land use and human population. *Biological Conservation* 123: 317–326.

Schärr, C., P. L. Vidale, D. Lüthi, C. Frei, C. Häberli, M. A. Liniger, et al. 2004. The role of increasing temperature variability in European summer heatwaves. *Nature* 427: 322–326.

Schemske, D. W., B. C. Husband, M. H. Ruckelshaus, C. Goodwillie, I. M. Parker, and J. M. Bishop. 1994. Evaluating approaches to the conservation of rare and endangered plants. *Ecology* 75: 584–606.

Schlaepfer, M. A., C. Hoover, and C. K. Dodd Jr. 2005. Challenges in evaluating the impact of the trade in amphibians and reptiles on wild populations. *BioScience* 55: 256–262.

Schmidt, J. C., R. H. Webb, R. A. Valdez, G. R. Marzolf, and L. E. Stevens. 1998. Science and values in river restoration in the Grand Canyon. *BioScience* 48: 735–747.

Schmidt, K. A., L. C. Nelis, N. Briggs, and R. S. Ostfeld. 2005. Invasive shrubs and songbird nesting success: effects of climate variability and predator abundance. *Ecological Applications* 15: 258–265.

Schmidtz, D. 2005. Using, respecting, and appreciating nature? *Conservation Biology* 19: 1672–1678.

Schmidtz, D. and E. Willott (eds.). 2001. *Environmental Ethics: What Really Matters, What Really Works*. Oxford University Press, New York.

Schmit, J. P., G. M. Mueller, P. R. Leacock, J. L. Mata, Q. Wu, and Y. Huang. 2005. Assessment of tree species richness as a surrogate for macrofungal species richness. *Biological Conservation* 121: 99–110.

Schneider, S. 1998. *Laboratory Earth: The Planetary Gamble We Can't Afford to Lose*. Basic Books, New York.

Scholes, R. J. and R. Biggs (eds.). 2004. *Ecosystem Services in Southern Africa: A Regional Assessment*. The Regional Scale Component of the Southern African Millennium Ecosystem Assessment. CSIR, Pretoria, South Africa.

Schonewald-Cox, C. M. 1983. Conclusions: Guidelines to management: A beginning attempt. *In* C. M. Schonewald-Cox, S. M. Chambers, B. MacBryde and L. Thomas (eds.), *Genetics and Conservation: A Reference for Managing Wild Animal and Plant Populations*, pp. 414–445. Benjamin/Cummings, Menlo Park, CA.

Schonewald-Cox, C. M. and M. Buechner. 1992. Park protection and public roads. *In* P. L. Fiedler and S. K. Jain (eds.), *Conservation Biology: The Theory and Practice of Nature Conservation, Preservation and Management*, pp. 373–396. Chapman and Hall, New York.

Schrope, M. 2001. Save our swamp. *Nature* 409: 128–130.

Schrott, G. R., K. A. With, and A. W. King. 2005. Demographic limitations on the ability of habitat restoration to rescue declining populations. *Conservation Biology* 19: 1181–1193.

Schultz, C. B. and P. C. Hammond. 2003. Using population viability analysis to develop recovery criteria for endangered insects: Case study of the Fender's Blue Butterfly. *Conservation Biology* 17: 1372–1385.

Schulz, H. N., T. Brinkhoff, T. G. Ferdelman, M. H. Marine, A. Teske, and B. B. Jorgensen. 1999. Dense populations of a giant sulfur bacterium in Namibian shelf sediments. *Science* 284: 493–495.

Schwartz, M. W. 1997. *Conservation in Highly Fragmented Landscapes*. Chapman and Hall, New York.

Schwartz, M. W. 1999. Choosing the appropriate scale of reserves for conservation. *Annual Review of Ecology and Systematics* 30: 83–108.

Schwartz, M. W., S. M. Hermann, and P. J. van Mantgem. 2000. Estimating the magnitude of decline of the Florida Torreya (*Torreya taxifolia* Arn.). *Biological Conservation* 95: 77–84.

Schwartzman S. and B. Zimmerman. 2005. Conservation alliances with indigenous peoples of the Amazon. *Conservation Biology* 19: 721–727.

Schwartzman, S., A. Moreira, and D. Nepstad. 2000. Rethinking tropical forest conservation: Perils in parks. *Conservation Biology* 14: 1351–1357.

Science and Spirit. 2001. www.science-spirit.org.

Scott, J. M., B. Csuti, and F. Davis. 1991. Gap analysis: An application of Geographic Information Systems for wildlife species. *In* D. J. Decker, M. E. Krasny, G. R. Goff, C. R. Smith, and D. W. Gross (eds.), *Challenges in the Conservation of Biological Resources: A Practitioner's Guide*, pp. 167–179. Westview Press, Boulder, CO.

Scott, J. M., F. W. Davis, R. G. McGhie, R. G. Wright, C. Groves, and J. Estes. 2001. Nature reserves: Do they capture the full range of America's biological diversity? *Ambio* 11: 999–1007.

Scott, J. M., D. D. Goble, J. A. Wiens, D. S. Wilcove, M. Bean, and T. Male. 2005. Recovery of imperiled species under the Endangered Species Act: the need for a new approach. *Frontiers in Ecology and the Environment* 3: 383–389.

Scott, M. E. 1988. The impact of infection and disease on animal populations: Implications for conservation biology. *Conservation Biology* 2: 40–56.

Sea World. 2000. Appendix: Population estimates. http://www.seaworld.org/infobooks/Baleen_estimatesbw.html.

Segal, J. M. 1999. *Graceful Simplicity: The Philosophy and Politics of the Alternative American Dream*. Berkeley, University of California Press.

Seidensticker, J., S. Christie, and P. Jackson (eds.). 1999. *Riding the Tiger: Tiger Conservation in Human Dominated Landscapes*. Cambridge University Press, London.

Sekercioglu, Ç. H., G. C. Daily, and P. R. Ehrlich. 2004. Ecosystem consequences of bird declines. *Proceedings of the National Academy of Sciences U.S.A.* 101: 18042–18047.

Semlitsch, R. D. and J. R. Bodie. 2003. Biological criteria for buffer zones around wetlands and riparian habitats for amphibians and reptiles. *Conservation Biology* 17: 1219–1228.

Sessions, G. (ed.). 1995. *Deep Ecology for the 21st Century: Readings on the Philosophy and Practice of the New Environmentalism*. Shambala Books, Boston.

Shafer, C. L. 1990. *Nature Reserves: Island Theory and Conservation Practice*. Smithsonian Institution Press, Washington, D.C.

Shafer, C. L. 1995. Values and shortcomings of small reserves. *BioScience* 45: 80–88.

Shafer, C. L. 1997. Terrestrial nature reserve design at the urban/rural interface. *In* M. W. Schwartz (ed.), *Conservation in Highly Fragmented Landscapes*, pp. 345–378. Chapman and Hall, New York.

Shafer, C. L. 1999. History of selection and system planning for U.S. natural area national parks and monuments: Beauty and biology. *Biodiversity and Conservation* 8: 189–204.

Shafer, C. L. 2001. Conservation biology trailblazers: George Wright, Ben Thompson, and Joseph Dixon. *Conservation Biology* 15: 332–344.

Shaffer, M. L. 1981. Minimum population sizes for species conservation. *BioScience* 31: 131–134.

Shankar, K., A. Hiremath, and K. Bawa. 2005. Linking biodiversity conservation and livelihoods in India. *Public Library of Science Biology* 3: 1879–1880.

Shanks, N. 2004. *God, the Devil, and Darwin: A Critique of Intelligent Design Theory*. Oxford University Press, New York.

Shanley, P. and L. Luz. 2003. The impacts of forest degradation on medicinal plant use and implications for health care in eastern Amazonia. *BioScience* 53: 573–584.

Shardlow M. and M. Harper. 2000. Compassion for competitors: saving wild arable plants. *Plant Talk*. 22/23: 39–42.

Sharpe, R. M. and D. S. Irvine. 2004. How strong is the evidence of a link between environmental chemicals and adverse effects on human reproductive health? *BioMedical Journal* 328: 447–451.

Sharrock, S. 2004. Databases and local action: Progress from BGCI on *ex situ* conservation. *Plant Talk*: 34–35.

Shepherd, G. 2004. *The Ecosystem Approach: Five Steps to Implementation*. IUCN, Gland, Switzerland.

Shi, D. E. 1985. *The Simple Life: Plain Living and High Thinking*. Oxford University Press, New York.

Shi, H., A. Singh, S. Kant, Z. Zhu, and E. Waller. 2005. Integrating habitat status, human population pressure, and protection status into biodiversity conservation priority setting. *Conservation Biology* 19: 1273–1285.

Shiganova, T. A. and Y. V. Bulgakova. 2000. Effect of gelatinous plankton on the Black and Azov Sea fish and their food resources. *ICES Journal of Marine Science* 57: 641–648.

Shultz, S., A. E. Dunham, K. V. Root, S. L. Soucy, S. D. Carroll, and L. R. Ginzburg. 1999. *Conservation Biology with RAMAS® EcoLab Software*. Sinauer Associates, Sunderland, MA.

Sigel, B. J., T. W. Sherry, and B. E. Young. 2006. Avian community response to lowland tropical rainforest isolation: 40 years of change at La Selva Biological Station, Costa Rica. *Conservation Biology* 20: 111–121.

Siitonen, P., A. Lehtinen, and M. Siitonen. 2005. Effects of forest edges on the distribution, abundance, and regional persistence of wood-rotting fungi. *Conservation Biology* 19: 250–260.

Simberloff, D. S. 1992. Do species-area curves predict extinction in fragmented forest? *In* T. C. Whitmore and J. A. Sayer (eds.), *Tropical Deforestation and Species Extinction*, pp. 75–89. Chapman and Hall, London.

Simberloff, D. S. 2003. How much information on population biology is needed to manage introduced species? *Conservation Biology* 17: 83–92.

Simberloff, D. S. and N. Gotelli. 1984. Effects of insularization on plant species richness in the prairie-forest ecotone. *Biological Conservation* 29: 27–46.

Simberloff, D. S., I. M. Parker, and P. N Windle. 2005. Introduced species policy, management, and future research needs. *Frontiers in Ecology and the Environment* 3: 12–20.

Simberloff, D. S., D. C. Schmitz, and T. C. Brown. (eds.). 1997. *Strangers in Paradise: Impact and Management of Nonindigenous Species in Florida*. Island Press, Washington, D.C.

Simberloff, D. S., J. A. Farr, J. Cox, and D. W. Mehlman. 1992. Movement corridors: Conservation bargains or poor investments? *Conservation Biology* 6: 493–505.

Simmons, R. E. 1996. Population declines, variable breeding areas and management options for flamingos in Southern Africa. *Conservation Biology* 10: 504–515.

Simpson, S. 2001. Fishy business. *Scientific American* 285: 82–89.

Singer, F. J., L. C. Zeigenfuss, and L. Spicer. 2001. Role of patch size, disease, and movement in rapid extinction of bighorn sheep. *Conservation Biology* 15: 1347–1354.

Singer, P. 1979. Not for humans only. *In* K. E. Goodpaster and K. M. Sayre (eds.), *Ethics and Problems of the Twenty-first Century*, pp. 191–206. University of Notre Dame, Notre Dame, IN.

Smart, S. M., R. G. H. Bunce, R. Marrs, M. LeDuc, L. G. Firbank, L. C. Maskell, et al. 2005. Large-scale changes in the abundance of common higher plant species across Britain between 1978, 1990, and 1998 as a consequence of human activity: Tests of hypothesised changes in trait representation. *Biological Conservation* 124: 355–371.

Smith, A. 1909. *An Inquiry into the Nature and Causes of the Wealth of Nations*. J. L. Bullock, (ed.). P. F. Collier & Sons, New York.

Smith, D. W. 2005. Ten years of Yellowstone wolves: 1995–2005. *Yellowstone Science* 13: 7–33.

Smith, D. W., K. M. Murphy, and D. S. Guernsey. 2001. *Yellowstone Wolf Project: Annual Report, 2000*. National Park Service, Yellowstone Center for Resources, Yellowstone National Park, Wyoming.

Smith, D. W., R. O. Peterson, and D. B. Houston. 2003. Yellowstone after wolves. *BioScience* 53: 330–340.

Smith, F. D. M., R. M. May, R. Pellew, T. H. Johnson, and K. R. Walter. 1993. How much do we know about the current extinction rate? *Trends in Ecology and Evolution* 8: 375–378.

Smith, T. B., S. Kark, C. J. Schneider, R. K. Wayne, and C. Moritz. 2001. Biodiversity hotspots and beyond: The need for preserving environmental transitions. *Trends in Ecology and Evolution* 16: 431.

Smith, V. H., G. D. Tilman, and J. C. Nekola. 1999. Eutrophication: impacts of excess nutrient inputs on freshwater, marine, and terrestrial ecosystems. *Environmental Pollution* 100: 179–196.

Smith, W. H. 2001. Pollution, overview. *In* S. A. Levin (ed.), *Encyclopedia of Biodiversity*, vol. 4, pp. 731–744. Academic Press, San Diego, CA.

Snelgrove, P. V. R. 2001. Marine sediments. *In* S. A. Levin (ed.). *Encyclopedia of Biodiversity*. Academic Press, San Diego, CA.

Snow, A. A., D. A. Andow, P. Gepts, E. M. Hallerman, A. Power, J. M. Tiedje, et al. 2005. Genetically engineered organisms and the environment: Current status and recommendations. *Ecological Applications* 15: 377–404.

Snyder, N. F., S. R. Derrickson, S. R. Beissinger, J. W. Wiley, T. B. Smith, W. D. Toone, et al. 1996. Limitations of captive breeding in endangered species recovery. *Conservation Biology* 10: 338–349.

Soares-Filho, B. S., D. C. Nepstad, L. M. Curran, G. C. Cerqueira, et al. 2006. Modelling conservation in the Amazon basin. *Nature* 440: 520–523.

Sobel, J. and C. Dahlgren. 2004. *Marine Reserves: A Guide to Science, Design and Use*. Island Press, Washington, D.C.

Soberón, J. 2004. Translating life's diversity: can scientists and policymakers learn to communicate better? *Environment* 46: 11–20.

Sorenson, L. G., Bradley, P. E., and M. Haynes Sutton. 2004. The West Indian Whistling-Duck and Wetlands Conservation Project: a model for species and wetlands conservation and education. *The Journal of Caribbean Ornithology*, Special Issue, pp. 72–80.

Soulé, M. E. 1980. Thresholds for survival: Maintaining fitness and evolutionary potential. *In* M. E. Soulé and B. A. Wilcox (eds.), *Conservation Biology: An Evolutionary-Ecological Perspective*, pp. 151–170. Sinauer Associates, Sunderland, MA.

Soulé, M. E. 1985. What is conservation biology? *BioScience* 35: 727–734.

Soulé, M. E. (ed.). 1987. *Viable Populations for Conservation*. Cambridge University Press, Cambridge.

Soulé, M. E. 1990. The onslaught of alien species and other challenges in the coming decades. *Conservation Biology* 4: 233–239.

Soulé, M. E. and G. H. Orians. (eds.). 2001. *Conservation Biology: Research Priorities for the Next Decade*. Island Press, Washington, D.C.

Soulé, M. E. and D. Simberloff. 1986. What do genetics and ecology tell us about the design of nature reserves? *Biological Conservation* 35: 19–40.

Soulé, M. E. and J. Terborgh. 1999. *Continental Conservation: Scientific Foundations of Regional Reserve Networks*. Island Press, Washington, D.C.

Soulé, M. E., J. A. Estes, J. Berger, and C. Martinez del Rio. 2003. Ecological effectiveness: Conservation goals for interactive species. *Conservation Biology* 17: 1238–1250.

Soulé, M. E., J. A. Estes, B. Miller, and D. L. Honnold. 2005. Strongly interacting species: Conservation policy, management, and ethics. *BioScience* 55: 168–176.

Spalding, M. D., C. Ravilious, and E. P. Green. 2001. *World Atlas of Coral Reefs*. University of California Press, Berkeley, CA.

Spielman, D., B. W. Brook, and R. Frankham. 2004. Most species are not driven to extinction before genetic factors impact them. *Proceedings of the National Academy of Sciences U.S.A.* 101: 15261–15264.

Spellerberg, I. F. 1994. *Evaluation and Assessment for Conservation: Ecological Guidelines for Determining Priorities for Nature Conservation*. Chapman and Hall, London.

Spellerberg, I. F. 2002. *Ecological Effects of Roads*. Science Publishers, Inc., Enfield, NH.

Spencer, C. N., B. R. McClelland, and J. A. Stanford. 1991. Shrimp stocking, salmon collapse and eagle displacement. *BioScience* 41: 14–21.

Speth, J. G. (ed.). 2003. *Worlds Apart: Globalization and the Environment*. Island Press, Washington, D.C.

Stankey, G. H. and B. Shindler. 2006. Formation of social acceptability judgments and their implications for management of rare and little-known species. *Conservation Biology* 20: 28–37.

Stanley, E. H. and M. W. Doyle. 2003. Trading off: The ecological effects of dam removal. *Frontiers in Ecology and the Environment* 1: 15–22.

Stanley-Price, M. R. 1989. *Animal Re-introductions: The Arabian Oryx in Oman*. Cambridge University Press, Cambridge.

Steadman, D. W. and P. S. Martin. 2003. The late Quaternary extinction and future resurrection of birds on Pacific Islands. *Earth Science Reviews* 61: 133–147.

Stearns, B. P. and S. C. Stearns. 1999. *Watching, From the Edge of Extinction*. Yale University Press, New Haven, CT.

Steffan-Dewenter, I. 2003. Importance of habitat area and landscape context for species richness of bees and wasps in fragmented orchard meadows. *Conservation Biology* 17: 1036–1044.

Stein, B. A. and S. R. Flack. 1997. *Species Report Card: The State of U.S. Plants and Animals*. The Nature Conservancy, Arlington, VA.

Stein, B. A., L. S. Kutner, and J. S. Adams (eds.). 2000. *Precious Heritage: The Status of Biodiversity in the United States*. Oxford University Press, New York.

Steinbeck, J. R., D. R. Schiel, and M. S. Foster. 2005. Detecting long-term change in complex communities: a case study from the rocky intertidal zone. *Ecological Applications* 15: 1813–1832.

Stephens, S. S., D. N. Koons, J. J. Rotella, and D. W. Willey. 2003. Effects of habitat fragmentation on avian nesting success: A review of evidence at multiple spatial scales. *Biological Conservation* 111: 101–110.

Stem, C., R. Margoluis, N. Salafsky, and M. Brown. 2005. Monitoring and evaluation in conservation: a review of trends and approaches. *Conservation Biology* 19: 295–309.

Steneck, R. S., M. H. Graham, B. J. Bourque, D. Corbett, J. M. Erlandson, J. A. Estes, et al. 2003. Kelp forest ecosystems: Biodiversity, stability, resilience, and future. *Environmental Conservation* 29: 436–459.

Steytler, N. S. and M. J. Samways. 1995. Biotope selection by adult male dragonflies (Odonata) at an artificial lake created for insect conservation in South Africa. *Biological Conservation* 72: 381–386.

Stockwell, C. A., A. P. Hendry, and M. T. Kinnison. 2003. Contemporary evolution meets conservation biology. *Trends in Ecology and Evolution* 18: 94–101.

Stohlgren, T. J. 2001. Endangered plants. In S. A. Levin (ed.), *Encyclopedia of Biodiversity*, vol. 2, pp. 465–478. Academic Press, San Diego, CA.

Stohlgren, T. J., D. A. Guenther, P. H. Evangelista, and N. Alley. 2005. Patterns of plant species richness, rarity, endemism, and uniqueness in an arid landscape. *Ecological Applications* 15: 715–725.

Stokes, D. and P. Morrison. 2003. GIS-based conservation planning. *Conservation in Practice* 4: 38–41.

Stolzenburg, W. 1996. Aquatic animals in danger. *Nature Conservancy* 46: 7.

Stone, C. P. and L. L. Loope. 1996. Alien species in Hawaiian national parks. In W. L. Halvorson and G. E. Davis (eds.), *Science and Ecosystem Management in the National Parks*, pp. 132–183. The University of Arizona Press, Tucson.

Stone, R. D. and C. D'Andrea. 2002. *Tropical Forests and the Human Spirit*. University of California Press, Berkeley, CA.

Strayer, D. L. 2001. Endangered freshwater invertebrates. In S. A. Levin (ed.), *Encyclopedia of Biodiversity*, vol. 2, pp. 425–440. Academic Press, San Diego, CA.

Struhsaker, T. T., P. J. Struhsaker, and K. S. Siex. 2005. Conserving Africa's rain forests: problems in protected areas and possible solutions. *Biological Conservation* 123: 45–54.

Stuart, S. N., J. S. Chanson, N. A. Cox, B. E. Young, A. S. L. Rodrigues, D. L. Fischman, et al. 2004. Status and trends of amphibian declines and extinctions worldwide. *Science* 306: 1783–1787.

Suding, K. N., K. L. Gross, and G. R. Houseman. 2004. Alternative states and positive feedbacks in restoration ecology. *Trends in Ecology and Evolution* 19: 46–53.

Summerville, K. S., M. J. Boulware, J. A. Veech, and T. O. Crist. 2003. Spatial variation in species diversity and composition of forest Lepidoptera in eastern deciduous forests of North America. *Conservation Biology* 17: 1045–1057.

Sutherland, W. J. (ed.). 1998. *Conservation Science and Action*. Blackwell Science, Oxford.

Sutherland, W. J. 2000. *The Conservation Handbook: Research, Management and Policy*. Blackwell Science, Ltd: Oxford.

Sutherland, W. J. and D. A. Hill. 1995. *Managing Habitats for Conservation*. Cambridge University Press, Cambridge.

Svarstad, H., H. C. Bugge, and S. S. Dhillion. 2000. From Norway to Novartis: Cyclosporin from *Tolypocladium inflatum* in an open access bioprospecting regime. *Biodiversity and Conservation* 9: 1521–1541.

Swetnam, T. W., C. D. Allen, and J. L. Betancourt. 1999. Applied historical ecology: using the past to manage the future. *Ecological Applications* 9: 1189–1206.

Swingland, I. R. 2003. *Capturing Carbon and Conserving Biodiversity*. EarthScan Publications Ltd., London.

Switalski, T. A., J. A. Bissonette, T. H. DeLuca, C. H. Luce, and M. A. Madej. 2004. Benefits and impacts of road removal. *Frontiers in Ecology and the Environment* 2: 21–28.

Szaro, R. C. and D. W. Johnston (eds.). 1996. *Biodiversity in Managed Landscapes: Theory and Practice*. Oxford University Press, New York

Tabarelli, M. and C. Gascon. 2005. Lessons from fragmentation research: improving management and policy guidelines for biodiversity conservation. *Conservation Biology* 19: 734–739.

Tait, C. J., C. B. Daniels, and R. S. Hill. 2005. Changes in species assemblages within the Adelaide metropolitan area, Australia, 1836–2002. *Ecological Applications* 15: 346–359.

Takacs, D. 1996. *The Idea of Biodiversity*. The Johns Hopkins University Press, Baltimore.

Tarasofsky, R. 2002. *Towards a mutually supportive relationship between the Convention on Biological Diversity and the World Trade Organization: An action guide*. IUCN, Gland, Switzerland.

Tautz, D., P. Arctander, A. Minelli, R. H. Thomas, and A. P. Vogler. 2003. A plea for DNA taxonomy. *Trends in Ecology and Evolution* 18: 70–74.

Taylor, L. 2000. *Plant based drugs and medicines*. Raintree Nutrition, Inc. Data from http://www.raintree.com/plantdrugs.htm.

Taylor, M. F. J., K. F. Suckling, and J. J. Rachlinski. 2005. The effectiveness of the Endangered Species Act: A quantitative analysis. *BioScience* 55: 360–366.

Taylor, V. J. and N. Dunstone (eds.). 1996. *The Exploitation of Mammal Populations*. Chapman and Hall, London.

Temperton, V. M., R. J. Hobbs, T. Nuttle, and S. Hall. (eds). 2004. *Assembly Rules and Restoration Ecology: Bridging the Gap Between Theory and Practice.* Island Press, Washington, D.C.

Temple, S. A. 1991. Conservation biology: New goals and new partners for managers of biological resources. *In* D. J. Decker, M. E. Krasny, G. R. Goff, C. R. Smith, and D. W. Gross (eds.). *Challenges in the Conservation of Biological Resources: A Practitioner's Guide,* pp. 45–54. Westview Press, Boulder, CO.

Terborgh, J. 1974. Preservation of natural diversity: The problem of extinction prone species. *BioScience* 24: 715–722.

Terborgh, J. 1999. *Requiem for Nature.* Island Press, Washington, D.C.

Terborgh, J. 2000. The fate of tropical forests: A matter of stewardship. *Conservation Biology* 14: 1358–1361.

Terborgh, J., L. C. Davenport, and C. Van Schaik. (eds.). 2002. *Making Parks Work: Identifying Key Factors to Implementing Parks in the Tropics.* Island Press, Covelo, CA.

Thapa, B. 1998. Debt-for-nature swaps: An overview. *International Journal of Sustainable Development and World Ecology* 5: 249–262.

Thapa, S. and B. Thapa. 2002. Debt-for-nature swaps: Potential applications in Nepal. *International Journal of Sustainable Development and World Ecology* 9: 239–255.

Theobald, D. M. 2004. Placing exurban land-use change in a human modification framework. *Frontiers in Ecology and the Environment* 2: 139–144.

Thiollay, J. M. 1989. Area requirements for the conservation of rainforest raptors and game birds in French Guiana. *Conservation Biology* 3: 128–137.

Thomas, A. 1995. Genotypic inference with the Gibbs sampler. *In* J. Ballou, M. Gilpin, and T. J. Foose (eds.), *Population Management for Survival and Recovery,* pp. 261–272. Columbia University Press, New York.

Thomas, C. D. and J. C. G. Abery. 1995. Estimating rates of butterfly decline from distribution maps: The effect of scale. *Biological Conservation* 73: 59–65.

Thomas, J. A., M. G. Telfer, D. B. Roy, C. D. Preston, J. J. D. Greenwood, J. Asher, et al. 2004. Comparative losses of British butterflies, birds, and plants and the global extinction crisis. *Science* 303: 1879–1881.

Thomas, K. S. 1991. *Living Fossil: The Story of the Coelocanth.* Norton, New York.

Thomashow, M. 1996. *Ecological Identity: Becoming a Reflective Environmentalist.* MIT Press, Cambridge.

Thomashow, M. 2002. *Bringing the Biosphere Home: Learning to Perceive Global Environmental Change.* Cambridge, MIT Press.

Thompson, D., I. Strange, M. Riddy, and C. D. Duck. 2005. The size and status of the population of southern sea lions *Otaria flavescens* in the Falkland Islands. *Biological Conservation* 121: 357–367.

Thoreau, H. D. 1863. *Excursions.* Tichnor and Fields, Boston, MA.

Thoreau, H. D. 1971. *Walden.* Princeton University Press, Princeton.

Thorne, E. T. and E. S. Williams. 1988. Disease and endangered species: The black-footed ferret as a recent example. *Conservation Biology* 2: 66–74.

Thrush, S. F., J. E. Hewitt, V. J. Cummings, J. I. Ellis, C. Hatton, A. Lohrer, and A. Norkko. 2004. Muddy water: Elevating sediment input to coastal and estuarine habitats. *Frontiers in Ecology and the Environment* 2: 299–306.

Tilman, D. 1999. The ecological consequences of change in biodiversity: A search for general principles. *Ecology* 80: 1455–1474.

Tilman, D. 2000. Causes, consequences, and ethics of biodiversity. *Nature* 405: 208–211.

Tilman, D., J. Fargione, B. Wolff, C. D'Antonio, A. Dobson, R. Howarth, et al. 2001. Forecasting agriculturally driven global environmental change. *Science* 292:281–284.

Timmer, V. and C. Juma. 2005. Biodiversity conservation and poverty reduction come together in the tropics: Lessons learned from the Equator Initiative. *Environment* 47: 25–44.

Tisdell, C, C. Wilson, and H. S. Nantha. 2005. Policies for saving a rare Australian glider: economics and ecology. *Biological Conservation* 123: 237–248.

Toledo, V. M. 2001. Indigenous peoples, biodiversity and. *In* S. A. Levin (ed.), *Encyclopedia of Biodiversity,* vol. 3, pp. 451–464. Academic Press, San Diego, CA.

Torchin, M. E and C. E. Mitchell. 2004. Parasites, pathogens, and invasions by plants and animals. *Frontiers in Ecology and the Environment* 4: 183–190.

Toth, L. A. and N. G. Aumen. 1994. Integration of multiple issues in environmental restoration and resource enhancement in south central Florida. *In* J. Cairns, Jr., T. V. Crawford, and H. Salwasser (eds.), *Implementing Integrated Environmental Management,* pp. 61–78. Virginia Polytechnic Institute and State University, Blacksburg, VA.

Totten, M., S. I. Pandya, and T. Janson-Smith. 2003. Biodiversity, climate, and the Kyoto Protocol: Risks and opportunities. *Frontiers in Ecology and the Environment* 1: 262–270.

Towne, E. G., D. C. Hartnett, and R. C. Cochran. 2005. Vegetation trends in tallgrass prairie from bison and cattle grazing. *Ecological Applications* 15:1550–1559.

Townsend, A. R., R. W. Howarth, F. A. Bazzaz, M. S. Booth, C. C. Cleveland, S. K. Collinge, et al. 2003. Human health effects of a changing global nitrogen cycle. *Frontiers in Ecology and the Environment* 1: 240–246.

TRAFFIC USA. World Wildlife Fund, Washington, D.C.

TransFair USA. 2004. Fair trade certification overview. http://www.transfairusa.org/content/certification/overview.php. 2005.

Tratalos, J. A. and T. J. Austin. 2001. Impacts of recreational SCUBA diving on coral communities of the Caribbean island of Grand Cayman. *Biological Conservation* 102: 67–75.

Troëng, S. and E. Rankin. 2005. Long-term conservation efforts contribute to positive green turtle *Chelonia mydas* nesting trend at Tortuguero, Costa Rica. *Biological Conservation* 121: 111–116.

Turner, M. G. 2005. Landscape ecology in North America: Past, present, and future. *Ecology* 86: 1967–1974.

Turner, M. G., R. H. Garner, and R. V. O'Neill. 2001. *Landscape Ecology in Theory and Practice: Pattern and Process.* Springer-Verlag, New York.

Turner, W., S. Spector, N. Gardiner, M. Fladeland, E. Sterling, and M. Steininger. 2003. Remote sensing for biodiversity science and conservation. *Trends in Ecology and Evolution* 18: 306–314.

Turner, W. R. and D. S. Wilcove. 2006. Adaptive decision rules for the acquisition of nature reserves. *Conservation Biology* 20: 527–537.

Tushabe, H., J. Kalema, A. Byaruhanga, J. Asasira, P. Ssegawa, A. Balmford, et al. 2006. A nationwide assessment of the biodiversity value of Uganda's Important Bird Areas network. *Conservation Biology* 20: 85–99

Tuxill, J. 1999. *Nature's Cornucopia: Our Stake in Plant Diversity.* World Watch Institute, Washington, D.C.

Twiss, J. R. and R. R. Reeves (eds.). 1999. *Conservation and Management of Marine Mammals.* Smithsonian Institution Press, Washington, D.C.

Union of Concerned Scientists. 1999. *Global Warming: Early Warning Signs.* Union of Concerned Scientists, Cambridge, MA.

United Nations. 1993a. *Agenda 21: Rio Declaration and Forest Principles.* Post-Rio Edition. United Nations Publications, New York.

United Nations. 1993b. *The Global Partnership for Environment and Development.* United Nations Publications, New York.

United Nations Millennium Project. 2005. *Investing in Development: A Practical Plan to Achieve the Millennium Development Goals.* United Nations Publications, New York.

United States Commission on Ocean Policy. 2004. An Ocean Blueprint for the 21st Century: Final Report of the U.S. Commission on Ocean Policy, Washington, D.C.

United States Fish and Wildlife Service. 2005. www.fws.gov.

Valette, J., D. Wysham, and N. Martinez. 2004. *A Wrong Turn From Rio: The World Bank's Road to Climate Catastrophe.* Sustainable Energy & Economy Network, Washington, D.C.

Valladares, G., A. Salvo, and L. Cagnolo. 2006. Habitat fragmentation effects on trophic processes of insect-plant food webs. *Conservation Biology* 20: 212–217.

Valutis, L. L. and J. M. Marzluff. 1999. The appropriateness of puppet-rearing birds for reintroduction. *Conservation Biology* 13: 584–591.

Van Andel, J. and J. Aronson. (eds.). 2005. *Restoration Ecology: the New Frontier*. Blackwell Publishing, Malden, MA.

Van Buskirk, J. and Y. Willi. 2004. Enhancement of farmland biodiversity within set-aside land. *Conservation Biology* 18: 987–994.

Vandeveer, D. and C. Pierce. 2002. *The Environmental Ethics and Policy Book: Philosophy, Ecology, Economics*. 3rd ed. Wadsworth Publishing Company, Belmont, CA.

Van Dover, C. L., C. R. German, K. G. Speer, L. M. Parson, and R. C. Vrijenhoek. 2002. Evolution and biogeography of deep-sea vent and seep invertebrates. *Science* 295: 1253–1257.

van Gemerden, B. S., R. S. Etienne, H. Olff, P. W. F. M. Hommel, and F. van Langevelde. 2005. Reconciling methodologically different biodiversity assessments. *Ecological Applications* 15: 1747–1760.

van Heezik, Y. and P. J. Seddon. 2005. Conservation education structure and content of graduate wildlife management and conservation biology programs: an international perspective. *Conservation Biology* 19: 7–14.

Van Wensveen, L. 2000. *Dirty Virtues: The Emergence of Ecological Virtue Ethics*. Prometheus, New York.

Van Wilgen, B. W., N. Govender, H. C. Biggs, D. Ntsala, and X. N. Funda. 2004. Response of savanna fire regimes to changing fire-management policies in a large African national park. *Conservation Biology* 18: 1533–1540.

Veith, M., J. Kosuch, R. Feldmann, H. Martens, and A. Seitz. 2000. A test for correct species declaration of frog legs imports from Indonesia into the European Union. *Biodiversity and Conservation* 9: 333–341.

Venevsky, S and I. Venevskaia. 2005. Hierarchical systematic conservation planning at the national level: Identifying national biodiversity hotspots using abiotic factors in Russia. *Biological Conservation* 124: 235–251.

Vergeer, P., E. Sonderen, and N. J. Ouborg. 2004. Introduction strategies put to the test: Local adaptation versus heterosis. *Conservation Biology* 18: 812–821.

Verhoeven, J. T. A., B. Arheimer, C. Yin, and M. M. Hefting. 2006. Regional and global concerns over wetlands and water quality. *Trends in Ecology and Evolution* 21: 96–103.

Vilas, C., E. San Miguel, R. Amaro, and C. Garcia. 2006. Relative contribution of inbreeding depression and eroded adaptive diversity to extinction risk in small populations of Shore Campion. *Conservation Biology* 20: 229–238.

Villa-Lobos, J. 2003. Landmark legislation protects imperiled U.S. plants. *Plant Talk* 32: 34–37.

Vilchis, L. I., M. J. Tegner, J. D. Moore, C. S. Friedman, K. L. Riser, T. T. Robbins, et al. 2005. Ocean warming effects on growth, reproduction, and survivorship of southern California abalone. *Ecological Applications* 15: 469–480.

Virtanen, P. 2003. Local management of global values: Community-based wildlife management in Zimbabwe and Zambia. *Society of Natural Resources* 16: 179–190.

Vitousek, P. M. 1994. Beyond global warming: Ecology and global change. *Ecology* 75: 1861–1876.

Vitousek, P. M., J. D. Aber, R. W. Howarth, G. E. Likens, P. A. Matson, D.W. Schindler, et al. 1997. Human alteration of the global nitrogen cycle: Sources and consequences. *Ecological Applications* 7: 737–750.

Volis, S., G. Bohrer, G. Oostermeiher, and P. Van Tienderen. 2005. Regional consequences of local population demography and genetics in relation to habitat management in *Gentiana pneumonanthe*. *Conservation Biology* 19: 357–367.

von Droste, B., H. Plachter, and M. Rossler (eds.). 1995. *Cultural Landscapes of Universal Value*. Gustav Fischer Verlag, New York.

Vredenburg, V. T. 2004. Reversing introduced species effects: Experimental removal of introduced fish leads to rapid recovery of a declining frog. *Proceedings of the National Academy of Sciences U.S.A.* 101: 7646–7650.

Walker, B. G., P. D. Boersma, and J. C. Wingfield. 2005. Physiological and behavioral differences in Magellanic penguin chicks in undisturbed and tourist-visited locations of a colony. *Conservation Biology* 19: 1571–1577.

Wallace, K., J. Callaway, and J. Zedler. 2005. Evolution of tidal creek networks in a high sedimentation environment: A 5-year experiment at Tijuana Estuary, California. *Estuaries* 28: 795–811.

Waller, G. (ed.). 1996. *Sealife: A Guide to the Marine Environment*. Smithsonian Institution Press, Washington, D.C.

Wallis de Vries, M. F. 2004. A quantitative conservation approach for the endangered butterfly *Maculinea alcon*. *Conservation Biology* 18: 489–499.

Walpole, M. J., H. J. Goodwin, and K. G. R. Ward. 2001. Pricing policy for tourism in protected areas: Lesson from Komodo National Park, Indonesia. *Conservation Biology* 15: 218–227.

Walters, M. J. 2004. No easy way out. *Conservation in Practice* 5: 20–27.

Walther, G. R., E. Post, P. Convey, A. Menzel, C. Parmesan, T. Beebee, et al. 2002. Ecological responses to recent climate change. *Nature* 416: 389–395.

Wang, J. 2004. Application of the one-migrant-per-generation rule to conservation management. *Conservation Biology* 18: 332–343.

Wang, R. and S. Bryant. 2003. The Three Gorges Dam: A look at the world's largest water resources project. *Water, Environment, and Technology*. 15: 28–33.

Wang, Z., B. Zhang, S. Zhang, X. Li, D. Liu, K. Song, et al. 2006. Changes of land use and of ecosystem service values in Sanjiang Plain, northeast China. *Environmental Monitoring and Assessment* 112: 69–91.

Waples, R. S., D. J. Teel, J. Myers, and A. Marshall. 2004. Life history divergence in Chinook salmon: Historic contingency and parallel evolution. *Evolution* 58: 386–403.

Wardle, D. A. and R. D. Bardgett. 2004. Human-induced changes in large herbivorous mammal density: the consequences for decomposers. *Frontiers in Ecology and the Environment* 2: 145–153.

Warren, M. S. 1991. The successful conservation of an endangered species, the heath fritillary butterfly *Mellicta athalia*, in Britain. *Biological Conservation* 55: 37–56.

Watling, L. and E. A. Norse. 1998. Disturbance of the seabed by mobile fishing gear: A comparison to forest clearcutting. *Conservation Biology* 12: 1180–1197.

Watson, L. H., H. E. Odendaal, T. J. Barry, and J. Pietersen. 2005. Population viability of Cape mountain zebra in Gamka Mountain Nature Reserve, South Africa: the influence of habitat and fire. *Biological Conservation* 122: 173–180.

Wayne, R. K. and P. A. Morin. 2004. Conservation genetics in the new molecular age. *Frontiers in Ecology and the Environment* 2: 89–97.

Weber, P. D. 1993. Reviving coral reefs. *In* L. R. Brown (ed.), *State of the World* 1993, pp. 42–60. Norton, New York.

Welch, E. B. and G. D. Cooke. 1990. Lakes. *In* W. R. Jordan III, M. E. Gilpin, and J. D. Aber (eds.), *Restoration Ecology: A Synthetic Approach to Ecological Research*, pp. 109–129. Cambridge University Press, Cambridge.

Wells, M. and K. Brandon. 1992. *People and Parks: Linking Protected Area Management with Local Communities*. The World Bank/WWF/USAID, Washington, D.C.

Wells, M. P. and T. O. McShane. 2004. Integrating protected area management with local needs and aspirations. *A Journal of the Human Environment* 33: 513–519.

Wells, S. and N. Hanna. 1992. *The Greenpeace Book on Coral Reefs*. Greenpeace, Washington, D.C.

Wenz, P. S. 2001. *Environmental Ethics Today*. Oxford University Press, New York.

Wesolowski, T. 2005. Virtual conservation: how the European Union is turning a blind eye to its vanishing primeval forests. *Conservation Biology* 19: 1349–1358.

West, J. M. and R. V. Salm. 2003. Resistance and resilience to coral bleaching: Implications for coral reef conservation and management. *Conservation of Biology* 17: 956–967.

Westemeier, R. L., J. D. Brown, S. A. Simpson, T. L. Esker, R. W. Jansen, J. W. Walk, et al. 1998. Tracking the long-term decline and recovery of an isolated population. *Science* 282: 1695–1698.

Western, D. 1989. Conservation without parks: Wildlife in the rural landscape. *In* D. Western and M. Pearl (eds.), *Conservation for the Twenty-first Century*, pp. 158–165. Oxford University Press, New York.

Westra L and B. E. Lawson. 2001. *Faces of Environmental Racism: Confronting Issues of Global Justice*. Lanham, MD, Rowman and Littlefield.

Whisenant, S. G. 1999. *Repairing Damaged Wetlands*. Cambridge University Press, Cambridge.

White, P. J. and R. A. Garrott. 2005. Yellowstone's ungulates after wolves—expectations, realizations, and predictions. *Biological Conservation* 125: 141–152.

White, P. S. 1996. Spatial and biological scales in reintroduction. *In* D. A. Falk, C. I. Millar, and M. Olwell (eds.), *Restoring Diversity: Strategies for Reintroduction of Endangered Plants*, pp. 49–86. Island Press, Washington, D.C.

White, P. S. and J. L. Walker. 1997. Approximating nature's variation: Selecting and using reference information in restoration ecology. *Restoration Ecology* 5: 338–349.

White, R. P., S. Murray, and M. Rohweder. 2000. *Pilot Assessment of Global Ecosystems: Grassland Ecosystems*. World Resources Institute, Washington, D.C.

Whiten, A. and C. Boesch. 2001. The cultures of chimpanzees. *Scientific American* 284: 61–67.

Whitmore, T. C. 1990. *An Introduction to Tropical Rain Forests*. Clarendon Press, Oxford.

Whitten, A. J., K. D. Bishop, S. V. Nash, and L. Clayton. 1987. One or more extinctions from Sulawesi, Indonesia? *Conservation Biology* 1: 42–48.

Wiersma, Y. F. and D. L. Urban. 2005. Beta diversity and nature reserve system design in the Yukon, Canada. *Conservation Biology* 19: 1262–1272.

Wiersma Y. F., T. D. Nudds, and D. H. Rivard. 2004. Models to distinguish effects of landscape patterns and human population pressures associated with species loss in Canadian national parks. *Landscape Ecology* 19: 773–786.

Wilcove, D. S. 2005. Ecology: enhanced: rediscovery of the ivory-billed woodpecker. *Science* 308: 1422–1423.

Wilcove, D. S. and L. Y. Chen. 1998. Management costs for endangered species. *Conservation Biology* 12: 1405–1407.

Wilcove, D. S. and J. Lee. 2004. Using economic and regulatory incentives to restore endangered species: Lessons learned from three new programs. *Conservation Biology* 18: 639–645.

Wilcove, D. S., M. McMillan, and K. C. Winston. 1993. What exactly is an endangered species? An analysis of the U.S. Endangered Species List: 1985–1991. *Conservation Biology* 7: 87–93.

Wilcove, D. S., M. J. Bean, R. Bonnie, and M. McMillan. 1996. *Rebuilding the Ark: Toward a More Effective Endangered Species Act for Private Land*. Environmental Defense Fund, Washington, D.C.

Wilcove, D. S., M. J. Bean, B. Long, W. J. Snape, and B. M. Beehler. 2004. The private side of conservation. *Frontiers and Ecology and Environment* 2: 326–331.

Wilcove, D. S., D. Rothstein, J. Dubow, A. Phillips, and E. Losos. 1998. Quantifying threats to imperiled species in the United States. *BioScience* 48: 607–615.

Wiles, G. J., J. Bart, R. E. Beck, Jr., and C. F. Aguon. 2003. Impacts of the brown tree snake: Patterns of decline and species persistence in Guam's avifauna. *Conservation Biology* 17: 1350–1360.

Wilkie, D. S., G. A., Morelli, J. Demmer, M. Starkey, P. Telfer, and M. Steil. 2006. Parks and people: assessing the human welfare effects of establishing protected areas for biodiversity conservation. *Conservation Biology* 20: 247–249.

Wilkie, D. S., M. Starkey, K. Abernethy, E. N. Effa, P. Telfer, and R. Godoy. 2005. Role of prices and wealth in consumer demand for bushmeat in Gabon, Central Africa. *Conservation Biology* 19: 268–274.

Willers, B. 1994. Sustainable development: A New World deception. *Conservation Biology* 8: 1146–1148.

Williams, G. E., J. W. Koebel, D. H. Anderson, S. G. Bousquin, D. J. Colangelo, J. L. Glenn, et al. 2005. Kissimmee River Restoration and Upper Basin Initiatives. *In* G. Redfield (ed.). *2005 South Florida Environmental Report*, Chapter 11. South Florida Water Management District, West Palm Beach, FL.

Williams, J. D. and R. M. Nowak. 1993. Vanishing species in our own backyard: Extinct fish and wildlife of the United States and Canada. *In* L. Kaufman and K. Mallory (eds.), *The Last Extinction*, pp. 107–140. MIT Press, Cambridge, MA.

Williams, P., D. Gibbons, C. Margules, A. Rebelo, et al. 1996. A comparison of richness hotspots, rarity hotspots and complementary areas for conserving the diversity of British birds. *Conservation Biology* 10: 155–174.

Willig, M. 2001. Latitude, common trends within. *In* S. A. Levin (ed.), *Encyclopedia of Biodiversity*, vol. 3, pp. 701–714. Academic Press, San Diego, CA.

Wilson, D. E. and R. F. Cole. 1998. *Measuring and Monitoring Biological Diversity: Standard Methods for Mammals*. Smithsonian Institution Press, Washington, D.C.

Wilson, E. O. 1989. Threats to biodiversity. *Scientific American* 261: 108–116.

Wilson, E. O. 1991. Rain forest canopy: The high frontier. *National Geographic* 180: 78–107.

Wilson, E. O. 1992. *The Diversity of Life*. The Belknap Press of Harvard University Press, Cambridge, MA.

Wilson, E. O. 2003. The encyclopedia of life. *Trends in Ecology and Evolution* 18: 77–80.

Wilson, E. O. and D. L. Perlmann. 1999. *Conserving Earth's Biodiversity*. Island Press, Washington, D.C.

Wirzba, N. 2003. *The Paradise of God: Renewing Religion in an Ecological Age*. Oxford University Press, Oxford.

Witoszek, N. and A. Brennan. 1999. *Philosophical Dialogues: Arne Naess and the Progress of Ecophilosophy*. Rowman and Littlefield, Lanham, MD.

Wofford J. E. B., R. E. Gresswell, and M. A. Banks. 2005. Influence of barriers to movement on within-watershed genetic variation of coastal cutthroat trout. *Ecological Applications* 15: 628–637.

Wohlforth, C. 2004. *The Whale and the Supercomputer: On the Northern Front of Climate Change*. North Point Press, New York.

Wolbarts, A. B. (ed.). 2001. *Solutions for an Environment in Peril*. Johns Hopkins University Press, Baltimore, MD.

Wolf, C. M., T. Garland, and B. Griffith. 1998. Predictors of avian and mammalian translocation success: Reanalysis with phylogenetically independent contrasts. *Biological Conservation* 86: 243–255.

Wolf, C. M., B. Griffith, C. Reed, and S. A. Temple. 1996. Avian and mammalian translocations: Update and reanalysis of 1987 survey data. *Conservation Biology* 10: 1142–1155.

Wolters M., A. Garbutt, and J. P. Bakker. 2005. Salt-marsh restoration: evaluating the success of de-embankments in north-west Europe. *Biological Conservation* 123: 249–268.

Woodard, C. 2000. *Ocean's End: Travels Through Endangered Seas*. Basic Books (Perseus Books Group), New York.

Woodford, J. 2000. *The Wollemi Pine*. Text Publishing House, Melbourne.

Woodhill, J. 2000. *Planning, Monitoring and Evaluating Programmes and Projects: An Introduction to Key Concepts, Approaches, and Terms*. IUCN, Gland, Switzerland.

World Bank. 2000a. *Supporting the Web of Life. The World Bank and Biodiversity: A Portfolio Update (1988–1999)*. The World Bank, Washington, D.C.

World Bank. 2000b. *The World Bank and The Global Environment: A Progress Report.* World Bank, Washington, D.C.

World Bank. 2004. *Ensuring the Future: The World Bank and Biodiversity (1998–2004).* The World Bank, Washington, D.C.

World Bank. 2005. *Going, Going, Gone: The Illegal Trade in Wildlife in East and Southeast Asia.* World Bank Environment and Social Development East Asia and Pacific Region Discussion Paper. http://siteresources.worldbank.org/INTEAPREGTOPENVIRONMENT/Resources/going-going-gone.pdf.

World Bank. 2006. *Mountains to Coral Reefs. The World Bank and Biodiversity 1988–2005.* World Bank, Washington, D.C.

World Commission on Environment and Development (WCED). 1987. *Our Common Future.* Oxford University Press, Oxford.

World Database on Protected Areas Consortium (WDPA). 2004. *2004 World Database on Protected Areas.* http://maps.geog.umd.edu/WDPA/index.html.

World Resources Institute (WRI). 1998. *World Resources 1998–1999.* Oxford University Press, New York.

World Resources Institute (WRI). 2000. *World Resources 2000–2001.* World Resources Institute, Washington, D.C.

World Resources Institute (WRI). 2003. *World Resources 2002–2004: Decisions for the Earth: Balance, voice, and power.* World Resources Institute, Washington, D.C.

World Resources Institute (WRI). 2005. *World Resources 2005: The Wealth of the Poor—Managing Ecosystems to Fight Poverty.* World Resources Institute, Washington, D.C.

World Wide Fund for Nature. 2004. *Living Planet Report 2004.* World Wide Fund for Nature, Gland.

World Wildlife Fund (WWF). 1999. *Religion and Conservation.* Full Circle Press, New Delhi.

World Wildlife Fund (WWF). 2000. *The Global 200 Ecoregions: A User's Guide.* WWF, Gland, Switzerland.

World Wildlife Fund (WWF). 2003. *Commercial Debt for Nature Swaps.* WWF Center for Conservation Finance http://worldwildlife.org/conservationfinance/swaps.cfm Switzerland. www.unep.org.

Worm, B., M. Sandow, A. Oschlies, H. K. Lotze, and R. A. Myers. 2005. Global patterns of predator diversity in the open oceans. *Science* 309: 1365–1369.

Wright, J. P., A. S. Flecker, and C. G. Jones. 2003. Local vs. landscape controls on plant species rickness in beaver meadows. *Ecology* 84: 3162–3173.

Wright, R., J. M. Scott, S. Mann, and M. Murray. 2001. Identifying unprotected and potentially at risk plant communities in the western USA. *Biological Conservation* 98: 97–106.

Wright, S. 1931. Evolution in Mendelian populations. *Genetics* 16: 97–159.

Wright, S. J., H. Zeballos, I. Domínguez, M. M. Gallardo, M. C. Moreno, and R. Ibánez. 2000. Poachers alter mammal abundance, seed dispersal, and seed predation in a Neotropical forest. *Conservation Biology* 14: 227–239.

Wu, J., J. Huang, X. Han, X. Gao, F. He, M. Jiang, et al. 2004. The Three Gorges Dam: An ecological perspective. *Frontiers in Ecology and the Environment* 2: 241–248.

Wunder, S. 1999. *Value Determinants of Plant Extractivism in Brazil.* Instituto de Pesquisa Econômica Aplicada, Rio de Janiero, Brazil.

Xie, P. 2003. Three Gorges Dam: Risk to ancient fish. *Science* 302: 1149–1150.

Yaffe, M. D. (ed.). 2001. *Judaism and Environmental Ethics: A Reader.* Lexington Books, Lanham, Md.

Yaffee, S. L. 1996. *Ecosystem Management in the United States: An Assessment of Current Experience.* Island Press, Washington, D.C.

Yaffee, S. L. 1999. Three faces of ecosystem management. *Conservation Biology* 13: 713–725.

Yamaoko, K., H. Moriyama, and T. Shigematsu. 1977. Ecological role of secondary forests in the traditional farming area in Japan. *Bulletin of Tokyo University* 20: 373–384.

Yates, C. J. and P. G. Ladd. 2005. Relative importance of reproductive biology and establishment ecology for persistence of a rare shrub in a fragmented landscape. *Conservation Biology* 19: 239–249.

Yodzis, P. 2001. Trophic levels. *In* S. A. Levin (ed.), *Encyclopedia of Biodiversity,* vol. 5, pp. 695–700. Academic Press, San Diego, CA.

Young, A. G. and G. M. Clarke (eds.). 2001. *Genetics, Demography, and Viability of Fragmented Populations.* Cambridge University Press, New York.

Young, B. E., S. N. Stuart, J. S. Chanson, N. A. Cox, and T. M. Boucher. 2004. *Disappearing Jewels: The Status of New World Amphibians.* NatureServe, Arlington, VA.

Young, T. P. 1994. Natural die-offs of large mammals: Implications for conservation. *Conservation Biology* 8: 410–418.

Young, T. P. 2000. Restoration ecology and conservation biology. *Biological Conservation* 92: 73–83.

Young T. P., T. M. Palmer, and M. E. Gadd. 2005. Competition and compensation among cattle, zebras, and elephants in a semi-arid savanna in Laikipia, Kenya. *Biological Conservation* 112: 251–259.

Young, W. 1995. A dump no more. *American Forests* 101: 58–59.

Zabel, R. W., M. D. Scheuerell, M. M. McClure, and J. G. Williams. 2006. The interplay between climate variability and density dependence in the population viability of Chinook salmon. *Conservation Biology* 20: 190–200.

Zacharias, M. A. and E. J. Gregr. 2005. Sensitivity and vulnerability in marine environments: an approach to identifying vulnerable marine areas. *Conservation Biology* 19: 86–97.

Zahler, P. 2003. Top-down meets bottom-up: conservation in a post-conflict world. *Conservation in Practice* 4: 23–29.

Zarin, D. J., E. A Davidson, E. Brondizio, I. C. G. Vieira, T. Sá, T. Feldpausch, et al. 2005. Legacy of fire slows carbon accumulation in Amazonian forest regrowth. *Frontiers in Ecology and the Environment* 3: 365–369.

Zavaleta, E. S. and K. B. Hulvey. 2004. Realistic species losses disproportionately reduce grassland resistance to biological invaders. *Science* 306: 1175–1177.

Zedler, J. B. 1996. Ecological issues in wetland mitigation: An introduction to the forum. *Ecological Applications* 6: 33–37.

Zedler, J. B. 2005. Restoring wetland plant diversity. A comparison of existing and adaptive approaches. *Wetlands Ecology and Management* 13: 5–14.

Zedler J. B. and J. C. Callaway. 2003. Adaptive restoration: a strategic approach for integrating research into restoration projects. *In* D. J. Rapport, W. L. Lasley, D. E. Rolston, N. O. Nielsen, C. O. Qualset, and A. B. Damania, (eds.), *Managing for Healthy Ecosystems.* Lewis Publishers, Boca Raton, FL.

Zedler, J. B., R. Lindig-Cisneros, C. Bonilla-Warford, and I. Woo. 2001. Restoration of biodiversity, overview. *In* S. A. Levin (ed.), *Encyclopedia of Biodiversity,* vol. 5, pp. 203–212. Academic Press, San Diego, CA.

Zhu, Y. Y., Y. Y. Wang, H. R. Che, and B. R. Lu. 2003. Conserving traditional rice varieties through management for crop diversity. *BioScience* 53: 158–162.

Zink, R. 2004. The role of subspecies in obscuring avian biological diversity and misleading conservation policy. *Proceedings of the Royal Society of London: Biological Sciences* 271: 561–564.

Zonneveld, I. S. and R. T. Forman (eds.). 1990. *Changing Landscapes: An Ecological Perspective.* Springer-Verlag, New York.

Zorn, P., W. Stephenson, and P. Grigoriev. 2001. An ecosystem management program and assessment process for Ontario National Parks. *Conservation Biology* 15: 353–362.

Index

About the Author

Richard B. Primack is a Professor of Biology at Boston University. He received his B.A. at Harvard University in 1972 and his Ph.D. at Duke University in 1976, and then was a postdoctoral fellow at the University of Canterbury. He has been a Visiting Professor at the University of Hong Kong and will be a Visiting Professor at Tokyo University in late 2006, and has been awarded Bullard and Putnam Fellowships from Harvard University and a Guggenheim Fellowship. Dr. Primack was President of the Association for Tropical Biology and Conservation and is currently Editor of the journal *Biological Conservation*. Eighteen foreign language editions of his textbooks have been produced, with local coauthors. He is an author of rain forest books, most recently *Tropical Rain Forests: An Ecological and Biogeographical Comparison* (with Richard Corlett). Dr. Primack's research interests include: the biological impacts of climate change; the loss of species in protected areas; tropical forest ecology and conservation; and conservation education. He is currently writing a popular book about changes in Concord since the time of Henry David Thoreau and *Walden*.

About the Book

Editor: Andrew D. Sinauer
Project Editor: Sydney Carroll
Production Manager: Christopher Small
Book Design: Joanne Delphia
Book Layout and Composition: Joanne Delphia
Cover Design: Jefferson Johnson
Book and Cover Manufacture: Courier Companies, Inc.